CONTEMPORARY APPROACHES TO PHILOSOPHY

Paul Moser AND Dwayne Mulder

Loyola University of Chicago

Macmillan Publishing Company
NEW YORK
Maxwell Macmillan Canada
TORONTO

Editor: Maggie Barbieri
Production Supervisor: France Burke
Production Manager: Su Levine
Text Designer: Eileen Burke
Cover Designer: Russ Maselli
Cover Illustration: Raffaello (1483–1520),
"Scuola di Atene," Collection of the
Vatican, Scala/Art Resource.
This book was set in Palatino by Americomp
and was printed and bound by Book Press.
The cover was printed by New England Book Components.

PRINTED IN THE UNITED STATES OF AMERICA

Macmillan Publishing Company
866 Third Avenue, New York, New York 10022

Macmillan Publishing Company is part of
the Maxwell Communication Group of Companies.

Maxwell Macmillan Canada, Inc.
1200 Eglinton Avenue East
Suite 200
Don Mills, Ontario M3C 3N1

LIBRARY OF CONGRESS CATALOGING-IN-PUBLICATION DATA

Moser, Paul K., 1957–
Contemporary approaches to philosophy / Paul Moser, Dwayne Mulder.
p. cm.
Includes bibliographical references.
ISBN 0-02-384171-0 (pbk.)
1. Philosophy. I. Mulder, Dwayne. II. Title.
B29.M619 1994
100—dc20 92-42195
CIP

Printing: 1 2 3 4 5 6 7 Year: 4 5 6 7 8 9 0

PREFACE

This book should help academic and nonacademic readers to answer the twofold question, "What is philosophy, and is it a worthwhile discipline?" It includes twenty-five selections on the nature of philosophy, from a variety of influential philosophical standpoints. The selections fall into these four categories: Pragmatism (Part I); Anglo-American Philosophy (Part II); Continental Philosophy (Part III); and Prospects for Philosophy (Part IV).

This collection can serve as a comprehensive textbook for any college course dealing with questions about the nature of philosophy. Readers already introduced to philosophy will perhaps gain the most from this book; but all the selections should be accessible, in the main, to middle-level undergraduate students and to educated nonacademic readers curious about the discipline of philosophy. None of the selections is technical or formal in approach. The selections can also benefit graduate students of philosophy and related disciplines.

The General Introduction introduces some themes from the philosophy of philosophy, or "metaphilosophy," and the section introductions summarize the book's selections. The summaries in the section introductions should help students identify some of the main points in the selections. The book concludes with a bibliography on metaphilosophy.

Our work on this book has benefited from comments from anonymous referees for Macmillan and from several colleagues at Loyola University of Chicago. These comments have improved the book, and we are grateful for them. Maggie Barbieri of Macmillan has been helpful throughout the process of completing the book. We hope that this collection heightens academic and nonacademic interest in metaphilosophy, if not in philosophy itself.

Paul Moser and Dwayne Mulder

CONTENTS

CONTEMPORARY APPROACHES TO PHILOSOPHY

GENERAL INTRODUCTION: PHILOSOPHY OF PHILOSOPHY

I. METAPHILOSOPHY

A philosopher is, let us say, anyone engaging in philosophical inquiry. What, however, is philosophical inquiry? Does such inquiry produce any definite results and, if so, what is the status of those results? Are they *true*? If so, how can they be *confirmed* as true? What, specifically, is the proper method for philosophical inquiry? Does the latter question, especially its use of 'proper', make sense? Such questions elicit fundamental disagreements among contemporary philosophers; and they motivate this book.

Contemporary approaches to the foregoing questions fall under the rather vague but widely used categories of *Anglo-American (analytic) philosophy, Continental philosophy,* and *pragmatism.* This book includes readings from each of these categories on the nature of philosophy. Bertrand Russell (1872–1970) and G. E. Moore (1873–1958), aided by major developments in modern logic, initiated an Anglo-American (analytic) rejection of British idealism in favor of a pluralistic realism based on "common sense uninfluenced by philosophy or theology." Their realism acknowledged the existence of a wide range of mind-independent facts countenanced by such common sense, thereby contradicting the idealist view of F. H. Bradley (1846–1924) that common sense relates us to mere appearance, not reality. Friedrich Nietzsche (1844–1900) set the stage for contemporary continental philosophy with his rejection of German idealism, especially the contrasting versions of Kant and Hegel. He emphasized the perspectival character of philosophy and introduced the genealogical method of tracing philosophical concepts back to their sources in the basic drives in human psychology. C. S. Peirce (1839–1914) founded American pragmatism, again largely as a reaction to parts of Hegel's idealist philosophy. Peirce's pragmatism stated that the meaning of a conception is exhausted by the experiential and practical effects of that conception's object.

Ancient, medieval, and classical modern philosophers worked with a significant variety of assumptions about what philosophy is. Recently, questions about the nature of philosophy have become a philosophical topic in their own right along with epistemology, metaphysics, value theory, and so on. C. I. Lewis, in his selection below, notes the importance of considerations about methods of philosophy:

> *The general character of any philosophy is likely to be determined by its initial assumptions and its methods. . . . [Therefore] it is right and proper that [a philosopher] should begin with some statement of program and method.*

In giving a "statement of program and method" and arguing for it, philosophers pursue the philosophy of philosophy, or *metaphilosophy.* We thus should distinguish between first-order and second-order philosophical inquiry. Epistemology, metaphysics, and value theory are among the first-order philosophical pursuits constituting the main activity of philosophers. Philosophical examination of such first-order pursuits moves inquiry to a higher, second-order level. For instance, epistemology, having the nature of knowledge as its own object, can itself become the object of higher-order philosophical inquiry. The latter inquiry concerns not the nature of knowledge directly, but rather the nature of epistemology: that is, the nature of the theory of knowledge. The distinction between philosophy and metaphilosophy resembles, in some ways, that between mathematics and metamathematics.

II. PLATO AND ARISTOTLE ON PHILOSOPHY

Although metaphilosophical disputes have had special prominence in the last century, they develop from the broader history of Western philosophy. Western philosophy originates in ancient Greece, where Plato and Aristotle set the stage, decisively, for much of subsequent philosophical inquiry. Ever since Plato and Aristotle, philosophers have pursued 'what is *X*?' questions. What is knowledge? What is meaning? What is being? What is justice? What is causation? What is free will? And so on. What, if anything, are such questions about, and how does one answer them? This is a fundamental metaphilosophical issue that divides numerous philosophers engaged in metaphysical, epistemological, or ethical inquiry; and it introduces the central question of the objectivity, or conceiving-independence, of entities, ideas, values, duties, and so on.

One might try to explain the nature of philosophy by explaining what leads people to pursue philosophy. Plato and Aristotle claim that wonder, or marvel, prompts people to philosophize (see *Theaetetus* 155d and *Metaphysics* 982b12). Wonder evidently produces philosophy, at least according to Plato and Aristotle, only when accompanied by a 'what is *X*?' question, or at least by a closely related question. This suggests that Plato and Aristotle do not think of wonder (*thauma*) as just a feeling of astonishment.

Aristotle illustrates his claim about philosophy with an example of people wondering initially at "obvious difficulties," and then advancing to "greater matters": for instance, matters about the genesis of the universe. Such wondering is no mere feeling of astonishment. Aristotle adds that a puzzled person who wonders considers himself ignorant, and that philosophy aims to escape from ignorance. Aristotle's "greater matters," by his own illustration, consist of unanswered questions about various phenomena (e.g., the moon, the sun, the stars). Thus, Aristotle apparently regards philosophy as beginning with wondering that includes, or at least prompts, questions of a certain sort, questions that typically take the form 'what is *X*?'

Plato and Aristotle evidently think of philosophical 'what is *X*?' questions as *essence-seeking*. For instance, Plato's question 'what is knowledge?' in the *Theaetetus* (146e) aims to identify what knowledge *itself* is; it does not aim for a list of the various sorts of knowledge. Similarly, his 'what is *X*?' questioning in the *Meno* (75a) aims for what is the same in, or common to, all *X*'s. It aims, in other words, for the essence (*ousia*) of *X* (*Meno* 72b; cf. *Euthyphro* 11a). Plato suggests that this aim involves providing a definition (*logos*) of the essence of *X* (*Republic* 534b). Aristotle, too, characterizes philosophy in terms of knowledge of essence, which in his view reduces to knowledge of definition (*Metaphysics* 983a27f.).

Both Plato and Aristotle, then, understand philosophical 'what is *X*?' questions as essense-seeking. Both understand definition as the way to identify essence. Both hold, accordingly, that philosophical 'what is *X*?' questions are definition-seeking and essence-seeking. The relevant definitions, according to Plato and Aristotle, are not stipulative; nor are they reports on conventional linguistic usage. They rather are *real* definitions: that is, essence-specifying definitions signifying the properties that locate something in its proper genus or species. Aristotle (*Categories* 2b28-3a5) is especially clear on this understanding of real definition.

A troublesome circle emerges now. If we explain essence in terms of what is captured by real definition, and then explain real definition in terms of what captures essence, we have made no explanatory mileage. We have only gone around in a circle. "This useless circle," according to Richard Robinson, "is the best that can be extracted from Aristotle when we ask what is meant by 'essence', and it is strong evidence that there is no such thing as essence in his sense of the word" (1954, p. 154). Regardless of whether Aristotle himself escaped this circle, we should ask whether other proponents of philosophical 'what is *X*?' questions can escape. If this circle is inescapable, those proponents will lack an informative account of the sort of questions supposedly definitive of philosophical inquiry. In that case, their account of what philosophy itself is will be inadequate. This is a straightforward illustration of the significance of metaphilosophical inquiry, and it extends to the origins of western philosophy in Plato and Aristotle.

III. REALISM

We may use the term 'essence-realist', or just 'realist', for any philosopher who, like Plato and Aristotle, holds that the correct answer to such a question as 'what is knowledge?' identifies certain essential features whose being essential is part of the *conceiving-independent* world. Such a realist denies that what *is* essential to something (e.g., knowledge) depends for its being essential on conceivers *taking*, or conceptualizing, it as essential. Following Plato and Aristotle, essence-realists regard the question 'what is knowledge?' as equivalent to this question: What is the conceiving-independent essence of knowledge?

The notion of conceiving-independence, according to various philosophers, amounts to the notion of *how things are* apart from *how conceivers take things to be.* Some anti-realists doubtful of intelligibility here overlook a relevant distinction between the conceiving-dependence of a notion and the conceiving-dependence of what that notion designates or subsumes. Even if the conditions for *imagining* how things are conceiving-independently always depend on conceivers, it may be that *what* is thus imagined is not similarly conceiving-dependent. A major concern of philosophers since the time of Plato is whether we can have knowledge of conceiving-independent reality. Various western philosophers have proposed methods for acquiring such knowledge, relying at times on such means as intellectual "intuition," "clear and distinct ideas," and "transcendental arguments." Some philosophers think of knowledge of conceiving-independent reality as "metaphysical," or "ontological," knowledge.

We have touched on attempts to rule out metaphysical knowledge via a claim that the concept of how things are conceiving-independently is unintelligible. Such attempts to eliminate metaphysics from philosophy derive from the logical positivist doctrines of Rudolf Carnap (1891–1970) and A. J. Ayer (1910–1989). We need to draw some distinctions to assess these attempts.

One might claim that, although the concept of how things are *as conceived* by some conceiver is intelligible, the concept of how things are apart from any conception is unintelligible. We may grant that whenever one conceives of something, one conceives of it in some more or less determinate way. One cannot conceive of a bookshelf, for example, without conceiving of it in some way: as being to the left of the desk, disorderly, or stacked full of books, for instance. Still, one can conceive of the bookshelf's remaining in *some determinate state* when no one is conceiving of it. We can conceive of a *situation* where the bookshelf exists while there is no conceiving of it, not even our own. The concept of this situation may depend on our conceiving, but the situation represented by this concept does not include any conceptual activity. What this concept is *about* is not necessarily conceiving-dependent, even if every concept is itself necessarily conceiving-dependent.

One cannot conceive of an object without conceiving of it in a more or less determinate way. One must conceive of it as an object *of a certain kind,* at the very least: say, a physical object or a temporal object. In this respect, it is impossible to conceive of something without conceptualizing it somehow. This consideration does not threaten the previous observation that one can conceive of a situation where the following obtains: a certain object exists and is featured in a determinate way but no one is conceiving of it as existing or as having certain features. It is doubtful, then, that we can eliminate metaphysics from philosophy by claiming that the concepts it employs are unintelligible pseudo-concepts. Nevertheless, there might be other problems threatening metaphysics.

IV. DEFENDING METAPHYSICAL CLAIMS

Metaphysical claims seem to rely on methodological considerations for their defense. Typically, one defends a metaphysical claim by indicating a method for testing that claim, showing that the method supports the claim, and arguing that the method succeeds in distinguishing metaphysical claims that capture conceiving-independent reality from those failing to do so. Therefore, the defense of a *methodological program* for philosophy would ideally avoid presuppositions that include metaphysical claims needing their own defense via a methodology. It is, however, difficult to avoid circularity at this level of reasoning. For example, if one wished to defend a philosophical method for acquiring metaphysical knowledge based on, say, some type of intellectual intuition, one would have to offer reasons for thinking that intellectual intuition *of that type* delivers truth regarding some aspect of conceiving-independent reality. At this point it is tempting and even common to refer to certain metaphysical claims *presumed* to be true to demonstrate that a certain type of intellectual intuition yields results in agreement with these claims and is, therefore, reliable. The same holds true for any other proposed method of acquiring metaphysical knowledge. One needs, however, some noncircular way to test the correctness or reliability of a proposed source of knowledge of how things are conceiving-independently, in order to defend philosophically the metaphysical claims that source produces.

What might one use as a standard for measuring (the correctness of claims produced by) a proposed source of knowledge of conceiving-independent situations? The desired standard cannot plausibly come from the alleged source of metaphysical knowledge we wish to test. Recall Wittgenstein's example of one's checking different copies of the same newspaper in order to confirm something it reported [cf. Wittgenstein (1953, §265)]. Testing a proposed source of metaphysical knowledge by some standard deriving from that source itself would tell us only whether the proposed source gives answers that "agree," in some appropriate sense, with all of its other deliverances. This would provide only internal assessment of the proposed source of metaphysical knowledge, whereas we need an external assessment, where "external" means "relevant to conceiving-independent reality."

We must ask whether there is some noncircular way of testing sources of belief as reliable measures of conceiving-independent reality. This issue raises the problem of testing a system of measurement itself. Some instruments might be unreliable for measuring. For example, a ruler made of a substance that expands significantly in heat and contracts significantly in cold would be unreliable for measuring things in very different temperatures. Similarly, a proposed source of metaphysical knowledge would be unreliable if it generated its own products or altered them relative to the "input" from conceiving-independent reality.

Skeptics will demand a noncircular method of testing a proposed source of metaphysical knowledge as a reliable measure of conceiving-independent reality. A noncircular method of testing for reliability is non-questionbegging: It does not simply *presume* an affirmative answer to a skeptic's familiar questions about reliability. Some of these questions concern the reliability, in any actual case, of our belief-forming processes (e.g., perception, introspection, memory, intuition, testimony) that sometimes produce belief in the existence of conceiving-independent reality. Some other familiar questions concern the reliability, in any actual case, of suitably coherent, explanatorily efficacious, or predictively successful belief regarding the existence of conceiving-independent reality.

Skeptics are not guilty here of this empty challenge: Give me a cogent noncircular argument, but do not use any premises. The pertinent challenge is rather: Give me cogent, *non*-questionbegging evidence to hold that your beliefs regarding the existence of conceiving-independent reality are objectively true. The demand is not that proponents of metaphysical knowledge forgo use of premises; it rather is just that they forgo use of *questionbegging* premises: premises that beg relevant questions about reliability motivating skepticism. A questionbegging argument from a proponent of metaphysical knowledge will not even begin to approach cogency for skeptics. Mere soundness of argument, then, is not at issue; *cogent*, non-questionbegging soundness is.

Questions under dispute in a philosophical context cannot attract non-questionbegging answers from mere *presumption* of the correctness of a disputed answer. If we allow such questionbegging in general, we can support *any* position we prefer: Simply beg the key question in any dispute regarding the preferred position. Given that strategy, argument becomes superfluous in the way circular argument is typically pointless. Questionbegging strategies promote an undesirable arbitrariness in philosophical debate. They are thus argumentatively inconclusive relative to the questions under dispute. This consideration is compatible with the view that what is questionbegging is always relative to a context of disputed issues, a context not necessarily shared by all inquirers. [For doubts about any purely formal criterion of vicious circularity in argument, see Sorensen (1991).]

Non-questionbegging evidence for a claim regarding the existence of conceiving-independent reality would be evidence yielding noncircular, or effective, discernment of the truth of a claim regarding the existence of conceiving-independent reality. We cannot effectively rely on *our* eyesight, for example, to test the objective reliability of our own eyesight. The familiar Snellen test for vision thus cannot effectively measure objectively reliable vision. Normal vision by the Snellen standard is based loosely on an assumed statistical average concerning human visual perceivers, not on considerations purporting to indicate objective reliability of vision. A skeptic will naturally question whether that statistical average is ever a reliable means to conceiving-independent reality. It is doubtful that we have any non-questionbegging evidence to hold that it is thus reliable. We cannot presume, in any case, the reliability of our vision to provide non-questionbegging evidence in favor of the reliability of our vision.

More generally, we cannot effectively rely on the deliverances of our belief-forming processes (e.g., perception, introspection, memory, intuition, testimony) to test the reliability of those processes regarding their accessing conceiving-independent facts. Appeal to the deliverances of those processes would beg the key question against an inquirer doubtful of the reliability of those deliverances and processes. The belief-forming processes in question need testing, with respect to their reliability, in order to yield non-questionbegging evidence for a claim to objective truth. Proponents of metaphysical knowledge (of the sort under consideration) claim to know conceiving-independent facts about external objects. A doubtful inquirer will naturally demand effective, non-questionbegging evidence for their claims. Questionbegging evidence will settle nothing in this philosophical dispute.

So far, then, we have claimed that a proposed source of metaphysical knowledge cannot effectively attest to its own reliability, much as the expanding and contracting ruler cannot effectively test *its own* reliability as a measuring device. In either case, one clearly would be relying on a method of testing which is itself included under the dispute.

In response to this observation, it seems natural to claim that there is some other test available. Using the analogy of the expanding and contracting ruler, one would like to say that we can test it easily enough by comparing its results to those of a ruler that has already been established as a reliable measuring instrument. This obviously gains us little or nothing, for we immediately confront the question of the reliability of *this* ruler. The case would be similar if one tried to establish the reliability of, say, sensory perception by appealing to "common sense." This of course only forces the question of the reliability of "common sense."

At this point, one will probably be tempted to extend the analogy with measurement in the following way. We can test the reliability of our ruler without appealing to any alternative measuring instrument that is equally in need of being tested. We can, for example, take one cold thing our (cold) ruler measured to be one meter and one hot thing our (hot) ruler measured to be one meter, and we can bring them side by side and *see* whether they are in fact the same length. We can run suitable variations on this experiment, of course, in order to establish conclusively whether this ruler is reliable (at least with respect to fluctuations due to temperature). Such processes embody what we *mean* by "measurement." Drawing on the analogy we've been using, one now feels assured that one can perform an analogous test on proposed sources of metaphysical knowledge. The analogy breaks down, however, at a crucial point, and if one fails to see this it can become a very misleading analogy. The disanalogy results from the fact that this test of the ruler relies on *perception* as an undisputed authority *external* to the established methods and processes of measurement. In the case of proposed sources of metaphysical knowledge, however, we have no such undisputed authority external to our cognitive processes. All of our knowing can be based only on some cognitive process or other, and no cognitive process lies outside the realm of dispute for the skeptic.

We can express this idea in another way. One consideration—perhaps employed only for the sake of argument by skeptics—indicates that a skeptic will not be successfully answered by proponents of metaphysical knowledge. Cognitively relevant access to *anything* by us humans depends on such a belief-forming process as perception, introspection, memory, or testimony. Any such process is subject to question regarding its reliability, and thus cannot itself deliver non-questionbegging support for its own reliability. Further, any such process will be incapable of providing non-questionbegging support for the reliability of some other cognitive process. This consideration applies likewise to any process or faculty (e.g., so-called "rational intuition") assumed to deliver synthetic *a priori* knowledge: substantive knowledge that does not depend on sensory or perceptual experience. We evidently cannot assume a position *independent* of our own cognitively relevant processes to deliver a non-questionbegging indication of the reliability of those processes. We can now see how this human cognitive predicament motivates skepticism about metaphysical knowledge. [See Moser (1993) for elaboration on this theme.]

A pragmatic defense of metaphysical knowledge, in terms of a belief's overall utility, faces a difficult question: What non-questionbegging evidence, if any, have we to affirm that a belief's overall pragmatic utility is ever a genuinely reliable means of access to what is objectively, or conceiving-independently, the case? It does no good here to note that it is pragmatically useful to regard pragmatic utility as a reliable means to objective truth. A skeptic, once again, seeks non-questionbegging evidence; and the pertinent issue concerns the (known) *correctness* of claims regarding conceiving-independent reality, not whether such claims are *useful.* Given the aforementioned human cognitive predicament, we can offer little hope for the needed non-questionbegging support on pragmatic grounds. *Pragmatic support* for a claim is one thing; *non-questionbegging evidence,* another. A skeptic demands the latter evidence, but despairs of ever achieving it.

Some proponents of metaphysical knowledge hold that the assumption of the existence of conceiving-independent reality (of a certain sort) is the best available explanation of our (subjectively described) *experience:* for example, our perceptual and sensory contents. [For different versions of an appeal to inference to best explanation, see Goldman (1988); Moser (1989); and Carruthers (1992).] These theorists rely on an "inference to the best explanation" to support metaphysical theses: in particular, theses about conceiving-independent reality. Explanation at this level seems different from familiar modes of explanation in science and everyday discourse. Explanation in science and everyday discourse works within the context of some more or less determinate ontology; but, if it aims to establish an ontology in a noncircular manner, inference to an explanation as a defense of a metaphysical thesis cannot work with any such context. When explanation works within an ontology, that ontology constrains what needs explanation, what counts as a satisfactory explanation, and what makes one explanation better than another. Regarding inference to a metaphysical thesis, in contrast, it is not clear what sets the pertinent constraints when one demands non-questionbegging support.

One might assume that experience requires a certain type of explanation of itself, but then one must specify how experience rules out certain explanations of itself. Criteria for explanatory satisfactoriness do not typically come from what is to be explained, but ordinarily come from something "antecedent" to what needs explanation. Wherever such constraints originate, however, skeptics about metaphysical theses will ask for non-questionbegging evidence for the assumption that a claim's satisfying certain standards for best explanation of experience (e.g., predictive power, simplicity, coherence, comprehensiveness) is ever a reliable indication of how things are conceiving-independently. We have seen that this is a tall order, given the aforementioned human cognitive predicament.

The following argument sums up the remarks above:

1. Metaphysical knowledge is, by definition, knowledge of how things are conceiving-independently.
2. Our effectively discerning that anyone has knowledge of conceiving-independent reality requires that we have effective, non-questionbegging access to conceiving-independent reality.
3. Finite conceivers, including ourselves, have access to anything only through cognitive processes subject to the effectively unanswerable question regarding whether they create or otherwise decisively influence what is thereby accessed; in short, we have no noncircular means of testing the reliability of our cognitive processes.
4. Hence, finite conceivers have no effective access to conceiving-independent reality.
5. Hence, finite conceivers cannot effectively discern whether they have metaphysical knowledge—even if they happen to have such knowledge.

Suppose that, following many philosophers, we demand a defense of accepted metaphysical theses that does not beg familiar skeptical questions about the reliability of cognitive processes. In that case, given the argument 1–5, we should withhold judgment on metaphysical theses about how things are conceiving-independently. From the standpoint of any kind of rationality prohibiting questionbegging reasons, one must remain an agnostic regarding conceiving-independent reality.

V. CONCEPTUAL ANALYSIS AND RELATIVISM

The claim that conceptual analysis can provide objective results in philosophy deserves special attention. We shall consider whether conceptual analysis can provide knowledge of some conceiving-independent facts.

Two broad strategies apply to the analysis of concepts. First, one can try to make explicit the implicit meaning a concept has in virtue of its use in some group of language-users: "ordinary" language-users, specialized language-users, and so on. This involves an attempt to identify the meaning of a concept in a way that captures some specified usage of a term designating that concept. The test for success or failure in this enterprise lies ultimately in an examination of well-established uses of certain terms to find whether those uses fall under the general conditions of the analysis. The second strategy for analysis consists in proposing, or recommending, one concept over others, even if this entails replacing a commonly used concept with some other concept: one more precise or even one significantly different [cf. Carnap (1950, p. 3), and Quine (1960, pp. 257–62)]. If, for example, the vast majority of people in a community use the term 'knowledge' in some cases for false beliefs with a particular sort of justification, an epistemologist might aim to exclude such usage by restricting use of the term to justified *true* belief. An important question in any such case concerns what justifies an epistemologist in dictating "appropriate" usage of a term.

Epistemologists using the first strategy will typically arrive at various analyses of knowledge. There are, for instance, theorists who systematically use the term 'knowledge' to allow for the inclusion of false beliefs [cf. Brown (1987, pp. 221–2)]. Many philosophers, however, systematically use 'knowledge' to exclude false belief. In addition, philosophers use 'knowledge' in ways encompassing various notions of justification, truth, and belief. Following the first strategy, then, philosophers arrive at different analyses of knowledge. [See Shope (1983) for illustration of the divergence in analyses of knowledge.] One problem with this strategy is that it delivers nothing more than a lexicographical listing of meanings corresponding to a variety of patterns of linguistic usage. It offers no way to evaluate the various meanings or to eliminate some while preserving one or another. Faced with a plethora of different analyses, one will naturally adopt the second strategy for conceptual analysis.

The second strategy faces the problem of justifying the recommendations of one concept over others. We have already mentioned Aristotle's doctrine of essence and definition. An Aristotelian philosopher might suggest that we can justify recommending one concept over another, if the former more accurately captures the essence of the thing it is a concept of. This would be to justify a concept by claiming that it is a real, essence-capturing definition. We have already noted a troublesome circle here that moves from definition to essence and back again. Let's briefly consider some other attempts to justify the use of one notion over another.

One might use considerations of logical consistency to rule out some meaning-ascriptions to terms. If one ascribes a meaning to a term in a certain analysis while simultaneously engaging in a pattern of usage violating that analysis, one may face a charge of inconsistency. If, for example, one analyzes the term 'sister' with just 'female sibling', one would invite a charge of inconsistency in applying 'sister' knowingly to a male or a non-sibling. The threatening inconsistency concerns an analysis and a use of a term, involving a conflict between one's theoretical commitments and one's actions.

Returning to the term 'knowledge', we should ask whether considerations of inconsistency can eliminate certain analyses. Consider a person using 'knowledge' to designate either false beliefs or true beliefs so long as they satisfy a particular justification condition—called justification*. One might contend that since this analysis includes a disjunction of the contradictory qualifiers 'true' and 'false', that disjunction can be eliminated, leaving us with an analysis of knowledge as belief having justification*. One might claim that 'knowledge', on this analysis, is *useless* as a result of its equivalence to 'belief with justification*'. This claim would, however, be debatable. 'Sister' is equivalent to 'female sibling', for example, but this does not make the former a useless term. On what basis, then, could one argue that 'knowledge' *should not* mean 'belief with justification*' and *should* mean 'true belief with justification*' (or something else)?

A typical philosopher will not be concerned about the mere term 'knowledge'; one can do what one will with it. What matters, according to many philosophers, is *the concept of knowledge,* for which 'knowledge' is merely a conventional designator. Epistemologists characteristically try to discover what the concept of knowledge is really like, that is, the *truth* about it. Part of what it is really like is its exclusion of false beliefs; or so the traditional story goes.

We should be cautious of any philosophical strategy that uncritically overlooks the significance of linguistic usage, taking terms in language to be merely conventional pointers, or designators. Such an uncritical attitude toward the functioning of language can easily foster what we call *the myth of the definite article:* It can lead one to think, for instance, that there is such a thing as *the* concept of knowledge. It fosters the belief that a term, 'knowledge', points out *the* concept of knowledge, and that the task of analyzing use of that term consists in correctly identifying the simple elements of *the* concept of knowledge. Taking terms to be mere pointers, designators, or names of something beyond linguistic usage is an essential part of a common strategy for distinguishing correct from incorrect analyses of a term.

If we eliminate the myth of the definite article, we can see that what concept a term designates depends on the meaning (or analysis) one gives the term; the pertinent concept does not independently determine the correctness of an analysis one gives the term. If one analyzes 'knowledge' as 'true belief with justification*', then the term designates a *different* concept from what it designates when analyzed as 'true belief with justification**' (where justification** differs from justification*). The term 'knowledge' does not designate a particular concept independently of the meaning one gives the term; nor can competing analyses (of knowledge, for instance) be evaluated as succeeding or failing to capture an independently identifiable concept (namely, *the* concept of knowledge). An analysis or some other form of assigning meaning determines what concept a term designates—at least for certain people; it thereby sets constraints for conceptual correctness for those people.

There can be different analyses of the same concept, or different concepts of the same thing. We could identify the concept of knowledge (by a convention) in terms of a notion of true belief with justification. Various analyses will meet the general standard set by the latter notion, so long as they include only concepts of true belief and justification. Analyses employing different conditions for justification will produce different concepts, although we can still call them different concepts of knowledge (generally conceived) in virtue of their *general* similarity. The different conditions for justification, in turn, are different conditions for the same thing, epistemic justification (generally conceived), in virtue of common constituents. The identification comes in virtue of common general conceptual constraints; the differentiation comes in virtue of differences at a certain level of conceptual specificity.

Conventions and theoretical purposes lead us to take a particular level of conceptual specificity (and no other) as identifying conditions for analyses' being of the same concept (or concepts' being about the same thing). Our purposes in inquiry set the conventions guiding our analyses. There is no way to determine the correct analysis of 'knowledge' apart from the purposes one has in using the term. These considerations support *conceptual instrumentalism,* the view that our concepts owe their preferability to our ends in inquiry. Given conceptual instrumentalism, we need not look to conceiving-independent situations to recommend one concept over others. We can look instead to an inquirer's purposes in formulating and wielding concepts. Such purposes can vary among inquirers; as a result, we can confront variability and relativity in concepts appropriate to inquiry. This *conceptual relativism* contributes to an explanation of various perennial disputes in philosophy. Many longstanding philosophical disputes, one may argue, arise from different philosophers using different specific notions of, for instance, knowledge, rationality, meaning, rightness, and goodness. If this is correct, we have cases not of genuine philosophical disagreement, but of people *talking about different matters,* at least at a level of specificity. [For more on this theme, see Moser (1993).]

In sum, then, we have introduced a central metaphilosophical question: Is it possible for philosophy to deliver non-questionbegging reasons in support of claims about how things are conceiving-independently? In other words, can metaphysicians *effectively* defend their claims against skeptical attacks? Many of the following selections deal directly with closely related issues. Some philosophers employ the more common term "objectivity" to describe the alleged goal of philosophy, and they ask about the possibility of establishing the "objective validity" of the results of philosophy. Among the philosophers included in this collection, some defend the possibility of objectivity (in some sense) in philosophy, while others attack the claim that philosophy can produce objective results. We have broached here some of the strategies of the former group: for example, pragmatic defenses, defenses based on broadly conceptual or logical analyses, and inferences to an explanation. We have tried to indicate central problems with these approaches relative to the goal of achieving knowledge of conceiving-independent facts.

Although we have not considered all strategies for defending objectivity, one should be able to use the central notion of a *non-questionbegging reason* relative to skeptical objections in appraising the strategies proposed in the following selections. One can also compare the anti-metaphysical positions included below with the argument we have given for withholding judgment on matters of what is the case conceiving-independently. The issues of the attainability of objectivity and the meaning of talk of objectivity run through all of these selections. In taking a stand on these issues, the philosophers represented herein are each taking a stand on the question of what philosophy *is*. They are therefore doing metaphilosophy, or the philosophy of philosophy.

References

Brown, Harold. 1987. *Observation and Objectivity.* New York: Oxford University Press.

Carnap, Rudolf. 1950. *Logical Foundations of Probability.* Chicago: University of Chicago Press.

Carruthers, Peter. 1992. *Human Knowledge and Human Nature.* Oxford: Oxford University Press.

Goldman, Alan. 1988. *Empirical Knowledge.* Berkeley: University of California Press.

Moser, Paul. 1989. *Knowledge and Evidence.* Cambridge: Cambridge University Press.

———. 1993. *Philosophy After Objectivity.* New York: Oxford University Press.

Quine, W. V. 1960. *Word and Object.* Cambridge, Mass.: The MIT Press.

Robinson, Richard. 1954. *Definition.* Oxford: Clarendon Press.

Shope, Robert. 1983. *The Analysis of Knowing.* Princeton: Princeton University Press.

Sorensen, Roy. 1991. " '*P*, Therefore, *P*' Without Circularity." *The Journal of Philosophy* 88, 245–66.

Wittgenstein, Ludwig. 1953. *Philosophical Investigations.* New York: Macmillan.

PART ONE

PRAGMATISM

The pragmatic approaches represented in this section emphasize the role of philosophizing subjects in philosophical activity. This emphasis typically joins with a rejection of any kind of objectivity in inquiry that transcends the influence of inquiring subjects. When pragmatists offer their characteristic pragmatic definition of "truth," they are changing the subject away from the question of whether philosophy can achieve objectivity of the sort noted in the General Introduction. The pragmatic theory of truth includes ineliminable reference to a subject. It thus offers a concept significantly different from a traditional correspondence theory of truth. Correspondence theories use a concept of objective, or conceiving-independent, truth. The key question for the pragmatists to answer, then, is: *Why* should one use a pragmatic rather than an objectivist concept of truth? Presumably, they would have to identify some problem with the objectivist concept and not simply ignore it.

Various pragmatists hold different views on meaningfulness. They appear also to give slightly different meaning to "meaningfulness." C. S. Peirce thinks that pragmatism shows metaphysical claims to be meaningless, whereas William James holds that pragmatism offers a method for resolving metaphysical disputes. Pragmatists agree, however, on the importance of relating meaningfulness to an understanding subject. They also agree on the fundamental role of the subject in *selecting* the most fundamental principles for interpreting experience.

In "What Pragmatism Is," C. S. Peirce claims that the method of philosophy should be more like the method of experimental science.
An experimentalist holds that any meaningful claim is a claim about what experiences one does or would have, given the execution of a certain experiment. Any claim that is not about some such thing is meaningless. Applying this to philosophy, Peirce formulates the thesis of *pragmatism* as the theory that the kind of meaning he calls the rational purport of a word or expression "lies exclusively in its conceivable bearing upon the conduct of life," and there is nothing more to it. Only experimental phenomena, involving interaction be-

tween an experimenter and the world, can have such a bearing on life. With this thesis, he claims to recognize the inseparability of human *purpose* from rational cognition.

Peirce coins the term *pragmaticism* for his own version of pragmatism. It explicitly begins, in its methodology, with the mental state in which one finds oneself as one begins philosophizing: roughly, a common sense view. Peirce aims to show that "almost every proposition of ontological metaphysics" is either meaningless or absurd. We can, according to Peirce, eliminate the problems of metaphysics, and the only remaining philosophical problems will yield to the observational methods of the sciences. Unlike positivism, pragmaticism does not eliminate philosophy altogether; it retains a "purified" philosophy, "a precious essence" of metaphysics, in order to illuminate science. Pragmaticism gives credence to our instinctive beliefs and is strongly realist.

William James gives his explanation of the pragmatic method in "What Pragmatism Means." He holds that a difference in meaning implies a practical difference, and thus that if there is no difference in practical consequences resulting from the truth of either of two claims, those claims do not differ in meaning. "There can *be* no difference anywhere that doesn't *make* a difference elsewhere." The method is a radical form of empiricism, emphasizing action and what is empirically concrete. James calls pragmatism anti-intellectualistic (not anti-intellectual), because it strongly opposes rationalistic tendencies to rely on *a priori* reasoning, necessities, first principles, etc. Pragmatism, by contrast, is open to the possibilities of nature and opposes dogma and the claim to finality of truth in our theories.

James outlines his pragmatic theory of truth. Truth, he says, is a property of beliefs or ideas, the property of helping us deal successfully with our experience and leading us successfully into new areas of experience. This is an *instrumentalist* theory of truth, and it opposes the objectivist truth, based on absolute correspondence to reality, of the rationalists. It takes truth to be a species of the good: that is, the good "in the way of belief" and for definite reasons. The pragmatic theory does not rule out the possibility of the truth of metaphysical or theological ideas, so long as they meet the pragmatist criterion of the right kind of usefulness. James thus sees the pragmatic method not as eliminating metaphysics, but as resolving metaphysical disputes that are otherwise interminable. One resolves such a dispute or assesses the truth of a metaphysical claim solely on the basis of the practical consequences of the ideas involved.

In "The Development of American Pragmatism," John Dewey characterizes what he calls "Pragmatism, Instrumentalism, or Experimentalism." He begins by reviewing Peirce's statement of pragmatism, noting the emphasis on clarifying the meaning of concepts and on the experimental, scientific method. Dewey fixes on the method of the scientific experimentalist as a paradigm for proper philosophical method in general. In clarifying a common misunderstanding of Peirce, Dewey says that "the modification of existence which results from [the application of concepts to existence] constitutes the true meaning of concepts." Such modification shows up in experimentation, and different meanings correspond to different possible applications of concepts to experience. Dewey also expresses the meaning of *truth* in terms of testing theories or hypotheses by experience. Dewey claims that James extended pragmatism because he wanted to apply the pragmatic method of clarifying meaning to more philosophical questions, especially religious or theological questions. James wished to emphasize the consequences for one's life of *accepting* one answer to a philosophical question rather than another. Dewey says that one of the most important consequences of applying the pragmatic method to traditional philosophical questions is the demonstration of the relevance of these questions to our lives.

In general, pragmatism is an extension of empiricism, but it focuses on consequences of philosophical doctrines rather than the empirical antecedents. In taking general concepts not as constructions out of past experience but as bases for organizing future experience, pragmatism opens up a creative role for reason in an indeterminate future yet to be made. Dewey connects pragmatism to the theory of evolution as follows: "The adaptations made by inferior organisms, for example their effective and coordinated responses to stimuli, become teleological in man and therefore give occasion to thought. . . . The function of intelligence is therefore not that of copying the objects of the environment, but rather of taking account of the way in which more effective and more profitable relations with these objects may be established in the future." Developing the theme of evolution, Dewey mentions his characteristic point that experimentalism or instrumentalism considers mutual effects between the human organism and its environment, taking them as unified in the system of nature. Dewey ends by identifying the continuity between Continental philosophy and American philosophy, while noting the latter's emphasis on the individual, subjectivity, freedom, and the practical.

C. I. Lewis, in "The Proper Method of Philosophy," gives a fundamental role to pragmatic considerations in his account of the nature of philosophy. The task of philosophy, he says, is to bring implicit principles by which we reason into clear and coherent expression. These principles are the fundamental *criteria of classification* and *principles of interpretation* of experience. These principles have a social and historical origin that depends on human interests and purposes; they are not simply dictated by experience. We bring these principles to experience; in this sense, they come prior to the accumulation of empirical data. For clarifying fundamental principles, Lewis recommends the *reflective method* rather than the speculative method. This method clarifies principles and concepts through close attention to language and criteria for the use of certain key terms, such as 'real'. It provides solvable, although perhaps difficult, problems for philosophy, whereas the speculative method may present unsolvable problems.

Lewis holds that philosophy should clarify *a priori* principles, and that there are no synthetic *a priori* truths. *A priori* principles are of our own making, since they are definitive or prescriptive statements, the result of a "legislative attitude" of the mind. They formulate an attitude of interpretation of experience, and operate in exactly the same way in metaphysics, ethics, and logic. This interpretive stance we generate entails that all experience can only be experience *from a certain point of view.* Such perspectival experience, according to Lewis, is the only content we have for philosophy. Interpretative principles are not fixed by anything wholly independent of us, but by social processes relative to our purposes. We select and justify them on the basis of their pragmatic usefulness relative to our interests, our purposes.

WHAT PRAGMATISM IS

Charles Sanders Peirce

1. The writer of this article has been led by much experience to believe that every physicist, and every chemist, and, in short, every master in any department of experimental science, has had his mind moulded by his life in the laboratory to a degree that is little suspected. The experimentalist himself can hardly be fully aware of it, for the reason that the men whose intellects he really knows about are much like himself in this respect. With intellects of widely different training from his own, whose education has largely been a thing learned out of books, he will never become inwardly intimate, be he on ever so familiar terms with them; for he and they are as oil and water, and though they be shaken up together, it is remarkable how quickly they will go their several mental ways, without having gained more than a faint flavor from the association. Were those other men only to take skillful soundings of the experimentalist's mind—which is just what they are unqualified to do, for the most part—they would soon discover that, excepting perhaps upon topics where his mind is trammelled by personal feeling or by his bringing up, his disposition is to think of everything just as everything is thought of in the laboratory, that is, as a question of experimentation. Of course, no living man possesses in their fullness all the attributes characteristic of his type: it is not the typical doctor whom you will see every day driven in buggy or coupé, nor is it the typical pedagogue that will be met with in the first schoolroom you enter. But when you have found, or ideally constructed upon a basis of observation, the typical experimentalist, you will find that whatever assertion you may make to him, he will either understand as meaning that if a given prescription for an experiment ever can be and ever is carried out in act, an experience of a given description will result, or else he will see no sense at all in what you say. If you talk to him as Mr. Balfour talked not long ago to the British Association saying that "the physicist . . . seeks for something deeper than the laws connecting possible objects of experience," that "his object is physical reality" unrevealed in experiments, and that the existence of such non-experiential reality "is the unalterable faith of science," to all such ontological meaning you will find the experimentalist mind to be color-blind. What adds to that confidence in this, which the writer owes to his conversations with experimentalists, is that he himself may almost be said to have inhabited a laboratory from the age of six until long past maturity; and having all his life associated mostly with experimentalists, it has always been with a confident sense of understanding them and of being understood by them.

That laboratory life did not prevent the writer (who here and in what follows simply exemplifies the experimentalist type) from becoming interested in methods of thinking; and when he came to read metaphysics, although much of it seemed to him loosely reasoned and determined by accidental prepossessions, yet in the writings of some philosophers, especially Kant, Berkeley, and Spinoza, he sometimes came upon strains of thought that recalled the ways of thinking of the laboratory, so that he felt he might trust to them; all of which has been true of other laboratory-men.

Endeavoring, as a man of that type naturally would, to formulate what he so approved, he framed the theory that a *conception,* that is, the rational purport of a word or other expression, lies exclusively in its conceivable bearing upon the conduct of life; so that, since obviously nothing that might not result from experiment can have any direct bearing upon conduct, if one can define accurately all the conceivable experimental phenomena which the affirmation or denial of a concept could imply, one will have therein a complete definition of the concept, and *there is absolutely nothing more in it.* For this doctrine he invented the name *pragmatism.* Some of his friends wished him to call it *practicism* or *practicalism* (perhaps on the ground that πρακτικός is better Greek than πραγματικός). But for one who had learned philosophy out of Kant, as the writer, along with nineteen out of every twenty experimentalists who have turned to philosophy, had done, and who still thought in Kantian terms most readily, *praktisch* and *pragmatisch* were as far apart as the two poles, the former belonging in a region of thought where no mind of the experimentalist type can ever make sure of solid ground under his feet, the latter expressing relation to some definite human purpose. Now quite the most striking feature of the new theory was its recognition of an inseparable connection between rational cognition and rational purpose; and that consideration it was which determined the preference for the name *pragmatism.*

2. Concerning the matter of philosophical nomenclature, there are a few plain considerations, which the writer has for many years longed to submit to the deliberate judgment of those few fellow-students of philosophy, who deplore the present state of that study, and who are intent upon rescuing it therefrom and bringing it to a condition like that of the natural sciences, where investigators, instead of contemning each the work of most of the others as misdirected from beginning to end, coöperate, stand upon one another's shoulders, and multiply incontestible results; where every observation is repeated, and isolated observations go for little; where every hypothesis that merits attention is subjected to severe but fair examination, and only after the predictions to which it leads have been remarkably borne out by experience is trusted at all, and even then only provisionally; where a radically false step is rarely taken, even the most faulty of those theories which gain wide credence being true in their main experiential predictions. To those students, it is submitted that no study can become scientific in the sense described, until it provides itself with a suitable technical nomenclature, whose every term has a single definite meaning universally accepted among students of the subject,

and whose vocables have no such sweetness or charms as might tempt loose writers to abuse them—which is a virtue of scientific nomenclature too little appreciated. It is submitted that the experience of those sciences which have conquered the greatest difficulties of terminology, which are unquestionably the taxonomic sciences, chemistry, mineralogy, botany, zoölogy, has conclusively shown that the one only way in which the requisite unanimity and requisite ruptures with individual habits and preferences can be brought about is so to shape the canons of terminology that they shall gain the support of *moral principle* and of every man's sense of decency; and that, in particular (under defined restrictions), the general feeling shall be that he who introduces a new conception into philosophy is under an obligation to invent acceptable terms to express it, and that when he has done so, the duty of his fellow-students is to accept those terms, and to resent any wresting of them from their original meanings, as not only a gross discourtesy to him to whom philosophy was indebted for each conception, but also as an injury to philosophy itself; and furthermore, that once a conception has been supplied with suitable and sufficient words for its expression, no other *technical* terms denoting the same things, considered in the same relations, should be countenanced. Should this suggestion find favor, it might be deemed needful that the philosophians in congress assembled should adopt, after due deliberation, convenient canons to limit the application of the principle. Thus, just as is done in chemistry, it might be wise to assign fixed meanings to certain prefixes and suffixes. For example, it might be agreed, perhaps, that the prefix *prope-* should mark a broad and rather indefinite extension of the meaning of the term to which it was prefixed; the name of a doctrine would naturally end in *-ism,* while *-icism* might mark a more strictly defined acception of that doctrine, etc. Then again, just as in biology no account is taken of terms antedating Linnæus—so in philosophy it might be found best not to go back of the scholastic terminology. To illustrate another sort of limitation, it has probably never happened that any philosopher has attempted to give a general name to his own doctrine without that name's soon acquiring in common philosophical usage, a signification much broader than was originally intended. Thus, special systems go by the names Kantianism, Benthamism, Comteanism, Spencerianism, etc., while transcendentalism, utilitarianism, positivism, evolutionism, synthetic philosophy, etc., have irrevocably and very conveniently been elevated to broader governments.

3. After awaiting in vain, for a good many years, some particularly opportune conjuncture of circumstances that might serve to recommend his notions of the ethics of terminology, the writer has now, at last, dragged them in over head and shoulders, on an occasion when he has no specific proposal to offer nor any feeling but satisfaction at the course usage has run without any canons or resolutions of a congress. His word "pragmatism" has gained general recognition in a generalized sense that seems to argue power of growth and vitality. The famed psychologist, James, first took it up, seeing that his "radical empiricism" substantially answered to the writer's definition of pragmatism, albeit with a certain difference in the point of view. Next, the admi-

rably clear and brilliant thinker, Mr. Ferdinand C. S. Schiller, casting about for a more attractive name for the "anthropomorphism" of his *Riddle of the Sphinx,* lit, in that most remarkable paper of his on *Axioms as Postulates,* upon the same designation as "pragmatism," which in its original sense was in generic agreement with his own doctrine, for which he has since found the more appropriate specification "humanism," while he still retains "pragmatism" in a somewhat wider sense. So far all went happily. But at present, the word begins to be met with occasionally in the literary journals, where it gets abused in the merciless way that words have to expect when they fall into literary clutches. Sometimes the manners of the British have effloresced in scolding at the word as ill-chosen—ill-chosen, that is, to express some meaning that it was rather designed to exclude. So then, the writer, finding his bantling "pragmatism" so promoted, feels that it is time to kiss his child good-by and relinquish it to its higher destiny; while to serve the precise purpose of expressing the original definition, he begs to announce the birth of the word "pragmaticism," which is ugly enough to be safe from kidnappers.[1]

Much as the writer has gained from the perusal of what other pragmatists have written, he still thinks there is a decisive advantage in his original conception of the doctrine. From this original form every truth that follows from any of the other forms can be deduced, while some errors can be avoided into which other pragmatists have fallen. The original view appears, too, to be a more compact and unitary conception than the others. But its capital merit, in the writer's eyes, is that it more readily connects itself with a critical proof of its truth. Quite in accord with the logical order of investigation, it usually happens that one first forms an hypothesis that seems more and more reasonable the further one examines into it, but that only a good deal later gets crowned with an adequate proof. The present writer having had the pragmatist theory under consideration for many years longer than most of its adherents, would naturally have given more attention to the proof of it. At any rate, in endeavoring to explain pragmatism, he may be excused for confining himself to that form of it that he knows best. In the present article there will be space only to explain just what this doctrine (which, in such hands as it has now fallen into, may probably play a pretty prominent part in the philosophical discussions of the next coming years), really consists in. Should the exposition be found to interest readers of *The Monist,* they would certainly be much more interested in a second article which would give some samples of the manifold applications of pragmaticism (assuming it to be true) to the solution of problems of different kinds. After that, readers might be prepared to take an interest in a proof that the doctrine is true—a proof which seems to the writer to leave no reasonable doubt on the subject, and to be the one contribution of value that he has to make to philosophy. For it would essentially involve the establishment of the truth of synechism.

The bare definition of pragmaticism could convey no satisfactory comprehension of it to the most apprehensive of minds, but requires the commentary to be given below. Moreover, this definition takes no notice of one or two other doctrines without the previous acceptance (or virtual acceptance) of which pragmaticism itself would be a nullity. They are included as a part of the pragmatism of Schiller, but the present writer prefers not to mingle different propositions. The preliminary propositions had better be stated forthwith.

The difficulty in doing this is that no formal list of them has ever been made. They might all be included under the vague maxim, "Dismiss make-believes." Philosophers of very diverse stripes propose that philosophy shall take its start from one or another state of mind in which no man, least of all a beginner in philosophy, actually is. One proposes that you shall begin by doubting everything, and says that there is only one thing that you cannot doubt, as if doubting were "as easy as lying." Another proposes that we should begin by observing "the first impressions of sense," forgetting that our very percepts are the results of cognitive elaboration. But in truth, there is but one state of mind from which you can "set out," namely, the very state of mind in which you actually find yourself at the time you do "set out"—a state in which you are laden with an immense mass of cognition already formed, of which you cannot divest yourself if you would; and who knows whether, if you could, you would not have made all knowledge impossible to yourself? Do you call it *doubting* to write down on a piece of paper that you doubt? If so, doubt has nothing to do with any serious business. But do not make believe; if pedantry has not eaten all the reality out of you, recognize, as you must, that there is much that you do not doubt, in the least. Now that which you do not at all doubt, you must and do regard as infallible, absolute truth. Here breaks in Mr. Make Believe: "What! Do you mean to say that one is to believe what is not true, or that what a man does not doubt is *ipso facto* true?" No, but unless he can make a thing white and black at once, *he* has to regard what he does not doubt as absolutely true. Now you, *per hypothesiu,* are that man. "But you tell me there are scores of things I do not doubt. I really cannot persuade myself that there is not some one of them about which I am mistaken." You are adducing one of your make-believe facts, which, even if it were established, would only go to show that doubt has a *limen,* that is, is only called into being by a certain finite stimulus. You only puzzle yourself by talking of this metaphysical "truth" and metaphysical "falsity," that you know nothing about. All you have any dealings with are your doubts and beliefs,[2] with the course of life that forces new beliefs upon you and gives you power to doubt old beliefs. If your terms "truth" and "falsity" are taken in such senses as to be definable in terms of doubt and belief and the course of experience (as for example they would be, if you were to define the "truth" as that to a belief in which belief would tend if it were to tend indefinitely toward absolute fixity), well and good: in that case, you are only talking about doubt and belief. But if by truth and falsity you mean something not definable in terms of doubt and belief in any way, then you are talking of entities of whose existence you can know nothing, and which Ockham's razor would clean shave off. Your problems would be greatly simplified, if, instead of saying that you want to know the "Truth," you were simply to say that you want to attain a state of belief unassailable by doubt.

Belief is not a momentary mode of consciousness; it is a habit of mind essentially enduring for some time, and mostly (at least) unconscious; and like other habits, it is (until it meets with some surprise that begins its dissolution) perfectly self-satisfied. Doubt is of an altogether contrary genus. It is not a habit, but the privation of a habit. Now a privation of a habit, in order to be anything at all, must be a condition of erratic activity that in some way must get superseded by a habit.

Among the things which the reader, as a rational person, does not doubt, is that he not merely has habits, but also can exert a measure of self-control over his future actions; which means, however, *not* that he can impart to them any arbitrarily assignable character, but, on the contrary, that a process of self-preparation will tend to impart to action (when the occasion for it shall arise), one fixed character, which is indicated and perhaps roughly measured by the absence (or slightness) of the feeling of self-reproach, which subsequent reflection will induce. Now, this subsequent reflection is part of the self-preparation for action on the next occasion. Consequently, there is a tendency, as action is repeated again and again, for the action to approximate indefinitely toward the perfection of that fixed character, which would be marked by entire absence of self-reproach. The more closely this is approached, the less room for self-control there will be; and where no self-control is possible there will be no self-reproach.

These phenomena seem to be the fundamental characteristics which distinguish a rational being. Blame, in every case, appears to be a modification, often accomplished by a transference, or "projection," of the primary feeling of self-reproach. Accordingly, we never blame anybody for what had been beyond his power of previous self-control. Now, thinking is a species of conduct which is largely subject to self-control. In all their features (which there is no room to describe here), logical self-control is a perfect mirror of ethical self-control—unless it be rather a species under that genus. In accordance with this, what you cannot in the least help believing is not, justly speaking, wrong belief. In other words, for you it is the absolute truth. True, it is conceivable that what you cannot help believing today, you might find you thoroughly disbelieve tomorrow. But then there is a certain distinction between things you "cannot" do, merely in the sense that nothing stimulates you to the great effort and endeavors that would be required, and things you cannot do because in their own nature they are insusceptible of being put into practice. In every stage of your excogitations, there is something of which you can only say, "I cannot think otherwise," and your experientially based hypothesis is that the impossibility is of the second kind.

There is no reason why "thought," in what has just been said, should be taken in that narrow sense in which silence and darkness are favorable to thought. It should rather be understood as covering all rational life, so that an experiment shall be an operation of thought. Of course, that ultimate state of habit to which the action of self-control ultimately tends, where no room is left for further self-control, is, in the case of thought, the state of fixed belief, or perfect knowledge.

Two things here are all-important to assure oneself of and to remember. The first is that a person is not absolutely an individual. His thoughts are what he is "saying to himself," that is, is saying to that other self that is just coming into life in the flow of time. When one reasons, it is that critical self that one is trying to persuade; and all thought whatsoever is a sign, and is mostly of the nature of language. The second thing to remember is that the man's circle of society (however widely or narrowly this phrase may be understood), is a sort of loosely compacted person, in some respects of higher rank than the person of an individual organism. It is these two things alone that render it possible for you—but only in the abstract, and in a Pickwickian sense—to distinguish between absolute truth and what you do not doubt.

Let us now hasten to the exposition of pragmaticism itself. Here it will be convenient to imagine that somebody to whom the doctrine is new, but of rather preternatural perspicacity, asks questions of a pragmaticist. Everything that might give a dramatic illusion must be stripped off, so that the result will be a sort of cross between a dialogue and a catechism, but a good deal liker the latter—something rather painfully reminiscent of Mangnall's *Historical Questions.*

Questioner: I am astounded at your definition of your pragmatism, because only last year I was assured by a person above all suspicion of warping the truth—himself a pragmatist—that your doctrine precisely was "that a conception is to be tested by its practical effects." You must surely, then, have entirely changed your definition very recently.

Pragmatist: If you will turn to Vols. VI and VII of the *Revue Philosophique,* or to the *Popular Science Monthly* for November 1877 and January 1878, you will be able to judge for yourself whether the interpretation you mention was not then clearly excluded. The exact wording of the English enunciation, (changing only the first person into the second), was: "Consider what effects that might conceivably have practical bearing you conceive the object of your conception to have. Then your conception of those effects is the WHOLE of your conception of the object."

Questioner: Well, what reason have you for asserting that this is so?

Pragmatist: That is what I specially desire to tell you. But the question had better be postponed until you clearly understand what those reasons profess to prove.

Questioner: What, then, is the *raison d'être* of the doctrine? What advantage is expected from it?

Pragmatist: It will serve to show that almost every proposition of ontological metaphysics is either meaningless gibberish—one word being defined by other words, and they by still others, without any real conception ever being reached—or else is downright absurd; so that all such rubbish being swept away, what will remain of philosophy will be a series of problems capable of investigation by the observational methods of the true sciences—the truth about which can be reached without those interminable misunderstandings and disputes which have made the highest of the positive sciences a mere amusement for idle intellects, a sort of chess—idle pleasure its purpose, and reading out of a book its method. In this regard, pragmaticism is a species of prope-positivism. But what distinguishes it from other species is, first, its retention of a purified philosophy; secondly, its full acceptance of the main body of our instinctive beliefs; and thirdly, its strenuous insistence upon the truth of scholastic realism (or a close approximation to that, well-stated by the late Dr. Francis Ellingwood Abbot in the Introduction to his *Scientific Theism*). So, instead of merely jeering at metaphysics, like other prope-positivists, whether by long drawn-out parodies or otherwise, the pragmaticist extracts from it a precious essence, which will serve to give life and light to cosmology and physics. At the same time, the moral applications of the doctrine are positive and potent; and there are many other uses of it not easily classed. On another occasion, instances may be given to show that it really has these effects.

Questioner: I hardly need to be convinced that your doctrine would wipe out metaphysics. Is it not as obvious that it must wipe out every proposition of science and everything that bears on the conduct of life? For you say that the only meaning that, for you, any assertion bears is that a certain experiment has resulted in a certain way: Nothing else but an experiment enters into the meaning. Tell me, then, how can an experiment, in itself, reveal anything more than that something once happened to an individual object and that subsequently some other individual event occurred?

Pragmatist: That question is, indeed, to the purpose—the purpose being to correct any misapprehensions of pragmaticism. You speak of an experiment in itself, emphasizing *"in itself."* You evidently think of each experiment as isolated from every other. It has not, for example, occurred to you, one might venture to surmise, that every connected series of experiments constitutes a single collective experiment. What are the essential ingredients of an experiment? First, of course, an experimenter of flesh and blood. Secondly, a verifiable hypothesis. This is a proposition[3] relating to the universe environing the experimenter, or to some well-known part of it and affirming or denying of this only some experimental possibility or impossibility. The third indispensable ingredient is a sincere doubt in the experimenter's mind as to the truth of the hypothesis.

Passing over several ingredients on which we need not dwell, the purpose, the plan, and the resolve, we come to the act of choice by which the experimenter singles out certain identifiable objects to be operated upon. The next is the external (or quasi-external) act by which he modifies those objects. Next, comes the subsequent *reaction* of the world upon the experimenter in a perception; and finally, his recognition of the teaching of the experiment. While the two chief parts of the event itself are the action and the reaction, yet the unity of essence of the experiment lies in its purpose and plan, the ingredients passed over in the enumeration.

Another thing: in representing the pragmaticist as making rational meaning to consist in an experiment (which you speak of as an event in the past), you strikingly fail to catch his attitude of mind. Indeed, it is not in an experiment, but in *experimental phenomena,* that rational meaning is said to consist. When an experimentalist speaks of a *phenomenon,* such as "Hall's phenomenon," "Zeemann's phenomenon" and its modification, "Michelson's phenomenon," or "the chessboard phenomenon," he does not mean any particular event that did happen to somebody in the dead past, but what *surely will* happen to everybody in the living future who shall fulfill certain conditions. The phenomenon consists in the fact that when an experimentalist shall come to *act* according to a certain scheme that he has in mind, then will something else happen, and shatter the doubts of sceptics, like the celestial fire upon the altar of Elijah.

And do not overlook the fact that the pragmaticist maxim says nothing of single experiments or of single experimental phenomena (for what is conditionally true *in futuro* can hardly be singular), but only speaks of *general kinds* of experimental phenomena. Its adherent does not shrink from speaking of general objects as real, since whatever is true represents a real. Now the laws of nature are true.

The rational meaning of every proposition lies in the future. How so? The meaning of a proposition is itself a proposition. Indeed, it is no other than the very proposition of which it is the meaning: it is a translation of it. But of the myriads of forms into which a proposition may be translated, what is that one which is to be called its very meaning? It is, according to the pragmaticist, that form in which the proposition becomes applicable to human conduct, not in these or those special circumstances, nor when one entertains this or that special design, but that form which is most directly applicable to self-control under every situation, and to every purpose. This is why he locates the meaning in future time; for future conduct is the only conduct that is subject to self-control. But in order that that form of the proposition which is to be taken as its meaning should be applicable to every situation and to every purpose upon which the proposition has any bearing, it must be simply the general description of all the experimental phenomena which the assertion of the proposition virtually predicts. For an experimental phenomenon is the fact asserted by the proposition that action of a certain description will have a certain kind of experimental result; and experimental results are the only results that can affect human conduct. No doubt, some unchanging idea may come to influence a man more than it had done; but only because some experience equivalent to an experiment has brought its truth home to him more intimately than before. Whenever a man acts purposively, he acts under a belief in some experimental phenomenon. Consequently, the sum of the experimental phenomena that a proposition implies makes up its entire bearing upon human conduct. Your question, then, of how a pragmaticist can attribute any meaning to any assertion other than that of a single occurrence is substantially answered.

Questioner: I see that pragmaticism is a thorough-going phenomenalism. Only why should you limit yourself to the phenomena of experimental science rather than embrace all observational science? Experiment, after all, is an uncommunicative informant. It never expiates: it only answers "yes" or "no"; or rather it usually snaps out "No," or, at best only utters an inarticulate grunt for the negation of its "no." The typical experimentalist is not much of an observer. It is the student of natural history to whom nature opens the treasury of her confidence, while she treats the cross-examining experimentalist with the reserve he merits. Why should your phenomenalism sound the meagre jews-harp of experiment rather than the glorious organ of observation?
Pragmaticist: Because pragmaticism is not definable as "thorough-going phenomenalism," although the latter doctrine may be a kind of pragmatism. The *richness* of phenomena lies in their sensuous quality. Pragmaticism does not intend to define the phenomenal equivalents of words and general ideas, but, on the contrary, eliminates their sential element, and endeavors to define the rational purport, and this it finds in the purposive bearing of the word or proposition in question.
Questioner: Well, if you choose so to make Doing the Be-all and the End-all of human life, why do you not make meaning to consist simply in doing? Doing has to be done at a certain time upon a certain object. Individual objects and single events cover all reality, as everybody knows, and as a practicalist ought to be the first to insight. Yet, your meaning, as you have described it, is *general.* Thus, it is of the nature of a mere word and not a reality. You say yourself that your meaning of a proposition is only the same proposition in another dress. But a practical man's meaning is the very thing he means. What do you make to be the meaning of "George Washington"?
Pragmaticist: Forcibly put! A good half dozen of your points must certainly be admitted. It must be admitted, in the first place, that if pragmaticism really made Doing to be the Be-all and the End-all of life, that would be its death. For to say that we live for the mere sake of action, as action, regardless of the thought it carries out, would be to say that there is no such thing as rational purport. Secondly, it must be admitted that every proposition professes to be true of a certain real individual object, often the environing universe. Thirdly, it must be admitted that pragmaticism fails to furnish any translation or meaning of a proper name, or other designation of an individual object. Fourthly, the pragmaticistic meaning is undoubtedly general; and it is equally indisputable that the general is of the nature of a word or sign. Fifthly, it must be admitted that individuals alone exist; and sixthly, it may be admitted that the very meaning of a word or significant object ought to be the very essence of reality of what it signifies. But when those admissions have been unreservedly made, you find the pragmaticist still constrained most earnestly to deny the force of your objection, you ought to infer that there is some consideration that has escaped you. Putting the admissions together, you will perceive that the pragmaticist grants that a proper name (although it is not customary to say that it has a *meaning*), has a certain denotative function peculiar, in each case, to that

name and its equivalents; and that he grants that every assertion contains such a denotative or pointing-out function. In its peculiar individuality, the pragmaticist excludes this from the rational purport of the assertion, although *the like* of it, being common to all assertions, and so, being general and not individual, may enter into the pragmaticistic purport. Whatever exists, *ex-sists,* that is, really acts upon other existents, so obtains a self-identity, and is definitely individual. As to the general, it will be a help to thought to notice that there are two ways of being general. A statue of a soldier on some village monument, in his overcoat and with his musket, is for each of a hundred families the image of its uncle, its sacrifice to the Union. That statue, then, though it is itself single, represents any one man of whom a certain predicate may be true. It is *objectively* general. The word "soldier," whether spoken or written, is general in the same way; while the name, "George Washington," is not so. But each of these two terms remains one and the same noun, whether it be spoken or written, and whenever and wherever it be spoken or written. This noun is not an existent thing: it is a *type,* or *form,* to which objects, both those that are externally existent and those which are imagined, may *conform,* but which none of them can exactly be. This is subjective generality. The pragmaticistic purport is general in both ways.

As to reality, one finds it defined in various ways; but if that principle of terminological ethics that was proposed be accepted, the equivocal language will soon disappear. For *realis* and *realitas* are not ancient words. They were invented to be terms of philosophy in the thirteenth century, and the meaning they were intended to express is perfectly clear. That is *real* which has such and such characters, whether anybody thinks it to have those characters or not. At any rate, that is the sense in which the pragmaticist uses the word. Now, just as conduct controlled by ethical reason tends toward fixing certain habits of conduct, the nature of which (as to illustrate the meaning, peaceable habits and not quarrelsome habits) does not depend upon any accidental circumstances, and *in that sense* may be said to be *destined;* so, thought, controlled by a rational experimental logic, tends to the fixation of certain opinions, equally destined, the nature of which will be the same in the end, however the perversity of thought of whole generations may cause the postponement of the ultimate fixation. If this be so, as every man of us virtually assumes that it is, in regard to each matter the truth of which he seriously discusses, then, according to the adopted definition of "real," the state of things which will be believed in that ultimate opinion is real. But, for the most part, such opinions will be general. Consequently, *some* general objects are real. (Of course, nobody ever thought that *all* generals were real; but the scholastics used to assume that generals were real when they had hardly any, or quite no, experiential evidence to support their assumption; and their fault lay just there, and not in holding that generals could be real.) One is struck with the inexactitude of thought even of analysts of power, when they touch upon modes of being. One will meet, for example, the virtual assumption that what is relative to thought cannot be real. But why not, exactly? *Red* is relative to sight, but the fact that this or that is in that relation to vision that we call being red is not *itself* relative to sight; it is a real fact.

Not only may generals be real, but they may also be *physically efficient,* not in every metaphysical sense, but in the common-sense acception in which human purposes are physically efficient. Aside from metaphysical nonsense, no sane man doubts that if I feel the air in my study to be stuffy, that thought may cause the window to be opened. My thought, be it granted, was an individual event. But what determined it to take the particular determination it did, was in part the general fact that stuffy air is unwholesome, and in part other *Forms,* concerning which Dr. Carus has caused so many men to reflect to advantage—or rather, *by* which, and the general truth concerning which Dr. Carus's mind was determined to the forcible enunciation of so much truth. For truths, on the average, have a greater tendency to get believed than falsities have. Were it otherwise, considering that there are myriads of false hypotheses to account for any given phenomenon, against one sole true one (or if you will have it so, against every true one), the first step toward genuine knowledge must have been next door to a miracle. So, then, when my window was opened, because of the truth that stuffy air is malsain, a physical effort was brought into existence by the efficiency of a general and non-existent truth. This has a droll sound because it is unfamiliar; but exact analysis is with it and not against it; and it has besides, the immense advantage of not blinding us to great facts—such as that the ideas "justice" and "truth" are, notwithstanding the iniquity of the world, the mightiest of the forces that move it. Generality is, indeed, an indispensable ingredient of reality; for mere individual existence or actuality without any regularity whatever is a nullity. Chaos is pure nothing.

That which any true proposition asserts is *real,* in the sense of being as it is regardless of what you or I may think about it. Let this proposition be a general conditional proposition as to the future, and it is a real general such as is calculated really to influence human conduct; and such the pragmaticist holds to be the rational purport of every concept.

Accordingly, the pragmaticist does not make the *summum bonum* to consist in action, but makes it to consist in that process of evolution whereby the existent comes more and more to embody those generals which were just now said to be *destined,* which is what we strive to express in calling them *reasonable.* In its higher stages, evolution takes place more and more largely through self-control, and this gives the pragmaticist a sort of justification for making the rational purport to be general.

There is much more in elucidation of pragmaticism that might be said to advantage, were it not for the dread of fatiguing the reader. It might, for example, have been well to show clearly that the pragmaticist does not attribute any different essential mode of being to an event in the future from that which he would attribute to a similar event in the past, but only that the practical attitude of the thinker toward the two is different. It would also have been well to show that the pragmaticist does not make Forms to be the *only* realities in the world, any more than he makes the reasonable purport of a word to be the only kind of meaning there is. These things are, however, implicitly involved in what has been said. There is only one remark concerning the pragmaticist's conception of the relation of his formula to the first principles of logic which need detain the reader.

Aristotle's definition of universal predication, which is usually designated (like a papal bull or writ of court, from its opening words), as the *Dictum de omni,* may be translated as follows: "We call a predication (be it affirmative or negative), *universal,* when, and only when, there is nothing among the existent individuals to which the subject affirmatively belongs, but to which the predicate will not likewise be referred (affirmatively or negatively, according as the universal predication is affirmative or negative)." The Greek is: λέγομεν δὲ τὸ κατὰ παντὸς κατηγορεῖσθαι ὅταν μηδὲν ᾗ λαβεῖν τῶν τοῦ ὑποκειμένου καθ' οὗ θάτερον οὐ λεχθήσεται καὶ τὸ κατὰ μηδενὸς ὡσαύτως. The important words "existent individuals" have been introduced into the translation (which English idiom would not here permit to be literal); but it is plain that existent individuals were what Aristotle meant. The other departures from literalness only serve to give modern English forms of expression. Now, it is well known that propositions in formal logic go in pairs, the two of one pair being convertible into another by the interchange of the ideas of antecedent and consequent, subject and predicate, etc. The parallelism extends so far that it is often assumed to be perfect; but it is not quite so. The proper mate of this sort to the *Dictum de omni* is the following definition of affirmative predication: We call a predication *affirmative* (be it universal or particular) when, and only when, there is nothing among the sensational effects that belong universally to the predicate which will not be (universally or particularly, according as the affirmative predication is universal or particular), said to belong to the subject. Now, this is substantially the essential proposition of pragmaticism. Of course, its parallelism to the *Dictum de omni* will only be admitted by a person who admits the truth of pragmaticism.

4. Suffer me to add one word more on this point. For if one cares at all to know what the pragmaticist theory consists in, one must understand that there is no other part of it to which the pragmaticist attaches quite as much importance as he does to the recognition in his doctrine of the utter inadequacy of action or volition or even of resolve or actual purpose, as materials out of which to construct a conditional purpose or the concept of conditional purpose. Had a purposed article concerning the principle of continuity and synthetising the ideas of the other articles of a series in the early volumes of *The Monist* ever been written, it would have appeared how, with thorough consistency, that theory involved the recognition that continuity is an indispensable element of reality, and that continuity is simply what generality becomes in the logic of relatives, and thus, like generality, and more than generality, is an affair of thought, and is the essence of thought. Yet even in its truncated condition, an

extra-intelligent reader might discern that the theory of those cosmological articles made reality to consist in something more than feeling and action could supply, inasmuch as the primeval chaos, where those two elements were present, was explicitly shown to be pure nothing. Now, the motive for alluding to that theory just here is, that in this way one can put in a strong light a position which the pragmaticist holds and must hold, whether that cosmological theory be ultimately sustained or exploded, namely, that the third category—the category of thought, representation, triadic relation, mediation, genuine thirdness, thirdness as such—is an essential ingredient of reality, yet does not by itself constitute reality, since this category (which in that cosmology appears as the element of habit) can have no concrete being without action, as a separate object on which to work its government, just as action cannot exist without the immediate being of feeling on which to act. The truth is that pragmaticism is closely allied to the Hegelian absolute idealism, from which, however, it is sundered by its vigorous denial that the third category (which Hegel degrades to a mere stage of thinking) suffices to make the world, or is even so much as self-sufficient. Had Hegel, instead of regarding the first two stages with his smile of contempt, held on to them as independent or distinct elements of the triune Reality, pragmaticists might have looked up to him as the great vindicator of their truth. (Of course, the external trappings of his doctrine are only here and there of much significance.) For pragmaticism belongs essentially to the triadic class of philosophical doctrines, and is much more essentially so than Hegelianism is. (Indeed, in one passage, at least, Hegel alludes to the triadic form of his exposition as to a mere fashion of dress.)

MILFORD, PA., September, 1904.

POSTSCRIPT. During the last five months, I have met with references to several objections to the above opinions, but not having been able to obtain the text of these objections, I do not think I ought to attempt to answer them. If gentlemen who attack either pragmatism in general or the variety of it which I entertain would only send me copies of what they write, more important readers they could easily find, but they could find none who would examine their arguments with a more grateful avidity for truth not yet apprehended, nor any who would be more sensible of their courtesy.

February 9, 1905.

NOTES

1. To show how recent the general use of the word "pragmatism" is, the writer may mention that, to the best of his belief, he never used it in copy for the press before to-day, except by particular request, in *Baldwin's Dictionary.* Toward the end of 1890, when this part of the *Century Dictionary* appeared, he did not deem that the word had sufficient status to appear in that work. But he has used it continually in philosophical conversation since, perhaps, the mid-seventies.
2. It is necessary to say that "belief" is throughout used merely as the name of the contrary

to doubt, without regard to grades of certainty nor to the nature of the proposition held for true, i.e., "believed."

3. The writer, like most English logicians, invariably uses the word *proposition* not as the Germans define their equivalent, *Satz,* as the language-expression of a judgment (*Urtheil*), but as that which is related to any assertion, whether mental and self-addressed or outwardly expressed, just as any possibility is related to its actualisation. The difficulty of the, at best, difficult problem of the essential nature of a Proposition has been increased, for the Germans, by their *Urtheil,* confounding, under one designation, the mental *assertion* with the *assertible.*

WHAT PRAGMATISM MEANS

William James

Some years ago, being with a camping party in the mountains, I returned from a solitary ramble to find everyone engaged in a ferocious metaphysical dispute. The *corpus* of the dispute was a squirrel—a live squirrel supposed to be clinging to one side of a tree-trunk; while over against the tree's opposite side a human being was imagined to stand. This human witness tries to get sight of the squirrel by moving rapidly round the tree, but no matter how fast he goes, the squirrel moves as fast in the opposite direction, and always keeps the tree between himself and the man, so that never a glimpse of him is caught. The resultant metaphysical problem now is this: *Does the man go round the squirrel or not?* He goes round the tree, sure enough, and the squirrel is on the tree; but does he go round the squirrel? In the unlimited leisure of the wilderness, discussion had been worn threadbare. Everyone had taken sides, and was obstinate; and the numbers on both sides were even. Each side, when I appeared, therefore appealed to me to make it a majority. Mindful of the scholastic adage that whenever you meet a contradiction you must make a distinction, I immediately sought and found one, as follows: "Which party is right," I said, "depends on what you *practically mean* by 'going round' the squirrel. If you mean passing from the north of him to the east, then to the south, then to the west, and then to the north of him again, obviously the man does go round him, for he occupies these successive positions. But if on the contrary you mean being first in front of him, then on the right of him, then behind him, then on his left, and finally in front again, it is quite as obvious that the man fails to go round him, for by the compensating movements the squirrel makes, he keeps his belly turned towards the man all the time, and his back turned away. Make the distinction, and there is no occasion for any farther dispute. You are both right and both wrong according as you conceive the verb 'to go round' in one practical fashion or the other."

Altho one or two of the hotter disputants called my speech a shuffling evasion, saying they wanted no quibbling or scholastic hair-splitting, but meant just plain honest English 'round,' the majority seemed to think that the distinction had assuaged the dispute.

I tell this trivial anecdote because it is a peculiarly simple example of what I wish now to speak of as *the pragmatic method.* The pragmatic method is primarily a method of settling metaphysical disputes that otherwise might be interminable. Is the world one or many?—fated or free?—material or spiritual?—here are notions either of which may or may not hold good of the world; and disputes over such notions are unending. The pragmatic method in such cases is to try to interpret each notion by tracing its respective practical consequences. What difference would it practically make to anyone if this notion rather than that notion were true? If no practical difference whatever can be traced, then the alternatives mean practically the same thing, and all dispute is idle. Whenever a dispute is serious, we ought to be able to show some practical difference that must follow from one side or the other's being right.

A glance at the history of the idea will show you still better what pragmatism means. The term is derived from the same Greek word πράγμα, meaning action, from which our words 'practice' and 'practical' come. It was first introduced into philosophy by Mr. Charles Peirce in 1878. In an article entitled 'How to Make Our Ideas Clear,' in the 'Popular Science Monthly' for January of that year[1] Mr. Peirce, after pointing out that our beliefs are really rules for action, said that, to develope a thought's meaning, we need only determine what conduct it is fitted to produce: that conduct is for us its sole significance. And the tangible fact at the root of all our thought-distinctions, however subtle, is that there is no one of them so fine as to consist in anything but a possible difference of practice. To attain perfect clearness in our thoughts of an object, then, we need only consider what conceivable effects of a practical kind the object may involve—what sensations we are to expect from it, and what reactions we must prepare. Our conception of these effects, whether immediate or remote, is then for us the whole of our conception of the object, so far as that conception has positive significance at all.

This is the principle of Peirce, the principle of pragmatism. It lay entirely unnoticed by anyone for twenty years, until I, in an address before Professor Howison's philosophical union at the University of California, brought it forward again and made a special application of it to religion. By that date (1898) the times seemed ripe for its reception. The word 'pragmatism' spread, and at present it fairly spots the pages of the philosophic journals. On all hands we find the 'pragmatic movement' spoken of, sometimes with respect, sometimes with contumely, seldom with clear understanding. It is evident that the term applies itself conveniently to a number of tendencies that hitherto have lacked a collective name, and that it has 'come to stay.'

To take in the importance of Peirce's principle, one must get accustomed to applying it to concrete cases. I found a few years ago that Ostwald, the illustrious Leipzig chemist, had been making perfectly distinct use of the principle of pragmatism in his lectures on the philosophy of science, tho he had not called it by that name.

"All realities influence our practice," he wrote me, "and that influence is their meaning for us. I am accustomed to put questions to my classes in this way: In what respects would the world be different if this alternative or that were true? If I can find nothing that would become different, then the alternative has no sense."

That is, the rival views mean practically the same thing, and meaning, other than practical, there is for us none. Ostwald in a published lecture gives this example of what he means. Chemists have long wrangled over the inner constitution of certain bodies called 'tautomerous.' Their properties seemed equally consistent with the notion that an instable hydrogen atom oscillates inside of them, or that they are instable mixtures of two bodies. Controversy raged; but never was decided. "It would never have begun," says Ostwald, "if the combatants had asked themselves what particular experimental fact could have been made different by one or the other view being correct. For it would then have appeared that no difference of fact could possibly ensue; and the quarrel was as unreal as if, theorizing in primitive times about the raising of dough by yeast, one party should have invoked a 'brownie,' while another insisted on an 'elf' as the true cause of the phenomenon."[2]

It is astonishing to see how many philosophical disputes collapse into insignificance the moment you subject them to this simple test of tracing a concrete consequence. There can *be* no difference anywhere that doesn't *make* a difference elsewhere—no difference in abstract truth that doesn't express itself in a difference in concrete fact and in conduct consequent upon that fact, imposed on somebody, somehow, somewhere and somewhen. The whole function of philosophy ought to be to find out what definite difference it will make to you and me, at definite instants of our life, if this world-formula or that world-formula be the true one.

There is absolutely nothing new in the pragmatic method. Socrates was an adept at it. Aristotle used it methodically. Locke, Berkeley and Hume made momentous contributions to truth by its means. Shadworth Hodgson keeps insisting that realities are only what they are 'known-as.' But these forerunners of pragmatism used it in fragments: they were preluders only. Not until in our time has it generalized itself, become conscious of a universal mission, pretended to a conquering destiny. I believe in that destiny, and I hope I may end by inspiring you with my belief.

Pragmatism represents a perfectly familiar attitude in philosophy, the empiricist attitude, but it represents it, as it seems to me, both in a more radical and in a less objectionable form than it has ever yet assumed. A pragmatist turns his back resolutely and once for all upon a lot of inveterate habits dear to professional philosophers. He turns away from abstraction and insufficiency, from verbal solutions, from bad *a priori* reasons, from fixed principles, closed systems, and pretended absolutes and origins. He turns towards concreteness and adequacy, towards facts, towards action, and towards power. That means the empiricist temper regnant, and the rationalist temper sincerely given up. It means the open air and possibilities of nature, as against dogma, artificiality and the pretence of finality in truth.

At the same time it does not stand for any special results. It is a method only. But the general triumph of that method would mean an enormous change in what I called in my last lecture the 'temperament' of philosophy. Teachers of the ultra-rationalistic type would be frozen out, much as the courtier type is frozen out in republics, as the ultramontane type of priest is frozen out in protestant lands. Science and metaphysics would come much nearer together, would in fact work absolutely hand in hand.

Metaphysics has usually followed a very primitive kind of quest. You know how men have always hankered after unlawful magic, and you know what a great part, in magic, *words* have always played. If you have his name, or the formula of incantation that binds him, you can control the spirit, genie, afrite, or whatever the power may be. Solomon knew the names of all the spirits, and having their names, he held them subject to his will. So the universe has always appeared to the natural mind as a kind of enigma, of which the key must be sought in the shape of some illuminating or power-bringing word or name. That word names the universe's *principle,* and to possess it is, after a fashion, to possess the universe itself. 'God,' 'Matter,' 'Reason,' 'the Absolute,' 'Energy,' are so many solving names. You can rest when you have them. You are at the end of your metaphysical quest.

But if you follow the pragmatic method, you cannot look on any such word as closing your quest. You must bring out of each word its practical cash-value, set it at work within the stream of your experience. It appears less as a solution, then, than as a program for more work, and more particularly as an indication of the ways in which existing realities may be *changed.*

Theories thus become instruments, not answers to enigmas, in which we can rest. We don't lie back upon them, we move forward, and, on occasion, make nature over again by their aid. Pragmatism unstiffens all our theories, limbers them up and sets each one at work. Being nothing essentially new, it harmonizes with many ancient philosophic tendencies. It agrees with nominalism for instance, in always appealing to particulars; with utilitarianism in emphasizing practical aspects; with positivism in its disdain for verbal solutions, useless questions, and metaphysical abstractions.

All these, you see, are *anti-intellectualist* tendencies. Against rationalism as a pretension and a method, pragmatism is fully armed and militant. But, at the outset, at least, it stands for no particular results. It has no dogmas, and no doctrines save its method. As the young Italian pragmatist Papini has well said, it lies in the midst of our theories, like a corridor in a hotel. Innumerable chambers open out of it. In one you may find a man writing an atheistic volume; in the next someone on his knees praying for faith and strength; in a third a chemist investigating a body's properties. In a fourth a system of idealistic metaphysics is being excogitated; in a fifth the impossibility of metaphysics is being shown. But they all own the corridor, and all must pass through it if they want a practicable way of getting into or out of their respective rooms.

No particular results then, so far, but only an attitude of orientation, is what the pragmatic method means. *The attitude of looking away from first things, principles, 'categories,' supposed necessities; and of looking towards last things, fruits, consequences, facts.*

So much for the pragmatic method! You may say that I have been praising it rather than explaining it to you, but I shall presently explain it abundantly enough by showing how it works on some familiar problems. Meanwhile the word pragmatism has come to be used in a still wider sense, as meaning also a certain *theory of truth.* I mean to give a whole lecture to the statement of that theory, after first paving the way, so I can be very brief now. But brevity is hard to follow, so I ask for your redoubled attention for a quarter of an hour. If much remains obscure, I hope to make it clearer in the later lectures.

One of the most successfully cultivated branches of philosophy in our time is what is called inductive logic, the study of the conditions under which our sciences have evolved. Writers on this subject have begun to show a singular unanimity as to what the laws of nature and elements of fact mean, when formulated by mathematicians, physicists and chemists. When the first mathematical, logical and natural uniformities, the first *laws,* were discovered, men were so carried away by the clearness, beauty and simplification that resulted, that they believed themselves to have deciphered authentically the eternal thoughts of the Almighty. His mind also thundered and reverberated in syllogisms. He also thought in conic sections, squares and roots and ratios, and geometrized like Euclid. He made Kepler's laws for the planets to follow; he made velocity increase proportionally to the time in falling bodies; he made the law of the sines for light to obey when refracted; he established the classes, orders, families and genera of plants and animals, and fixed the distances between them. He thought the archetypes of all things, and devised their variations; and when we rediscover any one of these his wondrous institutions, we seize his mind in its very literal intention.

But as the sciences have developed farther, the notion has gained ground that most, perhaps all, of our laws are only approximations. The laws themselves, moreover, have grown so numerous that there is no counting them; and so many rival formulations are proposed in all the branches of science that investigators have become accustomed to the notion that no theory is absolutely a transcript of reality, but that any one of them may from some point of view be useful. Their great use is to summarize old facts and to lead to new ones. They are only a man-made language, a conceptual shorthand, as someone calls them, in which we write our reports of nature; and languages, as is well known, tolerate much choice of expression and many dialects.

Thus human arbitrariness has driven divine necessity from scientific logic. If I mention the names of Sigwart, Mach, Ostwald, Pearson, Milhaud, Poincaré, Duhem, Ruyssen, those of you who are students will easily identify the tendency I speak of, and will think of additional names.

Riding now on the front of this wave of scientific logic Messrs. Schiller and Dewey appear with their pragmatistic account of what truth everywhere signifies. Everywhere, these teachers say, 'truth' in our ideas and beliefs means the same thing that it means in science. It means, they say, nothing but this, *that ideas (which themselves are but parts of our experience) become true just in so far as they help us to get into satisfactory relation with other parts of our experience,* to summarize them and get about among them by conceptual short-cuts instead of following the interminable succession of particular phenomena. Any idea upon which we can ride, so to speak; any idea that will carry us prosperously from any one part of our experience to any other part, linking things satisfactorily, working securely, simplifying, saving labor; is true for just so much, true in so far forth, true *instrumentally.* This is the 'instrumental' view of truth taught so successfully at Chicago, the view that truth in our ideas means their power to 'work,' promulgated so brilliantly at Oxford.

Messrs. Dewey, Schiller and their allies, in reaching this general conception of all truth, have only followed the example of geologists, biologists and philologists. In the establishment of these other sciences, the successful stroke was always to take some simple process actually observable in operation—as denudation by weather, say, or variation from parental type, or change of dialect by incorporation of new words and pronunciations—and then to generalize it, making it apply to all times, and produce great results by summating its effects through the ages.

The observable process which Schiller and Dewey particularly singled out for generalization is the familiar one by which any individual settles into *new opinions.* The process here is always the same. The individual has a stock of old opinions already, but he meets a new experience that puts them to a strain. Somebody contradicts them; or in a reflective moment he discovers that they contradict each other; or he hears of facts with which they are incompatible; or desires arise in him which they cease to satisfy. The result is an inward trouble to which his mind till then had been a stranger, and from which he seeks to escape by modifying his previous mass of opinions. He saves as much of it as he can, for in this matter of belief we are all extreme conservatives. So he tries to change first this opinion, and then that (for they resist change very variously), until at last some new idea comes up which he can graft upon the ancient stock with a minimum of disturbance of the latter, some idea that mediates between the stock and the new experience and runs them into one another most felicitously and expediently.

This new idea is then adopted as the true one. It preserves the older stock of truths with a minimum of modification, stretching them just enough to make them admit the novelty, but conceiving that in ways as familiar as the case leaves possible. An *outrée* explanation, violating all our preconceptions, would never pass for a true account of a novelty. We should scratch round industriously till we found something less eccentric. The most violent revolutions in an individual's beliefs leave most of his old order standing. Time and space, cause and effect, nature and history, and one's own biography remain untouched. New truth is always a go-between, a smoother-over of transitions. It marries old opinion to new fact so as ever to show a minimum of jolt, a maximum of continuity. We hold a theory true just in proportion to its success in solving this 'problem of maxima and minima.' But success in solving this problem is eminently a matter of approximation. We say this theory solves it on the whole more satisfactorily than that theory; but that means more satisfactorily to ourselves, and individuals will emphasize their points of satisfaction differently. To a certain degree, therefore, everything here is plastic.

The point I now urge you to observe particularly is the part played by the older truths. Failure to take account of it is the source of much of the unjust criticism leveled against pragmatism. Their influence is absolutely controlling. Loyalty to them is the first principle—in most cases it is the only principle; for by far the most usual way of handling phenomena so novel that they would make for a serious rearrangement of our preconceptions is to ignore them altogether, or to abuse those who bear witness for them.

You doubtless wish examples of this process of truth's growth, and the only trouble is their superabundance. The simplest case of new truth is of course the mere numerical addition of new kinds of facts, or of new single facts of old kinds, to our experience—an addition that involves no alteration in the old beliefs. Day follows day, and its contents are simply added. The new contents themselves are not true, they simply *come* and *are*. Truth is *what we say about* them, and when we say that they have come, truth is satisfied by the plain additive formula.

But often the day's contents oblige a rearrangement. If I should now utter piercing shrieks and act like a maniac on this platform, it would make many of you revise your ideas as to the probable worth of my philosophy. 'Radium' came the other day as part of the day's content, and seemed for a moment to contradict our ideas of the whole order of nature, that order having come to be identified with what is called the conservation of energy. The mere sight of radium paying heat away indefinitely out of its own pocket seemed to violate that conservation. What to think? If the radiations from it were nothing but an escape of unsuspected 'potential' energy, pre-existent inside of the atoms, the principle of conservation would be saved. The discovery of 'helium' as the radiation's outcome, opened a way to this belief. So Ramsay's view is generally held to be true, because, altho it extends our old ideas of energy, it causes a minimum of alteration in their nature.

I need not multiply instances. A new opinion counts as 'true' just in proportion as it gratifies the individual's desire to assimilate the novel in his experience to his beliefs in stock. It must both lean on old truth and grasp new fact; and its success (as I said a moment ago) in doing this, is a matter for the individual's appreciation. When old truth grows, then, by new truth's addition, it is for subjective reasons. We are in the process and obey the reasons. That new idea is truest which performs most felicitously its function of satisfying our double urgency. It makes itself true, gets itself classed as true, by the way it works; grafting itself then upon the ancient body of truth, which thus grows much as a tree grows by the activity of a new layer of cambium.

Now Dewey and Schiller proceed to generalize this observation and to apply it to the most ancient parts of truth. They also once were plastic. They also were called true for human reasons. They also mediated between still earlier truths and what in those days were novel observations. Purely objective truth, truth in whose establishment the function of giving human satisfaction in marrying previous parts of experience with newer parts played no rôle whatever, is nowhere to be found. The reasons why we call things true is the reason why they *are* true, for 'to be true' *means* only to perform this marriage-function.

The trail of the human serpent is thus over everything. Truth independent; truth that we *find* merely; truth no longer malleable to human need; truth incorrigible, in a word; such truth exists indeed superabundantly—or is supposed to exist by rationalistically minded thinkers; but then it means only the dead heart of the living tree, and its being there means only that truth also has its paleontology and its 'prescription,' and may grow stiff with years of veteran service and petrified in men's regard by sheer antiquity. But how plastic even the oldest truths nevertheless really are has been vividly shown in our day by the transformation of logical and mathematical ideas, a transformation which seems even to be invading physics. The ancient formulas are reinterpreted as special expressions of much wider principles, principles that our ancestors never got a glimpse of in their present shape and formulation.

Mr. Schiller still gives to all this view of truth the name of 'Humanism,' but, for this doctrine too, the name of pragmatism seems fairly to be in the ascendant, so I will treat it under the name of pragmatism in these lectures.

Such then would be the scope of pragmatism—first, a method; and second, a genetic theory of what is meant by truth. And these two things must be our future topics.

What I have said of the theory of truth will, I am sure, have appeared obscure and unsatisfactory to most of you by reason of its brevity. I shall make amends for that hereafter. In a lecture on 'common sense' I shall try to show what I mean by truths grown petrified by antiquity. In another lecture I shall expatiate on the idea that our thoughts become true in proportion as they successfully exert their go-between function. In a third I shall show how hard it is to discriminate subjective from objective factors in Truth's development. You may not follow me wholly in these lectures; and if you do, you may not wholly agree with me. But you will, I know, regard me at least as serious, and treat my effort with respectful consideration.

You will probably be surprised to learn, then, that Messrs. Schiller's and Dewey's theories have suffered a hailstorm of contempt and ridicule. All rationalism has risen against them. In influential quarters Mr. Schiller, in particular, has been treated like an impudent schoolboy who deserves a spanking. I should not mention this, but for the fact that it throws so much sidelight upon that rationalistic temper to which I have opposed the temper of pragmatism. Pragmatism is uncomfortable away from facts. Rationalism is comfortable only in the presence of abstractions. This pragmatist talk about truths in the plural, about their utility and satisfactoriness, about the success with which they 'work,' etc., suggests to the typical intellectualist mind a sort of coarse lame second-rate makeshift article of truth. Such truths are not real truth. Such tests are merely subjective. As against this, objective truth must be something non-utilitarian, haughty, refined, remote, august, exalted. It must be an absolute correspondence of our thoughts with an equally absolute reality. It must be what we *ought* to think, unconditionally. The conditioned ways in which we *do* think are so much irrelevance and matter for psychology. Down with psychology, up with logic, in all this question!

See the exquisite contrast of the types of mind! The pragmatist clings to facts and concreteness, observes truth at its work in particular cases, and generalizes. Truth, for him, becomes a class-name for all sorts of definite working-values in experience. For the rationalist it remains a pure abstraction, to the bare name of which we must defer. When the pragmatist undertakes to show in detail just *why* we must defer, the rationalist is unable to recognize the concretes from which his own abstraction is taken. He accuses us of *denying* truth; whereas we have only sought to trace exactly why people follow it and always ought to follow it. Your typical ultra-abstractionist fairly shudders at concreteness: other things equal, he positively prefers the pale and spectral. If the two universes were offered, he would always choose the skinny outline rather than the rich thicket of reality. It is so much purer, clearer, nobler.

I hope that as these lectures go on, the concreteness and closeness to facts of the pragmatism which they advocate may be what approves itself to you as its most satisfactory peculiarity. It only follows here the example of the sister-sciences, interpreting the unobserved by the observed. It brings old and new harmoniously together. It converts the absolutely empty notion of a static relation of 'correspondence' (what that may mean we must ask later) between our minds and reality, into that of a rich and active commerce (that anyone may follow in detail and understand) between particular thoughts of ours, and the great universe of other experiences in which they play their parts and have their uses.

But enough of this at present? The justification of what I say must be postponed. I wish now to add a word in further explanation of the claim I made at our last meeting, that pragmatism may be a happy harmonizer of empiricist ways of thinking, with the more religious demands of human beings.

Men who are strongly of the fact-loving temperament, you may remember me to have said, are liable to be kept at a distance by the small sympathy with facts which that philosophy from the present-day fashion of idealism offers them. It is far too intellectualistic. Old fashioned theism was bad enough, with its notion of God as an exalted monarch, made up of a lot of unintelligible or preposterous 'attributes'; but, so long as it held strongly by the argument from design, it kept some touch with concrete realities. Since, however, darwinism has once for all displaced design from the minds of the 'scientific,' theism has lost that foothold; and some kind of an immanent or pantheistic deity working *in* things rather than above them is, if any, the kind recommended to our contemporary imagination. Aspirants to a philosophic religion turn, as a rule, more hopefully nowadays towards idealistic pantheism than towards the older dualistic theism, in spite of the fact that the latter still counts able defenders.

But, as I said in my first lecture, the brand of pantheism offered is hard for them to assimilate if they are lovers of facts, or empirically minded. It is the absolutistic brand, spurning the dust and reared upon pure logic. It keeps no connexion whatever with concreteness. Affirming the Absolute Mind, which is its substitute for God, to be the rational presupposition of all particulars of fact, whatever they may be, it remains supremely indifferent to what the particular facts in our world actually are. Be they what they may, the Absolute will father them. Like the sick lion in Esop's fable, all footprints lead into his den, but *nulla vestigia retrorsum.* You cannot redescend into the world of particulars by the Absolute's aid, or deduce any necessary consequences of detail important for your life from your idea of his nature. He gives you indeed the assurance that all is well with *Him,* and for his eternal way of thinking; but thereupon he leaves you to be finitely saved by your own temporal devices.

Far be it from me to deny the majesty of this conception, or its capacity to yield religious comfort to a most respectable class of minds. But from the human point of view, no one can pretend that it doesn't suffer from the faults of remoteness and abstractness. It is eminently a product of what I have ventured to call the rationalistic temper. It disdains empiricism's needs. It substitutes a pallid outline for the real world's richness. It is dapper; it is noble in the bad sense, in the sense in which to be noble is to be inapt for humble service. In this real world of sweat and dirt, it seems to me that when a view of things is 'noble,' that ought to count as a presumption against its truth, and as a philosophic disqualification. The prince of darkness may be a gentleman, as we are told he is, but whatever the God of earth and heaven is, he can surely be no gentleman. His menial services are needed in the dust of our human trials, even more than his dignity is needed in the empyrean.

Now pragmatism, devoted tho she be to facts, has no such materialistic bias as ordinary empiricism labors under. Moreover, she has no objection whatever to the realizing of abstractions, so long as you get about among particulars with their aid and they actually carry you somewhere. Interested in no conclusions but those which our minds and our experiences work out together, she has no *a priori* prejudices against theology. *If theological ideas prove to have a value for concrete life, they will be true, for pragmatism, in the sense of being good for so much. For how much more they are true, will depend entirely on their relations to the other truths that also have to be acknowledged.*

What I said just now about the Absolute of transcendental idealism is a case in point. First, I called it majestic and said it yielded religious comfort to a class of minds, and then I accused it of remoteness and sterility. But so far as it affords such comfort, it surely is not sterile; it has that amount of value; it performs a concrete function. As a good pragmatist, I myself ought to call the Absolute true 'in so far forth,' then; and I unhesitatingly now do so.

But what does *true in so far forth* mean in this case? To answer, we need only apply the pragmatic method. What do believers in the Absolute mean by saying that their belief affords them comfort? They mean that since in the Absolute finite evil is 'overruled' already, we may, therefore, whenever we wish, treat the temporal as if it were potentially the eternal, be sure that we can trust its outcome, and, without sin, dismiss our fear and drop the worry of our finite responsibility. In short, they mean that we have a right ever and anon to take a moral holiday, to let the world wag in its own way, feeling that its issues are in better hands than ours and are none of our business.

The universe is a system of which the individual members may relax their anxieties occasionally, in which the don't-care mood is also right for men, and moral holidays in order—that, if I mistake not, is part, at least, of what the Absolute is 'known-as,' that is the great difference in our particular experiences which his being true makes for us, that is part of his cash-value when he is pragmatically interpreted. Farther than that the ordinary lay-reader in philosophy who thinks favorably of absolute idealism does not venture to sharpen his conceptions. He can use the Absolute for so much, and so much is very precious. He is pained at hearing you speak incredulously of the Absolute, therefore, and disregards your criticisms because they deal with aspects of the conception that he fails to follow.

If the Absolute means this, and means no more than this, who can possibly deny the truth of it? To deny it would be to insist that men should never relax, and that holidays are never in order.

I am well aware of how odd it must seem to some of you to hear me say that an idea is 'true' so long as to believe it is profitable to our lives. That it is *good,* for as much as it profits, you will gladly admit. If what we do by its aid is good, you will allow the idea itself to be good in so far forth, for we are the better for possessing it. But is it not a strange misuse of the word 'truth,' you will say, to call ideas also 'true' for this reason?

To answer this difficulty fully is impossible at this stage of my account. You touch here upon the very central point of Messrs. Schiller's, Dewey's and my own doctrine of truth, which I cannot discuss with detail until my sixth lecture. Let me now say only this, that truth is *one species of good,* and not, as is usually supposed, a category distinct from good, and co-ordinate with it. *The true is the name of whatever proves itself to be good in the way of belief, and good, too, for definite, assignable reasons.* Surely you must admit this, that if there were *no* good for life in true ideas, or if the knowledge of them were positively disadvantageous and false ideas the only useful ones, then the current notion that truth is divine and precious, and its pursuit a duty, could never have grown up or become a dogma. In a world like that, our duty would be to *shun* truth, rather. But in this world, just as certain foods are not only agreeable to our taste, but good for our teeth, our stomach and our tissues; so certain ideas are not only agreeable to think about, or agreeable as supporting other ideas that we are fond of, but they are also helpful in life's practical struggles. If there be any life that it is really better we should lead, and if there be any idea which, if believed in, would help us to lead that life, then it would be really *better for us* to believe in that idea, *unless, indeed, belief in it incidentally clashed with other greater vital benefits.*

'What would be better for us to believe'! This sounds very like a definition of truth. It comes very near to saying 'what we *ought* to believe': and in *that* definition none of you would find any oddity. Ought we ever not to believe what it is *better for us* to believe? And can we then keep the notion of what is better for us, and what is true for us, permanently apart?

Pragmatism says no, and I fully agree with her. Probably you also agree, as far as the abstract statement goes, but with a suspicion that if we practically did believe everything that made for good in our own personal lives, we should be found indulging all kinds of fancies about this world's affairs, and all kinds of sentimental superstitions about a world hereafter. Your suspicion here is undoubtedly well founded, and it is evident that something happens when you pass from the abstract to the concrete, that complicates the situation.

I said just now that what is better for us to believe is true *unless the belief incidentally clashes with some other vital benefit.* Now in real life what vital benefits is any particular belief of ours most liable to clash with? What indeed except the vital benefits yielded by *other beliefs* when these prove incompatible with the first ones? In other words, the greatest enemy of any one of our truths may be the rest of our truths. Truths have once for all this desperate instinct of self-preservation and of desire to extinguish whatever contradicts them. My belief in the Absolute, based on the good it does me, must run the gauntlet of all my other beliefs. Grant that it may be true in giving me a moral holiday. Nevertheless, as I conceive it,—and let me speak now confidentially, as it were, and merely in my own private person,—it clashes with other truths of mine whose benefits I hate to give up on its account. It happens to be associated with a kind of logic of which I am the enemy, I find that it entangles me in metaphysical paradoxes that are inacceptable, etc., etc. But as I have enough trouble in life already without adding the trouble of carrying these intellectual inconsistencies, I personally just give up the Absolute. I just *take* my moral holidays; or else as a professional philosopher, I try to justify them by some other principle.

If I could restrict my notion of the Absolute to its bare holiday-giving value, it wouldn't clash with my other truths. But we cannot easily thus restrict our hypotheses. They carry supernumerary features, and these it is that clash so. My disbelief in the Absolute means then disbelief in those other supernumerary features, for I fully believe in the legitimacy of taking moral holidays.

You see by this what I meant when I called pragmatism a mediator and reconciler and said, borrowing the word from Papini, that she 'unstiffens' our theories. She has in fact no prejudices whatever, no obstructive dogmas, no rigid canons of what shall count as proof. She is completely genial. She will entertain any hypothesis, she will consider any evidence. It follows that in the religious field she is at a great advantage both over positivistic empiricism, with its anti-theological bias, and over religious rationalism, with its exclusive interest in the remote, the noble, the simple, and the abstract in the way of conception.

In short, she widens the field of search for God. Rationalism sticks to logic and the empyrean. Empiricism sticks to the external senses. Pragmatism is willing to take anything, to follow either logic or the senses, and to count the humblest and most personal experiences. She will count mystical experiences if they have practical consequences. She will take a God who lives in the very dirt of private fact—if that should seem a likely place to find him.

Her only test of probable truth is what works best in the way of leading us, what fits every part of life best and combines with the collectivity of experience's demands, nothing being omitted. If theological ideas should do this, if the notion of God, in particular, should prove to do it, how could pragmatism possibly deny God's existence? She could see no meaning in treating as 'not true' a notion that was pragmatically so successful. What other kind of truth could there be, for her, than all this agreement with concrete reality?

In my last lecture I shall return again to the relations of pragmatism with religion. But you see already how democratic she is. Her manners are as various and flexible, her resources as rich and endless, and her conclusions as friendly as those of mother nature.

NOTES

1. Translated in the *Revue Philosophique* for January, 1879 (vol. vii).
2. 'Theorie und Praxis,' *Zeitsch, des Oesterreichischen Ingenieur u. ArchitectenVereines,* 1905, Nr. 4 u. 6. I find a still more radical pragmatism than Ostwald's in an address by Professor W. S. Franklin: "I think that the sickliest notion of physics, even if a student gets it, is that it is 'the science of masses, molecules and the ether.' And I think that the healthiest notion, even if a student does not wholly get it, is that physics is the science of the ways of taking hold of bodies and pushing them!" (*Science,* January 2, 1903.)

THE DEVELOPMENT OF AMERICAN PRAGMATISM

John Dewey

The purpose of this article is to define the principal theories of the philosophical movements known under the names of Pragmatism, Instrumentalism, or Experimentalism. To do this we must trace their historical development; for this method seems to present the simplest way of comprehending these movements and at the same time avoids certain current misunderstandings of their doctrines and of their aims.

The origin of Pragmatism goes back to Charles Sanders Peirce, the son of one of the most celebrated mathematicians of the United States, and himself very proficient in the science of mathematics; he is one of the founders of the modern symbolic logic of relations. Unfortunately Peirce was not at all a systematic writer and never expounded his ideas in a single system. The pragmatic method which he developed applies only to a very narrow and limited universe of discourse. After William James had extended the scope of the method, Peirce wrote an exposition of the origin of pragmatism as he had first conceived it; it is from this exposition that we take the following passages.

The term "pragmatic," contrary to the opinion of those who regard pragmatism as an exclusively American conception, was suggested to him by the study of Kant. In the "Metaphysics of Morals" Kant established a distinction between *pragmatic* and *practical.* The latter term applies to moral laws which Kant regards as *a priori,* whereas the former term applies to the rules of art and technique which are based on experience and are applicable to experience. Peirce, who was an empiricist, with the habits of mind, as he put it, of the laboratory, consequently refused to call his system "practicalism," as some of his friends suggested. As a logician he was interested in the art and technique of real thinking, and especially as far as pragmatic method is concerned in the art of making concepts clear, or of construing adequate and effective definitions in accord with the spirit of scientific method.

Following his own words, for a person "who still thought in Kantian terms most readily, *'praktisch'* and *'pragmatisch'* were as far apart as the two poles; the former belonging in a region of thought where no mind of the experimental type can ever make sure of solid ground under his feet, the latter expressing relation to some definite human purpose. Now quite the most striking feature of the new theory was its recognition of an inseparable connection between rational cognition and rational purpose."[1]

In alluding to the experimental type of mind, we are brought to the exact

Reprinted by permission of Southern Illinois University Press, from John Dewey, "The Development of American Pragmatism," in *John Dewey, the Later Works, 1925–1953,* Volume 2: 1925–1927, ed. Jo Ann Boydston, textual ed. Bridget A. Walsh, pp. 3–21. Carbondale and Edwardsville, Illinois: Southern Illinois University Press, 1984.

meaning given by Peirce to the word "pragmatic." In speaking of an experimentalist as a man whose intelligence is formed in the laboratory, he said: "Whatever assertion you may make to him, he will either understand as meaning that if a given prescription for an experiment ever can be and ever is carried out in act, an experience of a given description will result, or else he will see no sense at all in what you say." And thus Peirce developed the theory that "the rational purport of a word or other expression, lies exclusively in its conceivable bearing upon the conduct of life; so that, since obviously nothing that might not result from experiment can have any direct bearing upon conduct, if one can define accurately all the conceivable experimental phenomena which the affirmation or denial of a concept could imply, one will have therein a complete definition of the concept."[2]

The essay in which Peirce developed his theory bears the title: *How to make our Ideas Clear.*[3] There is a remarkable similarity here to Kant's doctrine in the efforts which he made to interpret the universality of concepts in the domain of experience in the same way in which Kant established the law of practical reason in the domain of the *a priori.* "The rational meaning of every proposition lies in the future. . . . But of the myriads of forms into which a proposition may be translated, what is that one which is to be called its very meaning? It is, according to the pragmatist, that form in which the proposition becomes applicable to human conduct, not in these or those special circumstances, nor when one entertains this or that special design, but that form which is most directly applicable to self-control under every situation, and to every purpose."[4] So also, "the pragmatist does not make the *summum bonum* to consist in action, but makes it to consist in that process of evolution whereby the existent comes more and more to embody generals. . . ."[5]—in other words—the process whereby the existent becomes, with the aid of action, a body of rational tendencies or of habits generalized as much as possible. These statements of Peirce are quite conclusive with respect to two errors which are commonly committed in regard to the ideas of the founder of pragmatism. It is often said of pragmatism that it makes action the end of life. It is also said of pragmatism that it subordinates thought and rational activity to particular ends of interest and profit. It is true that the theory according to Peirce's conception implies essentially a certain relation to action, to human conduct. But the rôle of action is that of an intermediary. In order to be able to attribute a meaning to concepts, one must be able to apply them to existence. Now it is by means of action that this application is made possible. And the modification of existence which results from this application constitutes the true meaning of concepts.

Pragmatism is, therefore, far from being that glorification of action for its own sake which is regarded as the peculiar characteristic of American life. It is also to be noted that there is a scale of possible applications of concepts to existence, and hence a diversity of meanings. The greater the extension of the concepts, the more they are freed from the restrictions which limit them to particular cases, the more is it possible for us to attribute the most general meaning to a term. Thus the theory of Peirce is opposed to every restriction of the meaning of a concept to the achievement of a particular end, and still more to a personal aim. It is still more strongly opposed to the idea that reason or thought should be reduced to being a servant of any interest which is pecuniary or too narrow. This theory was American in its origin in so far as it insisted on the necessity of human conduct and the fulfillment of some aim in order to clarify thought. But at the same time, it disapproves of those aspects of American life which make action an end in itself, and which conceive ends too narrowly and too practically. In considering a system of philosophy in its relation to national factors it is necessary to keep in mind not only the aspects of life which are incorporated in the system, but also the aspects against which the system is a protest. There never was a philosopher who has merited the name for the simple reason that he glorified the tendencies and characteristics of his social environment; just as it is also true that there never has been a philosopher who has not seized upon certain aspects of the life of his time and idealized them.

The work commenced by Peirce was continued by William James. In one sense James narrowed the application of Peirce's pragmatic method, but at the same time he extended it. The articles which Peirce wrote in 1878 commanded almost no attention from philosophical circles, which were then under the dominating influence of the neokantian idealism of Green, of Caird, and of the Oxford School, excepting those circles in which the Scottish philosophy of common sense maintained its supremacy. In 1898 James inaugurated the new pragmatic movement in an address entitled, *"Philosophical Conceptions and Practical Results,"* later reprinted in the volume, *"Collected Essays and Reviews."* Even in this early study one can easily notice the presence of those two tendencies to restrict and at the same time to extend early pragmatism. After having quoted the psychological remark of Peirce that "beliefs are really rules for action, and the whole function of thinking is but one step in the production of habits of action," and that every idea which we frame for ourselves of an object is really an idea of the possible effects of that object, he expressed the opinion that all these principles could be expressed more broadly than Peirce expressed them. "The ultimate test for us of what a truth means is indeed the conduct it dictates or inspires. But it inspires that conduct because it first foretells some particular turn to our experience which shall call for just that conduct from us. And I should prefer to express Peirce's principle by saying that the effective meaning of any philosophic proposition can always be brought down to some particular consequence, in our future practical experience, whether active or passive; the point lying rather in the fact that the experience must be particular, than in the fact that it must be active."[6] In an essay written in 1908 James repeats this statement and states that whenever he employs the term "the practical," he means by it, "the distinctively concrete, the individual, the particular and effective as opposed to the abstract, general and inert—'Pragmata' are things in their plurality—particular consequences can perfectly well be of a theoretic nature."[7]

William James alluded to the development which he gave to Peirce's expression of the principle. In one sense one can say that he enlarged the bearing of the principle by the substitution of particular consequences for the general rule or method applicable to future experience. But in another sense this substitution limited the application of the principle since it destroyed the importance attached by Peirce to the greatest possible application of the rule, or the habit of conduct—its extension to universality. That is to say, William James was much more of a nominalist than Peirce.

One can notice an extension of pragmatism in the above passage. James there alludes to the use of a method of determining the meaning of truth. Since truth is a term and has consequently a meaning, this extension is a legitimate application of pragmatic method. But it should be remarked that here this method serves only to make clear the meaning of the term, and has nothing to do with the truth of a particular judgment. The principal reason which led James to give a new color to pragmatic method was that he was preoccupied with applying the method to determine the meaning of philosophical problems and questions and that moreover, he chose to submit to examination philosophical notions of a theological or religious nature. He wished to establish a criterion which would enable one to determine whether a given philosophical question has an authentic and vital meaning or whether, on the contrary, it was trivial and purely verbal; and in the former case, what interests were at stake, when one accepts and affirms one or the other of two theses in dispute. Peirce was above all a logician; whereas James was an educator and wished to force the general public to realize that certain problems, certain philosophical debates have a real importance for mankind, because the beliefs which they bring into play lead to very different modes of conduct. If this important distinction is not grasped, it is impossible to understand the majority of the ambiguities and errors which belong to the later period in the pragmatic movement.

James took as an example the controversy between theism and materialism. It follows from this principle that if the course of the world is considered as completed, it is equally legitimate to assert that God or matter was its cause. Whether one way or the other, the facts are what they are, and it is they which determine whatever meaning is to be given to their cause. Consequently the name which we can give to this cause is entirely arbitrary. It is entirely different if we take the future into account. God then has the meaning of a power concerned with assuring the final triumph of ideal and spiritual values, and matter becomes a power indifferent to the triumph or defeat of these values. And our life takes a different direction according as we adopt one or the other of these alternatives. In the lectures on pragmatism published in 1907, he applies the same criticism to the philosophical problem of the One and the Many, that is to say of Monism and Pluralism, as well as to other questions. Thus he shows that Monism is equivalent to a rigid universe where everything is fixed and immutably united to others, where indetermination, free choice, novelty, and the unforeseen in experience have no place; a universe which demands the sacrifice of the concrete and complex diversity of things to the simplicity and nobility of an architectural structure. In what concerns our beliefs, Monism demands a rationalistic temperament leading to a fixed and dogmatic attitude. Pluralism, on the other hand, leaves room for contingence, liberty, novelty, and gives complete liberty of action to the empirical method, which can be greatly extended. It accepts unity where it finds it, but it does not attempt to force the vast diversity of events and things into a single rational mold.

From the point of view of an educator or of a student or, if you will, of those who are thoroughly interested in these problems, in philosophical discussions and controversies, there is no reason for contesting the value of this application of pragmatic method, but it is no less important to determine the nature of this application. It affords a means of discovering the implications for human life of philosophical conceptions which are often treated as of no importance and of a purely dialectical nature. It furnishes a criterion for determining the vital implications of beliefs which present themselves as alternatives in any theory. Thus as he himself said "the whole function of philosophy ought to be to find the characteristic influences which you and I would undergo at a determinate moment of our lives, if one or the other formula of the universe were true." However, in saying that the whole function of philosophy has this aim, it seems that he is referring rather to the teaching than to the construction of philosophy. For such a statement implies that the world formulas have already all been made, and that the necessary work of producing them has already been finished, so that there remains only to define the consequences which are reflected in life by the acceptance of one or the other of these formulas as true.

From the point of view of Peirce, the object of philosophy would be rather to give a fixed meaning to the universe by formulas which correspond to our attitudes or our most general habits of response to the environment; and this generality depends on the extension of the applicability of these formulas to specific future events. The meaning of concepts of "matter" and of "God" must be fixed before we can even attempt to reach an understanding concerning the value of our belief in these terms. Materialism would signify that the world demands on our part a single kind of constant and general habits; and God would signify the demand for another type of habits; the difference between materialism and theism would be tantamount to the difference in the habits required to face all the detailed facts of the universe. The world would be one in so far as it would be possible for us to form a single habit of action which would take account of all future existences and would be applicable to them. It would be many in so far as it is necessary for us to form several habits, differing from each other and irreducible to each other, in order to be able to meet the events in the world and control them. In short, Peirce wrote as a logician and James as a humanist.

William James accomplished a new advance in Pragmatism by his theory of the will to believe, or as he himself later called it, the right to believe. The discovery of the fundamental consequences of one or another belief has without fail a certain influence on that belief itself. If a man cherished novelty, risk, opportunity and a variegated esthetic reality, he will certainly reject any belief in Monism, when he clearly perceives the import of this system. But if, from the very start, he is attracted by esthetic harmony, classic proportions, fixity even to the extent of absolute security and logical coherence, it is quite natural that he should put faith in Monism. Thus William James took into account those motives of instinctive sympathy which play a greater rôle in our choice of a philosophic system than formal reasonings; and he thought that we would be rendering a service to the cause of philosophical sincerity if we would openly recognize the motives which inspire us. He also maintained the thesis that the greater part of philosophic problems and especially those which touch on religious fields are of such a nature that they are not susceptible of decisive evidence one way or the other. Consequently he claimed the right of a man to choose his beliefs not only in the presence of proofs or conclusive facts, but also in the absence of all evidence of this nature, and above all when he is forced to choose between one meaning or another, or when by refusing to choose, his refusal is itself equivalent to a choice. The theory of the will to believe gives rise to misunderstandings and even to ridicule; and therefore it is necessary to understand clearly in what way James used it. We are always obliged to act in any case; our actions and with them their consequences actually change according to the beliefs which we have chosen. Moreover it may be that, in order to discover the proofs which will ultimately be the intellectual justification of certain beliefs—the belief in freedom, for example, or the belief in God—it is necessary to begin to act in accordance with this belief.

In his lectures on Pragmatism, and in his volume of essays bearing the title *"The Meaning of Truth,"* which appeared in 1909, James extended the use of the pragmatic method to the problem of the nature of truth. So far we have considered the pragmatic method as an instrument in determining the meaning of words and the vital importance of philosophic beliefs. Now and then we have made allusion to the future consequences which are implied. James showed, among other things, that in certain philosophic conceptions, the affirmation of certain beliefs could be justified by means of the nature of their consequences, or by the differences which these beliefs make in existence. But then why not push the argument to the point of maintaining that the meaning of truth in general is determined by its consequences? We must not forget here that James was an empiricist before he was a pragmatist, and repeatedly stated that pragmatism is merely empiricism pushed to its legitimate conclusions. From a general point of view, the pragmatic attitude consists in "looking away from first things, principles, 'categories,' supposed necessities; and of looking towards last things, fruits, consequences, facts." It is only one step further to apply the pragmatic method to the problem of truth. In the natural sciences there is a tendency to identify truth in any particular case with a verification. The verification of a theory, or of a concept, is carried on by the observation of particular facts. Even the most scientific and harmonious physical theory is merely an hypothesis until its implications, deduced by mathematical reasoning or by any other kind of inference, are verified by observed facts. What direction therefore, must an empirical philosopher take who wishes to arrive at a definition of truth by means of an empirical method? He must, if he wants to apply this method, and without bringing in for the present the pragmatic formula, first find particular cases from which he then generalizes. It is therefore in submitting conceptions to the control of experience, in the process of verifying them, that one finds examples of what is called truth. Therefore the philosopher who applies this empirical method, without the least prejudice in favor of pragmatic doctrine, can be brought to conclude that truth "means" verification, or if one prefers, that verification either actual or possible, is the definition of truth.

In combining this conception of empirical method with the theory of pragmatism, we come upon other important philosophical results. The classic theories of truth in terms of the coherence or compatibility of terms, and of the correspondence of an idea with a thing, hereby receive a new interpretation. A merely mental coherence without experimental verification does not enable us to get beyond the realm of hypothesis. If a notion or a theory makes pretense of corresponding to reality or to the facts, this pretense cannot be put to the test and confirmed or refuted except by causing it to pass over into the realm of action and by noting the results which it yields in the form of the concrete observable facts to which this notion or theory leads. If, in acting upon this notion, we are brought to the fact which it implies or which it demands, then this notion is true. A theory corresponds to the facts because it leads to the facts which are its consequences, by the intermediary of experience. And from this consideration the pragmatic generalization is drawn that all knowledge is prospective in its results, except in the case where notions and theories after having been first prospective in their application, have already been tried out and verified. Theoretically, however, even such verifications or truths could not be absolute. They would be based upon practical or moral certainty, but they are always subject to being corrected by unforeseen future consequences or by observed facts which had been disregarded. Every proposition concerning truths is really in the last analysis hypothetical and provisional, although a large number of these propositions have been so frequently verified without fail that we are justified in using them as if they were absolutely true. But logically absolute truth is an ideal which cannot be realized, at least not until all the facts have been registered, or as James says "bagged," and until it is no longer possible to make other observations and other experiences.

Pragmatism, thus, presents itself as an extension of historical empiricism with this fundamental difference, that it does not insist upon antecedent phenomena but upon consequent phenomena; not upon the precedents but upon the possibilities of action, and this change in point of view is almost revolutionary in its consequences. An empiricism which is content with repeating facts already past has no place for possibility and for liberty. It cannot find room for general conceptions or ideas, at least no more than to consider them as summaries or records. But when we take the point of view of pragmatism we see that general ideas have a very different rôle to play than that of reporting and registering past experiences. They are the bases for organizing future observations and experiences. Whereas, for empiricism, in a world already constructed and determined, reason or general thought has no other meaning than that of summing up particular cases, in a world where the future is not a mere word, where theories, general notions, rational ideas have consequences for action, reason necessarily has a constructive function. Nevertheless the conceptions of reasoning have only a secondary interest in comparison with the reality of facts, since they must be confronted with concrete observations.[8]

Pragmatism thus has a metaphysical implication. The doctrine of the value of consequences leads us to take the future into consideration. And this taking into consideration of the future takes us to the conception of a universe whose evolution is not finished, of a universe which is still, in James' term, "in the making," "in the process of becoming," of a universe up to a certain point still plastic.

Consequently reason, or thought, in its more general sense, has a real, though limited function, a creative, constructive function. If we form general ideas and if we put them in action, consequences are produced which could not be produced otherwise. Under these conditions the world will be different from what it would have been if thought had not intervened. This consideration confirms the human and moral importance of thought and of its reflective operation in experience. It is therefore not true to say that James treated reason, thought and knowledge with contempt, or that he regarded them as mere means of gaining personal or even social profits. For him reason has a creative function, limited because specific, which helps to make the world other than it would have been without it. It makes the world really more reasonable; it gives to it an intrinsic value. One will understand the philosophy of James better if one considers it in its totality as a revision of English empiricism, a revision which replaces the value of past experience, of what is already given, by the future, by that which is mere possibility.

These considerations naturally bring us to the movement called instrumentalism. The survey which we have just made of James' philosophy shows that he regarded conceptions and theories purely as instruments which can serve to constitute future facts in a specific manner. But James devoted himself primarily to the moral aspects of this theory, to the support which it gave to "meliorism" and moral idealism, and to the consequences which followed from it concerning the sentimental value and the bearing of various philosophical systems, particularly to its destructive implications for monistic rationalism and for absolutism in all its forms. He never attempted to develop a complete theory of the forms or "structures" and of the logical operations which are founded on this conception. Instrumentalism is an attempt to constitute a precise logical theory of concepts, of judgments and inferences in their various forms, by considering primarily how thought functions in the experimental determinations of future consequences. That is to say, that it attempts to establish universally recognized distinctions and rules of logic by deriving them from the reconstructive or mediative function ascribed to reason. It aims to constitute a theory of the general forms of conception and reasoning, and not of this or that particular judgment or concept related to its own content, or to its particular implications.

As far as the historical antecedents of instrumentalism are concerned, two factors are particularly important, over and above this matter of experimental verification which we have already mentioned in connection with James. The first of these two factors is psychological, and the second is a critique of the theory of knowledge and of logic which has resulted from the theory proposed by neo-kantian idealism and expounded in the logical writings of such philosophers as Lotze, Bosanquet, and F. H. Bradley. As we have already said, neo-kantian influence was very marked in the United States during the last decade of the nineteenth century. I myself, and those who have collaborated with me in the exposition of instrumentalism, began by being neo-kantians, in the same way that Peirce's point of departure was kantianism and that of James was the empiricism of the British School.

The psychological tendencies which have exerted an influence on instrumentalism are of a biological rather than a physiological nature. They are closely related to the important movement whose promoter in psychology has been Doctor John Watson and to which he has given the name of Behaviourism. Briefly, the point of departure of this theory is the conception of the brain as an organ for the co-ordination of sense stimuli (to which one should add modifications caused by habit, unconscious memory, or what are called today "conditioned reflexes") for the purpose of effecting appropriate motor responses. On the basis of the theory of organic evolution it is maintained that the analysis of intelligence and of its operations should be compatible with the order of known biological facts, concerning the intermediate position occupied by the central nervous system in making possible responses to the environment, adequate to the needs of the living organism. It is particularly interesting to note that in the "Studies in Logical Theory" (1903), which was their first declaration, the instrumentalists recognized how much they owed to William James for having forged the instruments which they used, while at the same time, in the course of the studies, the authors constantly declared their belief in a close union of the "normative" principles of logic and the real processes of thought, in so far as these are determined by an objective or biological psychology and not by an introspective psychology of states of consciousness. But it is curious to note that the "instruments" to which allusion is made, are not the considerations which were of the greatest service to James. They precede his pragmatism and it is in one of the aspects of his "Principles of Psychology" that one must look for them. This important work (1890) really developed two distinct theses.

The one is a re-interpretation of introspective psychology, in which James denies that sensations, images and ideas are discreet and in which he replaces them by a continuous stream which he calls "the stream of consciousness." This conception necessitates a consideration of relations as an immediate part of the field of consciousness, having the same status as qualities. And throughout his "Psychology" James gives a philosophical tinge to this conception by using it in criticising the atomism of Locke and of Hume as well as the a-priorism of the synthesis of rational principles by Kant and his successors, among whom should be mentioned in England, Thomas Hill Green, who was then at the height of his influence.

The other aspect of his "Principles of Psychology" is of a biological nature. It shows itself in its full force in the criterion which James established for discovering the existence of mind. "The pursuance of future ends and the choice of means for their attainment are thus the mark and criterion of the presence of mentality in a phenomenon."[9] The force of this criterion is plainly shown in the chapter on Attention, and its relation to Interest considered as the force which controls it, and its teleological function of selection and integration; in the chapter on Discrimination and Comparison (Analysis and Abstraction), where he discusses the way in which ends to be attained and the means for attaining them evoke and control intellectual analysis; and in the chapter on Conception, where he shows that a general idea is a mode of signifying particular things and not merely an abstraction from particular cases or a super-empirical function,—that it is a teleological instrument. James then develops this idea in the chapter on reasoning where he says that "the only meaning of essence is teleological, and that classification and conception are purely teleological weapons of mind."

One might complete this brief enumeration by mentioning also the chapter of James' book in which he discusses the Nature of Necessary Truths and the Rôle of Experience, and affirms in opposition to Herbert Spencer, that many of our most important modes of perception and conception of the world of sensible objects are not the cumulative products of particular experience, but rather original biological sports, spontaneous variations which are maintained because of their applicability to concrete experiences after once having been created. Number, space, time, resemblance and other important "categories" could have been brought into existence, he says, as a consequence of some particular cerebral instability, but they could by no means, have been registered by the mind under some outside influence. Many significant and useless concepts also arise in the same manner. But the fundamental categories have been cumulatively extended and reinforced because of their value when applied to concrete instances and things of experience. It is therefore not the origin of a concept, it is its application which becomes the criterion of its value; and here we have the whole of pragmatism in embryo. A phrase of James' very well summarizes its import: "the popular notion that 'Science' is forced on the mind *ab extra,* and that our interests have nothing to do with its constructions, is utterly absurd."

Given the point of view which we have just specified, and the interest attaching to a logical theory of conception and judgment, there results a theory of the following description. The adaptations made by inferior organisms, for example their effective and co-ordinated responses to stimuli, become teleological in man and therefore give occasion to thought. Reflection is an indirect response to the environment, and the element of indirection can itself become great and very complicated. But it has its origin in biological adaptive behaviour and its ultimate function in its cognitive aspect is a prospective control of the conditions of its environment. The function of intelligence is therefore not that of copying the objects of the environment, but rather of taking account of the way in which more effective and more profitable relations with these objects may be established in the future.

How this point of view has been applied to the theory of judgment is too long a story to be told here. We shall confine ourselves here to saying that, in general, the "subject" of a judgment represents that portion of the environment to which a reaction must be made; the attribute represents the corresponding response or the habit or the manner in which one must behave towards the environment; the copula represents the organic and concrete act by which the connection is made between the fact and its signification; and finally the conclusion, or the definitive object of judgment, is simply the same situation transformed, a situation which implies a change as well in the original subject (including its mind) as in the environment itself. The new and harmonious unity thus attained verifies the bearing of the data which were at first chosen to serve as subject and of the concepts introduced into the situation during the process as teleological instruments for its elaboration. Until this final unification is attained the perceptual data and the conceptual principles, theories, are mere hypotheses from a logical point of view. Moreover, affirmation and negation are intrinsically a-logical: they are acts.

Such a summary survey can hardly pretend to be either convincing or suggestive. However, in noting the points of resemblance and difference between this phase of pragmatism and the logic of neo-Hegelian idealism, we are bringing out a point of great importance. According to the latter logic, thought constitutes in the last analysis its own object and even the universe. It is possible to affirm the existence of a series of forms of judgment, because our first judgments, which are nearest to sense, succeed in constituting objects in only a partial and fragmentary fashion, even to the extent of involving in their nature an element of contradiction. There results a dialectic which permits each inferior and partial type of judgment to pass into a more complete form until we finally arrive at the total judgment where the thought which comprehends the entire object or the universe as an organic whole of interrelated mental distinctions. It is evident that this theory magnifies the rôle of thought beyond all proportion. It is an objective and rational idealism which is opposed to and distinct from the subjective and perceptual idealism of Berkeley's school. Instrumentalism, however, assigns a positive function to thought, that of reconstituting the present stage of things instead of merely knowing them. As a consequence, there cannot be intrinsic degrees, or a hierarchy of forms of judgment. Each type has its own end, and its validity is entirely determined by its efficacy in the pursuit of its end. A limited perceptual judgment, adapted to the situation which has given it birth, is as true as is the most complete and significant philosophic or scientific judgment in its place. Logic, therefore, leads to a realistic metaphysics in so far as it accepts facts and events for what they are independently of thought, and to an idealistic metaphysics in so far as it contends that thought gives birth to distinctive acts which modify future facts and events in such a way as to render them more reasonable, that is to say, more adequate to the ends which we propose for ourselves. The ideal element is more accentuated by the inclusion progressively of social factors in human environment over and above natural factors; so that the needs which are fulfilled, the ends which are attained are no longer of a merely biological or particular character, but include also the ends and activities of other members of society.

It is natural that continental thinkers should be interested in American philosophy as it reflects, in a certain sense, American life. Thus it is clear after this rapid survey of the history of pragmatism that American thought merely continues European thought. We have imported our language, our laws, our institutions, our morals, and our religion from Europe, and we have adapted them to the new conditions of our life. The same is true of our ideas. For long years our philosophical thought was merely an echo of European thought. The pragmatic movement which we have traced in the present essay as well as neo-realism, behaviourism, the absolute idealism of Royce, the naturalistic idealism of Santayana, are all attempts at re-adaptation; but they are not creations *de novo*. They have their roots in British and European thought. Since these systems are re-adaptations they take into consideration the distinctive traits of the environment of American life. But as has already been said, they are not limited to reproducing what is worn and imperfect in this environment. They do not aim to glorify the energy and the love of action which the new conditions of American life exaggerated. They do not reflect the excessive mercantilism of American life. Without doubt all these traits of the environment have not been without a certain influence on American philosophical thought; our philosophy would not be national or spontaneous if it were not subject to this influence. But the fundamental idea which the movements of which we have just spoken, have attempted to express, is the idea that action and opportunity justify themselves only to the degree in which they render life more reasonable and increase its value. Instrumentalism maintains in opposition to many contrary tendencies in the American environment, that action should be intelligent and reflective, and that thought should occupy a central position in life. That is the reason for our insistence on the teleological phase of thought and knowledge. If it must be teleological in particular and not merely true in the abstract, that is probably due to the practical element which is found in all the phases of American life. However that may be, what we insist upon above all else is that intelligence be regarded as the only source and sole guarantee of a desirable and happy future. It is beyond doubt that the progressive and unstable character of American life and civilization has facilitated the birth of a philosophy which regards the world as being in continuous formation, where there is still place for indeterminism, for the new and for a real future. But this idea is not exclusively American, although the conditions of American life have aided this idea in becoming self-conscious. It is also true that Americans tend to underestimate the value of tradition and of rationality considered as an achievement of the past. But the world has also given proof of irrationality in the past and the irrationality is incorporated in our beliefs and our institutions. There are bad traditions as there are good ones: it is always important to distinguish. Our neglect of the traditions of the past, with whatever this negligence implies in the way of spiritual impoverishment of our life, has its compensation in the idea that the world is re-commencing and being re-made under our eyes. The future as well as the past can be a source of interest and consolation and give meaning to the present. Pragmatism and instrumental experimentalism bring into prominence the importance of the individual. It is he who is the carrier of creative thought, the author of action, and of its application. Subjectivism is an old story in philosophy; a story which began in Europe and not in America. But American philosophy, in the systems which we have expounded, has given to the subject, to the individual mind, a practical rather than an epistemological function. The individual mind is important because only the individual mind is the organ of modifications in traditions and institutions, the vehicle of experimental creation. One-sided and egoistic individualism in American life has left its imprint in our thought. For better or for worse, depending on the point of view, it has transformed the esthetic and fixed individualism of the old European culture into an active individualism. But the idea of a society of individuals is not foreign to American thought; it penetrates even our current individualism which is unreflective and brutal. And the individual which American thought idealises is not an individual *per se,* an individual fixed in isolation and set up for himself, but an individual who evolves and develops in a natural and human environment, an individual who can be educated.

If I were asked to give an historical parallel to this movement in American thought I would remind my reader of the French philosophy of the enlightenment. Every one knows that the thinkers who made that movement illustrious were inspired by Bacon, Locke, and Newton; what interested them was the application of scientific method and of the conclusions of an experimental theory of knowledge to human affairs, the critique and reconstruction of beliefs and institutions. As Höffding writes, they were animated "by a fervent faith in intelligence, progress, and humanity." And certainly they are not accused today, just because of their educational and social significance, of having sought to subordinate intelligence and science to ordinary utilitarian aims. They merely sought to free intelligence from its impurities and to render it sovereign. One can scarcely say that those who glorify intelligence and reason in the abstract, because of their value for those who find personal satisfaction in their possession, estimate intelligence more truly than those who wish to make it the sole and indispensable guide of intellectual and social life. When an American critic says of instrumentalism that it regards ideas as mere servants which make for success in life, he need only react, without reflection, on the ordinary verbal associations of the word "instrumental," as many others have reacted in the same manner to the use of the word "practical." Similarly a recent Italian writer after having said that pragmatism and instrumentalism are characteristic products of American thought, adds that these systems "regard intelligence as a mere mechanism of belief, and consequently attempt to reestablish the dignity of reason by making of it a machine for the production of beliefs useful to morals and society." This criticism does not hold. It is by no means the production of beliefs useful to morals and society which these systems pursue, but it is the formation of a faith in intelligence, as the one and indispensable belief necessary to moral and social life. The more one appreciates the intrinsic esthetic, immediate value of thought and of science, the more one takes into account what intelligence itself adds to the joy and dignity of life, the more one should feel grieved at a situation in which the exercise and joy of reason are limited to a narrow, closed and technical social group and the more one should ask how it is possible to make all participators in this inestimable wealth.

NOTES

1. *Monist,* vol. 15, p. 163.
2. *Monist,* vol. 15, p. 162.
3. *Popular Science Monthly,* 1878.
4. *Monist,* vol. 15, pp. 173–4.
5. *Monist,* vol. 15, p. 178.
6. *Collected Essays and Reviews,* p. 412.
7. *The Meaning of Truth,* pp. 209–210.

   In a footnote James gave an example of the errors which are committed in connection with the term "Practical" quoting M. Bourdeau who had written that "Pragmatism is an Anglo Saxon reaction against the intellectualism and rationalism of the Latin mind. . . . It is a philosophy without words, a philosophy of gestures and of facts, which abandons what is general and holds only to what is particular." In his lecture at California, James brought out the idea that his pragmatism was inspired to a considerable extent by the thought of the British philosophers, Locke, Berkeley, Hume, Mill, Bain, and Shadworth Hodgson. But he contrasted this method with German transcendentalism, and particularly with that of Kant. It is especially interesting to notice this difference between Peirce and James: the former attempted to give an experimental, not an *a priori* explanation of Kant, whereas James tried to develop the point of view of the British thinkers.
8. William James said in a happy metaphor, that they must be "cashed in," by producing specific consequences. This expression means that they must be able to become concrete facts. But for those who are not familiar with American idioms, James' formula was taken to mean that the consequences themselves of our rational conceptions must be narrowly limited by their pecuniary value. Thus Mr. Bertrand Russell wrote just recently that pragmatism is merely a manifestation of American commercialism.
9. *Psychology,* vol. I, p. 8.

THE PROPER METHOD OF PHILOSOPHY

Clarence Irving Lewis

The general character of any philosophy is likely to be determined by its initial assumptions and its method. When Descartes proposed to sweep the boards clean by doubting everything which admitted of doubt and announced the initial criterion of certainty to be the inner light of human reason, the distinguishing characteristics of the philosophic movement which resulted were thereby fixed. In similar fashion, the development from Locke to Hume is, for the most part, the logical consequence of the doctrine that the mind is a blank tablet on which experience writes. And when Kant proposed to inquire, not whether science is possible, but how it is possible, and identified the possibility of science with the validity of synthetic judgments *a priori*, the successive attempts of the nineteenth century to deduce the major philosophic truths as presuppositons of experience was foreordained.

Because method has this peculiar importance in philosophy, I believe that the reader of any philosophic book is entitled to know in advance what are the underlying convictions of this sort with which the writer sets out. It is right and proper that one should begin with some statement of program and method.

It is—I take it—a distinguishing character of philosophy that it is everybody's business. The man who is his own lawyer or physician, will be poorly served; but everyone both can and must be his own philosopher. He must be, because philosophy deals with ends, not means. It includes the questions, What is good? What is right? What is valid? Since finally the responsibility for his own life must rest squarely upon the shoulders of each, no one can delegate the business of answering such questions to another. Concerning the means whereby the valid ends of life may be attained, we seek expert advice. The natural sciences and the techniques to which they give rise, though they may serve some other interests also, are primarily directed to the discovery of such means. But the question of the ultimately valuable ends which shall be served, remains at once the most personal, and the most general of all questions.

And everyone *can* be his own philosopher, because in philosophy we investigate what we already know. It is not the business of philosophy, as it is of the natural sciences, to add to the sum total of phenomena with which men are acquainted. Philosophy is concerned with what is already familiar. To know in the sense of familiarity and to comprehend in clear ideas are, of course, quite different matters. Action precedes reflection and even precision of behavior commonly outruns precision of thought—fortunately for us. If it were not for this, naïve commonsense and philosophy would coincide, and there

Reprinted by permission of Andrew K. Lewis, from Clarence Irving Lewis, "Introduction," in C. I. Lewis, *Mind and the World Order,* pp. 1–35. New York: Charles Scribner's Sons, 1929. Corrected edition, New York: Dover Publications, 1956.

would be no problem. Just this business of bringing to clear consciousness and expressing coherently the principles which are implicitly intended in our dealing with the familiar, is the distinctively philosophic enterprise.

For instance, everybody knows the difference between right and wrong; if we had no moral sense, philosophy would not give us one. But who can state, with complete satisfaction to himself, the adequate and consistent grounds of moral judgment? Likewise, everyone knows the distinction of cogent reasoning from fallacy. The study of logic appeals to no criterion not already present in the learner's mind. That logical error is, in the last analysis some sort of inadvertance, is an indispensable assumption of the study. Even if it should be in some part an unwarranted assumption, we could not escape it, for the very business of learning through reflection or discussion presumes our logical sense as a trustworthy guide.

That the knowledge sought in ethics and in logic is, thus, something already implicit in our commerce with the familiar, has usually been recognized. But that the same is true in metaphysics, has not been equally clear. Metaphysics studies the nature of reality in general. Reality is presumably independent of any principles of ours, in a sense in which the right and the valid may not be. At least initial presumption to the contrary might be hopelessly prejudicial. Moreover, reality forever runs beyond the restricted field of familiar experience. What hope that cosmic riddles can be solved by self-interrogation! The secret which we seek may be in some field which is not yet adequately explored or even opened to investigation. Or it may be forever beyond the reach of human senses.

But it is not the business of philosophy to go adventuring beyond space and time. And so far as a true knowledge of the nature of reality depends on determining questions of phenomenal fact which are not yet settled, the philosopher has no special insight which enables him to pose as a prophet. We can do nothing but wait upon the progress of the special sciences. Or if speculate we must, at least such speculation is in no special sense the philosopher's affair. It is true that metaphysics has always been the dumping ground for problems which are only partly philosophic. Questions of the nature of life and mind, for example, are of this mixed sort. In part such issues wait upon further data from the sciences, from biology and physical-chemistry and psychology; in part they are truly philosophic, since they turn upon questions of the fundamental criteria of classification and principles of interpretation. No amassing of scientific data can determine these.

If, for example, the extreme behaviorists in psychology deny the existence of consciousness on the ground that analysis of the "mental" must always be eventually in terms of bodily behavior, then it is the business of philosophy to correct their error, because it consists simply in a fallacy of logical analysis. The analysis of any immediately presented *X* must always interpret this *X* in terms of its constant relations to other things—to *Y* and *Z*. Such end-terms of analysis—the *Y* and *Z*—will not in general be temporal or spatial constituents of *X*, but may be anything which bears a constant correlation with it. It is as if one should deny the existence of colors because, for purposes of exact investigation, the colors must be defined as frequencies of vibratory motion. In general terms, if such analysis concludes by stating X is a certain kind of Y–Z complex, hence X does not exist as a distinct reality," the error lies in overlooking a general characteristic of logical analysis—that it does not discover the "substance" or cosmic constituents of the phenomenon whose nature is analyzed but only the constant context of experience in which it will be found.

So far, then, as the divergence of psychological theories, from behaviorism which interprets mind in terms of physical behavior to theories of the subconscious which assimilate much of physiological activity to mind, represents no dispute about experimental fact but only disparity of definition and methodological criteria, psychology and metaphysics have a common ground. The delineation of the fundamental concepts "mind" and "mental" is a truly philosophic enterprise. A similar thing might be discovered in the case of other sciences.

Newly discovered scientific data might make such problems of fundamental concepts and classification easier—or more difficult—but of itself it cannot solve them because, in the nature of the case, they are antecedent to the investigation. Such concepts are not simply dictated by the findings of the laboratory, or by any sort of sense-experience. Their origin is social and historical and represents some enduring human interest. It is the human mind itself which brings them to experience, though the mind does not invent them in a vacuum or cut them from whole cloth. The tendency to forget that initial concepts are never merely dictated by empirical findings is precisely what accounts for the absurd prejudice—now happily obsolescent—that science is "just the report of facts." And this likewise helps to explain the common failure to distinguish between those cosmological speculations which are not philosophic at all, because they are merely guesses at which future observation or experiment may reveal, from the legitimate and necessary philosophic question of a coherent set of fundamental categories, such as "life" and "mind" and "matter," in terms of which experience may consistently and helpfully be interpreted.

It would, of course, be captious to reserve this problem of initial concepts to philosophers, even though we should remember that, since everybody is to be his own philosopher, this merely means reserving them as *general* problems. The expert in the scientific field will have his special competence with respect to them; but they are not his exclusive property, because they are to be resolved as much by criticism and reflection as by empirical investigation. Conversely, it would be pedantic if we should forbid the philosophic student to speculate concerning undetermined scientific fact. It is even questionable to deny the caption "metaphysics" to those cosmological and ontological problems which have this partly speculative and partly critical or reflective character. Historically their title to the name is fairly good. All I wish to point out is that there is a real distinction here between the speculative and the reflective elements; that this distinction coincides with a difference in the method by which resolution of the problem is to be sought; and that it is only the reflective element in such "metaphysical" problems which coincides in its nature and in the method of its solution with the problems of ethics and logic.

With this explanation, I hope I shall cause no confusion if I say that it is only so far as they are thus critical and reflective that the problems of ontology and cosmology are truly philosophic; and that metaphysics as a philosophic discipline is concerned with the nature of the real only so far as that problem is amendable to the reflective method and does not trench upon the field where only scientific investigation can achieve success. There are such reflective problems within any special science, and these may be said to constitute the philosophy of that science. There are also those problems of initial principle and criteria which are common to all the sciences and to the general business of life. These last are the problems of philosophy proper.

There is another sense in which metaphysics has often been speculative and departed from its proper philosophic business and method; that is, not by seeking to anticipate the science of the future, but through attempting by sheer force of rational reflection to transcend experience altogether. Dogmatism is out of fashion since Kant.[1] But that philosophic legerdemain which, with only experience for its datum, would condemn this experience to the status of appearance and disclose a reality more edifying, is still with us. The motives of this attitude are, indeed, ingrained in human nature, and I am reluctant to lay hands on that idealism which has played the rôle of Father Parmenides to all the present generation of philosophers. But at least we must observe that such metaphysics turns away from one type of problem which is real and soluble to another which may not be. Even if all experience be appearance, and all everyday thought and truth infected with contradiction, at least it must be admitted that some appearances are better than others. The mundane distinction of real and unreal *within* experience has its importance and calls for formulation of its criteria. It may be that Reality, with a capital *R*, the concrete-universal Reality which transcends all particular phenomena and underlies them, is a kind of philosophical *ignis fatuus*. Perhaps the idea "whole" applies only *within* experience, and no whole can validly be conceived except such as stands in contrast with something else and has concrete bounds. Perhaps the whole of Reality is, as Kant thought, an inevitable idea but also a necessarily empty one, to remind us forever of the more which is to be learned and connected with our previous knowledge. But whether this be so or not, there is the less ambitious and more important problem of determining the criteria by which the adjective "real" is correctly applied—the problem of the *abstract* universal. And if any be inclined to think that this question is too simple or too meager for a philosophic discipline, I shall hope to indicate his error.

A metaphysics which takes this as its problem will remain strictly within the reflective method. It will seek to determine the nature of the real, as ethics seeks to determine the good, and logic, the valid, purely by critical consideration of what does not transcend ordinary experience. That is, it will seek to *define* "reality," not to triangulate the universe. It will be concerned with the formulation of principles, but of principles already immanent in intelligent practice. A person with no sense of reality (other-worldly philosophers, for example) will not acquire one by the study of metaphysics. And by no possibility can such investigation reveal reality as something esoteric and edifying and transcendent of ordinary experience. Any metaphysics which portrays reality as something strangely unfamiliar or beyond the ordinary grasp, stamps itself as thaumaturgy, and is false upon the face of it.

The problem of a correctly conceived metaphysics, like the problem of ethics and of logic, is one to be resolved by attaining to clear and cogent self-consciousness. As it turns out, the problem of metaphysics is "the problem of the categories."[2] The reason for this lies in a curious complexity of the meaning of "reality." Logical validity is at bottom of one single type. And perhaps the good and the right are relatively simple in their ultimate nature. But the adjective "real" is systematically ambiguous and can have a single meaning only in a special sense. The ascription of reality to the content of any particular experience is always elliptical: some qualification—material reality, psychic reality, mathematical reality—is always understood. And whatever is real in one such sense will be unreal in others. Conversely, every given content of experience is a reality of some sort or other; so that the problem of distinguishing real from unreal, the principles of which metaphysics seeks to formulate, is always a problem of right understanding, or referring the given experience to its proper category. The mirage, for example, though not real trees and water, is a real state of atmosphere and light; to relegate it to the limbo of nothingness would be to obliterate a genuine item of the objective world. A dream is illusory because the dreamer takes its images for physical things; but to the psychologist, interested in the scientific study of the mental, just these experienced images, occurring in just this context of other circumstance, constitute a reality to be embraced under law and having its own indisputable place in the realm of fact. The content of every experience is real when it is correctly understood, and is that kind of reality which it is then interpreted to be. Metaphysics is concerned to reveal just that set of major classifications of phenomena, and just those precise criteria of valid understanding, by which the whole array of given experience may be set in order and each item (ideally) assigned its intelligible and unambiguous place.

So understood, the principles of the categories, which metaphysics seeks, stand, on the one side, in close relation to experience and can not meaningfully transcend it. But on the other side—or in a different sense—they stand above or before experience, and are definitive or prescriptive, and hence *a priori.*

Whatever principles apply to experience must be phrased in terms of experience. The clues to the categorial[3] interpretation—the correct understanding—of any presentation of sense must be empirical clues. If they are not contained within that segment of experience which constitutes the phenomenon itself, then they must be discoverable in its relation to other empirical fact. If the dream or illusion is not betrayed by internal evidence, then its true nature must be disclosed by the conjunction with what precedes or follows. But while the distinguishing marks of reality of any particular sort are thus experimental, the principles by which the interpretation or classification is made are prior to the experience in question. It is only because the mind is prepared to judge it real or unreal according as it bears or fails to bear certain marks, that interpretation of the given is possible at all, and that experience can be understood.

It is through reflective examination of experience (more particularly of our own part in it or attitude toward it) that we may correctly formulate these principles of the categories, since they are implicit in our practical dealings with the empirically given. But they are not empirical generalizations in the sense that some later experience may prove an exception and thus invalidate them. They formulate an attitude of interpretation or discrimination by which what would be exceptional is at once thrown out of court. For example, no experience of the physical can fail to bear those marks the absence of which would bar the given content of experience from interpretation as physical reality. The formulation of our deliberately taken, and consistently adhered to, attitude of interpretation constitutes a categorial *definition* of "the physical." Such a categorial definitive principle forbids nothing in the way of experience; it prohibits neither illusion nor senseless dream. Thus such principles are not material truths: they can be *a priori*—knowable with certainty in advance of experience—precisely because they impose no limitation upon the given but, as principles of interpretation, nevertheless condition it as a constituent of *reality*. It will be the thesis of a later chapter that the *a priori* has in general this same character of definitive principle, which does not limit the content of the given. We shall find in this nature of the *a priori* the solution of many traditional problems of the theory of knowledge.

So conceived, the principles which formulate criteria of the real, in its various types, are *a priori* in precisely the same sense as are the canons of ethics and of logic. Experience does not itself determine what is good or bad, or the nature of goodness, nor does it determine what is valid or invalid, or the nature of logical validity. Equally it does not determine what is real or unreal (in any particular sense), or the nature of reality. Experience does not categorize itself. The criteria of interpretation are of the mind; they are imposed upon the given by our active attitude.

The main business of a sound metaphysics is, thus, with the problem of the categories; the formulation of the criteria of reality, in its various types. It is to the shame of philosophy that these problems, which by their nature must be capable of precise solution since they require only persistent regard for fact and self-conscious examination of our own grounds of judgment, have been so generally neglected. Just this common disregard of verifiable fact and mundane criteria of the real is largely responsible for that quagmire of incertitude and welter of the irrelevant and vague which at present bears the name of metaphysics. The problems of the categories admit of as much real progress as those of logic; in fact, they are problems of the same general type. We may congratulate ourselves, I think, that a growing interest in such study, in this reflective or phenomenalistic or critical spirit, is one of the characteristics of the present period in philosophy.[4]

The definition of the real in general, and the picturing of reality as a whole, are subordinate matters; and perhaps, as has been suggested, the second of these is not possible. The word "real" has a single meaning, of course, in the same sense that "useful" or any other such elliptical term has a single meaning. Nothing is useful for every purpose, and perhaps everything is useful for some purpose. A definition of "useful" *in general* would not divide things into two classes, the useful and the useless. Nor could we arrive at such a definition by attempting to collect all useful things into a class and remark their common characters, since we should probably have everything in the class and nothing outside it to represent the useless. Instead, we should first have to consider the different types of usefulness or of useful things and then discover, if possible, what it is that characterizes the useful as contrasted with the useless in all these different cases. We should find, of course, that it was not some sense-quality but a relation to an end which was the universal mark of usefulness. Similarly, to arrive at a general definition of "the real" it would not do to lump together all sorts of realities in one class and seek directly for their common character. Everything in this class would be at once real, in some category, and unreal in others. And nothing would be left outside it. The subject of our generalization must be, instead, the distinction real–unreal in all the different categories. What definition of reality in general we might thus arrive at, we need not pause to inquire. Obviously it would be found to embrace some relation to empirical givenness in general or to our interpreting attitude, or to something involving both of these, rather than any particular and distinguishing empirical characteristics.

That in any case a successful definition of the real in general would not carry us far in any cosmological attempt to plumb the deeps of the universe, is evident from the fact that it would delimit reality in intension only, and would leave quite undetermined the particular content of reality *in extenso.* The total picture of reality can be drawn only when the last experience of the last man, and the final facts of science, are summed up. Why cosmology in this sense should be supposed to be the business of the philosopher—or of anyone else—I cannot see. In the nature of the case, it must be a coöperative enterprise, and presumably one that is always incomplete.

What we have here seen concerning the significance of "the real" will have its importance for certain topics discussed in later chapters. But our immediate interest in it lies in the fact that it brings metaphysics—which threatened to prove an exception—back into line with other branches of philosophy with respect to the method by which it should be pursued. It is only in and through the general course of human experience that we have a content for our philosophic thinking, and the significance of philosophic truth lies always in its application to experience. But it is experience from a certain point of view, or a certain aspect of it, with which we are concerned. Ethics cannot tell us how much of life is good, what particular sins are committed, or what proportion of men are moral; nor does metaphysics describe the course of the universe or determine the extent and the particulars of the real. It is the logical essence of goodness, the canons of validity, the criteria of the beautiful, and likewise, the principles of the distinction of real from unreal, that philosophy may hope to formulate. These criteria and principles, the mind itself brings to experience in its interpretation, its discriminations, and its evaluation of what is given. Thus philosophy is, so to speak, the mind's own study of itself in action; and the method of it is simply reflective. It seeks to formulate explicitly what from the beginning is our own creation and possession.

However, I should not like to appear to defend the notion that such analysis is a simple matter or that it requires only to express in precise terms the principles of common-sense. As has often enough been emphasized, common-sense is itself a naïve metaphysics and one which frequently breaks down on examination. Just as naïve morality may become confused before the dialectical attack, so common-sense categories of reality fail in crucial cases to meet the tests of consistency and accord with intelligent practice. It is true in metaphysics, as it is in ethics and in logic, that while valid principles must be supposed somehow implicit in the ordinary intercourse of mind with reality, they are not present in the sense of being fatally adhered to. If they were, the philosophic enterprise would have no practical value. Self-consciousness may be an end in itself, but if it did not have eventual influence upon human action it would be a luxury which humanity could not afford. That we coincide in our logical sense, does not make logic a work of supererogation. No more does coincidence in our ultimate sense of reality and in our categories render metaphysical discussion nugatory. Just as the study of logic may conduce to cogency of thought, and ethics contribute to greater clarity and consistency in moral judgment, so too the elucidation of metaphysical problems may contribute to the precision and adequacy of our interpretation of the real; it may even serve, on occasion, to work improvement in the concepts of the special sciences. Philosophy cannot be merely a verbally more precise rendering of common-sense, nor a direct generalization from actual practice. Though it rises from what is implicit in experience, its procedure must be critical, not descriptive. So far as it is to be of use, it must assume the function of sharpening and correcting an interpretation which has already entered into the fabric of that experience which is its datum. Logical principles aim to replace the uncritical moral sense, ethics, our naïve morality, and metaphysics, our unreflective ontological judgments. Such an enterprise is no simple matter of formulating the obvious.

The reflective method must, of course, be dialectical—in the Socratic-Platonic, not the Hegelian, sense. It accords with the Socratic presumption that the truth which is sought is already implicit in the mind which seeks it, and needs only to be elicited and brought to clear expression. It accords, further, in the recognition that it is definitions or "essences" which are the philosophic goal. And it likewise recognizes that the hope of agreement between minds, to be reached by philosophic discussion, must rest upon the presumption that this accord somehow exists already.

Historically, however, the dialectical method has been overlaid with all sorts of addenda, and perverted by extraneous assumptions which are fallacious. So that I should choose the name "reflective" as less liable to unwarranted interpretation. It does not follow from the dialectical method that the basis of the accord between minds represents some universal pattern of human reason, apart from the world of sense in which we live; nor that the mind has access to some realm of transcendent concepts which it recovers, of its own powers, at the instigation of experience; nor that agreement of minds presumes initial principles which are self-evident. It does not even follow that the agreement which we seek is already implicity complete in all respects. To all such notions there is an alternative, to account for this agreement between minds, which is simple and even obvious. The coincidence of our fundamental criteria and principles is the combined result of the similarity of human animals, and of their primal interests, and the similarities of the experience with which they have to deal. More explicitly, it represents one result of the interplay between these two; the coincidence of human modes of behavior, particularly when the interests which such behavior serves involve coöperation.

Our categories are guides to action. Those attitudes which survive the test of practice will reflect not only the nature of the active creature but the general character of the experience he confronts. Thus, indirectly, even what is *a priori* may not be an exclusive product of "reason," or made in Plato's heaven in utter independence of the world we live in. Moreover, the fact that man survives and prospers by his social habits serves to accentuate and perfect agreement in our basic attitudes. Our common understanding and our common world may be, in part, created in response to our need to act together and to comprehend one another. Critical discussion is but a prolongation of that effort which we make to extend the bounds of successful human coöperation. It is no more necessary to suppose that agreement in fundamental principles is completely ready-made than it is to suppose that infants must already have precisely those ideas which later they find words to express. Indeed our categories are almost as much a social product as in language, and in something like the same sense. It is only the *possibility* of agreement which must be antecedently presumed. The "human mind" is a coincidence of individual minds which partly, no doubt, must be native, but partly is itself created by the social process. Even that likeness which is native would seem to consist in capacities and tendencies to action, not in mental content or explicit modes of thought. That the categories are fundamental in such wise that the social process can neither create nor alter them, is a rationalistic prejudice without foundation. There is much which is profound and true in traditional conceptions of the *a priori*. But equally it should be clear that there is much in such conceptions which smacks of magic and superstitious nonsense. Particularly it is implausible that what is *a priori* can be rooted in a "rational nature of man" which is something miraculous and beyond the bounds of psychological analysis and genetic explanation.

It may be pointed out also that if we recognize critical reflection or dialectic as the only method which holds promise in philosophy, we do not thereby commit ourselves to the assumption that coherence or internal consistency is the only test, or a sufficient test, of philosophic truth. In philosophy, as elsewhere, consistency is only a negative test of truth; it is possible, however unlikely, to be consistently in error. Consistency would be a sufficient test only if we should suppose that there is nothing external to our logic which we must be true to. The reflective method does not take it for granted that all fact follows, Hegelian-fashion, from the logical structure of thought itself. As has been suggested, it does not even presuppose that what is *a priori* and of the mind—our categorial attitude of interpretation—is completely independent of the general character of experience.

It is of the essence of the dialectical or reflective method that we should recognize that proof, in philosophy, can be nothing more at bottom than persuasion. It makes no difference what the manner of presentation should be, whether deductive from initial assumptions, or inductive from example, or merely following the order dictated by clarity of exposition. If it be deductive, then the initial assumptions cannot coerce the mind. There are no propositions which are self-evident in isolation. So far as the deductive presentation hopes to convince of what was not previously believed, it must either seek out initial agreements from which it may proceed, or—as is more frequently the case—the deductively first propositions must be rendered significant and acceptable by exhibiting the cogency and general consonance with experience of their consequences. If the method be inductive from example, then the principles to be proved are implicit in the assumption that cited examples are veridical and typical and genuinely fall under the category to be investigated. There can be no Archimedean point for the philosopher. Proof, he can offer only in the sense of so connecting his theses as to exhibit their mutual support, and only through appeal to other minds to reflect upon their experience and their own attitudes and perceive that he correctly portrays them. If there be those minds which find no alternatives save certainty, apart from all appeal to prior fact, or skepticism, then to skepticism they are self-condemned. And much good may it do them! As philosophers, we have something we must be faithful to, even if that something be ourselves. If we are perverse, it is possible that our philosophy will consist of lies.

Already this introductory analysis of method is too long. But the conception of the *a priori* here suggested is a novel one: a little further discussion may have its value by way of anticipating briefly what is to follow.

If Philosophy is the study of the *a priori,* and is thus the mind's formulation of its own active attitudes, still the attitude which is the object of such study is one taken toward the content of an experience in some sense independent of and bound to be reflected in the attitude itself. What is *a priori*—it will be maintained—is prior to experience in almost the same sense that purpose is. Purposes are not dictated by the content of the given; they are our own. Yet purposes must take their shape and have their realization in terms of experience; the content of the given is not irrelevant to them. And purposes which can find no application will disappear. In somewhat the same fashion what is *a priori* and of the mind is prior to the content of the given, yet in another sense not altogether independent of experience in general.

It is an error common to rationalism and to pure empiricism that both attempt an impossible separation of something called the mind from something else called experience. Likewise both treat of knowledge as if it were a relation of the individual mind to external object in such wise that the existence of other minds is irrelevant; they do not sufficiently recognize the sense in which our truth is social. Traditional rationalism,[5] observing that any principles which should serve as ultimate criterion or determine categorial interpretation must be prior to and independent of the experience of which it applies, has supposed that such principles must be innate and so discoverable by some sort of direct inspection. If a canon of their truth is requisite, this must be supplied by something of a higher order than experience, such as self-evidence or the natural light of reason. The mistakes of this point of view are two. In the first place, it assumes that mind is immediate to itself in a sense in which the object of experience is not. But what other means have we of discovering the mind save that same experience in which also external objects are presented? And if the object transcends the experience of it, is not this equally true of the mind? The single experience exhausts the reality of neither. Any particular experience is a whole within which that part or aspect which represents the legislative or categorial activity of mind and that which is given content, independent of the mind's interpretation, are separable only by analysis. We have no higher faculty or more esoteric experience through which the mind discovers itself. And second, rationalism fallaciously assumes that what is prior to, or legislative for, the particular experience must be likewise independent of experience in general. Though categorial principle must, in the nature of the case, be prior to the particular experience, it nevertheless represents an attitude which the mind has taken in the light of past experience as a whole, and one which would even be susceptible of change if confronted with some pervasive alteration in the general character of what is presented. An example here may be of service: it is an *a priori* principle that physical things must have mass. By this criterion, they are distinguished from mirror-images and illusion. Since this is so, no particular experience could upset this principle, because any experience in which it should be violated would be repudiated as non-veridical or "not correctly understood." That is, by the principle itself, the phenomenon must be referred to some other category than the physical. In that sense, the truth of the principle is independent of the particular phenomenon. But a world in which we should experience phenomena having a persistence and independence not characteristic of imagination, and a coherence not characteristic of our dreams, but things which would still not be amendable to any gravitational generalizations, is entirely conceivable. In such a world our *a priori* principle would not be rendered false—since it is definitive of the physical; but the category "physical" might well be useless. (Incidentally it may be pointed out that this criterion of the physical is a historical and social product. Aristotle and the ancients knew it not.)

Though we bring the *a priori* principle, as criterion, to any particular experience, yet this legislative attitude of mind is clearly one which is taken because, our experience on the whole being what it is, this principle helps to render it intelligible, and behavior in accord with it is normally successful. The mind must bring to experience whatever serve as the criteria of interpretation—of the real, as of the right, the beautiful, and the valid. The content of experience cannot evaluate or interpret itself. Nevertheless the validity of such interpretation must reflect the character of experience in general, and meet the pragmatic test of value as a guide to action.

The fallacy of pure empiricism is the converse of that which rationalism commits. In seeking to identify the real with what is given in experience, apart from construction or interpretation by the mind, and to elicit general principles directly from the content of experience, empiricism condemns itself to a vicious circle. Experience as it comes to us contains not only the real but all the content of illusion, dream, hallucination, and misapprehension. When the empiricist supposes that laws or principles can be derived simply by generalization from experience, he *means* to refer only to *veridical* experience, forgetting that without the criterion of legislative principle experience cannot first be sorted into veridical and illusory.

It is this vicious circle which makes inevitable the historical dénouement of empiricism in Hume's skepticism. Berkeley pointed out that the real cannot be distinguished from the unreal by any relation between the idea in the mind and an independent object, but only by some relation within experience itself. In this, of course, he is right, whether we agree with his idealism or not: mind cannot transcend itself and discover a relation of what is in experience to what is not. Berkeley then seeks to indicate our actual empirical criteria: the real in experience is distinguished (1) by that independence of the will which is exhibited in the content of perception as contrasted with imagination, (2) by the greater liveliness of perception, (3) by the interconnection of veridical perceptions according to the "laws of nature." Obviously only the last of these is sufficient in critical cases such as hallucination and errors of observation. Hume wrecks the empiricist structure when he points out that such "laws of nature" cannot be derived by generalization from experience. For this, the distinction of necessary from contingent would be requisite. The basis of this distinction is not to be found in the content of experience; it is of the mind. Generalization from experience always presumes that the categorial interpretation already has been made. Laws which characterize all experience, of real and unreal both, are non-existent, and would in any case be worthless.

It is obvious that similar considerations hold for the other problems of philosophy. The nature of the good can be learned from experience only if the content of experience be first classified into good and bad, or grades of better and worse. Such classification or grading already involves the legislative application of the same principle which is sought. In logic, principles can be elicited by generalization from examples only if cases of valid reasoning have first been segregated by some criterion. It is this criterion which the generalization is required to disclose. In esthetics, the laws of the beautiful may be derived from experience only if the criteria of beauty have first been correctly applied.

The world of experience is not given in experience: it is constructed by thought from the data of sense. This reality which everybody knows reflects the structure of human intelligence as much as it does the nature of the independently given sensory content. It is a whole in which mind and what is given to mind already meet and are interwoven. The datum of our philosophic study is not the "buzzing, blooming confusion" on which the infant first opens his eyes, not the thin experience of immediate sensation, but the thick experience of every-day life.

This experience of *reality* exists only because the mind of man takes attitudes and makes interpretations. The buzzing, blooming confusion could not become reality for an oyster. A purely passive consciousness, if such can be conceived, would find no use for the concept of reality, because it would find none of the idea of the *un*real; because it would take no attitude that could be balked, and make no interpretation which conceivably could be mistaken.

On the other hand, we can discover mind and its principles only by analysis in this experience which we have. We cannot, unless dogmatically, construct experience from a hypothetical and transcendent mind working upon a material which likewise is something beyond experience. We can only discover mind and what is independently given to it by an analysis within experience itself. And it is only because mind has entered into the structure of the real world which we know and the experience of everyday, that analysis, or *any* attempted knowledge, may discover it.

In finding thus that the principles and criteria which philosophy seeks to formulate must be significant at once of experience and of our active attitudes, the reflective method inevitably is pragmatic also. Concepts and principles reveal themselves as instruments of interpretation; their meaning lies in the empirical consequences of the active attitude. The categories are ways of dealing with what is given to the mind, and if they had no practical consequences, the mind would never use them. Since philosophy seeks to formulate what is implicit in mind's every-day interpretations, we may test the significance of any philosophic principle, and pave the way for determining its truth, if we ask: How would experience be different if this should be correct than if it should be false? or, How differently should we orient ourselves to experience and deal with it if this should be so than if it should be not so?

Metaphysical issues which supposedly concern what is transcendent of experience altogether, must inevitably turn out to be issues wrongly taken. For example, if one say—as Mr. Broad has recently said[6]—that scientific reality of perduring electrons or what not, is something which at best is probable only, since it does not enter our direct experience of "sensa," then I think we may justly challenge him as Berkeley challenged Locke: Why not a world of sensa with *nothing* behind them? What makes "scientific reality" even probable if direct experience could be the same without its existence? Unless the modern physicist hopelessly deludes himself, does not the existence of electrons mean something verifiable in the laboratory? Otherwise, would he not be constrained to answer any question about electrons as Laplace is reputed to have answered Napoleon's question about God—that he had no need of this hypothesis? But if the existence or non-existence of "scientific reality" makes certain verifiable differences in experience, then these empirical criteria are the marks of the kind of reality which can be predicted of it. They are the "cash-value" of the category; they constitute what it means to be real in just the way that electrons can be real. "Scientific reality" is either an interpretation of certain parts and aspects of experience or it is a noise, signifying nothing.

The totality of the possible experiences in which any interpretation would be verified—the completest possible empirical verification which is conceivable—constitutes the entire meaning which that interpretation has. A predication of reality to what transcends experience completely and in every sense, is not problematic; it is nonsense.

Perhaps another illustration may make the point more clear. Occasionally philosophers amuse themselves by suggesting that the existences of things are intermittent; that they go out when we cease to notice them and come into being again at the moment of rediscovery. The answer is not given by any question-begging reference to the independent object or the conservation of matter. What we need to inquire is why this notion of permanent objects was ever invented. If nothing in experience would be different whether the existence of things should be intermittent or continuous, what character of experience is predicated by their "permanence"? When we have answered to such questions, we have discovered the whole meaning of "permanent existence" and nothing further, unless paradox of language, remains to be discussed. Reflection upon experience and our attitude to what is given cannot discover what is not implicitly already there—and there is nothing else which philosophic reflection can hope to disclose.

To sum up, then: The reflective method is empirical and analytic in that it recognizes experience in general as the datum of philosophy. But it is not empirical in the sense of taking this experience to coincide with data of sense which are merely given to the mind. Nor is it analytic in the sense of supposing that experience is complete and ready-made.

Rather, it finds that philosophy is particularly concerned with the part or aspect of experience which the mind contributes by its attitude of interpretation. In thus recognizing that the principles which are sought are in some sense *a priori*, it is rationalistic.

It is not rationalistic, however, in the sense of presuming the mind as a Procrustean bed into which experience is forced, or as an initial datum which can be assumed or its findings known apart from sense-experience. Nor does it presume the "rational human mind" as something completely identical in and native to all human beings, or as a transcendent entity which, even if it lived in some other world of sense, would still possess precisely the same categories and pattern of intelligence.

The reflective method is pragmatic in the same sense that it is empirical and analytic. It supposes that the categories and principles which it seeks must already be implicit in human experience and human attitude. The significance of such fundamental conceptions must always be practical because thought and action are continuous, and because no other origin of them can be plausible than an origin which reflects their bearing on experience. Further, it claims for philosophy itself the pragmatic sanction that reflection is but a further stretch of that critical examination of our own constructions and interpretations by which we free them from inconsistency and render them more useful. Since experience is not just given but is in part a product of the mind, philosophy itself may work some alteration of the active attitude by which the given in experience is met and moulded. But the reflective method is not, or need not be, pragmatic in the sense of supposing, as current pragmatism sometimes seems to do, that the categories of biology and psychophysics have some peculiar advantage for the interpretation of the practical attitudes of thought.

The reflective method necessarily leads to the repudiation of any reality supposed to be transcendent of experience altogether. A true philosophic interpretation must always follow the clues of the practical reasons for our predications. A philosophy which relegates any object of human thought to the transcendent, is false to the human interests which have created that thought, and to the experience which gives it meaning. Philosophic truth, like knowledge in general, is about experience, and not about something strangely beyond the ken of man, open only to the seer and the prophet. We all know the nature of life and of the real, though only with exquisite care can we tell the truth about them.

NOTES

1. Perhaps I should say, "*has been* out of fashion," since just now we are being treated to various new forms of dogmatism. But this, I take it, comes partly as a counsel of despair, and partly it represents a reaction against the often exaggerated claims of "idealism" and post-Kantian "criticism" to be able to proceed a priori without reference to particular results of the empirical sciences.
2. A more logical terminology would qualify this as the "categories of reality," and would distinguish these from the "categories of value."
3. "Categorial" is used throughout with the meaning "pertaining to the categories." This avoids possible confusion with "categorical," meaning specifically "unconditional, not hypothetical."
4. I have in mind, as examples, Whitehead's "Concept of Nature" and "Principles of Natural Knowledge," Russell's "Analysis of Mind," and Broad's "Scientific Thought."
5. The rationalism (if that term is justified) of post-Kantian idealism rests upon different assumptions and proceeds by different methods. It is not here in point.
6. "Scientific Thought," see esp. pp. 268 ff.

PART II

ANGLO-AMERICAN PHILOSOPHY

Anglo-American philosophy, as noted by Hilary Putnam in Part IV, has been greatly occupied by the question of how language "hooks on" to the world. More generally, it has been concerned with the question of what language is and how it functions. We could include logic under this concern with language, reversing Frege's inclusion of what we call the *philosophy of language* under the category of *logic,* but trying to emphasize the same general relationship.

The philosophers in this section all deal with the role of language and logic in philosophy. A central question is whether language of some sort (or a specific part of language) reveals anything about *how the world is.* Another important question is whether language is some sort of a useful tool for philosophy or rather a source of error. The relationship between philosophy and science is another common topic. This section presents a wide variety of positions, unified perhaps only by concerns with language, logic, and science and the roles these play in a proper philosophical method.

In "Logical Atomism," Bertrand Russell says that logic, not metaphysics, is fundamental in philosophy, and that differing philosophies should be characterized by their logics alone. As an example of differing philosophies, he mentions the philosophy of Leibniz based on the logical doctrine that every proposition has a subject and a predicate, in contrast with his philosophy of logical atomism based on the "new logic" of Peano and Frege. Philosophical problems are fundamentally problems of logic to be resolved by the technical methods of mathematical logic. Russell claims that philosophy has erred in using the "heroic method" common to speculative metaphysics and should rather emphasize greater care and accuracy. Russell offers, as an example of his method, the principle that one should, wherever possible, substitute logical constructions from known entities for inferences to unknown entities. Frege used this principle to replace the inference to the existence of cardinal numbers with the logical construction of a definition of cardinal numbers, and Russell used it in his theory of definite descriptions. In general, his method points out that our definitions of certain of our concepts lead us to infer that there are some unknown metaphysical entities when in fact there are only our logical constructions from directly experienced entities.

Russell emphasizes the influence of language on philosophy. Both the vocabulary and the syntax of natural languages can easily mislead us into assuming that certain words in our vocabulary must refer to real entities when in fact they do not. The subject-predicate syntax of our language leads us to believe that the world has a structure corresponding to it. Consequently, Russell advocates the construction of an ideal logical language preventing those inferences from the nature of language to the nature of the world that depend on the logical defects of natural language. Such a language could suggest what inferences from language to the structure of the world we may "reasonably" make: that is, those based on "what logic requires of a language which is to avoid contradiction."

Russell ends his essay with two further points. First, he argues that philosophy should get its "data" from science and that we should thus build our philosophy upon science. Second, Russell claims that the business of philosophy consists of logical analysis, followed by logical synthesis. The most important part of philosophy for him consists in the criticism and clarification of fundamental notions likely to be accepted uncritically.

G. E. Moore begins "What Is Philosophy?" by trying to characterize what he sees as the most important and interesting task of philosophy. He describes it as the attempt to give a general description of the universe as a whole and what exists in it. He then proceeds to set out some major philosophical views *as they relate to the views of common sense.* Moore sets out in detail what he takes to be the views of common sense, in order to make clear the extent to which certain philosophical positions violate common sense. He notes how common-sense views change from time to time. Current common sense, we are told, holds that there are material objects and acts of consciousness in the world, that they are related in certain definite ways, and that the existence of material objects does not depend on acts of consciousness apprehending them. Moore adds to this that it is a part of common sense to claim that we *know* all the things he has listed under common sense. He does not go on to claim that common sense says that we know *that we know* all these things, but simply that we believe that we know them all. Common sense does not amount to a general description of the whole universe, however, for it makes no claims about what *everything* in the universe is like, or about what *everything that we know* in the universe is like. Moore finds the views of common sense, taken as claims about everything that we know to be in the universe, to be very plausible. Although Moore does not explicitly state it here, he gives the views of common sense taken in this way the special philosophical status of a starting-point, just as he has taken them in this selection as a starting-point for the purposes of exposition. Philosophers can diverge from the views of common sense, Moore says, by accepting them but adding to them, by rejecting some or all of them in favor of contradictory views, or by keeping some and contradicting some. Moore ends this selection by characterizing the tasks of metaphysics, epistemology, logic, and ethics in relation to the general task of philosophy.

The selection from Ludwig Wittgenstein, entitled "Philosophy," comments both on the character of traditional philosophy and on the nature of Wittgensteinian "Philosophical Grammar." Wittgenstein uses various metaphors and illustrations to make his points.

According to Wittgenstein, the task of philosophy is to uncover false analogies in our language that lead to errors and prompt "philosophical" uneasiness and confusion. This task requires an overcoming of our will or desire to see things in a familiar, common way. It requires that we see things differently, not that we acquire new knowledge about abstruse matters.

The answers to philosophical difficulties must be ordinary and "homespun." For example, when a philosopher tells us we cannot step twice into the same river, we reply, "yes, we *can* step twice into the same river." Such comments show Wittgenstein's sympathy, at least in part, with Moore's attitude toward common sense; they also illustrate Wittgenstein's attitudes toward the ordinary use of language—attitudes that influenced the philosophical movement known as Ordinary Language (or Oxford) Philosophy. Traditional philosophy, Wittgenstein claims, runs into inextricable confusions because it diverges from the ordinary use of language without explicitly laying out the conditions for its new, technical usage.

Philosophy should strive for the perspicuous representation of our *grammar*. Grammar is the main object of our investigations. We aim at complete clarity, seeing connections between seemingly unrelated bits of language. Philosophy, as Wittgenstein sees it, should describe the actual use of language and lay everything out clearly before us. He adds that philosophical questions are like questions regarding the constitution of a certain society. That is, they are not like questions regarding mind-independent reality. Philosophy investigates language and thus the rules according to which *we decide* to use language. It tabulates the ordinary use of words in order to fix their meanings. A philosophical problem is an awareness of disorder in our concepts, and it can be solved (or rather, dissolved, "like a piece of sugar in water") by the ordering of our concepts.

The debate between A. J. Ayer and Frederick Copleston, entitled "Logical Positivism—A Debate," deals mainly with the question whether the statements of metaphysics are cognitively meaningful. Their other pertinent question is: Does philosophy consist only of conceptual analysis and criticism? Ayer would say that his view of philosophy is a result of his analysis of 'meaningfulness,' 'understanding,' 'explanation', etc. Copleston suggests, on the contrary, that the verification criterion of meaning is the result of Logical Positivism's wish to eliminate metaphysics from philosophy.

Ayer supports the principle of verification implying that only formal statements and empirically testable statements have cognitive significance. Using this principle, he argues that the statements of metaphysics, such as statements about the transcendent, lack cognitive significance. Metaphysicians put forth such statements as being both *necessary* (in some sense) and applicable to reality; but Ayer would claim that the *only* necessary statements are formal and thus lack applicability to reality. Ayer also uses his analysis of explanation to rule out metaphysical explanations, arguing that explanations must be falsifiable by empirical evidence but that metaphysical explanations are not. Ayer's defense of verificationism and his criticisms of metaphysics indicate that his main concern is to eliminate (philosophical) disputes in which none of the disputants knows what it would take, even in principle, to resolve the dispute.

Copleston defends a view of philosophy including more than conceptual analysis and criticism. He says that philosophy includes the task of "opening the mind to the Transcendent" and revealing the limits of science as a complete account of *reality*. He has a distinctive definition of 'cause,' which Ayer does not accept. Copleston holds that metaphysics consists of the search for the cause(s), in his sense, of the world of sense experience (of *contingent* being) as a whole. He says of cause, "[E]very being which has not in itself its reason of existence depends for its existence on an extrinsic reality which I call . . . cause." Giving such a cause constitutes a metaphysical explanation. Metaphysical explanations include statements that are "necessary or *certain*" and apply to reality. Copleston's defense of metaphysics seems to suggest that his fundamental concern is that contingent being be philosophically grounded in some self-grounding Being, and that we acknowledge truth and falsehood regarding metaphysical reality even if we are incapable of fully discerning it.

Copleston criticizes the verification criterion of meaning, contending that it presupposes a controversial philosophical position that cannot be demonstrated by the principle of verification itself. He infers that Ayer has failed to show that one must or should accept the principle. Copleston counters the principle with his own conditions for meaningfulness: A concept is meaningful if there is some experience relevant to its *formation*. Metaphysics is based on experience in that it involves intellectual reflection on experience, but it does not have to have empirically testable consequences. Metaphysical propositions are testable by rational discussion only. Copleston has the last word in this debate, and he saves his most powerful criticism of verificationism for it. He says that the principle itself is neither formal nor empirically testable, and that it is therefore meaningless by its own standard. Ayer eventually admitted this point (see, e.g., his "Introduction" in *Logical Positivism,* p. 15).

In "Empiricism, Semantics, and Ontology," Rudolf Carnap aims to show that using a language referring to abstract entities does not necessitate the acceptance of a particular ontology. In fact, such language use is compatible with empiricism and strictly scientific thinking.

In order to understand how this is so, one must make a fundamental distinction between two kinds of questions regarding the existence of entities. Our talk about entities of whatever sort goes on within a certain linguistic framework; if we desire to talk about a new sort of entities, we need to construct a new linguistic framework in which to do so. This involves the introduction of a general term for the new kind of entities and the introduction of variables of the new type. Questions about the existence of certain entities that are asked from *within* the linguistic framework are *internal questions* and are answerable by purely logical methods or by empirical methods. Examples include "Is there a white piece of paper on my desk?" and "Is there a prime number greater than a million?" The first is answered by empirical means, the second by logical means.

Going beyond internal questions, people sometimes ask *external questions* (philosophical questions) regarding the existence of the system of entities as a whole. For example, regarding the world of physical objects, we can ask the internal question, "Does this or that particular (kind of) thing exist?" or we can ask the external question, "Are there physical objects?" Carnap's main thesis is that we cannot answer the external questions as if they were internal, *theoretical* questions. Rather, these are *practical* questions requiring a practical decision of *choice* whether or not to accept and use a particular linguistic framework. Linguistic frameworks require no theoretical justification because their introduction does not imply any assertion about reality. This choice to introduce a framework is not based on the belief that it is "true" or "false" but on the degree of efficiency and usefulness the linguistic framework exhibits for our purposes. Carnap claims that ontological theses regarding the reality of the "thing world" or of any system of entities as a whole are pseudo-propositions because they cannot be answers to internal questions but are formed as if they were. Such claims are pseudo-propositions because one cannot think of any possible evidence that would be regarded as relevant by all involved and could decide the issue or at least support one answer over all others. Carnap ends with an injunction for tolerance: *"Let us be cautious in making assertions and critical in examining them, but tolerant in permitting linguistic forms."*

In "How I See Philosophy," Friedrich Waismann insists that philosophy is not science because there are *no proofs and no theorems* in philosophy. Philosophy provides *insight,* a new way of seeing things; it changes one's entire way of thinking. The method it employs is *discussion* and the use of *examples,* not proof. Further, there are in philosophy no questions that can be answered with a simple *Yes* or *No*. Philosophy does have many arguments, and it is the originality and persuasiveness of arguments that distinguishes great philosophy. But these arguments do not constitute proofs in the sense of scientific or mathematical proofs. There can be no proofs in philosophy because proofs always require premisses, and philosophers always immediately *question* each other's premisses, thus moving the discussion to a deeper level.

Waismann argues that the source of much of the philosopher's uneasiness and puzzlement is language. Language contains many false analogies producing profound mental discomfort for us. The problem in philosophy is not to find the answer to a given question but to find a *sense* for it. When we have found a clear sense for a question, the answer often is obvious. The error of many philosophers is to give an answer to a question before stopping to consider the question itself: in particular, what exactly it means.

The task of the philosopher is partly to *remind* others of how they have actually always used words in non-philosophical contexts. Although philosophical arguments are not deductive and thus do not prove, they do have force, Waismann claims. They have force by *reminding* us, at the appropriate time, of what we have already known. Philosophers also point out *absurdities* in inconsistent language use; they draw one's attention to one's own linguistic practice. It is characteristic of philosophical method that philosophers do not *force* their interlocutors. They simply try to make them *aware* of what they are doing.

Philosophical questions may pass into science as a result of being made more precise. When made clearer, philosophical questions become answerable. Waismann emphasizes the importance of the initial unclear questions as a necessary accompaniment of creative thinking and discovery. Unclear questions point the way for the construction of new meanings, new meaningful questions. Philosophers thus bring new questions into the world.

Roderick Chisholm, in "Philosophers and Ordinary Language," argues that ordinary language, of itself, does not have the philosophical significance that Norman Malcolm and like-minded ordinary-language philosophers give it. Chisholm grants that many philosophical statements do violate ordinary usage and thus can be misleading or seem more important than they are. Philosophers can even become entangled in verbal confusions as a result. Chisholm nonetheless argues against Malcolm's claim (in "Moore and Ordinary Language") that "any philosophical statement which violates ordinary language is false."

Chisholm begins by clarifying the meaning of "*incorrect* language usage." We must carefully distinguish *incorrect* from *mistaken* usage. Incorrect usage consists in using a word with an intensional meaning (as opposed to an extensional or denotational meaning) different from that of most people. Mistaken usage consists in the misapplication of a word to something that does not satisfy the conditions for that word's application. For example, if I spot a whale on a beach and call it a fish, this is *incorrect* language usage if I do not know the difference between whales and fish, but it is an example of *mistaken* usage if I know the difference but just do not know that this particular sea-dwelling creature is a whale rather than a fish. Keeping this distinction in mind, if we find out that a certain philosopher is using words incorrectly, it may well turn out, given the intensional meaning, that what is said is trivially true, whereas it appeared paradoxical before.

Chisholm identifies two linguistic theses in Malcolm's article. The first is that "if a philosophical statement is paradoxical, that is because it asserts the impropriety of an ordinary form of speech." In response, Chisholm maintains that there can be paradoxical philosophical statements that are empirical and not just about language. Further, when a philosopher does make a statement about language, it is typically a proposal for a certain usage, not an attempt to capture ordinary usage. As a proposal, it cannot be correct or incorrect. Malcolm's second thesis is that there are certain words in ordinary language whose use implies that they have a denotation: for example, words whose meaning can only be shown but not explained with other words. Chisholm responds that there are obvious ways of teaching and constraining the use of all such terms that do not imply the existence of something to which the words truly apply.

Karl Popper begins his article, "The Nature of Philosophical Problems and Their Roots in Science," by defending the claim that there *are* philosophical problems, contrary to what he says is the "present position of English philosophy," originating in Wittgenstein's later work, that there are no philosophical problems. Popper interprets Wittgenstein as saying that all genuine problems are scientific and that the apparent problems of philosophy are all pseudo-problems. Popper sees no point to a philosophy without problems to solve, and claims that since many interesting and exciting ideas can be introduced in language that might seem meaningless, we would be ill-advised to follow Wittgenstein's advice to eradicate all such statements. Popper agrees, however, with Wittgenstein that there is much *uselessly* meaningless philosophy that can be checked by linguistic analysis.

Popper also agrees with Wittgenstein that there are many pseudo-problems in philosophy, but he goes beyond Wittgenstein to advance his central claim that genuine philosophical problems *become* pseudo-problems when they are cut off from their roots in urgent problems *outside* philosophy. Thus, there are no *pure* philosophical problems, but only those that arise from non-philosophical problems. There are, accordingly, no unique philosophical methods for solving these problems. Any method that works for a particular problem is legitimate, and methods may vary depending on the *origin* of problems. A problem is "philosophical" if it is more closely connected with those discussed by traditional philosophy than with those discussed by some other discipline. Popper distinguishes philosophical from scientific activity, claiming that the former but not the latter includes *reflection* upon theories.

Popper uses historical examples from the philosophies of Plato and Kant to support his thesis. The lesson of these historical studies is that great dangers threaten (the kinds of danger that Wittgenstein made clear) if we try to understand philosophy in isolation from the non-philosophical problems with which it deals and from which it arises.

In "Semantic Ascent," W. V. Quine makes two central claims. First, he claims, contrary to Carnap's view, that the method of semantic ascent applies anywhere, not only in philosophy. Quine does, however, explain why it occurs much more often in philosophy. Second, he claims that there is no difference in kind between what the philosopher does and what natural scientists, mathematicians, and other theoreticians do.

In deciding what exists, Quine uses the method of semantic ascent, the shift from talk of things to talk of thing-words, from the material to the formal mode. He says that this method is especially characteristic of philosophical discussions, although he says the shift to discussing words can occur in theoretical discussions generally. Quine disagrees with Carnap's claim that non-philosophical theoretical questions have a non-verbal content or meaning that philosophical questions lack. In both cases, one answers the questions strictly on the basis of pragmatic considerations about linguistic frameworks.

Semantic ascent serves to clear up confused debates because it moves the discussion into a realm where all parties are more in agreement about the object of discussion (namely, words). Quine claims that semantic ascent figures in the natural sciences and mathematics as well as philosophy. Einstein's theory of relativity won out over its competitors partly because of its superiority when considered under semantic ascent as a piece of discourse.

The distinction between the philosopher and the scientist is merely a matter of degree; the philosopher deals with categories of greater breadth. The philosopher critically examines the scientist's acceptance of one or another realm of physical objects and makes explicit what has been tacitly assumed. The philosopher does *not,* according to Quine, differ from scientists and mathematicians by having a unique vantage point outside any conceptual scheme whatsoever. The philosopher's work, like the scientist's or mathematician's, *must* always go on within some conceptual system, and this system is always as much in need of philosophical scrutiny as any other.

Michael Dummett's central thesis, in "Can Analytical Philosophy Be Systematic, and Should It Be?," is that a systematic theory of meaning, a systematic account of the functioning of language that begs no questions by presupposing any semantic concepts, must be possible; he claims that such a theory would be the essential element in a philosophy of language serving as the foundation for all other philosophy.

Dummett's paper is primarily a response to claims from philosophers like Wittgenstein and Austin that the philosophy of language (and philosophy in general) cannot be systematic. According to Wittgenstein, philosophy does not establish truths but rectifies certain kinds of misunderstandings. According to Austin, philosophy is empirical research into the actual use of words and thus defies systematization.

Dummett claims that analytical philosophy has "very recently" (c. 1970–1975) undergone significant unification owing to three factors: (a) the widespread attention attracted by the work of Frege, (b) the dominance of contemporary American philosophy, and (c) the widespread dominance of the philosophy of language. Dummett defines analytic philosophy as post-Fregean philosophy. Frege altered our perspective by replacing epistemology with what he called logic (that includes what is now called philosophy of language). For analytic philosophy thus understood, philosophy of language is the foundation of all other philosophy because we can *analyze thought* only through the analysis of language.

Dummett argues that analytic philosophy must be systematic because the analysis of thought *via* the analysis of language *requires* that we make explicit the *general principles* that we *must* implicitly grasp in order to be able to use language. Dummett claims that it is the philosopher's task to give a systematic account of how language functions and acquires sense by making explicit those general principles. Frege laid the groundwork for this task. Future work in philosophy can and should be systematic in virtue of (a) its issuing in articulated theories and (b) its proceeding according to generally accepted methods and criteria for success.

LOGICAL ATOMISM

Bertrand Russell

The philosophy which I advocate is generally regarded as a species of realism, and accused of inconsistency because of the elements in it which seem contrary to that doctrine. For my part, I do not regard the issue between realists and their opponents as a fundamental one; I could alter my view on this issue without changing my mind as to any of the doctrines upon which I wish to lay stress. I hold that logic is what is fundamental in philosophy, and that schools should be characterized rather by their logic than by their metaphysic. My own logic is atomic, and it is this aspect upon which I should wish to lay stress. Therefore I prefer to describe my philosophy as "logical atomism," rather than as "realism," whether with or without some prefixed adjective.

A few words as to historical development may be useful by way of preface. I came to philosophy through mathematics, or rather through the wish to find some reason to believe in the truth of mathematics. From early youth, I had an ardent desire to believe that there can be such a thing as knowledge, combined with a great difficulty in accepting much that passes as knowledge. It seemed clear that the best chance of finding indubitable truth would be in pure mathematics, yet some of Euclid's axioms were obviously doubtful, and the infinitesimal calculus, as I was taught it, was a mass of sophisms, which I could not bring myself to regard as anything else. I saw no reason to doubt the truth of arithmetic, but I did not then know that arithmetic can be made to embrace all traditional pure mathematics. At the age of eighteen I read Mill's *Logic,* but was profoundly dissatisfied with his reasons for accepting arithmetic and geometry. I had not read Hume, but it seemed to me that pure empiricism (which I was disposed to accept) must lead to scepticism rather than to Mill's support of received scientific doctrines. At Cambridge I read Kant and Hegel, as well as Mr. Bradley's *Logic,* which influenced me profoundly. For some years I was a disciple of Mr. Bradley, but about 1898 I changed my views, largely as a result of arguments with G. E. Moore. I could no longer believe that knowing makes any difference to what is known. Also I found myself driven to pluralism. Analysis of mathematical propositions persuaded me that they could not be explained as even partial truths unless one admitted pluralism and the reality of relations. An accident led me at this time to study Leibniz, and I came to the conclusion (subsequently confirmed by Couturat's masterly researches) that many of his most characteristic opinions were due to the purely logical doctrine that every proposition has a subject and a predicate.

Reprinted by permission of Unwin Hyman, from Bertrand Russell, "Logical Atomism," in Russell, *Logic and Knowledge: Essays 1901–1950,* ed. Robert Charles Marsh, pp. 323–343. London: George Allen & Unwin, Ltd.; New York: The Macmillan Company, 1956.

This doctrine is one which Leibniz shares with Spinoza, Hegel, and Mr. Bradley; it seemed to me that, if it is rejected, the whole foundation for the metaphysics of all these philosophers is shattered. I therefore returned to the problem which had originally led me to philosophy, namely, the foundations of mathematics, applying to it a new logic derived largely from Peano and Frege, which proved (at least, so I believe) far more fruitful than that of traditional philosophy.

In the first place, I found that many of the stock philosophical arguments about mathematics (derived in the main from Kant) had been rendered invalid by the progress of mathematics in the meanwhile. Non-Euclidean geometry had undermined the argument of the transcendental aesthetic, Weierstrass had shown that the differential and integral calculus do not require the conception of the infinitesimal, and that, therefore, all that had been said by philosophers on such subjects as the continuity of space and time and motion must be regarded as sheer error. Cantor freed the conception of infinite number from contradiction, and thus disposed of Kant's antinomies as well as many of Hegel's. Finally Frege showed in detail how arithmetic can be deduced from pure logic, without the need of any fresh ideas or axioms, thus disproving Kant's assertion that "7 + 5 = 12" is synthetic—at least in the obvious interpretation of that dictum. As all these results were obtained, not by any heroic method, but by patient detailed reasoning, I began to think it probable that philosophy had erred in adopting heroic remedies for intellectual difficulties, and that solutions were to be found merely by greater care and accuracy. This view I have come to hold more and more strongly as time went on, and it has led me to doubt whether philosophy, as a study distinct from science and possessed of a method of its own, is anything more than an unfortunate legacy from theology.

Frege's work was not final, in the first place because it applied only to arithmetic, not to other branches of mathematics; in the second place because his premises did not exclude certain contradictions to which all past systems of formal logic turned out to be liable. Dr. Whitehead and I in collaboration tried to remedy these two defects, in *Principia Mathematica,* which, however, still falls short of finality in some fundamental points (notably the axiom of reducibility). But in spite of its shortcomings I think that no one who reads this book will dispute its main contention, namely, that from certain ideas and axioms of formal logic, by the help of the logic of relations, all pure mathematics can be deduced, without any new undefined idea or unproved propositions. The technical methods of mathematical logic, as developed in this book, seem to be very powerful, and capable of providing a new instrument for the discussion of many problems that have hitherto remained subject to philosophic vagueness. Dr. Whitehead's *Concept of Nature* and *Principles of Natural Knowledge* may serve as an illustration of what I mean.

When pure mathematics is organized as a deductive system—i.e. as the set of all those propositions that can be deduced from an assigned set of premises—it becomes obvious that, if we are to believe in the truth of pure mathematics, it cannot be solely because we believe in the truth of the set of premises. Some of the premises are much less obvious than some of their consequences, and are believed chiefly because of their consequences. This will be found to be always the case when a science is arranged as a deductive system. It is not the logically simplest propositions of the system that are the most obvious, or that provide the chief part of our reasons for believing in the system. With the empirical sciences this is evident. Electro-dynamics, for example, can be concentrated into Maxwell's equations, but these equations are believed because of the observed truth of certain of their logical consequences. Exactly the same thing happens in the pure realm of logic; the logically first principles of logic—at least some of them—are to be believed, not on their own account, but on account of their consequences. The epistemological question: "Why should I believe this set of propositions?" is quite different from the logical question: "What is the smallest and logically simplest group of propositions from which this set of propositions can be deduced?" Our reasons for believing logic and pure mathematics are, in part, only inductive and probable, in spite of the fact that, in their *logical* order, the propositions of logic and pure mathematics follow from the premises of logic by pure deduction. I think this point important, since errors are liable to arise from assimilating the logical to the epistemological order, and also, conversely, from assimilating the epistemological to the logical order. The only way in which work on mathematical logic throws light on the truth or falsehood of mathematics is by disproving the supposed antinomies. This shows that mathematics *may* be true. But to show that mathematics *is* true would require other methods and other considerations.

One very important heuristic maxim which Dr. Whitehead and I found, by experience, to be applicable in mathematical logic, and have since applied in various other fields, is a form of Ockham's razor. When some set of supposed entities has neat logical properties, it turns out, in a great many instances, that the supposed entities can be replaced by purely logical structures composed of entities which have not such neat properties. In that case, in interpreting a body of propositions hitherto believed to be about the supposed entities, we can substitute the logical structures without altering any of the detail of the body of propositions in question. This is an economy, because entities with neat logical properties are always inferred, and if the propositions in which they occur can be interpreted without making this inference, the ground for the inference fails, and our body of propositions is secured against the need of a doubtful step. The principle may be stated in the form: "Wherever possible, substitute constructions out of known entities for inferences to unknown entities."

The uses of this principle are very various, but are not intelligible in detail to those who do not know mathematical logic. The first instance I came across was what I have called "the principle of abstraction," or "the principle which dispenses with abstraction."[1] This principle is applicable in the case of any symmetrical and transitive relation, such as equality. We are apt to infer that such relations arise from possession of some common quality. This may or may not be true; probably it is true in some cases and not in others. But all the formal purposes of a common quality can be served by membership of the group of terms having the said relation to a given term. Take magnitude, for example. Let us suppose that we have a group of rods, all equally long. It is easy to suppose that there is a certain quality, called their length, which they all share. But all propositions in which this supposed quality occurs will retain their truth-value unchanged if, instead of "length of the rod *x*" we take "membership of the group of all those rods which are as long as *x*." In various special cases—e.g. the definition of real numbers—a simpler construction is possible.

A very important example of the principle is Frege's definition of the cardinal number of a given set of terms as the class of all sets that are "similar" to the given set—where two sets are "similar" when there is a one-one relation whose domain is the one set and whose converse domain is the other. Thus a cardinal number is the class of all those classes which are similar to a given class. This definition leaves unchanged the truth-values of all propositions in which cardinal numbers occur, and avoids the inference to a set of entities called "cardinal numbers," which were never needed except for the purpose of making arithmetic intelligible, and are now no longer needed for that purpose.

Perhaps even more important is the fact that classes themselves can be dispensed with by similar methods. Mathematics is full of propositions which seem to require that a class or an aggregate should be in some sense a single entity—e.g. the proposition "the number of combinations of n things any number at a time is 2^n." Since 2^n is always greater than n, this proposition leads to difficulties if classes are admitted because the number of classes of entities in the universe is greater than the number of entities in the universe, which would be odd if classes were some among entities. Fortunately, all the propositions in which classes appear to be mentioned can be interpreted without supposing that there are classes. This is perhaps the most important of all the applications of our principle. (See *Principia Mathematica,* *20.)

Another important example concerns what I call "definite descriptions," i.e. such phrases as "the even prime," "the present King of England," "the present King of France." There has always been a difficulty in interpreting such propositions as "the present King of France does not exist." The difficulty arose through supposing that "the present King of France" is the subject of this proposition, which made it necessary to suppose that he subsists although he does not exist. But it is difficult to attribute even subsistence to "the round square" or "the even prime greater than 2." In fact, "the round square does not subsist" is just as true as "the present King of France does not exist." Thus the distinction between existence and subsistence does not help us. The fact is that, when the words "the so-and-so" occur in a proposition, there is no corresponding single constituent of the proposition, and when the proposition is fully analysed the words "the so-and-so" have disappeared. An important consequence of the theory of descriptions is that it is meaningless to say "A exists" unless "A" is (or stands for) a phrase of the form "the so-and-so." If the so-and-so exists, and *x* is the so-and-so, to say "*x* exists" is nonsense. Existence, in the sense in which it is ascribed to single entities, is thus removed altogether from the list of fundamentals. The ontological argument and most of its refutations are found to depend upon bad grammar. (See *Principia Mathematica*, *14.)

There are many other examples of the substitution of constructions for inferences in pure mathematics, for example, series, ordinal numbers, and real numbers. But I will pass on to the examples in physics.

Points and instants are obvious examples: Dr. Whitehead has shown how to construct them out of sets of events all of which have a finite extent and a finite duration. In relativity theory, it is not points or instants that we primarily need, but event-particles, which correspond to what, in older language, might be described as a point at an instant, or an instantaneous point. (In former days, a point of space endured throughout all time, and an instant of time pervaded all space. Now the unit that mathematical physics wants has neither spatial nor temporal extension.) Event-particles are constructed by just the same logical process by which points and instants were constructed. In such constructions, however, we are on a different plane from that of constructions in pure mathematics. The possibility of constructing an event-particle depends upon the existence of sets of events with certain properties; whether the required events exist can only be known empirically, if at all. There is therefore no *a priori* reason to expect continuity (in the mathematical sense), or to feel confident that event-particles can be constructed. If the quantum theory should seem to demand a discrete space-time, our logic is just as ready to meet its requirements as to meet those of traditional physics, which demands continuity. The question is purely empirical, and our logic is (as it ought to be) equally adapted to either alternative.

Similar considerations apply to a particle of matter, or to a piece of matter of finite size. Matter, traditionally, has two of those "neat" properties which are the mark of a logical construction; first, that two pieces of matter cannot be at the same place at the same time; secondly, that one piece of matter cannot be in two places at the same time. Experience in the substitution of constructions for inferences makes one suspicious of anything so tidy and exact. One cannot help feeling that impenetrability is not an empirical fact, derived from observation of billiard-balls, but is something logically necessary. This feeling is wholly justified, but it could not be so if matter were not a logical construction. An immense number of occurrences coexist in any little region of space-time; when we are speaking of what is not logical construction, we find no such property as impenetrability, but, on the contrary, endless overlapping of the events in a part of space-time, however small. The reason that matter is impenetrable is because our definitions make it so. Speaking roughly, and merely so as to give a notion of how this happens, we may say that a piece of matter is all that happens in a certain track in space-time, and that we construct the tracks called bits of matter in such a way that they do not intersect. Matter is impenetrable because it is easier to state the laws of physics if we make our constructions so as to secure impenetrability. Impenetrability is a logically necessary result of definition, though the fact that such a definition is convenient is empirical. Bits of matter are not among the bricks out of which the world is built. The bricks are events, and bits of matter are portions of the structure to which we find it convenient to give separate attention.

In the philosophy of mental occurrences there are also opportunities for the application of our principle of constructions *versus* inferences. The subject, and the relation of a cognition to what is known, both have that schematic quality that arouses our suspicions. It is clear that the subject, if it is to be preserved at all, must be preserved as a construction, not as an inferred entity; the only question is whether the subject is sufficiently useful to be worth constructing. The relation of a cognition to what is known, again, cannot be a straightforward single ultimate, as I at one time believed it to be. Although I do not agree with pragmatism, I think William James was right in drawing attention to the complexity of "knowing." It is impossible in a general summary, such as the present, to set out the reasons for this view. But whoever has acquiesced in our principle will agree that here is *prima facie* a case for applying it. Most of my *Analysis of Mind* consists of applications of this principle. But as psychology is scientifically much less perfected than physics, the opportunities for applying the principle are not so good. The principle depends, for its use, upon the existence of some fairly reliable body of propositions, which are to be interpreted by the logician in such a way as to preserve their truth while minimizing the element of inference to unobserved entities. The principle therefore presupposes a moderately advanced science, in the absence of which the logician does not know what he ought to construct. Until recently, it would have seemed necessary to construct geometrical points; now it is event-particles that are wanted. In view of such a change in an advanced subject like physics, it is clear that constructions in psychology must be purely provisional.

I have been speaking hitherto of what it is *not* necessary to assume as part of the ultimate constituents of the world. But logical constructions, like all other constructions, require materials, and it is time to turn to the positive question, as to what these materials are to be. This question, however, requires as a preliminary a discussion of logic and language and their relation to what they try to represent.

The influence of language on philosophy has, I believe, been profound and almost unrecognized. If we are not to be misled by this influence, it is necessary to become conscious of it, and to ask ourselves deliberately how far it is legitimate. The subject-predicate logic, with the substance-attribute metaphysic, are a case in point. It is doubtful whether either would have been invented by people speaking a non-Aryan language; certainly they do not seem to have arisen in China, except in connection with Buddhism, which brought Indian philosophy with it. Again, it is natural, to take a different kind of instance, to suppose that a proper name which can be used significantly stands for a single entity; we suppose that there is a certain more or less persistent being called "Socrates," because the same name is applied to a series of occurrences which we are led to regard as appearances of this one being. As language grows more abstract, a new set of entities come into philosophy, namely, those represented by abstract words—the universals. I do not wish to maintain that there are no universals, but certainly there are many abstract words which do not stand for single universals—e.g. triangularity and rationality. In these respects language misleads us both by its vocabulary and by its syntax. We must be on our guard in both respects if our logic is not to lead to a false metaphysic.

Syntax and vocabulary have had different kinds of effects on philosophy. Vocabulary has most influence on common sense. It might be urged, conversely that common sense produces our vocabulary. This is only partially true. A word is applied at first to things which are more or less similar, without any reflection as to whether they have any point of identity. But when once usage has fixed the objects to which the word is to be applied, and tends to suppose that one word must stand for one object, which will be a universal in the case of an adjective or an abstract word. Thus the influence of vocabulary is towards a kind of platonic pluralism of things and ideas.

The influence of syntax, in the case of the Indo-European languages, is quite different. Almost any proposition can be put into a form in which it has a subject and a predicate, united by a copula. It is natural to infer that every fact has a corresponding form, and consists in the possession of a quality by a substance. This leads, of course, to monism, since the fact that there were several substances (if it were a fact) would not have the requisite form. Philosophers, as a rule, believe themselves free from this sort of influence of linguistic forms, but most of them seem to me to be mistaken in this belief. In thinking about abstract matters, the fact that the words for abstractions are no more abstract than ordinary words always makes it easier to think about the words than about what they stand for, and it is almost impossible to resist consistently the temptation to think about the words.

Those who do not succumb to the subject-predicate logic are apt to get only one step further, and admit relations of two terms, such as before-and-after, greater-and-less, right-and-left. Language lends itself to this extension of the subject-predicate logic, since we say "A precedes B," "A exceeds B," and so on. It is easy to prove that the fact expressed by a proposition of this sort cannot consist of the possession of a quality by a substance, or of the possession of two or more qualities by two or more substances. (See *Principles of Mathematics,* § 214). The extension of the subject-predicate logic is therefore right so far as it goes, but obviously a further extension can be proved necessary by exactly similar arguments. How far it is necessary to go up the series of three-term, four-term, five-term . . . relations I do not know. But it is certainly necessary to go beyond two-term relations. In projective geometry, for example, the order of points on a line or of planes through a line requires a four-term relation.

A very unfortunate effect of the peculiarities of language is in connection with adjectives and relations. All words are of the same logical type; a word is a class of series, of noises or shapes according as it is heard or read. But the meanings of words are of various different types; an attribute (expressed by an adjective) is of a different type from the objects to which it can be (whether truly or falsely) attributed; a relation (expressed perhaps by a preposition, perhaps by a transitive verb, perhaps in some other way) is of a different type from the terms between which it holds or does not hold. The definition of a logical type is as follows: A and B are of the same logical type if, and only if, given any fact of which A is a constituent, there is a corresponding fact which has B as a constituent, which either results by substituting B for A, or is the negation of what so results. To take an illustration, Socrates and Aristotle are of the same type, because "Socrates was a philosopher" and "Aristotle was a philosopher" are both facts; Socrates and Caligula are of the same type, because "Socrates was a philosopher" and "Caligula was not a philosopher" are both facts. To love and to kill are of the same type, because "Plato loved Socrates" and "Plato did not kill Socrates" are both facts. It follows formally from the definition that, when two words have meanings of different types, the relations of the words to what they mean are of different types; that is to say, there is not one relation of meaning between words and what they stand for, but as many relations of meaning, each of a different logical type, as there are logical types among the objects for which there are words. This fact is a very potent source of error and confusion in philosophy. In particular, it has made it extraordinarily difficult to express in words any theory of relations which is logically capable of being true, because language cannot preserve the difference of type between a relation and its terms. Most of the arguments for and against the reality of relations have been vitiated through this source of confusion.

At this point, I propose to digress for a moment, and to say, as shortly as I can, what I believe about relations. My own views on the subject of relations in the past were less clear than I thought them, but were by no means the views which my critics supposed them to be. Owing to lack of clearness in my own thoughts, I was unable to convey my meaning. The subject of relations is difficult, and I am far from claiming to be now clear about it. But I think certain points are clear to me. At the time when I wrote *The Principles of Mathematics,* I had not yet seen the necessity of logical types. The doctrine of types profoundly affects logic, and I think shows what, exactly, is the valid element in the arguments of those who oppose "external" relations. But so far from strengthening their main position, the doctrine of types leads, on the contrary, to a more complete and radical atomism than any that I conceived to be possible twenty years ago. The question of relations is one of the most important that arise in philosophy, as most other issues turn on it: monism and pluralism; the question whether anything is wholly true except the whole of truth, or wholly real except the whole of reality; idealism and realism, in some of their forms; perhaps the very existence of philosophy as a subject distinct from science and possessing a method of its own. It will serve to make my meaning clear if I take a passage in Mr. Bradley's *Essays on Truth and Reality,* not for controversial purposes, but because it raises exactly the issues that ought to be raised. But first of all I will try to state my own view, without argument.[2]

Certain contradictions—of which the simplest and oldest is the one about Epimenides the Cretan, who said that all Cretans were liars, which may be reduced to the man who says "I am lying"—convinced me, after five years devoted mainly to this one question, that no solution is technically possible without the doctrine of types. In its technical form, this doctrine states merely that a word or symbol may form part of a significant proposition, and in this sense have meaning, without being always able to be substituted for another word or symbol in the same or some other proposition without producing nonsense. Stated in this way, the doctrine may seem like a truism. "Brutus killed Caesar" is significant, but "Killed killed Caesar" is nonsense, so that we cannot replace "Brutus" by "killed," although both words have meaning. This is plain common sense, but unfortunately almost all philosophy consists in an attempt to forget it. The following words, for example, by their very nature, sin against it: attribute, relation, complex, fact, truth, falsehood, not, liar, omniscience. To give a meaning to these words, we have to make a détour by way of words or symbols and the different ways in which they may mean; and even then, we usually arrive, not at one meaning, but at an infinite series of different meanings. Words, as we saw, are all of the same logical type; therefore when the meanings of two words are of different types, the relations of the two words to what they stand for are also of different types. Attribute-words and relation-words are of the same type, therefore we can say significantly "attribute-words and relation-words have different uses." But we cannot say significantly "attributes are not relations." By our definition of types, since relations are relations, the form of words "attributes are relations" must be not false, but meaningless, and the form of words "attributes are not relations," similarly, must be not true, but meaningless. Nevertheless, the statement "attribute-words are not relation-words" is significant and true.

We can now tackle the question of internal and external relations, remembering that the usual formulations, on both sides, are inconsistent with the doctrine of types. I will begin with attempts to state the doctrine of external relations. It is useless to say "terms are independent of their relations," because "independent" is a word which means nothing. Two events may be said to be causally independent when no causal chain leads from one to the other; this happens, in the special theory of relativity, when the separation between the events is space-like. Obviously this sense of "independent" is irrelevant. If, when we say "terms are independent of their relations," we mean "two terms which have a given relation would be the same if they did not have it,"that is obviously false; for, being what they are, they have the relation, and therefore whatever does not have the relation is different. If we mean—as opponents of external relations suppose us to mean—that the relation is a third term which comes between the other two terms and is somehow hooked on to them, that is obviously absurd, for in that case the relation has ceased to be a relation, and all that is truly relational is the hooking of the relation to the terms. The conception of the relation as a third term between the other two sins against the doctrine of types, and must be avoided with the utmost care.

What, then, can we mean by the doctrine of external relations? Primarily this, that a relational proposition is not, in general, logically equivalent formally to one or more subject-predicate propositions. Stated more precisely: Given a relational propositional function "xRy," it is not in general the case that we can find predicates α, β, γ, such that, for all values of x and y, xRy is equivalent to $x\alpha$, $y\beta$, $(x, y)\gamma$ (where (x, y) stands for the whole consisting of x and y), or to any one or two of these. This, and this only, is what I mean to affirm when I assert the doctrine of external relations; and this, clearly, is at least part of what Mr. Bradley denies when he asserts the doctrine of internal relations.

In place of "unities" or "complexes," I prefer to speak of "facts." It must be understood that the word "fact" cannot occur significantly in any position in a sentence where the word "simple" can occur significantly, nor can a fact occur where a simple can occur. We must not say "facts are not simples." We can say, "The symbol for a fact must not replace the symbol for a simple, or vice versa, if significance is to be preserved." But it should be observed that, in this sentence, the word "for" has different meanings on the two occasions of its use. If we are to have a language which is to safeguard us from errors as to types, the symbol for a fact must be a proposition, not a single word or letter. Facts can be asserted or denied, but cannot be named. (When I say "facts cannot be named," this is, strictly speaking, nonsense. What can be said without falling into nonsense is: "The symbol for a fact is not a name.") This illustrates how meaning is a different relation for different types. The way to mean a fact is to assert it; the way to mean a simple is to name it. Obviously naming is different from asserting, and similar differences exist where more advanced types are concerned, though language has no means of expressing the differences.

There are many other matters in Mr. Bradley's examination of my views which call for reply. But as my present purpose is explanatory rather than controversial, I will pass them by, having, I hope, already said enough on the question of relations and complexes to make it clear what is the theory that I advocate. I will only add, as regards the doctrine of types, that most philosophers assume it now and then, and few would deny it, but that all (so far as I know) avoid formulating it precisely or drawing from it those deductions that are inconvenient for their systems.

I come now to some of Mr. Bradley's criticisms (*loc. cit* p. 280 ff.). He says:—

"Mr. Russell's main position has remained to myself incomprehensible. On the one side I am led to think that he defends a strict pluralism, for which nothing is admissible beyond simple terms and external relations. On the other side Mr. Russell seems to assert emphatically, and to use throughout, ideas which such a pluralism surely must repudiate. He throughout stands upon unities which are complex and which cannot be analysed into terms and relations. These two positions to my mind are irreconcilable, since the second, as I understand it, contradicts the first flatly."

With regard to external relations, my view is the one I have just stated, not the one commonly imputed by those who disagree. But with regard to unities, the question is more difficult. The topic is one with which language, by its very nature, is peculiarly unfitted to deal. I must beg the reader, therefore, to be indulgent if what I say is not exactly what I mean, and to try to see what I mean in spite of unavoidable linguistic obstacles to clear expression.

To begin with, I do not believe that there are complexes or unities in the same sense in which there are simples. I did believe this when I wrote *The Principles of Mathematics,* but, on account of the doctrine of types, I have since abandoned this view. To speak loosely, I regard simples and complexes as always of different types. That is to say, the statements "There are simples" and "There are complexes" use the words "there are" in different senses. But if I use the words "there are" in the sense which they have in the statement "there are simples," then the form of words "there are not complexes" is neither true nor false, but meaningless. This shows how difficult it is to say clearly, in ordinary language, what I want to say about complexes. In the language of mathematical logic it is much easier to say what I want to say, but much harder to induce people to understand what I mean when I say it.

When I speak of "simples" I ought to explain that I am speaking of something not experienced as such, but known only inferentially as the limit of analysis. It is quite possible that, by greater logical skill, the need for assuming them could be avoided. A logical language will not lead to error if its simple symbols (i.e. those not having any parts that are symbols, or any significant structure) all stand for objects of some one type, even if these objects are not simple. The only drawback to such a language is that it is incapable of dealing with anything simpler than the objects which it represents by simple symbols. But I confess it seems obvious to me (as it did to Leibniz) that what is complex must be composed of simples, though the number of constituents may be infinite. It is also obvious that the logical uses of the old notion of substance (i.e. those uses which do not imply temporal duration) can only be applied, if at all, to simples; objects of other types do not have that kind of being which one associates with substances. The essence of a substance, from the symbolic point of view, is that it can only be named—in old-fashioned language, it never occurs in a proposition except as the subject or as one of the terms of a relation. If what we take to be simple is really complex, we may get into trouble by naming it, when what we ought to do is to assert it. For example, if Plato loves Socrates, there is not an entity "Plato's love for Socrates," but only the fact that Plato loves Socrates. And in speaking of this as "a fact," we are already making it more substantial and more of a unity than we have any right to do.

Attributes and relations, though they may be not susceptible of analysis, differ from substances by the fact that they suggest a structure, and that there can be no significant symbol which symbolizes them in isolation. All propositions in which an attribute or a relation *seems* to be the subject are only significant if they can be brought into a form in which the attribute is attributed or the relation relates. If this were not the case, there would be significant propositions in which an attribute or a relation would occupy a position appropriate to a substance, which would be contrary to the doctrine of types, and would produce contradictions. Thus the proper symbol for "yellow" (assuming for the sake of illustration that this is an attribute) is not the single word "yellow," but the propositional function "x is yellow," where the structure of the symbol shows the position which the word "yellow" must have if it is to be significant. Similarly the relation "precedes" must not be represented by this one word, but by the symbol "x precedes y," showing the way in which the symbol can occur significantly. (It is here assumed that values are not assigned to x and y when we are speaking of the attribute or relation itself.)

The symbol for the simplest possible kind of fact will still be of the form "x is yellow" or "x precedes y," only that "x" and "y" will be no longer undetermined variables, but names.

In addition to the fact that we do not experience simples as such, there is another obstacle to the actual creation of a correct logical language such as I have been trying to describe. This obstacle is vagueness. All our words are more or less infected with vagueness, by which I mean that it is not always clear whether they apply to a given object or not. It is of the nature of words to be more or less general, and not to apply only to a single particular, but that would not make them vague if the particulars to which they applied were a definite set. But this is never the case in practice. The defect, however, is one which it is easy to imagine removed, however difficult it may be to remove it in fact.

The purpose of the foregoing discussion of an ideal logical language (which would of course be wholly useless for daily life) is twofold: first, to prevent inferences from the nature of language to the nature of the world, which are fallacious because they depend upon the logical defects of language; secondly, to suggest, by inquiring what logic requires of a language which is to avoid contradiction, what sort of a structure we may reasonably suppose the world to have. If I am right, there is nothing in logic that can help us to decide between monism and pluralism, or between the view that there are ultimate relational facts and the view that there are none. My own decision in favour of pluralism and relations is taken on empirical grounds, after convincing myself that the *a priori* arguments to the contrary are invalid. But I do not think these arguments can be adequately refuted without a thorough treatment of logical types, of which the above is a mere sketch.

This brings me, however, to a question of method which I believe to be very important. What are we to take as data in philosophy? What shall we regard as having the greatest likelihood of being true, and what as proper to be rejected if it conflicts with other evidence? It seems to me that science has a much greater likelihood of being true in the main than any philosophy hitherto advanced (I do not, of course, except my own). In science there are many matters about which people are agreed; in philosophy there are none. Therefore, although each proposition in a science may be false, and it is practically certain that there are some that are false, yet we shall be wise to build our philosophy upon science, because the risk of error in philosophy is pretty sure to be greater than in science. If we could hope for certainty in philosophy the matter would be otherwise, but so far as I can see such a hope would be chimerical.

Of course those philosophers whose theories, *prima facie,* run counter to science always profess to be able to interpret science so that it shall remain true on its own level, with that minor degree of truth which ought to content the humble scientist. Those who maintain a position of this sort are bound—so it seems to me—to show in detail how the interpretation is to be effected. In many cases, I believe that this would be quite impossible. I do not believe, for instance, that those who disbelieve in the reality of relations (in some such sense as that explained above) can possibly interpret those numerous parts of science which employ asymmetrical relations. Even if I could see no way of answering the objections to relations raised (for example) by Mr. Bradley, I should still think it more likely than not that some answer was possible, because I should think an error in a very subtle and abstract argument more probable than so fundamental a falsehood in science. Admitting that everything we believe ourselves to know is doubtful, it seems, nevertheless, that what we believe ourselves to know in philosophy is more doubtful than the detail of science, though perhaps not more doubtful than its most sweeping generalizations.

The question of interpretation is of importance for almost every philosophy, and I am not at all inclined to deny that many scientific results require interpretation before they can be fitted into a coherent philosophy. The maxim of "constructions *versus* inferences" is itself a maxim of interpretation. But I think that any valid kind of interpretation ought to leave the detail unchanged, though it may give a new meaning to fundamental ideas. In practice, this means that *structure* must be preserved. And a test of this is that all the propositions of a science should remain, though new meanings may be found for their terms. A case in point, on a nonphilosophical level, is the relation of the physical theory of light to our perceptions of colour. This provides different physical occurrences corresponding to different seen colours, and thus makes the structure of the physical spectrum the same as that of what we see when we look at a rainbow. Unless structure is preserved, we cannot validly speak of an interpretation. And structure is just what is destroyed by a monistic logic.

I do not mean, of course, to suggest that, in any region of science, the structure revealed at present by observation is exactly that which actually exists. On the contrary, it is in the highest degree probable that the actual structure is more fine-grained than the observed structure. This applies just as much to psychological as to physical material. It rests upon the fact that, where we perceive a difference (e.g. between two shades of colour), there is a difference, but where we do not perceive a difference it does not follow that there is not a difference. We have therefore a right, in all interpretation, to demand the preservation of observed differences, and the provision of room for hitherto unobserved differences, although we cannot say in advance what they will be, except when they can be inferentially connected with observed differences.

In science, structure is the main study. A large part of the importance of relativity comes from the fact that it has substituted a single four-dimensional manifold (space-time) for the two manifolds, three-dimensional space and one-dimensional time. This is a change of structure, and therefore has far-reaching consequences, but any change which does not involve a change of structure does not make much difference. The mathematical definition and study of structure (under the name of "relation-numbers") form Part IV of *Principia Mathematica.*

The business of philosophy, as I conceive it, is essentially that of logical analysis, followed by logical synthesis. Philosophy is more concerned than any special science with relations of different sciences and possible conflicts between them; in particular, it cannot acquiesce in a conflict between physics and psychology, or between psychology and logic. Philosophy should be comprehensive, and should be bold in suggesting hypotheses as to the universe which science is not yet in a position to confirm or confute. But these should always be presented *as* hypotheses, not (as is too often done) as immutable certainties like the dogmas of religion. Although, moreover, comprehensive construction is part of the business of philosophy, I do not believe it is the most important part. The most important part, to my mind, consists in criticizing and clarifying notions which are apt to be regarded as fundamental and accepted uncritically. As instances I might mention: mind, matter, consciousness, knowledge, experience, causality, will, time. I believe all these notions to be inexact and approximate, essentially infected with vagueness, incapable of forming part of any exact science. Out of the original manifold of events, logical structures can be built which will have properties sufficiently like those of the above common notions to account for their prevalence, but sufficiently unlike to allow a great deal of error to creep in through their acceptance as fundamental.

I suggest the following as an outline of a possible structure of the world; it is no more than an outline, and is not offered as more than possible.

The world consists of a number, perhaps finite, perhaps infinite, of entities which have various relations to each other, and perhaps also various qualities. Each of these entities may be called an "event"; from the point of view of old-fashioned physics, an event occupies a short finite time and a small finite amount of space, but as we are not going to have an old-fashioned space and an old-fashioned time, this statement cannot be taken at its face value. Every event has to a certain number of others a relation which may be called "compresence"; from the point of view of physics, a collection of compresent events all occupy one small region in space-time. One example of a set of compresent events is what would be called the contents of one man's mind at one time—i.e. all his sensations, images, memories, thoughts, etc., which can coexist temporally. His visual field has, in one sense, spatial extension, but this must not be confused with the extension of physical space-time; every part of his visual field is compresent with every other part, and with the rest of "the contents of his mind" at that time, and a collection of compresent events occupies a minimal region in space-time. There are such collections not only where there are brains, but everywhere. At any point in "empty space," a number of stars could be photographed if a camera were introduced; we believe that light travels over the regions intermediate between its source and our eyes, and therefore something is happening in these regions. If light from a number of different sources reaches a certain minimal region in space-time, then at least one event corresponding to each of these sources exists in this minimal region, and all these events are compresent.

We will define a set of compresent events as a "minimal region." We find that minimal regions form a four-dimensional manifold, and that, by a little logical manipulation, we can construct from them the manifold of space-time that physics requires. We find also that, from a number of different minimal regions, we can often pick out a set of events, one from each, which are closely similar when they come from neighbouring regions, and vary from one region to another according to discoverable laws. These are the laws of the propagation of light, sound, etc. We find also that certain regions in space-time have quite peculiar properties; these are the regions which are said to be occupied by "matter." Such regions can be collected, by means of the laws of physics, into tracks or tubes, very much more extended in one dimension of space-time than in the other three. Such a tube constitutes the "history" of a piece of matter; from the point of view of the piece of matter itself, the dimension in which it is most extended can be called "time," but it is only the private time of that piece of matter, because it does not correspond exactly with the dimension in which another piece of matter is most extended. Not only is space-time very peculiar within a piece of matter, but it is also rather peculiar in its neighbourhood, growing less so as the spatio-temporal distance grows greater; the law of this peculiarity is the law of gravitation.

All kinds of matter to some extent, but some kinds of matter (viz. nervous tissue) more particularly, are liable to form "habits," i.e. to alter their structure in a given environment in such a way that, when they are subsequently in a similar environment, they react in a new way, but if similar environments recur often, the reaction in the end becomes nearly uniform, while remaining different from the reaction on the first occasion. (When I speak of the reaction of a piece of matter to its environment, I am thinking both of the constitution of the set of compresent events of which it consists, and of the nature of the track in space-time which constitutes what we should ordinarily call its motion; these are called a "reaction to the environment" in so far as there are laws correlating them with characteristics of the environment.) Out of habit, the peculiarities of what we call "mind" can be constructed; a mind is a track of sets of compresent events in a region of space-time where there is matter which is peculiarly liable to form habits. The greater the liability, the more complex and organized the mind becomes. Thus a mind and a brain are not really distinct, but when we speak of a mind we are thinking chiefly of the set of compresent events in the region concerned, and of their several relations to other events forming parts of other periods in the history of the spatio-temporal tube which we are considering, whereas when we speak of a brain we are taking the set of compresent events as a whole, and considering its external relations to other sets of compresent events, also taken as wholes; in a word, we are considering the shape of the tube, not the events of which each cross-section of it is composed.

The above summary hypothesis would, of course, need to be amplified and refined in many ways in order to fit in completely with scientific facts. It is not put forward as a finished theory, but merely as a suggestion of the kind of thing that may be true. It is of course easy to imagine other hypotheses which may be true, for example, the hypothesis that there is nothing outside the series of sets of events constituting my history. I do not believe that there is any method of arriving at one sole possible hypothesis, and therefore certainty in metaphysics seems to me unattainable. In this respect I must admit that many other philosophies have the advantage, since in spite of their differences *inter se,* each arrives at certainty of its own exclusive truth.

NOTES

1. *Our Knowledge of the External World* (Open Court Co. and George Allen & Unwin, 1914), p. 42.
2. I am much indebted to my friend Wittgenstein in this matter. See his *Tractatus Logico-Philosophicus,* Kegan Paul, 1922. I do not accept all his doctrines, but my debt to him will be obvious to those who read his book.

WHAT IS PHILOSOPHY?

G. E. Moore

I want, as a start, to try to give you a general idea of what philosophy *is*: or, in other words, what sort of questions it is that philosophers are constantly engaged in discussing and trying to answer. I want to begin in this way for two reasons. In the first place, by doing this, I shall be giving you some idea of what the problems are which I myself mean to discuss in the rest of this course. And, in the second place, I think it is the best way of beginning any discussion of the main problems of philosophy. By attempting to give, first of all, a general sketch or outline of the whole subject, you point out how the different separate problems are connected with one another and can give a better idea of their relative importance.

I am going, then, first of all to try to give a description of the *whole* range of philosophy. But this is not at all an easy thing to do. It is not easy, because, when you come to look into the matter, you find that philosophers have in fact discussed an immense variety of different sorts of questions; and it is very difficult to give any general description, which will embrace *all* of these questions, and also very difficult to arrange them properly in relation to one another. I cannot hope really to do more than to indicate roughly the main sorts of questions with which philosophers are concerned, and to point out some of the most important connections between these questions. I will try to begin by describing those questions which seem to me to be the *most* important and the most generally interesting, and will then go on to those which are subordinate.

To begin with, it seems to me that the most important and interesting thing which philosophers have tried to do is no less than this; namely: To give a general description of the *whole* of the Universe, mentioning all the most important kinds of things which we *know* to be in it, considering how far it is likely that there are in it important kinds of things which we do not absolutely *know* to be in it, and also considering the most important ways in which these various kinds of things are related to one another. I will call all this, for short, 'Giving a general description of the *whole* Universe', and hence will say that the first and most important problem of philosophy is: To give a general description of the *whole* Universe. Many philosophers (though by no means all) have, I think, certainly tried to give such a description: and the very different descriptions which different philosophers have given are, I think, among the most important differences between them. And the problem is, it seems to me, plainly one which is peculiar to philosophy. There is no other science which

Reprinted by permission of Timothy Moore, from G. E. Moore, "What is Philosophy?" in Moore, *Some Main Problems of Philosophy*, pp. 1–27. London: George Allen & Unwin, Ltd.; New York: The Macmillan Company, 1953.

tries to say: Such and such kinds of things are the *only* kinds of things that there are in the Universe, or which we know to be in it. And I will now try to explain more clearly, by means of examples, exactly what I mean by this first problem—exactly what I mean by a general description of the *whole* Universe. I will try, that is, to mention the most important differences between the descriptions given by different philosophers. And I wish, for a particular reason, to begin in a particular way. There are, it seems to me, certain views about the nature of the Universe, which are held, now-a-days, by almost everybody. They are so universally held that they may, I think, fairly be called the views of Common Sense. I do not know that Common Sense can be said to have any views about the *whole* Universe: none of its views, perhaps, amount to this. But it has, I think, very definite views to the effect that certain kinds of things certainly are in the Universe, and as to some of the ways in which these kinds of things are related to one another. And I wish to begin by describing these views, because it seems to me that what is most amazing and most interesting about the views of many philosophers, is the way in which they go beyond or positively contradict the views of Common Sense: they profess to know that there are in the Universe most important kinds of things, which Common Sense does not profess to know of, and also they profess to know that there are *not* in the Universe (or, at least, that, if there are, we do not know it), things of the existence of which Common Sense is most sure. I think, therefore, you will best realise what these philosophical descriptions of the Universe really mean, by realising how very different they are from the views of Common Sense—how far, in some points, they go beyond Common Sense, and how absolutely, in others, they contradict it. I wish, therefore, to begin by describing what I take to be the most important views of Common Sense: things which we all commonly assume to be true about the Universe, and which we are sure that we know to be true about it.

To begin with, then, it seems to me we certainly believe that there are in the Universe enormous numbers of material objects, of one kind or another. We know, for instance, that there are upon the surface of the earth, besides our own bodies, the bodies of millions of other men; we know that there are the bodies of millions of other animals; millions of plants too; and, besides all these, an even greater number of inanimate objects—mountains, and all the stones upon them, grains of sand, different sorts of minerals and soils, all the drops of water in rivers and in the sea, and moreover ever so many different objects manufactured by men; houses and chairs and tables and railway engines, etc., etc. But, besides all these things upon the surface of the earth, there is the earth itself—an enormous mass of matter. And we believe too, nowadays, that the earth itself, and all that is in it or upon it, huge as it seems to us, is absurdly small in comparison with the whole material Universe. We are accustomed to the idea that the sun and moon and all the immense number of visible stars, are each of them great masses of matter, and most of them many times larger than the earth. We are accustomed, too, to the idea that they are situated at such huge distances from us that any distance from point to point upon the surface of the earth is absurdly small in comparison. All this we now believe about the material Universe: it is surely Common Sense to believe it all. But, as you know, there was a time when it was by no means Common Sense to believe some of these things: there was a time when nobody believed some of them. There was a time when there were not nearly so many men upon the earth as there are now; and when those who were upon it did not know how many there were. They believed only in the existence of a comparatively small number of human bodies beside their own; of a comparatively small number of animals and plants; and they had no idea how large the surface of the earth was. They believed, too, that the heavenly bodies were small compared to the earth, and at comparatively short distances from the earth. But I think I am right in saying we *now* believe that these primitive views about the material Universe were certainly wrong. We should say that we *know* that they were wrong: we have *discovered* that they were wrong: and this discovery is part of our progress in knowledge. But though there are thus *some* things about which the views of Common Sense have changed: yet, so far as concerns the point that there are in the Universe *a great number* of material objects, it has, so far as we know, remained the same. So far as we know, men have believed this almost as long as they have believed anything: they have always believed in the existence of a great many material objects.

But, now, besides material objects, we believe also that there are in the Universe certain phenomena very different from material objects. In short, we believe that we men, besides having bodies, also have *minds;* and one of the chief things which we mean, by saying we have *minds,* is, I think, this: namely, that we perform certain mental acts or acts of consciousness. That is to say, we see and hear and feel and remember and imagine and think and believe and desire and like and dislike and will and love and are angry and afraid, etc. These things that we do are all of them mental acts—acts of mind or acts of *consciousness:* whenever we do any of them, we are conscious of something: each of them partly consists in our being conscious of something in some way or other: and it seems to me that the thing of which we are most certain, when we say we are certain that we have minds, is that we do these things—that we perform these acts of consciousness. At all events we are certain that we do perform them and that these acts are something very different from material objects. To hear is not *itself* a material object, however closely it may be related to certain material objects; and so on with all the rest—seeing, remembering, feeling, thinking, etc. These things, these acts of consciousness are certainly not themselves material objects. And yet we are quite certain that there are immense numbers of them in the Universe. Every one of us performs immense numbers of them every day and all day long: we are perpetually seeing different things, hearing different things, thinking of different things, remembering different things. We cease to perform them only while we are asleep, without dreaming; and even in sleep, so long as we dream, we are performing acts of consciousness. There are, therefore, in the Universe at any moment millions of different acts of consciousness being performed by millions of different men, and perhaps also by many kinds of animals. It is, I think, certainly Common Sense to believe all this.

So far, then, we have seen that Common Sense believes that there are in the Universe, at least two different kinds of things. There are, to begin with, enormous numbers of material objects; and there are also a very great number of mental acts or acts of Consciousness.

But Common Sense has also, I think, certain very definite views as to the way in which these two kinds of things are related to one another. But, before I explain what these views are, I must first mention something which we believe to be true of absolutely *all* the material objects which I have mentioned—and, indeed, not only of them but of *all* objects, which we should commonly call material objects at all.

We believe, in fact, of all material objects, that each of them is, at any given moment, situated somewhere or other in something which we call *space.* And by saying that they are all of them in *space,* we mean, I think, at least two things. We mean, in the first place, that each of them is, at any given moment, at some definite *distance* from all the rest. It may be impossible practically to measure all these distances, or indeed to measure any of them absolutely exactly: but we believe that all of them could theoretically be measured, and expressed as so many miles or feet or inches, or such and such a fraction of an inch, down to those objects which are absolutely touching one another, and between which therefore the distance is nothing at all. We believe, for instance, that the earth is (roughly speaking) so many millions of miles distant from the sun in one direction, and many more millions of miles distant from the pole-star in another; and that just as there is, at any given moment, a definite distance between the sun and the earth, and between the pole-star and the earth, so there is also a definite distance between the sun and the pole-star, and similarly between any one of the heavenly bodies and all the rest. And so too between all the bodies on the surface of the earth, or any parts of these bodies: any two of them are, at any given moment, either touching one another, or else at some definite distance from one another—a distance which can be roughly expressed as so many miles or feet or inches or fractions of an inch. We believe, then, that it is true of all material objects that each is, at any given moment, at some definite distance from all the rest. This is one of the things which we mean by saying that they are all in space. But we mean, I think, *also* that each is distant from all the rest in some *direction* or other: in some one or other of a quite *definite* set of directions. And what this definite set of directions is, can, I think, be easily explained. We all know the shape of the figure which is called a sphere—the shape of a perfectly round ball. Now from the centre of a sphere a straight line can be drawn to each of the points upon its surface. Each of these straight lines, we should say, led in a different *direction* from the centre: this is what we mean by a direction. And moreover there are, we should say, absolutely no directions in which it is possible to move from the centre in a straight line *except* along one or other of these straight lines; if you are to move in a straight line from the centre of a sphere at all, you must go *towards* one or other of the points on its surface; and this is what I meant by speaking of a quite definite set of directions: all the possible directions in which you can go in a straight line from any given point form a quite definite set; namely, you must go along one or other of the straight lines leading from that point to some point on the surface of a sphere of which it is the centre. The second thing, then, which I say we believe about all material objects: is that starting from any point on any one of them, *all* the rest will lie upon one or other of this definite set of straight lines. If you consider all the straight lines which lead from any point to all the different points on the surface of a sphere enclosing it, absolutely every material object in the Universe will, at any given moment, lie on one or other of these straight lines; it will lie at some distance or other along one or other of them. There is, we should say, no other position in space which any material object could occupy; these straight lines will pass through every position in space; so that, if an object is in space at all it must be on one or other of them. This, therefore, is one of the things which we mean by saying that all material objects are situated in *space*. We mean, that is, when we talk of *the* space in which material objects lie and move, a space in which there are no other directions in which you can go from any point, except those which I have specified. We do, I think, certainly hold that all the material objects I have mentioned, do lie in such a space: that from any one of them all the rest must at any moment lie in one or other of these directions. And when we talk of 'material objects', we mean, I think, as a rule, only to include under this description objects of which this is true.

But, now, I introduced this account of what we believe about material objects, in order to explain what we believe about the *relation* of material objects to that other quite different sort of things, which I have called acts of consciousness or mental acts. Common Sense has, I said, some quite definite views about the way in which acts of consciousness in general are related to material objects, and I wish now to state what these views are.

We all, then, commonly believe, I think, that acts of consciousness are quite definitely *attached,* in a particular way, to some material objects, and quite as definitely not *attached* to others. And why I introduced my account of space, was in order to make more clear in what sense we believe acts of consciousness to be *attached* to certain material objects. We believe, I think, that our acts of consciousness—all those which we perform, so long as we are alive—are *attached* to our bodies, in the sense that they occur *in the same places* in which our bodies are. We all do, I think, constantly assume this in ordinary life, and assume it with the utmost certainty; although I believe most philosophers have held that, on the contrary, acts of consciousness do not occur in any place at all—that they are, simply, *nowhere—not* in space. But that we all do commonly assume it, that it is a belief of Common Sense, is, I think, pretty plain. I believe, for instance, that my acts of consciousness are taking place now in this room, where my body is. At the present moment I am hearing and seeing and thinking *here,* in this room. And when, just now, I travelled up to Waterloo by train, I believe that my mind and my acts of consciousness travelled with me. When the train and my body were at Putney, I was thinking and seeing at Putney. When the train and my body reached Clapham Junction, I was thinking and seeing at Clapham Junction. And so on with all the other places which I passed through. We all, I think, commonly assume, in this way, that our acts of consciousness take place, at any moment, *in the place* in which our bodies are at that moment. I do not mean to say that we have any definite idea as to exactly *where* in our bodies our acts of consciousness take place. I do not think we have. We should not be prepared to say whether they all took place at exactly the same spots in our bodies or whether different acts took place at different spots; nor should we be prepared to assign any particular spot as *the* spot at which a particular act took place. All that we do, I think, believe with certainty is that they all do take place somewhere or other in our bodies. At all events we all constantly talk as if we believed this. And I may illustrate the force of this belief which we now have, by contrasting it with a different belief which was formerly held. Some savages, I believe, used to hold that, sometimes when a man was dreaming, his mind or soul used to leave his body and go to some other place and watch what was going on in that place: that, therefore, while he was asleep, his acts of consciousness might be taking place at some place other than that where his body was. Now I think I am right in saying that it is no longer Common Sense to believe this. We commonly believe nowadays that, so long as we are alive, we can, at least normally, only think and see and hear and feel, *where* our bodies are. We believe, at least, that an immense number of acts of consciousness are attached, each of them, to some particular body, in the sense that they occur somewhere or other in that body. My acts of consciousness take place in my body; and yours take place in yours: and our minds (generally, at least) go with us, wherever our bodies go.

We believe, then, I think, that many acts of consciousness are attached to particular material objects, in the sense that they take place *where* those objects are. But I do not mean to say that this is the *only* sense in which we believe them to be attached to particular material objects. We also believe, no doubt, that many of them are *dependent* upon the changes which occur in our bodies. For instance, I only see, when certain changes take place in my eyes; I only hear, when certain changes take place in my ears; only think, perhaps, when certain changes take place in my brain. We certainly believe that many acts of consciousness are attached to particular bodies in this way also. But the simplest and most universal relation which we believe to hold between acts of consciousness and particular bodies is, I think, the one I have mentioned—namely, that they occur *where* those bodies are.

We believe, then, that acts of consciousness are attached to some material objects. But we believe, I think, no less certainly, that to the vast majority of material objects, *no* acts of consciousness are attached. We believe that they *are* attached to the living bodies of men—millions of different men—and, perhaps, of most animals; so that there is no lack of acts of consciousness in the Universe. But nevertheless to the vast majority of material objects we believe, I think, that *none* are attached. We are sure that chairs and tables and houses and mountains and stones do not really see or hear or feel or think or perform any other mental acts: we are sure that they are *not* conscious. We are sure too that the sun and moon and stars and earth are not conscious—that no conscious acts are attached to them, in the sense in which our conscious acts are attached to our bodies: *they* do not feel or hear or see, as *we* do. This, then, is one very important thing which we believe as to the relation between acts of consciousness and material objects: namely, that among the vast number of material objects in the Universe there are comparatively few to which acts of consciousness are attached; in other words, by far the greater number of the material objects in the Universe are *unconscious*. This, I think, may fairly be said to be the view of Common Sense nowadays. But this is another point in regard to which the present view of Common Sense differs a good deal from what it once was. There was, it seems pretty certain, a time when most men believed that acts of Consciousness *were* attached to logs of wood, and stones, and trees, and to the sun and moon and many other objects. They believed that spirits were at various times *in* these objects; and that while the spirits were in them, acts of consciousness often took place inside them: the spirit heard and saw and thought inside the log of wood, just as our minds hear and see and think inside our bodies. There was, then, a time when men commonly believed that consciousness was (for a time, at least) attached to many bodies, which we now believe to be unconscious. But even then, so far as I know, they always believed that there were, at any given time, many places in the Universe in which no acts of consciousness were going on. We, I think, only go much farther than this: we believe that, at any given time, the number of spots in which no act of consciousness is taking place is *immensely* larger than that of those in which an act of consciousness *is* taking place.

This, therefore, is one thing which we believe with regard to the relation between consciousness and material objects. But there are, I think, also two others which deserve to be mentioned. The first of these is this. We believe that we are at certain times conscious of certain material objects: we see, and feel, and think of them. But we believe with the utmost certainty that these material objects can and do continue to exist even when we are *not* conscious of them. We are, for instance, at this moment seeing certain material objects in this room. But we believe that they will continue to exist, even when we have all gone away and the room is shut up for the night and no one is seeing them. If I leave a room, for five minutes, in which a fire is burning, and then come back and find it burning still, I assume that it has been burning all the while I was away, and when no one was seeing it or feeling its heat, just as much as when I was there to see it. We all, I think, constantly assume with regard to material objects that they are, in this sense, wholly independent of our consciousness of them: they are all objects of a sort, which exist just as much when we are not conscious of them as when we are. We may, indeed, say of *all* material objects that they have three characteristics: (1) they are quite a different sort of thing from acts of consciousness, (2) they are all of them, at any given time, situated somewhere or other in space, and (3) they have this property which I have just mentioned—namely that they are a sort of thing, which exists when we are not conscious of it just as much as when we are. These three characteristics are not, I think, sufficient to define a material object: there may be other objects, which possess all three and yet are not material objects. But they are, I think, three of the most important characteristics which material objects have; and we should not call anything a material object, unless we meant to assert that it had all three.

A second thing, then, which we believe about the relation of consciousness to matter, is that matter is independent of our consciousness of it—that it exists even when we are not conscious of it; and we believe, too, that there are existing at any moment many more material objects, of which no man or animal is conscious, than material objects of which we are conscious. And the third thing which we believe about the relation of consciousness to matter is the following. We believe, namely, that there probably was a time when there were *no* acts of consciousness attached to any material objects on the earth: a time, when the earth was so hot that no living beings could exist upon it; and when therefore there could be no conscious beings on it either. And as regards human bodies and human consciousness we believe, I think, that this is not only probable, but certain. We believe that it is only for a comparatively limited time—*comparatively* limited, though amounting, perhaps, to several millions of years—that men have existed upon the earth: before that time, there were no bodies upon the earth which could be called human, and also no minds which could be called the minds of men; though there may have been minds and acts of consciousness belonging to other sorts of animals. And just as we believe that, at some time in the past, there were probably no conscious beings at all upon the earth, and certainly no beings with human consciousness; so we believe that there *may* come a time, in the future, when this will again be so. We should not indeed deny that, even when there was no consciousness on the earth, there *may* have been conscious beings elsewhere in the Universe, on other planets; we should not deny that there may be some now; nor should we deny that this may still be so, when (if ever) the time comes, when all consciousness upon the earth is again extinguished. But we should, I think, hold that there *may* have been, and may be again, long periods in the history of the material Universe, during which no consciousness was attached to any of the bodies in it—when no conscious acts were taking place anywhere in it. We believe, that is to say, that just as consciousness certainly is now attached to comparatively *few* among the material objects in the Universe, so there *may* have been in the past and *may* be again in the future, long periods when it was or will be attached to *none* at all. This is, I think, one belief of Common Sense with regard to the relation of consciousness to material objects; and, if it be so, it is certainly an important element in our general view of the Universe.

So far, then, the elements which I have tried to emphasize in the Common Sense view of the Universe, are these. Firstly, that there certainly are in the Universe two very different kinds of things, namely material objects and acts of consciousness. And secondly, as to the relation of these two kinds of things three points: the first (1) that conscious acts are attached to comparatively few among the material objects in the Universe; that the vast majority of material objects are unconscious. Indeed the only bodies to which we should say we know them with certainty to be attached are the living bodies of men, and perhaps other animals, upon the Earth. We should not deny that they *may* be attached also to other bodies on other planets: that there may on other planets be other living beings, which are conscious. But we should, I think, say that conscious acts certainly are not attached to the vast majority of the material objects in the Universe. This is one of our beliefs about the relation of acts of consciousness to material objects. A second is (2) that material objects are all of such a kind that they may exist, even when we are not conscious of them, and that many do in fact so exist. And the third is (3) that there *may* have been a time when acts of consciousness were attached to *no* material bodies anywhere in the Universe, and *may* again be such a time; and that there almost certainly was a time when there were no human bodies, with human consciousness attached to them, upon this earth.

And now there are only two other points in the views of Common Sense about the Universe, to which I wish to call attention.

The first is one, which I have constantly assumed in what I have already said, but which I wish now to mention expressly. It is this. That all material objects, and all the acts of consciousness of ourselves and other animals upon the earth, are in *time*. I say '*are* in time'; but, to speak more accurately I ought to say *either* have been in time *or* are so now *or* will be so in the future; *either* this, or else all three—*both* have been in time in the past, *and* are so now, *and* will be so in the future. For just one of the things which we mean by talking of 'time' is that there are such things as the past, the present and the future, and that there is a great difference between the three. None of the material objects in space and none of our acts of consciousness can, we hold, be truly said to *exist* at all, unless it exists *at the time at which we say so*; only those of them, for instance, which exist at the time at which I am now speaking can now be truly said to *exist* at all: of others it may be true that they *did* exist in the past or that they *will* exist in the future, but it cannot be true that they *do* exist. What I mean, then, when I say that all material objects and all our acts of consciousness are in time, is this: that each of them either did exist in the past, or exists now, or will exist in the future; *either* this, or else, all three: *both* did exist at some time in the past, does exist now, and will exist in the future. And I mean, too, that to say that a thing 'did exist' is something different from saying that it 'does exist' and both these again from saying that it 'will exist'; and that each of these different statements is in fact true of some things. I am, for instance, quite sure that there have been in the past many acts of consciousness, both of my own and those of other men; I am quite sure that many are existing now; and I am very certain, though less certain, that many will exist in the future. And so too of material objects: many have existed in the past, many do exist now, and many (in all probability) will exist in the future. I say we all commonly believe that these things are so. We believe that the three statements 'It *did* exist'; 'It *does* exist'; 'It *will* exist': are each of them true of many material objects and many acts of consciousness; the first true of some; the second true of others; and the third of still others; and of many, again, all three. And we believe also, that one or other of these statements is true of *all* of them; either this, or else in some instances that all three of them are true of one and the same thing: the sun or the earth, for instance, both *did* exist, *do* exist, and (probably) *will* exist. This, I say, is certainly the belief of Common Sense.

And there is only one other belief of Common Sense which I wish to mention: namely, this. We believe that we do really *know* all these things that I have mentioned. We *know* that there are and have been in the Universe the two kinds of things—material objects and acts of consciousness. We *know* that there are and have been in the Universe huge numbers of both. We *know* that many material objects exist when we are not conscious of them. We *know* that the vast majority of material objects are unconscious. We *know* that things of both kinds *have* existed in the past, which do not exist now, and that things of both kinds do exist now, which did *not* exist in the past. All these things we should, I think, certainly say that we *know*. And moreover we believe that we *know* an immense number of details about particular material objects and acts of consciousness, past, present and future. We know most, indeed, about the past; but a great deal about the present; and much also (though perhaps this is only probable knowledge) about the future. Indeed the sphere of most of the special sciences may be defined as being to give us detailed knowledge about particular objects of the kinds which I have been trying to define: that is to say, about material objects which are or have been somewhere or other in space, and about the acts of consciousness of men upon the earth. Most of the special sciences confine themselves to some particular group among objects of these two kinds; and we believe that they have been very successful in giving us a great deal of real knowledge about objects of these kinds. Astronomy, for instance, tells us about the heavenly bodies—their size and movements and composition and how they act upon one another. Physics and chemistry give us detailed knowledge about the composition of different kinds of material objects, and how they and their minute parts act upon one another. Biology gives us knowledge about the differences between different kinds of animals upon the earth. Botany about the differences between different kinds of plants. Physiology about the processes which go on in living bodies. Geology gives us knowledge about the present state and past history of the different layers of rock or soil of which the crust of the earth is composed. Geography gives us knowledge about the present distribution of land and water upon the surface of the earth; about the positions of mountains and rivers; about the different soils and climates of different parts of the earth. History and biography give us knowledge about the actions of different men and collections of men, which have existed upon the surface of the earth; and also about their acts of consciousness, what sorts of things they saw and heard and thought and believed. Finally Psychology deals specially with the acts of consciousness of men and to some extent to animals also; it tries to classify and distinguish the different kinds of mental acts which we perform, and to decide how these different acts are related to one another. All these sciences which I have mentioned are, you will observe, occupied exclusively with giving us information about the two kinds of objects which I have tried to define—namely, material objects in space, and the acts of consciousness of men and animals on the surface of the earth. And we certainly believe that all of them have succeeded in acquiring a great deal of real *knowledge* about objects of these kinds. We distinguish sharply, in each case, between things which are now absolutely known; things which were formerly believed, but believed wrongly; and things which we do not yet know. In the case of all these sciences, there are, we believe, an immense number of things which are now definitely known to be facts; a great many, which were formerly believed, but are now definitely known to be errors; and a great many which we do not know and perhaps never shall know. In all our ordinary talk, in all newspapers and in all ordinary books (by which I mean books *other* than philosophical books) we constantly assume that there is this distinction between what we know, what we wrongly believe, and what we are still in ignorance about: and we assume that an enormous number of truths about material objects and the acts of consciousness of men belong to the first class—the class of things absolutely *known*—known, that is, by some man on the surface of the earth. All this is, I think, certainly nowadays part of the belief of Common Sense about the Universe.

I have tried, then, to enumerate certain general beliefs about the Universe, which may, I think, be fairly said to be beliefs of Common Sense: beliefs which we almost all of us nowadays entertain; and I do not mean to say that these are the only views of Common Sense about the Universe; but only that they *are* views which it does hold—*some* of its principal beliefs. But now all of these beliefs taken together do not amount to a general description of the *whole* Universe: they are not a general description of the *whole* Universe, in the sense in which I said that the first problem of philosophy was to give us such a description. They consist in saying that there certainly *are* in the Universe certain large classes of things, and that these things are related to one another in certain ways. But what they do not say, as they stand, is that these large classes of things are the *only* classes of things which are in the Universe, or which we *know* to be in it: they do not say that everything which we know to be in the Universe belongs to one or other of these classes; they do not deny, as they stand, that there may be in the Universe, or may even be *known* to be in it, important classes of things which *do not* belong to any of the classes I have mentioned. For instance, Common Sense says, according to me: There are in the Universe two classes of things: There are material objects in space, and there are the acts of consciousness of living men and animals upon the surface of the earth. But, in order to convert these statements into a general description of the whole Universe, we should have to add one or other of two things. We should have to say *either: Everything* in the Universe belongs to one or other of these two classes; everything is either a material object in space, or an act of consciousness of some man or animal on the earth. And this would plainly, if any one said it, profess to be a general description of the *whole* Universe. Or else we might say: Everything which we *know* to be in the Universe, does belong to one or other of these two classes; though there *may* be in the Universe other things, which we do not know to be in it. And this also, I think, might fairly be said to be an attempt to give a general description of the whole Universe. It would, indeed, consist in saying that, in a sense, *no* such description can be given; since it would say that there may be in the Universe things which we do not know of and therefore cannot describe. But it *would* profess to give a general description of everything that we *know* to be in the Universe; and would be a thing which no one would say unless his object were to solve our first philosophical problem—namely, to give the best general description he could of the *whole* Universe.

Starting, therefore, from the view of Common Sense that there certainly are in the Universe (1) material objects in space and (2) the acts of consciousness of men and animals upon the earth, we might most simply get a general description of the Universe in one or other of two ways: Either by saying, these two kinds of things *are* the only kinds in the Universe; or by saying: they are the only kinds we *know* to be in it, *but* there may possibly also be others. And as regards the first of these two views, I doubt whether any one, on reflection, would be willing to accept it quite as it stands. The most obvious objection to it is that by asserting that there are no acts of consciousness in the Universe, except those of men and animals on the earth, it denies the possibility that there *may* be or have been on other planets living beings endowed with consciousness. And this is a possibility which almost everybody would think it rash to deny. But still, by slightly modifying it to allow of this possibility, we get a view which might, I think, seem very plausible to many people. We might, for instance, say: There really is not, and never has been anything in the Universe, except material objects in space, on the one hand, and acts of consciousness, more or less similar to those of men and animals, attached to living bodies more or less similar to theirs, on the other hand. This is, I think, really a plausible view of the Universe; at least as plausible as many that have been proposed by philosophers. But, no doubt, the second view is more plausible still: it does seem more plausible to add the proviso: These are the only things we *know* to be in it; *but* there *may* be other kinds of things unknown to us. And this, I think, is a view which really has been held by many people, philosophers and others. They have held, that is, that the only kinds of things which we *know* to be in the Universe are material objects in space, and the acts of consciousness of men and animals on the earth; while adding also that there *may* be other kinds of things unknown to us.

No doubt, philosophers who have said this or something like it, have not meant by it quite what they said. Those who hold that there are and *have been* in the Universe material objects in space, and that there are and have been acts of consciousness, can hardly deny that there certainly are in the Universe *also* at least two other things beside these—things which are neither material objects nor acts of consciousness—namely, Space and Time themselves. It must be admitted on this view that Space and Time themselves really *are*—that they are *something*; and it is obvious that they are *neither* material objects *nor* acts of consciousness. And similarly there may be in the Universe other kinds of things known to us, besides Space and Time, which are neither material objects nor yet acts of consciousness. For my part, I think, there certainly are several other kinds of things, and that it is one of the objects of philosophy to point them out. But those philosophers who have spoken as if material objects and acts of consciousness were the *only* kinds of things known by us to be in the Universe, have, I think, not really meant to deny this. They have meant, rather, that material objects and acts of consciousness are the only kinds of things known to us, which are in a certain sense *substantial*: substantial in a sense in which Space and Time themselves do not seem to be substantial. And I may say, at once, that, for my part, if we make suitable modifications of this sort, this view does seem to me to be a correct view. I hold, that is to say, that material objects in space, and the acts of consciousness of men and animals on the earth, really are the only *substantial* kinds of things *known* to us; though I should admit that there may possibly be others unknown to us; and though I think that there are certainly several *unsubstantial* kinds of things, which it is very important to mention, if we are to give a really complete general description of the *whole* Universe—Time and Space for instance.

One way, therefore, in which we might get a general description of the whole Universe, is by making additions to the views of Common Sense of the comparatively simple sort which I have just indicated. But many philosophers have held that any such view as this is very incorrect indeed. And different philosophers have held it to be incorrect in three different ways. They have either held that there certainly are in the Universe some most important kinds of things—*substantial* kinds of things—*in addition* to those which Common Sense asserts to be in it. Or else they have positively contradicted Common Sense: have asserted that some of the things which Common Sense supposes to be in it, are *not* in it, or else, that, if they are, we do not know it. Or else they have done *both*; both added and contradicted.

I wish now to give some examples of all three kinds of views. Both of those which *add* something very important to the views of Common Sense; and of those which *contradict* some of the views of Common Sense; and of those which do both.

To begin then with those which *add* something to the views of Common Sense.

There is, first of all, one view of this type which everybody has heard of. You all know, that enormous numbers of people, and not philosophers only, believe that there certainly is a God in the Universe: that, beside material objects and our acts of consciousness, there is also a Divine Mind, and the acts of consciousness of this mind; and that, if you are to give any complete description of the sum of things, of everything that is, you must certainly mention God. It might even be claimed that this view—the view that there is a God, is itself a view of Common Sense. So many people have believed and still do believe that there certainly is a God, that it might be claimed that this is a Common Sense belief. But, on the other hand, so many people now believe that, even if there is a God, we certainly do not *know* that there is one; that this also might be claimed as a view of Common Sense. On the whole, I think it is fairest to say, that Common Sense has *no* view on the question whether we do know that there is a God or not: that it neither asserts that we do know this, nor yet that we do not; and that, therefore, Common Sense has *no* view as to the Universe as a *whole*. We may, therefore, say that those philosophers who assert that there certainly *is* a God in the Universe do go *beyond* the views of Common Sense. They make a most important addition to what Common Sense believes about the Universe. For by a God is meant something so different both from material objects and from our minds, that to add that, besides these, there is also a God, is certainly to make an important addition to our view of the Universe.

And there is another view of this type, which also everybody has heard of. Everybody knows that enormous numbers of men have believed and still do believe that there *is* a future life. That is to say, that, besides the acts of consciousness attached to our bodies, while they are alive upon the earth, our minds go on performing acts of consciousness after the death of our bodies—go on performing acts of consciousness *not* attached to any living body on the surface of the earth. Many people believe that we *know* this: so many people believe it that, here again, as in the case of God, it might be claimed that this is a belief of Common Sense. But, on the other hand, so many people believe that, even if we have a future life, we certainly do not *know* that we have one; that here again it is perhaps fairest to say that Common Sense has no view on the point: that it asserts neither that we *do* know of a future life nor that we do *not*. This, therefore, also may be called an *addition* to the views of Common Sense; and certainly it is a most important addition. If there really are going on in the Universe at this moment, not only the acts of consciousness attached to the living bodies of men and animals on the surface of this earth, but also acts of consciousness performed by the minds of millions of men, whose bodies have long been dead—then certainly the Universe is a very different place from what it would be, if this were not the case.

Here, then, are two different views of the type which I describe as making important *additions* to the views of Common Sense, while not contradicting it. And there is only one other view of this type which I wish to mention. Some philosophers have held, namely, that there certainly is in the Universe, *something* else, beside material objects and our acts of consciousness, and something substantial too—but that we do not know what the nature of this something is—that it is something Unknown or Unknowable. This view, you see, must be carefully distinguished from that which I mentioned above as *not* going much beyond Common Sense: namely the view that there *may* be in the Universe, things which are neither material objects nor the acts of consciousness of men and animals, but that we do not know whether there are or not. There is a great difference between saying: There *may* be in the Universe some other kind of thing, but we do not know whether there is or not; and saying: There certainly *is* in the Universe some other important kind of thing, though we do not know *what* it is. This latter view may, I think, fairly be said to go a great way beyond the views of Common Sense. It asserts that in addition to the things which Common Sense asserts to be *certainly* in the Universe—namely, material objects in Space and the Acts of consciousness attached to living bodies—there *certainly* is something else besides, though we do not know what this something is. This view is a view which has, I think, been held by people who call themselves Agnostics; but I think it hardly deserves the name. To know, not only that there may be, but that there *certainly* is in the Universe something substantial besides material objects and our acts of consciousness is certainly to know a good deal. But I think it is a view that is not uncommonly held.

I have given, then, three examples of views which add to Common Sense without contradicting it and I now pass to the second type of views: those which contradict Common Sense, without *adding* to it; those which deny something which Common Sense professes to know, without professing to *know* anything, which Common Sense does *not* profess to know. I will call these, for the sake of a name, *sceptical views.*

Of this second type, there are, I think, two main varieties, both of which consist in saying that we do *not* know, certain things which Common Sense says we *do* know. No views of this type, I think, positively deny that there are in the Universe those things which Common Sense says certainly are in it: they only say that we simply do not know at all whether these things are in it or not; whereas Common Sense asserts quite positively that we *do* know that they are.

The first variety of this type is that which asserts that we simply do not know at all whether there are any material objects in the Universe at all. It admits that there *may* be such objects; but it says that none of us knows that there are any. It denies, that is to say, that we can know of the existence of any objects, which continue to exist when we are not conscious of them, except other minds and their acts of consciousness.

And the second view goes even further than this. It denies also that we can know of the existence of any minds or acts of consciousness except our own. It holds, in fact, that the only substantial kind of thing which any man can know to be in the Universe is simply his own acts of consciousness. It does not deny that there *may* be in the Universe other minds and even material objects too; but it asserts that, if there are, we cannot know it. This is, of course, an illogical position; since the philosopher who holds it, while asserting positively that no man can know of the existence of any other mind, also positively asserts that there are other men beside himself, who are all as incapable as he is of knowing the existence of any one else. But though it is illogical, it has been held. And it would cease to be illogical, if, instead of asserting that *no* man knows of the existence of any other mind, the philosopher were to confine himself to the assertion that *he* personally does not.

But now I come to the third type of views—views which depart *much* further from Common Sense than any that I have mentioned yet; since they *both* positively deny that there are in the Universe certain things, which Common Sense asserts certainly *are* in it, and *also* positively assert that there are in it certain kinds of things, which Common Sense does not profess to know of. Views of this type are, I may say, very much in favour among philosophers.

The chief views of this type may, I think, be divided into two classes: first, those whose contradiction of Common Sense merely consists in the fact that they positively deny the existence of space and material objects; and secondly, those which positively deny many other things as well. Both kinds, I must insist, do positively deny the existence of material objects; they say that there certainly *are* no such things in the Universe; not merely, like sceptical views, that we do not *know* whether there are or not.

First, then, for those views which merely contradict Common Sense by denying the existence of Space and material objects.

These views all, I think, start by considering certain things, which I will call the Appearances of material objects. And I think I can easily explain what I mean by this. You all know that, if you look at a church steeple from the distance of a mile, it has a different appearance from that which it has, when you look at it from the distance of a hundred yards; it looks smaller and you do not see it in many details which you see when you are nearer. These different appearances which the same material object may present from different distances and different points of view are very familiar to all of us: there certainly are such things in the Universe, as these things which I call Appearances of material objects. And there are two views about them, both of which might be held quite consistently with Common Sense, and between which, I think, Common Sense does not pronounce. It might be held that some, at least, among them really are parts of the objects,[1] of which they are appearances: really are situated in space, and really continue to exist, even when we are not conscious of them. But it might also be held, quite consistently with Common Sense, that *none* of these appearances are in space, and that they all exist only so long as they appear *to* some one: that, for instance, the appearance which the church tower presents to me on a particular occasion, exists only so long as I see it, and cannot be said to be in the same space with any material object or to be at any distance from any material object. All that it does insist on, I think, is that these appearances are appearances of material objects—of objects which do exist, when we are not conscious of them, and which *are* in space. Now the philosophers whose views I am now considering have, I think, all accepted the second of the two views about appearances, which I said were consistent with Common Sense—namely the view that these appearances only exist, so long as the person to whom they appear is seeing them, and that they are *not* in space. And they have then gone on to contradict Common Sense, by adding that these appearances are *not* appearances of material objects—that there are no material objects, for them to be appearances *of*.

And there are two different views of this kind, which have been held.

The first is the view of one of the most famous of English philosophers,

Bishop Berkeley. Berkeley's view may, I think, be said to have been that these Appearances are in fact not Appearances *of* anything at all. He himself says, indeed, that these Appearances are themselves material objects—that they are what we mean by material objects. He says that he is not denying the existence of matter, but only explaining what matter is. But he has been commonly held to have denied the existence of matter, and, I think, quite rightly. For he held that these Appearances do not exist except at the moment when we see them; and anything of which this is true can certainly not properly be said to be a material object: what we mean to assert, when we assert the existence of material objects, is certainly the existence of something which continues to exist even when we are *not* conscious of it. Moreover he certainly held, I think, that these appearances were not *all* of them in the same space: he held, for instance, that an appearance, which appears to me, was not at any distance or in any direction from an appearance which appears to you: whereas, as I have said, we should, I think, refuse to call anything a material object, which was not at some distance, in space, in some direction from all *other* material objects. I think, then, it may fairly be said that Berkeley denies the existence of any material objects, in the sense in which Common Sense asserts their existence. This is the way in which he contradicts Common Sense. And the way in which he *adds* to it, is by asserting the existence of a God, to whom, he thinks, there appear a set of appearances exactly like all of those which appear to us.

But Berkeley's view has not, I think, been shared by many other philosophers. A much commoner view is that these things which I have called the appearances of material objects, are in fact the appearances of *something,* but not, as Common Sense asserts, of material objects, but of minds or conscious beings. This view, therefore, both contradicts Common Sense, by denying the existence of material objects, and also goes beyond it by asserting the existence of immense numbers of minds, in addition to those of men and of animals. And it insists, too, that these minds are not in *space*: it is, it says, not true that they are at any distance in any direction from one another; they are, in fact, all simply *nowhere,* not in any place at all.

These views are, I think, startling enough. But there are other philosophers who have held views more startling still—who have held not only that space and material objects do not really exist, but also that time and our own conscious acts do not really exist either: that there are not really any such things in the Universe. At least, this is, I think, what many philosophers have meant. What they *say* is that all these four kinds of things, material objects, space, our acts of consciousness and time, are Appearances; that they are all of them Appearances *of* something else—either of some one thing, or else some collection of things, which is *not* a material object, nor an act of consciousness of ours, and which also is not in space nor yet in time. And, as you see, this proposition is ambiguous: whether it contradicts Common Sense or not depends on the question what these philosophers mean by calling these things Appearances. They might conceivably mean that these Appearances were just as real, as the things of which they are appearances; by asserting that they are Appearances of something else, they might only mean to assert that there is in the Universe something else *besides*—something to which these things are related in the same sort of way in which the appearance of a church-tower, which I see when I look at it from a distance, is related to the real church-tower. And, if they did only mean this, their views would merely be of the type of those that *add* to Common Sense: they would merely be asserting that, in addition to the things which Common Sense believes to be in the Universe, there is *also* something else *beside* or *behind* these things. But it seems to me quite plain that they do not really mean this. They do mean to maintain that matter and space and our acts of consciousness and time are *not* real in the sense in which Common Sense believes them to be real, and in which they themselves believe that the *something* else behind Appearances is real. And holding this, it seems to me that what they really mean is that these things are not real at all: that there are not really any such things in the Universe. What, I think, they really mean (though they would not all admit that they mean it) is something like this. There is a sense in which the pole-star, when we look at it, *appears* to be much smaller than the moon. We may say, then, that *what* appears—the *appearance,* in this case—is simply this: *that the pole-star is smaller than the moon*. But there simply *is* no such thing in the Universe as this which appears: the pole-star is *not* smaller than the moon: and, therefore, what appears to be in the Universe—namely, *that* it is smaller than the moon—is a simple nonentity—there is no such thing. It is in this sense, I think, that many philosophers have believed and still believe that not only matter and space but also our acts of consciousness and time simply do not exist: that there are no such things. They have believed that they are something which appears; but that what appears simply is *not* anything—that there is no such thing in the Universe. This, I think, is what they really mean, though they would not all admit that they mean it. And as to what they hold to be in the Universe, *instead of* the things which Common Sense holds to be in it, they have held different views. Some have held that it is a collection of different minds; others that it is one mind; others that it is something which is in some sense mental or spiritual, but which cannot be properly said either to be one mind or many.

These, then, are some of the views which have been held as to the nature of the Universe as a *whole*. And I hope these examples have made clear the sort of thing I mean by the first problem of philosophy—a *general* description of the whole Universe. Any answer to the problem must consist in saying one or other of three things: it must say *either* that certain large classes of things are the *only* kinds of things in the Universe, *i.e.,* that everything in it belongs to one or other of them; or else it must say that everything in the Universe is of one kind; or else it must say that everything which we *know* to be in the Universe belongs to some one of several classes or to some one class. And it must also, if it holds that there are several different classes of things, say something about the relation of these classes to one another.

This, then, is the first and most interesting problem of philosophy. And it seems to me that a great many others can be defined as problems bearing upon this one.

For philosophers have not been content simply to express their opinions as to what there is or is not in the Universe, or as to what we know to be in it or do not know to be in it. They have also tried to prove their opinions to be true. And with this, you see, a great many subordinate problems are opened up.

In order to prove, for instance, that any one of these views I have mentioned are true, you must both prove *it* and *also* refute all the others. You must prove either that there is a God, or that there is not, or that we do not know whether there is one or not. Either that there is a future life, or that there is not, or that we do not know whether there is one or not. And so on with all the other kinds of things I have mentioned: matter and space and time; and the minds of other men; and other minds, *not* the minds of men or animals. In order to prove that any particular view of the Universe is correct, you must prove, in the case of each of these things, either that they do exist, or that they do not, or that we do not know whether they do or not. And all these questions, you see, may be treated separately for their own sakes. Many philosophers, indeed, have not tried to give any general description of the *whole* Universe. They have merely tried to answer some one or more of these subordinate questions.

And there is another sort of subordinate questions, which ought, I think, to be specially mentioned. Many philosophers have spent a great deal of their time in trying to define more clearly what is the difference between these various sorts of things: for instance, what is the difference between a material object and an act of consciousness, between matter and mind, between God and man, etc. And these questions of definition are by no means so easy to answer as you might think. Nor must it be thought that they are mere questions of words. A good definition of the sorts of things you hold to be in the Universe, obviously adds to the clearness of your view. And it is not only a question of clearness either. When, for instance, you try to define what you mean by a material object, you find that there are several different properties which a material object might have, of which you had never thought before; and your effort to define may thus lead you to conclude that whole classes of things have certain properties, or have *not* certain others, of which you would never have thought, if you had merely contented yourself with asserting that there are material objects in the Universe, without enquiring what you meant by this assertion.

We may, then, say that a great class of subordinate philosophical problems consist in discussing whether the great classes of things I have mentioned do exist or do not, or whether we are simply ignorant as to whether they do or not; and also in trying to define these classes and considering how they are related to one another. A great deal of philosophy has consisted in discussing these questions with regard to God, a future life, matter, minds, Space and Time. And all these problems could be said to belong to that department of philosophy which is called Metaphysics.

But now we come to a class of questions which may be said to belong to other departments of philosophy, but which also have an evident bearing on the first main problem as to the general description of the Universe. One of the most natural questions to ask, when anybody asserts some fact, which you are inclined to doubt, is the question: How do you know that? And if the person answers the question in such a way as to shew that he has not learnt the fact in any one of the ways in which it is possible to acquire real knowledge, as opposed to mere belief, about facts of the sort, you will conclude that he does *not* really know it. In other words, we constantly assume in ordinary life that there are only a limited number of ways in which it is possible to acquire real *knowledge* of certain kinds of facts; and that if a person asserts a fact, which he has not learnt in any of these ways, then, in fact, he does not *know* it. Now philosophers also have used this sort of argument very largely. They have tried to classify exhaustively all the different kinds of ways in which we can know things; and have then concluded that, since certain things, which other philosophers have asserted or which they themselves formerly believed, are *not* known in any of these ways, therefore these things are not known at all.

Hence a large part of philosophy has, in fact, consisted in trying to classify completely all the different ways in which we can *know* things; or in trying to describe exactly particular ways of knowing them.

And this question—the question: How do we *know* anything at all? involves three different kinds of questions.

The first is of this sort. When you are asked: How do you know that? it may be meant to ask: What sort of a thing *is* your knowledge of it? What sort of a process goes on in your mind, when you *know* it? In what does this event, which you call a *knowing,* consist? This first question as to what sort of a thing knowledge is—as to what happens when we *know* anything—is a question which philosophy shares with psychology; but which many philosophers have tried to answer. They have tried to distinguish the different kinds of things, which happen in our minds, when we know different things; and to point out, what, if anything, is common to them all.

But there is, secondly, something else which may be meant; when it is asked what knowledge *is*. For we do not say that we *know* any proposition, for instance the proposition that matter exists, unless we mean to assert that this proposition is *true*: that it is *true* that matter exists. And hence there is included in the question what knowledge *is,* the question what is meant by saying that any proposition is *true.* This is a different question from the psychological question as to what happens in your mind, when you know anything; and this question as to what *truth* is has generally been said to be a question for *Logic,* in the widest sense of the term. And Logic, or at least parts of it, is reckoned as a department of philosophy.

And, finally, there is still another thing which may be meant, when it is asked: How do you know that? It may be meant, namely, what reason have you for believing it? or in other words, what other *thing* do you know, which *proves* this thing to be *true*? And philosophers have, in fact, been much occupied with this question also: the question what are the different ways in which a proposition can be proved to be true; what are all the different sorts of reasons which are good reasons for believing anything. This also is a question which is reckoned as belonging to the department of Logic.

There is, therefore, a huge branch of philosophy which is concerned with the different ways in which we know things; and many philosophers have devoted themselves almost exclusively to questions which fall under this head.

But finally, if we are to give a complete account of philosophy, we must mention one other class of questions. There is a department of philosophy which is called Ethics or ethical philosophy; and this department deals with a class of questions quite different from any which I have mentioned yet. We are all constantly in ordinary life asking such questions as: Would such and such a result be a good thing to bring about? or would it be a bad thing? Would such and such an action be a right action to perform or would it be a wrong one? And what ethical philosophy tries to do is to classify all the different sorts of things which *would* be good or bad, right or wrong, in such a way as to be able to say: Nothing would be good, unless it had certain characteristics, or one or other of certain characteristics; and similarly nothing would be bad, unless it had certain properties or one or other of certain properties: and similarly with the question, what sort of actions would be right, and what would be wrong.

And these ethical questions have a most important bearing upon our general description of the Universe in two ways.

In the first place, it is certainly one of the most important facts about the Universe that there are in it these distinctions of good and bad, right and wrong. And many people have thought that, from the fact that there are these distinctions, other inferences as to what is in the Universe can be drawn.

And in the second place, by combining the results of Ethics as to what *would* be good or bad, with the conclusions of Metaphysics as to what kinds of things there are in the Universe, we get a means of answering the question whether the Universe is, on the whole, good or bad, and how good or bad, compared with what it might be: a sort of question, which has in fact been much discussed by many philosophers.

To conclude, then, I think the above is a fair description of the sort of questions with which philosophers deal. And I shall try hereafter to say something about as many of the points which I have mentioned as I have space for. I propose to begin by considering some of the ways in which we know things. And first of all, I shall consider the question: How do we know of the existence of material objects, supposing that, as Common Sense supposes, we *do* know of their existence? And then, after considering *how* we know this, if we do know it, I shall go on to the question whether, in fact, we *do* know of their existence? trying to answer the principal objections of those philosophers, who have maintained that we certainly do not. In the course of this discussion we shall come upon a good many conclusions as to the sorts of ways in which we know things; and shall be in a better position to consider what *else* beside material objects we can know to exist.

I shall now, therefore, proceed to consider the most primitive sort of way in which we seem to have knowledge of material objects—that which we have by means of the senses—by seeing and hearing and feeling them.

NOTES

1. I should now say 'parts of the *surfaces* of the objects'. (1952)

PHILOSOPHY

Ludwig Wittgenstein

The following selection is a chapter from Wittgenstein's Big Typescript, *produced around 1933. Wittgenstein seems to have prepared it for publication, but he soon began making handwritten changes to the typescript and rewriting some of it. Parts of* The Big Typescript *ended up in works published posthumously, including* Philosophical Grammar *and* Philosophical Investigations *(some remarks from this article in particular appear among sections #111–133 in the* Investigations*). For a more thorough account of the history of* The Big Typescript, *see Anthony Kenny, "From the Big Typescript to the Philosophical Grammar,"* Acta Philosophica Fennica, *vol. 28 (1976), pp. 41–53.*

This selection appeared in print in the original German in Revue Internationale de Philosophie, *vol. 43 (1989), pp. 175–203. Heikki Nyman edited the original text for this publication and employed some mechanical devices to capture in print the handwritten notes and changes as well as the typewritten alternatives Wittgenstein had added to the typescript. These devices were preserved in the English translation by C. G. Luckhardt and M. A. E. Aue, which is reprinted here. Wittgenstein himself included alternate words or phrases in places either by enclosing them within the symbols //. . . .// behind the words for which they are an alternate or by typing them above those words. Nyman reproduced both of these devices in the published text. Nyman indicated the* handwritten *additions in his footnotes. Question marks above words or phrases and underlining indicate the handwritten additions of these marks in the typescript. Both indicate Wittgenstein's uncertainty about the adequacy of these expressions. Some marginal marks such as lines and crosses are not represented in the published text.*

—The Editors

86

DIFFICULTY OF PHILOSOPHY NOT THE INTELLECTUAL DIFFICULTY OF THE SCIENCES, BUT THE DIFFICULTY OF A CHANGE OF ATTITUDE. RESISTANCES OF THE *WILL* MUST BE OVERCOME.

As I have often said, philosophy does not lead me to any renunciation, since I do not abstain from saying something, but rather abandon a certain combination of words as senseless. In another sense, however, philosophy requires a resignation, but one of feeling and not of intellect. And maybe that is what makes it so difficult for many. It can be difficult not to use an expression, just as it is difficult to hold back tears, or an outburst of anger //rage//.

/(Tolstoy: the meaning (meaningfulness) of a subject lies in its being generally understandable. — That is true and false. What makes a subject difficult to understand—if it is significant, important—is not that some special instruction about abstruse things is necessary to understand it. Rather it is the contrast between the understanding of the subject and what most people want to see. Because of this the very things that are most obvious can become the most difficult to understand. What has to be overcome is not a difficulty of the intellect, but of the will.)/

Work on philosophy is—as work in architecture frequently is—actually more of a //a kind of// work on oneself. On one's own conception. On the way one sees things. (And what one demands of them.)

Roughly speaking, in //according to// the old conception—for instance that of the (great) western philosophers—there have been two kinds of problems in fields of knowledge //twofold kinds of problems. . . .//: essential, great, universal, and inessential quasi-accidental problems. And against this stands our conception, that there is no such thing as a great, essential problem in the sense of "problem" in the field of knowledge.

87

PHILOSOPHY SHOWS THE MISLEADING ANALOGIES IN THE USE OF OUR LANGUAGE.

Is grammar, as I use the word, only the description of the actual handling of language //languages//? So that its propositions could actually be understood as the propositions of a natural science?

That could be the descriptive science of speaking, in contrast to that of thinking.

Indeed, the rules of chess could be taken as propositions from the natural history of man. (As the games of animals are described in books on natural history.)

If I correct a philosophical mistake and say that this is the way it has always been conceived, but this is not the way it is, I always point to an analogy //I must always point to. . . .// that was followed, and show that this analogy is incorrect. //. . . . I must always point to an analogy according to which one had been thinking, but which one did not recognize as an analogy.//

The effect of a false analogy taken up into language: it means a constant battle and uneasiness (as it were, a constant stimulus). It is as if a thing seemed to be a human being from a distance, because we don't perceive anything definite, but from close up we see that it is a tree stump. The moment we move away a little and lose sight of the explanations, one figure appears to us; if after that we look more closely, we see a different figure; now we move away again, etc., etc.

(The irritating character of grammatical unclarity.)

Philosophizing is: rejecting false arguments.

The philosopher strives to find the liberating word, that is, the word that finally permits us to grasp what up until now[1] has intangibly weighed down our consciousness.

(It is as if one had a hair on one's tongue; one feels it, but cannot grasp //seize// it, and therefore cannot get rid of it.)

The philosopher delivers the word to us with which one //I// can express the thing and render it harmless.

(The choice of our words is so important, because the point is to hit upon the physiognomy of the thing exactly, because only the exactly aimed thought can lead to the correct track. The car must be placed on the tracks precisely so, so that it can keep rolling correctly.)

One of the most important tasks is to express all false thought processes so characteristically that the reader says, "Yes, that's exactly the way I meant it". To make a tracing of the physiognomy of every error.

Indeed we can only convict someone else of a mistake if he acknowledges that this really is the expression of his feeling. //. . . . if he (really) acknowledges this expression as the correct expression of his feeling.//

For only if he acknowledges it as such, is it the correct expression. (Psychoanalysis.)

What the other person acknowledges is the analogy I am proposing to him as the source of his thought.

88

WHERE DOES THE FEELING THAT OUR GRAMMATICAL INVESTIGATIONS ARE FUNDAMENTAL COME FROM?

(Questions of different kinds occupy us, for instance "What is the specific weight of this body", "Will the weather stay nice today", "Who[2] will come through the door next", etc. But among our questions there are those of a special kind. Here we have a different experience. The questions seem to be more fundamental than the others. And now I say: if we have this experience, then we have arrived at the limits of language.)[3]

Where does our investigation get its importance from, since it seems only to destroy everything interesting, that is, all that is great and important? (As it were all the buildings, leaving behind only bits of stone and rubble.)

Whence does this observation derive its importance:[4] the one that points out to us that a table can be used in more than one way, that one can think up a table that instructs one as to the use of a table? The observation that one can also conceive of an arrow as pointing from the tip to the tail, that I can use a model as a model in different ways?

What we do is to bring words back from their metaphysical to their correct[5] (normal) use in language.

(The man who said that one cannot step into the same river twice said something wrong; one c a n step into the same river twice.)

And this is what the solution of all philosophical difficulties looks like. Their[6] answers, if they are correct, must be homemade and ordinary.[7] But one must look at them in the proper spirit, and then it doesn't matter.[8]

Where do //did// the old philosophical problems get their importance from?

The law of identity, for example, seemed to be of fundamental importance. But now the proposition that this "law" is nonsense has taken over this importance.

I could ask: why do I sense a grammatical joke as being in a certain sense deep? (And that of course is what the depth of philosophy is.)

Why do we sense the investigation of grammar as being fundamental?

(When it has a meaning at all, the word "fundamental" can also mean something that is not metalogical, or philosophical.)[9]

The investigation of grammar is fundamental in the same sense in which we may call language fundamental—say its own foundation.

Our grammatical investigation differs from that of a philologist, etc.: what interests us, for instance, is the translation from one language into other languages we have invented. In general the rules that the philologist totally ignores are the ones that interest us. Thus we are justified in emphasizing this difference.

On the other hand it would be misleading to say that we deal with the essentials of grammar (he, with the accidentals).

"But that is only an external differentiation //an external difference//." I believe there is no other.

Rather we could say that we are calling something else grammar than he is. Even as we differentiate kinds of words where for him there is no difference (present).

The importance of grammar is the importance of language.

One could also call a word, for instance, 'red,' important insofar as it is used frequently and for important things, in contrast, for instance, to the word 'pipe-lid'. And then the grammar of the word 'red' is important because it describes the meaning of the word 'red'.

(All that philosophy can do is to destroy idols. And that means not creating a new one—for instance as in "absence of an idol".)

89

THE METHOD OF PHILOSOPHY: THE PERSPICUOUS REPRESENTATION OF GRAMMATICAL //LINGUISTIC// FACTS.
THE GOAL: THE TRANSPARENCY OF ARGUMENTS. JUSTICE.[10]

Someone has heard that the anchor of a ship is hauled up by a steam engine. He only thinks of the one that powers the ship (and because of which it is called a steamship) and cannot explain to himself what he has heard. (Perhaps the difficulty doesn't occur to him until later.) Now we tell him: No, it is not that steam engine, but besides it a number of other ones are on board, and one of these hoists the anchor.—Was his problem a philosophical one? Was it a philosophical one if he had already heard of the existence of other steam engines on the ship and only had to be reminded of it?—I believe his confusion has two parts: what the explainer tells him as fact the questioner could easily have conceived as a possibility by himself, and he could have posed his question in a definite form instead of in the form of a mere admission of confusion. He could have removed this part of his doubt by himself; however, reflection could not have instructed him about the facts. Or: the uneasiness that comes from not having known the truth was not removable by any ordering of his concepts.

The other uneasiness and confusion is characterized by the words "Something's wrong here" and the solution is characterized by (the words): "Oh, you don't mean *that* steam engine" or—in another case—". . . . By 'steam engine' you don't mean just a piston engine."

The work of the philosopher consists in assembling reminders for a particular purpose.

A philosophical question is similar to one about the constitution of a particular society.—And it would be as if a society came together without clearly written rules, but with a need for them: indeed also with an instinct following which they observed //followed// certain rules at their meetings; but this is made difficult by the fact that nothing is clearly expressed about this and no arrangement is made which clarifies //brings out clearly// the rules. Thus they in fact view one of them as president, but he doesn't sit at the head of the table and has no distinguishing marks, and that makes doing business difficult. Therefore we come along and create a clear order: we seat the president in a clearly identifiable spot, seat his secretary next to him at a little table of his own, and seat the other full members in two rows on both sides of the table, etc., etc.

If one asks philosophy: "*What* is—for instance—substance?" then one is asking for a rule. A general rule, which is valid for the word "substance", i.e., a rule according to which I have decided to play.—I want to say: the question "What is . . ." doesn't refer to a particular—practical—case, but we ask it sitting at our desks. Just remember the case of the law of identity in order to see that taking care of a philosophical problem is not a matter of pronouncing new truths about the subject of the investigation (identity).

The difficulty lies only[11] in understanding how establishing a rule helps us. Why it calms us after we have been so profoundly[12] uneasy. Obviously what calms us is that we see a system which (systematically) excludes those structures that have always made us uneasy, those we were unable to do anything with, and which we still?- thought we had to respect. Isn't the establishment of such a grammatical rule similar in this respect to the discovery of an explanation in physics, for instance, of the Copernican system? A similarity exists.—The strange thing about philosophical uneasiness and its resolution might seem to be that it is like the suffering of an ascetic who stood raising a heavy ball, amid groans, and whom someone released by telling him: "Drop it." One wonders: if these sentences make you uneasy and you didn't know what to do with them, why didn't you drop them earlier, what stopped you from doing it? Well, I believe it was the false system that he thought he had to accommodate himself to, etc.[13]

(The particular peace of mind that occurs when we can place other similar cases next to a case that we thought was unique, occurs again and again in our investigations when we show that a word doesn't have just one meaning (or just two), but is used in five or six different ways (meanings).)

Philosophical problems can be compared to locks on safes, which can be opened by dialing a certain word or number, so that no force can open the door until just this word has been hit upon, and once it is hit upon any child can open it. //.... and if it is hit upon, no effort at all is necessary to open the door// it//.//

The concepts of a perspicuous representation is of fundamental significance for us. It earmarks the form of account we give, the way we look at things. (A kind of '*Weltanschauung*', as is apparently typical of our time. Spengler.)

This perspicuous representation produces just that comprehension //understanding// which consists in "seeing connections". Hence the importance of intermediate cases// of finding intermediate cases.//

A sentence is completely logically analyzed when its grammar is laid out completely clearly. It might be written down or spoken in any number of ways.

Above all, our grammar is lacking in perspicuity.

Philosophy may in no way interfere with the real //actual// use of language //.... with what is really said//; it can in the end only describe it.

For it cannot give it any foundation either.

It leaves everything as it is.

It also leaves mathematics as it is (is now), and no mathematical discovery can advance it.

A "leading problem of mathematical logic" (Ramsey) is a problem of mathematics like any other.

(A simile is part of our edifice; but we cannot draw any conclusions from it either; it doesn't lead us beyond itself, but must remain standing as a simile. We can draw no inferences from it. As when we compare a sentence to a picture (in which case, what we understand by 'picture' must already have been established in us earlier //before//) or when I compare the application of language with, for instance, that of the calculus of multiplication.

Philosophy simply puts everything before us, and neither explains nor deduces anything.)

Since everything lies open to view there is nothing to explain either. For what might not lie open to view is of no interest to us. //. . . . , for what is hidden, for example, is . . . .//

The answer to the request for an explanation of negation is really: don't you understand it? Well, if you understand it, what is there left to explain, what business is there left for an explanation?

We must know what explanation means. There is a constant danger of wanting to use this word in logic in a sense that is derived from physics.

When[14] methodology talks about measurement, it does not say which material would be the most advantageous to make the measuring stick of in order to achieve this or that result: even though this too, after all, is part of the method of measuring. Rather this investigation is only interested in the circumstances under which we say that a length, the strength of a current (etc.) is measured. It wants to tabulate the methods which we already used and are familiar with, in order to determine the meaning of the words "length", "strength of current", etc.)

If one tried to advance theses in philosophy, it would never be possible to debate them, because everyone would agree to them.

Learning philosophy is really recollecting. We remember that we really used words in this way.[15]

The aspects of things //of language// which are philosophically most important are hidden because of their simplicity and familiarity.

(One is unable to notice something because it is always (openly) before one's eyes.)

The real foundations of his inquiry do not strike a man at all. Unless that fact has at some time struck him //he has become aware of it//. (Fraser, etc., etc.)

And this means he fails to be struck by what is most striking (powerful).

(One of the greatest impediments for philosophy is the expectation of new, deep //unheard of// elucidations.)

One might also give the name philosophy to what is possible //present// before all new discoveries and inventions.

This must also relate to the fact that I can't give any explanations of the variable "sentence". It is clear that this logical concept, this variable, must belong to the same order as the concept "reality" or "world."

If someone believes he has found the solution to the 'problem of life' and tried to tell himself that now everything is simple, then in order to refute himself he would only have to remember that there was a time when this 'solution' had not been found; but at that time too one had to be able to live, and in reference to this time the new solution appears like //as// a coincidence. And that's what happens to us in logic. If there were a 'solution' of logical (philosophical) problems then we would only have to call to mind that at one time they had not been solved (and then too one had to be able to live and think).—

All reflections can be carried out in a much more homemade manner than I used to do. And therefore no new words have to be used in philosophy, but rather the old common words of language are sufficient. //the old ones are sufficient//

(Our only task is to be just. That is, we must only point out and resolve the injustices of philosophy, and not posit new parties—and creeds.)

(It is difficult not to exaggerate in philosophy.)

(The philosopher exaggerates, shouts, as it were, in his helplessness, so long as he hasn't yet discovered the core of his confusion.)

The philosophical problem is an awareness of disorder in our concepts, and can be solved by ordering them.

A philosophical problem always has the form: "I simply don't know my way about."

As I do philosophy, its entire task consists in expressing myself in such a way that certain troubles //problems// disappear. ((Hertz.))

If I am correct, then philosophical problems must be completely solvable, in contrast to all others.

If I say: here we are at the limits of language, then it always seems //sounds// as if resignation were necessary, whereas on the contrary complete satisfaction comes, since no question remains.

The problems are dissolved in the actual sense of the word—like a lump of sugar in water.

/People who have no need for transparency in their argumentation are lost to philosophy./

90

PHILOSOPHY.
THE CLARIFICATION OF THE USE OF LANGUAGE. TRAPS OF LANGUAGE.

How is it that philosophy is such a complicated building //structure//. After all, it should be completely simple if it is that ultimate thing, independent of all experience, that it claims to be.—Philosophy unravels the knots in our thinking; hence its results must be simple, but its activity is as complicated as the knots that it unravels.

Lichtenberg: "Our entire philosophy is correction of the use of language, and therefore the correction of a philosophy, and indeed of the most general philosophy."

(The capacity[16] for philosophy consists[17] in the ability[18] to receive a strong and lasting impression from a grammatical fact.)[19]

Why are grammatical problems so tough and seemingly ineradicable?—Because they are connected with the oldest thought habits, i.e., with the oldest images that are engraved into our language itself. ((Lichtenberg.))

/Teaching philosophy involves the same immense difficulty as instruction in geography would have if a pupil brought with him a mass of false and far too simple //and falsely simplified// ideas about the course and connections of the routes of rivers //rivers// and mountain chains //mountains//./

/People are deeply imbedded in philosophical, i.e., grammatical confusions. And to free them from these presupposes pulling them out of the immensely manifold connections they are caught up in. One must so to speak regroup their entire language.—But this language came about //developed// as it did because people had—and have—the inclination to think in this way. Therefore pulling them out only works with those who live in an instinctive state of rebellion against //dissatisfaction with// language. Not with those who following all of their instincts live within the herd that has created this language as its proper expression./

Language contains the same traps for everyone; the immense network of well-kept //passable// false paths. And thus we see one person after another walking the same paths and we know already where he will make a turn, where he will keep on going straight ahead without noticing the turn, etc., etc.

Therefore wherever false paths branch off I should put up signs which help one get by the dangerous places.

One keeps hearing the remark that philosophy really makes no progress, that the same philosophical problems that had occupied the Greeks are still occupying us. But those who say that don't understand the reason it is //must be// so. The reason is that our language has remained the same and seduces us into asking the same questions over and over. As long as there is a verb 'to be' which seems to function like 'to eat' and 'to drink', as long as there are adjectives like 'identical', 'true', 'false', 'possible', as long as one talks about a flow of time and an expanse of space, etc., etc., humans will continue to bump up against the same mysterious difficulties, and stare at something that no explanation seems able to remove.

And this by the way satisfies a longing for the supra-natural //transcendental//, for in believing that they see the "limits of human understanding" of course they believe that they can see beyond it.

I read ". . . . philosophers are no nearer the meaning of 'Reality' than Plato got. . . ." What a strange state of affairs. How strange in that case that Plato could get that far at all! Or, that we were not able to get farther! Was it because Plato was so smart?

The conflict in which we constantly find ourselves when we undertake logical investigations is like the conflict of two people who have concluded a contract with each other, the last formulations of which are expressed in easily misunderstandable words, whereas the explanations of these formulations explain everything unmistakably. Now one of the two people has a short memory, constantly forgets the explanations, misinterprets the conditions of the contract, and continually gets //therefore continually runs// into difficulties. The other one constantly has to remind him of the explanations in the contract and remove the difficulty.

Remember what a hard time children have believing (or accepting) that a word really has //can have// two completely different meanings.

The aim of philosophy is to erect a wall at the point where language stops anyway.

The results of philosophy are the uncovering of one or another piece of plain nonsense, and are the bumps that the understanding has got by running its head up against the limits //the end// of language. These bumps let us understand //recognize// the value of the discovery.

What kind of investigation are we carrying out? Am I investigating the probability of cases that I give as examples, or am I investigating their actuality? No. I'm just citing what is possible and am therefore giving grammatical examples.

Philosophy is not laid down in sentences but in a language.

Just as laws only become interesting when there is an inclination to transgress them //when they are transgressed// certain grammatical rules are only interesting when philosophers want to transgress them.

Savages have games (that's what we call them, anyway) for which they have no written rules, no inventory of rules. Let's now imagine the activity of an explorer, who travels through the countries of these peoples and takes an inventory of their rules. This is completely analogous to what the philosopher does. ((But why don't I say: savages have languages (that's what we. . . .) . . . . without a written grammar?))[20]

91

WE DON'T ENCOUNTER PHILOSOPHICAL PROBLEMS AT ALL IN PRACTICAL LIFE (AS WE DO, FOR EXAMPLE, THOSE OF NATURAL SCIENCE). WE ENCOUNTER THEM ONLY WHEN WE ARE GUIDED NOT BY PRACTICAL PURPOSE IN FORMING OUR SENTENCES, BUT BY CERTAIN ANALOGIES WITHIN OUR LANGUAGE.

Language cannot express what belongs to the essence of the world. Therefore it cannot say that everything flows. Language can only say what we could also imagine differently.

That everything flows must lie in how language touches reality. Or better: that everything flows must lie in the nature of language. And, let's remember: in everyday life we don't notice that—as little as we notice the blurred edges of our visual field ("because we are so used to it", some will say). How, on what occasion, do we think we start noticing it? Isn't it when we want to form sentences in opposition to the grammar of time?

When someone says 'everything flows', we feel that we are hindered in pinning down the actual, actual reality. What goes on on the screen escapes us precisely because it is something going on. But we are describing something; and is that something else that is going on? The description is obviously linked to the very picture on the screen. There must be a false picture at the bottom of our feeling of helplessness. For what we want to describe we can describe.

Isn't this false picture that of a strip of film that runs by so quickly that we don't have any time to perceive a picture?

For in this case we would be inclined to chase after the picture. But in the course of something going on there is nothing analogous to that.

It is remarkable that in everyday life we never have the feeling that the phenomenon is getting away from us, that appearances are continually flowing, but only when we philosophize. This points to the fact that we are dealing here with a thought that is suggested to us through a wrong use of our language.

For the feeling is that the present vanishes into the past without our being able to stop it. And here we are obviously using the picture of a strip that constantly moves past us and that we can't stop. But of course it's just as clear that the picture is being misused. That one cannot say "time flows" if by "time" one means the possibility of change.

That we don't notice anything when we look around, look around in space, feel our own bodies, etc., etc., shows how natural these very things are to us. We don't perceive that we see space perspectivally or that the visual image is in some sense blurred near its edge. We don't notice this, and can never notice it, because it is *the* mode of perception. We never think about it, and it is impossible, because the form of our world has no contrary.

I wanted to say that it is odd that those who ascribe reality only to things and not to our mental images move so self-confidently in the world of imagination and never long to escape from it.

I.e., how self-evident is the given. Things would have to have come to a pretty pass for that to be just a tiny photograph taken from an oblique angle.

What is self-evident, *life*, is supposed to be something accidental, unimportant; by contrast something that normally I never worry my head about is what is real!

I.e., what one neither can nor wants to go beyond would not be the world.

Again and again there is the attempt to define the world in language and to display it—but that doesn't work. The self-evidence of the world is expressed in the very fact that language means only it, and can only mean it.

As language gets its way of meaning from what it means, from the world, no language is thinkable which doesn't represent this world.

In the theories and battles of philosophy we find words whose meanings are well-known to us from everyday life used in an ultraphysical sense.

When philosophers use a word and search for its meaning, one must always ask: is this word ever really used this way in the language which created it//for which it is created//?

Usually one will then find that it is not so, and that the word is used against //contrary to// its normal grammar. ("Knowing", "Being", "Thing".)

(Philosophers are often like little children,[21] who first scribble random[22] lines on a piece of paper with their pencils, and now //then// ask an adult "What is that?"—Here's how this happened: now and then the adult had drawn something for the child and said: "That's a man", "That's a house", etc. And then the child draws lines too, and asks: now what's that?)

92

METHOD OF PHILOSOPHY.
THE POSSIBILITY OF QUIET PROGRESS.

The real discovery is the one that makes me capable of stopping doing philosophy when I want to.

The one that gives philosophy peace, so that it is no longer //being// tormented by questions which bring itself in question.

Instead, we now demonstrate a method by examples; and one can break off the series of examples //and the series of examples can be broken off//.

But more correctly, one should say: Problems are solved (uneasiness //difficulties// eliminated), not a single problem.

Unrest in philosophy comes from philosophers looking at, seeing, philosophy all wrong, i.e., cut up into (infinite) vertical strips, as it were, rather than (finite) horizontal strips. This reordering of understanding creates the greatest difficulty. They want to grasp the infinite strip, as it were, and complain that //this// is not possible piece by piece. Of course it isn't, if by 'a piece' one understands an endless vertical strip. But it is, if one sees a horizontal strip as a piece //a whole, definite piece//.—But then we'll never get finished with our work! Of course //certainly// not, because it doesn't have an end.

(Instead of turbulent conjectures and explanations, we want to give quiet demonstrations[23] //statements// of linguistic facts //about linguistic facts//.) //we want the quiet noting[24] of linguistic facts.//

We must plow through the whole of language.

(When most people ought to[25] engage in a philosophical investigation, they act like someone who is looking for an object in a drawer very nervously. He throws papers out of the drawer—what he's looking for may be among them—leafs through the others hastily and sloppily. Throws some back into the drawer, mixes them up with the others, and so on. Then one can only tell him: Stop, if you look in that way, I can't help you look. First you have to start to examine one thing after another methodically, and in peace and quiet;

then I am willing to look with you and to direct myself with you as model in the method.

93

THE MYTHOLOGY IN THE FORMS OF OUR LANGUAGE. ((PAUL ERNST.))

In ancient rites we find the use of an extremely well-developed language of gestures.

And when I read Frazer, I would like to say again and again: All these processes, these changes of meaning, we have right in front of us even in our language of words. If what is hidden in the last sheaf is called the 'Cornwolf', as well as the sheaf itself, and also the man who binds it, then we recognize in this a linguistic process we know well.

The scapegoat, on which one lays one's sins, and who runs away into the desert with them—a false picture, similar to those that cause errors in philosophy.

I would like to say: nothing shows our kinship with those savages better, than that Frazer has at hand a word like "ghost" or "shade", which is so familiar to him and to us, to describe the views of these people.

(This is quite different than if he were to relate, for instance, that the savages imagined //imagine// that their head falls off when they have slain an enemy. Here our description would contain nothing superstitious or magical.)

Indeed, this oddity refers not only to the expressions "ghost" and "shade", and much too little is made of it that we include the words "soul" and "spirit" in our own educated vocabulary. Compared to this it is insignificant that we do not believe that our soul eats and drinks.

An entire mythology is laid down in our language.

Driving out death or killing death; but on the other hand it is portrayed as a skeleton, and therefore as dead itself, in a certain sense. "As dead as death." 'Nothing is as dead as death; nothing as beautiful as beauty itself!' The picture according to which reality is thought of here is that beauty, death,
are the pure (concentrated) substances they are
etc., is the pure (concentrated) substance, whereas in a beautiful object it is contained as an admixture.—And don't I recognize here my own observations about 'objects' and 'complex'? (Plato.)

The primitive forms of our language: noun, adjective and verb, show the simple picture into whose form language tries to force everything.

So long as one imagines the soul as a *thing*, a *body*, which is in our head, this hypothesis is *not* dangerous. The danger of our models does not lie in their imperfection and roughness, but in their unclarity (fogginess).

The danger sets in when we notice that the old model is not sufficient but then we don't change it, but only sublimate it, as it were. So long as I say the thought is in my head, everything is all right; things get dangerous when we say that the thought is not in my head, but in my spirit.

NOTES

1. Handwritten alternative: then.
2. In the original typescript: he. The initial letter "w" is a handwritten addendum.
3. Handwritten marginal note: belongs to "must", "can".
4. The typescript has: its importance:, the.
5. Handwritten alternative: normal. There is a handwritten wavy line under "correct".
6. Handwritten alternative: our.
7. Handwritten alternative: ordinary and trivial.
8. At the end of the remark there is the handwriting: < ["plain nonsense"].
9. The parentheses are a handwritten addition.
10. Under the title, in handwriting: ∀ p. 40/3?. This is a reference to page 40 of the typescript. Wittgenstein had apparently wanted to include a remark or a part of one from page 40 in page 414.
11. Handwritten alternative: now.
12. Handwritten alternative: deeply.
13. At the end of the remark there is a handwritten addition: hen and chalk trick.
14. Before the remark, in handwriting in the margin: VII 7.
15. In handwriting, in the margin: VII 164.
16. Handwritten alternative (with an unbroken wavy line under the original word): talent.
17. Handwritten alternative (with an unbroken wavy line under the original word): lies.
18. Handwritten alternative (elevated, with broken underlining): susceptibility.
19. Handwritten marginal remark: for 'humor', 'depth'.
20. In the typescript the parentheses are missing at the end of the remark.
21. Handwritten alternative: (Philosophers) often behave like little children. . . .
22. Handwritten alternative: some.
23. Handwritten alternative: reflection.
24. Originally in the manuscript: establishment.
25. Unclear textual point in the manuscript. The typewriting gives the impression that the original words "want to" were overstruck to produce "ought to".

LOGICAL POSITIVISM—A DEBATE

A. J. Ayer and F. C. Copleston

METAPHYSICS, ANALYTIC PHILOSOPHY AND SCIENCE

Ayer. Well, Father Copleston, you've asked me to summarize Logical Positivism for you and it's not very easy. For one thing, as I understand it, Logical Positivism is not a system of philosophy. It consists rather in a certain technique—a certain kind of attitude towards philosophic problems. Thus, one thing which those of us who are called logical positivists tend to have in common is that we deny the possibility of philosophy as a speculative discipline. We should say that if philosophy was to be a branch of knowledge, as distinct from the sciences, it would have to consist in logic or in some form of analysis, and our reason for this would be somewhat as follows. We maintain that you can divide propositions into two classes, formal and empirical. Formal propositions, like those of logic and mathematics, depend for their validity on the conventions of a symbol system. Empirical propositions, on the other hand, are statements of actual or possible observation, or hypotheses, from which such statements can be logically derived; and it is they that constitute science in so far as science isn't purely mathematical. Now our contention is that this exhausts the field of what may be called speculative knowledge. Consequently we reject metaphysics, if this be understood, as I think it commonly has been, as an attempt to gain knowledge about the world by non-scientific means. In as much as metaphysical statements are not testable by observation, we hold they are not descriptive of anything. And from this we should conclude that if philosophy is to be a cognitive activity it must be purely critical. It would take the form of trying to elucidate the concepts that were used in science or mathematics or in everyday language.

Copleston. Well, Professor Ayer, I can quite understand, of course, philosophers confining themselves to logical analysis if they wish to do so, and I shouldn't dream of denying or of belittling in any way its utility: I think it's obviously an extremely useful thing to do to analyse and clarify the concepts used in science. In everyday life, too, there are many terms used that practically have taken on an emotional connotation—"progressive" or "reactionary" or "freedom" or "the modern mind":—to make clear to people what's meant or what they mean by those terms, or the various possible meanings, is a very useful thing. But if the Logical Positivist means that logical analysis is the *only*

This debate took place on the Third Program of the British Broadcasting Corporation on June 13, 1949. It is reprinted by permission of A. J. Ayer's literary executors and Father Copleston, from A. J. Ayer and F. C. Copleston, "Logical Positivism—A Debate," in *A Modern Introduction to Philosophy*, Revised Edition, ed. Paul Edwards and Arthur Pap, pp. 726–756. New York: The Free Press, 1965.

function of philosophy—that's the point at which I should disagree with him. And so would many other philosophers disagree—especially on the Continent. Don't you think that by saying what philosophy is, one presupposes a philosophy, or takes up a position as a philosopher? For example, if one divides significant propositions into two classes, namely, purely formal propositions and statements of observation, one is adopting a philosophical position: one is claiming that there are no necessary propositions which are not purely formal. Moreover, to claim that metaphysical propositions, to be significant, should be verifiable as scientific hypotheses are verifiable is to claim that metaphysics, to be significant, should not be metaphysics.

Ayer. Yes, I agree that my position is philosophical, but not that it is metaphysical, as I hope to show later. To say what philosophy is, is certainly a philosophical act, but by this I mean that it is itself a question of philosophical analysis. We have to decide, among other things, what it is that we are going to call "philosophy" and I have given you my answer. It is not, perhaps, an obvious answer but it at least has the merit that it rescues philosophical statements from becoming either meaningless or trivial. But I don't suppose that we want to quarrel about how we're going to use a word, so much as to discuss the points underlying what you've just said. You would hold, I gather, that in the account I gave of the possible fields of knowledge something was left out.

Copleston. Yes.

Ayer. And that which is left out is what people called philosophers might well be expected to study?

Copleston. Yes, I should hold that philosophy, at any rate metaphysical philosophy, begins, in a sense, where science leaves off. In my personal opinion, one of the chief functions of metaphysics is to open the mind to the Transcendent—to remove the ceiling of the room, as it were, the room being the world as amenable to scientific handling and investigation. But this is not to say that the metaphysician is simply concerned with the Transcendent. Phenomena themselves (objects of what you would probably call "experience") can be considered from the metaphysical angle. The problem of universals, for instance, is a metaphysical problem. I say that metaphysical philosophy begins, *in a sense,* where science leaves off, because I do not mean to imply that the metaphysician cannot begin until science has finished its work. If this were so, the metaphysician would be quite unable to start. I mean that he asks other questions than those asked by the scientist and pursues a different method.

Ayer. To say that philosophy begins where science leaves off is perfectly all right if you mean that the philosopher takes the results of the scientist, analyses them, shows the logical connection of one proposition with another, and so on. But if you say that it leaps into a quite different realm—the realm which you describe as the "transcendent"—then I think I cease to follow you. And I think I can explain why I cease to follow you. I hold a principle, known as the principle of verification, according to which a statement intended to be a statement of fact is meaningful only if it's either formally valid, or some kind of observation is relevant to its truth or falsehood. My difficulty with your so-

called transcendent statements is that their truth or falsehood doesn't, it seems to me, make the slightest difference to anything that any one experiences.
Copleston. I don't care for the phrase "transcendent statement." I think myself that some positive descriptive statements about the Transcendent are possible; but, leaving that out of account, I think that one of the possible functions of the philosopher (a function which you presumably exclude) is to reveal the limits of science as a complete and exhaustive description and analysis of reality.
Ayer. Limits of science? You see I can quite well understand your saying that science is limited if you mean only that many more things may be discovered. You may say, for example, that the physics of the seventeenth century was limited in so far as physicists of the eighteenth, nineteenth and twentieth centuries have gone very much further.
Copleston. No, I didn't mean that at all. Perhaps I can illustrate what I mean in reference to anthropology. The biochemist can describe Man within his own terms of reference and up to a certain extent. But, although biochemistry may doubtless continue to advance, I see no reason to suppose that the biochemist will be able to give an exhaustive analysis of Man. The psychologist certainly would not think so. Now, one of the possible functions of a philosopher is to show how all these scientific analyses of man—the analyses of the biochemist, the empirical psychologist and so on—are unable to achieve the exhaustive analysis of the individual human being. Karl Jaspers, for example, would maintain that Man as free, i.e. precisely as free, cannot be adequately handled by any scientist who presupposes the applicability of the principle of deterministic causality and conducts his investigations with that presupposition in mind. I am not a follower of Karl Jaspers; but I think that to call attention to what he calls *Existenz* is a legitimate philosophical procedure.

METAPHYSICAL AND SCIENTIFIC EXPLANATION

Ayer. I do not see that you can know *a priori* that human behaviour is inexplicable. The most you can say is that our present stock of psychological hypotheses isn't adequate to explain certain features of it: and you may very well be right. But what more is required is better psychological investigation. We need to form new theories and test the theories by further observation, which is again the method of science. It seems to me that all you've said, when you've talked of the limits of science, is simply that a given science may not explain things, or explain as much as you would like to see explained. But that, which to me seems to be perfectly acceptable, is only a historical statement about a point which science has reached at a given stage. It doesn't show that there's room for a quite different kind of discipline, and you haven't made clear to me what that different kind of discipline which you reserve for the philosopher is supposed to be.
Copleston. Well, I think that one of the possible functions of the philosopher is to consider what is sometimes called the non-empirical or intelligible self.

There is an obvious objection, from your point of view, against the phrase "non-empirical self"; but I would like to turn to metaphysics in general. The scientists can describe various particular aspects of things, and all the sciences together can give, it is true, a very general description of reality. But the scientist, precisely as scientist, does not raise, for example, the question why anything is there at all. To raise this question is, in my opinion, one of the functions of the philosopher. You may say that the question cannot be answered. I think that it can; but, even if it could not be answered, I consider that it is one of the functions of the philosopher to show that there is such a problem. Some philosophers would say that metaphysics consists in raising problems rather than in answering them definitively; and, though I do not myself agree with the sheerly agnostic position, I think that there is value in raising the metaphysical problems, quite apart from the question whether one can or cannot answer them definitively. That is why I said earlier on that one of the functions of the philosopher is to open the mind to the Transcendent, to take the ceiling off the room—to use again a rather crude metaphor.

Ayer. Yes, but there's a peculiarity about these "why" questions. Supposing someone asks you "Why did the light go out?" You may tell him the light went out because there was a fuse. And he then says "Why does the light go out when it is fused?" Then perhaps you tell him a story about electrical connections, wires, and so on. That is the "how" story. Then, if he's not satisfied with that, you may give him the general theory of electricity which is again a "how" story. And then if he's not satisfied with that, you give him the general theory of electromagnetics, which is again a "how" story. You tell him that things function in this way at this level, and then your "why" answers are deductions from that. So that in the ordinary sense of a "why" question, putting a "why" question is asking for a "how" answer at a higher logical level—a more general "how" answer. Well now if you raise this question with regard to the world as a whole, you're asking for what? The most general possible theory?

Copleston. No, the metaphysical question I have in mind is a different sort of question. If I ask, for example, how the earth comes to be in its present condition, I expect an answer which refers to empirical causes and conditions. There I quite agree with you. I go to the astronomer for an answer. And if one persists in asking such questions, I dare say one could, in theory, go back indefinitely. At least, I am prepared to admit the possibility. But if I ask why there are phenomena at all, why there is something rather than nothing, I am not asking for an answer in terms of empirical causes and conditions. Even if the series of phenomena did go back indefinitely, without beginning, I could still raise the question as to why the infinite series of phenomena exists, how it comes to be there. Whether such a question can be answered or not is obviously another matter. But if I ask whether anything lies behind phenomena, whether anything is responsible for the series, finite or infinite, of phenomena, the answer—supposing that there is an answer—must, in my opinion, refer to a reality beyond or behind phenomena. But in any case to ask why any finite phenomena exist, why there is something rather than nothing, is to ask a different sort of question from the question why water tends to flow downhill rather than uphill.

Ayer. But my objection is that your very notion of an explanation of all phenomena is self-contradictory.

Copleston. What is the contradiction?

Ayer. The contradiction is, I think, that if you accept my interpretation of what "why" questions are, then asking a "why" question is always asking for a more general description; and asking for the "why" of that is asking for a more general description still. And then you say, "Give me an answer to a 'why' which doesn't take the form of a description," and that's a contradiction. It's like saying "Give me a description more general than any description, which itself is not a description." And clearly nobody can do that.

Copleston. That is not the question I am asking. There would be a contradiction if I did not distinguish between a scientific question and a metaphysical question, but a metaphysical question concerns the intelligible structure of reality in so far as it is *not* amenable to the investigation by the methods of empirical science. It seems to me that when I propose a metaphysical question you ask me to re-state the question as though it were a scientific question. But, if I could do that, the question would not be a metaphysical question, would it?

Ayer. Well, what form would your metaphysical question take?

Copleston. Well, in my opinion, the existence of phenomena in general requires some explanation, and I should say explanation in terms of a transcendent reality. I maintain that this is a possible philosophical question. Whatever the answer may be, it obviously cannot consist in a further description of phenomena. Aristotle asserted that philosophy begins with wonder. If someone feels no wonder at the existence of the physical world, he is unlikely to ask any questions about its existence as such.

Ayer. If you say anything of that kind, it still means that you're treating your transcendent reality, or rather the statements about your transcendent reality, in the same way as a scientific hypothesis. It becomes a very, very general scientific hypothesis. Only you want to say it's not like a scientific hypothesis. Why not? I suppose it's because you can't test it in any way. But if you can't test it in any way, then you've not got an explanation and you haven't answered my question.

Copleston. Well, at this point I should like to remark that you're presupposing that one must be able to test every hypothesis in a certain way. I do not mean to allow that every metaphysical statement is a hypothesis; but even if it were, it would not be scientifically testable without ceasing to be a metaphysical statement. You seem to me to reject from the beginning the reflective work of the intellect on which rational metaphysics depends. Neither Spinoza nor Fichte nor Hegel nor St. Thomas Acquinas supposed that one could investigate scientifically what they respectively believed to be the metaphenomenal reality. But each of them thought that intellectual reflection can lead the mind to postulate that reality.

Ayer. Well in one sense of the words, of course it can. You can penetrate disguises. If something's heavily camouflaged you can understand that it's there even if you can't see it. That's because you know what it would be like to see it independently of seeing it in disguise. Now your kind of penetration is a very queer one, because you say you can discern things lying behind other things with simply no experience of stripping off the disguise and coming across the thing undisguised.

Copleston. It's not exactly a question of a disguise. I can strip off camouflage and see the camouflaged thing with my eyes. But no metaphysician would pretend that one could see a metaphenomenal reality with the eyes: it can be apprehended only by an intellectual activity, though that activity must, of necessity, begin with the objects of sense-experience and introspection. After all, you yourself *reflect on* the data of experience: your philosophy does not consist in stating atomic experiences.

Ayer. No indeed it doesn't. Since I hold that philosophy consists in logical analysis, it isn't in my view a matter of stating experiences at all: if by stating experiences you mean just describing them.

Copleston. It seems to me that we are discussing my particular brand of metaphysics rather than Logical Positivism. However, I should maintain that the very ability to raise the question of the existence of the world (or of the series of phenomena, if you like) implies a dim awareness of the non-self-sufficiency of the world. When this awareness becomes articulate and finds expression, it may lead to a metaphysical speculation, to a conscious thinking of contingent existence *as such.* And I should maintain that an intellectual apprehension of the nature of what I call contingent being as such involves an apprehension of its relatedness to self-grounded Being. Some philosophers (Hegel among them, I think) would hold that one cannot think finite being *as such* without implicitly thinking the Infinite. The words "as such" are, I should say, important. I can perfectly well think of a cow, for example, without thinking of any metaphysical reality; but if I abstract from its characteristics as a cow and think of it merely as contingent being, I pass into the sphere of metaphysics.

Ayer. But it's precisely questions like this question about the world as a whole that I think we should rule out. Supposing you asked a question like "Where do all things come from?" Now that's a perfectly meaningful question as regards any given event. Asking where it came from is asking for a description of some event prior to it. But if you generalize that question, it becomes meaningless. You're then asking what event is prior to all events. Clearly no event can be prior to all events, because if it's a member of the class of all events it must be included in it and therefore can't be prior to it. Let me give another instance which illustrates the same point. One can say of any one perception that it's a hallucination, meaning by this that it isn't corroborated by one's own further perceptions or by those of other people, and that makes sense. Now, some people, and philosophers too, I'm afraid, want to generalize this and say with a profound air: "Perhaps all our experiences are hallucinatory." Well, that

of course becomes meaningless. In exactly the same way I should say that this question of where does it all come from isn't meaningful.
Copleston. It isn't meaningful if the only meaningful questions are those which can be answered by the methods of empirical science, as you presuppose. In my opinion, you are unduly limiting "meaningfulness" to a certain restricted kind of meaningfulness. Now, the possibility of raising the question of the Absolute seems to depend largely on the nature of relations. If one denies that one can discern any implication or internal relation to the existing phenomena considered as such, then a metaphysic of the absolute becomes an impossible thing. If the mind can discern such a relation, then I think a metaphysic of the Absolute is possible.
Ayer. Metaphysic of the Absolute? I am afraid my problem still is, What questions are being asked? Now supposing one were to ask, Is the world dependent on something outside itself? Would you regard that as a possible question?
Copleston. Yes I think it's a possible question.
Ayer. Well then you're using a very queer sense of causation, aren't you? Because in the normal sense in which you talk of one event being dependent or consequent on another, you'd be meaning that they had some kind of temporal relation to each other. In fact, normally if one uses the word causation one is saying that the later event is dependent on the earlier, in the sense that all cases of the earlier are also cases of the later. But now you can't be meaning that, because if you were you'd be putting your cause in the world.
Copleston. Well now, aren't you presupposing the validity of a certain philosophical interpretation of causality? It may be true or false; but it is a philosophical view, and it is not one which I accept.
Ayer. But surely on any view of causality, the causal relation holds between things that happen, and presumably anything that happens is in the world. I don't know what you mean by your other-worldly reality, but if you make it a cause you automatically bring this supposed reality into the world.
Copleston. It would bring the world into relation with the reality; and personally I should not dream of adopting any metaphysic which did not start with experience of this world. But the relating of the world to a Being outside the world would not bring that Being into the world. Incidentally, I have just used the word "outside." This illustrates admirably the inadequacy of language for expressing metaphysical ideas. "Outside" suggests distance in space, "independent" would be better. But I should like to make some remarks about this use of the word "cause." I am very glad you brought the question up. First of all, as far as I understand the use of the term by scientists, causal laws would mean for them, I suppose, statistical generalizations from observed phenomena. At least this would be one of the meanings, I think.
Ayer. That makes it rather more genetic than it need be. I mean the question is not really where these scientific expressions have come from, but what use they're put to. Let us say that they are generalizations which refer to observable events or phenomena, if you will.

Copleston. I agree, of course, that one cannot use the principle of causality, if understood in a sense which involves references to phenomena exclusively, in order to transcend phenomena. Supposing, for example, that I understood by the principle of causality the proposition that the initial state of every phenomenon is determined by a preceding phenomenon or by preceding phenomena, quite apart from the fact that it may not apply even to all phenomena. But what I understand by the philosophic principle of causality is the general proposition that every being which has not in itself its reason for existence depends for its existence on an extrinsic reality which I call, in this connection, cause. This principle says nothing as to the character of the cause. It may be free or not free. Therefore it cannot be refuted by infra-atomic indeterminism, if there is such a thing, any more than it is refuted by the free acts of men. Some philosophers would probably say that this principle has only subjective necessity; but I don't hold this view myself, nor do I see any very cogent reason for holding it. Moreover, though the principle is, in a sense, presupposed by the scientist when he traces the connection between a phenomenal effect and a phenomenal cause, the principle mentions not phenomenal causes, but an extrinsic reality. If one is speaking of all beings which have not in themselves the reason for their existence, the extrinsic reality in question must transcend them. To my way of thinking the philosophic principle of causality is simply an implication of the intelligibility of phenomena, if these are regarded as contingent events.

Ayer. Well then, again I think I should accuse you of the fallacy of misplaced generalization. You see, what is the intelligibility of phenomena? You can understand sentences; you can understand an argument; they can be intelligible or not. But what is the understanding of phenomena? Even a particular one, let alone all phenomena? Well I think you could give a sense to understanding a particular phenomenon. You would recognize some description of it as an accurate description, and then understanding the phenomenon would be a matter of explaining this description, that is, of deducing it from some theory. Now, you say, are all phenomena intelligible? Does that mean that you are looking for a single theory from which every true proposition can be deduced? I doubt if you could find one, but even if you did, you'd want that theory again, wouldn't you, to be explained in its turn, which gives you an infinite regress? You see, phenomena just happen, don't they? Is there a question of their being intelligible or not intelligible?

Copleston. No, phenomena don't "just happen." I didn't "just happen." If I did, my existence would be unintelligible. And I'm not prepared to acquiesce in the idea that the series of phenomena, even if infinite, just happens, unless you can give me a good reason for doing so. I think you can legitimately raise the question why there is finite existence as such. Whether it's answerable or not is another pair of shoes.

Ayer. Well, I quite agree that many metaphysicians have supposed themselves to be asking and answering questions of this kind. But I still want to say that I don't regard these as genuine questions, nor do I regard the answers as intelligible. For example, let us take the case of someone who says that the answer is that Reality is the Absolute expressing itself. I say such an answer explains nothing because I can do nothing with it, and I don't know what it would be like for such a proposition to be true. I should say the same about all statements of this kind.

Copleston. And why should it be necessary to do anything with a proposition?

Ayer. Because you put this up as a hypothesis, and a hypothesis is supposed to explain.

Copleston. An explanation is meant to explain, certainly. What I meant was that there is no reason why we should be able to deduce "practical" consequences from it.

Ayer. Well, if you don't get practical answers what kind of answers do you get?

Copleston. Theoretical answers, of course. I should have thought, as a simple-minded historian of philosophy, that one has been given a good many metaphysical answers. They cannot all be true; but the answers are forthcoming all the same.

Ayer. Yes, but the trouble still is that these answers are given not as explanations of any particular event, but of all events. And I wonder if this notion of an explanation of all events isn't itself faulty. When I explain something by telling you that *this* is the way it works, I thereby exclude other possibilities. So that any genuine explanation is compatible with one course of events, and incompatible with another. That, of course, is what distinguishes one explanation from another. But something which purported to explain all events, not merely all events that did occur, but any event that could occur, would be empty as an explanation because nothing would disagree with it. You might explain all events as they do occur, provided you allowed the possibility that if they occurred differently your explanation would be falsified. But the trouble with these so-called metaphysical explanations is that they don't merely purport to explain what does happen, but to serve equally for anything that could conceivably happen. However you changed your data, the same explanation would still hold, but that makes it as an explanation absolutely vacuous.

Copleston. I think that what you are demanding is that any explanation of the existence of phenomena should be a scientific hypothesis. Otherwise you will not recognize it as an explanation. This is to say, "All explanations of facts are of the type of scientific hypothesis or they are not explanations at all." But the explanation of all finite beings cannot be a scientific explanation, i.e. in the technical use of the word "scientific." But it can be a rational explanation all the same. "Rational" and "scientific" are not equivalent terms, and it is a prejudice to think that they are equivalent.

Ayer. But does a non-scientific explanation explain anything? Let me take an example. Suppose someone said that the explanation for things happening as they did was that it answered the purposes of the deity. Now I should say that would only be meaningful if you could show that events going this way rather

than that way answered his purpose. But if you're going to say that whatever happens is going to answer his purpose, then it becomes useless as an explanation. In fact it's not an explanation at all. It becomes empty of significance because it's consistent with everything.
Copleston. If I seek the explanation of the world, I am considering an ontological question, and what I am looking for is an ontological explanation and not simply a logical explanation.

NECESSARY AND CONTINGENT PROPOSITIONS

Ayer. Now I think I get more of what you're saying. But aren't you asking for something contradictory? You see, so long as an explanation is contingent, that is something that might be otherwise logically, you're going to say it's not a sufficient explanation. So that you want for your proposition something that is logically necessary. But of course once your proposition becomes logically necessary it is a purely formal one, and so doesn't explain anything. So what you want is to have a proposition that is both contingent and necessary, contingent in so far as it's got to describe the world, necessary in so far as it's not just something happening to be, but something that must be. But that's a contradiction in terms.
Copleston. There is a contradiction only if one grants an assumption of yours which I deny. A proposition which is applicable to a contingent thing or event is not necessarily a contingent proposition. Nor is the proposition that it is contingent an analytic or self-evident proposition. In any case I'm not seeking the ontological explanation of the world in a proposition.
Ayer. But shouldn't you be?
Copleston. Why should one be?
Ayer. Well, what is explanation except a matter of deriving one proposition from another? But perhaps you prefer to call your ontological principle a fact. Then what you're asking for is a fact that is at one and the same time contingent and necessary, and you can't have it.
Copleston. Why should it at one and the same time be contingent and necessary?
Ayer. It's got to be contingent in order to do for an explanation. It's got to be necessary because you're not satisfied with anything contingent.
Copleston. I shouldn't admit that it's got to be contingent in order to do its work of explanation. I'd say that it didn't do its work of explanation if it was contingent.
Ayer. But how possibly could you derive anything empirical from a necessary proposition?
Copleston. I am not attempting to derive an empirical thing from a necessary proposition. I do attempt, however, to render empirical things intelligible by reference to an absolute or necessary being.

Ayer. But surely a necessary being can only be one concerning which the proposition that it exists is necessary?
Copleston. The proposition would be necessary, yes. But it doesn't follow that one can discern its necessity. I'm not holding, for instance, the ontological argument for the existence of God, though I do believe that God's existence is the ultimate ontological explanation of phenomena.
Ayer. Well now, ultimate in what sense? In the sense that you can't find a more general proposition from which it can be deduced?
Copleston. An ultimate principle or proposition is obviously not deducible—if you must speak of propositions instead of beings.
Ayer. Well, it is better so.
Copleston. The world doesn't consist of contingent propositions, though things may be expressed in contingent propositions. Nor should I say that a necessary being consists of necessary propositions.
Ayer. No, of course I shouldn't say that the world consists of propositions: it's very bad grammar, bad logical grammar. But the words necessary and contingent, which you introduced, do apply to propositions in their ordinary logical acceptance.
Copleston. Yes, they do apply to propositions, but I do not accept the position that all necessary or certain propositions are tautologies. I think that there are necessary or certain propositions which also apply to things.
Ayer. Yes, but not in any different sense. A statement to the effect that a being is necessary could be translated into a statement that a proposition referring to that being was necessary. Now you've got into the difficulty that from a logically necessary proposition, which I should say meant a *formally* valid proposition, and therefore a materially empty proposition, you want to derive a proposition with material content. You do want to have it both ways, you want to have statements, facts if you like, which are both contingent and necessary, and that, of course, you can't have. And a metaphysician can't have it either.
Copleston. But, you see, I do not believe that all certain propositions are only formally valid, in the sense of being tautologies. I am not saying that there are propositions which are both necessary and contingent: what I am saying is that there are, in my opinion, propositions which are certain and which are yet applicable to reality. If the reality in question happens to be contingent, that doesn't make the proposition contingent, if by contingent you mean an uncertain empirical hypothesis.
Ayer. Well, then I must protest I *don't* understand your use of the word "necessary." You see, it seems to me we've got a fairly clear meaning for "logically necessary"; propositions that are formally valid, I should call logically necessary; and I can understand "causally necessary." I should say that events are linked by causal necessity when there is some hypothesis, not itself logically necessary, from which their connection is deducible. Now you want to introduce a third sense of necessity, which is the crucial sense for you, which isn't either of those, but is—what?

THE NATURE OF LOGICAL NECESSITY

Copleston. By a necessary proposition I mean a *certain* proposition. You may say that there are no certain propositions which are applicable to reality; but that is another matter. Earlier in our discussion I distinguished at least two senses of the principle of causality. I regard the philosophic version as certain. In other words, besides purely logical propositions and what you would, I think, call empirical hypotheses, I believe that there are metaphysical propositions which are certain. Now take the principle of contradiction. I think that there is a metaphysical version of the principle which is not simply what is sometimes called "a law of thought," but is rather imposed on the mind by its experience of being, or, better, by its reflection on its experience of being. But I presume that you would say that the principle is only formal. Well, it seems to me that if it's purely formal, then I ought to admit there's a possibility of this piece of paper being white and not white at the same time. I can't think it, but I ought, I think, on your assumption, to admit the abstract possibility of it. But I can't think it, I can't admit its abstract possibility.
Ayer. Well, if you tell me that the paper is both white and not-white, of course you don't tell me anything about fact, do you?
Copleston. Well, no, I should say that is because one can't admit the possibility of its being both white and not-white at the same time.
Ayer. You can't admit that possibility, given existing conventions, about the use of the word "not," but of course you could perfectly well introduce a convention by which it would be meaningful. Supposing you chose, when the paper was grey, to say it was white and not-white. Then you would have altered your logic. But given that you're using a logic in which you exclude "p and not-p," then of course you exclude the paper's being white and not-white.
Copleston. A logic in which you don't exclude "p and not-p" may have uses; but I do not see that any significant statement can be made about this piece of paper in such a logic. It seems to me that if the principle of contradiction is purely formal and tautological, that I ought to admit the possibility of its being white—what I *call* white—of its being white and not-white at the same time; but I can't think that.
Ayer. No, of course you can't. You shouldn't be expected to, because to think that would be to use symbols in a way not in accordance with the conventions under which that particular group of symbols are to be used. But of course you could describe the same experience in a different sort of logic; you could introduce a different grammar of color-classification which allowed you to say that the paper was and was not a certain color, for example in the case where the color is changing. Certain Hegelians want to do that, and we have no call to stop them. There's no particular advantage in doing it, because you can equally well describe the phenomenon in the Aristotelian logic; but if, in the case where it's changing its color you like to say that it's both white and not-white, that's all right, so long as it's understood how your terms are being used.

Copleston. It seems to me that it would be the nature of the thing itself that forced me to speak in a certain way. If I have before me Smith and Jackson, I can't think of Smith being Smith-and-Jackson at the same time. I should say that it's not merely a law of thought or an analytic tautology that forces me to say that, but the nature of the things themselves.
Ayer. I agree that such conventions are based on empirical facts, the nature of your experiences, and adapted to meet them; but you can again quite easily imagine circumstances in which you would be inclined to change your logic in that respect. Certain neurotic phenomena might very well incline one to say that Smith had acquired some of Jackson's personality, and then if such things were very common, you might get a new usage of "person," according to which you could have two different persons inhabiting one body, or one person inhabiting different bodies.
Copleston. Well, I can agree to speak about things using any terms I like, I suppose: I can agree to call this paper red, when I know that it's white, but that in no way alters the nature of the paper.
Ayer. No. No one is claiming that it does. The fact is that the paper looks as it does. If you have a symbol system which you use to describe those facts, then that symbol system will itself have certain conventions, governing the use of certain symbols in it. Now I think in any given symbol system I could separate what I call the logical expressions, and the descriptive expressions. Words like "not," I should say, were logical expressions.
Copleston. Supposing one had another logical system. Is there any rule of speaking within that system? And suppose now you are using a three-valued logic. You could perfectly well use that to describe what you now describe, could you?
Ayer. Yes, the difference would be that you couldn't make certain inferences that you now make. Thus, from the fact that the paper was *not* not-white you couldn't then infer that it was white: you could only infer that it was either white or the intermediate state, which you would choose to describe, not by a separate word, which brings you back to your two-valued system, but by saying both white and not-white.
Copleston. My point is that there are, in my opinion, certain propositions which are founded on an experience of reality and which are not, therefore, simply formal propositions or tautologies. If one wishes to keep within the sphere of purely formal logic one can, on this understanding, employ a three-valued logic. But purely formal propositions are not likely to help one in metaphysics. No doubt you would say "Hear, hear." But I admit, and you do not, propositions which are certain and yet not purely formal. Some people would call such propositions "synthetic *a priori* propositions," but I do not care for the phrase myself, on account of its association with the philosophy of Kant. However, the issue between us is in any case whether or not there are propositions which are certain and which yet apply to reality; and I do not think that the introduction of the three-valued logic really affects the point. I have no wish to deny that there may be propositions which *are* purely formal. But I am

convinced of the existence of valid metaphysical propositions. However, I should like to raise another question, in order to get your views on it. Perhaps you would help me to attain clarity in the matter. My question is this. Within a three-valued system of logic is there any rule of consistency at all?
Ayer. Yes. Otherwise it wouldn't be a system of logic.
Copleston. Then does it not seem that there is at least one proto-proposition which governs all possible systems of logic?
Ayer. No, that doesn't follow.
Copleston. Well, supposing in a system without the principle of contradiction one simply disregarded the principles of consistency within the system. Would you say then that one was contradicting oneself?
Ayer. No, because in that sense the notion of contradiction as you understand it wouldn't apply.
Copleston. Well, would you say one was at variance with the rules of the game?
Ayer. Yes, you wouldn't be playing that game.
Copleston. Then there *are* some laws, if one likes to speak in that way, that govern all games?
Ayer. No, there are no laws that govern all games, but each game has a certain set of laws governing it.
Copleston. Well, consistency, or observation of law, within a game, whatever these laws may be, is itself, it seems to me, a kind of proto-principle.
Ayer. What's common to all of them is that if the game is conducted in accordance with certain rules, then if you don't observe those rules, you're not playing that game, though possibly some other.
Copleston. And are you producing unintelligible statements?
Ayer. Whether the statements were intelligible or not, of course, would depend on whether they could be interpreted as counters in some other game.
Copleston. Ah, but within the game itself . . .
Ayer. No, they would not be.
Copleston. Well then, it does seem to me that there is, at any rate, a principle of consistency, which seems to me to be a kind of proto-proposition governing all reasoning.
Ayer. Well, take it this way. Take it in the case of chess, or bridge. Now you might play bridge, and revoke.
Copleston. Yes.
Ayer. And if it's done once, occasionally, that's considered to be a slip, and you haven't stopped playing bridge. But supposing now you make revoking a general habit, and nobody worries, you're allowed to revoke when you please, then you're playing some different game. Now possibly you might be able to determine the rules of that game too.
Copleston. Yes.
Ayer. Well now, exactly the same with logic, you see: in an ordinary, say Aristotelian, logic, certain moves are allowed.
Copleston. Necessitated, I should say. Yes.

Ayer. And certain moves, including admitting contradictories, are disallowed.
Copleston. Well?
Ayer. Now supposing you have a game which breaks those rules, then you have a different game.
Copleston. Granted. But I don't admit that all logics are games, in the sense that no logic applies to reality or that all possible logics apply equally well. I see no *reason* to say this. If one did say it, the statement would be a philosophical, even a metaphysical, statement, and therefore, I suppose, according to your view, technically meaningless. However, supposing that they are games, there is a certain architectonic governing the playing of those games.
Ayer. No. All you can say is, not that there's any given rule that must be observed in every game, because there isn't, but that in any game there must be some rule. And it is an empirical question which logic is the most useful. Compare the case of alternative geometries.
Copleston. Observance of consistency seems to me to mean something more than "Unless you observe the rules of the game you do not observe the rules of the game." It means, "If you contradict yourself, that is, if you contradict your premises and definitions, you do not reason significantly." That is not an arbitrary or conventional principle, I should suggest.
Ayer. But surely all that you are saying is that in a language, namely the one we are now using, where one of the principles of correct reasoning is the observance of the law of non-contradiction, anyone who violates this law isn't reasoning correctly. That is certainly a valid statement, but it *is* conventional.

THE RELATION OF LANGUAGE TO PHILOSOPHY

Copleston. I should like to know what you, as a logical positivist, think about the relation of language to philosophy. Would you say that philosophy depends on language, in the sense that philosophical ideas depend on grammatical and syntactical structure?
Ayer. Not quite in that sense, but I think that philosophy can be said to be about language.
Copleston. And you think that to some extent it depends on the language you use to do it in?
Ayer. What you can imagine to be possible depends very much upon what kind of symbol system you're using. Yes.
Copleston. Can you give me an illustration of the way in which philosophy depends on language?
Ayer. Well, I should say, for example, that the belief of Western philosophers in substance was very much bound up with the subject-predicate form of most sentences in Western languages.
Copleston. In that case it's a question of empirical investigation, isn't it? I mean as to whether that is the case or not. And we should find, if the theory is true, that if the grammatical and syntactical structure of different languages

is different, philosophical problems raised in those languages are different. Surely you can translate the Western philosophical problems into some quite primitive non-European languages. And where difficulty in doing so arises, this is not owing to the grammatical and syntactical structure of the language in question, but owing to the absence of the abstract expression which will correspond to the Western idea. It seems to me that the ideas come before the expression. To say that the expression governs the ideas and the formation of the ideas, is to put the cart before the horse.

Ayer. The idea comes before the expression? As an image, or something of that sort?

Copleston. Sometimes, of course, it will be an image, but I'm a little doubtful whether all ideas are accompanied by images. But let us take your concrete example, substance. Presumably the Greeks got the idea of substance before they applied the word "ousia" to it. Let's take a test case. Aristotle wrote in greek, Avicenna and Averroes in Arabic, and Maimonides, partly at least, in Hebrew. Well, if the theory of the dependence of philosophy on language is true, it ought, I think, to be empirically provable that the difference between the philosophies of Aristotle, Avicenna, Averroes and Maimonides were due to differences in the grammatical and syntactical structures of the languages they respectively employed. As far as I know that's never been shown. It seems to me that the differences are due to quite other causes, partly theological.

Ayer. Maybe. But I still maintain that philosophers have been influenced by language. Of course the interesting thing now is not to find out why they said what they did, but evaluate what it was they were saying, and how far it was significant or true. Now I do think it rather queer that people have been so inclined to believe in substance with no empirical evidence about it whatsoever. I think the grammatical distinction of subject and predicate may be one cause, but I admit that I haven't made the empirical investigation. This is only a conjecture. Similarly I should expect people with ideographic languages to be less concerned about the problem of universals, for example, not being easily able to isolate abstract words.

Copleston. Yes, in some cases I should think it would be due not to deficiency of language so much as to direction of interest.

Ayer. And then you get things like the tendency to treat all words as names.

Copleston. Yes, I know. I mean, I'm not trying to adopt an extreme position. I should question any such extreme position, which I understand you don't hold, as that philosophical problems are simply due to the form of the language which the philosophers who raised those problems used. But I don't wish to deny that some philosophers have been misled by language. For example, if one supposes that to every word there is a corresponding thing, that to redness, for example, there corresponds a redness which is different from the redness of a rose, or any particular red thing; then I should say that the philosopher was misled by language. What I would emphasize would be that this question of the influence of language on philosophy is simply a question of empirical investigation in any given case. The dogmatic *a priori* statement concerning the influence of language on philosophy should be studiously avoided.

Ayer. I agree that it's an empirical question how our own philosophical problems have grown up. But that doesn't affect my contention that the method of solving these problems is that of linguistic analysis.

THE PRINCIPLE OF VERIFIABILITY

Copleston. Well, perhaps we'd better attend to your principle of verifiability. You mentioned the principle of verification earlier. I thought possibly you'd state it, Professor, would you?

Ayer. Yes. I'll state it in a fairly loose form, namely that to be significant a statement must be either, on the one hand, a formal statement, one that I should call analytic, or on the other hand empirically testable, and I should try to derive this principle from an analysis of understanding. I should say that understanding a statement meant knowing what would be the case if it were true. Knowing what would be the case if it were true means knowing what observations would verify it, and that in turn means being disposed to accept certain situations as warranting the acceptance or rejection of the statement in question. From which there are two corollaries: one, which we've been talking about to some extent, that statements to which no situations are relevant one way or the other are ruled out as non-factual; and, secondly, that the content of the statement, the cash value, to use James's term, consists of a range of situations, experiences, that would substantiate or refute it.

Copleston. Thank you. Now I don't want to misinterpret your position, but it does seem to me that you are presupposing a certain philosophical position. What I mean is this. If you say that any factual statement, in order to be meaningful, must be verifiable, and if you mean by "verifiable" verifiable by sense-experience, then surely you are presupposing that all reality is given in sense-experience. If you are presupposing this, you are presupposing that there can be no such thing as a metaphysical reality. And if you presuppose this, you are presupposing a philosophical position which cannot be demonstrated by the principle of verification. It seems to me that logical positivism claims to be what I might call a "neutral" technique, whereas in reality it presupposes the truth of positivism. Please pardon my saying so, but it looks to me as though the principle of verifiability were excogitated partly *in order* to exclude metaphysical propositions from the range of meaningful propositions.

Ayer. Even if that were so, it doesn't prove it invalid. But, to go back, I certainly should not make any statement about *all* reality. That is precisely the kind of statement that I use my principle in order not to make. Nor do I wish to restrict experience to sense experience: I should not at all mind counting what might be called introspectible experiences, or feelings, mystical experiences if you like. It would be true, then, that people who haven't had certain experiences won't understand propositions which refer to them; but that I don't mind either. I can quite well believe that you have experiences different from mine. Let us assume (which after all is an empirical assumption) that you have even a sense different from mine. I should be in the position of the blind man, and then I should admit that statements which are unintelligible to me might be meaningful for you. But I should then go on to say that the factual content of your statements *was* determined by the experiences which counted as their verifiers or falsifiers.

Copleston. Yes, you include introspection, just as Hume did. But my point is that you assume that a factually informative statement is significant only if it is verifiable, at least in principle, by direct observation. Now obviously the existence of a metaphysical reality is not verifiable by direct observation, unless you are willing to recognize a purely intellectual intuition as observation. I am not keen on appealing to intuition, though I see no compelling reason to rule it out from the beginning. However, if you mean by "verifiable" verifiable by direct sense-observation and/or introspection, you seem to me to be ruling out metaphysics from the start. In other words, I suggest that acceptance of the principle of verifiability, as you appear to understand it, implies the acceptance of philosophical positivism. I should probably be prepared to accept the principle if it were understood in a very wide sense, that is, if "verifiable by experience" is understood as including intellectual intuition and also as meaning simply that some experience, actual or conceivable, is relevant to the truth or falsity of the proposition concerned. What I object to is any statement of the principle of verifiability which tacitly assumes the validity of a definite philosophical position.

Now, you'd make a distinction, I think, between analytic statements on the one hand, and empirical statements, and metaphysical and ethical statements on the other. Or at any rate metaphysical statements; leave ethical out of it. You'd call the first group cognitive, and the second emotive. Is that so?

Ayer. I think the use of the word emotive is not very happy, although I have used it in the past, because it suggests that they're made with emotion, which isn't necessarily the case; but I accept what you say, if you mean by "emotive" simply "non-cognitive."

Copleston. Very well. I accept, of course, your substitution of "non-cognitive" for "emotive." But my objection still remains. By cognitive statements I presume that you mean statements which satisfy the criterion of meaning, that is to say, the principle of verifiability: and by non-cognitive statements I presume you mean statements which do not satisfy that criterion. If this is so, it seems to me that when you say that metaphysical statements are non-cognitive you are not saying much more than that statements which do not satisfy the principle of verifiability do not satisfy the principle of verifiability. In this case, however, no conclusion follows as to the significance or non-significance of metaphysical propositions. Unless, indeed, one has previously accepted your philosophical position; that is to say, unless one has first assumed that they are non-significant.

Ayer. No, it's not as simple as that. My procedure is this: I should claim that the account I've given you of what understanding a statement is, is the account that does apply to ordinary common-sense statements, and to scientific statements, and then I would give a different account of how mathematical statements functioned, and a different account again of value-judgments.
Copleston. Yes.
Ayer. I then say that statements which don't satisfy these conditions are not significant, not to be understood; and I think you can quite correctly object that by putting my definitions together, all I come down to saying is that statements that are not scientific or common-sense statements are not scientific or common-sense statements. But then I want to go further and say that I totally fail to understand—again, I'm afraid, using my own use of understanding: what else can I do?—I fail to understand what these other non-scientific statements and non-common-sense statements, which don't satisfy these criteria, are supposed to be. Someone may say he understands them, in some sense of understanding other than the one I've defined. I reply, It's not clear to me what this sense of understanding is, nor, *a fortiori* of course, what it is he understands, nor how these statements function. But of course you may say that in making it a question of how these statements function, I'm presupposing my own criterion.
Copleston. Well, then, in your treatment of metaphysical propositions you are either applying the criterion of verifiability or you are not. If you are, then the significance of metaphysical propositions is ruled out of court *a priori,* since the truth of the principle of verifiability, as it seems to be understood by you, inevitably involves the non-significance of such propositions. In this case the application of the criterion to concrete metaphysical propositions constitutes a proof neither of the nonsignificance of these propositions nor of the truth of the principle. All that is shown, it seems to me, is that metaphysical propositions do not satisfy a definite assumed criterion of meaning. But it does not follow that one must accept that criterion of meaning. You may legitimately say, if you like, "I will accept as significant factual statements only those statements which satisfy these particular demands"; but it does not follow that I, or anyone else, has to make those particular demands before we are prepared to accept a statement as meaningful.
Ayer. What I do is to give a definition of certain related terms: understanding, meaningful, and so on. I can't force you to accept them, but I can perhaps make you unhappy about the consequences of not accepting them. What I should do is this. I should take any given proposition, and show how it functioned. In the case of a scientific hypothesis, I would show that it had a certain function, namely that, with other premises, you could deduce certain observational consequences from it. I should then say, This is how this proposition works, this is what it does, this is what it amounts to. I then take a mathematical proposition and play a slightly different game with that, and show that it functions in a certain way, in a calculus, in a symbolic system. You then present me with

these other statements, and I then say: On the one hand, they have no observational consequences; on the other hand, they aren't statements of logic. All right. So you understand them. I have given a definition of understanding according to which they're not, in my usage of the term, capable of being understood. Nevertheless you reject my definition. You're perfectly entitled to, because you can give understanding a different meaning if you like. I can't stop you. But now I say, Tell me more about them. In what sense are they understood? They're not understood in my sense. They aren't parts of a symbolic system. You can't do anything with them, in the sense of deriving any observational consequences from them. What *do* you want to say about them? Well, you may just want to say, "They're facts," or something of that sort. Then again I press you on your use of the word "facts."

Copleston. You seem to me to be demanding that in order for a factual statement to be significant one must be able to deduce observational consequences from it. But I do not see why this should be so. If you mean directly observable consequences, you appear to me to be demanding too much. In any case are there not some propositions which are not verifiable, even in principle, but which would yet be considered by most people to have meaning and to be either true or false? Let me give an example. I don't want to assume the mantle of a prophet, and I hope that the statement is false; but it is this: "Atomic warfare will take place, and it will blot out the entire human race." Now, most people would think that this statement has meaning; it means what it says. But how could it possibly be verified empirically? Supposing it were fulfilled, the last man could not say with his last breath, "Copleston's prediction has been verified," because he would not be entitled to say this until he was dead, that is, until he was no longer in a position to verify the statement.

Ayer. It's certainly practically unverifiable. You can't be man, surviving all men. On the other hand, there's no doubt it describes a possible situation. Putting the observer outside the story, one knows quite well what it would be like to observe devastation, and fail to observe any men. Now it wouldn't necessarily be the case that, in order to do that, one had to observe oneself. Just as, to take the case of the past, there were dinosaurs before there were men. Clearly, no man saw that, and clearly I, if I am the speaker, can't myself verify it: but one knows what it would be like to have observed animals and not to have observed men.

Copleston. The two cases are different. In regard to the past we have empirical evidence. For example, we have fossils of dinosaurs. But in the case of the prediction I mentioned there would be nobody to observe the evidence and so to verify the proposition.

Ayer. In terms of the evidence, of course, it becomes very much easier for me. That would be too easy a way of getting out of our difficulty, because there is also evidence for the atomic thing.

Copleston. Yes, but there would be no evidence for the prediction that it will blot out the human race, even if one can imagine the state of affairs that would verify it. Thus by imagining it, one's imagining oneself into the picture.

Ayer. No, no.
Copleston. Yes, yes. One can imagine the evidence and one can imagine oneself verifying it; but, in point of fact, if the prediction were fulfilled there would be no one there to verify. By importing yourself imaginatively into the picture, you are canceling out the condition of the fulfillment of the prediction. But let us drop the prediction. You have mentioned imagination. Now, what I should prefer to regard as the criterion of the truth or falsity of an existential proposition is simply the presence or absence of the asserted fact or facts, quite irrespective of whether I can know whether there are corresponding facts or not. If I can at least imagine or conceive the facts, the existence of which would verify the proposition, the proposition has significance for me. Whether I can or cannot know that the facts correspond is another matter.
Ayer. I don't at all object to your use of the word "facts" so long as you allow them to be observable facts. But take the contrary case. Suppose I say "There's a 'drogulus' over there," and you say "What?" and I say "Drogulus," and you say "What's a drogulus?" Well, I say "I can't describe what a drogulus is, because it's not the sort of thing you can see or touch, it has no physical effects of any kind, but it's a disembodied being." And you say, "Well how am I to tell if it's there or not?" and I say "There's no way of telling. Everything's just the same if it's there or it's not there. But the fact is it's there. There's a drogulus there standing just behind you, spiritually behind you." Does that make sense?
Copleston. It seems to me to do so. I should say that to state that there is a drogulus in the room or not is true or false, provided that you can—that you, at any rate, have some idea of what is meant by a drogulus; and if you can say to me it's a disembodied spirit, then I should say that the proposition is either true or false whether one can verify it or not. If you said to me "By drogulus I merely mean the word 'drogulus,' and I attach no other significance to it whatsoever," then I should say that it isn't a proposition any more than if I said "piffle" was in the room.
Ayer. That's right. But what is "having some idea" of something? I want to say that having an idea of something is a matter of knowing how to recognize it. And you want to say that you can have ideas of things even though there's no possible situation in which you could recognize them, because nothing would count as finding them. I would say that I understand the words "angel," "table," "cloth," "drogulus," if I'm disposed to accept certain situations as verifying the presence or absence of what the word is supposed to stand for. But you want to admit these words without any reference to experience. Whether the thing they are supposed to stand for exists or not, everything is to go on just the same.
Copleston. No. I should say that you can have an idea of something if there's some experience that's relevant to the formation of the idea, not so much to its verification. I should say that I can form the idea of a drogulus or a disembodied spirit from the idea of body and the idea of mind. You may say that there's no mind and there's no spirit, but at any rate there are, as you'll admit, certain internal experiences of thinking and so on which at any rate account for

the formation of the idea. Therefore I can say I have an idea of a drogulus or whatever it is, even though I'm quite unable to know whether such a thing actually exists or not.
Ayer. You would certainly not have to know that it exists, but you would have to know what would count as its existing.
Copleston. Yes. Well, if you mean by "count as its existing" that there must be some experience relevant to the formation of the idea, then I should agree.
Ayer. Not to the formation of the idea, but to the truth or falsity of the propositions in which it is contained.

ARE STATEMENTS ABOUT GOD MEANINGFUL?

Copleston. The word "metaphysics" and the phrase "metaphysical reality" can have more than one meaning: but when I refer to a metaphysical reality in our present discussion, I mean a being which in principle, and not merely in fact, transcends the sphere of what can be sensibly experienced. Thus God is a metaphysical reality. Since God is *ex hypothesi* immaterial, He cannot *in principle* be apprehended by the senses. May I add two remarks? My first remark is that I do not mean to imply that no sense-experience is in any way relevant to establishing or discovering the existence of a metaphysical reality. I certainly do believe that metaphysics must be based on experiences of some sort. But metaphysics involves intellectual reflection on experience: no amount of immediate sense-experience will disclose the existence of a metaphysical reality. In other words, there is a half-way house between admitting only the immediate data of experience and on the other hand leaping to the affirmation of a metaphysical reality without any reference to experience at all. You yourself reflect on the data of experience. The metaphysician carries that reflection a stage further. My second remark is this: Because one cannot have a sense-experience of a metaphysical reality, it does not follow that one could not have another type of experience of it. And if anyone has such an experience, it does not mean that the metaphysical reality is deprived, as it were, of its metaphysical character and becomes non-metaphysical. I think that this is an important point.
Ayer. Yes, but asking are there metaphysical realities isn't like asking are there still wolves in Asia, is it? It looks as if you've got a clear usage for metaphysical reality, and are then asking "Does it occur or not? Does it exist or not?" and as if I'm arbitrarily denying that it exists. My difficulty is not in answering the question "Are there, or are there not, metaphysical realities?" but in understanding what usage is being given to the expression "metaphysical reality." When am I to count a reality as metaphysical? What would it be like to come upon a metaphysical reality? That's my problem. It isn't that I arbitrarily say there can't be such things, already admitting the use of the term, but that I'm puzzled about the use of the term. I don't know what people who say there are metaphysical realities *mean* by it.

Copleston. Well, that brings us back to the beginning, to the function of philosophy. I should say that one can't simply raise in the abstract the question "Are there metaphysical realities?" Rather one asks, "Is the character of observable reality of such a kind that it leads one to postulate a metaphysical reality, a reality beyond the physical sphere?" If one grants that it is, even then one can only speak about that metaphysical reality within the framework of human language. And language is after all primarily developed to express our immediate experience of surrounding things, and therefore there's bound to be a radical inadequacy in any statements about a metaphysical reality.
Ayer. But you're trying to have it both ways, you see. If it's something that you say doesn't have a meaning in my language, then I don't understand it. It's no good saying "Oh well, of course it really has a meaning," because what meaning could it have except in the language which it's used?
Copleston. Let's take a concrete example. If I say, for example, "God is intelligent," well, you may very well say to me "What meaning can you give to the word 'intelligent,' because the only intelligence you have experienced is the human intelligence, and are you attributing that to God?" And I should have to say no, because I'm not. Therefore, if we agreed to use the word intelligent simply to mean human intelligence, I should have to say "God is not intelligent"; but when I said that a stone is not intelligent, I should mean that a stone was, speaking qualitatively, less than intelligent. And when I said that God was intelligent, I should mean that God was more than intelligent, even though I could give no adequate account of what that intelligence was in itself.
Ayer. Do you mean simply that he knows more than any given man knows? But to what are you ascribing this property? You haven't begun to make that clear.
Copleston. I quite see your point, of course. But what you are inviting me to do is to describe God in terms which will be as clear to you as the terms in which one might describe a familiar object of experience, or an unfamiliar object which is yet so like to familiar objects that it can be adequately described in terms of things which are already familiar to you. But God is *ex hypothesi* unique; and it is quite impossible to describe Him adequately by using concepts which normally apply to ordinary objects of experience. If it were possible, He would not be God. So you are really asking me to describe God in a manner which would be possible only if He were not God. I not only freely admit that human ideas of God are inadequate, but also affirm that this must be so, owing to the finitude of the human intellect and to the fact that we can come to a philosophical knowledge of God only through reflection on the things we experience. But it does not follow that we can have *no* knowledge of God, though it does follow that our philosophical knowledge of God cannot be more than analogical.
Ayer. Yes, but in the case of an ordinary analogy, when you say that something is like something else you understand what both things are. But in this case if you say something is analogical, I say "analogical of what?" And then you don't tell me of what. You merely repeat the first term of analogy. Well I

got no analogy. It's like saying that something is "taller than," and I say "taller than?" and you repeat the first thing you say. Then I understand it's taller than itself, which is nonsense.

Copleston. I think that one must distinguish physical analogy and metaphysical analogy. If I say that God is intelligent, I do not say so simply because I want to call God intelligent, but either because I think that the world is such that it must be ascribed in certain aspects at least to a Being which can be described in human terms only as intelligent, or because I am satisfied by some argument that there exists an Absolute Being and then deduce that that Being must be described as intelligent. I am perfectly aware that I have no adequate idea of what that intelligence is in itself. I am ascribing to God an attribute which, translated into human terms, must be called intelligence. After all, if you speak of your dog as intelligent, you are using the word in an analogous sense, and it has some meaning for you, even though you do not observe the dog's physical operations. Mathematicians who speak of multidimensional space have never observed such a space; but presumably they attach some meaning to the term. When we speak of "extra-sensory perception" we are using the word "perception" analogously.

Ayer. Yes, but mathematical physicists do test their statements by observation, and I know what counts as a case of extra-sensory perception. But in the case of your statements I don't know what counts. Of course you *might* give them an empirical meaning, you might say that by "God is intelligent" you meant that the world had certain features. Then we'd inspect it to see if it had these features or not.

Copleston. Well of course I should prefer to start from the features of the world before going to God. I shouldn't wish to argue from God to the features of the world. But to keep within your terms of reference of empiricism, well then I'd say that if God is personal, then He's capable, for example, of entering into relationship with human beings. And it's possible to find human beings who claim to have a personal intercourse with God.

Ayer. Then you've given your statement a perfectly good empirical meaning. But it would then be like a scientific theory, and you would be using this in exactly the same way as you might use a concept like electron to account for, explain, predict, a certain range of human experience, namely, that certain people did have these experiences which they described as "entering into communion with God." Then one would try to analyse it scientifically, find out in what conditions these things happened, and then you might put it up as a theory. What you'd have done would be psychology.

Copleston. Well, as I said, I was entering into your terms of reference. I wouldn't admit that when I say God is personal I merely mean that God can enter into intercourse with human beings. I should be prepared to say that He was personal even if I had no reason for supposing that He entered into intercourse with human beings.

Ayer. No, but it's only in that case that one has anything one can control. The facts are that these human beings have these experiences. They describe these experiences in a way which implies more than that they're having these experiences. But if one asks what more, then what answer does one get? Only, I'm afraid, a repetition of the statement that was questioned in the first place.

Copleston. Let's come back to this religious experience. However you subsequently interpret the religious experience, you'd admit that it was relevant to the truth or falsity of the proposition that, say, God existed.

Ayer. Relevant in so far as the proposition that God existed is taken as a description or prediction of the occurrence of these experiences. But not, of course, relevant to any inference you might want to draw, such as that the world was created, or anything of that kind.

Copleston. No, we'll leave that out. All I'm trying to get at is that you'd admit that the proposition "God exists" could be a meaningful form of metaphysical proposition.

Ayer. No, it wouldn't then be a metaphysical proposition. It'd be a perfectly good empirical proposition like the proposition that the unconscious mind exists.

Copleston. The proposition that people have religious experiences would be an empirical proposition; and the proposition that God exists would also be an empirical proposition, provided that all I meant by saying that God exists was that some people have a certain type of experience. But it is *not* all I mean by it. All I originally said was that if God is personal, then one of the consequences would be that He could enter into communication with human beings. If He does so, that does not make God an empirical reality, in the sense of not being a metaphysical reality. God can perfectly well be a metaphysical reality, that is, independent of *physis* or nature, even if intelligent creatures have a non-sensible experience of Him. However, if you wish to call metaphysical propositions empirical propositions, by all means do so. It then becomes a question of terminology.

Ayer. No. I suggest that you're trying to have it both ways. You see, you allow me to give these words, these shapes or noises, an empirical meaning. You allow me to say that the test whereby what you call God exists or not is to be that certain people have experiences, just as the test for whether the table exists or not is that certain people have experiences, only the experiences are of a different sort. Having got that admission you then shift the meaning of the words "God exists." You no longer make them refer simply to the possibility of having these experiences, and so argue that I have admitted a metaphysical proposition, but of course I haven't. All I've admitted is an empirical proposition, which you've chosen to express in the same words as you also want to use to express your metaphysical proposition.

Copleston. Pardon me, but I did not say that the test whereby what I call God exists or not is that certain people have certain experiences. I said that if God exists, one consequence would be that people could have certain experiences. However, even if I accept your requirements, it follows that in one case at least you are prepared to recognize the word "God" as meaningful.

Ayer. Of course I recognize it as meaningful if you give it an empirical meaning, but it doesn't follow there's any empirical evidence for the truth of your metaphysical proposition.

AGAIN: ARE THERE METAPHYSICAL EXPLANATIONS?

Copleston. But then I don't claim that metaphysical propositions are not in some way founded on reflection on experience. In a certain sense I should call myself an empiricist, but I think that your empiricism is too narrow. Another point. You will not allow a factual statement to be significant unless it is verifiable. Now, suppose I say that we both have immortal souls. If we have, then the proposition will be empirically verified in due course. Are you then prepared to admit that my statement that we both have immortal souls is a significant statement? If you are not prepared, is this because you demand a particular kind of verification and reject any other type? Such an attitude would not seem to me to be warranted. And I don't see that thereby any statement about reality to which one concludes via the experience is deprived of its metaphysical character, and introduced into the empirical sphere.

Ayer. Oh, surely. Let us take a case of a common-sense proposition, such as that there is a glass of water in front of us. The evidence of that is my seeing it, touching it. But of course the meaning of that proposition, the factual content of that proposition, isn't exhausted by any one particular piece of evidence of that sort. I may be having a hallucination. What my proposition predicts is more evidence of the same kind. It isn't that my seeing what I do is evidence for the existence of something totally unobservable. I go beyond the immediate evidence only in so far as I take this experience to be one of an indefinite series of experiences of seeing, touching it, etc., which my statement covers. Equally, in the case of your statement I should want to say that if you want to treat it empirically, you must then treat it as predicting, in exactly the same way, in certain conditions, religious experiences. What it will mean will be the possibility of further religious experiences.

Copleston. It's this predicting that I don't like, because it doesn't seem to me that even a scientific proposition necessarily consists in a prediction. Surely it's explicative, and also can be simply explicative, not necessarily a prediction.

Ayer. But isn't it explicative in the sense that it links up with a particular phenomenon, or with lots and lots of other ones that either will occur, have occurred, or would occur in certain circumstances? Take the case of physics. Do you want a world of electrons somehow behind the perceptual world? Is that what you're after?

Copleston. No. We'll take the electronic theory. I should have thought that its function was to explain certain phenomena; that it originated in an endeavour to explain certain phenomena or, more generally, that it is part of the attempt

to discover the constitution of matter. I should not describe it as an attempt to predict events, except secondarily perhaps.
Ayer. Oh, I don't want to make the prediction a practical question, but I do want to say that understanding phenomena is a matter of lining them, of grouping them, and that the test of an explanation is that it applies to the hitherto unobserved cases. Suppose I am describing the path of a body and I draw a graph. Then the test of my having explained the observations is that hitherto unobserved points fall on the line I draw.
Copleston. Then my idea of metaphysics would be that of explaining, as I said at the beginning, the series of phenomena, so that the reasoning would rise out of the phenomena themselves, or out of things themselves. In that sense it would be based on experience, even though the term of the reasoning might not itself be an object of experience. I can understand your ruling out all that reflective enquiry and reasoning that constitutes metaphysics, but if you rule it out it would seem to me to be in virtue of a presupposed philosophy.
Ayer. No, I want to say that I rule out nothing as an explanation so long as it explains. I make no statements about what is real and what is not real. That seems to me again an empirical question. My objection to the kind of statements that we've agreed to call metaphysical is that they don't explain.
Copleston. That's a matter for detailed argument and detailed discussion of some particular argument. It's distinct, it seems to me, from the question of meaning. I can quite imagine somebody saying, "Your argument for, say, the existence of God is false. Your principles on which you're arguing are quite false." And if so, there's a conclusion.
Ayer. No, I don't want to say it isn't an accurate explanation. What I want to say is that it isn't an explanation at all. That's to say it doesn't even purport to do the work that an explanation does, simply because any given observation or situation is compatible with it. Now if you want to say that you are using the word in some peculiar sense, of course I can't stop you, but equally I should say that (a) it isn't the ordinary sense, and (b) that this peculiar sense hasn't been made clear to me.
Copleston. But you see I consider that the existence of what we call the world not only is compatible with God's existence, but demands the conclusion that God exists. I may have misunderstood you: but you seem to me to be saying that if the proposition that God exists means anything, one should be able to deduce some observation-statement from it. If you mean by deducing an observation-statement deducing a thing, I certainly do not think that one can do this. I believe that the existence of God can be inferred from the existence of the world, but I do not think that the world can be deduced from God. Spinoza might think otherwise, of course. If you are demanding that I should deduce the world from God, if I am to make the proposition "God exists" significant, you are demanding that I should adopt a particular idea of God and of creation. For, if one could deduce the world from God,

creation would be necessary, and God would create necessarily. If I say that I cannot deduce observation-statements from the existence of God, it is not because I have no idea of God, but because my idea of God will not permit me to say this.
Ayer. You said that the existence of the world demands the conclusion that God exists. Do you mean that this conclusion follows logically, or follows causally?
Copleston. I should say causally. I'm certainly not going to say that God exists means that a world exists, if by that you mean that the world follows necessarily from God, but given the world then I should say that there is a necessary relationship.
Ayer. Logical or causal?
Copleston Causal.
Ayer. Well, then we're back on the point we've already been over, aren't we?—this difficulty of a notion of causation that isn't the ordinary notion of causation, a notion that's still totally unexplained.
Copleston. On the contrary. I mentioned earlier on that what I mean by the principle of causality is that anything which comes into existence owes that existence to an extrinsic reality, which I term "cause." Incidentally, this notion of causality is much more like the ordinary notion of causation than the phenomenalistic notion which you would regard as the scientific notion. However, I agree that we are back where we were, namely at the question whether there are any principles which can be called certain metaphysical principles. That seems to me one of the chief issues between logical positivist and the metaphysician.

SUMMARY OF THE MAJOR DISAGREEMENTS

Ayer. It seems to me, indeed, that this has been my quarrel with you all along, that you fail to supply any rules for the use of your expressions. I am not asking for explicit definitions. All that I require is that some indication be given of the way in which the expression relates to some possible experience. It is only when a statement fails to refer, even indirectly, to anything observable that I wish to dismiss it as metaphysical. It is not necessary that the observations should actually be made. There are cases, as you have pointed out, where for practical, or even for theoretical, reasons, the observations could not in fact be made. But one knows what it would be like to make them. The statements which refer to them may be said to be verifiable in principle, if not in fact. To put the point more simply, I understand a statement of fact if I know what to look for on the supposition that it is true. And my knowing what to look for is itself a matter of my being able to interpret the statement as referring at least to some possible experience.

Now, you may say, indeed you have said, that this is all entirely arbitrary.

The principle of verifiability is not itself a descriptive statement. Its status is that of a persuasive definition. I am persuaded by it, but why should you be? Can I prove it? Yes, on the basis of other definitions. I have, in fact, tried to show you how it can be derived from an analysis of understanding. But if you are really obstinate, you will reject these other definitions too. So it looks as if we reach a deadlock. But let us then see in what positions we are left. I claim for my method that it does yield valuable results in the way of analysis, and with this you seem disposed to agree. You do not deny the importance of the analytic method in philosophy, nor do you reject all the uses to which I put it. Thus you accept in the main the account that I give of empirical propositions. You have indeed objected to my treatment of the propositions of logic, but there I think that I am in the right. At least I am able to account for their validity: whereas on your view it is utterly mysterious. The main difference between us is that you want to leave room for metaphysics. But now look at the results you get. You put forward your metaphysical statements as ultimate explanations of fact, but you admit that they are not explanations, in any accepted sense of the term, and you cannot say in what sense they are explanations. You cannot show me how they are to be tested, and you seem to have no criterion for deciding whether they are true or false. This being so, I say they are unintelligible. You say, No, you understand them; but for all the good they do you (I mean cognitively, not emotionally) you might just as well abandon them. This is my case against your metaphysical statements. You may decline to be persuaded by it, but what sort of a case can you make for them? I leave the last word to you.

Copleston. I have enjoyed our discussion very much. I have contended that a metaphysical idea has meaning if some experience is relevant to the formation of that idea, and that a rational metaphysic is possible if there are, as I think there are, principles which express an intellectual apprehension of the nature of being. I think that one *can* have an intellectual experience—or intuition if you like—of being. A metaphysical proposition is testable by rational discussion, but not by purely empirical means. When you say that metaphysical propositions are meaningless because they are unverifiable in your sense, I do not think that this amounts to more than saying that metaphysics are not the same thing as empirical science. In short, I consider that logical positivism, apart from its theory of analytic propositions, simply embodies the notion of nineteenth-century positivism that the terms "rational" and "scientific" have the same extension. This notion may correspond to a popular prejudice, but I see no adequate reason for accepting it.

I still find it difficult to understand the status of the principle of verification. It is either a proposition or no proposition. If it is, it must be, on your premises, either a tautology or an empirical hypothesis. If the former, no conclusion follows as to metaphysics. If the latter, the principle itself would require verification. But the principle of verification cannot itself be verified. If, however, the principle is not a proposition, it must, on your premises, be meaningless. In any case, if the meaning of an existential proposition consists, according to the principle, in its verifiability, it is impossible, I think, to escape an infinite regress, since the verification will itself need verification, and so on indefinitely. If this is so, then all propositions, including scientific ones, are meaningless.

EMPIRICISM, SEMANTICS, AND ONTOLOGY

Rudolf Carnap

1. THE PROBLEM OF ABSTRACT ENTITIES

Empiricists are in general rather suspicious with respect to any kind of abstract entities like properties, classes, relations, numbers, propositions, etc. They usually feel much more in sympathy with nominalists than with realists (in the medieval sense). As far as possible they try to avoid any reference to abstract entities and to restrict themselves to what is sometimes called a nominalistic language, i.e., one not containing such references. However, within certain scientific contexts it seems hardly possible to avoid them. In the case of mathematics, some empiricists try to find a way out by treating the whole of mathematics as a mere calculus, a formal system for which no interpretation is given or can be given. Accordingly, the mathematician is said to speak not about numbers, functions, and infinite classes, but merely about meaningless symbols and formulas manipulated according to given formal rules. In physics it is more difficult to shun the suspected entities, because the language of physics serves for the communication of reports and predictions and hence cannot be taken as a mere calculus. A physicist who is suspicious of abstract entities may perhaps try to declare a certain part of the language of physics as uninterpreted and uninterpretable, that part which refers to real numbers as space-time coordinates or as values of physical magnitudes, to functions, limits, etc. More probably he will just speak about all these things like anybody else but with an uneasy conscience, like a man who in his everyday life does with qualms many things which are not in accord with the high moral principles he professes on Sundays. Recently the problem of abstract entities has arisen again in connection with semantics, the theory of meaning and truth. Some semanticists say that certain expressions designate certain entities, and among these designated entities they include not only concrete material things but also abstract entities, e.g., properties as designated by predicates and propositions as designated by sentences.[1] Others object strongly to this procedure as violating the basic principles of empiricism and leading back to a metaphysical ontology of the Platonic kind.

It is the purpose of this article to clarify this controversial issue. The nature and implications of the acceptance of a language referring to abstract entities will first be discussed in general; it will be shown that using such a language does not imply embracing a Platonic ontology but is perfectly compatible with empiricism and strictly scientific thinking. Then the special question of the role of abstract entities in semantics will be discussed. It is hoped that the clarification of the issue will be useful to those who would like to accept abstract

Reprinted by permission of *Revue Internationale de Philosophie,* from Rudolf Carnap, "Empiricism, Semantics, and Ontology," *Revue Internationale de Philosophie* 4 (1950), pp. 20–40.

entities in their work in mathematics, physics, semantics, or any other field; it may help them to overcome nominalistic scruples.

2. LINGUISTIC FRAMEWORKS

Are there properties, classes, numbers, propositions? In order to understand more clearly the nature of these and related problems, it is above all necessary to recognize a fundamental distinction between two kinds of questions concerning the existence or reality of entities. If someone wishes to speak in his language about a new kind of entities, he has to introduce a system of new ways of speaking, subject to new rules; we shall call this procedure the construction of a linguistic *framework* for the new entities in question. And now we must distinguish two kinds of questions of existence: first, questions of the existence of certain entities of the new kind *within the framework;* we call them *internal questions;* and second, questions concerning the existence or reality *of the system of entities as a whole,* called *external questions.* Internal questions and possible answers to them are formulated with the help of the new forms of expressions. The answers may be found either by purely logical methods or by empirical methods, depending upon whether the framework is a logical or a factual one. An external question is of a problematic character which is in need of closer examination.

The world of things. Let us consider as an example the simplest kind of entities dealt with in the everyday language: the spatio-temporally ordered system of observable things and events. Once we have accepted the thing language with its framework for things, we can raise and answer internal questions, e.g., "Is there a white piece of paper on my desk?", "Did King Arthur actually live?", "Are unicorns and centaurs real or merely imaginary?", and the like. These questions are to be answered by empirical investigations. Results of observations are evaluated according to certain rules as confirming or disconfirming evidence for possible answers. (This evaluation is usually carried out, of course, as a matter of habit rather than a deliberate, rational procedure. But it is possible, in a rational reconstruction, to lay down explicit rules for the evaluation. This is one of the main tasks of a pure, as distinguished from a psychological, epistemology.) The concept of reality occurring in these internal questions is an empirical, scientific, non-metaphysical concept. To recognize something as a real thing or event means to succeed in incorporating it into the system of things at a particular space-time position so that it fits together with the other things recognized as real, according to the rules of the framework.

From these questions we must distinguish the external question of the reality of the thing world itself. In contrast to the former questions, this question is raised neither by the man in the street nor by scientists, but only by philosophers. Realists give an affirmative answer, subjective idealists a negative one, and the controversy goes on for centuries without ever being solved.

And it cannot be solved because it is framed in a wrong way. To be real in the scientific sense means to be an element of the system; hence this concept cannot be meaningfully applied to the system itself. Those who raise the question of the reality of the thing world itself have perhaps in mind not a theoretical question as their formulation seems to suggest, but rather a practical question, a matter of a practical decision concerning the structure of our language. We have to make the choice whether or not to accept and use the forms of expression in the framework in question.

In the case of this particular example, there is usually no deliberate choice because we all have accepted the thing language early in our lives as a matter of course. Nevertheless, we may regard it as a matter of decision in this sense: we are free to choose to continue using the thing language or not; in the latter case we could restrict ourselves to a language of sense-data and other "phenomenal" entities, or construct an alternative to the customary thing language with another structure, or, finally, we could refrain from speaking. If someone decides to accept the thing language, there is no objection against saying that he has accepted the world of things. But this must not be interpreted as if it meant his acceptance of a *belief* in the reality of the thing world; there is no such belief or assertion or assumption, because it is not a theoretical question. To accept the thing world means nothing more than to accept a certain form of language, in other words, to accept rules for forming statements and for testing, accepting, or rejecting them. The acceptance of the thing language leads, on the basis of observations made, also to the acceptance, belief, and assertion of certain statements. But the thesis of the reality of the thing world cannot be among these statements, because it cannot be formulated in the thing language or, it seems, in any other theoretical language.

The decision of accepting the thing language, although itself not of a cognitive nature, will nevertheless usually be influenced by theoretical knowledge, just like any other deliberate decision concerning the acceptance of linguistic or other rules. The purposes for which the language is intended to be used, for instance, the purpose of communicating factual knowledge, will determine which factors are relevant for the decision. The efficiency, fruitfulness, and simplicity of the use of the thing language may be among the decisive factors. And the questions concerning these qualities are indeed of a theoretical nature. But these questions cannot be identified with the question of realism. They are not yes-no questions but questions of degree. The thing language in the customary form works indeed with a high degree of efficiency for most purposes of everyday life. This is a matter of fact, based upon the content of our experiences. However, it would be wrong to describe this situation by saying: "The fact of the efficiency of the thing language is confirming evidence for the reality of the thing world"; we should rather say instead: "This fact makes it advisable to accept the thing language".

The system of numbers. As an example of a system which is of a logical rather than a factual nature let us take the system of natural numbers. The framework for this system is constructed by introducing into the language new expressions with suitable rules: (1) numerals like "five" and sentence forms like "there are five books on the table"; (2) the general term "number" for the new entities, and sentence forms like "five is a number"; (3) expressions for properties of numbers (e.g., "odd", "prime"), relations (e.g., "greater than"), and functions (e.g. "plus"), and sentence forms like "two plus three is five"; (4) numerical variables ("*m*", "*n*", etc.) and quantifiers for universal sentences ("for every *n*, . . .") and existential sentences ("there is an *n* such that . . .") with the customary deductive rules.

Here again there are internal questions, e.g., "Is there a prime number greater than a hundred?" Here, however, the answers are found, not by empirical investigation based on observations, but by logical analysis based on the rules for the new expressions. Therefore the answers are here analytic, i.e., logically true.

What is now the nature of the philosophical question concerning the existence or reality of numbers? To begin with, there is the internal question which, together with the affirmative answer, can be formulated in the new terms, say, by "There are numbers" or, more explicitly, "There is an *n* such that *n* is a number". This statement follows from the analytic statement "five is a number" and is therefore itself analytic. Moreover, it is rather trivial (in contradistinction to a statement like "There is a prime number greater than a million", which is likewise analytic but far from trivial), because it does not say more than that the new system is not empty; but this is immediately seen from the rule which states that words like "five" are substitutable for the new variables. Therefore nobody who meant the question "Are there numbers?" in the internal sense would either assert or even seriously consider a negative answer. This makes it plausible to assume that those philosophers who treat the question of the existence of numbers as a serious philosophical problem and offer lengthy arguments on either side, do not have in mind the internal question. And, indeed, if we were to ask them: "Do you mean the question as to whether the framework of numbers, *if* we were to accept it, would be found to be empty or not?", they would probably reply: "Not at all; we mean a question *prior* to the acceptance of the new framework". They might try to explain what they mean by saying that it is a question of the ontological status of numbers; the question whether or not numbers have a certain metaphysical characteristic called reality (but a kind of ideal reality, different from the material reality of the thing world) or subsistence or status of "independent entities". Unfortunately, these philosophers have so far not given a formulation of their question in terms of the common scientific language. Therefore our judgment must be that they have not succeeded in giving to the external question and to the possible answers any cognitive content. Unless and until they supply a clear cognitive interpretation, we are justified in our suspicion that their question is a pseudo-question, that is, one disguised in the form of a theoretical question while in fact it is non-theoretical; in the present case it is the practical problem whether or not to incorporate into the language the new linguistic forms which constitute the framework of numbers.

The system of propositions. The variables, "*p*", "*q*", etc., are introduced with a rule to the effect that any (declarative) sentence may be substituted for a variable of this kind; this includes, in addition to the sentences of the original thing language, also all general sentences with variables of any kind which may have been introduced into the language. Further, the general term "proposition" is introduced. "*p* is a proposition" may be defined by "*p* or not *p* " (or by any other sentence form yielding only analytic sentences). Therefore, every sentence of the form "... is a proposition" (where any sentence may stand in the place of the dots) is analytic. This holds, for example, for the sentence:

(a) "Chicago is large is a proposition".

(We disregard here the fact that the rules of English grammar require not a sentence but a that-clause as the subject of another sentence; accordingly, instead of (a) we should have to say "That Chicago is large is a proposition".) Predicates may be admitted whose argument expressions are sentences; these predicates may be either extensional (e.g., the customary truth-functional connectives) or not (e.g., modal predicates like "possible", "necessary", etc.). With the help of the new variables, general sentences may be formed, e.g.,

(b) "For every *p*, either *p* or not-*p*".
(c) "There is a *p* such that *p* is not necessary and not-*p* is not necessary".
(d) "There is a *p* such that *p* is a proposition".

(c) and (d) are internal assertions of existence. The statement "There are propositions" may be meant in the sense of (d); in this case it is analytic (since it follows from (a)) and even trivial. If, however, the statement is meant in an external sense, then it is non-cognitive.

It is important to notice that the system of rules for the linguistic expressions of the propositional framework (of which only a few rules have here been briefly indicated) is sufficient for the introduction of the framework. Any further explanations as to the nature of the propositions (i.e., the elements of the system indicated, the values of the variables "*p*", "*q*", etc.) are theoretically unnecessary because, if correct, they follow from the rules. For example, are propositions mental events (as in Russell's theory)? A look at the rules shows us that they are not, because otherwise existential statements would be of the form: "If the mental state of the person in question fulfils such and such conditions, then there is a *p* such that ...". The fact that no references to mental conditions occur in existential statements (like (c), (d), etc.) shows that propositions are not mental entities. Further, a statement of the existence of linguistic entities (e.g., expressions, classes of expressions, etc.) must contain a reference to a language. The fact that no such reference occurs in the existential statements here, shows that propositions are not linguistic entities. The fact that in these statements no reference to a subject (an observer or knower) occurs (nothing like: "There is a *p* which is necessary for Mr. *X*"), shows that the propositions (and their properties, like necessity, etc.) are not subjective. Although characterizations of these or similar kinds are, strictly speaking, unnecessary, they may nevertheless be practically useful. If they are given, they should be understood, not as ingredient parts of the system, but merely as marginal notes with the purpose of supplying to the reader helpful hints or convenient pictorial associations which may make his learning of the use of the expressions easier than the bare system of the rules would do. Such a characterization is analogous to an extrasystematic explanation which a physicist sometimes gives to the beginner. He might, for example, tell him to imagine the atoms of a gas as small balls rushing around with great speed, or the electromagnetic field and its oscillations as quasi-elastic tensions and vibrations in an ether. In fact, however, all that can accurately be said about atoms or the field is implicitly contained in the physical laws of the theories in question.[2]

The system of thing properties. The thing language contains words like "red", "hard", "stone", "house", etc., which are used for describing what things are like. Now we may introduce new variables, say "*f*", "*g*", etc., for which those words are substitutable and furthermore the general term "property". New rules are laid down which admit sentences like "Red is a property", "Red is a color", "These two pieces of paper have at least one color in common" (i.e., "There is an *f* such that *f* is a color, and . . ."). The last sentence is an internal assertion. It is of an empirical, factual nature. However, the external statement, the philosophical statement of the reality of properties—a special case of the thesis of the reality of universals—is devoid of cognitive content.

The systems of integers and rational numbers. Into a language containing the framework of natural numbers we may introduce first the (positive and negative) integers as relations among natural numbers and then the rational numbers as relations among integers. This involves introducing new types of variables, expressions substitutable for them, and the general terms "integer" and "rational number".

The system of real numbers. On the basis of the rational numbers, the real numbers may be introduced as classes of a special kind (segments) of rational numbers (according to the method developed by Dedekind and Frege). Here again a new type of variables is introduced, expressions substitutable for them (e.g., "$\sqrt{2}$"), and the general term "real number".

The spatio-temporal coordinate system for physics. The new entities are the space-time points. Each is an ordered quadruple of four real numbers, called its coordinates, consisting of three spatial and one temporal coordinates. The physical state of a spatio-temporal point or region is described either with the help of qualitative predicates (e.g., "not") or by ascribing numbers as values of a physical magnitude (e.g., mass, temperature, and the like). The step from the system of things (which does not contain space-time points but only extended objects with spatial and temporal relations between them) to the physical coordinate system is again a matter of decision. Our choice of certain features, although itself not theoretical, is suggested by theoretical knowledge, either logical or factual. For example, the choice of real numbers rather than rational numbers or integers as coordinates is not much influenced by the facts of experience but mainly due to considerations of mathematical simplicity. The restriction to rational coordinates would not be in conflict with any experimental knowledge we have, because the result of any measurement is a rational number. However, it would prevent the use of ordinary geometry (which says, e.g., that the diagonal of a square with the side I has the irrational value $\sqrt{2}$) and thus lead to great complications. On the other hand, the decision to use three rather than two or four spatial coordinates is strongly suggested, but still not forced upon us, by the result of common observations. If certain events allegedly observed in spiritualistic séances, e.g., a ball moving out of a sealed box, were confirmed beyond any reasonable doubt, it might seem advisable to use four spatial coordinates. Internal questions are here, in general, empirical questions to be answered by empirical investigations. On the other hand, the external questions of the reality of physical space and physical time are pseudo-questions. A question like "Are there (really) space-time points?" is ambiguous. It may be meant as an internal question; then the affirmative answer is, of course, analytic and trivial. Or it may be meant in the external sense: "Shall we introduce such and such forms into our language?"; in this case it is not a theoretical but a practical question, a matter of decision rather than assertion, and hence the proposed formulation would be misleading. Or finally, it may be meant in the following sense: "Are our experiences such that the use of the linguistic forms in question will be expedient and fruitful?" This is a theoretical question of a factual, empirical nature. But it concerns a matter of degree; therefore a formulation in the form "real or not?" would be inadequate.

3. WHAT DOES ACCEPTANCE OF A KIND OF ENTITIES MEAN?

Let us now summarize the essential characteristics of situations involving the introduction of a new kind of entities, characteristics which are common to the various examples outlined above.

The acceptance of a new kind of entities is represented in the language by the introduction of a framework of new forms of expressions to be used according to a new set of rules. There may be new names for particular entities of the kind in question; but some such names may already occur in the language before the introduction of the new framework. (Thus, for example, the thing language contains certainly words of the type of "blue" and "house" before the framework of properties is introduced; and it may contain words like "ten" in sentences of the form "I have ten fingers" before the framework of numbers is introduced.) The latter fact shows that the occurrence of constants of the type in question—regarded as names of entities of the new kind after the new framework is introduced—is not a sure sign of the acceptance of the new kind of entities. Therefore the introduction of such constants is not to be regarded as an essential step in the introduction of the framework. The two essential steps are rather the following. First, the introduction of a general term, a predicate of higher level, for the new kind of entities, permitting us to say of any particular entity that it belongs to this kind (e.g., "Red is a *property*", "Five is a *number*"). Second, the introduction of variables of the new type. The new entities are values of these variables; the constants (and the closed compound expressions, if any) are substitutable for the variables.[3] With the help of the variables, general sentences concerning the new entities can be formulated.

After the new forms are introduced into the language, it is possible to formulate with their help internal questions and possible answers to them. A question of this kind may be either empirical or logical; accordingly a true answer is either factually true or analytic.

From the internal questions we must clearly distinguish external questions, i.e., philosophical questions concerning the existence or reality of the total system of the new entities. Many philosophers regard a question of this kind as an ontological question which must be raised and answered *before* the introduction of the new language forms. The latter introduction, they believe, is legitimate only if it can be justified by an ontological insight supplying an affirmative answer to the question of reality. In contrast to this view, we take the position that the introduction of the new ways of speaking does not need any theoretical justification because it does not imply any assertion of reality. We may still speak (and have done so) of "the acceptance of the new entities" since this form of speech is customary; but one must keep in mind that this phrase does not mean for us anything more than acceptance of the new framework, i.e., of the new linguistic forms. Above all, it must not be interpreted as referring to an assumption, belief, or assertion of "the reality of the entities". There is no such assertion. An alleged statement of the reality of the system of entities is a pseudo-statement without cognitive content. To be sure, we have to face at this point an important question; but it is a practical, not a theoretical question; it is the question of whether or not to accept the new linguistic forms. The acceptance cannot be judged as being either true or false because it is not an assertion. It can only be judged as being more or less expedient, fruitful, conducive to the aim for which the language is intended. Judgments of this kind supply the motivation for the decision of accepting or rejecting the kind of entities.[4]

Thus it is clear that the acceptance of a linguistic framework must not be regarded as implying a metaphysical doctrine concerning the reality of the entities in question. It seems to me due to a neglect of this important distinction that some contemporary nominalists label the admission of variables of abstract types as "Platonism".[5] This is, to say the least, an extremely misleading terminology. It leads to the absurd consequence, that the position of everybody who accepts the language of physics with its real number variables (as a language of communication, not merely as a calculus) would be called Platonistic, even if he is a strict empiricist who rejects Platonic metaphysics.

A brief historical remark may here be inserted. The non-cognitive character of the questions which we have called here external questions was recognized and emphasized already by the Vienna Circle under the leadership of Moritz Schlick, the group from which the movement of logical empiricism originated. Influenced by ideas of Ludwig Wittgenstein, the Circle rejected both the thesis of the reality of the external world and the thesis of its irreality as pseudo-statements;[6] the same was the case for both the thesis of the reality of universals (abstract entities, in our present terminology) and the nominalistic thesis that they are not real and that their alleged names are not names of anything but merely *flatus vocis.* (It is obvious that the apparent negation of a pseudo-statement must also be a pseudo-statement. It is therefore not correct to classify the members of the Vienna Circle as nominalists, as is sometimes done. However, if we look at the basic anti-metaphysical and pro-scientific attitude of most nominalists (and the same holds for many materialists and realists in the modern sense), disregarding their occasional pseudo-theoretical formulations, then it is, of course, true to say that the Vienna Circle was much closer to those philosophers than to their opponents.

4. ABSTRACT ENTITIES IN SEMANTICS

The problem of the legitimacy and the status of abstract entities has recently again led to controversial discussions in connection with semantics. In a semantical meaning analysis certain expressions in a language are often said to designate (or name or denote or signify or refer to) certain extra-linguistic entities.[7] As long as physical things or events (e.g., Chicago or Caesar's death) are taken as designata (entities designated), no serious doubts arise. But strong objections have been raised, especially by some empiricists, against abstract entities as designata, e.g., against semantical statements of the following kind:

(1) "The word 'red' designates a property of things";
(2) "The word 'color' designates a property of properties of things";
(3) "The word 'five' designates a number";
(4) "The word 'odd' designates a property of numbers";
(5) "The sentence 'Chicago is large' designates a proposition".

Those who criticize these statements do not, of course, reject the use of the expressions in question, like "red" or "five"; nor would they deny that these expressions are meaningful. But to be meaningful, they would say, is not the same as having a meaning in the sense of an entity designated. They reject the belief, which they regard as implicitly presupposed by those semantical statements, that to each expression of the types in question (adjectives like "red", numerals like "five", etc.) there is a particular real entity to which the expression stands in the relation of designation. This belief is rejected as incompatible with the basic principles of empiricism or of scientific thinking. Derogatory labels like "Platonic realism", "hypostatization", or "Fido–Fido principle" are attached to it. The latter is the name given by Gilbert Ryle to the criticized belief, which, in his view, arises by a naïve inference of analogy: just as there is an entity well known to me, viz. my dog Fido, which is designated by the name "Fido", thus there must be for every meaningful expression a particular entity to which it stands in the relation of designation or naming, i.e., the relation exemplified by "Fido"–Fido. The belief criticized is thus a case of hypostatization, i.e., of treating as names expressions which are not names. While "Fido" is a name, expressions like "red", "five", etc., are said not to be names, not to designate anything.

Our previous discussion concerning the acceptance of frameworks enables us now to clarify the situation with respect to abstract entities as designata. Let us take as an example the statement:

(a) " 'Five' designates a number".

The formulation of this statement presupposes that our language L contains the forms of expressions which we have called the framework of numbers, in particular, numerical variables and the general term "number". If L contains these forms, the following is an analytical statement in L:

(b) "Five is a number".

Further, to make the statement (a) possible, L must contain an expression like "designates" or "is a name of" for the semantical relation of designation. If suitable rules for this term are laid down, the following is likewise analytic:

(c) " 'Five' designates five".

(Generally speaking, any expression of the form " '. . .' designates . . . " is an analytic statement provided the term ". . ." is a constant in an accepted framework. If the latter condition is not fulfilled, the expression is not a statement.) Since (a) follows from (c) and (b), (a) is likewise analytic.

Thus it is clear that *if* someone accepts the framework of numbers, then he must acknowledge (c) and (b) and hence (a) as true statements. Generally speaking, if someone accepts a framework for a certain kind of entities, then he is bound to admit the entities as possible designata. Thus the question of the admissibility of entities of a certain type or of abstract entities in general as designata is reduced to the question of the acceptability of the linguistic framework for those entities. Both the nominalistic critics, who refuse the status of designators or names to expressions like "red", "five", etc., because they deny the existence of abstract entities, and the skeptics, who express doubts concerning the existence and demand evidence for it, treat the question of existence as a theoretical question. They do, of course, not mean the internal question; the affirmative answer to *this* question is analytic and trivial and too obvious for doubt or denial, as we have seen. Their doubts refer rather to the system of entities itself; hence they mean the external question. They believe that only after making sure that there really is a system of entities of the kind in question are we justified in accepting the framework by incorporating the linguistic forms into our language. However, we have seen that the external question is not a theoretical question but rather the practical question whether or not to accept those linguistic forms. This acceptance is not in need of a theoretical justification (except with respect to expediency and fruitfulness), because it does not imply a belief or assertion. Ryle says that the "Fido"–Fido principle is "a grotesque theory". Grotesque or not, Ryle is wrong in calling it a theory. It is rather the practical decision to accept certain frameworks. Maybe Ryle is historically right with respect to those whom he mentions as previous representatives of the principle, viz. John Stuart Mill, Frege, and Russell. If these philosophers regarded the acceptance of a system of entities as a theory, an assertion, they were victims of the same old, metaphysical confusion. But it is certainly wrong to regard *my* semantical method as involving a belief in the reality of abstract entities, since I reject a thesis of this kind as a metaphysical pseudo-statement.

The critics of the use of abstract entities in semantics overlook the fundamental difference between the acceptance of a system of entities and an internal assertion, e.g., an assertion that there are elephants or electrons or prime numbers greater than a million. Whoever makes an internal assertion is certainly obliged to justify it by providing evidence, empirical evidence in the case of electrons, logical proof in the case of the prime numbers. The demand for a theoretical justification, correct in the case of internal assertions, is sometimes wrongly applied to the acceptance of a system of entities. Thus, for example, Ernest Nagel asks for "evidence relevant for affirming with warrant that there are such entities as infinitesimals or propositions". He characterizes the evidence required in these cases—in distinction to the empirical evidence in the case of electrons—as "in the broad sense logical and dialectical". Beyond this no hint is given as to what might be regarded as relevant evidence. Some nominalists regard the acceptance of abstract entities as a kind of superstition or myth, populating the world with fictitious or at least dubious entities, analogous to the belief in centaurs or demons. This shows again the confusion mentioned, because superstition or myth is a false (or dubious) internal statement.

Let us take as example the natural numbers as cardinal numbers, i.e., in contexts like "Here are three books". The linguistic forms of the framework of numbers, including variables and the general term "number", are generally used in our common language of communication; and it is easy to formulate explicit rules for their use. Thus the logical characteristics of this framework are sufficiently clear (while many internal questions, i.e., arithmetical questions, are, of course, still open). In spite of this, the controversy concerning the external question of the ontological reality of the system of numbers continues. Suppose that one philosopher says: "I believe that there are numbers as real entities. This gives me the right to use the linguistic forms of the numerical framework and to make semantical statements about numbers as designata of numerals". His nominalistic opponent replies: "You are wrong; there are no numbers. The numerals may still be used as meaningful expressions. But they are not names, there are no entities designated by them. Therefore the word "number" and numerical variables must not be used (unless a way were found to introduce them as merely abbreviating devices, a way of translating them into the nominalistic thing language)." I cannot think of any possible evidence that would be regarded as relevant by both philosophers, and therefore, if actually found, would decide the controversy or at least make one of the opposite theses more probable than the other. (To construe the numbers as classes or properties of the second level, according to the Frege-Russell method, does, of course, not solve the controversy, because the first philosopher would affirm and the second deny the existence of the system of classes or properties of the second level.) Therefore I feel compelled to regard the external question as a pseudo-question, until both parties to the controversy offer a common interpretation of the question as a cognitive question; this would involve an indication of possible evidence regarded as relevant by both sides.

There is a particular kind of misinterpretation of the acceptance of abstract entities in various fields of science and in semantics, that needs to be cleared up. Certain early British empiricists (e.g., Berkeley and Hume) denied the existence of abstract entities on the ground that immediate experience presents us only with particulars, not with universals, e.g., with this red patch, but not with Redness or Color-in-General; with this scalene triangle, but not with Scalene Triangularity or Triangularity-in-General. Only entities belonging to a type of which examples were to be found within immediate experience could be accepted as ultimate constituents of reality. Thus, according to this way of thinking, the existence of abstract entities could be asserted only if one could show either that some abstract entities fall within the given, or that abstract entities can be defined in terms of the types of entity which are given. Since these empiricists found no abstract entities within the realm of sense-data, they either denied their existence, or else made a futile attempt to define universals in terms of particulars. Some contemporary philosophers, especially English philosophers following Bertrand Russell, think in basically similar terms. They emphasize a distinction between the data (that which is immediately given in consciousness, e.g., sense-data, immediately past experiences, etc.) and the constructs based on the data. Existence or reality is ascribed only to the data; the constructs are not real entities; the corresponding linguistic expressions are merely ways of speech not actually designating anything (reminiscent of the nominalists' *flatus vocis*). We shall not criticize here this general conception. (As far as it is a principle of accepting certain entities and not accepting others, leaving aside any ontological, phenomenalistic and nominalistic pseudo-statements, there cannot be any theoretical objection to it.) But if this conception leads to the view that other philosophers or scientists who accept abstract entities thereby assert or imply their occurrence as immediate data, then such a view must be rejected as a misinterpretation. References to space-time points, the electromagnetic field, or electrons in physics, to real or complex numbers and their functions in mathematics, to the excitatory potential or unconscious complexes in psychology, to an inflationary trend in economics, and the like, do not imply the assertion that entities of these kinds occur as immediate data. And the same holds for references to abstract entities as designata in semantics. Some of the criticisms by English philosophers against such references give the impression that, probably due to the misinterpretation just indicated, they accuse the semanticist not so much of bad metaphysics (as some nominalists would do) but of bad psychology. The fact that they regard a semantical method involving abstract entities not merely as doubtful and perhaps wrong, but as manifestly absurd, preposterous and grotesque, and that they show a deep horror and indignation against this method, is perhaps to be explained by a misinterpretation of the kind described. In fact, of course, the semanticist does not in the least assert or imply that the abstract entities to which he refers can be experienced as immediately given either by sensation or by a kind of rational intuition. An assertion of this kind would indeed be very dubious psychology. The psychological question as to which kinds of entities do and which do not occur as immediate data is entirely irrelevant for semantics, just as it is for physics, mathematics, economics, etc., with respect to the examples mentioned above.[8]

5. CONCLUSION

For those who want to develop or use semantical methods, the decisive question is not the alleged ontological question of the existence of abstract entities but rather the question whether the use of abstract linguistic forms or, in technical terms, the use of variables beyond those for things (or phenomenal data), is expedient and fruitful for the purposes for which semantical analyses are made, viz. the analysis, interpretation, clarification, or construction of languages of communication, especially languages of science. This question is here neither decided nor even discussed. It is not a question simply of yes or no, but a matter of degree. Among those philosophers who have carried out semantical analyses and thought about suitable tools for this work, beginning with Plato and Aristotle and, in a more technical way on the basis of modern logic, with C. S. Peirce and Frege, a great majority accepted abstract entities. This does, of course, not prove the case. After all, semantics in the technical sense is still in the initial phases of its development, and we must be prepared for possible fundamental changes in methods. Let us therefore admit that the nominalistic critics may possibly be right. But if so, they will have to offer better arguments than they have so far. Appeal to ontological insight will not carry much weight. The critics will have to show that it is possible to construct a semantical method which avoids all references to abstract entities and achieves by simpler means essentially the same results as the other methods.

The acceptance or rejection of abstract linguistic forms, just as the acceptance or rejection of any other linguistic forms in any branch of science, will finally be decided by their efficiency as instruments, the ratio of the results achieved to the amount and complexity of the efforts required. To decree dogmatic prohibitions of certain linguistic forms instead of testing them by their success or failure in practical use, is worse than futile; it is positively harmful because it may obstruct scientific progress. The history of science shows examples of such prohibitions based on prejudices deriving from religious, mythological, metaphysical, or other irrational sources, which slowed up the developments for shorter or longer periods of time. Let us learn from the lessons of history. Let us grant to those who work in any special field of investigation the freedom to use any form of expression which seems useful to them; the work in the field will sooner or later lead to the elimination of those forms which have no useful function. *Let us be cautious in making assertions and critical in examining them, but tolerant in permitting linguistic forms.*

NOTES

1. The terms "sentence" and "statement" are here used synonymously for declarative (indicative, propositional) sentences.
2. In my book *Meaning and Necessity* (Chicago, 1947) I have developed a semantical method which takes propositions as entities designated by sentences (more specifically, as intensions of sentences). In order to facilitate the understanding of the systematic development, I added some informal, extra-systematic explanations concerning the nature of propositions. I said that the term "proposition" "is used neither for a linguistic expression nor for a subjective, mental occurrence, but rather for something objective that may or may not be exemplified in nature. . . . We apply the term 'proposition' to any entities of a certain logical type, namely, those that may be expressed by (declarative) sentences in a language" (p. 27). After some more detailed discussions concerning the relation between propositions and facts, and the nature of false propositions, I added: "It has been the purpose of the preceding remarks to facilitate the understanding of our conception of propositions. If, however, a reader should find these explanations more puzzling than clarifying, or even unacceptable, he may disregard them" (p. 31) (that is, disregard these extra-systematic explanations, not the whole theory of the propositions as intentions of sentences, as one reviewer understood). In spite of this warning, it seems that some of those readers who were puzzled by the explanations, did not disregard them but thought that by raising objections against them they could refute the theory. This is analogous to the procedure of some laymen who by (correctly) criticizing the ether picture or other visualizations of physical theories, thought they had refuted those theories. Perhaps the discussions in the present paper will help in clarifying the role of the system of linguistic rules for the introduction of a framework for entities on the one hand, and that of extra-systematic explanations concerning the nature of the entities on the other.
3. W. V. Quine was the first to recognize the importance of the introduction of variables as indicating the acceptance of entities. "The ontology to which one's use of language commits him comprises simply the objects that he treats as falling . . . within the range of values of his variables" ("Notes on Existence and Necessity", *Journal of Philosophy,* 40 (1943), p. 118; compare also his "Designation and Existence", *Journal of Philosophy,* 36 (1939), 702–9, and "On Universals", *Journal of Symbolic Logic,* 12 (1947), 74–84).
4. For a closely related point of view on these questions see the detailed discussions in Herbert Feigl, "Existential Hypotheses", *Philosophy of Science,* 17 (1950), 35–62.
5. Paul Bernays, "Sur le platonisme dans les mathématiques" (*L'Enseignement math.,* 34 (1935), 52–69). W. V. Quine, see previous note and a recent paper, "On What There Is", *Review of Metaphysics,* 2 (1948), 21–38. Quine does not acknowledge the distinction which I emphasize above, because according to his general conception there are no sharp boundary lines between logical and factual truth, between questions of meaning and questions of fact, between the acceptance of a language structure and the acceptance of an assertion formulated in the language. This conception, which seems to deviate considerably from

customary ways of thinking, will be explained in his article, "Semantics and Abstract Objects", *Proceedings of the American Academy of Arts and Sciences,* 80 (1951), 90–96. When Quine in the article, "On What There Is", classifies my logicistic conception of mathematics (derived from Frege and Russell) as "platonic realism" (p. 33), this is meant (according to a personal communication from him) not as ascribing to me agreement with Plato's metaphysical doctrine of universals, but merely as referring to the fact that I accept a language of mathematics containing variables of higher levels. With respect to the basic attitude to take in choosing a language form (an "ontology" in Quine's terminology, which seems to me misleading), there appears now to be agreement between us: "the obvious counsel is tolerance and an experimental spirit" ("On What There Is", p. 38).

6. See Carnap, *Scheinprobleme in der Philosophie; das Fremdpsychische und der Realismusstreit,* Berlin, 1928. Moritz Schlick, *Positivismus und Realismus,* reprinted in *Gesammelte Aufsätze,* Wien, 1938.
7. See *Introduction to Semantics,* Studies in Semantics, Vol. I (Cambridge, Mass., 1942); *Meaning and Necessity* (Chicago, 1947). The distinction I have drawn in the latter book between the method of the name-relation and the method of intension and extension is not essential for our present discussion. The term "designation" is used in the present article in a neutral way; it may be understood as referring to the name-relation or to the intension-relation or to the extension-relation or to any similar relations used in other semantical methods.
8. Wilfrid Sellars ("Acquaintance and Description Again", in *Journal of Philosophy,* 46 (1949), 496–504; see pp. 502 f.) analyzes clearly the roots of the mistake "of taking the designation relation of semantic theory to be a reconstruction of *being present to an experience*".

HOW I SEE PHILOSOPHY

Friedrich Waismann

1. WHAT philosophy is? I don't know, nor have I a set formula to offer. Immediately I sit down to contemplate the question I am flooded with so many ideas, tumbling over one another, that I cannot do justice to all of them. I can merely make an attempt, a very inadequate one, to sketch with a few strokes what the lie of the land seems to me to be, tracing some lines of thought without entering upon a close-knit argument.

It is, perhaps easier to say what philosophy is not than what it is. The first thing, then, I should like to say is that philosophy, as it is practiced today, is very unlike science; and this in three respects: in philosophy there are no proofs; there are no theorems; and there are no questions which can be decided, Yes or No. In saying that there are no proofs I do not mean to say that there are no arguments. Arguments certainly there are, and first-rate philosophers are recognized by the originality of their arguments; only these do not work in the sort of way they do in mathematics or in the sciences.

There are many things beyond proof: the existence of material objects, of other minds, indeed of the external world, the validity of induction, and so on. Gone are the days when philosophers were trying to prove all sorts of things: that the soul is immortal, that this is the best of all possible worlds and the rest, or to refute, by 'irrefutable' argument and with relish, materialism, positivism and what not. Proof, refutation—these are dying words in philosophy, though G. E. Moore still 'proved' to a puzzled world that it exists. What can one say to this—save, perhaps, that he is a great prover before the Lord?

But can it be *proved* that there are no proofs in philosophy? No; for one thing, such a proof, if it were possible, would by its very existence establish what it was meant to confute. But why suppose the philosopher to have an I.Q. so low as to be unable to learn from the past? Just as the constant failure of attempts at constructing a perpetual motion machine has in the end led to something positive in physics, so the efforts to construct a philosophical 'system', going on for centuries and going out of fashion fairly recently, tell their tale. This, I think, is part of the reason why philosophers today are getting weaned from casting their ideas into deductive moulds, in the grand style of Spinoza.

What I want to show in this article is that it is quite wrong to look at philosophy as though it had for its aim to provide theorems but had lamentably failed to do so. The whole conception changes when one comes to realize that what philosophers are concerned with is something different—neither

Reprinted by permission of Waismann's literary executors and the publisher, from F. Waismann, "How I See Philosophy," in Waismann, *How I See Philosophy,* ed. Rom Harré, pp. 1–38. London: Macmillan and Co. Ltd.; New York: St. Martin's Press, 1968.

discovering new propositions nor refuting false ones nor checking and rechecking them as scientists do. For one thing, proofs require premisses. Whenever such premisses have been set up in the past, even tentatively, the discussion at once challenged them and shifted to a deeper level. Where there are no proofs there are no theorems either. (To write down lists of propositions 'proved' by Plato or Kant: a pastime strongly to be recommended.) Yet the failure to establish a sort of Euclidean system of philosophy based on some suitable 'axioms' is, I submit, neither a mere accident nor a scandal but deeply founded in the nature of philosophy.

Yet there are questions; (and arguments). Indeed, a philosopher is a man who senses as it were hidden crevices in the build of our concepts where others only see the smooth path of commonplaceness before them.

Questions but no answers? Decidedly odd. The oddness may lessen when we take a look at them at closer range. Consider two famous examples: Achilles and the tortoise, and the astonishment of St Augustine when confronted with the fact of memory. He is amazed, not at some striking feat of memory, but at there being such a thing as memory at all. A sense-impression, say a smell or a taste, floats before us and disappears. One moment it is here and the next it is gone. But in the galleries of the memory pale copies of it are stored up after its death. From there I can drag them out when and as often as I wish, like, and yet strangely unlike, the original—unlike in that they are not perishable like the momentary impression: what was transitory has been arrested and has achieved duration. But who can say how this change comes about?

Here the very fact of memory feels mystifying in a way in which ordinary questions asking for information do not; and *of course* it is not a factual question. What is it?

From Plato to Schopenhauer philosophers are agreed that the source of their philosophizing is wonder. What gives rise to it is nothing recondite and rare but precisely those things which stare us in the face: memory, motion, general ideas. (Plato: What does 'horse' mean? A singular particular horse? No, for it may refer to *any* horse; *all* the horses, the total class? No, for we may speak of this or that horse. But if it means neither a single horse nor all horses, what *does* it mean?) The idealist is shaken in just the same way when he comes to reflect that he has, in Schopenhauer's words, 'no knowledge of the sun but only of an eye that sees a sun, and no knowledge of the earth but only of a hand that feels an earth'. Can it be, then, that nothing whatever is known to us except our own consciousness?

In looking at such questions, it seems as if the mind's eye were growing dim and as if everything, even that which ought to be absolutely clear, was becoming oddly puzzling and unlike its usual self. To bring out what seems to be peculiar to these questions one might say that they are not so much questions as tokens of a profound uneasiness of mind. Try for a moment to put yourself into the frame of mind of which Augustine was possessed when he asked: How is it possible to measure time? Time consists of past, present and future. The past can't be measured, it is gone; the future can't be measured, it is not yet here; and the present can't be measured, it has no extension. Augustine knew of course how time is measured and this was not his concern. What puzzled him was how it is *possible* to measure time, seeing that the past hour cannot be lifted out and placed alongside the present hour for comparison. Or look at it this way: what is measured is in the past, the measuring is in the present: how can that be?

The philosopher as he ponders over some such problem has the appearance of a man who is deeply disquieted. He seems to be straining to grasp something which is beyond his powers. The words in which such a question presents itself do not quite bring out into the open the real point—which may, perhaps more aptly, be described as the recoil from the incomprehensible. If, on a straight railway journey, you suddenly come in sight of the very station you have just left behind, there will be terror, accompanied perhaps by slight giddiness. That is exactly how the philosopher feels when he says to himself, 'Of course time can be measured; but how *can* it?' It is as though, up to now, he had been passing heedlessly over the difficulties, and now, all of a sudden, he notices them and asks himself in alarm, 'But how can that be?' That is a sort of question which we only ask when it is the very facts themselves which confound us, when something about them strikes us as preposterous.

Kant, I fancy, must have felt something of the sort when he suddenly found the existence of geometry a puzzle. Here we have propositions as clear and transparent as one would wish, prior, it seems, to all experience; at the same time they apply miraculously to the real world. How is that possible? Can the mind, unaided by experience, in some dark manner actually fathom the properties of real things? Looked upon in this way, geometry takes on a disturbing air.

We all have our moments when something quite ordinary suddenly strikes us as queer—for instance, when time appears to us as a curious thing. Not that we are often in this frame of mind; but on some occasions, when we look at things in a certain way, unexpectedly they seem to change as though by magic: they stare at us with a puzzling expression, and we begin to wonder whether they can possibly be the things we have known all our lives.

'Time flows' we say—a natural and innocent expression, and yet one pregnant with danger. It flows 'equably', in Newton's phrase, at an even rate. What can this mean? When something moves, it moves with a definite speed (and speed means: rate of change in time). To ask with what speed time moves, i.e. to ask how quickly time changes in time, is to ask the unaskable. It also flows, again in Newton's phrase, 'without relation to anything external'. How are we to figure that? Does time flow on irrespective of what happens in the world? Would it flow on even if everything in heaven and on earth came to a sudden standstill as Schopenhauer believed? For if this were not so, he said, time would have to stop with the stopping of the clock and move with the clock's movement. How odd: time flows at the same rate and yet without speed; and perhaps even without anything to occur in it. The expression is puzzling in another way. 'I can never catch myself being in the past or in the future', someone might say; 'whenever I think or perceive or breathe the word "now", I am in the present; therefore I am *always* in the present.' In saying this, he may think of the present moment as a bridge as it were from which he is looking down at the 'river of time'. Time is gliding along underneath the bridge, but the 'now' does not take part in the motion. What was future passes into the present (is just below the bridge) and then into the past, while the onlooker, the 'self' or the 'I', is always in the present. 'Time flows *through* the "now" ', he may feel to be a quite expressive metaphor. Yes, it sounds all right—until he suddenly comes to his senses and, with a start, realizes, 'But surely the moment flies?' (Query: How to succeed in wasting time? Answer: In this way, for instance—by trying, with eyes closed or staring vacantly in front of oneself, to catch the present moment as it is flitting by.) He may come now to look at matters in a different way. He sees himself advancing through time towards the future, and with this goes a suggestion of being active, just as at other times he may see himself floating down the stream whether he likes it or not. 'What exactly is it that is moving—the events in time or the present moment?', he may wonder. In the first case, it looks to him as if time were moving while he stands still; in the second case as if he were moving through time. 'How exactly is it?', he may say in a dubious voice, 'Am I always in the present? Is the present always eluding me?' Both ring true in a way; but they contradict each other. Again, does it make sense to ask, 'At what time is the present moment?' Yes, no doubt; but how *can* it, if the 'now' is but the fixed point from which the dating of any event ultimately receives its sense?

So he is pulled to and fro: 'I am always in the present, yet it slips through my fingers; I am going forward in time—no, I am carried down the stream.' He is using different pictures, each in its way quite appropriate to the occasion; yet when he tries to apply them jointly they clash. 'What a queer thing time must be', he may say to himself with a puzzled look on his face, 'what after all *is* time?'—expecting, half-expecting perhaps, that the answer will reveal to him time's hidden essence. Ranged beyond the intellectual are deeper levels of uneasiness—terror of the inevitability of time's passage, with all the reflections upon life that this forces upon us. Now all these anxious doubts release themselves in the question, 'What is time?' (*En passant* this is a hint that *one* answer will never do—will never remove all these doubts that break out afresh on different levels and yet are expressed in the same form of words.)

As we all know what time is, and yet cannot say what it is, it feels mystifying; and precisely because of its elusiveness it catches our imagination. The more we look at it the more we are puzzled: it seems charged with paradoxes. 'What is time? What is this being made up of movement only without anything that is moving?' (Schopenhauer.) How funny to have it bottled up! 'I've got here in my hand the most potent, the most enigmatic, the most fleeting of all essences—Time.' (Logan Pearsall Smith of an hour-glass.) For Shelley it is an 'unfathomable sea! whose waves are years', a 'shoreless flood', for Proust—well, why not leave something to the reader?

But isn't the answer to this that what mystifies us lies in the *noun* form 'the time'? Having a notion embodied in the form of a noun almost irresistibly makes us turn round to look for what it is 'the name of'. We are trying to catch the shadows cast by the opacities of speech. A wrong analogy absorbed into the forms of our language produces mental discomfort (and the feeling of discomfort, when it refers to language, is a profound one). 'All sounds, all colours . . . evoke indefinite and yet precise emotions, or, as I prefer to think, call down among us certain disembodied powers whose footsteps over our hearts we call emotions' (W. B. Yeats).

Yet the answer is a prosaic one: don't ask what time is but how the *word* 'time' is being used. Easier said than done; for if the philosopher rectifies the use of language, ordinary language has 'the advantage of being in possession of declensions', to speak with Lichtenberg, and thus renews its spell over him, luring him on into the shadow chase. It is perhaps only when we turn to languages of a widely different grammatical structure that the way towards such possibilities of interpretation is entirely barred. 'It is highly probable that philosophers within the domain of the Ural-Altaic languages (where the subject-concept is least developed) will look differently "into the world" and be found on paths of thought different from those of the Indo-Europeans or Mussulmans' (Nietzsche).

2. It may be well at this point to remind ourselves that the words 'question' and 'answer', 'problem' and 'solution' are not always used in their most trite sense. It is quite obvious that we often have to do something very different to find the way out of a difficulty. A problem of politics is solved by adopting a certain line of action, the problems of novelists perhaps by the invention of devices for presenting the inmost thoughts and feelings of their characters; there is the painter's problem of how to suggest depth or movement on the canvas, the stylistic problem of expressing things not yet current, not yet turned into cliché; there are a thousand questions of technology which are answered, not by the discovery of some truth, but by a practical achievement; and there is of course the 'social question'. In philosophy, the real problem is not to find the answer to a given question but to find a sense for it.

To see in what the 'solution' of such a 'problem' consists let us start with Achilles who, according to Zeno, is to this day chasing the tortoise. Suppose that Achilles runs twice as fast as the tortoise. If the tortoise's start is 1, Achilles will have to cover successively 1, $\frac{1}{2}$, $\frac{1}{4}$, $\frac{1}{8}$, . . . ; this series is endless: so he can never catch the tortoise. 'Nonsense!' (a mathematician's voice), 'the sum of the infinite series is finite, namely 2, and that settles it.' Though perfectly true, his remark is not to the point. It does not remove the sting from the puzzle, the disconcerting idea, namely, that however far we go in the series there is always a next term, that the lead the tortoise has in the race, though naturally getting smaller and smaller, yet never ceases to be: there *can* be no moment when it is strictly zero. It is *this* feature of the case, I suggest, that we do not understand and which throws us into a state of confusion.

But look at it this way. Suppose that we apply the same sort of argument to a minute, then we shall have to argue in some such way as this. Before the minute can be over the first half of it must elapse, then one-quarter of it, then one-eighth of it, and so on *ad infinitum*. This being an endless process, the minute can never come to an end. Immediately we have the argument in this form, the blunder leaps to the eye: we have been confusing two senses of 'never', a temporal and a non-temporal one. While it is quite correct to say that the sequence 1, $\frac{1}{2}$, $\frac{1}{4}$, $\frac{1}{8}$, . . . never ends, this sense of the word 'never' has nothing whatever to do with time. All it means is that there is no last term in the series, or (what comes to the same) that to any term, no matter how far out in the sequence, a successor can be constructed according to the simple rule 'halve it': that is what is meant here by 'never'; whereas in saying, for instance, that man will never find out anything to avert death, 'never' is meant in the sense 'at no time'. It is clear that the mathematical assertion concerning the possibility of going on in the sequence by forming new terms according to the rule does not state anything about actual occurrences in time. The mistake should really be obvious: in saying that, since the start is getting progressively smaller and yet can never cease to be, Achilles can never catch the tortoise, we jump from the mathematical, *non*-temporal to the temporal sense. Had there been two different words in our language to make these senses the confusion could never have arisen, and the world would be poorer for one of its most attractive paradoxes. But the same word is, as a matter of course, used with different meanings. Result: something like a conjuring trick. While our attention is diverted, while 'in our mind's eye', we stare fixedly at Achilles as he is speeding along, with each big bound diminishing his distance from the tortoise, the one sense is so innocuously palmed off for the other as to escape notice.

This way of bringing out the fallacy also holds when the other key term is used for presenting the puzzle. As there will 'always' be a next term in the sequence, i.e. a next step in the scheme of subdividing the race-course (the word 'always' looking just as spotless and innocent) we readily fall into the trap of concluding that the tortoise will 'always' be ahead of Achilles, eternally to be chased by his pursuer.

Many are the types of bewilderment: there is the obsessional doubt—can I ever know that other people have experiences, that they see, hear and feel as I do? Can I be sure that memory does not always deceive me? Are there really material objects and not only sense-impressions 'of' them? There is the doubt-like uneasiness—what sort of being is possessed by numbers? There is the anxiety doubt—are we really free? This doubt has taken many different forms, one of which I shall single out for discussion—the question, namely, whether the law of excluded middle, when it refers to statements in the future tense, forces us into a sort of logical Predestination. A typical argument is this. If it is true now that I shall do a certain thing tomorrow, say, jump into the Thames, then no matter how fiercely I resist, strike out with hands and feet like a madman, when the day comes I cannot help jumping into the water; whereas, if this prediction is false now, then whatever efforts I may make, however many times I may nerve and brace myself, look down at the water and say to myself, 'One, two, three—', it is impossible for me to spring. Yet that the prediction is either true or false is itself a necessary truth, asserted by the law of excluded middle. From this the startling consequence seems to follow that it is already now decided what I shall do tomorrow, that indeed the entire future is somehow fixed, logically preordained. Whatever I do and whichever way I decide, I am merely moving along lines clearly marked in advance which lead me towards my appointed lot. We are all, in fact, marionettes. If we are not prepared to swallow *that,* then—and there is a glimmer of hope in the 'then'—there is an alternative open to us. We need only renounce the law of excluded middle for statements of this kind, and with it the validity of ordinary logic, and all will be well. Descriptions of what will happen are, at present, neither true nor false. (This sort of argument was actually propounded by Lukasiewicz in favour of a three-valued logic with 'possible' as a third truth-value alongside 'true' and 'false'.[1])

The way out is clear enough. The asker of the question has fallen into the error of so many philosophers: of giving an answer before stopping to consider the question. For is he clear what he is asking? He seems to suppose that a statement referring to an event in the future is at present undecided, neither true nor false, but that when the event happens the proposition enters into a sort of new state, that of being true. But how are we to figure the change from 'undecided' to 'true'? Is it sudden or gradual? At what moment does the statement 'it will rain tomorrow' begin to be true? When the first drop falls to the ground? And supposing that it will not rain, when will the statement begin to be false? Just at the end of the day, at 12 P.M. sharp? Supposing that the event *has* happened, that the statement *is* true, will it remain so for ever? If so, in what way? Does it remain uninterruptedly true, at every moment of day and night? Even if there were no one about to give it any thought? Or is it true only at the moments when it is being thought of? In that case, how long does it remain true? For the duration of the thought? We wouldn't know how to answer these questions; this is due not to any particular ignorance or stupidity on our part but to the fact that something has gone wrong with the way the words 'true' and 'false' are applied here.

If I say, 'It is true that I was in America', I am saying that I was in America and no more. That in uttering the words 'It is true that—' I take responsibility upon myself is a different matter that does not concern the present argument. The point is that in making a statement prefaced by the words 'It is true that' I do not *add* anything to the factual information I give you. *Saying* that something is true is not *making* it true: cf. the criminal lying in court, yet every time he is telling a lie protesting, his hand on his heart, that he is telling the truth.

What is characteristic of the use of the words 'true' and 'false' and what the pleader of logical determinism has failed to notice is this. 'It is true' and 'it is false', while they certainly have the force of asserting and denying, are not descriptive. Suppose that someone says, 'It is true that the sun will rise tomorrow' all it means is that the sun will rise tomorrow: he is not regaling us with an extra-description of the trueness of what he says. But supposing that he were to say instead, 'It is true *now* that the sun will rise tomorrow', this would boil down to something like 'The sun will rise tomorrow now'; which is nonsense. To ask, as the puzzle-poser does, 'Is it true or false *now* that such-and-such will happen in the future?' is not the sort of question to which an answer can be given: which *is* the answer.

This sheds light on what has, rather solemnly, been termed the 'timelessness of truth'. It lies in this: that the clause 'it is true that—' does not allow of inserting a date. To say of a proposition like 'Diamond is pure carbon' that it is true on Christmas Eve would be just as poor a joke as to say that it is true in Paris and not in Timbuctoo. (This does not mean that we cannot say in certain circumstances, 'Yes, it was true in those days' as this can clearly be paraphrased without using the word 'true'.)

Now it begins to look a bit less paradoxical to say that when a philosopher wants to dispose of a question the one thing he must not do is: to give an answer. A philosophic question is not solved: it *dis*solves. And in what does the 'dissolving' consist? In making the meaning of the words used in putting the question so clear to ourselves that we are released from the spell it casts on us. Confusion was removed by calling to mind the use of language or, so far as the use *can* be distilled into rules, the rules: it therefore *was* a confusion about the use of language, or a confusion about rules. It is here that philosophy and grammar meet.

There is one further point that needs elucidation. When we say of a given assertion, e.g. 'It is raining', that it is true we can hardly escape the impression that we say something 'about' the assertion, namely, that it has the property of trueness. To make such a statement seems, then, to say *more* than what was asserted originally, namely, that it is raining and that this assertion is true. That, however, leads to queer consequences. For in which sense does it say more? Consider first under which circumstances it would be appropriate to say of two given propositions that the one says 'more' than the other. 'This is red' says more than 'this is coloured' for the obvious reason that anyone can conclude from the first statement to the second but no one reversely; similarly 'today is Tuesday' says more than 'today is a weekday'. The criterion, then, suggests itself that, given two propositions p and q, p says more than q, if $\sim p \cdot q$ is meaningful and $p \cdot \sim q$ contradictory. The holder of the view that 'p is true' says more than p (p standing e.g. for 'It is raining'), may now be challenged to explain what he means by that. Is he using the word 'more' in the sense just explained? If so, the curious consequence ensues that it must *make sense* to assert the conjunction $\sim p \cdot p$, that is, in our case, 'It is not true that it is raining and it is raining'. Since this obviously is not what he had in mind, what *does* he mean? We are not contradicting him; we merely remind him of how these words have always been used by him, in non-philosophical contexts that is, and then point out that, if he still wants to use them in this sense, to say what he wanted to say lands him in an absurdity. All we do is to make him aware of his own practice. We abstain from any assertion. It is for him to explain what he means. Not that he cannot do it. In ascribing truth to a given statement, he might say, he wants to express perhaps either (i) that it is 'in accordance with fact' or something of the sort; or (ii) that he *knows* that it is true. In the first case he is faced with the same dilemma, namely, that it must make sense to say, 'It is not in accordance with the facts that it is raining and it is raining'; in the second fresh difficulties are breaking out. For one thing, the words 'it is true that—', when uttered by different people, would then mean different things; for another, and this is more fatal to the advocate of fatalism, in construing the words in this sense, he cuts the ground from under his own feet. No one would then be worried by the question whether, supposing that it is false now that he will write a certain letter tomorrow, it follows that it will really be impossible for him to write that letter, that this line of conduct is barred to him, logically barred. For since 'it is false now' means in the new sense 'he doesn't know yet' nothing follows and the whole question evaporates.

My reason for going into this tangle at some length is that the method applied in unravelling it presents some interesting features. First, we don't *force* our interlocutor. We leave him free to choose, accept or reject any way of using his words. He may depart from ordinary usage—language is not untouchable—if it is only in this way that he can explain himself. He may even use an expression one time in this, another time in that, way. The only thing we insist upon is that he should be aware of what he is doing. If we strictly adhere to this method—going over the argument, asking him at each step whether he is willing to use an expression in a certain way, if not, offering him alternatives, but leaving the decisions to him and only pointing out what their consequences are—no dispute can arise. Disputes arise only if certain steps in this procedure are omitted so that it looks as if we had made an assertion, adding to the world's woes a new apple of discord. This would be the true way of doing philosophy undogmatically. The difficulty of this method lies in presenting the subject in a manner which can easily be taken in—in arranging the cases and the ways in which they are connected through intermediate links so that we can gain a clear synoptic view of the whole.

Second, we do not use arguments in order to prove or disprove any 'philosophic view'. As we have no views we can afford to look at things as they are.

Next, we only describe; we do not 'explain'. An explanation, in the sense of a deductive proof, cannot satisfy us because it pushes the question 'Why just these rules and no other ones?' only one stage back. In following that method, we do not *want* to give reasons. All we do is to describe a use or tabulate rules. In doing this, we are not making any discoveries: there is nothing to be discovered in grammar. Grammar is autonomous and not dictated by reality. Giving reasons, bound as it is to come to an end and leading to something which cannot further be explained, *ought* not to satisfy us. In grammar we never ask the question 'why?'

But isn't the result of this that philosophy itself 'dissolves'? Philosophy eliminates those questions which *can* be eliminated by such a treatment. Not all of them, though: the metaphysician's craving that a ray of light may fall on the mystery of the existence of this world, or on the incomprehensible fact that it is comprehensible, or on the 'meaning of life'—even if such questions *could* be shown to lack a clear meaning or to be devoid of meaning altogether, they are *not silenced.* It does nothing to lessen the dismay they arouse in us. There is something cheap in 'debunking' them. The heart's unrest is not to be stilled by logic. Yet philosophy is not dissolved. It derives its weight, its grandeur, from the significance of the questions it destroys. It overthrows idols, and it is the importance of these idols which gives philosophy its importance.

Now it can perhaps be seen why the search for answers fitting the moulds of the questions fails, is *bound* to fail. They are not real questions asking for information but 'muddles felt as problems' (Wittgenstein) which wither away when the ground is cleared. If philosophy advances, it is not by adding new propositions to its list, but rather by transforming the whole intellectual scene and, as a consequence of this, by reducing the number of questions which befog and bedevil us. Philosophy so construed is one of the great liberating forces. Its task is, in the words of Frege, 'to free the spirit from the tyranny of words by exposing the delusions which arise, almost inevitably, through the use of a word language'.

3. What, only criticism and no meat? The philosopher a fog dispeller? If that were all he was capable of I would be sorry for him and leave him to his devices. Fortunately, this is not so. For one thing, a philosophic question, if pursued far enough, may lead to something positive—for instance, to a more profound understanding of language. Take the sceptical doubts as to material objects, other minds, etc. The first reaction is perhaps to say: these doubts are idle. Ordinarily, when I doubt whether I shall finish this article, after a time my doubt comes to an end. I cannot go on doubting for ever. It's the destiny of doubt to die. But the doubts raised by the sceptic never die. Are they doubts? Are they pseudo-questions? They appear so only when judged by the twin standards of common sense and common speech. The real trouble lies deeper: it arises from the sceptic casting doubt on the very facts which underlie the use of language, those permanent features of experience which make concept formation possible, which in fact are precipitated in the use of our most common words. Suppose that you see an object in front of you quite clearly, say, a pipe, and when you are going to pick it up it melts into thin air, then you may feel, 'Lord, I'm going mad' or something of the sort (unless the whole situation is such that you have reason to suspect that it was some clever trick). But what, the sceptic may press now, if such experiences were quite frequent? Would you be prepared to *dis*solve the connection between different sense experiences which form the hard core of our idea of a solid object, to *un*do what language has done—to part with the category of thing-hood? And would you then be living in a phenomenalist's paradise with colour patches and the other paraphernalia of the sense-datum theory, in a disobjected, desubstantialized world? To say in such circumstances, 'Look, it's just tabling now' would be a joke (for even in the weakened verb forms 'tabling', 'chairing' an element of the thing-category lingers on). That is why the sceptic struggles to express himself in a language which is not fit for this purpose. He expresses himself misleadingly when he says that he doubts such-and-such *facts*: his doubts cut so deep that

they affect the fabric of language itself. For what he doubts is already embodied in the very forms of speech, e.g. in what is condensed in the use of thing-words. The moment he tries to penetrate those deep-sunken layers, he undermines the language in which he ventilates his qualms—with the result that he seems to be talking nonsense. He is not. But in order to make his doubts fully expressible, language would first have to go into the melting-pot. (We can get a glimmering of what is needed from modern science where all the long-established categories—thinghood, causality, position—had to be revolutionized. This required nothing less than the construction of some new language, not the expression of new facts with the old one.)

If we look at the matter in this way the attitude of the sceptic is seen in a new light. He considers possibilities which lie far outside the domain of our current experience. If his doubts are taken seriously, they turn into observations which cast a new and searching light on the subsoil of language, showing what possibilities are open to our thought (though not to ordinary language), and what paths might have been pursued if the texture of our experience were different from what it is. These problems are not spurious: they make us aware of the vast background in which any current experiences are embedded, and to which language has adapted itself; thus they bring out the unmeasured sum of experience stored up in the use of our words and syntactical forms.

For another thing, a question may decide to go in for another career than dissolving: it may pass into science. Frege, for instance, was prompted to his inquiries by philosophical motives, namely, to find a definite answer to the question about the nature of arithmetical truths—whether they are analytic or synthetic, *a priori* or *a posteriori.* Starting from this question and pursuing it with all possible rigour, he was led to unearth a whole mine of problems of scientific nature; and proceeding along these lines, he came to fashion a new instrument, a logic, which in delicacy and range and power far surpassed anything that went by this name before, a subject revealing to this day new and unexpected depths. True, the question from which Frege set out was not too clearly defined owing to the imprecise nature of the Kantian terms in which it was expressed.

A whole chapter might be written on the fate of questions, their curious adventures and transformations—how they change into others and in the process remain, and yet do not remain, the same. The original question may split and multiply almost like a character in a dream play. To mention just a few examples: can logic be characterized completely in a formal way, i.e. without bringing in any extraneous ideas such as the use of language and all that goes with it? Can arithmetic be characterized in any such way, entirely 'from within'? Or will any interpretation include some *Erdenrest* of the empiric? These questions have given rise to extensive research on mathematical interpretation of formal systems. The query how far logical intuition is correct has ramified into a bunch of questions pertaining to the theory of logical types, the axiom of choice, etc., indeed to a far more fundamental issue, namely, whether ordinary logic itself is 'right' as contrasted with the system of inferences evolved by the intuitionists. Or again, are there undecidable questions in mathematics, not in the restricted sense of Gödel, but undecidable in an absolute sense? Are there natural limits to generalization? It is interesting to watch how from a question of this sort, not too precise, somewhat blurred, new and better defined questions detach themselves, the parent question—in Frege's case philosophic *par excellence*—giving rise to a scientist's progeny.

Now something else must be noted—how these questions become, not only precise, but clear (which is not the same thing). To illustrate, can the infinity represented by all natural numbers be compared with the infinity represented by all points in space? That is, can the one be said to be less than, or equal to, the other? When it was first asked, the question had no clear sense—perhaps no sense at all. Yet it guided G. Cantor in his ingenious search. Before set theory was discovered—or should I rather say 'invented'?—the question acted as a sort of signpost pointing vaguely to some so far uncharted region of thought. It is perhaps best characterized by saying that it guides our imagination in a given direction, stimulates research along new lines. Such questions do not 'dissolve': they are solved, only not in the existing system of thought but rather by constructing a new conceptual system—such as set theory—where the intended and faintly anticipated sense finds its full realization. They are therefore of the nature of incitements to the building of such systems, they point from the not-yet-meaningful to the meaningful.

The question is the first groping step of the mind in its journeyings that lead towards new horizons. The genius of the philosopher shows itself nowhere more strikingly than in the new kind of question he brings into the world. What distinguishes him and gives him his place is the passion of questioning. That his questions are at times not so clear is perhaps of not so much moment as one makes of it. There is nothing like clear thinking to protect one from making discoveries. It is all very well to talk of clarity, but when it becomes an obsession it is liable to nip the living thought in the bud. This, I am afraid, is one of the deplorable results of Logical Positivism, not foreseen by its founders, but only too striking in some of its followers. Look at these people, gripped by a clarity neurosis, haunted by fear, tongue-tied, asking themselves continually, 'Oh dear, now does this make perfectly good sense?' Imagine the pioneers of science, Kepler, Newton, the discoverers of non-Euclidean geometry, of field physics, the unconscious, matter waves or heaven knows what, imagine them asking themselves this question at every step—this would have been the surest means of sapping any creative power. No great discoverer has acted in accordance with the motto, 'Everything that can be said can be said clearly'. And some of the greatest discoveries have even emerged from a sort of primordial fog. (Something to be said for the fog. For my part, I've always suspected that clarity is the last refuge of those who have nothing to say.)

The great mind is the great questioner. An example in point is Kant's problem 'How is geometry possible?' The way to its solution was only opened up through the rise of the 'axiomatic method'. Seeing that the axioms of geometry are capable of an indefinite number of different interpretations and that the particular way they may be interpreted is irrelevant to deductive purposes,

Hilbert separated what belongs to the logical form of the axioms from what belongs to their intuitional (or other) content and turned the whole question by saying: a point, a straight line, etc., may be anything that satisfies the axioms. As the business of deduction hinges only on the relations in which the basic terms stand to each other and not on the 'content' we associate with them, and as these relations are fully set out in the axioms, the axioms in their totality determine what a 'point', a 'line', etc., is so far as it is sufficient for deductive needs. Through the rise of this technique it became apparent that the word 'geometry', as understood by Kant, covers, in fact, two totally different sciences, mathematical and physical geometry. It was the failure to distinguish between them that produced Kant's perplexity. 'So far as the laws of mathematics refer to reality, they are not certain; and so far as they are certain, they do not refer to reality' (Einstein). Kant's credit lies in having *seen* that there is a problem, not in having solved it.

But here a new problem presents itself: How do we know what will satisfy a given question? More generally: How does the answer fit the question? Questions of the current sort ('What is the right time?') show already by their form what sort of answer to expect. They are, so to speak, cheques with a blank to be filled; yet not always so: Augustine's question, 'How is it possible to measure time?' or Kant's question, 'How is geometry possible?' do not trace out the form of the answer. There is no *obvious* link between question and answer, any more than there is in the case of asking 'What is a point?' When Hilbert's idea—that the axioms of geometry jointly provide the 'implicit definition' of the basic terms—was first propounded it came totally unexpected; no one had ever thought of that before; on the contrary, many people had an uneasy feeling, as if this were a way of evading the issue rather than an answer, amongst them no less a man than Frege. He thought the problem still unsolved.

Now is there anything one can do to make a man like Frege see that the axiomatic method provides the correct answer? Can it, for example, be *proved* to him? The point to which attention must now be drawn, though it should really be obvious, is that such a proof cannot be given, and it cannot because he, the asker, has first to be turned round to see the matter differently. What is required is a change of the entire way of thinking. Indeed, anyone who is puzzled by this problem and yet refuses to accept Hilbert's solution only betrays that he has got stuck in the groove hollowed out by the form in which the question is put. 'A point is—' he begins and then stops. What is to be done to help him to get out of the groove or, better still, to make him shift for himself when he feels 'cramped' in it, is a *discussion,* not a proof.

Frege behaves not so very unlike a man mystified by the question, 'What is time?' We may suggest converting the latter into the question how the word 'time' is being used (which would bring him down to earth). But aren't we cheating him? We seem to be holding out the answer to *one* question, but not to that one which he was asking. He may suspect that we are trying to fob him off with the second best we have in store, his original question still remaining an enigma. Similarly Frege: he considered it a scandal that the questions 'What is a point?', 'What is a number?' were still unanswered.

In either of these cases, the aim of a discussion, in the absence of a proof, can only be to change the asker's attitude. We may, for instance, scrutinize similar, or partially similar, cases, point out that the form of the answer is not always that of the question; by going patiently over such cases, the vast background of analogies against which the question is seen will slowly change. The turning up of a wide field of language loosens the position of certain standards which are so ingrained that we do not see them for what they are; and if we do this in an effective manner, a mind like Frege's will be released from the obsession of seeking strainingly for an answer to fit the mould. Arguments are used in such a discussion, though not as proofs but rather as means to make him see things he had not noticed before: e.g. to dispel wrong analogies, to stress similarities with other cases and in this way to bring about something like a shift of perspective. However, there is no way of proving him wrong or bullying him into mental acceptance of the proposal: when all is said and done the decision is his.

But here more is at stake than loosening a cramped position—it is a question of escaping the domination of linguistic forms. How often are we merely following the channels carved out by numberless repetition of the same modes of expression—as when we say, unsuspectingly, 'Time flows' and are, when confronted (say) with Augustine's paradox, suddenly shocked out of complacency. Existing language, by offering us only certain stereotyped moulds of expression, creates habits of thought which it is almost impossible to break. Such a mould is, e.g. the actor-action scheme of the Indo-European languages. How deep their influence is can perhaps be surmised from Descartes' conclusion from thinking to the presence of an agent, an ego, different from the thinking, that does the thinking—a conclusion so natural and convincing to us because it is supported by the whole weight of language. Frege's obsession with the question 'What is a number?' is another case. As we can speak of '*the* number five', five, Frege argued, must be the proper name of an entity, a sort of Platonic crystal, indicated by means of the definite article. (A Chinese pupil of mine once informed me that Frege's question is unaskable in Chinese, 'five' being used there only as a numeral in contexts like 'five friends', 'five boats', etc.) Again, when we say of a given statement that it is true, we seem to be saying something 'about' it—evidence of the power of the subject-predicate cliché. Indeed, so strong is the temptation to construe it in this way, namely, as a statement about a statement, that the idea of a different interpretation scarcely occurs to us. It is important to notice that in doing so we assimilate the expression into analogical forms; but it is no less important to notice that none of these analogies needs to be present to our minds: it is enough if they make themselves felt in a dim, inarticulated way. Such patterns have an effect on us like thousands of explicit analogies: they act upon us, one might say, like a field of force, a language field, that draws our mental gaze in a certain direction.

And, I venture to add, it is precisely because of the fleeting, half-formed, shadow-like nature of these analogies that it is almost impossible to escape their influence. If we are taken in by them, it is our fault. A philosopher, instead of preaching the righteousness of ordinary speech, should learn to be on his guard against the pitfalls ever present in its forms. To use a picture: just as a good swimmer must be able to swim up-stream, so the philosopher should master the unspeakably difficult art of thinking up-speech, against the current of clichés.

Now for another point. When we dissuade a man like Frege from his search, we seem to be hindering him from reaching the aim he set out to reach. Does our discussion clash, then, with his search? And, if so, in which way? First of all, in no clearly definable way; for he is not yet clearly aware what he is aiming at, and the discussion brings him gradually to see things in a different light. How is this change brought about? Well, he first saw the question in analogy with other ones, and these analogies are, one by one, destroyed; or rather, in the course of the discussion they are seen to be misleading. In proportion as the whole conceptual background changes, he comes to see that something is wrong with the way he put his question, that the attainment of his object is no longer satisfying. It is not that he gives up because he has tried very hard, but in vain, and has now got tired: no, he gives up because he 'sees' the question differently. And in what does *this* consist? Well, in the fact that he is now well aware of the analogies which were misleading him, that he sees the question against a different linguistic background (a 'figure' sometimes changes when it is seen against a different 'ground'), that a certain strain disappears and that he says, with a sigh of relief, 'Yes, that's it'.

The philosopher contemplates things through the prism of language and, misled (say) by some analogy, suddenly sees things in a new strange light. We can cope with these problems only by digging down to the soil from which they spring. What we do is to light up the mental background from which the question has detached itself; in a clearer perception of some of the crucial concepts the question transforms itself into another one. Not that it has been answered in the current sense. Rather we have removed the factors that prompted the question by a more profound and penetrating analysis. The essence of this process is that it leads the questioner on to some new aspect—and leads him with his spontaneous consent. He agrees to be thus led and therefore ends by abandoning his search. We cannot constrain anyone who is unwilling to follow the new direction of a question; we can only extend the field of vision of the asker, loosen his prejudices, guide his gaze in a new direction: but all this can be achieved only with his consent.

By our critical analysis we try to counteract the influence of the language field, or (what comes to the same) we may help the questioner to gain a deeper insight into the nature of what he is seeking first of all—make him see the build of the concepts and the moulds in which he expresses the question. What matters is more like changing his outlook than proving to him some theorem; or more like increasing his insight. Insight cannot be lodged in a theorem, and this is the deeper reason why the deductive method is doomed to fail: insight cannot be demonstrated by proof.

What it comes to in the end is that the asker of the question, in the course of the discussion, has to make a number of *decisions.* And this makes the philosophical procedure so unlike a logical one. He compares, for instance, the case before him with analogous ones and has to *judge* how far these analogies hold. That is, it is for him to decide how far he is willing to accept these analogies: he has not, like a slave, to follow blindly in their track.

Science is rich in questions of this type. They are not scientific questions properly and yet they exercise scientists, they are philosophic questions and yet they do not exercise philosophers.

What I have wanted to say in this section and have not said, or only half-said:

(1) Philosophy is not only criticism of language: so construed, its aim is too narrow. It is criticizing, dissolving and stepping over *all* prejudices, loosening all rigid and constricting moulds of thought, no matter whether they have their origin in language or somewhere else.
(2) What is essential in philosophy is the breaking through to a *deeper insight*—which is something positive—not merely the dissipation of fog and the exposure of spurious problems.
(3) Insight cannot be lodged in a theorem, and it can therefore not be demonstrated.
(4) Philosophic arguments are, none of them, logically *compelling*: they really screen what actually happens—the quiet and patient undermining of categories over the whole field of thought.
(5) Their purpose is to open our eyes, to bring us to see things in a new way—from a wider standpoint unobstructed by misunderstandings.
(6) The essential difference between philosophy and logic is that logic *constrains* us while philosophy leaves us free: in a philosophic discussion we are led, step by step, to change our angle of vision, e.g. to pass from one way of putting a question to another, and this with our spontaneous agreement—a thing profoundly different from deducing theorems from a given set of premisses. Misquoting Cantor one might say: the essence of philosophy lies in its freedom.

4. There is a notion that philosophy is an exercise of the intellect and that philosophic questions can be settled by argument, and conclusively if one only knew how to set about it. What seems to me queer, however, is that I cannot find any really good hard argument; and more than that, the example just discussed must make it doubtful whether any compelling argument *can* be found. Out of this plight I incline to come to a new and somewhat shocking conclusion: that the thing cannot be done. No philosopher has ever proved anything. The whole claim is spurious. What I have to say is simply this. Philosophic arguments are not deductive; therefore they are not rigorous; and therefore they don't prove anything. Yet they have force.

Before going into the matter, I want to show, quite summarily first, how implausible the view is that rigorous arguments are applied in philosophy. A first alarming sign can perhaps already be seen in the notorious fact that the ablest minds disagree, that what is indisputable to the one seems to have no force in the eyes of the other. In a clear system of thought such differences are impossible. That they exist in philosophy is weighty evidence that the arguments have none of the logical rigour they have in mathematics and the exact sciences.

Next, arguments, in the way they are thought of, must contain inferences, and inferences must start somewhere. Now where is the philosopher to look for his premisses? To science? Then he will 'do' science, not philosophy. To statements of everyday life? To particular ones? Then he will never be able to advance a single step beyond them. To general statements? If so, a number of questions raise their ugly heads. By what right does he pass from 'some' to 'all'? ('To Generalize is to be an Idiot', W. Blake.) Can he be sure that his premisses are stated with such clarity and precision that not a ghost of a doubt can creep in? Can he be sure that they contain meat, are not analytic, vacuous, definitions in disguise and the like? Can he be sure that they are true? (How *can* he?) And even supposing, what is not the case, that all these requirements could be met, there is still another task looming before him when it comes to developing the consequences: can he be sure how to operate with the terms? (How *can* he?) I am not letting out a secret when I say that the ordinary rules of logic often break down in natural speech—a fact usually hushed up by logic books. Indeed, the words of common language are so elastic that anyone can stretch their sense to fit his own whims; and with this their 'logic' is queered. (Plenty of scope for a 'natural logic': 'we know that we are *unhappy;* so we *are* unhappy. We *know* that we are unhappy; so we are *great.'* (Pascal.) 'If she had perished, she had perished': does this entail that she has not perished? If so, by what rule? 'If I believed that I should be very silly indeed': does this, or does this not, entail that I don't believe it? Natural language holds logical problems of its own, lots of them.)

This brings me to another point. Ordinary language simply has not got the 'hardness', the logical hardness, to cut axioms in it. It needs something like a metallic substance to carve a deductive system out of it such as Euclid's. But common speech? If you begin to draw inferences it soon begins to go 'soft' and fluffs up somewhere. You may just as well carve cameos on a cheese *soufflé.* (My point is: language is plastic, yielding to the will to express, even at the price of some obscurity. Indeed, how could it ever express anything that does not conform to the cliché? If logicians had their way, language would become as clear and transparent as glass, but also as brittle as glass: and what would be the good of making an axe of glass that breaks the moment you use it?) But language is not hard. And that is why it is dangerous in philosophy to hunt for premisses instead of just going over the ground, standing back and saying: look.

Most philosophic arguments, to ignore constructions *à la* Spinoza, hinge on such points as what 'can' and what 'cannot' be said or what sort of question it is 'proper' and what sort of question it would be 'inappropriate' to ask. Much skill and ingenuity has been spent in elucidating such questions as to whether a certain metaphor is 'natural', a certain diction 'fitting'. It would not be right to burke the point that considerations such as these, while apparently pertaining to matters of style, contribute in fact largely to the forcefulness of an argument, indeed play a very real and decisive part in the way they make us look at the subject. In going over, examining and comparing the various modes of expression that centre around certain key notions, for instance, 'imagination', 'memory', 'pleasure', we catch the first glimpse of what is sometimes called the 'logic' of these notions. Now can any of these things be proved? Can it be proved, for example, that a certain diction is 'fitting'? (Remember, no such thing as a definition of a 'well-formed formula'.) No philosopher has ever made so much as an attempt. Everyone uses words in this way and he leaves it at that; and rightly so. For what sort of reasons *could* he give anyway? Here already, at the very threshold, the idea of a philosophic proof begins to ring hollow.

'Ah, but the ordinary use of language.' All right; but even so, it is not that one 'cannot' use language differently. To illustrate: 'frozen music'—does this 'tell' you anything? Perhaps not; yet a saying like 'Architecture is frozen music' (Goethe) drives the point home. To say 'The arms are full of blunted memories' sounds odd, until you come upon it in Proust's contexts. The 'will to understand' does not even flinch before those bogies of the logician, contradictions: it transforms them, wresting a new sense from the apparent nonsense. ('Dark with excess of light', 'the luminous gloom of Plato'—just to remind the reader of two examples of Coleridge.) There are about 303 reasons why we sometimes express ourselves in a contradiction, and understandably so.

Result: it cannot even be proved that a given expression is natural, a metaphor fitting, a question proper (or unaskable), a collocation of words expressive (or devoid of meaning). Nothing of the sort can be demonstrated.

Two other points reinforce what has been said. What we sometimes do in a philosophical discussion is not argue at all but simply raise lots of questions—a method brilliantly employed by Ryle. Indeed, a volley of perplexing questions can certainly not be described as an argument and *a fortiori* not as a logical one, yet it is no less effective in making one turn back in recoil to consider one's views. Lastly, though on the surface the philosopher seems to be engaged in much the same thing as a logician is, for instance, in testing an argument for any loose links in it or in building up an argument, this should not mislead us. For if he were to construct rigorous proofs, where are the theorems established by them? What has he to show as the fruit of his labours?

I have not raised any of these questions wantonly; they force themselves on everyone who tries to arrive at a clear and unbiased view of the matter. Should these difficulties not have their origin in the nature of philosophy itself?

5. I proceed now to consider philosophic arguments, especially those which are regarded as constituting a decisive advance, to see whether they give

us any reason for modifying the view advocated here. There are only a few classical cases. One of them is Hume's celebrated argument to show that the relation of cause and effect is intrinsically different from that of ground and consequence. Now in what does this 'proof' consist? He *reminds* us of what we have always known: that, while it is self-contradictory to assert the ground and deny the consequence, no such contradiction arises in assuming that a certain event, the 'cause', may be followed not by its usual effect but by some other event. If it is asked 'Is this a proof?' what is one to say? It certainly is not the sort of proof to be found in a deductive system. Much of the same applies to Berkeley's argument when he tells us that, try as he might, he cannot call up in his mind an abstract idea of a triangle, of just a triangle with no particular shape, any more than he can conceive the idea of a man without qualities. Is this a proof? He points out the obvious. (Only it wants a genius to see it.)

To take my own argument against logical fatalism, it is not strict. The decisive step consists in following a certain analogy with other cases. It is analogical, not logical. Similarly the argument used against Zeno is not conclusive. (I have no space to enlarge upon that.)

Now for two more examples, one of the current sort of argument applied today by philosophers, the other taken from Aristotle.

When we say of someone that he 'sees' or 'hears' an aeroplane, or 'descries' or 'detects' a lark in the sky, or again that he 'tastes' or 'smells' roast pork, we do not ascribe to him an activity. That 'seeing' is not a sort of doing can be illustrated, e.g. by calling attention to the fact that we don't use the continuous present tense. We say 'I see the clock', not 'I am seeing the clock' (save G. E. Moore, who, oddly enough, regularly says that he 'is seeing his right hand'), whereas it is perfectly correct to say 'I am looking at the clock, listening to its ticking', and so in the other cases. Again, while it is proper to say 'I have forgotten to post the letter', no one would say 'I have forgotten to see the letter-box'. There is no sense in asking you, when you look at me, whether your seeing is easy or difficult, quick or slowish, careful or heedless, whether you see me deliberately and whether you have now finished seeing me. So, it is argued, perceiving is not a doing (an argument used by myself in lectures).

The point to be laboured is that this argument is not conclusive. Odd as it sounds, 'I have finished seeing you' *may* be said, though only in very special circumstances. A man with impaired eyesight who, unable to take in the shape as a whole, has perhaps to scan the face bit by bit in search of some characteristic marks might say, and understandably, 'Now I have finished seeing you'. We too are occasionally in a not much better position, as when, in magnesium light, we look at some scene, and afterwards complain, 'Too quick, I couldn't take it in'. It would seem then that there is no more than a difference in degree between this case and the normal ones. Odd cases, certainly; but what would you think of a mathematician whose theorems collapse when applied to slightly out-of-the-way curves?

For my next example I choose pleasure. Aristotle, in criticizing Plato[2], pointed out that if pleasure were a process going on in time I could enjoy something swiftly or slowly—an argument which is almost a bombshell in its destructive power. Certainly, to speak in such terms is very odd and sounds absurd. Yet, if I strain my imagination, I can perhaps bring myself to conceive of a set of circumstances under which it would not be entirely unnatural to say such a thing. In listening to music, for example, when I am following a slow and gentle movement, my enjoying it appears in some respects to be different from what I get when listening to an exciting piece of music. The very quality of my enjoyment seems to change as if something of the slow and gentle or of the wild, intoxicating flow of the music had entered into it. If I say, in the one case, that I was enjoying it leisurely like basking in the sun or sipping wine, in the other that I was suddenly carried away, breathlessly following its onrush and enjoying it like a storm at sea—does this sound like sheer nonsense? So there does seem to be a time factor in pleasure.

Amongst the most powerful weapons in the philosopher's armoury are *reductio ad absurdum* and infinite regress arguments. Before proceeding to an appraisal of these forms of reasoning, it will be well to consider how they work in their home land, mathematics.

Let me choose as a typical case the proof that $\sqrt{2}$ is irrational. If it were a rational number, we could find two integers m and n such that

$$m^2 = 2n^2 \quad (1)$$

We may then argue as follows. As m^2 is even, m must be even; hence $m = 2m_1$. Substitution yields

$$2m_1^2 = n^2. \quad (2)$$

As n^2 is even, n must be even; hence $n = 2n_1$. Substitution yields

$$m_1^2 = 2n_1^2. \quad (3)$$

If, then, two integers m and n exist which stand in the relation (1), they must have halves which stand in exactly the same relation (3), and these must have halves which stand in the same relation, and so on *ad infinitum;* which is plainly impossible, m and n being finite. Therefore the tentative assumption (1) cannot hold, and $\sqrt{2}$ cannot be rational. Q.E.D. This is the prototype of a refutation by infinite regress.

Arguments of this type have been applied outside mathematics. However, when I come to look at them a bit more closely I begin to hesitate. An example will illustrate my doubts. An argument propounded against the use of mechanical models is this. If the elastic properties of matter can be explained as being due to electric forces with which the molecules act on each other, it surely is pointless to explain the action of the electric forces as being due to the elastic properties of a mechanical medium, the 'ether'. To do this is to go round in a circle: elasticity is explained in terms of electric force, and electric force in terms of elasticity; while the attempt to break out of the circle by supposing that the elasticity of the ether is due to 'electric forces' acting between the ether particles and these to the elastic properties of a second-order ether is to be pushed into an infinite series of reduction steps. Thus the mechanistic programme is faced with a dilemma both horns of which are equally fatal.

A formidable argument—or is it? I can well imagine an undaunted champion of the lost cause retort: 'Not a bit of a regress. Yes, the ether is elastic, not, however, in the sense in which a spring is: while elasticity of matter can be reduced to electric force, elasticity of the ether, being an ultimate postulate of the theory, cannot be reduced any further.' And with this the argument falls to the ground.

But this is unconvincing, it will be said. I agree; I am not such an imbecile as to plead for retaining mechanical models and the rest. My point is only to see whether this 'refutation' is compelling. *It isn't.* The advocate of models is not forcibly dislodged from his position. There is, it would seem, always a way of getting out of the dilemma—of wriggling out if you like—which foils the argument. What is shown in it is merely that to cling to models of this sort becomes, in the circumstances, very unnatural. But to say that something is unnatural is not to say that it is logically impossible: yet this is what the argument should establish. In the mathematical proof cited above no loophole was left for wriggling out. The whole deduction was a 'chain of adamant'—precisely the sort of thing the argument under review is not.

Consider now a similar argument. There cannot be any such thing as volitions, it has been said. Volitions were called in by theorists to provide causes not only for what we (intentionally) do but also for mental processes or operations such as controlling an impulse, paying heed to something, and the like. As a consequence of this, acts of will were supposed to be the sort of thing the presence of which makes an action 'voluntary', or which—somehow, in some unfathomable way—'gets itself translated' into a bodily or mental act. In fine, volitions were thought of as causes as well as effects of other, mental or physical, occurrences. Now the dilemma: if my pulling of the trigger were the result of a mental act of 'willing to pull the trigger', what of this mental act itself? Was it willed or unwilled? If unwilled, it cannot be called voluntary and therefore not a volition; if willed, then we must suppose, according to the theory, that it results from a prior act, namely, 'willing to will to pull the trigger', and that from another, *ad infinitum,* leaving no possibility for me ever to start.

Brilliant as the argument is, the point to be brought up here is only whether it is logically fatal. Does it really prove that the assumption of acts of willing involves an infinite regress? A believer in such acts need not be cowed into submission. To ask of volitions whether they are themselves voluntary or involuntary acts, he may say, is plain nonsense. Only an *action* can be voluntary or involuntary, not an act of will. It is just the point that an act of will is an act of will and does not issue from any anterior act of will, any more than, in order to recall a thing I must first recall what I want to recall, and before I can even do that I must recall that I want to recall what I want to recall, and so on *ad infinitum.* Just as I can recall a thing without need to call in an act of recalling what I want to recall, so my pulling the trigger may be the direct result of an act of will without the latter issuing from a parent act of will. Thus the whole argument apparently crumbles away.

This is meant not to belittle the argument or detract from its force, but only to get clear as to *what sort* of force it has. If it were conclusive, it would, with its destructive power, do away with a good many more acts and states of mind, not only with volitions—with intending and desiring, for instance. Indeed, precisely similar arguments can be constructed 'to deal with them'. Intention: though clearly not the sort of thing to be classed as a simple 'act', it yet seems somehow to 'connect' with what goes on in us before we carry it into action—such as considering, planning, hesitating, choosing. I may, let us say, intend to find a flaw in a given argument, and when I subsequently turn it over in my mind, this will be the result of my intention. Some mental operations, then, *can* arise from an intention, they are 'intended'. So what of the intention itself? Is it intended or unintended? If the intention is not intended, it is not the intention, and if it is intended it must be due to another intention, and this to yet another *ad infinitum.* Similarly in the case of desire. Suppose that I feel a desire for a certain thing, is this desire itself desired or undesired? Either answer lands us in absurdities.

If the strength of the argument were to lie in its structure it would, with its devastating effect, apply after the exchange of some of its terms for other ones, e.g. 'volition' for 'intention'—provided, of course, that certain other circumstances essential to the reasoning are the same. Yet, while the first argument sounds, to say the least, very plausible, no one will be duped by its caricatures. So if it *has* any force it cannot owe it to its structure and consequently cannot be of a logical sort. It is meant to refute the existence of a kind of mental thrust; but then we should remember that to prove the non-existence of something is always a precarious business. 'No one has ever proved the non-existence of Apollo or Aphrodite' it has been observed; too much weight, then, need perhaps not be laid on this particular case. What is disturbing, however, is the ease with which arguments can be cast into pseudo-deductive moulds. And it is this fact to which I wish to call attention by examining the argument. As has been shown in the preceding discussion, it is not an isolated case. No philosophic argument ends with a Q.E.D. However forceful, it never forces. There is no bullying in philosophy, neither with the stick of logic nor with the stick of language.

6. In throwing such strong doubts on the power of arguments as used by philosophers I may seem to deny them any value whatever. But such is not my intention. Even if they are lacking in logical rigour this certainly has not prevented an original thinker from using them successfully, or from bringing out something not seen before or not seen so clearly. So in the case I have dis-

cussed: something *is* seen in that argument, something *is* made clear, though perhaps not quite in the sense intended by the arguer. If so, something very important has been left out from the picture.

Perhaps our objections have been doing injustice to philosophic arguments. They were, quite mistakenly as I hope to have shown, supposed to be proofs and refutations in a strict sense. But what the philosopher does is something else. *He builds up a case.* First, he makes you see all the weaknesses, disadvantages, shortcomings of a position; he brings to light inconsistencies in it or points out how unnatural some of the ideas underlying the whole theory are by pushing them to their farthest consequences; and this he does with the strongest weapons in his arsenal, reduction to absurdity and infinite regress. On the other hand, he offers you a new way of looking at things not exposed to those objections. In other words, he submits to you, like a barrister, all the facts of his case, and you are in a position of a judge. You look at them carefully, go into the details, weigh the pros and cons and arrive at a verdict. But in arriving at a verdict you are not following a deductive highway, any more than a judge in the High Court does. Coming to a decision, though a rational process, is very unlike drawing conclusions from given premisses, just as it is very unlike doing sums. A judge has to judge, we say, implying that he has to use discernment in contrast to applying, machine-like, a set of mechanical rules. There are no computing machines for doing the judge's work nor could there be any—a trivial yet significant fact. When the judge reaches a decision this may be, and in fact often is, a rational result, yet not one obtained by deduction; it does not simply follow from such-and-such: what is required is insight, judgement. Now, in arriving at a verdict, you are like a judge in that you are not carrying out a number of formal logical steps: you have to use discernment, e.g. to descry the pivotal point. Considerations such as these make us see what is already apparent in the use of 'rational', that this term has a wider range of application than what can be established deductively. To say that an argument can be rational and yet not deductive is not a sort of contradiction as it would inevitably be in the opposite case, namely, of saying that a deductive argument need not be rational.

This alters the whole picture. The point to be emphasized is that a philosopher may see an important truth and yet be unable to demonstrate it by formal proof. But the fact that his arguments are not logical does nothing to detract from their rationality. To return to our previous example, the argument used against volition, though it is not what it professes to be, logically destructive, nevertheless has a force difficult to resist. Now to what is this due? It does not need much acumen to find the answer. It is the whole arrangement of so many felicitous examples, preceding the argument, and their masterly analysis, which breathes life into its bare bones; aided greatly by the fact that the connection between a mental thrust and a bodily movement is allowed to remain a mystery. The unsatisfactoriness of this position, together with the amassing of hosts of unanswerable questions and very striking examples—this makes the argument so convincing.

What do you find in reading Ryle or Wittgenstein? Lots of examples with little or no logical bone in between. Why so many examples? They speak for themselves; they are usually more transparent than the trouble maker; each one acts as an analogy; together they light up the whole linguistic background with the effect that the case before us is seen in the light they produce. Indeed, examples aptly arranged are often more convincing and, above all, of a more lasting effect than an argument which is anyhow spidery. Not that the 'proofs' proffered are valueless: a *reductio ad absurdum* always points to a knot in thought, and so does an infinite regress. But they *point* only. The real strength lies in the examples. All the proofs, in a good book on philosophy, could be dispensed with, without its losing a whit of its convincingness. To seek, in philosophy, for rigorous proofs is to seek for the shadow of one's voice.

In order to forestall misinterpretations which will otherwise certainly arise I have to concede one point: arguments on a small scale, containing a few logical steps only, may be rigorous. The substance of my remarks is that the conception of a whole philosophical view—from Heraclitus to Nietzsche or Bradley—is never a matter of logical steps. A *weltanschauung* like any of these or even a new approach like that of Wittgenstein is never 'arrived at', in particular it is not deduced, and once found it can neither be proved nor refuted by strictly logical reasoning; though arguments may play a part in making them acceptable. But some authors have disdained even that.

The one remaining question to be asked is this: if the philosopher's views cannot be derived from any premisses, how has he ever arrived at them? How can he get to a place to which no road is leading? This leads to a new and deeper problem.

7. To ask, 'What is your aim in philosophy?' and to reply, 'To show the fly the way out of the fly-bottle' is . . . well, honour where it is due, I suppress what I was going to say; except perhaps this. There is something deeply exciting about philosophy, a fact not intelligible on such a negative account. It is not a matter of 'clarifying thoughts' nor of 'the correct use of language' nor of any other of these damned things. What is it? Philosophy is many things and there is no formula to cover them all. But if I were asked to express in one single word what is its most essential feature I would unhesitatingly say: vision. At the heart of any philosophy worth the name is vision, and it is from there it springs and takes its visible shape. When I say 'vision' I mean it: I do not want to romanticize. What is characteristic of philosophy is the piercing of that dead crust of tradition and convention, the breaking of those fetters which bind us to inherited preconceptions, so as to attain a new and broader way of looking at things. It has always been felt that philosophy should reveal to us what is hidden. (I am not quite insensitive to the dangers of such a view.) Yet from Plato to Moore and Wittgenstein every great philosopher was led by a sense of vision: without it no one could have given a new direction to human thought or opened windows into the not-yet-seen. Though he may be a good technician, he will not leave his marks on the history of ideas. What is decisive is a new way of seeing and, what goes with it, the will to transform the whole

intellectual scene. This is the real thing and everything else is subservient to it.

Suppose that a man revolts against accepted opinion, that he feels 'cramped' in its categories; a time may come when he believes, rightly or wrongly, that he has freed himself of these notions; when he has that sense of sudden growth in looking back at the prejudices which held him captive; or a time when he believes, rightly or wrongly, that he has reached a vantage point from which things can be seen to be arranged in clear and orderly patterns while difficulties of long standing dissolve as though by magic. If he is of a philosophic cast of mind he will argue this out with himself and then, perhaps, try to impart what has dawned on him to others. The arguments he will offer, the attacks he will make, the suggestions he will advance are all devised for one end: to win other people over to his own way of looking at things, to change the whole climate of opinion. Though to an outsider he appears to advance all sorts of arguments, this is not the decisive point. What is decisive is that he has seen things from a new angle of vision. Compared to that everything else is secondary. Arguments come only afterwards to lend support to what he has seen. 'Big words, not every philosopher, etc.': but where should one get one's bearings if not from the masters? And besides, once tradition has given way there is always ample scope for specialists to reduce some 'pockets of resistance'. Unpalatable though it may be, behind the arguments so well-planned, so neat and logical, something else is at work, a will to transform the entire way of thinking. In arguing for his view, the philosopher will, almost against his will, have to undermine current categories and clichés of thinking by exposing the fallacies which underly the established views he is attacking; and not only this, he may go so far as to question the canons of satisfactoriness themselves. In this sense, philosophy is the retesting of the standards. In every philosopher lives something of the reformer. That is the reason why any advance in science when it touches the standards is felt to be of philosophic significance, from Galileo to Einstein and Heisenberg.

If there is any truth in this, the relation of logic and philosophy appears in a new light. What is at issue is not a conflict between a formal and a less formal or informal logic, nor between the behaviour of technical and everyday concepts, but something radically different. It is the difference between drawing a conclusion and seeing, or making one see, a new aspect.

To put the matter in a nutshell, a philosophic argument does more and does less than a logical one: less in that it never establishes anything conclusively; more in that, if successful, it is not content to establish just one isolated point of truth, but effects a change in our whole mental outlook so that, as a result of that, myriads of such little points are brought into view or turned out of sight, as the case may be. Are illustrations necessary? Once Hume had exposed the fallacies of his predecessors when dealing with the notion of causality he had made it impossible for anyone to think along the lines of Spinoza whose world looks to us as strange as the moon. Suppose that you look at a picture-puzzle: at first you can see it in only a maze of lines; then, suddenly, you recognize a human face. Can you now, having discovered the face, see the lines as before? Clearly not. As with the maze of lines, so with the muddle cleared up by Hume: to recapture the mood of the past, to travel back into the fog has become impossible—one of the big difficulties of understanding the history of philosophy. It is for the same reason that the rise of the linguistic technique in our day has put an end to the great speculative systems of the past.

A philosophy is an attempt to unfreeze habits of thinking, to replace them by less stiff and restricting ones. Of course, these may in time themselves harden, with the result that they clog progress: Kant, the *Alleszermalmer* to his contemporaries, yet proudly upholding his table of categories—which appear to us unduly narrow. The liberator of yesterday may turn into the tyrant of tomorrow.

It can now be seen that the philosopher is not doing what the logician does, only less competently, but doing something altogether different. A philosophic argument is not an *approximation* of a logical one nor is the latter the ideal the philosopher is striving for. Such an account totally misdescribes what really takes place. Philosophy is not an exercise in formal logic, philosophic arguments are not chains of logical inference, only bungled ones, nor can they by any effort be recast into deductive moulds. What is being confused here is the scientist's aim to find new truths and the philosopher's aim to gain insight. As the two things are so entirely out of scale it is small wonder that the philosopher cannot move in the logician's armour. Not even if the logician himself is fighting the battle. The clash over the law of excluded middle in mathematics is a clash between two parties, each in possession of clear and precisely defined concepts. Yet there seems to be no way of settling the dispute by cogent argument. If it were true that philosophical troubles arise from the loose nature of our everyday concepts, why should such conflicts break out in the exactest of the sciences?

There have never been any absolutely cogent reasons for parting with the law of excluded middle, accepting Darwinism, giving up the Ptolemaic system or renouncing the principle of causality. If any of these things could be demonstrated how does it come that there are always partisans of the 'lost causes'? Are they like the unlucky circle-squarers, wasting their time in trying to do what has been shown to be logically impossible? The truth is that conflicts of this type cannot be resolved, not entirely, either by adducing factual evidence or by logical demonstration. Both sides, of course, bring up arguments in the combat but they are not decisive. These are battles never lost and never won irrevocably. It is a typical situation, a recurrent theme in the history of human thought.

Whenever science arrives at a crucial stage where the fundamental notions become uncertain and are held as it were in solution, disputes of an odd kind are breaking out. The mere fact that leading scientists, in spite of differences in temperament, outlook, etc., take part in them, feel bound to do so, should make us reflect. Now what the protagonists avowedly or unavowedly are trying to do is to win their fellow scientists over to their own way of thinking; and to the degree to which their arguments are attempts at changing the whole intellectual attitude they take on a philosophical character. Is this coincidence?

8. I have so far spoken of 'seeing a new aspect' without making an attempt to explain the term. I hope now to do so, though only perfunctorily, by giving one or two illustrations. There is a sort of paradox connected with the idea of certain discoveries. Descartes, for instance, was the discoverer of analytic geometry. But could he seek for it? To say that he spent years looking for it sounds downright absurd. What we are inclined to say in such a case is: to seek for analytic geometry is not possible—first because it was not seen and then because it was seen. But if he could not seek, how could he find? This leads us straight to the heart of the matter.

Consider first an entirely imaginary case. In the propositional calculus, as it was built up by Frege, two primitive ideas occur, 'not' and 'or'. It was later discovered by Sheffer that the whole calculus can be based on one single idea (his 'stroke' function). Of what kind was this discovery? Suppose that Frege, by a curious chance, had written all his logical axioms in the form

$$\sim(\ldots.) \mathbf{v} \sim(\ldots.)$$

i.e. as a sum of two negations, but had none the less mistakenly believed that *two* symbols were required for expressing these laws, namely '~' and '**v**'. Imagine now that someone else looking at these formulae is struck by what, on our assumption, has escaped Frege, namely that they all have one and the same structure and require therefore only one symbol. In what exactly does his discovery consist? In his *seeing* the formulae in a new way, in his reading a new structure into them. What matters is his apprehension: so long as he does not see the structure of a new system in the old one he has not got it. Anyone may look at the formulae and yet not perceive what Sheffer has perceived, the occurrence of an identical structure. *This* is the discovery, not the introducing of a special symbol for a combination of the old ones. It would have been quite enough, for instance, had Sheffer merely pointed out the constant recurrence of this structure in all the laws without providing his 'stroke'; that is inessential.

This example may illustrate what is meant by the 'seeing of a new aspect'. Seeing such an aspect is often the core of a new discovery. If you look at the formulae, the moment you notice the new structure in them they suddenly seem to change—a phenomenon akin to seeing a figure, say, a drawn cube differently, now as solid and protruding, now as hollow and receding. The one pattern suddenly 'jumps' into the other. Similarly in our case, there are also differences; thus the new aspect, once it has dawned, can steadily be held in mind and has not that perceptual instability. The apprehension of a new pattern in the formulae seems to hold in it actually more of a visual experience, anyhow to be more closely akin to it than it might at first appear. Seeing and interpreting, looking and thinking seem as it were to fuse here.

If it is now asked whether it is possible for anyone to *seek* for the new aspect, what is one to reply? Well, that something *can* be seen in a new way is seen only when it *is* seen in this way. That an aspect is possible is seen only when the aspect has already flashed and not before: that's why the finding cannot be anticipated, not even by the greatest genius. It always comes unbidden and, as it would seem, in a sudden flash.

To take another case, is the calculation

$$(5+3)^2=5^2+2\cdot5\cdot3+3^2$$

at the same time a proof that

$$(2+3)^2=2^2+2\cdot2\cdot3+3^2?$$

Yes and no—depending on how you look at it. (Does it strike you that the 2 in the middle term is a 'structural' 2, deriving not from the special numbers but from the general form of the operation?) A man, while reckoning with special numbers only, may yet conceivably do algebra if he sees the special sums in a new way, as the expressions of a general law. (Discovery of algebra as the discovery of an aspect of numerical calculation.)

What goes for these more or less trivial cases goes for Descartes and also for Einstein and Hilbert. They were unable to seek, Einstein for a conceptual gap in the idea of simultaneity, Hilbert for the axiomatic method. Though these discoveries are of a different order altogether, the principle underlying them is the same. None of them has ever 'arrived' at his view because he was never travelling. They did not seek, they found (like Picasso). And that is so wrong with the whole way in which such discoveries are so often presented—as if they were the result of a 'method' or 'procedure', as if the great men arrived at their solutions by drawing logical inferences. This leaves out the most essential thing—the flashing of a new aspect which is *non*-inferential. The moments of seeing cannot be foreseen, any more than they can be planned, forced, controlled, or summoned by will-power.

Is there any truth in what I am saying? I shall not argue. Instead, let me remind you of some observations which will be familiar to you. It is notorious that a philosophy is not made, it grows. You don't choose a puzzle, you are shocked into it. Whoever has pondered some time over some dark problem in philosophy will have noticed that the solution, when it comes, comes with a suddenness. It is not through working very hard towards it that it is found. What happens is rather that he suddenly sees things in a new light—as if a veil had been lifted that screened his view, or as if the scales had fallen from his eyes, leaving him surprised at his own stupidity not to have seen what was there quite plain before him all the time. It is less like finding out something and more like maturing, outgrowing preconceived notions.

To give just one example of vision in philosophy: Wittgenstein saw through a big mistake of his time. It was then held by most philosophers that the nature of such things as hoping and fearing, or intending, meaning and understanding could be discovered through introspection, while others, in particular psychologists, sought to arrive at an answer by experiment, having only obscure notions as to what their results meant. Wittgenstein changed the whole approach by saying: what these words mean shows itself in the way they are used—the nature of understanding reveals itself in grammar, not in experiment. This was at the time quite a revelation and came to him, as far as I remember, suddenly.

The view advocated here is that at the living centre of every philosophy is a vision and that it should be judged accordingly. The really important questions to be discussed in the history of philosophy are not whether Leibniz or Kant were consistent in arguing as they did but rather what lies behind the systems they have built. And here I want to end with a few words on metaphysics.

To say that metaphysics is nonsense *is* nonsense. It fails to acknowledge the enormous part played at least in the past by those systems. Why this is so, why they should have such a hold over the human mind I shall not undertake here to discuss. Metaphysicians, like artists, are the antennae of their time: they have a flair for feeling which way the spirit is moving. (There is a Rilke poem about it[3].) There is something visionary about great metaphysicians as if they had the power to see beyond the horizons of their time. Take, for instance, Descartes's work. That it has given rise to endless metaphysical quibbles is certainly a thing to hold against it. Yet if we attend to the spirit rather than to the words I am greatly inclined to say that there is a certain grandeur in it, a prophetic aspect of the comprehensibility of nature, a bold anticipation of what has been achieved in science at a much later date. The true successors of Descartes were those who translated the spirit of this philosophy into deeds, not Spinoza or Malebranche but Newton and the mathematical description of nature. To go on with some hairsplitting as to what substance is and how it should be defined was to miss the message. It was a colossal mistake. A philosophy is there to be lived out. What goes into the word dies, what goes into the work lives.

NOTES

1. Cf. *Polish Logic 1920–39,* edited by Storrs McCall (Oxford, 1967), Papers I, II and III.
2. Aristotle, *Nicomachean Ethics,* Bk. x, ch. 3.
3. This probably refers to *Die Sonette an Orpheus,* Part I, no. 12 (ed. R.H.).

PHILOSOPHERS AND ORDINARY LANGUAGE

Roderick M. Chisholm

THE POINT of a philosophical symposium on ordinary language, I take it, is to discuss certain contemporary views about the relation between ordinary language and philosophy. Among these are: (1) that many apparently important philosophical statements "violate" ordinary language in that they use it incorrectly; (2) that such statements are misleading and often seem comparatively unimportant when formulated correctly; and (3) that "any philosophical statement which violates ordinary language is false." The first two of these theses seem to me to be true, but the third seems to be false; accordingly, I shall restrict this paper to an examination of the third.[1]

The clearest defense of this thesis is to be found in Norman Malcolm's important paper, "Moore and Ordinary Language," in Volume IV of the "Library of Living Philosophers." Malcolm describes and defends what he takes to be G. E. Moore's method of defending ordinary language "against its philosophical violators."[2] "The philosophizing of most of the more important philosophers," according to Malcolm, "has consisted in their more or less subtly repudiating ordinary language";[3] but Moore, sensing that "any philosophical statement which violates ordinary language is false,"[4] has devised a method of refuting such statements. "The essence of Moore's technique of refuting philosophical statements consists in pointing out that these statements *go against ordinary language.*[5] Whether this is in fact Moore's technique need not concern us.

Most philosophical views, it seems to me *cannot* be refuted so easily. My hope, in criticizing this paper, which Malcolm wrote a number of years ago, is to elicit clarification of what is surely one of the most significant movements in contemporary philosophy. I shall first discuss the concept of correctness and then I shall examine two linguistic theories upon which Malcolm bases the thesis.

I

Let us begin by asking how we would show that a philosopher is using language *incorrectly.* Suppose we have found an epistemologist who holds that *certainty* is very difficult to attain: he tells us that, although people may *believe* that there is furniture in the room or that the earth has existed for hundreds of years past, no one can be *certain* that such beliefs are true. We might point out

Reprinted from Roderick M. Chisholm, "Philosophers and Ordinary Language," *Philosophical Review* 60 (1951), pp. 317–328.

to him that people *do* call such beliefs "certain"; we might go on to note that, ordinarily, one would apply the word "uncertain" only to beliefs of a much more problematic sort, for instance to conjectures about the weather; we might add that, if anyone were to teach a child the meaning of the words "certain" and "uncertain," he would never cite as an *uncertain* belief the one about the furniture; and so on. This sort of technique, which is frequently used, would show that the epistemologist disagrees with most people about the denotation of the word "certain," since he does not apply that word to the beliefs to which it is ordinarily applied. But would it show that he is using the word incorrectly? To see that it would not, let us consider a different case. A fifteenth-century geographer might have pointed out to Columbus that ordinarily people apply the word "flat" and not the word "round" to the earth; that they apply the word "round" to entities of quite a different sort, possibly to peaches and olives; that if a man wanted to teach his children the meaning of the word "round" he would never cite the earth as an example; and so on. But, Malcolm holds, this would not show that Columbus was using language incorrectly, since in this case ordinary people were making a *mistake* and Columbus was not.[6]

If we are thus to distinguish between *mistaken* usage and *incorrect* usage, we need, apparently, some such concept as that of *connotation* or *intension* for describing incorrectness. In the Columbus case, where *mistaken* usage was involved, we may assume that the word "round," as well as the word "flat," had the same intension for each of the persons concerned. Thus it is possible to say that the disagreement was unlike those which often arise because someone uses language incorrectly. For example, people sometimes argue over the question "Is a whale a fish?" and yet seem to be in agreement about the properties of whales; usually, in such cases, the word "fish" does *not* have the same intension for each of the persons concerned. In the whale case, unlike the Columbus case, at least one person is using language incorrectly. It is possible, therefore, that our epistemologist is using the word "certain" correctly, even though he disagrees with most people concerning its denotation. For it may be that, although his language is correct, he is mistaken about the facts. Or, as he might insist, it may be that his language is correct and that, as in the Columbus case, ordinary people are mistaken about the facts.[7]

To say that someone uses a word correctly, then, is to say, in part at least, that it has for him the same intension it has for most people.[8] Language as it is ordinarily used cannot be incorrect since "correct language" is synonymous with "ordinary language"; "ordinary language *is* correct language."[9] Thus the principal way to find out whether someone is using a word incorrectly would be to find out what intension the word has for him and what it has ordinarily, and then to compare intensions.[10] It is not enough, then, to provide a technique which merely shows that the philosopher disagrees with most people concerning the *denotation* of a word.

But when, finally, we *have* learned that a philosopher is using words incorrectly, what follows? Suppose the epistemologist does use the word "certain" incorrectly; he uses it, not as it is ordinarily used, but, say, to refer to a type of cognition which it would be logically impossible for any man to attain. Clearly, when we have pointed this out, we have not *refuted* him. To be sure, now that we *understand* him, we are no longer shocked by his statement that "certain," in his sense, does not apply to beliefs about the furniture. In all probability his statement which formerly seemed paradoxical now seems trivial and uninteresting. But we have not refuted him, since we have not shown that what he is saying is *false.* Indeed we now see, what we had not seen before, that what he is saying is *true,* since, presumably, our beliefs about the furniture *do not* have what he calls "certainty."[11]

Malcolm believes, however, that "a philosophical statement cannot be paradoxical and not be false."[12] We must look further, then, if we are to find a technique of refutation. This brings us to the first of the two theories mentioned above.

II

According to the first theory, "if a philosophical statement is paradoxical, that is because it asserts the impropriety of an ordinary form of speech."[13] The philosopher who says "Nothing is certain" may *seem* to be concerned, not with language, but with knowledge and belief; according to the theory, however, his statements are *really* "disguised linguistic statements."[14] He may not even realize that they are disguised; what the philosopher does may be "concealed from himself as well as from others."[15] And similarly for the other paradoxical philosophers: e.g., those who deny the reality of space and time; those who hold that no material thing exists unperceived; those who hold we cannot be certain there are other minds; those who hold, as Russell does, that we see, not external objects, but only parts of our brains; and so on. It is important to realize, moreover, that this theory is intended to apply not merely to those philosophers who are out to "entertain, dazzle, and bewilder the customers"; according to Malcolm, "the philosophizing of *most* of the more important philosophers has consisted in their more or less subtly repudiating ordinary language."[16] Thus, wherever we find a philosophy which is really a disguised attack upon ordinary language, we have only to remove the disguise and refute the philosophy (if it is false) by purely linguistic considerations.

This technique evidently involves three steps, each of them very doubtful, it seems to me. (1) First we show that the philosophical statement is not an "empirical statement," that it does not concern the "empirical facts." (2) From this it will follow, according to the theory, that the philosopher is really trying to tell us something about language. (3) Then, with the philosopher's disguise thus removed, an easy refutation is at hand.

(1) What does it mean to say, of a statement, that it does not concern the "empirical facts"? No meaning is provided for the technical term "empirical" (or "empirical facts"), and it seems to be used in a number of different ways.

When Malcolm says that a philosopher's statement is not *empirical,* he usually means that, in the (incorrect) sense in which the philosopher interprets his statement, its denial is contradictory. In other words, in the (incorrect) language the philosopher uses, his paradoxical statements are *necessary.* And Malcolm has shown with considerable care and ingenuity that many philosophical statements *are* nonempirical in this sense; among these are many statements which have been made about certainty.[17] But it is very difficult to see the justification for saying, as our theory would require, that *all* of the paradoxical statements of philosophy are statements which in the language of the philosophers are necessary. After all, for every paradoxical philosophical statement which is necessary, in a philosopher's language, we can find a variant of it, equally paradoxical, which is not necessary in that language. Suppose, for example, our philosopher uses "know" (incorrectly) to describe a type of cognition which one can have only of one's own experience. Then he may say, for example, "No one can know the content of anyone else's experience," and this paradoxical statement, let us assume, will turn out to be *necessary,* in his language. But suppose "Jones is other than his grocer" is *not* necessary in that language. Then the paradoxical statement "Jones can never know the content of his grocer's mind" will not be necessary; hence we will have a paradoxical philosophical statement which is yet *empirical,* on the present account.

The other possible meanings of "empirical" do not fare much better. We might, for example, interpret it to mean the same as "capable of being supported by evidence."[18] But in *this* sense probably *all* of the paradoxical statements cited are empirical, since each is supposed by *some* evidence, however inadequate; the epistemologist reminds us that people *do* make mistakes, even when they feel certain; Russell reminds us of the speed of light, its effects in the brain, and so on.[19] And if we take the term "empirical" even more narrowly to mean, say, "translatable into a phenomenalistic language," perhaps we can show that none of the statements cited is empirical; but now the problem is to show that the ordinary statements of science and common sense *are* empirical, in this narrow sense. In short, the success of the program we are discussing will depend upon showing that there is a sense of the term "empirical" attributable to the statements of common sense and the sciences and not to those of the paradoxical philosophers. The difficulty of the program is not lessened, of course, if for the technical term "empirical" we substitute some other, say "factual" or "informational," or some combination, such as "conveying information about empirical matters of fact."

(2) The second general problem is that of showing that the disputes, instigated by paradoxical philosophers, are really linguistic. If we *do* find that a philosophical dispute does not concern the "empirical facts" (in some significant sense), may we conclude that the disputants therefore disagree about "what language shall be used to describe those facts?" It seems clear to me that we cannot. Even in the whale case, the most we have a right to conclude is that people *use* language differently and *mistakenly believe* that they are in disagreement about the facts. From the fact that they *use* words differently, it does not

at all follow that they have different *beliefs* concerning which use is more nearly correct. Possibly, like people who use different regional accents, they have *no* beliefs about the correctness or other virtues of their different uses. Nor does it even follow that they have what Stevenson calls a disagreement in *attitude* concerning their respective uses; they might be people who are tolerant linguistically. Of course it may be, as is often intimated, that the linguistic difference is symptomatic of some significant subconscious disagreement. And some philosophers (though not Malcolm, so far as I know) are interested in speculating about the motives *other* philosophers may have for using one locution rather than another.[20] But the most a psychiatrist could tell us about our problem is that a philosopher might *say* one thing, while wishing, subconsciously or otherwise, for something else, possibly wishing that he were *saying* something else. But it would be incorrect to describe this fact by saying that the philosopher is "really asserting" the something else. From the fact that people use language differently, then, it does not follow that they disagree about language.

(3) The third problem is that of providing a refutation. Suppose (to discount all of the foregoing) we agree that the paradoxical philosophers really *are* trying to convey something about the "propriety" of ordinary language; the epistemologist is saying that it is "incorrect" or "improper" to ascribe certainty to beliefs about material things; or Russell is stating "that it is really a more correct way of speaking to say that you see a part of your brain than to say that you see the postman,"[21] and so on. Do we now have a technique of refutation?

Unfortunately there is still room for doubt concerning what it is, according to the theory we are examining, that the paradoxical philosophers are supposed to be trying to say. We may choose between two quite different types of interpretation. According to the first, the epistemologist is saying that ordinary people never *do* use the word "certain" to refer to beliefs about material things; Russell is saying that people ordinarily talk the way *he* likes to talk in his philosophical writings, that when they look at the mailman or the sun they say "I see a part of my brain" and that they never say "I see the sun" or "I see the mailman." The other shocking philosophical views would be interpreted similarly; when philosophers seem to deny the existence of time, or of space, or of matter, and such like, what they are really trying to tell us is that people ordinarily talk in these paradoxical ways. This interpretation of Malcolm's thesis, however implausible it may seem, is suggested by the fact that the term "correct language," as we have seen, is to be taken to mean language as it is ordinarily used; thus if someone says that a certain way of speaking is the *correct* way, he means it is the *ordinary* way. The paradoxical philosophers, then, would really be trying to tell us how people ordinarily use words. If *this* is the true interpretation of what the paradoxical philosophers are saying, then, clearly, we *can* refute their views by appealing to the facts of ordinary language, for it is obvious that people *do not* talk in these strange ways. But it is also obvious, it seems to me, that the philosophers are not trying to *say* that they do. The epistemologist is not contending, even subconsciously, that ordinarily people do not use the word "certain." And surely what Russell is fond of telling us is *not* that the ordinary man never *says* that he sees the sun, but that he *does* say it and that when he does he is mistaken. Moreover, I can not believe that *this* is the sort of view which is being attributed to Russell and the others. It is more plausible to suppose that the alternative interpretation is intended: these philosophers are not trying to *describe* ordinary language; they are *proposing* that we change it. This is the way Lazerowitz would interpret them: according to him, paradoxical philosophical statements should be in the "language of proposal" rather than in the "language of assertion."[22] The epistemologist is proposing that we change the meaning of "certain" and Russell is proposing that we use the word "see" in a different way: "Henceforth let us say that we see our brains and not that we see the mailman." This is the alternative to saying that the paradoxical philosophers are really trying to *describe* ordinary language. But if we decide that they are merely making *proposals,* then, once again, we are without a method of refutation, since, as Lazerowitz puts it, proposals "have no refutation."[23] A proposal may be ill-advised, but *being* a proposal it is neither true nor false and hence cannot be refuted.

Thus we haven't yet found a general technique for showing that the paradoxical statements of philosophy are false.

III

Malcolm's second linguistic theory, if true, does provide us with a method of refutation. This theory, which is of quite a different sort from the one we have been discussing, concerns the psychology of language. There are words in ordinary language, Malcolm believes, whose *use* implies that they have a denotation. That is to say, from the fact that they are used in ordinary language, we may infer that there is something to which they truly apply. Of course, this is not true of all words; from the fact that the word "God" and the word "ghost" have an ordinary use, we may not infer that there is a God or that there are ghosts. But, Malcolm believes, from the fact that "expressions like 'earlier,' 'later,' 'to the left of,' 'behind,' 'above,' 'material things,' 'it is possible that,' 'it is certain that' "[24] have a use, we *may* infer that there is something to which they truly apply. And thus if we know that such words *are* used in ordinary language, we may say of any philosopher who says there are *no* cases of certainty or *no* material things, etc. that he is mistaken. These philosophical words, according to Malcolm, are expressions the meanings of which must be shown; they cannot be explained to people "in terms of the meanings of words which they already know."[25]

> *In the case of all expressions the meanings of which must be* shown *and cannot be explained, as can the meaning of "ghost," it follows, from the fact that they are ordinary expressions in the language, that there have been*

> many *situations of the kind which they describe; otherwise so many people could not have learned the correct use of those expressions. Whenever a philosophical paradox asserts, therefore, with regard to such an expression, that always when that expression is used the use of it produces a false statement, then to prove that the expression is an ordinary expression is completely to refute the paradox.*[26]

Let us assume for the moment that this theory is true. What philosophers can we refute with it? Not an epistemologist who says we cannot be certain of beliefs about material things; he can deny the certainty of all such beliefs and still be immune, provided only that he allows us an occasional instance of certainty, say, for example, in the case of sense-data or elementary arithmetic. For the technique applies only to those philosophers who hold there are *no* instances to which the philosophical words in question apply. And if we *could* find a philosopher who said, "Nothing is certain," or who said "The word 'certain' interpreted in its ordinary sense, has no denotation," we could not refute *him* by this method, unless we knew he was using these words correctly. If our epistemologist, for example, were to say, "Nothing is certain," the technique would not apply, since we happen to know that *he* uses the word "certain" incorrectly and *not* as it is understood in ordinary language. This technique, then, would seem to apply normally to cases in which these special words are being used *correctly,* not to cases in which they are used incorrectly.[27] Thus we have yet to find how a proof of linguistic incorrectness can provide us with a method of refutation. The technique applies most obviously to those philosophers who, using ordinary language correctly make false statements about it— or, rather, make statements which *would* be false if this theory were true.

What reason is there for believing then, that these philosophically interesting words, such as "certain," "material thing," and the others listed above, can be explained only ostensively, that is to say, by exhibiting instances of their application? It is difficult to imagine how this type of explanation could be achieved, for example, in the case of "it is possible that," which Malcolm cites. It is even more difficult to imagine how we could produce instances of the true application of "fictitious," "imaginary," "nothing," "nonexistent," and "impossible," which he does not cite. The philosopher whom we are refuting by this method may tell us that ordinary people learn the meaning of "certain," "material thing," and so on, by whatever method they learn the meaning of such words as "impossible" and "nothing." He may tell us, for instance, that people have recourse to some "method of contrast"; we learn the meaning of "impossible" by having it contrasted with "possible." Similarly, he might say we learn the meaning of "certain" by having it contrasted with "doubtful." And there may be other methods of conveying the meanings of words. There might be a "method of limits": one might convey the meaning of "perfect circle" by exhibiting a sequence of shapes which seem to approach circularity as a limit.[28] Similarly, if there are no cases of certainty, one might convey the meaning of "certain" by arranging conjectures or opinions in such a series. And there could even be a "method of illusion." Suppose, for example, we teach a child the meaning of the word "courage" by showing him someone calmly accepting situations which we mistakenly believe he regards as dangerous. If the child also has this mistaken belief, he may be able to abstract the quality of courage in the manner required; but, since the belief is mistaken, the ostensive explanation has been accomplished without exhibiting an instance of the true application of the word. It might well be that some of the philosophically interesting words have been learned in this fashion. The skeptic might tell us that we have learned the meaning of "certain" by observing situations (i.e., beliefs) which we mistakenly took to have characteristics they did not have in fact. McTaggart probably would have said that this is the way we learn the meaning of the expression "material thing." And doubtless a study of the psychology of language would reveal still other ways of explaining the meanings of words. Such suggestions as these are not likely to seem unacceptable to one who can accept a paradoxical philosophy.

Our philosopher, therefore, should not have great difficulty in countering this type of refutation. And probably it is just as well: most philosophers are ready enough, as it is, to infer entities answering to the expressions which occur in ordinary language.

Thus we have failed to find sufficient reason for believing that "any philosophical statement which violates ordinary language is false."

Many philosophical statements *do* violate ordinary language; as a result, they are misleading, they may seem more important than they are, and philosophers may become entangled in verbal confusions. One of Mr. Malcolm's valuable contributions has been to show us how readily all of this does occur. But for the rest, so far as I can see, ordinary language does not have the philosophical significance which he and others attribute to it.

NOTES

1. Read at the annual meeting of the American Philosophical Association, University of Toronto, December 27–29, 1950.

2. Norman Malcolm, "Moore and Ordinary Language," *The Philosophy of G. E. Moore,* ed. P. A. Schilpp ("The Library of Living Philosophers," vol. IV; Evanston and Chicago, Northwestern University, 1942), p. 368.

3. *Ibid.,* p. 365.

4. *Ibid.,* p. 368.

5. *Ibid.,* p. 349.

6. "There are two ways in which a person may be wrong when he makes an empirical statement. First he may be making a mistake as to what the empirical facts are. Second, he may know all right what the empirical facts are, but may use the wrong language to describe those facts.

We might call the first 'being mistaken about the facts,' and the second 'using incorrect language' or 'using improper language' or 'using wrong language.' . . . [When people] said that the earth was flat, they were wrong. The way in which their statement was wrong was that they were making a mistake about the facts, not that they were using incorrect language; they were using perfectly correct language to describe what they thought to be the case. In the sense in which they said what was wrong, it is perfectly possible for *everyone* to say what is wrong" (*Ibid.*, p. 356).

7. Compare C. A. Campbell, "Common-Sense Propositions and Philosophical Paradoxes," *Aristotelian Society Proceedings*, XLV (1944–1945); also Morris Weitz, "Philosophy and the Abuse of Language," *Journal of Philosophy*, XLIV (1947), 533–546.

8. The *intension* of a word, say "horse," for some person, might be said to comprise those characteristics which it is necessary for him to believe an object to have before he will refer to it as a "horse" (or apply the word "horse" to it). Compare C. I. Lewis, *An Analysis of Knowledge and Valuation*, p. 43.

9. Malcolm, "Moore and Ordinary Language," p. 357.

10. Malcolm and others have suggested that correctness can sometimes be determined without elaborate lexicographical investigation. For example, if we can show that the epistemologist so uses "certain" that the ordinary statement "I am certain it's raining" is contradictory, his use is probably incorrect, since, if Malcolm is right, people do not ordinarily make statements which are contradictory. A similar short cut is available in connection with words which "operate in pairs, e.g., 'large' and 'small,' 'animate' and 'inanimate,' 'vague' and 'clear,' 'certain' and 'probable.' In their use in ordinary language a member of a pair requires it opposite—for animate is *contrasted* with inanimate, . . ." etc. ("Moore and Ordinary Language," p. 364. Compare Alice Ambrose, "Moore's Proof of an External World," also in *The Philosophy of G. E. Moore.*) However, it would be hazardous to suppose, whenever we find such a pair, that each member denotes something. Compare such pairs as "real" and "unreal," "possible" and "impossible," "actual" and "fictitious," "angels" and "devils," "elect" and "damned," "Creation" and "Creator," "mortals" and "immortals," and so on.

Some have held that the principal business of philosophy is the difficult task of finding out and making articulate the ordinary intensions of words such as "certain" and the like. Compare C. J. Ducasse, *Philosophy as a Science.*

11. Compare J. L. Cobitz, "The Appeal to Ordinary Language," *Analysis, XI* (1950), 9–11; also Norman Malcolm, "Certainty and Empirical Statements," *Mind*, LI (1942), 18–46, esp. p. 25. When we show that the epistemologist's statement is trivial, we may not refute him, but possibly we will *silence* him. One of the more important contributions of Malcolm and others concerned with correctness has been to show that many philosophical statements may be trivialized in this way.

12. "Moore and Ordinary Language," p. 361.

13. *Ibid.*, p. 362.

14. *Ibid.*, p. 354.

15. Morris Lazerowitz, "The Existence of Universals," *Mind*, LV (1946), 1–24; the quotation appears on p. 23.

16. "Moore and Ordinary Language," p. 365 (my italics). Malcolm holds, consistently, that the *denials* of the paradoxical philosophies—Moore's defense of common sense, for example—are also disguised linguistic statements. But these assert the "propriety" rather than the "impropriety" of ordinary language.

17. See Malcolm's "Certainty and Empirical Statements"; also his "The Verification Argument," *Philosophical Analysis*, ed. Max Black (Ithaca, New York, Cornell University Press, 1950).

18. In "Certainty and Empirical Statements" Malcolm seems to interpret "empirical" this way; cf. p. 20. In that paper he seems also to use "empirical statements" synonymously with

"statement which makes sense"; cf. p. 33. The expression "making sense," of course, involves the same difficulties as does "empirical."

19. Whether the evidence is *good,* is another point. Malcolm has pointed out, in fact, that it *is not* very good. See "Certainty and Empirical Statements," p. 42. On this point, compare Ralph M. Blake, "Can Speculative Philosophy Be Defended?" *Philos. Rev.,* LII (1943), 127–134.

20. Compare B. A. Farrell's critical discussion, "An Appraisal of Therapeutic Positivism," *Mind,* LV (1946), 25–48, 133–150. In addition to the works cited there, see Morris Lazerowitz, "Strong and Weak Verification, II," *Mind,* LIX (1950), 345–357; "Are Self-Contradictory Expressions Meaningless?" *Philos. Rev.,* LVIII (1949), 563–584. See also various papers by John Wisdom, particularly *Aristotelian Society Proceedings,* XXXVII (1936–1937); also J. Findlay, "Some Reactions to Recent Cambridge Philosophy," *Australasian Journal of Psychology and Philosophy,* XVIII (1940), 193–211.

21. Malcolm, "Moore and Ordinary Language," p. 350.

22. Morris Lazerowitz, "Moore's Paradox," *The Philosophy of G. E. Moore,* p. 391. Lazerowitz also applies this interpretation to those who, like Moore, deny the paradoxical views. Moore comments: "Mr. Lazerowitz concludes that when, for instance, I tried to show that time is not unreal, all that I was doing was to recommend that we should not use certain expressions in a different way from that in which we do! If this is all I was doing, I was certainly making a huge mistake, for I certainly did not think it was all. And I do not think so now." ("A Reply to My Critics," *The Philosophy of G. E. Moore,* p. 675).

23. "Moore's Paradox," p. 376.

24. "Moore and Ordinary Language," p. 360.

25. *Ibid.,* p. 360.

26. *Ibid.,* p. 361. Compare Max Black, *Language and Philosophy* (Ithaca, New York, Cornell University Press, 1949), pp. 16–17.

27. Of course, one could provide an *incorrect* formulation for the view that some of these words, as ordinarily used, have no denotation. And if we could find a philosopher who held such a view and formulated it incorrectly, the technique *would* apply to him.

28. Compare C. D. Broad, *Five Types of Ethical Theory,* pp. 57–59.

THE NATURE OF PHILOSOPHICAL PROBLEMS AND THEIR ROOTS IN SCIENCE

K. R. Popper

1

It was after some hesitation that I decided to take as my point of departure the present position of English philosophy. For I believe that the function of a scientist or of a philosopher is to solve scientific or philosophical problems, rather than to talk about what he or other philosophers are doing or might do. Even an unsuccessful attempt to solve a scientific or philosophical problem, if it is an honest and devoted attempt, appears to me more significant than any discussion of a question such as 'What is science?' or 'What is philosophy?'. And even if we put this latter question, as we should, in the somewhat improved form 'What is the character of philosophical problems?', I for one should not bother much about it; I should feel that it has little weight if compared with even such a minor problem of philosophy, as, say, the question whether every discussion must always proceed from 'assumptions' or 'suppositions' which themselves are beyond argument.[1]

When describing 'What is the character of philosophical problems?' as a somewhat improved form of 'What is philosophy?', I wished to hint at one of the reasons for the futility of the current controversy concerning the nature of philosophy—the naive belief that there is an entity such as 'philosophy', or perhaps 'philosophical activity', and that it has a certain character or 'nature'. The belief that there is such a thing as physics, or biology, or archaeology, and that these 'studies' or 'disciplines' are distinguishable by the subject matter which they investigate, appears to me to be a residue from the time when one believed that a theory had to proceed from a definition of its own subject matter.[2] But subject matter, or kinds of things, or classes of things, do not, I hold, constitute a basis for the distinction of disciplines. Disciplines are distinguished partly for historical reasons and reasons of administrative convenience (such as the organization of teaching and of appointments), partly because the theories which we construct to solve our problems have a tendency[3] to grow into unified systems. But all this classification and distinction is a comparatively unimportant and superficial affair. *We are not students of subject matter but students of problems.* And problems may cut right across the borders of any subject matter or discipline.

Obvious as this fact may appear to some people, it is so important for our present discussion that it is worth while to illustrate it by an example. It hardly

Reprinted by permission of the *British Journal for the Philosophy of Science* and the author, from Karl Popper, "The Nature of Philosophical Problems and Their Roots in Science," *British Journal for the Philosophy of Science* 3 (1952), pp. 124–156.

needs mentioning that a problem posed to a geologist such as the assessment of the chances of finding deposits of oil or of uranium in a certain district needs for its solution the help of theories and techniques usually classified as mathematical, physical, and chemical. It is, however, less obvious that even a more 'basic' science such as atomic physics may have to make use of a geological survey, and of geological theories and techniques, if it wishes to solve a problem arising in one of its most abstract and fundamental theories; for example, the problem of testing predictions concerning the relative stability or instability of atoms of an even or odd atomic number.

I am quite ready to admit that many problems, even if their solution involves the most diverse disciplines, nevertheless 'belong', in some sense, to one or another of the traditional disciplines; for example, the two problems mentioned 'belong' clearly to geology and physics respectively. This is due to the fact that each of them arises out of a discussion which is characteristic of the tradition of the discipline in question. It arises out of the discussion of some theory, or out of empirical tests bearing upon a theory; and theories, as opposed to subject matter, may constitute a discipline (which might be described as a somewhat loose cluster of theories undergoing a process of challenge, change, and growth). But this does not alter the view that the classification into disciplines is comparatively unimportant, and that we are students, not of disciplines, but of problems.

But are there philosophical problems? The present position of English philosophy, which I shall take as my point of departure, originates, I believe, from the late Professor Ludwig Wittgenstein's influential doctrine that there are none; that all genuine problems are scientific problems; that the alleged problems of philosophy are pseudo-problems; that the alleged propositions or theories of philosophy are pseudo-propositions or pseudo-theories; that they are not false (if false,[4] their negations would be true propositions or theories) but strictly meaningless combinations of words, no more meaningful than the incoherent babbling of a child who has not yet learned to speak properly.[5]

As a consequence, philosophy cannot contain any theories. Its true nature, according to Wittgenstein, is not that of a theory, but that of an activity. The task of all genuine philosophy is that of unmasking philosophical nonsense, and of teaching people to talk sense.

My plan is to take this doctrine[6] of Wittgenstein's as my starting point (section 2). I shall try (in section 3) to explain it; to defend it, to some extent; and to criticise it. And I shall support all this (in sections 4 to 6) by some examples from the history of scientific ideas.

But before proceeding to carry out this plan, I wish to reaffirm my conviction that a philosopher should philosophise, that is, try to solve philosophic problems, rather than talk about philosophy. If Wittgenstein's doctrine is true, then nobody can, in this sense, philosophise. If this were my opinion, I would give up philosophy. But it so happens that I am not only deeply interested in certain philosophical problems (I do not much care whether they are 'rightly' called 'philosophical problems'), but possessed by the belief that I may even contribute—if only a little, and only by hard work—to their solution. And my only excuse for talking here about philosophy—instead of philosophising—is, in the last resort, my hope that, in carrying out my programme for this address, an opportunity will offer itself of doing a little philosophising, after all.

2

Ever since the rise of Hegelianism there has existed a dangerous gulf between science and philosophy. Philosophers were accused—rightly, I believe—of 'philosophising without knowledge of fact', and their philosophies were described as 'mere fancies, even imbecile fancies'.[7] Although Hegelianism was the leading influence in England and on the Continent, opposition to it, and contempt of its pretentiousness, never died out completely. Its downfall was brought about by a philosopher who, like Leibniz, Kant, and J. S. Mill before him, had a sound knowledge of science, especially mathematics. I am speaking of Bertrand Russell.

Russell is also the author of the classification (closely related to his famous *theory of types*) which is the basis of Wittgenstein's view of philosophy, the classification of the expressions of a language into

(1) *True statements*
(2) *False statements*
(3) *Meaningless expressions,* among which there are statement-like sequences of words, which may be called 'pseudo-statements'.

Russell operated with this distinction in connection with the solution of the logical paradoxes which he discovered. It was essential, for this solution, to distinguish, more especially, between (2) and (3). We might say, in ordinary speech, that a false statement, like '3 times 4 equals 173' or 'All cats are cows', is meaningless. Russell, however, reserved this characterisation for expressions such as '3 times 4 are cows' or 'All cats equal 173', that is, for expressions which are better not described as false statements (as can easily be seen from the fact that their *prima facie* negations, for example, 'Some cats do not equal 173' are no more satisfactory than the original expressions) but as pseudo-statements.

Russell used this distinction mainly for the elimination of the paradoxes (which, he indicated, were meaningless pseudo-statements). Wittgenstein went further. Led, perhaps, by the feeling that what philosophers, especially Hegelian philosophers, were saying was somewhat similar to the paradoxes of logic, he used Russell's distinction in order to denounce all philosophy as meaningless.

As a consequence, there could be no genuine philosophical problems. All alleged philosophical problems could be classified into four classes:[8] (1) those which are purely logical or mathematical, to be answered by logical or mathematical propositions, and therefore not philosophical; (2) those which are factual, to be answered by some statement of the empirical sciences, and therefore again not philosophical; (3) those which are combinations of (1) and (2), and therefore, again, not philosophical; and (4) meaningless pseudo-problems such as 'Do all cows equal 173?' or 'Is Socrates identical?' or 'Does an invisible, untouchable, and apparently altogether unknowable Socrates exist?'

Wittgenstein's idea of eradicating philosophy (and theology) with the help of an adaption of Russell's theory of types was ingenious and original (and more radical even than Comte's positivism which it resembles closely).[9] This idea became inspiration of the powerful modern school of language analysts who have inherited his belief that there are no genuine philosophical problems, and that all a philosopher can do is to unmask and dissolve the linguistic puzzles which have been proposed by traditional philosophy.

My own view of the matter is that only as long as I have genuine philosophical problems to solve shall I continue to take an interest in philosophy. I fail to understand the attraction of a philosophy without problems. I know, of course, that many people talk nonsense; and it is conceivable that it should become one's task (an unpleasant one) to unmask somebody's nonsense, for it may be dangerous nonsense. But I believe that some people have said things which were not very good sense, and certainly not very good grammar, but which are at the same time highly interesting and exciting, and perhaps more worth listening to than the good sense of others. I may mention the differential and integral calculus which, especially in its early forms, was, no doubt, completely paradoxical and nonsensical by Wittgenstein's (and other) standards; which became, however, reasonably well founded as the result of some hundred years of great mathematical efforts; but whose foundations even at this very moment are still in need, and in the process, of clarification.[10] We might remember, in this context, that it was the contrast between the apparent absolute precision of mathematics and the vagueness and imprecision of philosophical language which deeply impressed the earlier followers of Wittgenstein. But had there been a Wittgenstein to use his weapons against the pioneers of the calculus, and had he succeeded in the eradication of their nonsense, where their contemporary critics (such as Berkeley who was, fundamentally, right) failed, then he would have strangled one of the most fascinating and philosophically important developments in the history of thought. Wittgenstein once wrote: 'Whereof one cannot speak, thereof one must be silent.' It was, if I remember rightly, Erwin Schroedinger who replied: 'But it is only here that speaking becomes interesting.' The history of the calculus—and perhaps of his own theory[11]—bears him out.

No doubt, we should all train ourselves to speak as clearly, as precisely, as simply, and as directly as we can. But I believe that there is not a classic of science, or of mathematics, or indeed a book worth reading that could not be shown, by a skillful application of the technique of language analysis, to be full of meaningless pseudo-propositions and what some people might call 'tautologies'.

3

But I have promised to say something in defence of Wittgenstein's views. What I wish to say is, first, that there is much philosophical writing (especially in the Hegelian school) which may justly be criticised as meaningless verbiage; secondly, that this kind of irresponsible writing was checked, for a time at least, by the influence of Wittgenstein and the language analysts (although it is likely that the most wholesome influence in this respect was the example of Russell who, by the incomparable charm and the clarity of his writings, established the fact that subtlety of content was compatible with lucidity and unpretentiousness of style).

But I am prepared to admit more. In partial defence of Wittgenstein's view, I am prepared to defend the following two theses.

My first thesis is that every philosophy, and especially every philosophical 'school', is liable to degenerate in such a way that its problems become practically indistinguishable from pseudo-problems, and its cant, accordingly, practically indistinguishable from meaningless babble. This, I shall try to show, is a consequence of philosophical inbreeding. The degeneration of philosophical schools is the consequence of the mistaken belief that one can philosophise without being compelled to turn to philosophy *by problems which arise outside philosophy*—in mathematics, for example, or in cosmology, or in politics, or in religion, or in social life. To put it in other words, my first thesis is this. *Genuine philosophical problems are always rooted in urgent problems outside philosophy, and they die if these roots decay.* In their efforts to solve them, philosophers are liable to pursue what looks like a philosophical method or like a technique or like an unfailing key to philosophical success.[12] But no such methods or techniques exist; philosophical methods are unimportant, and any method is legitimate if it leads to results capable of being rationally discussed. What matters is neither methods nor techniques—nothing but a sensitiveness to problems, and a consuming passion for them; or as the Greeks said, the gift of wonder.

There are those who feel the urge to solve a problem, those for whom the problem becomes real, like a disorder which they have to get out of their system.[13] They will make a contribution even if they use a method or a technique. But there are others who do not feel this urge, who have no serious and pressing problem but who nevertheless produce exercises in fashionable methods, and for whom philosophy is *application* (of whatever insight or technique you like) rather than *search.* They are luring philosophy into the bog of pseudo-problems and verbal puzzles; either by offering us pseudo-problems for real ones (the danger which Wittgenstein saw), or by persuading us to concentrate upon the endless and pointless task of unmasking what they rightly or wrongly take for pseudo-problems (the trap into which Wittgenstein fell).

My second thesis is that what appears to be the *prima facie* method of teaching philosophy is liable to produce a philosophy which answers Wittgenstein's description. What I mean by '*prima facie* method of teaching philosophy', and what would seem to be the only method, is that of giving the beginner (whom we take to be unaware of the history of mathematical, cosmological, and other ideas of science as well as of politics) the works of the great philosophers to read; say, of Plato and Aristotle, Descartes and Leibniz, Locke, Berkeley, Hume, Kant, and Mill. What is the effect of such a course of reading? A new world of astonishingly subtle and vast *abstractions* opens itself to the reader, abstractions of an extremely high and difficult level. Thoughts and arguments are put before his mind which sometimes are not only hard to understand, but whose relevance remains obscure since he cannot find out what they may be relevant to. Yet the student knows that these are the great philosophers, that this is the way of philosophy. Thus he will make an effort to adjust his mind to what he believes (mistakenly, as we shall see) to be their way of thinking. He will attempt to speak their queer language, to match the torturous spirals of their argumentation, and perhaps even tie himself up in their curious knots. Some may learn these tricks in a superficial way, others may begin to become genuinely fascinated addicts. Yet I feel that we ought to respect the man who, having made his effort, comes ultimately to what may be described as Wittgenstein's conclusion: 'I have learned the jargon as well as anybody. It is very clever and captivating. In fact, it is dangerously captivating; for the simple truth about the matter is that it is much ado about nothing—just a lot of nonsense.'

Now I believe such a conclusion to be grossly mistaken; it is, however, the almost inescapable result, I contend of the *prima facie* method of teaching philosophy here described. (I do not deny, of course, that some particularly gifted students may find very much more in the works of the great philosophers than this story indicates—and without deceiving themselves.) For the chance of finding out the extra-philosophical problems (the mathematical, scientific, moral and political problems) which inspired these great philosophers is very small indeed. These problems can be discovered, as a rule, only by studying the history of, for example, scientific ideas, and especially the problem-situation in mathematics and the sciences of the period in question; and this, in turn, presupposes a considerable acquaintance with mathematics and science. Only an understanding of the contemporary problem-situation in the sciences can enable the student of the great philosophers to understand that they tried to solve urgent and concrete problems; problems which, they found, could not be dismissed. And only after understanding this fact can a student attain a different picture of the great philosophies—one which makes full sense of the apparent nonsense.

I shall try to establish my two theses with the help of examples; but before turning to these examples, I wish to summarise my theses, and to balance my account with Wittgenstein.

My two theses amount to the contention that philosophy is deeply rooted in non-philosophical problems; that Wittengstein's negative judgment is correct, by and large, as far as philosophies are concerned which have forgotten their extra-philosophical roots; and that these roots are easily forgotten by philosophers who 'study' philosophy, instead of being forced into philosophy by the pressure of non-philosophical problems.

My view of Wittgenstein's doctrine may be summed up as follows. It is true, by and large, that pure philosophical problems do not exist; for indeed, the purer a philosophical problem becomes, the more is lost of its original sense, significance, or meaning, and the more liable is its discussion to degenerate into empty verbalism. On the other hand, there exist not only genuine scientific problems, but genuine philosophical problems. Even if, upon analysis, these problems turn out to have factual components, they need not be classified as belonging to science. And even if they should be soluble by, say, purely logical means, they need not be classified as purely logical or tautological. Analogous situations arise in physics. For example, the explanation or prediction of certain spectral terms (with the help of a hypothesis concerning the structure of atoms) may turn out to be soluble by purely mathematical calculations. But this, again, does not imply that the problem belonged to pure mathematics rather than to physics. We are perfectly justified in calling a problem 'physical' if it is connected with problems and theories which have been traditionally discussed by physicists (such as the problems of the constitution of matter), even if the means used for its solution turn out to be purely mathematical. As we have seen, the solution of problems may cut through the boundary of many sciences. Similarly, a problem may be rightly called 'philosophical' if we find that, although originally it may have arisen in connection with, say, atomic theory, it is more closely connected with the problems and theories which have been discussed by philosophers than with theories nowadays treated by physicists. And again, it does not matter in the least what kind of methods we use in solving such a problem. Cosmology, for example, will always be of great philosophical interest, even though by some of its methods it has become closely allied to what is perhaps better called 'physics'. To say that, since it deals with factual issues, it must belong to science rather than to philosophy, is not only pedantic but clearly the result of an epistemological, and thus of a philosophical, dogma. Similarly, there is no reason why a problem soluble by logical means should be denied the attribute 'philosophical'. It may well be typically philosophical, or physical, or biological. For example, logical analysis played a considerable part in Einstein's special theory of relativity; and it was, partly, this fact which made this theory philosophically interesting, and which gave rise to a wide range of philosophical problems connected with it.

Wittgenstein's doctrine turns out to be the result of the thesis that all genuine statements (and therefore all genuine problems) can be classified into one of two exclusive classes: factual statements (*synthetic a posteriori*), and logical statements (*analytic a priori*). This simple dichotomy, although extremely valuable for the purposes of a rough survey, turns out to be for many purposes too simple.[14] But although it is, as it were, specially designed to exclude the existence of philosophical problems, it is very far from achieving even this aim;

for even if we accept the dichotomy, we can still claim that factual or logical or mixed problems may turn out, in certain circumstances, to be philosophical.

4

I now turn to my first example: *Plato and the Crisis in Early Greek Atomism.*

My thesis here is that Plato's central philosophical doctrine, the so-called Theory of Forms or Ideas, cannot be properly understood except in an extra-philosophical context[15]; more especially in the context of the critical problem situation in Greek science[16] (mainly in the theory of matter) which developed as a consequence of *the discovery of the irrationality of the square root of two.* If my thesis is correct, then Plato's theory has not so far been fully understood. (Whether a 'full' understanding can ever be achieved is, of course, most questionable.) But the more important consequence would be that it can never be understood by philosophers trained in accordance with the *prima facie* method described in the foregoing section—unless, of course, they are specially and *ad hoc* informed of the relevant facts (which they may have to accept on authority).

It is well known[17] that Plato's Theory of Forms is historically as well as in its content closely connected with the Pythagorean theory that all things are, in essence, numbers. The details of this connection, and the connection between Atomism and Pythagoreanism, are perhaps not so well known. I shall therefore tell the whole story in brief, as I see it at present.

It appears that the founder of the Pythagorean order or sect was deeply impressed by two discoveries. The first discovery was that a *prima facie* purely qualitative phenomenon such as musical harmony was, in essence, based upon the purely numerical ratios 1 : 2 ; 2 : 3 ; 3 : 4. The second was that the 'right' or 'straight' angle (obtainable for example by folding a leaf twice, so that the two folds form a cross) was connected with the purely numerical ratios 3 : 4 : 5, or 5 : 12 : 13 (the sides of rectangular triangles). These two discoveries, it appears, led Pythagoras to the somewhat fantastic generalisation that all things are, in essence, numbers, or ratios of numbers; or that number was the ratio (*logos = reason*), the rational essence of things, or their real nature.

Fantastic as this idea was, it proved in many ways fruitful. One of its most successful applications was to simple geometrical figures, such as squares, rectangular and isosceles triangles, and also to certain simple solids, such as pyramids. The treatment of some of these geometrical problems was based upon the so-called *gnōmōn.*

This can be explained as follows. If we indicate a square by four dots,

$$\begin{matrix} \bullet & \bullet \\ \bullet & \bullet \end{matrix}$$

we may interpret this as the result of adding three dots to the one dot on the upper left corner. These three dots are the first *gnōmōn*; we may indicate it thus:

By adding a second *gnōmōn*, consisting of five more dots, we obtain

One sees at once that every number of the sequence of the odd numbers, 1, 3, 5, 7 . . . , each forms a *gnōmōn* of a square, and that the sums 1, 1 + 3, 1 + 3 + 5, 1 + 3 + 5 + 7, . . . are the square numbers, and that, if n is the (number of dots in the) side of a square, its area (total number of dots = n^2) will be equal to the sum of the first n odd numbers.

As with the treatment of squares, so with the treatment of isosceles triangles.

Here each *gnōmōn* is a last horizontal line of points, and each element of the sequence 1, 2, 3, 4 . . . is a *gnōmōn*. The 'triangular numbers' are the sums 1 + 2; 1 + 2 + 3; 1 + 2 + 3 + 4, etc., that is, the sums of the first n natural numbers. By putting two such triangles side by side

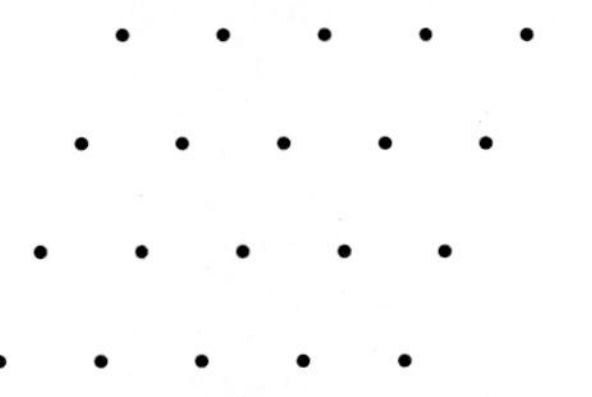

we obtain the parallelogram with the horizontal side $n + 1$ and the other side n, containing $n(n + 1)$ dots. Since it consists of two isosceles triangles, its number is $2(1 + 2 + \ldots + n)$, so that we obtain the equation

(3) $$1 + 2 + \ldots + n = \tfrac{1}{2} n\,(n + 1)$$

and

$$(4) \qquad d(1 + 2 + \ldots + n) = \tfrac{d}{2}\, n\,(n + 1).$$

From this it is easy to obtain the general formula for the sum of an arithmetical series.

We also obtain 'oblong numbers', that is the numbers of oblong rectangular figures, of which the simplest is

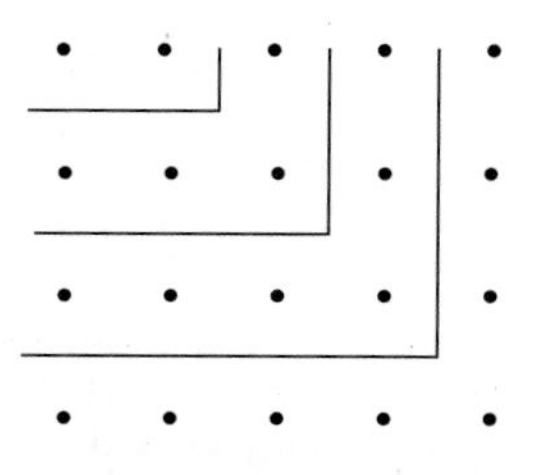

with the oblong numbers 2 + 4 + 6 . . . , i.e. the *gnōmōn* of an oblong is an even number, and the oblong numbers are the sums of the even number.

These considerations were extended to solids; for example, by summing the first triangular number, pyramid numbers were obtained. But the main application was to plain figures, or shapes, or 'Forms'. These, it was believed, are characterised by the appropriate sequence of numbers, and thus by the numerical ratios of the consecutive numbers of the sequence. In other words, *'Forms' are numbers or ratios of numbers.* On the other hand, not only shapes of things, but also abstract properties, such as harmony, and 'straightness' are numbers. In this way, the general theory that numbers are the rational essences of all things, is arrived at with some plausibility.

It is very probable that the development of this view was influenced by the similarity of the dot-diagrams with the diagram of a constellation such as the Lion, or the Scorpion, or the Virgo. If a Lion is an arrangement of dots, it must have a number. In this way the belief seems to have arisen that the numbers, or 'Forms', are heavenly shapes of things.

One of the main elements of this early theory was the so-called 'Table of Opposites', based upon the fundamental distinction between odd and even numbers. It contains such things as

ONE	MANY
ODD	EVEN
MALE	FEMALE
REST (BEING)	CHANGE (BECOMING)
DETERMINATE	INDETERMINATE
SQUARE	OBLONG
STRAIGHT	CROOKED
RIGHT	LEFT
LIGHT	DARKNESS
GOOD	BAD

In reading through this strange table one gets some idea of the working of the Pythagorean mind, and why not only the 'Forms' or shapes of geometrical figures were considered to be numbers, in essence, but also abstract ideas, such as Justice and, of course, Harmony, and Health, Beauty and Knowledge. The table is interesting also because it was taken over, with very little alteration, by Plato. Plato's famous theory of 'Forms' or 'Ideas' may indeed be described, somewhat roughly, as the doctrine that the 'Good' side of the Table of Opposites constitutes an (invisible) Universe, a Universe of Higher Reality, of the Unchanging and Determinate 'Forms' of all things, and that True and Certain Knowledge (*epistēmē* = *scientia* = *science*) can be of this Unchanging and Real Universe only, while the visible world of change and flux in which we live and die, the world of generation and destruction, the world of experience, is only a kind of reflection or copy of that Real World. It is only a world of appearance, of which no True and Certain Knowledge can be obtained. What can be obtained in the place of Knowledge (*epistēmē*) are only the plausible but uncertain and prejudiced opinions (*doxa*) of fallible mortals.[18] In his interpretation of the Table of Opposites, Plato was influenced by Parmenides, the man who stimulated the development of Democritus' atomic theory.

Returning now to the original Pythagorean view, there is one thing in it which is of decisive importance for our story. It will have been observed that the Pythagorean emphasis upon Number was fruitful from the point of view of the development of scientific ideas. This is often but somewhat loosely expressed by saying that the Pythagoreans encouraged numerical scientific measurements. Now the point which we must realise is that, for the Pythagoreans, all this was *counting rather than measuring*. It was the counting of numbers, of invisible essences or 'Natures' which were Numbers of little dots or stigmata. Admittedly, we cannot count these little dots directly, since they are invisible. What we actually do is not to count the Numbers or Natural Units, but to measure, i.e. to count arbitrary visible units. But the significance of measurements was interpreted as revealing, indirectly, the true *Ratios of the Natural Units or of the Natural Numbers.*

Thus Euclid's methods of proving the so-called 'Theorem of Pythagoras' (Euclid's I, 47) according to which, if a is the side of a triangle opposite to its right angle between b and c,

$$a^2 = b^2 + c^2, \qquad (1)$$

was completely foreign to the spirit of Pythagorean mathematics. In spite of the fact that the theorem was known to the Babylonians and geometrically proved by them, neither Pythagoras nor Plato appear to have known the general *geometrical* proof; for the problem for which they offered the solutions, the *arithmetical* one of finding the integral solutions for the sides of rectangular triangles, can be easily solved, if (1) is known by the formula (m and n are natural numbers, and $m > n$)

$$a = m^2 + n^2;\ b = 2mn;\ c = m^2 - n^2. \tag{2}$$

But formula (2) was unknown to Pythagoras and even to Plato. This emerges from the tradition according to which Pythagoras proposed the formula

$$a = 2m(m + 1) + 1;\ b = 2.m(m + 1);\ c = 2m + 1 \tag{3}$$

which can be read off the *gnōmōn* of the square numbers, but which is less general than (2), since it fails, for example, for 8 : 15 : 17. To Plato, who is reported to have improved Pythagoras' formula (3), is attributed another formula which still falls short of the general solution (2).

We now come to the discovery of the *irrationality of the square root of two.* According to tradition, this discovery was made within the Pythagorean order, but was kept secret. (This is suggested by the old term for 'irrational', '*arrhētos*', that is, 'unspeakable', which might well have meant 'the unspeakable mystery'.) This discovery struck at the root of Pythagoreanism; for it meant that such a simple geometrical entity as the diagonal d of the square with the side a could demonstrably not be characterised by *any* ratio of natural numbers; $d : a$ was *no ratio.* The tradition has it that the member of the school who gave away the secret was killed for his treachery. However this may be, there is little doubt that the realisation of the fact that irrational magnitudes (they were, of course, not recognised as numbers) existed, and that their existence could be proved, led to the downfall of the Pythagorean order.

The Pythagorean theory, with its dot-diagrams, contains, no doubt, the suggestion of a very primitive atomism. How far the atomic theory of Democritus was influenced by Pythagoreanism is difficult to assess. Its main influences came, one can say for certain, from the Eleatic School: from Parmenides and from Zeno. The basic problem of this school, and of Democritus, was that of the rational understanding of *change.* (I differ here from the interpretations of Cornford and others.) I think that this problem derives from Ionian rather than from Pythagorean thought, and that it has remained the fundamental problem of Natural Philosophy.

Although Parmenides himself was not a physicist (as opposed to his great Ionian predecessors), he may be described, I believe, as having fathered *theoretical physics.* He produced an anti-physical theory which, however, was the first hypothetical-deductive system. And it was the beginning of a long series of such systems of physical theories each of which was an improvement on its predecessor. As a rule the improvement was found necessary by the realisation that the earlier system was falsified by certain facts of experience. Such an empirical refutation of the consequences of a deductive system leads to efforts at its reconstruction, and thus to a new and improved theory which, as a rule, clearly bears the mark of its ancestry, of the older theory as well as of the refuting experience.

These experiences or observations were, we shall see, very crude at first, but they became more and more subtle as the theories became more and more capable of accounting for the cruder observations. In the case of Parmenides' theory, the clash with observation was so obvious that it would seem perhaps fanciful to describe the theory as the first hypothetical-deductive system of physics. We may, therefore, describe it as the last pre-physical deductive system, whose falsification gave rise to the first truly physical theory, the atomistic theory of Democritus.

Parmenides' theory is simple. He finds it impossible to understand change or movement rationally, and concludes that there is really no change—or that change is only apparent. But before we indulge in feelings of superiority, in the face of such a hopelessly unrealistic theory, we should first realise that there is a serious problem here. If a thing X changes, then clearly it is no longer the same thing X. On the other hand, we cannot say that X changes without implying that X persists during the change; that it is the same thing X, at the beginning and at the end of the change. Thus, it appears that we arrive at a contradiction, and that the idea of a thing that changes, and therefore the idea of change, is impossible.

All this sounds very philosophical and abstract, and so it is. But it is a fact that the difficulty here indicated has never ceased to make itself felt in the development of physics.[19] And a deterministic system such as that of Einstein's field theory might even be described as a four-dimensional version of Parmenides' unchanging three-dimensional universe. For, in a sense, no change occurs in Einstein's four-dimensional block-universe. Everything is there just as it is, in its four-dimensional *locus*; change becomes a kind of 'apparent' change; it is 'only' the observer who, as it were, glides along his world-line and becomes successively conscious of the different *loci* along this world-line, that is, of his spatio-temporal surrounding. . . .

To return from this new Parmenides to the older father of theoretical physics, we may present his deductive theory roughly as follows.

(1) Only what is, is.
(2) What is not does not exist.
(3) Non-being, that is, the void, does not exist.
(4) The world is full.
(5) The world has no parts; it is one huge block (because it is full).
(6) Motion is impossible (since there is no empty space into which anything could move).

The conclusions (5) and (6) were obviously contradicted by facts. Thus Democritus argued from the falsity of the conclusion to that of the premises:

(6′) There is motion (thus motion is possible).
(5′) The world has parts; it is not one, but many.
(4′) Thus the world cannot be full.[20]
(3′) The void or (non-being) exist.

So far the theory had to be altered. With regard to being, or to the many existing things (as opposed to the void), Democritus adopted Parmenides' theory that they had no parts. They were indivisible (atoms), because they were full, because they had no void inside.

The central point of this theory is that it gives a rational account of change. The world consists of empty space (the void) with atoms in it. The atoms do not change; they are Parmenidean indivisible block universes in miniature.[21] All change is due to rearrangement of atoms in space. Accordingly, *all change is movement.* Since the only kind of novelty possible is novelty of arrangement, it is, in principle, possible *to predict all future changes in the world,* provided we manage to predict the motion of mass-points.

Democritus' theory of change was of tremendous importance for the development of physical science. It was partly accepted by Plato, who retained much of atomism but explained change not only by unchanging yet moving atoms, but also by the 'Forms' which were subject neither to change nor to motion. But it was condemned by Aristotle who taught in its stead that all change was the unfolding of the inherent potentialities of essentially unchanging *substances.* But although Aristotle's theory of substances as the subjects of change became dominant, it proved barren;[22] and Democritus' theory that all change must be explained by movement became the tacitly accepted official programme of physics down to our own day. It is still part of the philosophy of physics, in spite of the fact that physics itself has outgrown it (to say nothing of the biological and social sciences). For with Newton, in addition to moving mass-points, *forces* of changing intensity (and direction) enter the scene. True, these changes can be explained as due to, or dependent upon, motion, that is upon the changing position of particles, but they are nevertheless not identical with the changes in position; owing to the square law, the dependence is not even a linear one. And with Faraday and Maxwell, changing fields of forces become as important as material atomic particles. That our modern atoms turn out to be composite is a minor matter; from Democritus' point of view, not our atoms but rather our elementary particles would be real atoms—except that these too turn out to be liable to change. Thus we have a most interesting situation. A philosophy of change, designed to meet the difficulty of understanding change rationally, serves sciences for thousands of years, but is ultimately superseded by the development of science itself; and this fact passes practically unnoticed by philosophers who are busily denying the existence of philosophical problems.

Democritus' theory was a marvellous achievement. It provided a theoretical framework for the explanation of most of the empirically known properties of matter (discussed already by the Ionians), such as compressibility, degrees of hardness and resilience, rarefaction and condensation, coherence, disintegration, combustion, and many others. But apart from being important as an explanation of the phenomena of experience, the theory was important in other ways. First, it established the methodological principle that a deductive theory or explanation must 'save the phenomena', that is, must be in agreement with experience. Secondly, it showed that a theory may be speculative, and based upon the fundamental (Parmenidean) principle that the world as it must be understood by argumentative thought turns out to be different from the world of *prima facie* experience, from the world as seen, heard, smelled, tasted, touched;[23] and that such a speculative theory may nevertheless accept the empiricist 'criterion' that it is the visible that decides the acceptance or rejection of a theory of the invisible[24] (such as the atoms). This philosophy has remained fundamental to the whole development of physics, and has continued to conflict with all 'relativistic'[25] and 'positivistic'[26] tendencies.

Furthermore, Democritus' theory led to the first successes of the method of exhaustion (the forerunner of the calculus of integration), since Archimedes himself acknowledged that Democritus was the first to formulate the theory of the volumes of cones and pyramids.[27] But perhaps the most fascinating element in Democritus' theory is his doctrine of the quantisation of space and time. I have in mind the doctrine, now extensively discussed,[28] that there is a shortest distance and a smallest time interval, that is to say, distances in space and time (elements of length and time, Democritus' *ameres*[29] in contradistinction to his atoms) such that no smaller ones are measurable.

5

Democritus' atomism was developed and expounded as a point for point reply[30] to the detailed arguments of his Eleatic predecessors, of Parmenides and of his pupil, Zeno. Especially Democritus' theory of atomic distances and time intervals is the direct result of Zeno's arguments, or more precisely, of the rejection of Zeno's conclusions. But nowhere in Zeno is there an allusion to the discovery of irrationals.

We do not know the date of the proof of the irrationality of the square root of two, or the date when the discovery became publicly known. Although there existed a tradition ascribing it to Pythagoras (sixth century B.C.), and although some authors[31] call it the 'theorem of Pythagoras', there can be little doubt that the discovery was not made, and certainly not publicly known, before 450 B.C., and probably not before 420. Whether Democritus knew about it is uncertain. I now feel inclined to believe that he did not; and that the title of Democritus' two lost books, *Peri alogōn grammōn kai kastōn,* should be translated *On Illogical Lines and Full Bodies* (*Atoms*),[32] and that these two books do not contain any reference to the problem of irrationality.[33]

My belief that Democritus did not know about irrationalities is based on the fact that there are no traces of a defence of his theory against the fatal blow which it received from this discovery. For the blow was as fatal to Atomism as it was to Pythagoreanism. Both theories were based on the doctrine that all measurement is, ultimately, counting of natural units, so that every measurement must be reducible to pure numbers. The distance between any two atomic points must, therefore, consist of a certain number of atomic distances; thus all distances must be commensurable. But this turns out to be impossible even in the simple case of the distances between the corners of a square, because of the incommensurability of its diagonal with its side.

It was Plato who realised this fact, and who in the *Laws* stressed its importance in the strongest possible terms, denouncing his compatriots for their failure to realise what it meant. It is my contention that his whole philosophy, and especially his theory of 'Forms' or 'Ideas', was influenced by it.

Plato was very close to the Pythagoreans as well as to the Eleatic Schools; and although he appears to have felt antipathetic to Democritus, he was himself an atomist of a kind. (Atomist teaching remained as one of the school traditions of the Academy.[34]) This is not surprising in view of the close relation between Pythagorean and atomistic ideas. But all this was threatened by the discovery of the irrational. I suggest that Plato's main contribution to science sprang from his realisation of the problem of the irrational, and from the modification of Pythagoreanism and atomism which he undertook in order to rescue science from a catastrophic situation.

He realised that the purely arithmetical theory of nature was defeated, and that a new mathematical method for description and explanation of the world was needed. Thus he encouraged the development of an autonomous geometrical method which found its fulfilment in the 'Elements' of the Platonist Euclid.

What are the facts? I shall try to put them all briefly together.

(1) Pythagoreanism and atomism in Democritus' form were both fundamentally based on arithmetic, that is on counting.

(2) Plato emphasised the catastrophic character of the discovery of the irrationals.

(3) He inscribed over the door of the Academy: 'Nobody untrained in geometry may enter my house'. But *geometry,* according to Plato's immediate pupil Aristotle as well as to Euclid, treats of incommensurables or irrationals, in contradistinction to *arithmetic* which treats of 'the odd and the even'.

(4) Within a short time after Plato's death, his school produced, in Euclid's *Elements,* a work whose main point was that it freed mathematics from the 'arithmetical' assumption of commensurability or rationality.

(5) Plato himself contributed to this development, and especially to the development of solid geometry.

(6) More especially, he gave in the *Timaeus* a specifically geometrical version of the formerly purely arithmetical atomic theory, that is, a version which constructed the elementary particles (the famous Platonic bodies) out of triangles which incorporated the irrational square roots of two and of three. (See below.) In most other respects, he preserved both Pythagorean ideas as well as some of the most important ideas of Democritus.[35] At the same time, he tried to eliminate Democritus' void; for he realised that motion remains possible even in a 'full' world, provided motion is conceived as of the character of vortices in a liquid. Thus he retained some of the most fundamental ideas of Parmenides.[36]

(7) Plato encouraged the construction of geometrical models of the world, and especially models explaining the planetary movements. Euclid's geometry was not intended as an exercise in pure geometry (as now usually assumed), but as a *theory of the world.* Ever since[37] Plato and Euclid, but not before, it has been taken for granted that geometry (rather than arithmetic) is the fundamental instrument of all physical explanations and descriptions, of the theory of matter as well as of cosmology.[38]

These are the historical facts. They go a long way, I believe, to establish my contention that what I have described as the *prima facie* method of philosophy cannot lead to an understanding of the problems which inspired Plato. Nor can it lead to an appreciation of what may be justly claimed to be his greatest philosophical achievement, the geometrical theory of the world which became the basis of the works of Euclid, Aristarchus, Archimedes, Copernicus, Kepler, Galileo, Descartes, Newton, Maxwell, and Einstein.

But is this achievement properly described as philosophical? Does it not rather belong to physics—a factual science—and to pure mathematics—a branch, Wittgenstein's school would contend, of tautological logic?

I believe that we can at this stage see fairly clearly why Plato's achievement (although it has no doubt its physical, its logical, its mixed, and its nonsensical components) was a philosophical achievement; why at least part of his philosophy of nature and of physics has lasted and, I believe, will last.

What we find in Plato and his predecessors is the conscious construction and invention of a new approach towards the world and towards the knowledge of the world. This approach transforms a fundamentally theological idea, *the idea of explaining the visible world by a postulated invisible world,*[39] into the fundamental instrument of theoretical science. The idea was explicitly formulated by Anaxagoras and Democritus[40] as the principle of investigations into the nature of matter or body; visible matter was to be explained by hypotheses about invisibles, about an *invisible structure which is too small to be seen.* With Plato, this idea is consciously accepted and generalised; the visible world of change is ultimately to be explained by an invisible world of unchanging 'Forms' (or substances or essences, or 'natures'—as we shall see, geometrical shapes or figures).

Is this idea about the invisible structure of matter a physical or a philosophical idea? If a physicist *acts* upon this theory, that is to say, if he accepts it, perhaps even without becoming conscious of it, by accepting the traditional problems of his subject, as presented by the problem-situation with which he is confronted; and if he, so acting, produces a new specific theory of the structure of matter; then I should not call him a philosopher. But if he reflects upon it, and, for example, rejects it (like Berkeley or Mach), preferring a phenomenological or positivistic physics to the theoretical and somewhat theological approach, then he may be called a philosopher. Similarly, those who consciously searched for the theoretical approach, who constructed it, and who explicitly formulated it, and thus transferred the hypothetical-deductive method from the field of theology to that of physics, were philosophers, even though they were physicists in so far as they acted upon their own precepts and tried to produce actual theories of the invisible structure of matter.

But I shall not pursue the question as to the proper application of the label 'philosophy' any further; for this problem, which is Wittgenstein's problem, clearly turns out to be one of linguistic usage, a pseudo-problem which by now must be rapidly developing into a bore to my audience. But I wish to add a few more words on Plato's theory of Forms or Ideas, or more precisely, on point (6) of the list of historical facts given above.

Plato's theory of the structure of matter can be found in the *Timaeus.* It has at least a superficial similarity with the modern theory of solids which interprets them as crystals. His physical bodies are composed of invisible elementary particles of various shapes, the shapes being responsible for the macroscopic properties of visible matter. The shapes of the elementary particles, in their turn, are determined by the shapes of the plane figures which form their sides. And these plane figures, in their turn, are ultimately all composed by *two* elementary triangles, viz. the half-square (*or isosceles* rectangular) triangle which incorporates the *square root of two,* and the half-equilateral rectangular triangle which incorporates the *square-root of three,* both of them irrationals.

These triangles, in their turn, are described as the copies[41] of unchanging 'Forms' or 'Ideas', which means that specifically *geometrical* 'Forms' are admitted into the company of the Pythagorean *arithmetical* Form-Numbers.

There is little doubt that the motive of this construction is the attempt to solve the crisis of atomism by incorporating the irrationals into the last elements of which the world is built. Once this has been done, the difficulty of the existence of irrational distances is overcome.

But why did Plato choose just these two triangles? I have elsewhere[42] expressed the view, as a conjecture, that Plato believed that all other irrationals might be obtained by adding to the rationals multiples of the square roots of two and three. I now feel quite confident that the crucial passage in the *Timaeus* clearly implies this doctrine (which was mistaken, as Euclid later showed). For in the passage in question, Plato says quite clearly that '*All* triangles are derived from two, each having a right angle', going on to specify these two as the half-square and half-equilateral. But this can only mean, in the context, that *all* triangles can be composed by combining these two, a view which is equivalent to the mistaken theory of the relative commensurability of all irrationals with sums of rationals and the square roots of two and three.[43]

But Plato did not pretend that he had a proof of the theory in question. On the contrary, he says that he assumes the two triangles as principles 'in accordance with an account which combines probable conjecture with necessity'. And a little later, after explaining that he takes the half-equilateral triangle as the second of his principles, he says, 'The reason is too long a story; but if anybody should test this matter, and prove that it has this property' (I suppose the property that all other triangles can be composed of these two) 'then the prize is his, with all our good will'.[44] The language is somewhat obscure, and no doubt the reason is that Plato lacked a proof of his conjecture concerning these two triangles, and felt it should be supplied by somebody.

The obscurity of the passage had the strange effect that Plato's quite clearly stated choice of triangles to introduce irrationals into his world of Forms seems to have escaped notice, in spite of Plato's emphasis upon the problem in other places. And this fact, in turn, may perhaps explain why Plato's Theory of Forms could appear to Aristotle to be fundamentally the same as the Pythagorean theory of form-numbers,[45] and why Plato's atomism appeared to Aristotle merely as a comparatively minor variation of that of Democritus. Aristotle, in spite of his association of arithmetic with the odd and even, and of geometry with the irrational, does not appear to have taken the problem of the irrationals seriously. It appears that he took Plato's reform programme for geometry for granted; it had been partly carried out by Eudoxus before Aristotle entered the Academy, and Aristotle was only superficially interested in mathematics. He never alludes to the inscription on the Academy.

To sum up, it seems probable that Plato's theory of Forms was, like his theory of matter, a re-statement of the theories of his predecessors, the Pythagoreans and Democritus respectively, in the light of his realisation that the existence of irrationals demanded the emancipation of geometry from arithmetic. By encouraging this emancipation, Plato contributed to the development of Euclid's system, the most important and influential deductive theory ever constructed. By his adoption of geometry as the theory of the world, he provided Aristarchus, Newton, and Einstein with their intellectual toolbox. The calamity of Greek atomism was thus transformed into a momentous achievement. But Plato's scientific interests are partly forgotten. The problem-situation in science which gave rise to his philosophical problems is little understood. And his greatest achievement, the geometrical theory of the world, has influenced our world-picture to such an extent that we unconsciously take it for granted.

6

One example never suffices. As my second example, out of a great many interesting possibilities, I choose Kant. His *Critique of Pure Reason* is one of the most difficult books ever written. Kant wrote in undue haste, and about a problem which, I shall try to show, was insoluble. Nevertheless it was not a pseudo-problem, but an inescapable problem which arose out of the contemporary situation of physical theory.

His book was written for people who knew some Newtonian stellar dynamics and who had at least some idea of its history—of Copernicus, Tycho Brahe, Kepler, and Galileo.

It is perhaps hard for intellectuals of our own day, spoilt and blasé as we are by the spectacle of scientific success, to realise what Newton's theory meant, not just for Kant, but for any eighteenth century thinker. After the unmatched daring with which the Ancients had tackled the riddle of the Universe, there had come a period of long decay, recovery, and then a staggering success. Newton had discovered the long sought secret. His geometrical theory, based on and modelled after Euclid, had been at first received with great misgivings, even by its own originator.[46] The reason was that the gravitational force of attraction was felt to be 'occult', or at least something which needed an explanation. But although no plausible explanation was found (and Newton scorned recourse to *ad-hoc* hypotheses), all misgivings had disappeared long before Kant made his own important contribution to Newtonian theory, 78 years after the *Principia.*[47] No qualified judge[48] of the situation could doubt any longer that the theory was true. It had been tested by the most precise measurements, and it had always been right. It had led to the prediction of minute deviations from Kepler's laws, and to new discoveries. In a time like ours, when theories come and go like the buses in Piccadilly, and when every schoolboy has heard that Newton has long been superseded by Einstein, it is hard to recapture the sense of conviction which Newton's theory inspired, or the sense of elation, and of liberation. A *unique event* had happened in the history of thought, one which could never be repeated: the first and final discovery of the absolute truth about the universe. An age-old dream had come true. Mankind had obtained *knowledge,* real, certain, indubitable, and demonstrable knowledge—divine *scientia* or *epistēmē,* and not merely *doxa,* human opinion.

Thus for Kant, Newton's theory was simply true, and the belief in its truth remained unshaken for a century after Kant's death. Kant to the end accepted what he and everybody else took for a fact, the attainment of *scientia* or *epistēmē.* At first he accepted it without question. This state he called his 'dogmatic slumber'. He was roused from it by Hume.

Hume had taught that there would be no such thing as certain knowledge of universal laws, or *epistēmē*; that all we knew was obtained with the help of observation which could be only of particulars, so that our knowledge was uncertain. His arguments were convincing (and he was, of course, right). But here was the fact, or what appeared as a fact—Newton's attainment of *epistēmē.*

Hume roused Kant to the realisation of the near absurdity of what he never doubted to be a fact. Here was a problem which could not be dismissed. How could a man have got hold of such knowledge? Knowledge which was general, precise, mathematical, demonstrable, indubitable, and yet explanatory of observed facts?

Thus arose the central problem of the *Critique*: 'How is pure natural science possible?'. By 'pure natural science'—*scientia, epistēmē*—Kant means, simply, Newton's theory.

Although the *Critique* is badly written, and although it abounds in bad grammar, this problem was not a linguistic puzzle. Here was knowledge. How could we ever attain it? The question was inescapable. But it was also insoluble. For the apparent fact of the attainment of *epistēmē* was no fact. As we now know, or believe, Newton's theory is no more than a marvelous hypothesis, an astonishingly good approximation; unique indeed, but not as divine truth, only as a unique invention of a human genius; not *epistēmē*, but belonging to the realm of *doxa*. With this, Kant's problem, 'How is pure natural science possible', collapses, and the most disturbing of his perplexities disappear.

Kant's proposed solution of his insoluble problem consisted of what he proudly called his 'Copernican Revolution' of the problem of knowledge. Knowledge—*epistēmē*—was possible because we are not passive receptors of sense data, but their active digesters. By digesting and assimilating them, we form and organise them into a Universe. In this process, we impose upon the material presented to our senses the mathematical laws which are part of our digestive and organising mechanism. Thus our intellect does not discover universal laws in nature, but it prescribes its own laws and imposes them upon nature.

This theory is a strange mixture of absurdity and truth. It is as absurd as the mistaken problem it attempts to solve; for it proves too much, being designed to prove too much. According to Kant's theory, 'pure natural science' is not only *possible;* although he does not realise this, it becomes the *necessary result* of our mental outfit. For if the fact of our attainment of *epistēmē* can be explained at all by the fact that our intellect legislates for and imposes its own laws upon nature, then the first of these two facts cannot be contingent any more than the second. Thus the problem is no longer how Newton could make his discovery but how everybody else could have failed to make it. How is it that our digestive mechanism did not work much earlier?

This is a patently absurd consequence of Kant's idea. But to dismiss it offhand, and to dismiss his problem as a pseudo-problem is not good enough. For we can find an element of truth in his idea (and a much needed correction of some Humean views), after reducing his problem to its proper dimensions. His question, we now know, or believe we know, should have been: 'How are successful hypotheses possible?' And our answer, in the spirit of his Copernican Revolution, might, I suggest, be something like this: Because, as you said, we are not passive receptors of sense data, but active organisms. Because we react to our environment not always merely instinctively, but sometimes consciously, and freely. Because we can invent myths, stories, theories; because we have a thirst for explanation, an insatiable curiosity, a wish to know. Because we not only invent stories and theories, but try them out and see whether they work and how they work. Because by a great effort, by trying hard and erring often, we may sometimes, if we are lucky, succeed in hitting upon a story, an explanation, which 'saves the phenomena'; perhaps by making up a myth about 'invisibles', such as atoms or gravitational forces, which explain the visible. Because knowledge is an adventure of ideas. These ideas, it is true, are produced by us, and not by the world around us; they are not merely the traces of repeated sensations or stimuli or what not; here you were right. But we are more active and free than even you believed; for similar observations or similar environmental situations do not, as your theory implied, produce similar explanations in different men. Nor is the fact that we originate our theories, and that we attempt to impose them upon the world, an explanation of their success, as you believed. For the overwhelming majority of our theories, of our freely invented ideas, are unsuccessful; they do not stand up to searching tests, and are discarded as falsified by experience. Only a very few of them succeed, for a time, in the competitive struggle for survival.[49]

7

Few of Kant's successors appear ever to have clearly understood the precise problem-situation which gave rise to his work. There were two such problems for him, Newton's dynamics of the heavens, and the absolute standards of human brotherhood and justice to which the French revolutionaries appealed, or, as Kant puts it, 'the starry heavens above me, and the moral law within me'. But Kant's starry heavens are seldom identified as an allusion to Newton.[50] From Fichte onward,[51] many have copied Kant's 'method' and the dreadful style of his *Critique.* But most of these imitators have forgotten Kant's original interests and problems, busily trying either to tighten, or else to explain away, the Gordian knot in which Kant, through no fault of his own, had tied himself up.

We must beware of mistaking the well-nigh senseless and pointless subtleties of the imitators for the pressing and genuine problems of the pioneer. We should remember that his problem, although not an empirical one in the ordinary sense, nevertheless turned out, unexpectedly, to be in some sense factual (Kant called such facts 'transcendental'), since it arose from an apparent but non-existent instance of a *scientia* or *epistēmē.* And we should, I submit, seriously consider the suggestion that Kant's answer, in spite of its partial absurdity, contained the nucleus of a philosophy of science.

NOTES

1. I call this a minor problem because I believe that it can easily be solved, by refuting the ('relativistic') doctrine indicated in the text.
2. This view is part of what I have called ''essentialism'. Cf. for example my *Open Society,* ch. II, or 'The Poverty of Historicism I' (*Economica* N.S., 1944, II, No. 42).
3. This tendency can be explained by the principle that theoretical explanations are the more satisfactory the better they can be supported by *independent* evidence. (This somewhat cryptic remark cannot, I fear, be amplified in the present context.)
4. It is of particular importance in this connection to realise that Wittgenstein's use of the term 'meaningless' is *not* the usual and somewhat vague one according to which an absurdly false assertion (such as '2 + 3 = 5.427' or 'I can play Bach on the adding machine') may be called 'meaningless'. He called a statement-like expression 'meaningless' only if it is not a properly constructed statement at all, and therefore neither true nor false. Wittgenstein himself gave the example: 'Socrates is identical'.
5. Since Wittgenstein described his own *Tractatus* as meaningless (see also the next footnote), he distinguished, at least by implication, between revealing and unimportant

nonsense. But this does not affect his main doctrine which I am discussing, the non-existence of philosophical problems. (A discussion of other doctrines of Wittgenstein's can be found in the Notes to my *Open Society*, esp. notes 26, 46, 51, and 52 to ch. II.)

6. It is easy to detect at once one flaw in this doctrine: the doctrine, it may be said, is itself a philosophic theory, claiming to be true, and not to be meaningless. This criticism, however, is a little too cheap. It might be countered in at least two ways. (1) One might say that the doctrine is indeed meaningless *qua* doctrine, but not *qua* activity. (This is the view of Wittgenstein, who said at the end of his *Tractatus Logico-Philosophicus* that whoever understood the book must realise at the end that it was itself meaningless, and must discard it like a ladder, after having used it to reach the desired height.) (2) One might say that the doctrine is not a philosophical but an empirical one, that it states the historical fact that all 'theories' proposed by philosophers are in fact ungrammatical; that they do not, in fact, conform to the rules inherent in those languages in which they appear to be formulated, that this defect turns out to be impossible to remedy; and that every attempt to express them properly has lead to the loss of their philosophic character (and revealed them, for example, as empirical truisms, or as false statements). These two counter arguments rescue, I believe, the threatened consistency of the doctrine, which in this way indeed becomes 'unassailable', as Wittgenstein puts it by the kind of criticism referred to in this note. (See also the next note but one.)
7. The two quotations are not the words of a scientific critic, but, ironically enough, Hegel's own characterisation of the philosophy of his friend and forerunner Schelling. Cf. my *Open Society*, note 4 (and text) to ch. 12.
8. Wittgenstein still upheld the doctrine of the non-existence of philosophical problems in the form here described when I saw him last (in 1946, when he presided over a stormy meeting of the Moral Science Club in Cambridge, on the occasion of my reading a paper on 'Are there Philosophical Problems?'). Since I had never seen any of his unpublished manuscripts which were privately circulated by some of his pupils, I had been wondering whether he had modified what I here call his 'doctrine'; but I found his views on this most fundamental and influential point of his teaching unchanged.
9. Cf. note 52 (2) to ch. 11 of my *Open Society*.
10. I am alluding to G. Kreisel's recent construction of a monotone bounded sequence of rationals every term of which can be actually computed, but which does not possess a computable limit—in contradiction to what appears to be the *prima facie* interpretation of the classical theorem of Bolzano and Weierstrass, but in agreement with Brouwer's doubts about this theorem. Cf. *Journal of Symbolic Logic*, 1952, vol. 17, p. 57.
11. Before Max Born proposed his famous probability interpretation, Schroedinger's wave equation was, some might contend, meaningless.
12. It is very interesting that the imitators were always inclined to believe that the 'master' did his work with the help of a secret method or a trick. It is reported that in J. S. Bach's days some musicians believed that he possessed a secret formula for the construction of fugue themes.
13. I am alluding to a remark by Professor Gilbert Ryle, who says on page 9 of his *Concept of Mind*: 'Primarily I am trying to get some disorders out of my own system.'
14. Already in my *Logik der Forschung* (Vienna, 1935), I pointed out that a theory such as Newton's may be *interpreted* either as factual or as consisting of implicit definitions (in the sense of Poincaré and Eddington), and that the interpretation which a physicist adopts exhibits itself in his *attitude* towards tests which go against his theory rather than in what he says. The dogma of the simple dichotomy has been recently attacked, on very different lines, by F. H. Heinemann (*Proc. of the Xth Intern. Congress of Philosophy* (Amsterdam, 1949), Fasc. 2, 629, Amsterdam, 1949), by W. van O. Quine, and by Morton G.

White. It may be remarked, again from a different point of view, that the dichotomy applies, in a precise sense, only to a formalised language, and therefore is liable to break down for those languages in which we must speak prior to any formalisation, i.e. in those languages in which all the traditional problems were conceived. Some members of the school of the language analysts, however, still believe it a sound method to unmask a theory as 'tautological'.

15. In my *Open Society and Its Enemies,* I have tried to explain in some detail another extra-philosophical root of the same doctrine, viz. a political root. I also discussed there (in note 9 to ch. 6 of the revised 4th edition, 1952) the problem with which I am concerned in the present section, but from a somewhat different angle. The note referred to and the present section partly overlap; but they are largely supplementary to each other. Relevant references (esp. to Plato) omitted here will be found there.
16. There are historians who deny that the term 'science' can be properly applied to any development which is older than the sixteenth or even the seventeenth century. But quite apart from the fact that controversies about labels should be avoided, there can, I believe, no longer be a doubt nowadays about the astonishing similarity, not to say identity, of the aims, interests, activities, arguments, and methods, of, say, Galileo and Archimedes, or Copernicus and Plato, or Kepler and Aristarchus (the 'Copernicus of antiquity'). And any doubt concerning the extreme age of scientific observation, and of careful computations based upon observation, has been dispelled nowadays by the discovery of new evidence concerning the history of ancient astronomy. We can now draw not only a parallel between Tycho and Hipparchus, but even one between Hansen (1857) and Cidenas the Chaldean (314 B.C.), whose computations of the 'constants for the motion of Sun and Moon' are without exception comparable in precision to those of the best nineteenth-century astronomers, 'Cidenas' value for the motion of the Sun from the Node (0′.5 to great), although inferior to Brown's, is superior to at least one of the most widely used modern values', wrote J. K. Fotheringham in 1928, in his most admirable article 'The Indebtedness of Greek to Chaldean Astronomy' (*The Observatory,* 1928, 51, No. 653), upon which my contention concerning the age of astronomy is based.
17. From Aristotle's *Metaphysics.*
18. Plato's distinction (*epistēmē* vs. *doxa*) derives, I think, from Parmenides (*truth* vs. *seeming*). Plato clearly realised that all knowledge of the visible world, the changing world of appearance, consists of *doxa;* that it is tainted by uncertainty even if it utilises the *epistēmē,* the knowledge of the unchanging 'Forms' and of pure mathematics, to the utmost, and even if it interprets the visible world with the help of a theory of the invisible world. Cf. *Crarylus,* 439b ff., *Rep.* 476d ff.; and especially *Timaeus,* 29b ff., where the distinction is applied to those parts of Plato's own theory which we should nowadays call 'physics' or 'cosmology', or, more generally, 'natural science'. They belong, Plato says, to the realm of *doxa* (in spite of the fact that science = *scientia* = *epistēmē;* cf. my remarks on this problem in *The Philosophical Quarterly,* April 1952, p. 168). For a different view concerning Plato's relation to Parmenides, see Sir David Ross, *Plato's Theory of Ideas,* Oxford, 1951, p. 164.
19. This may be seen from Emile Myerson's *Identity and Reality,* one of the most interesting philosophical studies of the development of physical theories.
20. The inference from the existence of motion to that of a void does not follow, because Parmenides' inference from the fullness of the world to the impossibility of motion does not follow. Plato seems to have been the first to see, if only dimly, that in a full world circular or vortex-like motion is possible, provided that there is a liquid-like medium in the world. (Peas can move with the vortices of pea-soup.) This idea, first offered somewhat half-heartedly in the *Timaeus,* becomes the basis of Cartesianism and of the light-ether theory as it was held down to 1905.

21. Democritus' theory admitted also large block-atoms, but the vast majority of his atoms were invisibly small.
22. The barrenness of the 'essentialist' (cf. note 2 above) theory of substance is connected with its anthropomorphism; for substances (as Locke saw) take their plausibility from the experience of a self-identical but changing and unfolding self. But although we may welcome the fact that Aristotle's substances have disappeared from *physics,* there is nothing wrong, as Professor Hayek says, in thinking anthropomorphically about *man;* and there is no reason why they should disappear from psychology.
23. Cf. Democritus, Diels, fragm. 11 (cf. Anaxagoras, Dield fragm. 21; see also fragm. 7).
24. Cf. Sextus Empiricus, *Adv. mathem.* (Bekker) vii. 140, p. 221, 23B.
25. 'Relativistic' in the sense of philosophical relativism, e.g. of Protagoras' *homo mensura* doctrine. It is, unfortunately, still necessary to emphasise that Einstein's theory has nothing in common with philosophical relativism.
26. Such as those of Bacon; the theory (but fortunately not the practice) of the early *Royal Society;* and in our time, of Mach (who opposed atomic theory); and of the sense-data theorists.
27. Cf. Diels, fragm. 155, which must be interpreted in the light of Archimedes (ed. Heiberg) II^2, p. 428 f. Cf. S. Luria's most important article 'Die Infinitesimalmethode der antiken Atomisten' (*Quellen & Studien zur Gesch. d. Math.* Abt. B. Bd. 2, Heft 2 (1932), p. 142).
28. Cf. A. March, *Natur und Erkenntnis,* Vienna, 1948, p. 193 f.
29. Cf. S. Luria, *op. cit.,* esp. pp. 148 ff., 172 ff.
30. This point for point reply is preserved in Aristotle's *On Generation and Corruption,* 316a 14 ff., a very important passage first identified as Democritean by I. Hammer Jensen in 1910 and carefully discussed by Luria who says (*op. cit.* 135) of Parmenides and Zeno: 'Democritus borrows their deductive arguments, but he arrives at the opposite conclusion.'
31. Cf. G. H. Hardy and H. M. Wright, *Introduction of the Theory to Numbers* (1938), pp. 39, 42, where a very interesting historical remark on Theodorus' proof, as reported in Plato's *Theacteteus,* will be found.
32. Rather than *On Irrational Lines and Atoms,* as I translated in note 9 to ch. 6 of my *Open Society* (revised ed.). What is probably meant by the title (considering Plato's passage mentioned in the next note) might, I think, be best rendered by '*On Crazy Distances and Atoms'.* Cf. H. Vogt, *Bibl. Math.,* 1910, 10, 147, and S. Luria, *op. cit.* pp. 168 ff. where it is convincingly suggested that (Arist.) *De insec. lin.* 968b 17 and Plutarch, *De comm. notit.,* 38, 2, p. 1078 f., contain traces of Democritus' work. According to these sources, Democritus' argument was this. *If lines are infinitely divisible,* then they are composed of an infinity of ultimate units and are therefore *all* related like $\infty{:}\infty$, that is to say, they are all 'non-comparable' (there is no proportion). Indeed, if lines are considered as classes of points, the 'number' (potency) of the points of a line is, according to modern views, equal for all lines, whether the lines are finite or infinite. This fact has been described as 'paradoxical' (for example, by Bolzano) and might well have been described as 'crazy' by Democritus. It may be noted that, according to Brouwer, even the classical theory of the *measure* of a continuum leads to fundamentally the same results; since he asserts that all classical continua have zero measure, the absence of a ratio is here expressed by 0:0. Democritus' result (and his theory of *ameres*) appears to be inescapable as long as geometry is based on the Pythagorean *arithmetical method,* i.e. on the counting of dots.
33. This would be in keeping with the fact mentioned in the note cited from the *Open Society,* that the term '*alogos*' is only much later known to be used for 'irrational', and that Plato who

(*Repub.* 534d) alludes to Democritus' title, nevertheless never uses '*alogos*' as a synonym for '*arrhētos*'.

34. See S. Luria, esp. on Plutarch, *loc. cit.*
35. Plato took over, more especially, Democritus' theory of vortices (Diels, fragm. 167, 164; cf. Anaxagoras, Diels 9; and 12, 13); see also the next footnote, and his theory of what we nowadays would call gravitational phenomena (Diels, 164; Anaxagoras, 12, 13, 15, and 2)—a theory which, slightly modified by Aristotle, was ultimately discarded by Galileo.
36. Plato's reconciliation of atomism and the theory of the *plenum* ('nature abhors a void') became of the greatest importance for the history of physics down to our own day. For it influenced Descartes strongly, became the basis of the theory of ether and light, and thus ultimately, via Huyghens and Maxwell, of de Broglie's and of Schroedinger's wave mechanics.
37. The only exception is the partial reappearance of arithmetical methods in the New Quantum Theory, e.g. in the electron shell theory of the periodic system based upon Pauli's exclusion principle.

    Concerning the modern tendency towards what is sometimes called 'arithmetisation of geometry' (a tendency which is hardly characteristic of all modern work on geometry), it should be noted that there is little similarity with the Pythagorean approach since *infinite sequences* of natural numbers are its main instrument rather than the natural numbers themselves.
38. For a similar view of Plato's and Euclid's influence, see G. F. Hemens, *Proc. of the Xth Intern. Congress of Philosophy* (Amsterdam 1949), Fasc. 2, 847.
39. Cf. Homer's explanation of the visible world before Troy with the help of the invisible world of the Olympus. The idea loses, with Democritus, some of its theological character (which is still strong in Parmenides, although less so in Anaxagoras) but regains it with Plato, only to lose it soon afterwards.
40. See the references given above.
41. For the process by which the triangles are stamped out of space (the 'mother') by the ideas (the 'father'), cf. my *Open Society,* note 15 to ch. 3, and the references there given, as well as note 9 to ch. 6.
42. In the last quoted note.
43. In the note referred to I also conjectured that it was the close approximation of the sum of these two square roots to π which encouraged Plato in his mistaken theory. Although I have no new evidence, I believe that this conjecture is much strengthened by the view that Plato in fact believed in the mistaken theory described here.
44. The two quotations are from the *Timaeus,* 53c/d and 542/b.
45. I believe that our consideration may throw some light on the problem of Plato's famous 'two principles'—'The One' and 'The Indeterminate Dyad'. The following interpretation develops a suggestion made by van der Wielen (*De Ideegetallen van Plato,* 1941, p. 132 f.) and brilliantly defended against van der Wielen's own criticism by Ross (Plato's *Theory of Ideas,* p. 201). We assume that the 'Indeterminate Dyad' is a straight line or distance, not to be interpreted as a unit distance, or as having yet been measured at all. We assume that a point (limit, *monas,* 'One') is placed successively in such positions that it divides the Dyad according to the ratio I:n, for any natural number n. Then we can describe the 'generation' of the numbers as follows. For $n = 1$, the Dyad is divided into two parts whose ratio is I:I. This may be interpreted as the 'generation' of Twoness out of Oneness and the Dyad, since we have divided the Dyad into *two* equal parts. Having thus 'generated' the number 2, we can divide the Dyad according to the ratio I:2 (and the larger section, as before, according to the ratio I:I), thus generating *three* equal parts and the number 3; generally, the 'generation' of a number n gives rise to a division of the Dyad

in the ratio $1:n$, and with this, to the 'generation' of the number $n + 1$. (And in each state intervenes the 'One', the point which introduces a limit or form or measure into the otherwise 'indeterminate' Dyad, afresh, to create the new number; this remark is intended to strengthen Ross' case against van der Wielen's.)

Now it should be noted that this procedure, although it 'generates' (in the first instance, at least) only the series of natural numbers, nevertheless contains a *geometrical* element—the division of a line, first into two equal parts, and then into two parts according to a certain proportion $1:n$. Both kinds of division are in need of geometrical methods, and the second, more especially, needs a method such as Eudoxus' Theory of Proportions. Now I suggest that Plato began to ask himself why he should not divide the Dyad also in the proportion of $1:\sqrt{2}$ and of $1:\sqrt{3}$. This, he must have felt, was a departure from the method by which the natural numbers are generated; it is less 'arithmetical' still, and it needs more specifically 'geometrical' methods. But it would 'generate', in the place of natural numbers, linear elements in the proportion $1:\sqrt{2}$ and $1:\sqrt{3}$, which may be identical with the 'atomic lines' (*Metaphysics,* 992a19) from which the atomic triangles are constructed. At the same time, the characterisation of the Dyad as 'indeterminate' would become highly appropriate, in view of the Pythagorean attitude (cf. Philolaos, Diels fragm. 2 and 3) towards the irrational. (Perhaps the name 'The Great and the Small' began to be replaced by 'The Indeterminate Dyad' when irrational proportions were generated in addition to rational ones.)

Assuming this view to be correct, we might conjecture that Plato approached slowly (beginning in the *Hippias Major,* and thus long before the *Republic*—as opposed to a remark made by Ross *op. cit.*, top of page 56) to the view that *the irrationals are numbers,* since both the natural numbers and the irrationals are 'generated' by similar and essentially geometric processes. But once this view is reached (and it was first reached, it appears, in the *Epinomis* 990d–e, whether or not this work is Plato's), then even the irrational triangles of the *Timaeus* become 'numbers' (i.e. characterised by numerical, if irrational, propositions). But with this, the peculiar contribution of Plato, and the difference between his and the Pythagorean theory, is liable to become indiscernible; and this may explain why it has been lost sight of, even by Aristotle.

46. See Newton's letter to Bentley, 1693.
47. The so-called Kant-Laplacean Hypothesis published by Kant in 1755.
48. There had been some very pertinent criticism (especially by Leibniz and Berkeley) but in view of the success of the theory it was—I believe rightly—felt that the critics had somehow missed the point of the theory. We must not forget that even today the theory still stands, with only minor modifications, as an excellent first (or, in view of Kepler, perhaps as a second) approximation.
49. The ideas of this 'answer' were elaborated in my *Logik der Forschung* (1935).
50. That this identification is corrected may be seen from the last ten lines of the penultimate paragraph of the *Critique of Practical Reason.*
51. Cf. my *Open Society,* note 58 to ch. 12.

SEMANTIC ASCENT

W. V. Quine

Part of our concern here has been with the question what a theory's commitments to objects consist in, and of course this second-order question is about words. But what is noteworthy is that we have talked more of words than of objects even when most concerned to decide what there really is: what objects to admit on our own account.

This would not have happened if and insofar as we had lingered over the question whether in particular there are wombats, or whether there are unicorns. Discourse about non-linguistic objects would have been an excellent medium in which to debate those issues. But when the debate shifts to whether there are points, miles, numbers, attributes, propositions, facts, or classes, it takes on an in some sense philosophical cast, and straightaway we find ourselves talking of words almost to the exclusion of the non-linguistic objects under debate.

Carnap has long held that the questions of philosophy, when real at all, are questions of language; and the present observation would seem to illustrate his point. He holds that the philosophical questions of what there is are questions of how we may most conveniently fashion our "linguistic framework," and not, as in the case of the wombat or unicorn, questions about extralinguistic reality.[1] He holds that those philosophical questions are only apparently about sorts of objects, and are really pragmatic questions of language policy.

But why should this be true of the philosophical questions and not of theoretical questions generally? Such a distinction of status is of a piece of the notion of analyticity, and as little to be trusted. After all, theoretical sentences in general are defensible only pragmatically; we can but assess the structural merits of the theory which embraces them along with sentences directly conditioned to multifarious stimulations. How then can Carnap draw a line across this theoretical part and hold that the sentences this side of the line enjoy non-verbal content or meaning in a way that those beyond the line do not? His own appeal to convenience of linguistic framework allows pragmatic connections across the line. What other sort of connection can be asked anywhere, short of direct conditioning to non-verbal stimulations?

Yet we do recognize a shift from talk of objects to talk of words as debate progresses from existence of wombats and unicorns to existence of points, miles, classes, and the rest. How can we account for this? Amply, I think, by proper account of a useful and much used manoeuvre which I shall call *semantic ascent.*

Reprinted by permission of The Massachusetts Institute of Technology and the author, from W. V. Quine, "Semantic Ascent," in Quine, *Word and Object,* pp. 270–276. Cambridge, Massachusetts: The MIT Press, 1960.

It is the shift from talk of miles to talk of 'mile'. It is what leads from the material (*inhaltlich*) mode into the formal mode, to invoke an old terminology of Carnap's. It is the shift from talking in certain terms to talking about them. It is precisely the shift that Carnap thinks of as divesting philosophical questions of a deceptive guise and setting them forth in their true colors. But this tenet of Carnap's is the part that I do not accept. Semantic ascent, as I speak of it, applies anywhere.[2] 'There are wombats in Tasmania' might be paraphrased as ' 'Wombat' is true of some creatures in Tasmania', if there were any point in it. But it does happen that semantic ascent is more useful in philosophical connections than in most, and I think I can explain why.

Consider what it would be like to debate over the existence of miles without ascending to talk of 'mile'. "Of course there are miles. Wherever you have 1760 yards you have a mile." "But there are no yards either. Only bodies of various lengths." "Are the earth and moon separated by bodies of various lengths?" The continuation is lost in a jumble of invective and question-begging. When on the other hand we ascend to 'mile' and ask which of its contexts are useful and for what purposes, we can get on; we are no longer caught in the toils of our opposed uses.

The strategy of semantic ascent is that it carries the discussion into a domain where both parties are better agreed on the objects (viz., words) and on the main terms concerning them. Words, or their inscriptions, unlike points, miles, classes, and the rest, are tangible objects of the size so popular in the marketplace, where men of unlike conceptual schemes communicate at their best. The strategy is one of ascending to a common part of two fundamentally disparate conceptual schemes, the better to discuss the disparate foundations. No wonder it helps in philosophy.

But it also figures in the natural sciences. Einstein's theory of relativity was accepted in consequence not just of reflections on time, light, headlong bodies, and the perturbations of Mercury, but of reflections also on the theory itself, as discourse, and its simplicity in comparison with alternative theories. Its departure from classical conceptions of absolute time and length is too radical to be efficiently debated at the level of object talk unaided by semantic ascent. The case was similar, if in lesser degrees, for the disruptions of traditional outlook occasioned by the doctrines of molecules and electrons. These particles come after wombats and unicorns, and before points and miles, in a significant gradation.

The device of semantic ascent has been used much and carefully in axiomatic studies in mathematics, for the avoidance, again, of question-begging. In axiomatizing some already familiar theory, geometry say, one used to be in danger of imagining that he had deduced some familiar truth of the theory purely from his axioms when actually he had made inadvertent use of further geometrical knowledge. As a precaution against this danger, a device other than semantic ascent was at first resorted to: the device of disinterpretation. One feigned to understand only the logical vocabulary and not the distinctive terms of the axiom system concerned. This was an effective way of barring information extraneous to the axioms and thus limiting one's inferences to what the axioms logically implied. The device of disinterpretation had impressive side effects, some good, such as the rise of abstract algebra, and some bad, such as the notion that in pure mathematics "we never know what we are talking about, nor whether what we are saying is true."[3] At any rate, with Frege's achievement of a full formalization of logic, an alternative and more refined precaution against question-begging became available to axiomatic studies; and it is a case, precisely, of what I am calling semantic ascent. Given the deductive apparatus of logic in the form of specified operations on notational forms, the question whether a given formula follows logically from given axioms reduces to the question whether the specified operations on notational forms are capable of leading to that formula from the axioms. An affirmative answer to such a question can be established without disinterpretation, yet without fear of circularity, indeed without using the terms of the theory at all except to talk about them and the operations upon them.

We must also notice a further reason for semantic ascent in philosophy. This further reason holds also, and more strikingly, for logic; so let us look there first. Most truths of elementary logic contain extralogical terms; thus 'If all Greeks are men and all men are mortal . . .'. The main truths of physics, in contrast, contain terms of physics only. Thus whereas we can expound physics in its full generality without semantic ascent, we can expound logic in a general way only by talking of forms of sentences. The generality wanted in physics can be got by quantifying over non-linguistic objects, while the dimension of generality wanted for logic runs crosswise to what can be got by such quantification. It is a difference in shape of field and not in content; the above syllogism about the Greeks need owe its truth no more peculiarly to language than other sentences do.

There are characteristic efforts in philosophy, those coping e.g. with perplexities of lion-hunting or believing, that resemble logic in their need of semantic ascent as a means of generalizing beyond examples.[4] Not that I would for a moment deny that when the perplexities about lion-hunting or believing and its analogues are cleared up they are cleared up by an improved structuring of discourse; but the same is true of an advance in physics. The same is true even though the latter restructuring be led up to (as often happens) within discourse of objects, and not by semantic ascent.

For it is not as though considerations of systematic efficacy, broadly pragmatic considerations, were operative only when we make a semantic ascent and talk of theory, and factual considerations of the behavior of objects in the world were operative only when we avoid semantic ascent and talk within the theory. Considerations of systematic efficacy are equally essential in both cases; it is just that in the one case we voice them and in the other we are tacitly guided by them. And considerations of the behavior of objects in the world, even behavior affecting our sensory surfaces by contact or radiation, are likewise essential in both cases.

There are two reasons why observation is felt to have no such bearing on logic and philosophy as it has on theoretical physics. One is traceable to misapprehensions about semantic ascent. The other is traceable to curriculum classifications. This latter factor tends likewise to make one feel that observation has no such bearing on mathematics as it has on theoretical physics. Theoretical assertions in physics, being terminologically physics, are generally conceded to owe a certain empirical content to the physical observations which, however indirectly, they help to systematize, whereas laws of so-called logic and mathematics, however useful in systematizing physical observations, are not considered to pick up any empirical substance thereby. A more reasonable attitude is that there are merely variations in degree of centrality to the theoretical structure, and in degree of relevance to one or another set of observations.

Earlier I spoke of dodges whereby philosophers have thought to enjoy the systematic benefits of abstract objects without suffering the objects. There is one more such dodge in what I have been inveighing against in these last pages: the suggestion that the acceptance of such objects is a linguistic convention distinct somehow from serious views about reality.

The question what there is is a shared concern of philosophy and most other non-fiction genres. The descriptive answer has been given only in part, but at some length. A representative assortment of land masses, seas, planets, and stars have been individually described in the geography and astronomy books, and an occasional biped or other middle-sized object in the biographies and art books. Description has been stepped up by mass production in zoology, botany, and mineralogy, where things are grouped by similarities and described collectively. Physics, by more ruthless abstraction from differences in detail, carries mass description farther still. And even pure mathematics belongs to the descriptive answer to the question what there is; for the things about which the question asks do not exclude the numbers, classes, functions, etc., if such there be, whereof pure mathematics treats.

What distinguishes between the ontological philosopher's concern and all this is only breadth of categories. Given physical objects in general, the natural scientist is the man to decide about wombats and unicorns. Given classes, or whatever other broad realm of objects the mathematician needs, it is for the mathematician to say whether in particular there are any even prime numbers or any cubic numbers that are sums of pairs of cubic numbers. On the other hand it is scrutiny of this uncritical acceptance of the realm of physical objects itself, or of classes, etc., that devolves upon ontology. Here is the task of making explicit what had been tacit, and precise what had been vague; of exposing and resolving paradoxes, smoothing kinks, lopping off vestigial growths, clearing ontological slums.

The philosopher's task differs from the others', then, in detail; but in no such drastic way as those suppose who imagine for the philosopher a vantage point outside the conceptual scheme that he takes in charge. There is no such cosmic exile. He cannot study and revise the fundamental conceptual scheme of science and common sense without having some conceptual scheme, whether the same or another no less in need of philosophical scrutiny, in which to work. He can scrutinize and improve the system from within, appealing to coherence and simplicity; but this is the theoretician's method generally. He has recourse to semantic ascent, but so has the scientist. And if the theoretical scientist in his remote way is bound to save the eventual connections with non-verbal stimulation, the philosopher in his remoter way is bound to save them too. True, no experiment may be expected to settle an ontological issue; but this is only because such issues are connected with surface irritations in such multifarious ways, through such a maze of intervening theory.

NOTES

1. Carnap, "Empiricism, Semantics, and Ontology."
2. In a word, I reject Carnap's doctrine of "quasi-syntactic" or "pseudo-object" sentences, but accept his distinction between the material and the formal mode. See his *Logical Syntax,* 63–64. (It was indeed I, if I may reminisce, who in 1934 proposed 'material mode' to him as translation of his German.)
3. Russell, *Mysticism and Logic and Other Essays,* p. 75. The essay in question dates from 1901, and happily the aphorism expressed no enduring attitude on Russell's part. But the attitude expressed has been widespread.
4. Wittgenstein's characteristic style, in his later period, consisted in avoiding semantic ascent by sticking to the examples.

CAN ANALYTICAL PHILOSOPHY BE SYSTEMATIC, AND SHOULD IT BE?

Michael Dummett

The term 'analytical philosophy' denotes, not a school, but a cluster of schools, sharing certain basic presuppositions, but different amongst themselves in every other possible way. As in all movements, its most bitter quarrels have been internal ones. When I was a student at Oxford in the late 1940's, the dominant philosophical influence was that of RYLE; and, despite the fact that RYLE had started his career as the English exponent of the philosophy of HUSSERL, and had in 1929 published a critical but highly respectful review of *Sein und Zeit,* the enemy, at the time when I was a student, was not HEIDEGGER; HEIDEGGER was perceived only as a figure of fun, too absurd to be taken seriously as a threat to the kind of philosophy practised at Oxford. The enemy was, rather, CARNAP: he it was who was seen in RYLE'S Oxford as the embodiment of philosophical error, above all, as the exponent of a false philosophical methodology. Of course, the CARNAP whom RYLE taught us to reject was a caricature of the real CARNAP; but, so strong was this prejudice, that it took me, for one, many years to realise that there is much worthy of study in CARNAP'S writings. Nothing can more vividly illustrate the contrast between the philosophical atmosphere in which my British contemporaries grew up and that in which American philosophers of the same generation developed: for in the United States CARNAP was accepted as the leader of the analytical school, and the most influential American practitioners of analytical philosophy, from QUINE down, are people whose philosophical formation was CARNAPian, and whose thought can be understood only as the outcome of a painful effort to scrutinise and correct certain of CARNAP'S fundamental doctrines.

The divergence of tradition between analytical philosophy as practised on one side of the Atlantic and on the other bears strongly upon the question we have to examine. It would be ridiculous to address the question, 'Can analytical philosophy be systematic?', to the author of *Der logische Aufbau der Welt;* and, though few American philosophers have followed their mentor so closely as to produce such rivals to that work as NELSON GOODMAN'S *Structure of Appearance,* most are unanimous in regarding philosophy, with QUINE, as at least cognate with the natural sciences, as part of the same general enterprise as they. In those English philosophical circles dominated by the later WITTGENSTEIN or by AUSTIN, on the other hand, the answer given to this question was a resounding 'No': for them, the attempt to be systematic in philosophy was the primal error, founded upon a total misconception of the character of the subject.

Reprinted by permission of the author, from Michael Dummett, "Can Analytical Philosophy Be Systematic, and Should It Be?" *Hegel-Studien,* Beiheft 17 (1977), pp. 305–326.

The reason lay in what was thought to be the fundamental discovery, enunciated in WITTGENSTEIN's *Tractatus* (*Abhandlung*), of the nature of philosophy: philosophy is not a science. Here 'science' is used in the most general way, to embrace any discipline (art history, for example) whose aim is to arrive at and establish *truths.* According to WITTGENSTEIN, both in his earlier and his later phases, this is *not* the object of philosophy. Chemistry aims to discover chemical truths, and history to discover historical truths, but the successful outcome of philosophy is not a number of true propositions whose truth was not known before. Philosophy is concerned, not to establish truths of a very general kind, not even truths which can be arrived at by ratiocination alone, but to rectify certain kinds of misunderstanding, the misunderstandings we have of our own concepts; and this means our misunderstanding of our own language, since to possess a concept is to be the master of a certain fragment of language. Human language is an instrument of enormous complexity, and our mastery of it is largely an implicit mastery: we are able to employ it in practice, but, when we try to give an explicit account of that practice, we commit gross errors. Because it is in our nature to be reflective, to try to explain all that we observe, we do not rest content with being able to make practical use of our language for the ordinary transactions of life, but try to frame hypotheses about the general principles according to which that language functions; or, mistakenly regarding language as a mere external covering with which the thought is clothed, we attempt to strip off this outer clothing and penetrate to the pure thought beneath. In doing this, we are like savages gaping at a machine whose working they have not the background to comprehend: we form fantastic misconceptions of the way our language works. Like all our thought, these misconceptions are themselves expressed in language; but language, when it is made to serve such a purpose, is like an engine racing while disconnected—it does no work, not even the wrong work; it does not issue even in propositions which are to be denied and replaced by true ones, but merely expresses characteristic kinds of intellectual confusion the only remedy for which is extended and patient treatment, in the sense in which a doctor treats an illness. It is this treatment which is the proper work of the philosopher; and a large part of it will consist in drawing the sufferer's attention to the actual, often humdrum, facts about our employment of language, facts of which he is of course already aware, but which he had overlooked in the excitement generated by the misleading picture which had gripped his mind. If this is the nature of philosophy, then evidently it cannot be systematic. There can be no means by which every possible misunderstanding can be blocked off in advance; each must be treated as we encounter it. And, even when we are concerned with the eradication of some specific misconception, we shall not accomplish it by substituting some correct theory for a mistaken one, because we are not operating in a region where theories are required at all. What we are aiming to do is to substitute a clear vision for a distorted one. What there is to be seen is not a matter for philosophy at all, but for science, for empirical observation; the philosopher has no more business saying what there is to be seen than does the oculist:

what he is trying to prevent is a frame of mind in which whatever is seen is grotesquely misinterpreted. In so far as the philosopher has any business at all to state what there is to be seen, the facts which he has to recall will not be ones that the philosopher has discovered, but, rather, very familiar facts known to everybody, and he will recall them only because they fit badly into the theory, or pseudo-theory, in which the conceptual confusion is embodied. But such recalling of familiar facts, particularly facts about language, will not of itself provide a sufficient treatment of the confusion, because, until the confusion is removed, they will themselves be misperceived; the philosopher has to grapple with the seductive reasoning which so compulsively engendered the misunderstanding in the first place, or by which it defends itself against criticism. But the philosopher's reasoning does not issue, like the mathematician's, in theorems which he can then enunciate; when he has unpicked the tangle, and the strands lie separated from one another, he has finished his work: then we see the world aright. There is, however, nothing that we can state as the result of the philosopher's work: an undistorted vision is not itself an object of sight.

The AUSTINian reason for rejecting system in philosophy is less powerful than WITTGENSTEIN's, and needs less attention, partly because it no longer seems in the least attractive, and partly because, to a greater extent than with other philosophers, AUSTIN's practice failed to tally with his official methodology. His official view was this: philosophical problems are to be resolved by attention to the actual uses of words; so we may as well set about studying the uses of words without keeping our eyes on the problems, which will take care of themselves, that is, evaporate, if we do our work satisfactorily. Philosophy, on this view, is not a therapy but an empirical study: we have to describe, in detail, particular uses of particular words. But it is not a systematic study, because its subject-matter is incapable of systematisation; we cannot arrange our results into some aesthetically satisfying deductive theory, because they form only a collection of loosely connected *particular* facts, as particular as those entered in the dictionary.

I began by remarking that the term 'analytical philosophy' covers the work of philosophers of exceedingly diverse views and approaches: but, striking as these divergences have been in the past, my remark probably applies less to the strictly contemporary scene than it does to any time in the past. There has been a very considerable rapprochement between the various branches of analytical philosophy; and this has been due to three interconnected facts. First, the ever more widespread knowledge of and attention to the work of FREGE. Up to, say, 1950, the influence of FREGE upon analytical philosophy had been very great, but it had been exerted largely at second hand, transmitted through a few rare, though influential, philosophers who had studied him directly—CHURCH, CARNAP, RUSSELL and, above all, WITTGENSTEIN; and so, for the most part, FREGE's doctrines reached others only as understood by those writers, and not clearly distinguished from their own opinions. Now, a quarter-century later, and a half-century after FREGE's death, every serious philosophy student in Britain or the United States acknowledges a thorough study of FREGE's writings as essential to a philosophical education; and the shift in perspective—and not merely in historical perspective—brought about by the recognition of FREGE as the fountain-head of analytical philosophy, rather than supposing it to have begun with RUSSELL, or with WITTGENSTEIN, or with the Vienna Circle, has had a profound, and unifying, effect. Secondly, the work of contemporary American philosophers is at the present moment far more influential in Britain than it has ever been before; for the first time since I have been at Oxford, and probably for the first time since the influence of HEGEL was predominant there, work done in philosophy further away than Cambridge has come to occupy the centre of the stage. Finally, as cause or consequence of the first two, the focus of interest within the subject has altered. For several decades, the most vigorous branch of philosophy within Britain was philosophical psychology—the study of questions concerning motive, intention, pleasure, and the like: now it is the philosophy of language. Formerly, the most usual appellation for the type of philosophy practised at Oxford was 'linguistic philosophy': but that no more implied that its adherents worked principally upon questions concerning language than the name 'logical positivism' implied that the principal contribution of the members of that school was to logic. Just as for the positivists logic was an instrument, not the field of study, so for linguistic philosophy the study of language was for the most part a means and not an end. In part this was due to the idea that no general doctrine about language was needed as a basis for the investigation, by linguistic means, of philosophically problematic concepts, in part to the idea that such a doctrine was needed, but had already been attained. Neither idea would find much favour now: the philosophy of language is seen both as that part of the subject which underlies all the rest, and as that which it is currently most fruitful to investigate.

This tendency within analytical philosophy is recent only so far as British philosophy is concerned: it represents an alignment of the British with the American school; and I should like to declare myself wholly in sympathy with it. In saying this, I am not wishing to endorse particular doctrines currently popular amongst American philosophers of language—linguistic holism, the rejection of a substantive distinction between sense and reference, the causal theory of reference, or possible-worlds semantics, all of which appear to me mistaken in whole or part—but only their general orientation. In order to give my reasons for this, I must pose the question what distinguishes analytical philosophy, in all its manifestations, from other schools.

A succinct definition would be: analytical philosophy is post-FREGEan philosophy. FREGE's fundamental achievement was to alter our perspective in philosophy, to replace epistemology, as the starting-point of the subject, by what he called 'logic'. What FREGE called 'logic' included, but only as a proper part, what everyone else, before and since, has called 'logic': it also embraced precisely what is now called 'philosophy of language'. That would have sounded odd to FREGE, for he almost always used the word 'Sprache' to mean 'natural language', and he had a strong contempt for natural language; but, even were that contempt completely justified, so that, as he believed, we have, for the purpose of serious philosophical study, to replace natural language by an artificially devised language purged of its defects, FREGE's work has the interest that he claims for it only if the resulting formalised language is a more perfect instrument for doing the same thing as that which we normally do by means of natural language, and if, therefore, in studying the formalised language, we are studying the ideal which natural language strives after, but fails to attain. Thus we may characterise analytical philosophy as that which follows FREGE in accepting that the philosophy of language is the foundation of the rest of the subject.

For FREGE, as for all subsequent analytical philosophers, the philosophy of language is the foundation of all other philosophy because it is only by the analysis of language that we can analyse thought. Thoughts differ from all else that is said to be among the contents of the mind in being wholly communicable: it is of the essence of thought that I can convey to you the very thought I have, as opposed to being able to tell you merely something about what my thought is like. It is of the essence of thought, not merely to be communicable, but to be communicable, without residue, by means of language. In order to understand thought, it is necessary, therefore, to comprehend the means by which thought is expressed. If the philosopher attempts, in the manner I mentioned earlier, to strip thought of its linguistic clothing and penetrate to its pure naked essence, he will merely succeed in confusing the thought itself with the subjective inner accompaniments of thinking. We communicate thoughts by means of language because we have an implicit understanding of the working of language, that is, of the principles governing the use of language; it is these principles, which relate to what is open to view in the employment of language, unaided by any supposed contact between mind and mind other than via the medium of language, which endow our sentences with the senses that they carry. In order to analyse thought, therefore, it is necessary to make explicit those principles, regulating our use of language, which we already implicitly grasp.

This task has both a general and a particular aspect. In its general aspect, our concern is with the fundamental outlines of an account of how language functions: and that constitutes the philosophy of language, which is accordingly that philosophical theory which is the foundation of all the rest. But, in its particular aspects, we may be concerned with the analysis of thoughts concerning this or that particular subject-matter, or involving this or that cluster of concepts: and these are the branches of philosophy which spring out of the parent stem. Unless our general account of language is on the right lines, the analysis which, in particular branches of philosophy, we give of special types of sentence or special forms of expression is liable to be defective, which is why the philosophy of language lies at the base of the entire structure; this, of course, does not mean that all work in other parts of philosophy ought to cease until a fully adequate philosophy of language has been attained. FREGE himself did not make the claim that the only task of philosophy is the analysis of thought, and hence of language—that was left for WITTGENSTEIN to enunciate in the *Tractatus;* but by his practice in the one particular branch of philosophy in which he worked, the philosophy of mathematics, he left little doubt that that was his view; the very same grounds on which he resisted the intrusion of psychological considerations into what he called 'logic', namely that thought is objective and common to all, whereas mental processes are private and subjective, are given by him for keeping them out of the philosophy of mathematics. The proper philosophical study of mathematics proceeds by analysing the language of mathematics. Only one who persisted in confusing thoughts with inner mental processes would think that this involved diverting our attention from the *objects* of mathematics to the *experience* of mathematical activity; experience does not come into it at all, and, as for mathematical objects, the philosopher will need to talk about these in so far as it is necessary to do so in order to give an adequate account of mathematical language. The difference between the mathematician and the philosopher of mathematics is not that the former is concerned with mathematical objects and the latter is concerned only with the inner experiences of the mathematician, but that the mathematician is concerned to establish the truth or falsity of mathematical statements, while the philosopher is concerned with the way in which they are endowed with sense. There is no reason to suppose that FREGE would have adopted any different attitude to any other branch of philosophy, if he had chosen to work in it.

In the foregoing remarks, I have attempted an account of certain fundamental views, expressly advocated by FREGE or implicit in his philosophical method, which may also be claimed, with some plausibility, to be shared by all practitioners of analytical philosophy; but, even if I have succeeded, in practice the effect of these common beliefs on the work of the various analytical philosophers has been very different. FREGE and the early WITTGENSTEIN both made direct contributions to the philosophy of language: but, when we reach the Vienna Circle, we have to do with philosophers whose interest in the subject was no longer much for its own sake, but rather because they saw it as an armoury from which they could draw weapons that would arm them for combat in other areas of philosophy. The principle of verification was for them a sword with which they could slay numberless metaphysical dragons; but now that we look back, it is difficult to see how, out of that principle, could be fashioned a coherent philosophy of language, or theory of meaning, at all. It was not in itself even the summary of a theory of meaning, but a consequence claimed to follow from some theory even the outline of which was never once clearly formulated. And, if this is to be said of the positivists, something even stronger holds for the 'ordinary language' school dominant for a period at Oxford. They jettisoned the slogan 'Meaning is the method of verification' for the slogan, borrowed from WITTGENSTEIN, 'Meaning is use': but, while the former slogan hinted at some unitary theory of meaning, a key concept in terms of which a general model could be given for the understanding of a sentence, the latter slogan was expressly used to reject the idea that a uniform account is possible. Only particularity was acceptable; a general theory was a *fatuus ignis,* generated by the philosopher's vain hopes of finding a pattern where none existed. All that a philosopher ought to try to do was to explain the 'use' of each sentence, one by one; for that was all that can be done.

Now, whatever be the right account of language, such a conception can be recognised offhand as wrong, for the obvious reason that we do not learn sentences one by one. It would fit a code of signals, the significance of each of which has to be learned separately, but not a language. It should hardly need pointing out to anyone, least of all to a school of philosophers who prided themselves on their attention to language, that we understand a sentence by understanding the words that compose it and the principles according to which they are put together. But the fact is that there is no formulation of the doctrine of total particularism advocated by this school that will fit that basic fact; for it is *sentences,* not words, that have a 'use' in the intended sense, sentences by means of which, in WITTGENSTEIN's terminology, we 'make a move in the language-game'. Any workable account of language must, therefore, represent a mastery of language as consisting in a grasp of some principles not relating to complete individual sentences, even if these consist solely of principles relating to individual words and to modes of sentence-construction. A grasp of such principles will *issue* in a knowledge of the 'use' that can be made of any given sentence of the language; but it will not be *constituted* by such knowledge. The question is what are the principles an implicit grasp of which composes an understanding of the language; and to answering this question the 'ordinary language' school had virtually nothing to contribute.

The rejection of generality, the insistence on concentrating on the 'use' of each individual sentence, led to the giving of accounts of 'use' which were often remarkably superficial, even when subtle. They were superficial, because they employed psychological and semantic concepts which a theory of meaning has no right to presuppose as already understood, because it can be expected to explain them; what else, after all, could anyone do but invoke such concepts if presented with some complex sentence and asked to describe its 'use'? So they would freely employ such a notion as that of expressing attitude, or conveying a belief, or rejecting a question, without the slightest consciousness that it is the business of the philosophy of language to explain what it is to do any one of these things. Nowhere is this more evident than in the constant use that was made of concepts of truth and falsity, as needing no explanation: for these are concepts which have their home in the theory of meaning, which will have been fully elucidated only when we have understood the role which they have to play in a correct theory of meaning for language; and yet they were employed in descriptions of 'use', and disputes were conducted over whether they should be applied to this or that sentence, under given conditions, or at all, not merely as if it were perfectly clear what is the connection between truth and meaning, but as if there were nothing to be known, and hence nothing capable of being said, about that connection.

Moreover, particularism led to superficiality for another reason, which can be most tersely stated by saying that it promoted a conscious disregard for the distinction between semantic and pragmatic aspects. (I do not myself care for the 'semantic'/'pragmatic' terminology; but that is because I think it obscures the differences between several distinct distinctions.) Anyone not in the grip of a theory, asked to explain the meaning of a sentence like 'Either he is your brother or he is not' or 'I know that I am here', would be disposed to begin by distinguishing what the sentence literally said from what, in particular circumstances, someone might seek to convey by uttering it; but, from the standpoint of the orthodox 'ordinary language' doctrine, only the latter notion was legitimate—*it* was what constituted the 'use' of the sentence; and, if no circumstances could be excogitated, however bizarre, in which it might actually be uttered for some genuine purpose, then the sentence 'had no use' and was therefore meaningless. As for the former notion—that of what the sentence literally said—that was spurious, an illegitimate byproduct of the attempt to construct a theory of meaning in terms of general concepts. It was this, of course, more than anything else which led hostile observers to form the impression of the activities of 'ordinary language' philosophers as the practice of a solemn frivolity.

Naturally, so grotesquely false a methodology could not be consistently adhered to by intelligent people. In consequence, in place of the general semantic concepts which had been expelled in the original determination to pay attention to nothing but the actual 'use' of particular sentences, new ones, such as the celebrated notion of presupposition, or that of conversational implicature, or AUSTIN's distinctions between illocutionary and perlocutionary force, etc., were invented by the 'ordinary language' philosophers themselves; and, in the process, 'ordinary language' philosophy ceased to exist, almost without anyone noticing that it had. An era had ended, not with a bang, but a whimper; and the moment was propitious for the American counter-attack.

The doctrines of 'ordinary language' philosophy were a caricature, but not a gross caricature, of the views of the later WITTGENSTEIN, from whom, as I remarked, the slogan 'Meaning is use' was borrowed. No-one can say about WITTGENSTEIN that, in his later phase, he neglected the philosophy of language, that he used ideas about meaning only as a tool to attack problems in other areas of philosophy: large tracts of the *Philosophische Untersuchungen* are directly devoted to the philosophy of language. The most immediately obvious difference between his conception of 'use' and that of the 'ordinary language' school is that he emphatically did not envisage a description of use as making free appeal to psychological and semantic concepts: what he meant by 'use' is most readily seen from the analogy which he draws in the *Untersuchungen* with an account of the use of money. To understand the significance, that is, the conventional significance, of a coin involves understanding the *institution* of money; what would be needed to convey that significance to someone who came from a society in which money was unknown would be a description of the whole practice in which the transference of coins is embedded; such a description is therefore also needed if we wish to make explicit what it is that, in grasping the significance of a coin, we implicitly apprehend. A description of the institution of money that would serve this purpose would presuppose no economic concepts: it would give an account of what actually happens in terms of what is open to observation by someone innocent of such concepts. In the same way, what WITTGENSTEIN conceived of as constituting an account of the use of language is illustrated by the 'language-games' which he described in the *Brown Book* and elsewhere. In these, some very rudimentary language, or fragment of a language conceived of as existing in isolation, is displayed as being actually spoken: what is described is the complex of activities with which utterances of sentences of the language are interwoven; and, again, the description does not invoke psychological or semantic concepts, but is couched entirely in terms of what is open to outward view.

This conception of a language-game illustrates for us what WITTGENSTEIN would consider to be an adequate account of the functioning of an entire actual language: such an account would, again, consist of a description of the language-game in which the language played a role, and would differ in principle from those described by Wittgenstein only in its immensely greater complexity. It is important to notice the difference between this idea and the conception of a theory of meaning that can be derived from FREGE. Both are agreed that what is required is a description of the conventional principles which govern the *practice* of speaking the language, a description which does not invoke the notion of a sentence's expressing a thought, but, rather, displays that which renders any given sentence the expression of a particular thought. But, for FREGE, the institution of language is autonomous. A sentence expresses the thought it does in virtue of our being able to derive the condition for its truth in a particular way from its composition out of its constituent words; and the notion of truth can be understood only by grasping the various highly general types of linguistic practice that consist in uttering a sentence, with a given truth-condition, in accordance with one or another convention that determines the linguistic art effected by the utterance—that of asserting that the condition for the truth of the sentence is fulfilled, for example, or that of asking whether it is fulfilled. Hence, on this account, it is largely irrelevant to our capacity to speak a language such as that which we have that we are able to engage in non-linguistic activities: we could speak much the same kind of language if we were a sort of intelligent and sentient trees, who could observe the world and utter sounds, but could engage in no other type of action. For WITTGENSTEIN, on the other hand, it is essential to our language that its employment is interwoven with our non-linguistic activities. In the language-games which he describes, what confers meaning on the linguistic utterances is their immediate and direct connection with other actions; for instance, the builder asks for a certain number of stones of a certain shape, and they are passed to him. What makes it difficult for us to see that it is *use,* in this sense, which confers meaning on the sentences of our actual language, or, better, in which their meaning consists, is the remoteness of the connection between linguistic activities (for example, that on which I am now engaged) and non-linguistic ones; it is nevertheless this connection which endows our words with the meanings they have.

Now this idea, striking as it is as a first and, if correct, fundamental, insight, remains in WITTGENSTEIN largely programmatic. FREGE did not, indeed, complete the task of giving even a general sketch of the kind of theory of meaning which he favoured: notoriously, his discussions of the notion of sense supply arguments for holding that we need a theory of sense rather than merely a theory of reference, but do not provide any general model for what we should take a speaker's grasp of the sense of a word of a given logical category to consist in; nor is it clear to what extent he thought it possible to give a non-circular account of the conventions governing the various types of linguistic act such as assertion, or how, if at all, such an account is to be framed. Nevertheless, despite these lacunae, we have an outline of the general form which a FREGEan theory of meaning must assume, sufficiently clear for us to be able to discuss the plausibility of the claim that by this means an adequate account of the functioning of a language can be given. But, of the sort of theory of meaning favoured by WITTGENSTEIN, we have no such outline: we do not know how to begin to set about constructing such a theory. The difficulty lies with those utterances which would normally be classed as assertoric. A command, after all, is aimed at eliciting a direct non-verbal response, a question at eliciting a verbal one. True enough, in the actual case, an utterance of either of these kinds may fail to elicit the response it aims at, and, at least in the case of commands, an adequate description of the linguistic institution must include a general statement of the consequences of the hearer's failure to respond in the way called for. But an assertoric utterance is not, in the general case, aimed at evoking a specific response; how the hearer responds will depend on many things, in particular upon his desires and his existing beliefs. That is not to deny that an assertion will often have effects upon behaviour, and, in the long run, upon non-verbal behaviour; but it does cast doubt upon the possibility of giving an account of the meanings of assertoric sentences directly in terms of their connections with non-linguistic activities. WITTGENSTEIN was not intending merely to make some observations about what it is that *ultimately* gives significance to our language. If that had been all that he had in mind, it could be accommodated within a FREGEan framework. The connection between language and extra-linguistic reality would in that case be assured by the principles which govern the conditions for the truth of our sentences; the effect which an assertion might have upon the conduct of a hearer could then be indirectly accounted for by his grasp of this connection, taken together with his wants and his capacities for action. But it is plain from several passages in the *Untersuchungen* that WITTGENSTEIN intended, in this respect, flatly to oppose FREGE's conception of meaning. In particular, the concept of *assertion*, considered as a type of linguistic act capable of being described in a manner uniform with respect to the truth-conditions of any sentence used to make an assertion, is to be rejected. Our difficulty is, not merely that WITTGENSTEIN has shown us no compelling reason why we must reject it, but that he has not given us any indication of what we are to put in its place.

The particularism which was so marked a feature of the official doctrine of the 'ordinary language' school, though it became less and less discernible in their practice, took its source from WITTGENSTEIN. It was part of FREGE's doctrine that, since a sentence is the smallest unit of language by the utterance of which it is possible to *say* anything, the meaning of a word is to be explained in terms of the contribution it makes to the meaning of each *particular* sentence from the meanings of the word that compose it, but the *general* notion of sentence-meaning is prior to that of word-meaning. This idea has not been challenged by WITTGENSTEIN or anyone else. Now suppose that we face the task of giving a general account of the meanings of the expressions of a language. We might begin by dividing into large categories the sentences of the language, on the basis of the different kinds of linguistic act—assertion, question, command, etc.—that are effected by uttering them; for, it would be natural to think, if sentence-meaning is to be taken as primary, we had better first distinguish types of sentence-meaning as possessed by sentences employed for such very different purposes. Now, for any given sentence, there will be two moments in the understanding of its meaning: the recognition of it as belonging to a particular category, and the grasp of its individual content, whereby it is distinguished from other sentences in the same category. Thus, if one sentence serves to give a command, and another to voice a wish, we must know these facts about the categories to which they belong if we are to understand them; and to know that involves knowing what it is, in general, to give a command or to express a wish. In order to understand those sentences, we must also grasp their individual contents: we must know *which* command the one conveys and *which* wish the other expresses; and this will, in each case, be determined by the composition of the sentence out of its constituent words.

The difficulty now is that, if the sentences in each category possess a different type of sentence-meaning from those in any other category, and if the meaning of a word consists in the contribution it makes to determining the meaning of a sentence containing it, it appears that the words in an imperative sentence must have a meaning of a quite different kind from the same words when they occur in an optative sentence; and this is absurd. The escape from such an intolerable conclusion is provided by the obvious fact that most words in any sentence serve to determine, not the category to which it belongs, but its individual content as against that of other members of the category, together with the idea that the individual content of a sentence is determined in a uniform manner, regardless of its category. Thus it seems natural to suggest that, granted that we know the category to which each sentence belongs, we know the individual content of an imperative sentence by knowing in what circumstances the command it conveys will have been obeyed, and that we know the individual content of an optative sentence by knowing in what circumstances the wish it expresses will have been fulfilled. In this way, we may think of the individual content of a sentence of most of the other categories as being determined by associating with that sentence a certain range of circumstances, the *significance* of that association depending upon the category in question. We thus arrive at the distinction, originally drawn by FREGE, between the *sense* (Sinn) of a sentence and the *force* (Kraft) attached to it. Those constituents of the sentence which determine its sense associate a certain state of affairs with the sentence; that feature of it which determines the force with which it is uttered fixes the conventional significance of the utterance in relation to that state of affairs (i.e., according as the speaker is asserting that the state of affairs obtains, asking whether it obtains, commanding that it should obtain, expressing a wish that it obtain, etc.).

It is difficult to see how a systematic theory of meaning for a language is possible without acknowledging the distinction between sense and force, or one closely similar. Whether the categories I have used as examples—assertoric, interrogative, imperative and optative—are legitimate ones, or ought to be replaced by some others, is a secondary question; in this context, even the question whether the notion of the sense of a sentence which I have just sketched is correct is secondary. What seems essential is that we should have some division of sentential utterances into a determinate range of categories, according to the type of linguistic act effected by the utterance; that there should be some notion of the sense of a sentence, considered as an ingredient in its meaning and as capable of being shared by sentences belonging to different categories; that the notion of sense be such that, once we know both the category to which a sentence belongs and the sense which it carries, then we have an essential grasp of the significance of an utterance of the sentence; and that, for each category, it should be possible to give a uniform explanation of the linguistic act effected by uttering a sentence of that category, in terms of its sense, taken as given. I do not think that we have, at present, any conception of what a theory of meaning for a language would look like if it did not conform to this pattern.

It is, however, just this conception which WITTGENSTEIN attacks. He does not stop at rejecting the claim that all assertoric sentences form a single category, of which a uniform account can be given: he denies that *any* surveyable list of types of linguistic act can be arrived at. This is precisely to deny that the distinction between sense and force is available to simplify the task of explaining the meanings of sentences by distinguishing two different components of their meanings: our theory of meaning must, for each individual sentence, issue in a direct account of the conventional significance of an utterance of that sentence, rather than one derived from a general description of the use of sentences of some general category to which it belongs. Not only do we not know in the least how to set about devising a theory of meaning in conformity with this maxim, but it leads to that neglect of the difference between semantic and pragmatic considerations which I noted in the practice of the 'ordinary language' philosophers.

WITTGENSTEIN's deliberately unsystematic philosophical method makes it difficult to be certain what his intention was. Did he have in mind some theory of meaning of a completely different kind from that proposed by FREGE? Or did he reject the whole idea of a systematic theory of meaning? I should not myself attempt to answer these questions; I think it better to approach WITTGENSTEIN's later work bearing in mind different possible interpretations, without always trying to decide which is the intended one; frequently, his ideas will be found fruitful and stimulating under all possible interpretations of them. But the fact of the matter is that, powerful and penetrating as are many of his discussions of detailed questions in philosophy, including ones relating to language, we do not know how to go about extracting from his later writings any coherent general philosophy of language. The idea—if it *is* WITTGENSTEIN's idea—that no systematic theory of meaning is possible is not merely one which is, at the present stage of enquiry, defeatist, but one that runs counter to obvious facts. The fact that anyone who has a mastery of any given language is able to understand an infinity of sentences of that language, an infinity which is, of course, principally composed of sentences which he has never heard before, is one emphasised not only by the modern school of linguists, headed by CHOMSKY, but by WITTGENSTEIN himself; and this fact can hardly be explained otherwise than by supposing that each speaker has an implicit grasp of a number of general principles governing the use in sentences of words of the language. If, then, there exist such general principles of which every speaker has an implicit grasp, and which serve to confer on the words of the language their various meanings, it is hard to see how there can be any theoretical obstacle to making those principles explicit; and an explicit statement of those principles an implicit grasp of which constitutes the mastery of the language would be, precisely, a complete theory of meaning for the language. On the other hand, if what WITTGENSTEIN intended was some theory of meaning of a wholly new kind, there is not sufficient indication in his writings for us to be able to reconstruct even the general outlines of such a new type of theory. It is undoubtedly the case that, given a sufficient background of the beliefs and desires of both speaker and hearer, the making of an assertoric utterance will frequently have an effect upon the non-linguistic behaviour of the hearer, and register the speaker's commitment to some course of action: but, just because these effects and this commitment depend so heavily upon the varying background, it appears impossible to see how a theory of meaning could be constructed which explained the meanings of assertoric sentences in terms of a direct connection between the utterance of such sentences and the non-linguistic behaviour of the speaker and hearer. That is simply to say that the language-games devised by WITTGENSTEIN to give an account of some very small fragments of language do not appear a promising model for a systematic account of an entire language; and, if after all they are, WITTGENSTEIN has not himself shown us how we are to be guided by these models.

Even amongst the analytical school, WITTGENSTEIN was, during his life-time, a highly controversial figure. Some believed him to be the discoverer of the definitively correct method of philosophy; for them, he had charted the course which, henceforward, all must take who wished to practise the subject, if their contribution was to be of any value. To others, his work was confused, his ideas erroneous, and his influence disastrous. No-one not imbued with prejudice could deny that his personal intellectual capacity was that of a genius;

unfortunately, this in no way settles the value of his contribution to philosophy, since genius may as often lead men astray on to a false path as it may set them on a correct but hitherto undiscovered track. Only now have we reached a moment at which it is beginning to be possible to arrive at an evaluation of WITTGENSTEIN's work that can be generally agreed, at least among members of the analytical school. My own opinion is that he will come to be seen as an immensely fertile source of important and often penetrating philosophical ideas, whose work nevertheless does not constitute, as he and his followers believed that it did, and as FREGE's work undoubtedly did, a solid foundation for future work in philosophy. By this I mean particularly that, although many of his detailed ideas remain interesting and important for us, his example, as regards the *style* in which he practised philosophy, is not to be imitated. This style was the outcome, not only of his unique personality, but also of his general doctrines about the nature of philosophy itself. As I explained earlier, these general doctrines hinge upon the contention that philosophy is not concerned with any topic about which a systematic theory is possible; it seeks to remove, not ignorance or false beliefs, but conceptual confusion, and therefore has nothing positive to set in place of what it removes. As I have said, I do not feel certain from WITTGENSTEIN's observations about language and about meaning that he held a systematic theory of meaning for a language to be an impossibility in principle; the strongest ground for attributing to him such a view is that it appears to be the only premiss from which his thesis about the nature of philosophy could be legitimately derived. I have already given my reasons for supposing that, on the contrary, a systematic theory of meaning must be possible; and, even if it should prove in the end not to be possible, we certainly have no adequate insight at present into what makes it impossible, and shall therefore learn much that is of the greatest value if we continue for the time being in our endeavours to construct such a theory.

If this analysis is correct, the most urgent task that philosophers are now called upon to carry out is to devise what I have been calling a 'systematic theory of meaning', that is to say, a systematic account of the functioning of language which does not beg any questions by presupposing as already understood any semantic concepts, even such familiar ones as those of truth and of assertion. Such an account will necessarily take the form of a *theory,* because it is evident that the mastery of a language involves the implicit apprehension of a vast complex of interconnections, and does not merely consist in a number of in principle isolable practical abilities. We are by no means as yet agreed even upon the general form which such a theory of meaning ought to take; but, thanks primarily to FREGE, we understand enough both about the underlying syntactical structure of our language and about what is demanded of a theory of meaning to be able to undertake the investigation as a collective enterprise to the same extent that advance in the sciences is also the result of co-operative endeavour. These remarks apply directly only to the philosophy of language, not to other branches of philosophy; but I speak as a member of the analytical school of philosophy, of which I have already observed that the characteristic tenet is that the philosophy of language is the foundation for all the rest of philosophy. This is not to suggest that work in all other branches of philosophy must wait upon the completion of a satisfactory theory of meaning; intellectual construction is not like architecture, in that we do not, in the former case, need to complete the foundation before work on the upper storeys can begin. But it does mean, I think, that the correctness of any piece of analysis carried out in another part of philosophy cannot be fully determined until we know with reasonable certainty what form a correct theory of meaning for our language must take. I am maintaining that we have now reached a position where the search for such a theory of meaning can take on a genuinely scientific character; this means, in particular, that it can be carried on in such a way, not, indeed, that disputes do not not arise, but that they can be resolved to the satisfaction of everyone, and, above all, that we may hope to bring the search within a finite time to a successful conclusion. The history of the subject indeed makes it very tempting to adopt the frequently expressed view that there are never any agreed final conclusions in philosophy; but, few as they may be, there exist counter-examples to this thesis, examples, that is, of solutions to what were once baffling problems that have now been accepted as part of the established stock of knowledge; for such an example, we need look no further than to FREGE's resolution, by means of the quantifier-variable notation, of the logic of generality. Whether, once we have attained an agreed theory of meaning, the other parts of philosophy will then also take on a similarly scientific character, or whether they will continue to be able to be explored only in the more haphazard manner that has been traditional in philosophy for many centuries, I do not claim to know.

It will have been noticed that I have slipped into discussing simultaneously whether or not, from the standpoint of the analytical school, future work in philosophy can and ought to be systematic in two distinct senses of 'systematic'. In one sense, a philosophical investigation is systematic if it is intended to issue in an articulated theory, such as is constituted by any of the great philosophical 'systems' advanced in the past by philosophers like SPINOZA or KANT. In the other sense, a philosophical investigation is systematic if it proceeds according to generally agreed methods of enquiry, and its results are generally accepted or rejected according to commonly agreed criteria. These two senses in which it may be asked whether or not philosophy can and ought to be systematic are independent of one another. Most, perhaps all, the natural sciences are systematic in both senses; but history, for example, is systematic only in the second sense, namely that there are agreed methods of investigation and agreed criteria for testing what are claimed as results of such investigation, and not in the first sense, since historical research does not issue in any articulated theory. When, in the past, philosophy has been systematic, it has generally been systematic in the first sense only, not in the second: I have been advancing the view that, at least in the philosophy of language, philosophy ought henceforward to be systematic in both senses. The subject-matter of this part of philosophy demands an articulated theory; and we have reached a stage in our investigations at which that minimum has been established which makes it possible for future research to proceed according to more or less agreed methods of enquiry, and for its results to be judged in accordance with generally accepted standards.

For those who value it at all, it has always been something of a scandal that philosophy has, through most of its history, failed to be systematic in the second sense, to such an extent that the question, 'Can there be progress in philosophy?', is a perennial one. If philosophy is regarded, as most of its practitioners have regarded it, as one—perhaps the most important—sector in the quest for truth, it is then amazing that, in all its long history, it should not yet have established a generally accepted methodology, generally accepted criteria of success and, therefore, a body of definitively achieved results. (On the same assumption, it is to be expected that the truths discovered by philosophical enquiry should permit themselves to be arranged into an articulated theory or system, that is, that philosophy should be systematic in the first of the two senses, since the manifold interconnections between one part of philosophy and another are a matter of common philosophical experience; but this expectation gives rise to no scandal, since, as already remarked, the work of individual philosophers has frequently resulted in the creation of just such theories or systems.) We should expect any activity which has as its goal the establishment of truths to be systematic in the *second* sense, precisely because it is of the essence of the concept of truth that truth should be an objective feature of the propositions to which it attaches; wherever commonly agreed criteria for the correctness of a proposition appear to be lacking, we naturally entertain the suspicion that the proposition cannot rightly be supposed even to be capable of possessing the property of being true. (The step from saying that there exists no agreed standard by which the correctness of a proposition may be judged to saying that there is no notion of objective truth which may be applied to that proposition is, however, far from being a certain one; it remains an as yet unresolved question within the theory of meaning—which, as already remarked, is where the concept of truth has its home—what is the exact relation between the notion of truth and our capacity for recognising a proposition as true.) In any case, even if the apparent failure of philosophers to make their subject systematic in the second sense does not lead us to doubt whether it is the business of philosophy to arrive at truths at all, the whole enterprise seems somewhat pointless if its goal cannot be attained or, at least, cannot be attained to the satisfaction of most of its practitioners. What is the use of conducting any enquiry if it cannot be told when the results of that enquiry have been achieved? In this respect, philosophy shows at great disadvantage when compared with mathematics; both appear to represent different sectors in the quest for truth, both appear to proceed solely by means of ratiocination, but mathematics has amassed a great body of established results, while philosophy appears to engender nothing but unending disagreements. It is this scandalous situation which renders attractive such a conception of philosophy, as not being, after all, in the least concerned with establishing true propositions, as that held by

WITTGENSTEIN; on such a view, there may indeed be progress in philosophy, namely as philosophers become better at curing conceptual confusions, without there being any body of established doctrine to show for that progress.

I have contended in this lecture for a more traditional view of the character of philosophy than WITTGENSTEIN's, a view, namely, that does indeed accept it for what it purports to be, a sector in the quest for truth. If that claim is accepted, then the fact that philosophy failed, throughout most of its long history, to achieve a systematic methodology does indeed cry out for explanation; and I shall not here attempt to give any adequate explanation of this remarkable fact. From WITTGENSTEIN himself we have a striking analogy to illustrate how it is that we may claim that progress occurs in philosophy, even though so little remains settled. He compares philosophical activity with the task of rearranging in systematic order the books of a great library hitherto haphazardly disposed: in carrying out such a rearrangement, a vital step may be taken by placing a number of volumes together on a single shelf, even though they remain there only temporarily, and, when the final arrangement is completed, none of those particular books remain on that shelf or together on any shelf. The illuminating power of this analogy does not depend upon WITTGENSTEIN's particular conception of the nature of philosophy, and it could be applied, though with much less force, to some of the sciences; but that does not explain why the analogy is so much more apt when it is applied to philosophy than to any other intellectual discipline. Presumably, the analogy is liable to apply most fittingly to those subjects which remain in their early stages; so what needs explanation—an explanation which I have already said I am not going to attempt to offer—is how it comes about that philosophy, although as ancient as any other subject and a great deal more ancient than most, should have remained for so long 'in its early stages'. The 'early stages' of any discipline are, presumably, to be characterised as those in which its practitioners have not yet attained a clear view of its subject-matter and its goals. If the thesis for which I have contended in this lecture is correct, philosophy has only just very recently struggled out of its early stage into maturity: the turning-point was the work of FREGE, but the widespread realisation of the significance of that work has had to wait for half a century after his death, and, at that, is still confined only to the analytical school. Such a claim may at first sight appear preposterous, until we remember that logic, as a subject, is almost as ancient as philosophy, and that it, too, came of age only with the work of FREGE. What has given philosophy its historical unity, what has characterised it over all the centuries as a single subject, is the range of questions which philosophers have attempted to answer: there has been comparatively little variation in what has been recognised as constituting a philosophical problem. What has fluctuated wildly is the way in which philosophers have in general characterised the range of problems with which they attempt to deal, and the kind of reasoning which they have accepted as providing answers to these problems. Sometimes philosophers have claimed that they were investigating, by purely rational means, the most general properties of the universe;

sometimes, that they have been investigating the workings of the human mind; sometimes, again, that they have been providing, when these exist, justifications for our various claims to knowledge concerning different types of subject-matter. Only with FREGE was the proper object of philosophy finally established: namely, first, that the goal of philosophy is the analysis of the structure of *thought;* secondly, that the study of *thought* is to be sharply distinguished from the study of the psychological process of *thinking;* and, finally, that the only proper method for analysing thought consists in the analysis of *language.* As I have argued, the acceptance of these three tenets is common to the entire analytical school; but, during the interval between FREGE's time and now, there have been within that school many somewhat wayward misinterpretations and distortions of FREGE's basic teaching, and it has taken nearly a half-century since his death for us to apprehend clearly what the real task of philosophy, as conceived by him, involves.

I know that it is reasonable to greet all such claims with scepticism, since they have been made many times before in the history of philosophy. Just because the scandal caused by philosophy's lack of a systematic methodology has persisted for so long, it has been a constant preoccupation of philosophers to remedy that lack, and a repeated illusion that they had succeeded in doing so. HUSSERL believed passionately that he at last held the key which would unlock every philosophical door; the disciples of KANT ascribed to him the achievement of at last devising a correct philosophical methodology; SPINOZA believed that he was doing for philosophy what EUCLID had done for geometry; and, before him, DESCARTES supposed that he had uncovered the one and only proper philosophical method. I have mentioned only a few of many examples of this illusion; for any outsider to philosophy, by far the safest bet would be that I was suffering from a similar illusion in making the same claim for FREGE. To this I can offer only the banal reply which any prophet has to make to any sceptic: time will tell.

PART III

CONTINENTAL PHILOSOPHY

The selections in this section are all concerned with highlighting the subjectivity, or perspectival character, of philosophy. More fundamentally, they address the question of the meanings of "subjectivity" and "objectivity," and they investigate possible origins of what has been included under the term "objectivity." The philosophers represented in this section experiment with various meanings for these terms and with the relationships between their meanings. They all agree in a fundamental criticism of traditional philosophy: They reject the claim that philosophy achieves objectivity in a sense that elevates it above all other human enterprises. They differ, however, in their view about what exactly philosophy should be once the tradition has been rejected.

In "On the Prejudices of Philosophers," Friedrich Nietzsche begins by attacking what he calls dogmatism as an improper method for attaining the truth, on the ground that it has never yet attained truth. Such philosophizing has been based on popular superstition (for example, the "soul superstition"), seduction by grammar, or illegitimate generalizations. The greatest and most dangerous error of philosophy so far was Plato's invention of the pure spirit and the good *as such.* This was an error because it denied *perspective,* the "basic condition of all life."

The typical prejudice of metaphysicians is the claim that the greatest aspects of life (truth, beauty, selfless deeds, moral excellence, etc.) could not have arisen out of this "paltry world" (the world of contingent being) that consists only of the worst components of life—delusion and lust. Metaphysicians thus claim that we can explain the good only if it came from some other realm, the realm of Being. This prejudice, according to Nietzsche, leads to the value of *truth* above all. Nietzsche wants to put into question the will to truth, asking what it is in us that really wants truth. Pure concepts (such as "cause" and "effect") are conventional fictions used for the purpose of communication and designation. One should not use them for metaphysical explanation. The value of promoting and cultivating life is higher than the value of truth. For example, synthetic *a priori* judgments are among the falsest judgments but have a great value for our present life. Without accepting certain "lies" (e.g., our cognitive systems of ordering experience), one could not live. Philosophers think of themselves as critical, systematic, and independent in their pursuit of "truth." In fact, they all follow down the same path, "revolve in the same orbit." It is the "innate systematic structure and relationship of their concepts" that leads them all down the same path. They are guided in their philosophy by language and grammar, wherein concepts are expressed. Grammar determines the possible world-interpretations for them and excludes others. For example, the ego as the subject of the act of thought is a supposition supported by a grammatical habit that requires an agent for any act, a supposition invoked to explain and interpret thought.

Philosophers pretend to reach their conclusions strictly on the basis of supporting arguments, but in fact accept their conclusions on the basis of assumptions or prejudices while supporting their positions with arguments only after the fact. Philosophy has always been the personal confession or testimony of its author, who aims to expound his or her *values,* and develops a system that is supposed to support those values.

In his early work, "Phenomenology," Edmund Husserl says that philosophical thinking concerns itself with the problem of whether and how cognition gets at things as they are in themselves. We cannot begin with the "natural thinking" of science, or we will end up in contradiction. Rather, we must begin with an "ultimate, clear, and inherently consistent insight into the essence of cognition." A critique of cognition is a prior condition for the possibility of metaphysics. The method for such a critique is the phenomenological method, where phenomenology is the general doctrine of essences.

The first step for phenomenology is to begin with cognitions that are beyond doubt. We begin with *cogitationes,* bare acts of *reflection* on cognition. These *cogitationes* are special because they are immanent and thus do not introduce the problem of how cognition can transcend or reach beyond itself. To get at the immanent, the philosopher must execute a *phenomenological reduction,* excluding all transcendent positing. The philosopher's basis must be a kind of "seeing" or direct insight, more fundamental than demonstration.

The second step for phenomenology is required because the pure phenomena left after the phenomenological reduction are not sufficient for our purposes: that is, to yield universally valid findings. We need to reduce these further, via *eidetic reduction,* to obtain universals, essences. Here we can directly inspect the universal, or essential, structures found in phenomena.

At the third step for phenomenology we notice that the absolutely self-given separates into appearance and that which appears, and does so *within* pure immanence. Consciousness *constitutes* something that is not identical to the *cogitatio* itself and is not a transcendent object. Such "constitution of intentional objects" exhibits essential structures that differentiate perceiving, imagining, remembering, etc. The *task of philosophy* is to trace out and analyze all forms of givenness and all correlations between the phenomena of cognition and the objects of cognition (intentional objects). This makes up an analysis of the inherent structure of the pure phenomena that remain after the phenomenological and eidetic reductions.

In "Philosophy," a later work, Husserl states that the goal of philosophy has traditionally been universal, definitive knowledge of the world as it is in itself, but there is no definitively certain starting-point for reaching knowledge of the world as it is in itself. No matter how "harmonious" an experience may be, there is always the possibility that it is an illusion.

We *begin* in our philosophizing, not with certain knowledge of a thing in itself, but with the "life-world," as Husserl calls it in the *Crisis of the European Sciences and Transcendental Phenomenology.* Experience gives us an "I," a "you," a "we," a community of other egos. It is this community of conscious life, the common lived world, that is our basis in philosophy for grounding knowledge. It gives us *corrected experience.* We correct and interpret our experience by comparing it with that of other egos, but experience remains essentially relative.

Husserl claims that philosophy (except for idealism) has always gone astray by employing the naturalistic-scientific sense of objectivity. Philosophy must realize that the world is always given only as subjectively relative. It takes on meaning only through subjectivity; and the notion of the world as it is in itself arises purely out of subjectivity. Phenomenology is a philosophy restricting itself, via the *phenomenological reduction,* to actual subjectivity.

Philosophy develops one's reason. This development moves by stages of self-reflection in philosophy. Eventually one develops to the point of forming the idea of autonomy, of a reasonable self-responsible "I," still inseparably correlated with the community, however. This is the discovery of absolute intersubjectivity; philosophy must start from the world as the whole of mankind (the life-world). Philosophy is the infinite cycle of discovering its own unsatisfactory relativity and driving on further to reach a higher rationality. Full rationality, however, always lies out at the horizon, receding with each of our advances. It is an infinite regulating ideal. Philosophy is self-understanding that takes a person as part of mankind, which is eternally striving toward reason.

In "The End of Philosophy and the Task of Thinking," Martin Heidegger claims that philosophy (as metaphysics) has entered its final stage. Its task has been to examine Being as the ultimate ground of beings. Philosophy (metaphysics) has reached its end not as a mere stopping but as a completion, a gathering into its most extreme possibility. Plato's thinking has dominated all of Western philosophy, and his thinking is paradigmatically metaphysical. With the 19th-century reversal of Platonism in Marx and Nietzsche, philosophy as metaphysics reaches completion, all possible permutations of the program having been run.

There remains a not yet realized task of thinking at the end of philosophy, a task found at the *beginning* of philosophy. It is preparatory thinking that merely prepares one for a possible course. It is a preparation for the possibility that humanity will overcome its technological, scientific, and industrial character. This thinking has as its task the determination of that which is still controversial for thinking, its "matter." This involves understanding the call "to the things themselves" and the *method* appropriate to it. Hegel and Husserl proposed a method for philosophy that required reduction to absolute *subjectivity* as the matter of philosophy, as the "sole absolute being."

The method of absolute subjectivity contains the original preparatory position of philosophy within it as buried and "unthought." The unthought within the method and matter of philosophy is "opening" or "clearing," *aletheia* as found in Parmenides, an openness that *makes possible* the appearing and showing of things and the possibility of truth. It is the opening for everything that is present, for all presence. All philosophical thinking, method, intuition, and evidence depend on the opening as their precondition.

What *aletheia* is as such remains unheeded, concealed. The task of thinking at the end of philosophy is to pursue the self-concealing opening of presence, to surrender to the *matter* of thinking.

In "Existentialism," Jean-Paul Sartre characterizes existentialism as a philosophical doctrine setting the methodological stricture that "existence precedes essence, or . . . that subjectivity must be the starting point." Sartre's philosophical method rejects the idea of a predetermined human nature whose realization functions as an independent *telos,* or goal, of human life. He rejects the long-standing philosophical doctrine that the essence of being human precedes actual human existence and serves to define what it is to be human. He also rejects a determinism that might go along with this. According to Sartre, we define ourselves: We freely create our own essences through our existence and the choices we make in playing out that existence. We do this from our own subjective perspectives, not in reference to an objectively determined essence of *a priori* guidelines. Consequently, we must take responsibility for what we are, for our essence, individually and collectively. The universal subjectivity in defining our essence entails, according to Sartre, that "it is impossible for man to transcend human subjectivity," that it is part of the universal human condition that we cannot escape our own limited, subjective perspective. This claim has implications for philosophical method; for it rules out from the start any method that aspires to objectivity, replacing it with intersubjectivity, and it heavily emphasizes subjective interpretation. The responsibility attaching to each individual decision (in virtue of the freedom to create our essence) attaches equally to philosophical decisions made from the subjective standpoint. All philosophizing is thus infused with the same ethical responsibility to humanity that characterizes more practical decision-making.

In "What is Phenomenology?" Maurice Merleau-Ponty aims to clarify what phenomenology is, in response to a number of apparent contradictions in interpretations of Husserl's work. The main problem of interpreting phenomenology is characterizing its attitude toward the world. It seems both to separate the philosopher from the world and at the same time immerse the philosopher in the world. It seems to take the world as it is lived as a starting point, but also to produce the world as the product of consciousness.

Merleau-Ponty responds that phenomenology is primarily a manner of thinking. It addresses itself always only to description of the world as lived from a particular point of view. The world taken in this way is directly accessible. It is not the product of analysis, but the source of all analysis and explanation. The world is not something the subject constructs, but it is always there, given to the subject, as an absolute and primordial point of departure. Perception, consequently, is not a science or act but the background for all conscious acts.

The phenomenological reduction, then, is the apprehension of the world purely as the world-as-meaning. One becomes aware of the nature of the world only by suspending one's recognition of our essential relationships with the world as a being-in-the-world. The essence of the world is what it is for us prior to any thematization or analysis. The eidetic reduction gets at that essence by trying to "make reflection emulate the unreflective life of consciousness." The unreflective life of consciousness, then, always operates within the lifeworld that is the philosopher's ultimate concern.

In "Nietzsche, Genealogy, History," Michel Foucault describes the genealogical method for unearthing the history of "invasions, struggles, plundering, disguises, and ploys" lying beneath our words. The study of philosophy requires meticulous examination of the systems involved and how they exhibit different powers at work in the development of history. The genealogical method does not search for the origins of things in their essences, but reveals that there is something very different that lies behind things. We find behind them complex constructions gradually built through a historical process from diverse elements. The tools of reason, such as our central philosophical concepts, resulted from struggles among philosophers for intellectual conquest. Genealogy finds, for example, the beginnings of value systems in systems of domination embodied in sets of rules or obligations. It is the role of the genealogist to expose the diverse elements and beginnings of philosophical notions. Genealogy records the history of moral and metaphysical concepts as a series of interpretations, and *interpretation* is "the violent or surreptitious appropriation of a system of rules, which in itself has no essential meaning." It finds the beginnings of philosophical concepts not in the objective truth of being but in the accidental, the heterogeneity of what happens to have been.

Genealogical history emphasizes that the present is not a privileged point in historical development. The present contains merely the current episodes within a long continuing series of development. Genealogy is distinguished from history in the traditional sense by its refusal to strive for a suprahistorical perspective employing absolute standards. It places what is taken as absolute within a process, searching out what is discontinuous rather than trying to identify something constant. It focuses on what is closest, not on distant ideals. Genealogical history follows Nietzsche by always affirming the dependence of knowledge on a limited human perspective.

In "Deconstruction and the Other," Jacques Derrida explains his deconstructive technique, a technique for reading (primarily philosophical) texts, that is supposed to expose characteristics beyond the usual "intended meaning of the writer." He says that the "site" of his work is not properly philosophical; he seeks a "non-philosophical site from which to question philosophy" through the deconstruction of philosophical texts. He wants to achieve a vantage, or perspective, where philosophy can "appear to itself as other than itself" in order that it may reflect on itself in an original manner. This vantage, or "non-site," cannot itself be captured within philosophy proper. He claims that the problematic of *writing,* found in any text, is crucial in the "deconstruction of metaphysics." Deconstruction is not one general method, however, because each text determines its own laws of reading. Deconstruction does work in general to expose the philosophical and theoretical presuppositions at work in any general method of textual criticism.

Derrida's approach to metaphysics is heavily influenced by Heidegger's attempts to "overcome" Greek metaphysics and to retrieve the original task of thinking. Derrida is also influenced by the genealogical and genetic methods of Nietzsche and Freud in his formulation of an approach to philosophy that is itself not part of philosophy proper. Achieving such an approach is, according to Derrida, necessary for achieving "true radicality" in deconstruction. From this non-site, philosophy and non-philosophical literature are not isolable, neither taking precedence over the other. Derrida deconstructs *texts,* and tries to expose philosophy as literary, as a kind of writing.

Derrida objects to criticisms claiming that he aims to suspend or eliminate the reference of language. He is, in fact, centrally concerned with the "other" of language; and he aims to expose the complexity of the question of reference. Derrida objects to the claim that deconstruction is nihilistic: It is "not an enclosure in nothingness, but an openness towards the other."

In "Philosophy as Stand-In and Interpreter," Jürgen Habermas agrees with recent critics of philosophy who claim that it can no longer assume the role of a final judge over all other disciplines, "ushering them to their proper places." Philosophy does not have a privileged position of authority from which it can oversee and order the various areas of human culture. Habermas thinks that philosophy can work *with* other disciplines and remain distinctive in so far as it deals with universal topics and raises universal, although fallible, claims. He describes philosophy as a "stand-in" holding a place open within the empirical sciences for empirical theories with strong universalistic claims that those sciences might not otherwise address. In addition, philosophy can serve as a mediator, or "interpreter," between disciplines of empirical research becoming so specialized that communication between those disciplines and the general public is problematic. Philosophy, according to Habermas, is the cultural tradition that "ranges across *the whole spectrum*" of the lifeworld, overcoming the isolation, for example, of science, morals, and art.

Habermas emphasizes the role of reason for all philosophizing, claiming that it is always constrained to follow the best available arguments. Habermas disagrees with the present-day "dismissive goodbye and good riddance" to philosophy. He deals with three versions of such a farewell to philosophy, the therapeutic, the heroic, and the salvaging farewell. He argues that philosophy cannot be eliminated, and that the part that must remain includes argumentation and justificatory dispute. Agreement reached through argumentation is the only criterion of validity for *any* of our judgments, according to Habermas.

ON THE PREJUDICES OF PHILOSOPHERS

Friedrich Nietzsche

1

The will to truth, which is still going to tempt us to many a hazardous enterprise; that celebrated veracity of which all philosophers have hitherto spoken with reverence: what questions this will to truth has already set before us! What strange, wicked, questionable questions! It is already a long story—yet does it not seem as if it has only just begun? Is it any wonder we should at last grow distrustful, lose our patience, turn impatiently away? That this sphinx should teach us too to ask questions? *Who* really is it that here questions us? *What* really is it in us that wants 'the truth'?—We did indeed pause for a long time before the question of the origin of this will—until finally we came to a complete halt before an even more fundamental question. We asked after the *value* of this will. Granted we want truth: *why not rather* untruth? And uncertainty? Even ignorance?—The problem of the value of truth stepped before us—or was it we who stepped before this problem? Which of us is Oedipus here? Which of us sphinx? It is, it seems, a rendezvous of questions and question-marks.—And, would you believe it, it has finally almost come to seem to us that this problem has never before been posed—that we have been the first to see it, to fix our eye on it, to *hazard* it? For there is a hazard in it and perhaps there exists no greater hazard.

2

'How *could* something originate in its antithesis? Truth in error, for example? Or will to truth in will to deception? Or the unselfish act in self-interest? Or the pure radiant gaze of the sage in covetousness? Such origination is impossible; he who dreams of it is a fool, indeed worse than a fool; the things of the highest value must have another origin *of their own*—they cannot be derivable from this transitory, seductive, deceptive, mean little world, from this confusion of desire and illusion! In the womb of being, rather, in the intransitory, in the hidden god, in the "thing in itself"—*that* is where their cause must lie and nowhere else!'—This mode of judgement constitutes the typical prejudice by which metaphysicians of all ages can be recognized; this mode of evaluation stands in the background of all their logical procedures; it is on account of this their 'faith' that they concern themselves with their 'knowledge', with something that is at last solemnly baptized 'the truth'. The fundamental faith of the metaphysicians is *the faith in antithetical values.* It has not occurred to even the most cautious of them to pause and doubt here on the threshold, where however it was most needful they should: even if they *had* vowed to themselves '*de omnibus dubitandum*'. For it may be doubted, firstly whether there exists any antitheses at all, and secondly whether these popular evaluations and value-antitheses, on which the metaphysicians have set their seal, are not perhaps merely foreground valuations, merely provisional perspectives, perhaps moreover the perspectives of a hole-and-corner, perhaps from below, as it were frog-perspectives, to borrow an expression employed by painters. With all the value that may adhere to the true, the genuine, the selfless, it could be possible that a higher and more fundamental value for all life might have to be ascribed to appearance, to the will to deception, to selfishness and to appetite. It might even be possible that *what* constitutes the value of those good and honoured things resides precisely in their being artfully related, knotted and crocheted to these wicked, apparently antithetical things, perhaps even in their being essentially identical with them. Perhaps!—But who is willing to concern himself with such dangerous perhapses! For that we have to await the arrival of a new species of philosopher, one which possesses tastes and inclinations opposite to and different from those of its predecessors—philosophers of the dangerous 'perhaps' in every sense.—And to speak in all seriousness: I see such new philosophers arising.

3

Having kept a close eye on philosophers and read between their lines for a sufficient length of time, I tell myself: the greater part of conscious thinking must still be counted among the instinctive activities, and this is so even in the case of philosophical thinking; we have to learn differently here as we have learned differently in regard to heredity and the 'innate'. Just as the act of being born plays no part in the procedure and progress of heredity, so 'being conscious' is in no decisive sense the *opposite* of the instinctive—most of a philosopher's conscious thinking is secretly directed and compelled into definite channels by his instincts. Behind all logic too and its apparent autonomy there stand evaluations, in plainer terms physiological demands for the preservation of a certain species of life. For example, that the definite shall be of greater value than the indefinite, appearance of less value than 'truth': but such valuations as these could, their regulatory importance for *us* notwithstanding, be no more than foreground valuations, a certain species of *niaiserie* which may be necessary precisely for the preservation of beings such as us. Assuming, that is to say, that it is not precisely man who is the 'measure of things'. . .

4

The falseness of a judgement is to us not necessarily an objection to a judgement: it is here that our new language perhaps sounds strangest. The question is to what extent it is life-advancing, life-preserving, species-preserving, perhaps even species-breeding; and our fundamental tendency is to assert that the falsest judgements (to which synthetic judgements *a priori* belong) are the most indispensable to us, that without granting as true the fictions of logic, without measuring reality against the purely invented world of the unconditional and self-identical, without a continual falsification of the world by means of numbers, mankind could not live—that to renounce false judgements would be to renounce life, would be to deny life. To recognize untruth as a condition of life: that, to be sure, means to resist customary value-sentiments in a dangerous fashion; and a philosophy which ventures to do so places itself, by that act alone, beyond good and evil.

5

What makes one regard philosophers half mistrustfully and half mockingly is not that one again and again detects how innocent they are—how often and how easily they fall into error and go astray, in short their childishness and childlikeness—but that they display altogether insufficient honesty, while making a mighty and virtuous noise as soon as the problem of truthfulness is even remotely touched on. They pose as having discovered and attained their real opinions through the self-evolution of a cold, pure, divinely unperturbed dialectic (in contrast to the mystics of every rank, who are more honest and more stupid than they—these speak of 'inspiration'): while what happens at bottom is that a prejudice, a notion, an 'inspiration', generally a desire of the heart sifted and made abstract, is defended by them with reasons sought after the event—they are one and all advocates who do not want to be regarded as such, and for the most part no better than cunning pleaders for their prejudices, which they baptize 'truths'—and *very* far from possessing the courage of the conscience which admits this fact to itself, very far from possessing the good taste of the courage which publishes this fact, whether to warn a foe or a friend or out of high spirits and in order to mock itself. The tartuffery, as stiff as it is virtuous, of old Kant as he lures us along the dialectical bypaths which lead, more correctly, mislead, to his 'categorical imperative'—this spectacle makes us smile, we who are fastidious and find no little amusement in observing the subtle tricks of old moralists and moral-preachers. Not to speak of that hocus-pocus of mathematical form in which, as if in iron, Spinoza encased and masked his philosophy—'the love of *his* wisdom', to render that word fairly and squarely—so as to strike terror into the heart of any assailant who should dare to glance at that invincible maiden and Pallas Athene—how much personal timidity and vulnerability this masquerade of a sick recluse betrays!

6

It has gradually become clear to me what every great philosophy has hitherto been: a confession on the part of its author and a kind of involuntary and unconscious memoir; moreover, that the moral (or immoral) intentions in every philosophy have every time constituted the real germ of life out of which the entire plant has grown. To explain how a philosopher's most remote metaphysical assertions have actually been arrived at, it is always well (and wise) to ask oneself first: what morality does this (does *he*—) aim at? I accordingly do not believe a 'drive to knowledge' to be the father of philosophy, but that another drive has, here as elsewhere, only employed knowledge (and false knowledge!) as a tool. But anyone who looks at the basic drives of mankind to see to what extent they may in precisely this connection have come into play as *inspirational* spirits (or demons and kobolds—) will discover that they have all at some time or other practised philosophy—and that each one of them would be only too glad to present *itself* as the ultimate goal of existence and as the legitimate *master* of all the other drives. For every drive is tyrannical: and it is as *such* that it tries to philosophize.—In the case of scholars, to be sure, in the case of really scientific men, things may be different—'better', if you will—there may really exist something like a drive to knowledge there, some little independent clockwork which, when wound up, works bravely on *without* any part of the scholar's other drives playing any essential part. The scholar's real 'interests' therefore generally lie in quite another direction, perhaps in his family or in making money or in politics; it is, indeed, almost a matter of indifference whether his little machine is set up in this region of science or that, whether the 'promising' young worker makes himself into a good philologist or a specialist in fungus or a chemist—he is not *characterized* by becoming this or that. In the philosopher, on the contrary, there is nothing whatever impersonal; and, above all, his morality bears decided and decisive testimony to *who he is*—that is to say, to the order of rank the innermost drives of his nature stand in relative to one another.

7

How malicious philosophers can be! I know of nothing more venomous than the joke Epicurus allowed himself to make against Plato and the Platonists: he called them *Dionysiokolakes.* The literal and foreground meaning of this word is 'flatterers of Dionysus', that is to say, tyrants' hangers-on and lickspittles; in addition, however, it is as much as to say 'they are all *actors,* there is nothing genuine about them' (for *Dionysiokolax* was a popular term for an actor). And the latter meaning is really the piece of malice that Epicurus discharged at Plato: he was annoyed by the grandiose manner, the *mise en scène* of which Plato and his pupils were masters—of which Epicurus was not a master! He, the old schoolteacher from Samos who sat hidden in his little garden at Athens and wrote three hundred books—who knows, perhaps out of rage at Plato and ambitious envy of him?—It took a century for Greece to find out who this garden god Epicurus had been.—Did it find out?—

8

In every philosophy there is a point at which the philosopher's 'conviction' appears on the scene: or, to put it in the words of an ancient Mystery:

adventavit asinus,
pulcher et fortissimus.

9

You want to *live* 'according to nature'. O you noble Stoics, what fraudulent words! Think of a being such as nature is, prodigal beyond measure, indifferent beyond measure, without aims or intentions, without mercy or justice, at once fruitful and barren and uncertain; think of indifference itself as a power—how *could* you live according to such indifference? To live—is that not precisely wanting to be other than this nature? Is living not valuating, preferring, being unjust, being limited, wanting to be different? And even if your imperative 'live according to nature' meant at bottom the same thing as 'live according to life'—how could you *not* do that? Why make a principle of what you yourselves are and must be?—The truth of it is, however, quite different: while you rapturously pose as deriving the canon of your law from nature, you want something quite the reverse of that, you strange actors and self-deceivers! Your pride wants to prescribe your morality, your ideal, to nature, yes to nature itself, and incorporate them in it; you demand that nature should be nature 'according to the Stoa' and would like to make all existence exist only after your own image—as a tremendous eternal glorification and universalization of Stoicism! All your love of truth notwithstanding, you have compelled yourselves for so long and with such persistence and hypnotic rigidity to view nature *falsely*, namely Stoically, you are no longer capable of viewing it in any other way—and some abysmal arrogance infects you at last with the Bedlamite hope that, *because* you know how to tyrannize over yourselves—Stoicism is self-tyranny—nature too can be tyrannized over: for is the Stoic not a *piece* of nature? . . . But this is an old and never-ending story: what formerly happened with the Stoics still happens today as soon as a philosophy begins to believe in itself. It always creates the world in its own image, it cannot do otherwise; philosophy is this tyrannical drive itself, the most spiritual will to power, to 'creation of the world', to *causa prima.*

10

The zeal and subtlety, I might even say slyness, with which the problem 'of the real and apparent world' is set upon all over Europe today makes one think hard and prick up one's ears; and anyone who hears in the background only a 'will to truth' and nothing more, certainly does not enjoy the best of hearing. In rare and isolated cases such a will to truth, some extravagant and adventurous courage, a metaphysician's ambition to maintain a forlorn position, may actually play a part and finally prefer a handful of 'certainty' to a whole cartful of beautiful possibilities; there may even exist puritanical fanatics of conscience who would rather lie down and die on a sure nothing than on an uncertain something. But this is nihilism and the sign of a despairing, mortally weary soul, however brave the bearing of such a virtue may appear. In the case of stronger, livelier thinkers who are still thirsty for life, however, it seems to be different: when they take sides *against* appearance and speak even of 'perspective' with an arrogant disdain, when they rank the credibility of their own body about as low as the credibility of the ocular evidence which says 'the earth stands still', and thus with apparent good humour let slip their firmest possession (for what is believed in more firmly today than the body?)—who knows whether they are at bottom trying to win back something that was formerly an even *firmer* possession, some part or other of the old domain of the faith of former times, perhaps 'the immortal soul', perhaps 'the old God', in short ideas by which one could live better, that is to say more vigorously and joyfully, than by 'modern ideas'? There is *distrust* of these modern ideas in this outlook, there is disbelief in all that has been constructed yesterday and today; there is perhaps in addition a little boredom and mockery which can no longer endure the bric-à-brac of concepts of the most various origin such as so-called positivism brings to the market today; the disgust of a more fastidious taste at the village-fair motleyness and patchiness of all these reality-philosophasters in whom there is nothing new or genuine except this motleyness. In this, it seems to me, we ought to acknowledge that these sceptical anti-realists and knowledge-microscopists of today are in the right: the instinct which makes them recoil from *modern* reality stands unrefuted—what do we care about the retrograde bypaths they choose! The essential thing about them is *not* that they want to go 'back', but that they want to—get *away.* A little strength, soaring, courage, artistic power *more,* and they would want to go *up and away*—and not back!

11

It seems to me that there is today an effort going on everywhere to distract attention from the actual influence exercised on German philosophy by Kant and, in particular, prudently to gloss over the value he set upon himself. Kant was first and foremost proud of his table of categories; with this table in his hand he said: 'This is the hardest thing that could ever be undertaken on behalf of metaphysics.'—But let us understand this 'could be'! He was proud of having *discovered* a new faculty in man, the faculty of synthetic judgements *a priori*. Granted he deceived himself in this: the evolution and rapid burgeoning of German philosophy none the less depended on this pride of his and on the eager rivalry of the whole younger generation to discover, if possible, something of which to be still prouder—and in any event 'new faculties'!—But let us stop and reflect: it is time we did so. Kant asked himself: how are synthetic judgements *a priori possible?*—and what, really, did he answer? *By means of a faculty*: but unfortunately not in a few words, but so circumspectly, venerably, and with such an expenditure of German profundity and flourishes that the comical *niaiserie allemande* involved in such an answer was overlooked. People even lost their heads altogether on account of this new faculty, and the rejoicing reached its climax when Kant went on further to discover a moral faculty in man—for at that time the Germans were still moral and by no means practitioners of *Realpolitik*.—The honeymoon time of German philosophy arrived; and the young theologians of the College of Tübingen went straightaway off into the bushes—all in search of 'faculties'. And what did they not find—in that innocent, rich, still youthful era of German spirit, to which the malicious fairy, romanticism, piped and sang, in those days when he was not yet able to distinguish between 'finding' and 'inventing'! They found above all a faculty for the 'supra-sensible': Schelling baptized it intellectual intuition, and therewith satisfied the most heartfelt longings of his Germans, which longings were fundamentally pious. One can do no greater wrong to this whole high-spirited and enthusiastic movement, which was really youthfulness however boldly it disguised itself in hoary and senile concepts, then to take it seriously and, an even worse injustice, to treat it with moral indignation; it is enough to say that one grew older—and the dream disappeared. A time came when one rubbed one's eyes: one is still rubbing them today. One had been dreaming: and the first and foremost of the dreamers was—old Kant. 'By means of a faculty'—he had said, or at least meant. But is that—an answer? An explanation? Or is it not rather merely a repetition of the question? How does opium induce sleep? 'By means of a faculty', namely the *virtus dormitivia*—replies the doctor in Molière,

> *quia est in eo virtus dormitiva,*
> *cujus est natura sensus assoupire.*

But answers like that belong in comedy, and it is high time to replace the Kantian question 'how are synthetic judgements *a priori* possible?' with another question: 'why is belief in such judgements *necessary?*'"—that is to say, it is time to grasp that, for the purpose of preserving beings such as ourselves, such judgements must be *believed* to be true; although they might of course still be *false* judgements! Or more clearly, crudely and basically: synthetic judgements *a priori* should not 'be possible' at all: we have no right to them, in our mouths they are nothing but false judgements. But belief in their truth is, of course, necessary as foreground belief and ocular evidence belonging to the perspective optics of life.—Finally, in considering the enormous influence 'German philosophy'—I hope you understand its right to inverted commas?—has exercised throughout Europe, one cannot doubt that a certain *virtus dormitiva* has played a part in it: the noble idlers, the virtuous, the mystics, the artists, the three-quarter Christians and the political obscurantists of all nations were delighted to possess, thanks to German philosophy, an antidote to the still overwhelming sensualism which had overflowed out of the previous century into this, in short—'*sensus assoupire*' . . .

12

As for materialistic atomism, it is one of the best-refuted things there are; and perhaps no scholar in Europe is still so unscholarly today as to accord it serious significance except for handy everyday use (as an abbreviated means of expression)—thanks above all to the Pole Boscovich who, together with the Pole Copernicus, has been the greatest and most triumphant opponent of ocular evidence hitherto. For while Copernicus persuaded us to believe, contrary to all the senses, that the earth does *not* stand firm, Boscovich taught us to abjure belief in the last thing of earth that 'stood firm', belief in 'substance', in 'matter', in the earth-residuum and particle atom: it was the greatest triumph over the senses hitherto achieved on earth.—One must, however, go still further and also declare war, a remorseless war of the knife, on the 'atomistic need' which, like that more famous 'metaphysical need', still goes on living a dangerous after-life in regions where no one suspects it—one must also first of all finish off that other and more fateful atomism which Christianity has taught best and longest, the *soul atomism.* Let this expression be allowed to designate that belief which regards the soul as being something indestructible, eternal, indivisible, as a monad, as an *atomon*: *this* belief ought to be ejected from science! Between ourselves, it is not at all necessary by that same act to get rid of 'the soul' itself and thus forgo one of the oldest and most venerable of hypotheses: as is often the way with clumsy naturalists, who can hardly touch 'the soul' without losing it. But the road to new forms and refinements of the soul-hypothesis stands open: and such conceptions as 'mortal soul' and 'soul as multiplicity of the subject' and 'soul as social structure of the drives and emotions' want henceforth to possess civic rights in science. To be sure, when the *new* psychologist puts an end to the superstition which has hitherto flourished around the soul-idea with almost tropical luxuriance, he has as it were thrust himself out into a new wilderness and a new mistrust—it may be that the older psychologists had a merrier and more comfortable time of it—: ultimately, however, he sees that, by precisely that act, he has also condemned himself to *inventing* the new—and, who knows? perhaps to *finding* it.—

13

Physiologists should think again before postulating the drive to self-preservation as the cardinal drive in an organic being. A living thing desires above all to *vent* its strength—life as such is will to power—: self-preservation is only one of the indirect and most frequent *consequences* of it.— In short, here as everywhere, beware of *superfluous* teleological principles!—such as is the drive to self-preservation (we owe it to Spinoza's inconsistency). For this is a requirement of method, which has essentially to be economy of principles.

14

It is perhaps just dawning on five or six minds that physics too is only an interpretation and arrangement of the world (according to our own requirements, if I may say so!) and *not* an explanation of the world: but in so far as it is founded on belief in the senses it passes for more than that and must continue to do so for a long time to come. It has the eyes and the hands on its side, it has ocular evidence and palpability on its side: and this has the effect of fascinating, persuading, *convincing* an age with fundamentally plebeian tastes—for it instinctively follows the canon of eternal, popular sensualism. What is obvious, what has been 'explained'? Only that which can be seen and felt—thus far has every problem to be scrutinized. Obversely: it was precisely in opposition to palpability that the charm of the Platonic mode of thinking, which was a *noble* mode of thinking, consisted—on the part of men who perhaps rejoiced in even stronger and more exacting senses than our contemporaries possess, but who knew how to experience a greater triumph in mastering them: which they did by means of pale, cold, grey conceptual nets thrown over the motley whirl of the senses—the mob of the senses, as Plato called them. This overcoming and interpretation of the world in the manner of Plato involved a kind of *enjoyment* different from that which the physicists of today offer us, or from that offered us by the Darwinists and anti-teleologists among the labourers in physiology, with their principle of the 'smallest possible effort' and the greatest possible stupidity. 'Where man has nothing more to see or grasp he has nothing more to do'—that is certainly a different imperative from the Platonic, but for an uncouth industrious race of machinists and bridge-builders of the future, which has nothing but *course* work to get through, it may well be the right one.

15

If one is to pursue physiology with a good conscience one is compelled to insist that the organs of sense are *not* phenomena in the sense of idealist philosophy: for if they were they could not be causes! Sensualism therefore is at least a regulative hypothesis, certainly a heuristic principle.—What? and others even go so far as to say that the external world is the work of our organs? But then our body, as a piece of this external world, would be the work of our organs! But then our organs themselves would be—the work of our organs! This, it seems to me, is a complete *reductio ad absurdum,* supposing that the concept *causa sui* is something altogether absurd. Consequently the external world is *not* the work of our organs—?

16

There are still harmless self-observers who believe 'immediate certainties' exist, for example 'I think' or, as was Schopenhauer's superstition, 'I will': as though knowledge here got hold of its object pure and naked, as 'thing in itself', and no falsification occurred either on the side of the subject or on that of the object. But I shall reiterate a hundred times that 'immediate certainty', like 'absolute knowledge' and 'thing in itself', contains a *contradictio in adjecto*: we really ought to get free from the seduction of words! Let the people believe that knowledge is total knowledge, but the philosopher must say to himself: when I analyse the event expressed in the sentence 'I think', I acquire a series of rash assertions which are difficult, perhaps impossible, to prove—for example, that it is *I* who think, that it has to be something at all which thinks, that thinking is an activity and operation on the part of an entity thought of as a cause, that an 'I' exists, finally that what is designated by 'thinking' has already been determined—that I *know* what thinking is. For if I had not already decided that matter within myself, by what standard could I determine that what is happening is not perhaps 'willing' or 'feeling'? Enough: this 'I think' presupposes that I *compare* my present state with other known states of myself in order to determine what it is: on account of this retrospective connection with other 'knowledge' at any rate it possesses no immediate certainty for me.—In place of the 'immediate certainty' in which the people may believe in the present case, the philosopher acquires in this way a series of metaphysical questions, true questions of conscience for the intellect, namely: 'Whence do I take the concept of thinking? Why do I believe in cause and effect? What gives me the right to speak of an "I", and even of an "I" as cause, and finally of an "I" as cause of thought?' Whoever feels able to answer these metaphysical questions straight away with an appeal to a sort of *intuitive* knowledge, as he does who says: 'I think, and know that this at least is true, actual and certain'—will find a philosopher today ready with a smile and two question-marks. 'My dear sir,' the philosopher will perhaps give him to understand, 'it is improbable you are not mistaken: but why do you want the truth at all?—

17

As for the superstitions of the logicians, I shall never tire of underlining a concise little fact which these superstitious people are loath to admit—namely, that a thought comes when 'it' wants, not when 'I' want; so that it is a *falsification* of the facts to say: the subject 'I' is the condition of the predicate 'think'. *It* thinks: but that this 'it' is precisely that famous old 'I' is, to put it mildly, only an assumption, an assertion, above all not an 'immediate certainty'. For even with this 'it thinks' one has already gone too far: this 'it' already contains an *interpretation* of the event and does not belong to the event itself. The inference here is in accordance with the habit of grammar: 'thinking is an activity, to every activity pertains one who acts, consequently—'. It was more or less in accordance with the same scheme that the older atomism sought, in addition to the 'force' which acts, that little lump of matter in which it resides, out of which it acts, the atom; more rigorous minds at last learned to get along without this 'residuum of earth', and perhaps we and the logicians as well will one day accustom ourselves to getting along without that little 'it' (which is what the honest old 'I' has evaporated into).

18

It is certainly not the least charm of a theory that it is refutable: it is with precisely this charm that it entices subtler minds. It seems that the hundred times refuted theory of 'free will' owes its continued existence to this charm alone—: again and again there comes along someone who feels he is strong enough to refute it.

19

Philosophers are given to speaking of the will as if it were the best-known thing in the world; Schopenhauer, indeed, would have us understand that the will alone is truly known to us, known completely, known without deduction or addition. But it seems to me that in this case too Schopenhauer has done only what philosophers in general are given to doing: that he has taken up a *popular prejudice* and exaggerated it. Willing seems to me to be above all something *complicated,* something that is a unity only as a word—and it is precisely in this *one* word that the popular prejudice resides which has overborne the always inadequate caution of the philosophers. Let us therefore be more cautious for once, let us be 'unphilosophical'—let us say: in all willing there is, first of all, a plurality of sensations, namely the sensation of the condition we *leave,* the sensation of the condition towards which we *go,* the sensation of this 'leaving' and 'going' itself, and then also an accompanying muscular sensation which, even without our putting 'arms and legs' in motion, comes into play through a kind of habit as soon as we 'will'. As feelings, and indeed many varieties of feeling, can therefore be recognized as an ingredient of will, so, in the second place, can thinking: in every act of will there is a commanding thought—and do not imagine that this thought can be separated from the 'willing', as though will would then remain over! Thirdly, will is not only a complex of feeling and thinking, but above all an *affect*: and in fact the affect of command. What is called 'freedom of will' is essentially the affect of superiority over him who must obey: 'I am free, "he" must obey'—this consciousness adheres to every will, as does that tense attention, that straight look which fixes itself exclusively on *one* thing, that unconditional evaluation 'this and nothing else is necessary now', that inner certainty that one will be obeyed, and whatever else pertains to the state of him who gives commands. A man who *wills*—commands something in himself which obeys or which he believes obeys. But now observe the strangest thing of all about the will—about this so complex thing for which people have only *one* word: inasmuch as in the given circumstances we at the same time command *and* obey, and as the side which obeys knows the sensations of constraint, compulsion, pressure, resistance, motion which usually begin immediately after the act of will; inasmuch as, on the other hand, we are in the habit of disregarding and deceiving ourselves over this duality by means of the synthetic concept 'I', so a whole chain of erroneous conclusions and consequently of false evaluations of the will itself has become attached to the will as such—so that he who wills believes wholeheartedly that willing *suffices* for action. Because in the great majority of cases willing takes place only when the effect of the command, that is to say obedience, that is to say the action, was to be *expected,* the *appearance* has translated itself into the sensation, as if there were here a *necessity of effect.* Enough: he who wills believes with a tolerable degree of certainty that will and action are somehow one—he attributes the success, the carrying out of the willing, to the will itself, and thereby enjoys an increase of that sensation of power which all success brings with it. 'Freedom of will'—is the expression for that complex condition of pleasure of the person who wills, who commands and at the same time identifies himself with the executor of the command—who as such also enjoys the triumph over resistances involved but who thinks it was his will itself which overcame these resistances. He who wills adds in this way the sensations of pleasure of the successful executive agents, the serviceable 'underwills' or under-souls—for our body is only a social structure composed of many souls—to his sensations of pleasure as commander. *L'effet, c'est moi*: what happens here is what happens in every well-constructed and happy commonwealth: the ruling class identifies itself with the successes of the commonwealth. In all willing it is absolutely a question of commanding and obeying, on the basis, as I have said already, of a social structure composed of many 'souls': on which account a philosopher should claim the right to include willing as such within the field of morality: that is, of morality understood as the theory of the relations of dominance under which the phenomenon 'life' arises.—

20

That individual philosophical concepts are not something arbitrary, something growing up autonomously, but on the contrary grow up connected and related to one another; that, however suddenly and arbitrarily they appear to emerge in the history of thought, they none the less belong just as much to a system as do the members of the fauna of a continent: that fact is in the end also shown in the fact that the most diverse philosophers unfailingly fill out again and again a certain basic scheme of *possible* philosophies. Under an invisible spell they always trace once more the identical orbit: however, independent of one another they may feel, with their will to criticism or systematism, something in them leads them, something drives them in a definite order one after another: it is precisely that innate systematism and relationship of concepts. Their thinking is in fact not so much a discovering as a recognizing, a remembering, a return and home-coming to a far-off, primordial total household of the soul out of which those concepts once emerged—philosophizing is to that extent a species of atavism of the first rank. The singular family resemblance between all Indian, Greek and German philosophizing is easy enough to explain. Where there exists a language affinity it is quite impossible, thanks to the common philosophy of grammar—I mean thanks to unconscious domination and directing by similar grammatical functions—to avoid everything being prepared in advance for a similar evolution and succession of philosophical systems: just as the road seems to be barred to certain other possibilities of world interpretation. Philosophers within the domain of the Ural-Altaic languages (in which the concept of the subject is least developed) will in all probability look 'into the world' differently and be found on different paths from the Indo-Germans and Moslems: the spell of definite grammatical function and racial conditions.—So much by way of retort to Locke's superficiality with regard to the origin of ideas.

21

The *causa sui* is the best self-contradiction hitherto imagined, a kind of logical rape and unnaturalness: but mankind's extravagant pride has managed to get itself deeply and frightfully entangled with precisely this piece of nonsense. For the desire for 'freedom of will' in that metaphysical superlative sense which is unfortunately still dominant in the minds of the half-educated, the desire to bear the whole and sole responsibility for one's actions and to absolve God, world, ancestors, chance, society from responsibility for them, is nothing less than the desire to be precisely that *causa sui* and, with more than Münchhausen temerity, to pull oneself into existence out of the swamp of nothingness by one's own hair. Assuming it is possible in this way to get beyond the peasant simplicity of this celebrated concept 'free will' and banish it from one's mind, I would then ask whoever does that to carry his 'enlightenment' a step further and also banish from his mind the contrary of that unnatural concept 'free will': I mean 'unfree will', which amounts to an abuse of cause and effect. One ought not to make 'cause' and 'effect' *into material things,* as natural scientists do (and those who, like them, naturalize in their thinking—), in accordance with the prevailing mechanistic stupidity which has the cause press and push until it 'produces an effect'; one ought to employ 'cause' and 'effect' only as pure *concepts,* that is to say as conventional fictions for the purpose of designation, mutual understanding, *not* explanation. In the 'in itself' there is nothing of 'causal connection', of 'necessity', of 'psychological unfreedom'; there 'the effect' *does not* 'follow the cause', there no 'law' rules. It is *we* alone who have fabricated causes, succession, reciprocity, relativity, compulsion, number, law, freedom, motive, purpose; and when we falsely introduce this world of symbols into things and mingle it with them as though this symbol-world were an 'in itself', we once more behave as we have always behaved, namely *mythologically.* 'Unfree will' is mythology: in real life it is only a question of *strong* and *weak* wills.—It is almost always a symptom of what is lacking in himself when a thinker detects in every 'causal connection' and 'psychological necessity' something of compulsion, exigency, constraint, pressure, unfreedom: such feelings are traitors, the person who has them gives himself away. And, if I have observed correctly, 'unfreedom of will' is in general conceived as a problem from two completely antithetical standpoints but always in a profoundly *personal* manner: one will at no price give up his 'responsibility', his belief in *himself,* the personal right to *his* deserts (the vain races belong here—), the other, on the contrary, will not be responsible for anything, to blame for anything, and out of an inner self-contempt wants to be able to *shift off* his responsibility for himself somewhere else. This latter, when he writes books, tends today to espouse the cause of the criminal; his most pleasing disguise is a kind of socialist sympathy. And the fatalism of the weak-willed is indeed beautified to an astonishing degree when it can present itself as '*la religion de la souffrance humaine*': that is *its* 'good taste'.

22

You must pardon me as an old philologist who cannot refrain from the maliciousness of putting his finger on bad arts of interpretation: but 'nature's conformity to law' of which you physicists speak so proudly, as though—it exists only thanks to your interpretation and bad 'philology'—it is not a fact, not a 'text', but rather only a naïve humanitarian adjustment and distortion of meaning with which you go more than halfway to meet the democratic instincts of the modern soul! 'Everywhere equality before the law—nature is in this matter no different from us and no better off than we': a nice piece of mental reservation in which vulgar hostility towards everything privileged and autocratic, as well as a second and more subtle atheism, lie once more disguised. '*Ni dieu, ni maître*'—that is your motto too: and therefore 'long live the law of nature!'—isn't that so? But, as aforesaid, that is interpretation, not text; and someone could come along who, with an opposite intention and art of interpretation, knew how to read out of the same nature and with regard to the same phenomena the tyrannically ruthless and inexorable enforcement of power-demands—an interpreter who could bring before your eyes the universality and unconditionality of all 'will to power' in such a way that almost any word and even the word 'tyranny' would finally seem unsuitable or as a weakening and moderating metaphor—as too human—and who none the less ended by asserting of this world the same as you assert of it, namely that it has a 'necessary' and 'calculable' course, but *not* because laws prevail in it but because laws are absolutely *lacking,* and every power draws its ultimate consequences every moment. Granted this too is only interpretation, and you will be eager enough to raise this objection?—well, so much the better.—

23

All psychology has hitherto remained anchored to moral prejudices and timidities: it has not ventured into the depths. To conceive it as morphology and the *development-theory of the will to power,* as I conceive it—has never yet so much as entered the mind of anyone else: in so far as it is permissible to see in what has hitherto been written a symptom of what has hitherto been kept silent. The power of moral prejudices has penetrated deep into the most spiritual world, which is apparently the coldest and most free of presuppositions—and, as goes without saying, has there acted in a harmful, inhibiting, blinding, distorting fashion. A genuine physio-psychology has to struggle with unconscious resistances in the heart of the investigator, it has 'the heart' against it: even a theory of the mutual dependence of the 'good' and the 'wicked' impulses causes, as a more refined immorality, revulsion to a conscience still strong and hearty—and even more a theory of the derivation of all good impulses from wicked ones. Supposing, however, that someone goes so far as to regard the emotions of hatred, envy, covetousness, and lust for domination as life-conditioning emotions, as something which must fundamentally and essentially be present in the total economy of life, consequently must be heightened further if life is to be heightened further—he suffers from such a judgement as from seasickness. And yet even this hypothesis is as far from being the strangest and most painful in this tremendous, still almost unexplored realm of dangerous knowledge—and there are in fact a hundred good reasons why everyone should keep away from it who—*can!* On the other hand: if your ship *has* been driven into these seas, very well! Now clench your teeth! Keep your eyes open! Keep a firm hand on the helm!—We sail straight over morality and *past* it, we flatten, we crush perhaps what is left of our own morality by venturing to voyage thither—but what do *we* matter! Never yet has a *deeper* world of insight revealed itself to daring travellers and adventurers: and the psychologist who in this fashion 'brings a sacrifice'—it is *not* the *sacrifizio dell'intelletto,* on the contrary!—will at least be entitled to demand in return that psychology shall again be recognized as the queen of the sciences, to serve and prepare for which the other sciences exist. For psychology is now once again the road to the fundamental problems.

PHENOMENOLOGY AND PHILOSOPHY

Edmund Husserl

PHENOMENOLOGY

Natural thinking in science and everyday life is untroubled by the difficulties concerning the possibility of cognition. *Philosophical thinking* is circumscribed by one's position toward the problems concerning the possibility of cognition. The perplexities in which reflection about the possibility of a cognition that "gets at" the things themselves becomes entangled: How can we be sure that cognition accords with things as they exist in themselves, that it "gets at them"? What do things in themselves care about our ways of thinking and the logical rules governing them? These are laws of how we think; they are psychological laws—Biologism, psychological laws as laws of adaptation.

Absurdity: to begin with, when we think naturally about cognition and fit it and its achievements into the natural ways of thinking which pertains to the sciences we arrive at theories that are appealing at first. But they end in contradiction or absurdity—Inclination to open scepticism.

Even this attempt to look at these problems scientifically we can call "theory of knowledge." At any rate what emerges is the idea of a theory of knowledge as a science which solves the above-mentioned difficulties, gives us an ultimate, clear, therefore inherently consistent insight into the essence of cognition and the possibility of its achievements. The critique of cognition in this sense is the condition of the possibility of a metaphysics.

The *method* of the critique of cognition is the phenomenological method, phenomenology as the general doctrine of essences, within which the science of the essence of cognition finds its place.

What sort of method is this? How can a science of cognition be established if cognition in general, what cognizing means and can accomplish, is questioned? What method can here reach the goal?

A. THE FIRST STEP IN THE PHENOMENOLOGICAL ORIENTATION

(1) Right away we become dubious whether such a science is at all possible. If it questions all cognition, every cognition chosen as a starting point is questioned. How then can it ever begin?

This, however, is only a specious difficulty. In "being called into question," cognition is neither *disavowed* nor regarded as in *every* sense doubtful. The question is about some accomplishments imputed to cognition, whereas in fact it is even an open question whether the difficulties pertain to all possible types of cognition. At any rate, if the theory of knowledge is to concern itself with the possibility of cognition it must have cognitions of the possibilities of cognition which, as such, are beyond question; indeed, cognitions in the fullest sense, cognitions about which absolutely no doubt of their having reached their objects is possible. If we are uncertain or unclear as to how it is possible for cognition to reach its object, and we are inclined to doubt that such a thing is possible, we must, first of all, have before us indubitable examples of cognitions or possible cognitions which really reach, or would reach, their respective objects. At the outset we must not take anything as a cognition just because it seems to be one; otherwise we would have no possible, or what comes to the same thing, no sensible objective.

Here the *Cartesian method of doubt* provides a starting point. Without doubt there is *cogitatio,* there is, namely, the mental process during the [subject's] undergoing it and in a simple reflection upon it. The seeing, direct grasping and having of the *cogitatio* is already a cognition. The *cogitationes* are the first absolute data.

(2) What follows naturally is our *first question in the theory of knowledge*: What distinguishes the certainty in these examples from the uncertainty in other instances of alleged cognition? Why is there in certain cases a tendency toward scepticism and toward asking the sceptical question: How can cognition reach a being, and why is there not this doubt and this difficulty in connection with the *cogitationes?*

People answer at first—that is indeed the answer ready at hand—in terms of the pair of concepts or words *immanence* and *transcendence.* The "seeing" cognition of the *cogitatio* is immanent. The cognition belonging to the objective sciences, the natural sciences and the sciences of culture (*Geisteswissenschaften*) and on closer inspection also the mathematical sciences, is transcendent. Involved in the objective sciences is the *doubtfulness of transcendence,* the question: How can cognition reach beyond itself? How can it reach a being that is not to be found within the confines of consciousness? There is not this difficulty with the "seeing" cognition of the *cogitatio.*

(3) Next, one is inclined to interpret, as if this were obvious, immanence as genuine immanence (*reelle Immanenz*) and even perhaps to interpret it psychologically, as *immanence in something real* (*reale Immanenz*): the object of cognition too, is within the cognition process as a real actuality, or in the [stream of] ego-consciousness of which the mental process is a part. That the cognition act can hit upon and find its object in the same [stream of] consciousness and within the same real here and now, that is what is taken for granted. The neophyte will say, at this point, that the immanent is in me, the transcendent outside of me.

On a closer view, however, *genuine immanence* (*reelle Immanenz*) differs from *immanence in the sense of self-givenness as constituted in evidence* (*Evidenz*). The genuinely immanent (*reell Immanente*) is taken as the indubitable just on account of the fact that it presents nothing else, "points" to nothing "outside" itself, for what is here intended is fully and adequately given in itself. Any self-givenness other than that of the genuinely immanent (*reell Immanente*) is not yet in view.

(4) So for the moment no distinction is made. The first step toward clarity now is this: the genuinely immanent (*reell Immanentes*), or what would here mean the same, the adequately self-given, is beyond question. I may make use of it. That which is transcendent (not genuinely immanent) I may not use. Therefore, I must accomplish a *phenomenological reduction*: I must *exclude all that is transcendently posited.*

Why? [Because] if I am in the dark as to how cognition can reach that which is transcendent, not given in itself but "intended as being outside," no cognition or science of the transcendent can help to dispel the darkness. What I want is *clarity.* I want to understand *the possibility* of that reaching. But this, if we examine its sense, signifies: I want to come face to face with the essence of the possibility of that reaching. I want to make it given to me in an act of "seeing." A "seeing" cannot be demonstrated. The blind man who wishes to see cannot be made to see by means of scientific proofs. Physical and physiological theories about colors give no "seeing" (*schauende*) clarity about the meaning of color as those with eyesight have it. If, therefore, the critique of cognition is a science, as it doubtless is in the light of these considerations, a science which is to clarify all species and forms of cognition, *it can make no use of any science of the natural sort.* It cannot tie itself to the conclusions that any natural science has reached about what is. For it they remain in question. As far as the critique of cognition is concerned, all the sciences are only *phenomena of science.* Every tie of that sort signifies a defective μετάβασις (foundation). This comes about only by way of a mistaken but often seductive *shifting between problems*: between explaining cognition as a fact of nature in psychological and scientific terms and elucidating cognition in terms of its essential capabilities to accomplish its task. Accordingly, if we are to avoid this confusion and remain constantly mindful of the meaning of the question concerning these capabilities, we need *phenomenological reduction.*

This means: everything transcendent (that which is not given to me immanently) is to be assigned the index zero, i.e., its existence, its validity is not to be assumed as such, except at most as *the phenomenon of a claim to validity.* I am to treat all sciences only as phenomena, hence not as systems of valid truths, not as premises, not even as hypotheses for me to reach truth with. This applies to the whole of psychology and the whole of natural science. Meanwhile, the proper *meaning of our principle* is in the constant challenge to stay with the objects as they are in question *here* in the critique of cognition and not to confuse the problems *here* with quite different ones. The elucidation of the ways in which cognition is possible does not depend upon the ways of objective science. To bring knowledge to evident self-givenness and to seek to view the nature of its accomplishment does not mean to deduce, to make inductions, to calculate, etc. It is not the same as eliciting, with reasons, novel things from things already given or purportedly given.

B. THE SECOND LEVEL OF THE PHENOMENOLOGICAL ORIENTATION

We now need a *new stratum of considerations* in order to achieve a higher level of clarity about the nature of phenomenological research and its problems.

(1) First, the Cartesian *cogitatio* already requires the phenomenological reduction. The psychological phenomenon in psychological apperception and objectification is not a truly absolute datum. The truly absolute datum is the *pure phenomenon,* that which is reduced. The mentally active ego, the object, man in time, the thing among things, etc., are not absolute data; hence man's mental activity as his activity is no absolute datum either. *We abandon finally the standpoint of psychology, even of descriptive psychology.* And so what is also *reduced* is the question which initially drove us: no longer how can I, this man, contact in my mental processes something existing in itself, perhaps out there, beyond me; but we now replace this hitherto ambiguous question, unstable and complex, because of its transcendent burden, with the *pure basic question*: How can the pure phenomenon of cognition reach something which is not immanent to it? How can the absolute self-givenness of cognition reach something not self-given and how is this reaching to be understood?

At the same time the concept of *genuine immanence* (*reellen Immanenz*) is reduced. It no longer signifies immanence in something *real* (*reale Immanenz*), the immanence in human consciousness and in the real (*realen*) psychic phenomenon.

(2) Once we have the "seen" phenomena, it seems that we already have a phenomenology, a science of these phenomena.

But as soon as we begin there, we notice a certain constriction. / The field of absolute phenomena—taken one at a time—does not seem to be enough to fulfill our intentions. What good are single "seeings" to us, no matter how securely they bring our *cogitationes* to self-givenness? At first it seems beyond question that on the basis of these "seeings" we can undertake logical operations, can compare, contrast, subsume under concepts, predicate, although, as appears later, behind these operations stand new objectives. But even if what here seems beyond question were taken for granted and considered no further, we could not understand how we could here arrive at universally valid findings of the sort we need.

But one thing seems to help us along: *eidetic abstraction.* It yields inspectable universals, species, essences, and so it seems to provide the redeeming idea: for do we not seek "seeing" clarity about the essence of cognition? Cognition belongs to the sphere of *cogitationes.* Accordingly, we must through "seeing" bring its universal objects into the consciousness of the universal. Thus it becomes possible to have a doctrine about the essence of cognition.

We take this step in agreement with a tenet of Descartes's concerning *clear and distinct perceptions.* The "existence" of the *cogitatio* is guaranteed by its absolute *self-givenness,* by its givenness in *pure evidence* (*Evidenz*). Whenever we have pure evidence (*Evidenz*), the pure viewing and grasping of something objective directly and in itself, we have the same guarantees, the same certainties.

This step gave us a new objectivity as absolutely given, i.e., the *objectivity of essences;* and as to begin with the logical acts which find expression in assertions based upon what is intuited remain unnoticed, so now we get the field of *assertions about essences,* viz., of what is generally the case as given in pure "seeing." That is to say at first undifferentiated from the individually given universal objects.

(3) Yet do we now have everything; do we have the fully delineated phenomenology and the clear self-evidence to put us in the position of having what we need for the critique of cognition? And are we clear about the issues to be resolved?

No, the step we took leads us further. It makes clear to us in the first place that *genuine* (*reell*) *immanence* (and the same is true of transcendence) is but a special case of the *broader concept of immanence as such.* No longer is it a commonplace and taken on face value that *the absolutely given* and the *genuinely immanent* are one and the same. For that which is universal is absolutely given but is not genuinely immanent. *The act of cognizing* the universal is something singular. At any given time, it is a moment in the stream of consciousness. *The universal itself,* which is given in evidence (*Evidenz*) within the stream of consciousness is nothing singular but just a universal, and in the genuine (*reellen*) sense it is transcendent.

Consequently, the idea of *phenomenological reduction* acquires a more immediate and more profound determination and a clearer meaning. It means not the exclusion of the genuinely transcendent (perhaps even in some psychologico-empirical sense), but the exclusion of the transcendent as such as something to be accepted as existent, i.e., everything that is not evident givenness in its true sense, that is not absolutely given to pure "seeing." But, of course, everything of what we said remains. Inductive or deductive scientific conclusions or facets, etc., from hypotheses, facts, axioms, remain excluded and are allowed only as "phenomena"; and the same with all reference to any "knowing" and "cognition": inquiry must concern itself always with *pure "seeing"* and, therefore, not with the genuinely immanent. It is inquiry within the sphere of pure evidence, inquiry into essences. We also said that its field is the *a priori within absolute self-givenness.*

Thus the field is now characterized. It is a field of absolute cognitions, within which the ego and the world and God and the mathematical manifolds and whatever else may be a scientifically objective matter are held in abeyance, cognitions which are, therefore, also not dependent on these matters, which are valid in their own right, whether we are sceptics with regard to the others or not. All that remains as it is. The root of the matter, however, is *to grasp the meaning of the absolutely given, the absolute clarity of the given,* which excludes every meaningful doubt, in a word, *to grasp the absolutely "seeing" evidence which gets hold of itself.* To a certain extent in the discovery of all this lies the historical significance of the Cartesian method of doubt. But for Descartes to discover and to abandon were the same. We do nothing but clearly formulate and develop consistently what was always implicit in this age-old project. We part company in this connection with psychologistic interpretations of evidence in terms of feelings.

C. THE THIRD LEVEL OF THE PHENOMENOLOGICAL ORIENTATION

Once more we need a new level of considerations, to give us greater clarity about the meaning of phenomenology and to develop further its problems.

How far does self-givenness reach? Is it contained in the givenness of the *cogitatio* and in the ideations which grasp it in its generality? Our phenomenological sphere, the sphere of absolute clarity, of immanences in the true sense, reaches no farther than self-givenness reaches.

We are once again led somewhat deeper, and in depths lie the obscurities and in the obscurities lie the problems.

Everything seemed at first simple and hardly requiring hard work. The prejudice about immanence as genuine immanence, as if the latter were what mattered, one may cast off, and yet one remains at first wedded to genuine immanence, at least in a certain sense. It seems, at first, that in "seeing" essences we have only to grasp in its generality the genuinely immanent in the *cogitationes* and to establish the connections rooted in essences. This, too, seems an easy matter. We reflect; we look back at our own acts; we appraise their genuine contents, as they are, only under phenomenological reduction. This appears to be the sole difficulty. And now, of course, there is nothing further than to lift that which is "seen" into consciousness of universality.

The matter, however, becomes less cozy when we take a closer look at the data. First, the *cogitationes,* which we regard as simple data and in no way mysterious, hide all sorts of transcendencies.

If we look closer and notice how in the mental process, say of [perceiving] a sound, even after phenomenological reduction, *appearance and that which appears stand in contrast,* and this *in the midst of pure givenness,* hence in the midst of true immanence, then we are taken aback. Perhaps the sound lasts. We have there the patently given unity of the sound and its duration with its temporal phases, the present and the past. On the other hand, when we reflect, the phenomenon of enduring sound, itself a temporal phenomenon, has its own now-phase and past phases. And if one picks out a now-phase of the phenomenon there is not only the objective now of the sound itself, but the now of the sound is but a point in the duration of a sound.

Detailed analyses will be given in the course of our special tasks. The above suggestion is enough to call attention to a new point: that the phenomenon of sound perception, even as evident and reduced, demands within the immanent a distinction between *appearance* and *that which appears.* We thus have two absolute data, the givenness of the appearing and the givenness of the object; and the object within this immanence is not immanent in the sense of genuine immanence; it is not a concrete part (*Stück*) of the appearance, i.e., the past phases of the enduring sound are now still objective and yet they are not genuinely contained in the present moment of the appearance. Therefore, we also find in the case of the phenomenon of perception what we found in the case of consciousness of universals, namely, that it is a consciousness which constitutes something self-given which is not contained within what is occurring [in the world] and is not at all found as *cogitatio.*

At the lowest level of reflection, the naive level, at first it seems as if evidence were a matter of simple "seeing," a mental inspection without a character of its own, always one and the same and in itself undifferentiated: the "seeing" just "sees" the things (*Sachen*), the things are simply there and in the truly evident "seeing" they are there in consciousness, and "seeing" is simply to "see" them. Or, to use our previous simile: a direct grasping or taking or pointing to something that simply is and is there. All difference is thus in the things that exist in themselves and have their differences through themselves.

And now how different the "seeing" of things shows itself to be on closer analysis. Even if we retain under the heading of attention the notion of an undifferentiated and in itself no further describable "seeing," it is, nevertheless, apparent that it really makes no sense at all to talk about things which are "simply there" and just need to be "seen." On the contrary, this "simply being there" consists of certain mental processes of specific and changing structure, such as perception, imagination, memory, predication, etc., and in them the things are not contained as in a hull or vessel. Instead, the things come to be *constituted* in these mental processes, although in reality they are not at all to be found in them. For "things to be given" is for them to be *exhibited* (represented) as so and so in such phenomena. And this is not to say that the things once more exist in themselves and "send their representatives into consciousness." This sort of thing cannot occur to us within the sphere of phenomenological reduction. Instead, the things are and are given in appearance and in virtue of the appearance itself; though they are, or are taken as, individually separable from the appearance, they are essentially inseparable from it insofar as the single appearance (the consciousness of the given) is not in question.

Thus this marvelous correlation between the *phenomenon of cognition* and the *object of cognition* reveals itself everywhere. Now let us notice that the task of phenomenology, or rather the area of its tasks and inquiries, is no such trivial things as merely looking, merely opening one's eyes. Already in the first and simplest cases, in the lowest forms of cognition, the greatest difficulties confront pure analysis and the inspection of essences. It is easy to talk of correlation in general but it is very difficult to clarify the way in which an object of cognition *constitutes* itself in cognition. And the task if just this: within the framework of pure evidence (*Evidenz*) or self-givenness *to trace all forms of givenness and all correlations* and to conduct an elucidatory analysis. Of course, to do this we need to take account not only of single acts but also of their complexities, of the consistency or inconsistency of their connections and of the intentions (*Teleologien*) apparent in them. These connections are not conglomerations but distinctively connected and as it were congruent unities, and unities of cognition, which, as unities of cognition have also their unitary objective correlates. Thus they belong themselves to the *cognitive acts,* their types are cognition types, their native forms are forms of thought and forms of intuition (the word not here to be taken in its Kantian sense).

It now remains to trace step by step the data in all their modifications, those that are, properly speaking, data and those that are not, the simple and the compounded ones, those that so to say are constituted at once and those that essentially are built up stepwise, those that are absolutely valid and those that in the process of cognition acquire givenness and validity in an unlimited progression.

We finally arrive in this way at an understanding of how the transcendent real object can be met (can be known in its nature) in the cognitive act as that which one primarily means by it, and how the sense of this meaning is filled out step by step in a developing cognitive context (if only it has the proper forms which belong to the constitution of the object of experience). We then understand how the object of experience is progressively constituted, and how this manner of being constituted is prescribed. We understand that such a stepwise constitution is required by the very essence of the experienced object.

Along this path one approaches the methodological forms which determine all the sciences and are constitutive of all scientifically given objects, and so also the elucidation of the theory of science and with it implicitly the elucidation of all the sciences; however, only implicitly, i.e., it is only once this enormous work of elucidation has been accomplished that the critique of cognition will be fit to become a critique of the specialized sciences and thereby to evaluate them metaphysically.

These then are the problems of givenness, the problems of the *constitution of objects of all sorts within cognition.* The phenomenology of cognition is the science of cognitive phenomena in two senses. On the one hand it has to do with cognitions as appearances, presentations, acts of consciousness in which this or that object is presented, is an object of consciousness, passively or actively. On the other hand, the phenomenology of cognition has to do with these objects as presenting themselves in this manner. The word "phenomenon" is ambiguous in virtue of the essential correlation between *appearance and that which appears.* Φαινόμενον (phenomenon) in its proper sense means that which appears, and yet it is by preference used for the appearing itself, for the subjective phenomenon (if one may use this expression which is apt to be misunderstood in the vulgar psychological sense).

In reflection, the *cogitatio,* the appearing itself, becomes an object, and this encourages the rise of ambiguity. Finally, we need not repeat once more that in speaking about investigating the objects and modes of cognition, we also mean investigation into essences, which, in the sphere of the absolutely given, exhibits in a general way the ultimate meaning, the possibility, the essence of the objectivity of cognition and of the cognition of objects.

It goes without saying that the *general phenomenology of reason* has to solve also the parallel problems of the correlation between *valuing* and the *things valued,* etc. If the word "phenomenology" were used so broadly as to cover the analysis of everything self-given, the incoherent data would become coherent: analyzing sense-given entities according to their various kinds, etc.—the common element is then in the methodology of the analysis of essences within the sphere of immediate evidence.

PHILOSOPHY

The task which the philosopher puts to himself, his life-goal as a philosopher: universal science of the world, universal, definitive knowledge, the universe of truths in themselves about the world, the world in itself. What about this goal and its attainability? Can I begin with a truth, a definitive truth? A definitive truth, a truth through which I can assert something about something that is in itself and be indubitably certain of its definitiveness? If I already had such "immediately self-evident" truths, then I could perhaps mediately derive new ones from them. But where do I have them? Is any entity in itself so indubitably certain to me through immediate experience that I could, in accord with this experience, with descriptive concepts which immediately fit this experience or the content of this experience, express immediate truths in themselves? But what about any and every experience of what is in the world, experience of what I am immediately certain of as existing spatiotemporally? It is certain; but this certainty can modalize itself, it can become doubtful, it can dissolve in the course of experience into illusion: no immediate experiential assertion gives me an entity as what it is in itself but only something meant with certainty that must verify itself in the course of my experiencing life. But the verification which lies merely in the harmonious character of actual experience does not prevent the possibility of illusion.

Experiencing—in general, living as an ego (thinking, valuing, acting)—I am necessarily an "I" that has its "thou," its "we," its "you"—the "I" of the

Reprinted by permission of Northwestern University Press, from Edmund Husserl, "Philosophy as Mankind's Self-Reflection: the Self-Realization of Reason," in Husserl, *The Crisis of European Sciences and Transcendental Phenomenology,* trans. David Carr, pp. 335–341. Evanston, Illinois: Northwestern University Press, 1970.

personal pronouns. And equally necessarily, I am and we are, in the community of egos, correlates of everything to which we address ourselves as existing in the world, which we always presuppose as being commonly experienceable in addressing ourselves to it, naming it, speaking about it, grounding our knowledge, and which as such is there for us, is actual, is valid for us in the community of conscious life as a life which is not individually isolable but is internally communalized. But this is always such that the world is our common world, necessarily having ontic validity; yet in particular matters I can enter into contradiction with others, into doubt and negation of being, similarly to the way I do this with myself. Now where and how do I have something that exists definitively in itself? [Corrected] experience—either as communal experience and reciprocal correction or as one's own personal experience and self-correction—does not change the relativity of experience; even as communal experience it is relative, and thus all descriptive assertions are necessarily relative, and all conceivable inferences, deductive or inductive, are relative. How can thinking achieve anything but relative truths? The man of everyday life is after all not without reason; he is a thinking being, he has the καθόλον, unlike the animal, hence he has language, description, he makes inferences, he asks questions of truth, he verifies, argues, and decides in a rational way—but does the whole idea of "truth in itself" have a meaning for him? Is this [idea], together with its correlate, what exists in itself, not a philosophical invention? But it is not a fiction, not a dispensable invention without significance, but one which raises—or is called to raise—man to a new level in a new historical development [*Historizität*] of human life. A historical development whose entelechy is this new idea and the philosophical or scientific praxis belonging to it, the method of a new sort of scientific thinking.

"In-itself" means as much as "objective," at least in the way that the objective is opposed in the exact sciences to the merely subjective, the latter being understood as that which merely indicates something objective or that in which something objective is supposed merely to appear. It is merely a phenomenon of something objective; to come to know the objective by recognizing it within the phenomena and to determine it through objective concepts and truths, this is the task.

But the sense of the task thus posed and of its presuppositions, that is, the presuppositions of all method, has never been seriously considered and itself investigated in a scientific manner, in an ultimately responsible manner, so that one has not even become clear on the fact that the sense of natural-scientific objectivity, or of the task and method of natural science, is fundamentally and essentially different from the sense of objectivity, task, and method in the humanistic disciplines. This is as true of psychology as it is of the so-called concrete humanistic disciplines. One has expected the same objectivity from psychology as from physics, and because of this a psychology in the full and actual sense has been quite impossible; for an objectivity after the fashion of natural science is downright absurd when applied to the soul, to subjectivity, whether as an individual subjectivity, individual person, and individual life or as communally historical subjectivity, as social subjectivity in the broadest sense.

This is the ultimate sense of the objection that one must make to the philosophies of all times—with the exception of the philosophy of idealism, which of course failed in its method: that it was not able to overcome the naturalistic objectivism which was from the beginning and always remained a very natural temptation. As I said, only idealism, in all its forms, attempts to lay hold of subjectivity as subjectivity and to do justice to the fact that the world is never given to the subject and the communities of subjects in any other way than as the subjectively relative valid world with particular experiential content and as a world which, in and through subjectivity, takes on ever new transformations of meaning; and that even the apodictically persisting conviction of one and the same world, exhibiting itself subjectively in changing ways, is a conviction motivated purely within subjectivity, a conviction whose sense—the world itself, the actually existing world—never surpasses the subjectivity that brings it about. But idealism was always too quick with its theories and for the most part could not free itself from hidden objectivistic presuppositions; or else, as speculative idealism, it passed over the task of interrogating, concretely and analytically, actual subjectivity, i.e., subjectivity as having the actual phenomenal world in intuitive validity—which, properly understood, is nothing other than carrying out the phenomenological reduction and putting transcendental phenomenology into action. This explains, by the way, why I call the phenomenology I have developed transcendental and why I speak in it of transcendental subjectivity. For when Kant gives the old word a new meaning through his critique of reason, one can easily convince oneself that the quite different idealism of Berkeley and Hume, indeed any idealism, looked at more closely, has the same thematic field and poses questions within this field which are only differently formulated.

Reason is the specific characteristic of man, as a being living in personal activities and habitualities. This life, as personal life, is a constant becoming through a constant intentionality of development. What becomes, in this life, is the person himself. His being is forever becoming; and in the correlation of individual-personal and communal-personal being this is true of both, i.e., of the [individual] man and of unified human civilizations.

Human personal life proceeds in stages of self-reflection and self-responsibility from isolated occasional acts of this form to the stage of universal self-reflection and self-responsibility, up to the point of seizing in consciousness the idea of autonomy, the idea of a resolve of the will to shape one's whole personal life into the synthetic unity of a life of universal self-responsibility and, correlatively, to shape oneself into the true "I," the free, autonomous "I" which seeks to realize his innate reason, the striving to be true to himself, to be able to remain identical with himself as a reasonable "I"; but there is an inseparable correlation here between individual persons and communities by virtue of their inner immediate and mediate interrelatedness in all their interests—interrelated in both harmony and conflict—and also in the necessity of allowing individual-personal reason to come to ever more perfect realization only as communal-personal reason and vice versa.

The universally, apodictically grounded and grounding science arises now as the necessarily highest function of mankind, as I said, namely, as making possible mankind's development into a personal autonomy and into an all-encompassing autonomy for mankind—the idea which represents the driving force of life for the highest stage of mankind.

Thus philosophy is nothing other than [rationalism], through and through, but it is rationalism differentiated within itself according to the different stages of the movement of intention and fulfillment; it is *ratio in the constant movement of self-elucidation,* begun with the first breakthrough of philosophy into mankind, whose innate reason was previously in a state of concealment, of nocturnal obscurity.

The image of the dawn characterizes Greek philosophy in its beginning stage, the first elucidation through the first cognitive conception of "what is" as universe, as world of what is; following soon after this, in a subjective direction of gaze, is the correlative discovery of long-familiar man as the subject of the world, this subject being conceived, however, as man within mankind, who is related through his reason to the totality of being and to himself. From the viewpoint of merely external historical scholarship, with its focus upon men existing in the world and upon the philosophies as theoretical constructs (systems of propositions), the history of philosophy is [merely] one cultural configuration among others and, in its external, faded sequence (which the historical point of view—*lucus a non lucendo*—calls a development), a causal process occurring in the world, in the world's space-time.

Seen from the inside, however, it is a struggle of the generations of philosophers, who are the bearers of this spiritual development, living and surviving in spiritual community, in the constant struggle of "awakened" reason to come to itself, to an understanding of itself, to a reason which concretely understands itself in understanding the existing world, existing in its whole universal truth. [To say that] philosophy, science in all its forms, is rational—that is a tautology. But in all its forms it is on its way to a higher rationality; it is rationality which, discovering again and again its unsatisfying relativity, is driven on in its toils, in its will to attain the true and full rationality. But finally it discovers that this rationality is an idea residing in the infinite and is *de facto* necessarily [only] on the way; but [it discovers] also that there is a final form here which is at the same time the beginning form of a new sort of infinity and relativity—this, however, in a double sense of discovery which signifies, historically, two epochs of beginning and advance.

The first is the epoch in which the demand of apodicticity is discovered and for the first time lucidly taken up into the will by a historically individualized philosophical personality: that is, Descartes, as the initiator of the historical epoch of the modern period. The discovery is submerged for a time, lapsing into misinterpretation; [but] it is relatively fruitful even under this misinterpretation, taking effect in the sciences of rationalism, its a priori and empirical sciences. The consciousness of the inadequacy of this philosophy arouses reaction: apart from the sensationalistic and finally skeptical philosophy (Hume) there is the Kantian and subsequent transcendental philosophy—in which the transcendental primal motive, however, the motive which arises out of the demand for apodicticity, is still not aroused.

The up-and-down of the historical movements—newly strengthened empiricist sensationalism and skepticism, newly strengthened rationalism in the older scientific style, German Idealism and the reaction against it—all this together characterizes the first epoch, that of the whole "modern period." The second period is the renewed beginning, as the reappropriation of the Cartesian discovery, the fundamental demand of apodicticity; and in this beginning, through the changed historical situation (to which all the fateful developments and philosophies of the first epoch belong), there arise forces of motivation, a radical thinking-through of the genuine and imperishable sense of apodicticity (apodicticity as a fundamental problem), the exhibiting of the true method of an apodictically grounded and apodictically progressing philosophy; and included within this is the discovery of the radical contrast between what is usually called apodictic knowledge and what, in the transcendental understanding, outlines the primal ground and the primal method of all philosophy. It is precisely with this that there begins a philosophy with the deepest and most universal self-understanding of the philosophizing ego as the bearer of absolute reason coming to itself, of the same ego as implicating, in his apodictic being-for-himself, his fellow subjects and all possible fellow philosophers; [this is] the discovery of absolute intersubjectivity (objectified in the world as the whole of mankind), as that in which reason, in obscurity, in elucidation, in the movement of lucid self-understanding, is in infinite progress; the discovery of the necessary concrete manner of being of absolute (in the ultimate sense, transcendental) subjectivity in a transcendental life of constant "world-constitution"; the new discovery, correlative to this, of the "existing world," whose ontic meaning, as transcendentally constituted, results in a new meaning for what, in the earlier stages, was called world, world-truth, world-knowledge; but within this a new meaning is also given to human existence: [man's] existence in the spatiotemporally pregiven world as the self-objectification of transcendental subjectivity and its being, its constituting life; what follows this is the ultimate self-understanding of man as being responsible for his own human being: his *self-understanding as being in being called to a life of apodicticity,* not only in abstractly practicing apodictic science in the usual sense but [as being mankind] which realizes its whole concrete being in apodictic freedom by becoming apodictic mankind in the whole active life of its reason—through which it is human; as I said, mankind understanding itself as rational, understanding that it is rational in seeking to be rational; that this signifies an infinity of living and striving toward reason; that reason is precisely that which man *qua* man, in his innermost being, is aiming for, that which alone can satisfy him, make him "blessed"; that reason allows for no differentiation into "theoretical," "practical," "aesthetic," or whatever; that being human is teleological being and an ought-to-be, and that this teleology holds sway in each and every activity and project of an ego; that through self-understanding in all this it can know the apodictic *telos*; and that this knowing, the ultimate self-understanding, has no other form than self-understanding according to a priori principles as self-understanding in the form of philosophy.

THE END OF PHILOSOPHY AND THE TASK OF THINKING

Martin Heidegger

The title designates the attempt at a reflection which persists in questioning. The questions are paths to an answer. If the answer could be given, the answer would consist in a transformation of thinking, not in a propositional statement about a matter at stake.

The following text belongs to a larger context. It is the attempt undertaken again and again ever since 1930 to shape the question of Being and Time in a more primal way. This means; to subject the point of departure of the question in *Being and Time* to an immanent criticism. Thus it must become clear to what extent the *critical* question of what the matter of thinking is, necessarily and continually belongs to thinking. Accordingly, the name of the task of *Being and Time* will change.

We are asking:

1. What does it mean that philosophy in the present age has entered its final stage?
2. What task is reserved for thinking at the end of philosophy?

1. *WHAT DOES IT MEAN THAT PHILOSOPHY IN THE PRESENT AGE HAS ENTERED ITS FINAL STAGE?*

Philosophy is metaphysics. Metaphysics thinks being as a whole—the world, man, God—with respect to Being, with respect to the belonging together of beings in Being. Metaphysics thinks beings as being in the manner of representational thinking which gives reasons. For since the beginning of philosophy and with that beginning, the Being of beings has showed itself as the ground (*arche, aition*). The ground is from where beings as such are what they are in their becoming, perishing and persisting as something that can be known, handled and worked upon. As the ground, Being brings beings to their actual presencing. The ground shows itself as presence. The present of presence consists in the fact that it brings what is present each in its own way to presence. In accordance with the actual kind of presence, the ground has the character of grounding as the ontic causation of the real, as the transcendental making possible of the objectivity of objects, as the dialectical mediation of the movement of the absolute Spirit, of the historical process of production, as the will to power positing values.

What characterizes metaphysical thinking which grounds the ground for beings is the fact that metaphysical thinking departs from what is present in its presence, and thus represents it in terms of its ground as something grounded.

What is meant by the talk about the end of philosophy? We understand the end of something all too easily in the negative sense as a mere stopping, as the lack of continuation, perhaps even as decline and impotence. In contrast, what we say about the end of philosophy means the completion of metaphysics. However, completion does not mean perfection as a consequence of which philosophy would have to have attained the highest perfection at its end. Not only do we lack any criterion which would permit us to evaluate the perfection of an epoch of metaphysics as compared with any other epoch. The right to this kind of evaluation does not exist. Plato's thinking is no more perfect than Parmenides'. Hegel's philosophy is no more perfect than Kant's. Each epoch of philosophy has its own necessity. We simply have to acknowledge the fact that a philosophy is the way it is. It is not our business to prefer one to the other, as can be the case with regard to various *Weltanschauungen.*

The old meaning of the word "end" means the same as place: "from one end to the other" means: from one place to the other. The end of philosophy is the place, that place in which the whole of philosophy's history is gathered in its most extreme possibility. End as completion means this gathering.

Throughout the whole history of philosophy, Plato's thinking remains decisive in changing forms. Metaphysics is Platonism. Nietzsche characterizes his philosophy as reversed Platonism. With the reversal of metaphysics which was already accomplished by Karl Marx, the most extreme possibility of philosophy is attained. It has entered its final stage. To the extent that philosophical thinking is still attempted, it manages only to attain an epigonal renaissance and variations of that renaissance. Is not then the end of philosophy after all a cessation of thinking? To conclude this would be premature.

As a completion, an end is the gathering into the most extreme possibilities. We think in too limited a fashion as long as we expect only a development of recent philosophies of the previous style. We forget that already in the age of Greek philosophy a decisive characteristic of philosophy appears: the development of sciences within the field which philosophy opened up. The development of the sciences is at the same time their separation from philosophy and the establishment of their independence. This process belongs to the completion of philosophy. Its development is in full swing today in all regions of beings. This development looks like the mere dissolution of philosophy, and is in truth its completion.

It suffices to refer to the independence of psychology, sociology, anthropology as cultural anthropology, to the role of logic as logistics and semantics. Philosophy turns into the empirical science of man, of all of what can become the experiential object of his technology for man, the technology by which he establishes himself in the world by working on it in the manifold modes of making and shaping. All of this happens everywhere on the basis and according to the criterion of the scientific discovery of the individual areas of beings.

No prophecy is necessary to recognize that the sciences now establishing themselves will soon be determined and guided by the new fundamental science which is called cybernetics.

This science corresponds to the determination of man as an acting social being. For it is the theory of the steering of the possible planning and arrangement of human labor. Cybernetics transforms language into an exchange of news. The arts become regulated-regulating instruments of information.

The development of philosophy into the independent sciences which, however, interdependently communicate among themselves ever more markedly, is the legitimate completion of philosophy. Philosophy is ending in the present age. It has found its place in the scientific attitude of socially active humanity. But the fundamental characteristic of this scientific attitude is its cybernetic, that is, technological character. The need to ask about the modern technology is presumably dying out to the same extent that technology more definitely characterizes and regulates the appearance of the totality of the world and the position of man in it.

The sciences will interpret everything in their structure that is still reminiscent of the origin from philosophy in accordance with the rules of science, that is, technologically. Every science understands the categories upon which it remains dependent for the articulation and delineation of its area of investigation as working hypotheses. Their truth is measured not only by the effect which their application brings about within the progress of research.

Scientific truth is equated with the efficiency of these effects.

The sciences are now taking over as their own task what philosophy in the course of its history tried to present in part, and even there only inadequately, that is, the ontologies of the various regions of beings (nature, history, law, art). The interest of the sciences is directed toward the theory of the necessary structural concepts of the coordinated areas of investigation. "Theory" means now: supposition of the categories which are allowed only a cybernetical function, but denied any ontological meaning. The operational and model character of representational-calculative thinking becomes dominant.

However, the sciences still speak about the Being of beings in the unavoidable supposition of their regional categories. They just don't say so. They can deny their origin from philosophy, but never dispense with it. For in the scientific attitude of the sciences, the document of their birth from philosophy still speaks.

The end of philosophy proves to be the triumph of the manipulable arrangement of a scientific-technological world and of the social order proper to this world. The end of philosophy means: the beginning of the world civilization based upon Western European thinking.

But is the end of philosophy in the sense of its development to the sciences also already the complete realization of all the possibilities in which the thinking of philosophy was posited? Or is there a *first* possibility for thinking apart from the *last* possibility which we characterized (the dissolution of philosophy in the technologized sciences), a possibility from which the thinking of philosophy would have to start out, but which as philosophy it could nevertheless not experience and adopt?

If this were the case, then a task would still have to be reserved for thinking in a concealed way in the history of philosophy from its beginning to its end, a task accessible neither to philosophy as metaphysics nor, and even less so, to the sciences stemming from philosophy. Therefore we ask:

2. *WHAT TASK IS RESERVED FOR THINKING AT THE END OF PHILOSOPHY?*

The mere thought of such a task of thinking must sound strange to us. A thinking which can be neither metaphysics nor science?

A task which has concealed itself from philosophy since its very beginning, even in virtue of that beginning, and thus has withdrawn itself continually and increasingly in the time to come?

A task of thinking which—so it seems—includes the assertion that philosophy has not been up to the matter of thinking and has thus become a history of mere decline?

Is there not an arrogance in these assertions which desires to put itself above the greatness of the thinkers of philosophy?

This suspicion easily suggests itself. But it can as easily be removed. For every attempt to gain insight into the supposed task of thinking finds itself moved to review the whole of the history of philosophy. Not only this, but it is even forced to think the historicity of that which grants a possible history to philosophy.

Because of this, that supposed thinking necessarily falls short of the greatness of the philosophers. It is less than philosophy. Less also because the direct or indirect effect of this thinking on the public in the industrial age, formed by technology and science, is decisively less possible to this thinking than it was in the case of philosophy.

But above all, the thinking in question remains slight because its task is only of a preparatory, not of a founding character. It is content with awakening a readiness in man for a possibility whose contour remains obscure, whose coming remains uncertain.

Thinking must first learn what remains reserved and in store for thinking to get involved in. It prepares its own transformation in this learning.

We are thinking of the possibility that the world civilization which is just now beginning might one day overcome the technological-scientific-industrial character as the sole criterion of man's world sojourn. This may happen not of and through itself, but in virtue of the readiness of man for a determination which, whether listened to or not, always speaks in the destiny of man which has not yet been decided. It is just as uncertain whether world civilization will soon be abruptly destroyed or whether it will be stabilized for a long time, in a stabilization, however, which will not rest in something enduring, but rather establish itself in a sequence of changes, each of which presenting the latest fashion.

The preparatory thinking in question does not wish and is not able to predict the future. It only attempts to say something to the present which was already said a long time ago precisely at the beginning of philosophy and for that beginning, but has not been explicitly thought. For the time being, it must be sufficient to refer to this with the brevity required. We shall take a directive which philosophy offers as an aid in our undertaking.

When we ask about the task of thinking, this means in the scope of philosophy: to determine that which concerns thinking, which is still controversial for thinking, which is the controversy. This is what the word "matter" means in the German language. It designates that with which thinking has to do in the case at hand, in Plato's language *to pragma auto* (cf. "The Seventh Letter" 341 C7).

In recent times, philosophy has of its own accord expressly called thinking "to the things themselves." Let us mention two cases which receive particular attention today. We hear this call "to the things themselves" in the "Preface" which Hegel has placed before his work which was published in 1807, *System of Science,*[1] first part: "The Phenomenology of Spirit." This preface is not the preface to the *Phenomenology,* but to the *System of Science,* to the whole of philosophy. The call "to the things themselves" refers ultimately—and that means: according to the matter, primarily—to the *Science of Logic.*

In the call "to the things themselves," the emphasis lies on the "themselves." Heard superficially, the call has the sense of a rejection. The inadequate relations to the matter of philosophy are rejected. Mere talk about the purpose of philosophy belongs to these relations, but so does mere reporting about the results of philosophical thinking. Both are never the real totality of philosophy. The totality shows itself only in its becoming. This occurs in the developmental presentation of the matter. In the presentation, theme and method coincide. For Hegel, this identity is called: the idea. With the idea, the matter of philosophy "itself" comes to appear. However, this matter is historically determined: subjectivity. With Descartes' *ego cogito,* says Hegel, philosophy steps on firm ground for the first time where it can be at home. If the *fundamentum absolutum* is attained with the *ego cogito* as the distinctive *subiectum,* this means: The subject is the *hypokeimenon* which is transferred to consciousness, what is truly present, what is unclearly enough called "substance" in traditional language.

When Hegel explains in the Preface (ed. Hoffmeister, p. 19), "The true (in philosophy) is to be understood and expressed not as substance, but just as much as subject," then this means: The Being of beings, the presence of what is present, is only manifest and thus complete presence when it becomes present as such for itself in the absolute Idea. But since Descartes, *idea* means: *perceptio.* Being's coming to itself occurs in speculative dialectic. Only the movement of the idea, the method, is the matter itself. The call "to the thing itself" requires a philosophical method appropriate in it.

However, what the matter of philosophy should be is presumed to be decided from the outset. The matter of philosophy as metaphysics is the Being of beings, their presence in the form of substantiality and subjectivity.

A hundred years later, the call "to the thing itself" again is uttered in Husserl's treatise *Philosophy as Exact Science.* It was published in the first volume of the journal *Logos* in 1910–11 (pp. 289 ff.). Again, the call has at first the sense of a rejection. But here it aims in another direction than Hegel's. It concerns naturalistic psychology which claims to be the genuine scientific method of investigating consciousness. For this method blocks access to the phenomena of intentional consciousness from the very beginning. But the call "to the thing itself" is at the same time directed against historicism which gets lost in treatises about the standpoints of philosophy and in the ordering of types of philosophical *Weltanschauungen.* About this Husserl says in italics (*ibid.*, p. 340): *"The stimulus for investigation must start not with philosophies, but with issues and problems."*

And what is at stake in philosophical investigation? In accordance with the same tradition, it is for Husserl as for Hegel the subjectivity of consciousness. For Husserl, the *Cartesian Meditations* were not only the topic of the Parisian lectures in February, 1920. Rather, since the time following the *Logical Investigations,* their spirit accompanied the impassioned course of his philosophical investigations to the end. In its negative and also in its positive sense, the call "to the thing itself" determines the securing and development of method. It also determines the procedure of philosophy by means of which the matter itself can be demonstrated as a datum. For Husserl, "the principle of all principles" is first of all not a principle of content, but one of method. In his work published in 1913,[2] Husserl devoted a special section (section 24) to the determination of "the principle of all principles." "No conceivable theory can upset this principle," says Husserl (*ibid,.* p. 44).

"The principle of all principles" reads:

> *that every primordial dator Intuition is a source of authority* (Rechtsquelle) *for knowledge, that whatever presents itself in "Intuition" in primordial form* (*as it were in its bodily reality*)*, is simply to be accepted as it gives itself out to be, though only within the limits in which it then presents itself.*

"The principle of all principles" contains the thesis of the precedence of method. This principle decides what matter alone can suffice for the method. "The principle of principles" requires reduction to absolute subjectivity as the matter of philosophy. The transcendental reduction to absolute subjectivity gives and secures the possibility of grounding the objectivity of all objects (the Being of this being) in its valid structure and consistency, that is, in its constitution, in and through subjectivity. Thus transcendental subjectivity proves to be "the sole absolute being" (*Formal and Transcendental Logic,* 1929, p. 240). At the same time, transcendental reduction as the method of "universal science" of the constitution of the Being of beings has the same mode of being as this absolute being, that is, the manner of the matter most native to philosophy. The method is not only directed toward the matter of philosophy. It does not just belong to the matter as a key belongs to a lock. Rather, it belongs to the matter because it is "the matter itself." If one wanted to ask: Where does "the principle of all principles" get its unshakable right, the answer would have to be: from transcendental subjectivity which is already presupposed as the matter of philosophy.

We have chosen a discussion of the call "to the thing itself" as our guideline. It was to bring us to the path which leads us to a determination of the task of thinking at the end of philosophy. Where are we now? We have arrived at the insight that for the call "to the thing itself," what concerns philosophy as its matter is established from the outset. From the perspective of Hegel and Husserl—and not only from their perspective—the matter of philosophy is subjectivity. It is not the matter as such that is controversial for the call, but rather its presentation by which the matter itself becomes present. Hegel's speculative dialectic is the movement in which the matter as such comes to itself, comes to its own presence. Husserl's method is supposed to bring the matter of philosophy to its ultimately originary givenness, that means: to its own presence.

The two methods are as different as they could possibly be. But the matter as such which they are to present is the same, although it is experienced in different ways.

But of what help are these discoveries to us in our attempt to bring the task of thinking to view? They don't help us at all as long as we do not go beyond a mere discussion of the call and ask what remains unthought in the call "to the thing itself." Questioning in this way, we can become aware how something which it is no longer the matter of philosophy to think conceals itself precisely where philosophy has brought its matter to absolute knowledge and to ultimate evidence.

But what remains unthought in the matter of philosophy as well as in its method? Speculative dialectic is a mode in which the matter of philosophy comes to appear of itself and for itself, and thus becomes presence. Such appearance necessarily occurs in some light. Only by virtue of light, i.e., through brightness, can what shines show itself, that is, radiate. But brightness in its turn rests upon something open, something free which might illuminate it here and there, now and then. Brightness plays in the open and wars there with darkness. Wherever a present being encounters another present being or even only lingers near it—but also where, as with Hegel, one being mirrors itself in another speculatively—there openness already rules, open region is in play. Only this openness grants to the movement of speculative thinking the passage through that which it thinks.

We call this openness which grants a possible letting-appear and show "opening." In the history of language, the German word "opening" is a borrowed translation of the French *clairière.* It is formed in accordance with the older words *Waldung* (foresting) and *Feldung* (fielding).

The forest clearing (opening) is experienced in contrast to dense forest, called "density" (*Dickung*) in older language. The substantive "opening" goes back to the verb "to open." The adjective *licht* "open" is the same word as "light." To open something means: To make something light, free and open, e.g., to make the forest free of trees at one place. The openness thus originating is the clearing. What is light in the sense of being free and open has nothing in common with the adjective "light," meaning "bright"—neither linguistically nor factually.[3] This is to be observed for the difference between openness and light. Still, it is possible that a factual relation between the two exists. Light can stream into the clearing, into its openness, and let brightness play with darkness in it. But light never first creates openness. Rather, light presupposes openness. However, the clearing, the opening, is not only free for brightness and darkness, but also for resonance and echo, for sounding and diminishing of sound. The clearing is the open for everything that is present and absent.

It is necessary for thinking to become explicitly aware of the matter called opening here. We are not extracting mere notions from mere words, e.g., "opening," as it might easily appear on the surface. Rather, we must observe the unique matter which is adequately named with the name "opening." What the word designates in the connection we are now thinking, free openness, is a "primal phenomenon," to use a word of Goethe's. We would have to say a primal matter. Goethe notes (*Maxims and Reflections,* n. 993): "Look for nothing behind phenomena: they themselves are what is to be learned." This means: The phenomenon itself, in the present case the opening, sets us the task of learning from it while questioning it, that is, of letting it say something to us.

Accordingly, we may suggest that the day will come when we will not shun the question whether the opening, the free open, may not be that within which alone pure space and ecstatic time and everything present and absent in them have the place which gathers and protects everything.

In the same way as speculative dialectical thinking, originary intuition and its evidence remain dependent upon openness which already dominates, upon the opening. What is evident is what can be immediately intuited. *Evidentia* is the word which Cicero uses to translate the Greek *enargeia,* that is, to transform it into the Roman. *Enargeia,* which has the same root as *argentum* (silver), means that which in itself and of itself radiates and brings itself to light. In the Greek language, one is not speaking about the action of seeing, about *videre,* but about that which gleams and radiates. But it can only radiate if openness has already been granted. The beam of light does not first create the opening, openness, it only traverses it. It is only such openness that grants to giving and receiving at all what is free, that in which they can remain and must move.

All philosophical thinking which explicitly or inexplicitly follows the call "to the thing itself" is already admitted to the free space of the opening in its movement and with its method. But philosophy knows nothing of the opening.

Philosophy does speak about the light of reason, but does not heed the opening of Being. The *lumen naturale,* the light of reason, throws light only on openness. It does concern the opening, but so little does it form it that it needs it in order to be able to illuminate what is present in the opening. This is true not only of philosophy's *method,* but also and primarily of its *matter,* that is, of the presence of what is present. To what extent the *subiectum,* the *hypokeimenon,* that which already lies present, thus what is present in its presence is constantly thought also in subjectivity cannot be shown here in detail. Refer to Heidegger, *Nietzsche,* vol. 2 (1961), pp. 429 ff.

We are concerned now with something else. Whether or not what is present is experienced, comprehended or presented, presence as lingering in openness always remains dependent upon the prevalent opening. What is absent, too, cannot be as such unless it presences in the *free space of the opening.*

All metaphysics including its opponent positivism speaks the language of Plato. The basic word of its thinking, that is, of his presentation of the Being of beings, is *eidos, idea:* the outward appearance in which beings as such show themselves. Outward appearance, however, is a manner of presence. No outward appearance without light—Plato already knew this. But there is no light and no brightness without the opening. Even darkness needs it. How else could we happen into darkness and wander through it? Still, the opening as such as it prevails through Being, through presence, remains unthought in philosophy, although the opening is spoken about in philosophy's beginning. How does this occur and with which names? Answer:

In Parmenides' reflective poem which, as far as we know, was the first to reflect explicitly upon the Being of beings, which still today, although unheard, speaks in the sciences into which philosophy dissolves. Parmenides listens to the claim:

> . . . *kreo de se panta puthestha*
> *emen aletheies eukukleos atremes etor*
> *ede broton doxas, tais ouk emi pistis alethes.*
> Fragment I, 28 ff.
> . . . but you should learn all:
> the untrembling heart of unconcealment, well-rounded
> and also the opinions of mortals,
> lacking the ability to trust what is unconcealed.[4]

Aletheia, unconcealment, is named here. It is called well-rounded because it is turned in the pure sphere of the circle in which beginning and end are everywhere the same. In this turning, there is no possibility of twisting, deceit and closure. The meditative man is to experience the untrembling heart of unconcealment. What does the word about the untrembling heart of unconcealment mean? It means unconcealment itself in what is most its own, means the place of stillness which gathers in itself what grants unconcealment to begin with. That is the opening of what is open. We ask: openness for what? We have already reflected upon the fact that the path of thinking, speculative and intuitive, needs the traversable opening. But in that opening rests possible radiance, that is, the possible presencing of presence itself.

What prior to everything else first grants unconcealment in the path on which thinking pursues one thing and perceives it: *hotos estin . . . einai:* that presence presences. The opening grants first of all the possibility of the path to presence, and grants the possible presencing of that presence itself. We must think *aletheia,* unconcealment, as the opening which first grants Being and thinking and their presencing to and for each other. The quiet heart of the opening is the place of stillness from which alone the possibility of the belonging together of Being and thinking, that is, presence and perceiving, can arise at all.

The possible claim to a binding character or commitment of thinking is grounded in this bond. Without the preceding experience of *aletheia* as the opening, all talk about committed and non-committed thinking remains without foundation. Where does Plato's determination of presence as *idea* have its binding character from? With regard to what is Aristotle's interpretation of presencing as *energeia* binding?

Strangely enough, we cannot even ask these questions always neglected in philosophy as long as we have not experienced what Parmenides had to experience: *aletheia,* unconcealment. The path to it is distinguished from the street on which the opinion of mortals must wander around. *Aletheia* is nothing mortal, just as little as death itself.

It is not for the sake of etymology that I stubbornly translate the name *aletheia* as unconcealment, but for the matter which must be considered when we think that which is called Being and thinking adequately. Unconcealment is, so to speak, the element in which Being and thinking and their belongings together exist. *Aletheia* is named at the beginning of philosophy, but afterward it is not explicitly thought as such by philosophy. For since Aristotle it became the task of philosophy as metaphysics to think beings as such ontotheologically.

If this is so, we have no right to sit in judgment over philosophy, as though it left something unheeded, neglected it and was thus marred by some essential deficiency. The reference to what is unthought in philosophy is not a criticism of philosophy. If a criticism is necessary now, then it rather concerns the attempt which is becoming more and more urgent ever since *Being and Time* to ask about a possible task of thinking at the end of philosophy. For the question now arises, late enough: Why is *aletheia* not translated with the usual name, with the word "truth"? The answer must be:

Insofar as truth is understood in the traditional "natural" sense as the correspondence of knowledge with beings demonstrated in beings, but also insofar as truth is interpreted as the certainty of the knowledge of Being, *aletheia,* unconcealment in the sense of the opening may not be equated with truth. Rather, *aletheia,* unconcealment thought as opening, first grants the possibility of truth. For truth itself, just as Being and thinking, can only be what it is in the element of the opening. Evidence, certainty in every degree, every kind of verification of *veritas* already move *with* that *veritas* in the realm of the prevalent opening.

Aletheia, unconcealment thought as the opening of presence, is not yet truth. Is *aletheia* then less than truth? Or is it more because it first grants truth as *adequatio* and *certitudo,* because there can be no presence and presenting outside of the realm of the opening?

This question we leave to thinking as a task. Thinking must consider whether it can even raise this question at all as long as it thinks philosophically, that is, in the strict sense of metaphysics which questions what is present only with regard to its presence.

In any case, one thing becomes clear: To raise the question of *aletheia,* of unconcealment as such, is not the same as raising the question of truth. For this reason, it was inadequate and misleading to call *aletheia* in the sense of opening, truth.[5] The talk about the "truth of Being" has a justified meaning in Hegel's *Science of Logic,* because here truth means the certainty of absolute knowledge. But Hegel also, as little as Husserl, as little as all metaphysics, does not ask about Being as Being, that is, does not raise the question how there can be presence as such. There is presence only when opening is dominant. Opening is named with *aletheia,* unconcealment, but not thought as such.

The natural concept of truth does not mean unconcealment, not in the philosophy of the Greeks either. It is often and justifiably pointed out that the word *alethes* is already used by Homer only in the *verba dicendi,* in statement and thus in the sense of correctness and reliability, not in the sense of unconcealment. But this reference means only that neither the poets nor everyday language usage, not even philosophy see themselves confronted with the task of asking how truth, that is, the correctness of statements, is granted only in the element of the opening of presence.

In the scope of this question, we must acknowledge the fact that *aletheia,* unconcealment in the sense of the opening of presence, was originally only experienced as *orthotes,* as the correctness of representations and statements. But then the assertion about the essential transformation of truth, that is, from unconcealment to correctness, is also untenable.[6] Instead we must say: *Aletheia,* as opening of presence and presenting in thinking and saying, originally comes under the perspective of *homoiosis* and *adaequatio,* that is, the perspective of adequation in the sense of the correspondence of representing with what is present.

But this process inevitably provokes another question: How is it that *aletheia,* unconcealment, appears to man's natural experience and speaking *only* as correctness and dependability? Is it because man's ecstatic sojourn in the openness of presencing is turned only toward what is present and the existent presenting of what is present? But what else does this mean than that presence as such, and together with it the opening granting it, remain unheeded? Only what *aletheia* as opening grants is experienced and thought, not what it is as such.

This remains concealed. Does this happen by chance? Does it happen only as a consequence of the carelessness of human thinking? Or does it happen because self-concealing, concealment, *lethe* belongs to *a-letheia,* not just as an addition, not as shadow to light, but rather as the heart of *aletheia*? And does not even a keeping and preserving rule in this self-concealing of the opening of presence from which unconcealment can be granted to begin with, and thus what is present can appear in its presence?

If this were so, then the opening would not be the mere opening of presence, but the opening of presence concealing itself, the opening of a self-concealing sheltering.

If this were so, then with these questions we would reach the path to the task of thinking at the end of philosophy.

But isn't this all unfounded mysticism or even bad mythology, in any case a ruinous irrationalism, the denial of *ratio*?

I return to the question: What does *ratio, nous, noein,* perceiving (*Vernunft—Vernehmen*) mean? What does ground and principle and especially principle of all principles mean? Can this ever be sufficiently determined unless we experience *aletheia* in a Greek manner as unconcealment and then, above and beyond the Greek, think it as the opening of self-concealing? As long as *ratio* and the rational still remain questionable in what is their own, talk about irrationalism is unfounded. The technological scientific rationalization ruling the present age justifies itself every day more surprisingly by its immense results. But these results say nothing about what the possibility of the rational and the irrational first grants. The effect proves the correctness of technological scientific rationalization. But is the manifest character of what-is exhausted by what is demonstrable? Doesn't the insistence on what is demonstrable block the way to what-is?

Perhaps there is a thinking which is more sober than the irresistible race of rationalization and the sweeping character of cybernetics. Presumably it is precisely this sweeping quality which is extremely irrational.

Perhaps there is a thinking outside of the distinction of rational and irrational still more sober than scientific technology, more sober and thus removed, without effect and yet having its own necessity. When we ask about the task of this thinking, then not only this thinking, but also the question about it is first made questionable. In view of the whole philosophical tradition, this means:

We all still need an education in thinking, and before that first a knowledge of what being educated and uneducated in thinking means. In this respect, Aristotle gives us a hint in Book IV of his *Metaphysics* (1006a ff.). It reads: *esti gar apaideusia to me gignoskein tinon dei zetein apodeixin kai tinon ou dei.* "For it is uneducated not to have an eye for when it is necessary to look for a proof, and when this is not necessary."

This sentence demands careful reflection. For it is not yet decided in what way that which needs no proof in order to become accessible to thinking is to be experienced. Is it dialectical mediation or originary intuition or neither of the two? Only the peculiar quality of that which demands of us above all else to be admitted can decide about that. But how is this to make the decision possible for us before we have not admitted it? In what circle are we moving here, inevitably?

Is it the *eukukleos alethein,* well-founded unconcealment itself, thought as the opening?

Does the name for the task of thinking then read instead of *Being and Time:* Opening and Presence?

But where does the opening come from and how is it given? What speaks in the "It gives"?

The task of thinking would then be the surrender of previous thinking to the determination of the matter of thinking.

NOTES

1. *Wissenschaft, scientia,* body of knowledge, not "science" in the present use of that word. For German Idealism, science is the name for philosophy. (Tr.)
2. English edition: *Ideas* (New York: Collier Books, 1962). (Tr.)
3. Both meanings exist in English for light. The meaning Heidegger intends is related to lever (i.e., alleviate, lighten a burden). (Tr.)
4. Standard translation: "It is needful that you should learn of all matters—both the unshaken heart of well-rounded truth and the opinions of mortals which lack true belief." (Tr.)
5. How the attempt to think a matter can at times stray from that which a decisive insight has already shown, is demonstrated by a passage from *Being and Time* (1927) (p. 262, New York: Harper & Row, 1962). To translate this word (*aletheia*) as "truth," and, above all, to define this expression conceptually in theoretical ways, is to cover up the meaning of what the Greeks made "self-evidently" basic for the terminological use of aletheia as a prephilosophical way of understanding it.
6. This statement has profound implications for Heidegger's book *Platons Lehbre von der Wahrheit.* (Tr.)

EXISTENTIALISM

Jean-Paul Sartre

What is meant by the term *existentialism?*

Most people who use the word would be rather embarrassed if they had to explain it, since, now that the word is all the rage, even the work of a musician or painter is being called existentialist. A gossip columnist in *Clartés* signs himself *The Existentialist,* so that by this time the word has been so stretched and has taken on so broad a meaning, that it no longer means anything at all. It seems that for want of an advance-guard doctrine analogous to surrealism, the kind of people who are eager for scandal and flurry turn to this philosophy which in other respects does not at all serve their purposes in this sphere.

Actually, it is the least scandalous, the most austere of doctrines. It is intended strictly for specialists and philosophers. Yet it can be defined easily. What complicates matters is that there are two kinds of existentialist; first, those who are Christian, among whom I would include Jaspers and Gabriel Marcel, both Catholic; and on the other hand the atheistic existentialists, among whom I class Heidegger, and then the French existentialists and myself. What they have in common is that they think that existence precedes essence, or, if you prefer, that subjectivity must be the starting point.

Just what does that mean? Let us consider some object that is manufactured, for example, a book or a paper-cutter: here is an object which has been made by an artisan whose inspiration came from a concept. He referred to the concept of what a paper-cutter is and likewise to a known method of production, which is part of the concept, something which is, by and large, a routine. Thus, the paper-cutter is at once an object produced in a certain way and, on the other hand, one having a specific use; and one can not postulate a man who produces a paper-cutter but does not know what it is used for. Therefore, let us say that, for the paper-cutter, essence—that is, the ensemble of both the production routines and the properties which enable it to be both produced and defined—precedes existence. Thus, the presence of the paper-cutter or book in front of me is determined. Therefore, we have here a technical view of the world whereby it can be said that production precedes existence.

When we conceive God as the Creator, He is generally thought of as a superior sort of artisan. Whatever doctrine we may be considering, whether one like that of Descartes or that of Leibnitz, we always grant that will more or less follows understanding or, at the very least, accompanies it, and that when God creates He knows exactly what He is creating. Thus, the concept of man

Reprinted by permission of Philosophical Library, excerpted from Jean-Paul Sartre, "Existentialism," in Sartre, *Existentialism and Human Emotions,* trans. Bernard Frechtman, pp. 12–40. New York: Philosophical Library, 1957.

in the mind of God is comparable to the concept of paper-cutter in the mind of the manufacturer, and, following certain techniques and a conception, God produces man, just as the artisan, following a definition and a technique, makes a paper-cutter. Thus, the individual man is the realization of a certain concept in the divine intelligence.

In the eighteenth century, the atheism of the *philosophes* discarded the idea of God, but not so much for the notion that essence precedes existence. To a certain extent, this idea is found everywhere; we find it in Diderot, in Voltaire, and even in Kant. Man has a human nature; this human nature, which is the concept of the human, is found in all men, which means that each man is a particular example of a universal concept, man. In Kant, the result of this universality is that the wild-man, the natural man, as well as the bourgeois, are circumscribed by the same definition and have the same basic qualities. Thus, here too the essence of man precedes the historical existence that we find in nature.

Atheistic existentialism, which I represent, is more coherent. It states that if God does not exist, there is at least one being in whom existence precedes essence, a being who exists before he can be defined by any concept, and that this being is man, or, as Heidegger says, human reality. What is meant here by saying that existence precedes essence? It means that, first of all, man exists, turns up, appears on the scene, and, only afterwards, defines himself. If man, as the existentialist conceives him, is indefinable, it is because at first he is nothing. Only afterward will he be something, and he himself will have made what he will be. Thus, there is no human nature, since there is no God to conceive it. Not only is man what he conceives himself to be, but he is also only what he wills himself to be after this thrust toward existence.

Man is nothing else but what he makes of himself. Such is the first principle of existentialism. It is also what is called subjectivity, the name we are labeled with when charges are brought against us. But what do we mean by this, if not that man has a greater dignity than a stone or table? For we mean that man first exists, that is, that man first of all is the being who hurls himself toward a future and who is conscious of imagining himself as being in the future. Man is at the start a plan which is aware of itself, rather than a patch of moss, a piece of garbage, or a cauliflower; nothing exists prior to this plan; there is nothing in heaven: man will be what he will have planned to be. Not what he will want to be. Because by the word "will" we generally mean a conscious decision, which is subsequent to what we have already made of ourselves. I may want to belong to a political party, write a book, get married; but all that is only a manifestation of an earlier, more spontaneous choice that is called "will." But if existence really does precede essence, man is responsible for what he is. Thus, existentialism's first move is to make every man aware of what he is and to make the full responsibility of his existence rest on him. And when we say that a man is responsible for himself, we do not only mean that he is responsible for his own individuality, but that he is responsible for all men.

The word subjectivism has two meanings, and our opponents play on the two. Subjectivism means, on the one hand, that an individual chooses and makes himself; and, on the other, that it is impossible for man to transcend human subjectivity. The second of these is the essential meaning of existentialism. When we say that man chooses his own self, we mean that every one of us does likewise; but we also mean by that that in making this choice he also chooses all men. In fact, in creating the man that we want to be, there is not a single one of our acts which does not at the same time create an image of man as we think he ought to be. To choose to be this or that is to affirm at the same time the value of what we choose, because we can never choose evil. We always choose the good, and nothing can be good for us without being good for all.

If, on the other hand, existence precedes essence, and if we grant that we exist and fashion our image at one and the same time, the image is valid for everybody and for our whole age. Thus, our responsibility is much greater than we might have supposed, because it involves all mankind. If I am a workingman and choose to join a Christian trade-union rather than be a communist, and if by being a member I want to show that the best thing for man is resignation, that the kingdom of man is not of this world, I am not only involving my own case—I want to be resigned for everyone. As a result, my action has involved all humanity. To take a more individual matter, if I want to marry, to have children; even if this marriage depends solely on my own circumstances or passion or wish, I am involving all humanity in monogamy and not merely myself. Therefore, I am responsible for myself and for everyone else. I am creating a certain image of man of my own choosing. In choosing myself, I choose man.

This helps us understand what the actual content is of such rather grandiloquent words as anguish, forlornness, despair. As you will see, it's all quite simple.

First, what is meant by anguish? The existentialists say at once that man is anguish. What that means is this: the man who involves himself and who realizes that he is not only the person he chooses to be, but also a lawmaker who is, at the same time, choosing all mankind as well as himself, can not help escape the feeling of his total and deep responsibility. Of course, there are many people who are not anxious; but we claim that they are hiding their anxiety, that they are fleeing from it. Certainly, many people believe that when they do something, they themselves are the only ones involved, and when someone says to them, "What if everyone acted that way?" they shrug their shoulders and answer, "Everyone doesn't act that way." But really, one should always ask himself, "What would happen if everybody looked at things that way?" There is no escaping this disturbing thought except by a kind of double-dealing. A man who lies and makes excuses for himself by saying "not everybody does that," is someone with an uneasy conscience, because the act of lying implies that a universal value is conferred upon the lie.

Anguish is evident even when it conceals itself. This is the anguish that

Kierkegaard called the anguish of Abraham. You know the story: an angel has ordered Abraham to sacrifice his son; if it really were an angel who has come and said, "You are Abraham, you shall sacrifice your son," everything would be all right. But everyone must first wonder, "Is it really an angel, and am I really Abraham? What proof do I have?"

There was a madwoman who had hallucinations; someone used to speak to her on the telephone and give her orders. Her doctor asked her, "Who is it who talks to you?" She answered, "He says it's God." What proof did she really have that it was God? If an angel comes to me, what proof is there that it's an angel? And if I hear voices, what proof is there that they come from heaven and not from hell, or from the subconscious, or a pathological condition? What proves that they are addressed to me? What proof is there that I have been appointed to impose my choice and my conception of man on humanity? I'll never find any proof or sign to convince me of that. If a voice addresses me, it is always for me to decide that this is the angel's voice; if I consider that such an act is a good one, it is I who will choose to say that it is good rather than bad.

Now, I'm not being singled out as an Abraham, and yet at every moment I'm obliged to perform exemplary acts. For every man, everything happens as if all mankind has its eyes fixed on him and were guiding itself by what he does. And every man ought to say to himself, "Am I really the kind of man who has the right to act in such a way that humanity might guide itself by my actions?" And if he does not say that to himself, he is masking his anguish.

There is no question here of the kind of anguish which would lead to quietism, to inaction. It is a matter of a simple sort of anguish that anybody who has had responsibilities is familiar with. For example, when a military officer takes the responsibility for an attack and sends a certain number of men to death, he chooses to do so, and in the main he alone makes the choice. Doubtless, orders come from above, but they are too broad; he interprets them, and on this interpretation depend the lives of ten or fourteen or twenty men. In making a decision he can not help having a certain anguish. All leaders know this anguish. That doesn't keep them from acting; on the contrary, it is the very condition of their action. For it implies that they envisage a number of possibilities, and when they choose one, they realize that it has value only because it is chosen. We shall see that this kind of anguish, which is the kind that existentialism describes, is explained, in addition, by a direct responsibility to the other men whom it involves. It is not a curtain separating us from the action, but is part of action itself.

When we speak of forlornness, a term Heidegger was fond of, we mean only that God does not exist and that we have to face all the consequences of this. The existentialist is strongly opposed to a certain kind of secular ethics which would like to abolish God with the least possible expense. About 1880, some French teachers tried to set up a secular ethics which went something like this: God is a useless and costly hypothesis; we are discarding it; but, meanwhile, in order for there to be an ethics, a society, a civilization, it is essential that certain values be taken seriously and that they be considered as having an *a priori* existence. It must be obligatory, *a priori,* to be honest, not to lie, not to beat your wife, to have children, etc., etc. So we're going to try a little device which will make it possible to show that values exist all the same, inscribed in a heaven of ideas, though otherwise God does not exist. In other words—and this, I believe, is the tendency of everything called reformism in France—nothing will be changed if God does not exist. We shall find ourselves with the same norms of honesty, progress, and humanism, and we shall have made of God an outdated hypothesis which will peacefully die off by itself.

The existentialist, on the contrary, thinks it very distressing that God does not exist, because all possibility of finding values in a heaven of ideas disappears along with Him; there can no longer be an *a priori* Good, since there is no infinite and perfect consciousness to think it. Nowhere is it written that the Good exists, that we must be honest, that we must not lie; because the fact is we are on a plane where there are only men. Dostoievsky said, "If God didn't exist, everything would be possible." That is the very starting point of existentialism. Indeed, everything is permissible if God does not exist, and as a result man is forlorn, because neither within him nor without does he find anything to cling to. He can't start making excuses for himself.

If existence really does precede essence, there is no explaining things away by reference to a fixed and given human nature. In other words, there is no determinism, man is free, man is freedom. On the other hand, if God does not exist, we find no values or commands to turn to which legitimize our conduct. So, in the bright realm of values, we have no excuse behind us, nor justification before us. We are alone, with no excuses.

That is the idea I shall try to convey when I say that man is condemned to be free. Condemned, because he did not create himself, yet, in other respects is free; because, once thrown into the world, he is responsible for everything he does. The existenialist does not believe in the power of passion. He will never agree that a sweeping passion is a ravaging torrent which fatally leads a man to certain acts and is therefore an excuse. He thinks that man is responsible for his passion.

The existentialist does not think that man is going to help himself by finding in the world some omen by which to orient himself. Because he thinks that man will interpret the omen to suit himself. Therefore, he thinks that man, with no support and no aid, is condemned every moment to invent man. Ponge, in a very fine article, has said, "Man is the future of man." That's exactly it. But if it is taken to mean that this future is recorded in heaven, that God sees it, then it is false, because it would really no longer be a future. If it is taken to mean that, whatever a man may be, there is a future to be forged, a virgin future before him, then this remark is sound. But then we are forlorn.

To give you an example which will enable you to understand forlornness better, I shall cite the case of one of my students who came to see me under the following circumstances: his father was on bad terms with his mother, and, moreover, was inclined to be a collaborationist; his older brother had been killed in the German offensive of 1940, and the young man, with somewhat immature but generous feelings, wanted to avenge him. His mother lived alone with him, very much upset by the half-treason of her husband and the death of her older son; the boy was her only consolation.

The boy was faced with the choice of leaving for England and joining the Free French Forces—that is, leaving his mother behind—or remaining with his mother and helping her to carry on. He was fully aware that the woman lived only for him and that his going-off—and perhaps his death—would plunge her into despair. He was also aware that every act that he did for his mother's sake was a sure thing, in the sense that it was helping her to carry on, whereas every effort he made toward going off and fighting was an uncertain move which might run aground and prove completely useless; for example, on his way to England he might, while passing through Spain, be detained indefinitely in a Spanish camp; he might reach England or Algiers and be stuck in an office at a desk job. As a result, he was faced with two very different kinds of action: one, concrete, immediate, but concerning only one individual; the other concerned an incomparably vaster group, a national collectivity, but for that very reason was dubious, and might be interrupted en route. And, at the same time, he was wavering between two kinds of ethics. On the one hand, an ethics of sympathy, of personal devotion; on the other, a broader ethics, but one whose efficacy was more dubious. He had to choose between the two.

Who could help him choose? Christian doctrine? No. Christian doctrine says, "Be charitable, love your neighbor, take the more rugged path, etc., etc." But which is the more rugged path? Whom should he love as a brother? The fighting man or his mother? Which does the greater good, the vague act of fighting in a group, or the concrete one of helping a particular human being to go on living? Who can decide *a priori?* Nobody. No book of ethics can tell him. The Kantian ethics says, "Never treat any person as a means, but as an end." Very well, if I stay with my mother, I'll treat her as an end and not as a means; but by virtue of this very fact, I'm running the risk of treating the people around me who are fighting, as means; and, conversely, if I go to join those who are fighting, I'll be treating them as an end, and, by doing that, I run the risk of treating my mother as a means.

If values are vague, and if they are always too broad for the concrete and specific case that we are considering, the only thing left for us is to trust our instincts. That's what this young man tried to do; and when I saw him, he said, "In the end, feeling is what counts. I ought to choose whichever pushes me in one direction. If I feel that I love my mother enough to sacrifice everything else for her—my desire for vengeance, for action, for adventure—then I'll stay with her. If, on the contrary, I feel that my love for my mother isn't enough, I'll leave."

But how is the value of a feeling determined? What gives his feeling for his mother value? Precisely the fact that he remained with her. I may say that I like so-and-so well enough to sacrifice a certain amount of money for him, but I may say so only if I've done it. I may say "I love my mother well enough to remain with her" if I have remained with her. The only way to determine the value of this affection is, precisely, to perform an act which confirms and defines it. But, since I require this affection to justify my act, I find myself caught in a vicious circle.

On the other hand, Gide has well said that a mock feeling and a true feeling are almost indistinguishable; to decide that I love my mother and will remain with her, or to remain with her by putting on an act, amount somewhat to the same thing. In other words, the feeling is formed by the acts one performs; so, I can not refer to it in order to act upon it. Which means that I can neither seek within myself the true condition which will impel me to act, nor apply to a system of ethics for concepts which will permit me to act. You will say, "At least, he did go to a teacher for advice." But if you seek advice from a priest, for example, you have chosen this priest; you already knew, more or less, just about what advice he was going to give you. In other words, choosing your adviser is involving yourself. The proof of this is that if you are a Christian, you will say, "Consult a priest." But some priests are collaborating, some are just marking time, some are resisting. Which to choose? If the young man chooses a priest who is resisting or collaborating, he has already decided on the kind of advice he's going to get. Therefore, in coming to see me he knew the answer I was going to give him, and I had only one answer to give: "You're free, choose, that is, invent." No general ethics can show you what is to be done; there are no omens in the world. The Catholics will reply, "But there are." Granted—but, in any case, I myself choose the meaning they have.

When I was a prisoner, I knew a rather remarkable young man who was a Jesuit. He had entered the Jesuit order in the following way: he had had a number of very bad breaks; in childhood, his father died, leaving him in poverty, and he was a scholarship student at a religious institution where he was constantly made to feel that he was being kept out of charity; then, he failed to get any of the honors and distinctions that children like; later on, at about eighteen, he bungled a love affair; finally, at twenty-two, he failed in military training, a childish enough matter, but it was the last straw.

This young fellow might well have felt that he had botched everything. It was a sign of something, but of what? He might have taken refuge in bitterness or despair. But he very wisely looked upon all this as a sign that he was not made for secular triumphs, and that only the triumphs of religion, holiness, and faith were open to him. He saw the hand of God in all this, and so he entered the order. Who can help seeing that he alone decided what the sign meant?

Some other interpretation might have been drawn from this series of setbacks; for example, that he might have done better to turn carpenter or revolutionist. Therefore, he is fully responsible for the interpretation. Forlornness implies that we ourselves choose our being. Forlornness and anguish go together.

As for despair, the term has a very simple meaning. It means that we shall confine ourselves to reckoning only with what depends upon our will, or on the ensemble of probabilities which make our action possible. When we want something, we always have to reckon with probabilities. I may be counting on the arrival of a friend. The friend is coming by rail or street-car; this supposes that the train will arrive on schedule, or that the street-car will not jump the track. I am left in the realm of possibility; but possibilities are to be reckoned with only to the point where my action comports with the ensemble of these possibilities, and no further. The moment the possibilities I am considering are not rigorously involved by my action, I ought to disengage myself from them, because no God, no scheme, can adapt the world and its possibilities to my will. When Descartes said, "Conquer yourself rather than the world," he meant essentially the same thing.

The Marxists to whom I have spoken reply, "You can rely on the support of others in your action, which obviously has certain limits because you're not going to live forever. That means: rely on both what others are doing elsewhere to help you, in China, in Russia, and what they will do later on, after your death, to carry on the action and lead it to its fulfillment, which will be the revolution. You even *have* to rely upon that, otherwise you're immoral." I reply at once that I will always rely on fellow-fighters insofar as these comrades are involved with me in a common struggle, in the unity of a party or a group in which I can more or less make my weight felt; that is, one whose ranks I am in as a fighter and whose movements I am aware of at every moment. In such a situation, relying on the unity and will of the party is exactly like counting on the fact that the train will arrive on time or that the car won't jump the track. But, given that man is free and that there is no human nature for me to depend on, I can not count on men whom I do not know by relying on human goodness or man's concern for the good of society. I don't know what will become of the Russian revolution; I may make an example of it to the extent that at the present time it is apparent that the proletariat plays a part in Russia that it plays in no other nation. But I can't swear that this will inevitably lead to a triumph of the proletariat. I've got to limit myself to what I see.

Given that men are free and that tomorrow they will freely decide what man will be, I can not be sure that, after my death, fellow-fighters will carry on my work to bring it to its maximum perfection. Tomorrow, after my death, some men may decide to set up Fascism, and the others may be cowardly and muddled enough to let them do it. Fascism will then be the human reality, so much the worse for us.

Actually, things will be as man will have decided they are to be. Does that mean that I should abandon myself to quietism? No. First, I should involve myself; then, act on the old saw, "Nothing ventured, nothing gained." Nor does it mean that I shouldn't belong to a party, but rather that I shall have no illusions and shall do what I can. For example, suppose I ask myself, "Will socialization, as such, ever come about?" I know nothing about it. All I know is that I'm going to do everything in my power to bring it about. Beyond that, I can't count on anything. Quietism is the attitude of people who say, "Let others do what I can't do." The doctrine I am presenting is the very opposite of quietism, since it declares, "There is no reality except in action." Moreover, it goes further, since it adds, "Man is nothing else than his plan; he exists only to the extent that he fulfills himself; he is therefore nothing else than the ensemble of his acts, nothing else than his life."

According to this, we can understand why our doctrine horrifies certain people. Because often the only way they can bear their wretchedness is to think, "Circumstances have been against me. What I've been and done doesn't show my true worth. To be sure, I've had no great love, no great friendship, but that's because I haven't met a man or woman who was worthy. The books I've written haven't been very good because I haven't had the proper leisure. I haven't had children to devote myself to because I didn't find a man with whom I could have spent my life. So there remains within me, unused and quite viable, a host of propensities, inclinations, possibilities, that one wouldn't guess from the mere series of things I've done."

Now, for the existentialist there is really no love other than one which manifests itself in a person's being in love. There is no genius other than one which is expressed in works of art; the genius of Proust is the sum of Proust's works; the genius of Racine is his series of tragedies. Outside of that, there is nothing. Why say that Racine could have written another tragedy, when he didn't write it? A man is involved in life, leaves his impress on it, and outside of that there is nothing. To be sure, this may seem a harsh thought to someone whose life hasn't been a success. But, on the other hand, it prompts people to understand that reality alone is what counts, that dreams, expectations, and hopes warrant no more than to define a man as a disappointed dream, as miscarried hopes, as vain expectations. In other words, to define him negatively and not positively. However, when we say, "You are nothing else than your life," that does not imply that the artist will be judged solely on the basis of his works of art; a thousand other things will contribute toward summing him up. What we mean is that a man is nothing else than a series of undertakings, that he is the sum, the organization, the ensemble of the relationships which make up these undertakings.

When all is said and done, what we are accused of, at bottom, is not our pessimism, but an optimistic toughness. If people throw up to us our works of fiction in which we write about people who are soft, weak, cowardly, and sometimes even downright bad, it's not because these people are soft, weak, cowardly, or bad; because if we were to say, as Zola did, that they are that way because of heredity, the workings of environment, society, because of biological or psychological determinism, people would be reassured. They would say, "Well, that's what we're like, no one can do anything about it." But when the existentialist writes about a coward, he says that this coward is responsible for his cowardice. He's not like that because he has a cowardly heart or lung or brain; he's not like that on account of his physiological make-up; but he's like that because he has made himself a coward by his acts. There's no such thing as a cowardly constitution; there are nervous constitutions; there is poor blood, as the common people say, or strong constitutions. But the man whose blood is poor is not a coward on that account, for what makes cowardice is the act of renouncing or yielding. A constitution is not an act; the coward is defined on the basis of the acts he performs. People feel, in a vague sort of way, that this coward we're talking about is guilty of being a coward, and the thought frightens them. What people would like is that a coward or a hero be born that way.

One of the complaints most frequently made about *The Ways of Freedom*[1] can be summed up as follows: "After all, these people are so spineless, how are you going to make heroes out of them?" This objection almost makes me laugh, for it assumes that people are born heroes. That's what people really want to think. If you're born cowardly, you may set your mind perfectly at rest; there's nothing you can do about it; you'll be cowardly all your life, whatever you may do. If you're born a hero, you may set your mind just as much at rest; you'll be a hero all your life; you'll drink like a hero and eat like a hero. What the existentialist says is that the coward makes himself cowardly, that the hero makes himself heroic. There's always a possibility for the coward not to be cowardly any more and for the hero to stop being heroic. What counts is total involvement; some one particular action or set of circumstances is not total investment.

Thus, I think we have answered a number of the charges concerning existentialism. You see that it can not be taken for a philosophy of quietism, since it defines man in terms of action; nor for a pessimistic description of man—there is no doctrine more optimistic, since man's destiny is within himself; nor for an attempt to discourage man from acting, since it tells him that the only hope is in his acting and that action is the only thing that enables a man to live. Consequently, we are dealing here with an ethics of action and involvement.

Nevertheless, on the basis of a few notions like these, we are still charged with immuring man in his private subjectivity. There again we're very much misunderstood. Subjectivity of the individual is indeed our point of departure, and this for strictly philosophic reasons. Not because we are bourgeois, but because we want a doctrine based on truth and not a lot of fine theories, full of hope but with no real basis. There can be no other truth to take off from than this: *I think; therefore, I exist.* There we have the absolute truth of consciousness becoming aware of itself. Every theory which takes man out of the moment in which he becomes aware of himself is, at its very beginning, a theory which confounds truth, for outside the Cartesian *cogito,* all views are only probable, and a doctrine of probability which is not bound to a truth dissolves into thin air. In order to describe the probable, you must have a firm hold on the true. Therefore, before there can be any truth whatsoever, there must be an absolute truth; and this one is simple and easily arrived at; it's on everyone's doorstep; it's a matter of grasping it directly.

Secondly, this theory is the only one which gives man dignity, the only one which does not reduce him to an object. The effect of all materialism is to treat all men, including the one philosophizing, as objects, that is, as an ensemble of determined reactions in no way distinguished from the ensemble of qualities and phenomena which constitute a table or a chair or a stone. We definitely wish to establish the human realm as an ensemble of values distinct from the material realm. But the subjectivity that we have thus arrived at, and which we have claimed to be truth, is not a strictly individual subjectivity, for we have demonstrated that one discovers in the *cogito* not only himself, but others as well.

The philosophies of Descartes and Kant to the contrary, through the *I think* we reach our own self in the presence of others, and the others are just as real to us as our own self. Thus, the man who becomes aware of himself through the *cogito* also perceives all others, and he perceives them as the condition of his own existence. He realizes that he can not be anything (in the sense that we say that someone is witty or nasty or jealous) unless others recognize it as such. In order to get any truth about myself, I must have contact with another person. The other is indispensable to my own existence, as well as to my knowledge about myself. This being so, in discovering my inner being I discover the other person at the same time, like a freedom placed in front of me which thinks and wills only for or against me. Hence, let us at once announce the discovery of a world which we shall call intersubjectivity; this is the world in which man decides what he is and what others are.

Besides, if it is impossible to find in every man some universal essence which would be human nature, yet there does exist a universal human condition. It's not by chance that today's thinkers speak more readily of man's condition than of his nature. By condition they mean, more or less definitely, the *a priori* limits which outline man's fundamental situation in the universe. Historical situations vary; a man may be born a slave in a pagan society or a feudal lord or a proletarian. What does not vary is the necessity for him to exist in the world, to be at work there, to be there in the midst of other people, and to be mortal there. The limits are neither subjective nor objective, or, rather, they have an objective and a subjective side. Objective because they are to be found everywhere and are recognizable everywhere; subjective because they are *lived* and are nothing if man does not live them, that is, freely determine his existence with reference to them. And though the configurations may differ, at least none of them are completely strange to me, because they all appear as attempts either to pass beyond these limits or recede from them or deny them or adapt to them. Consequently, every configuration, however individual it may be, has a universal value.

Every configuration, even the Chinese, the Indian, or the Negro, can be understood by a Westerner. "Can be understood" means that by virtue of a situation that he can imagine, a European of 1945 can, in like manner, push himself to his limits and reconstitute within himself the configuration of the Chinese, the Indian, or the African. Every configuration has universality in the sense that every configuration can be understood by every man. This does not at all mean that this configuration defines man forever, but that it can be met with again. There is always a way to understand the idiot, the child, the savage, the foreigner, provided one has the necessary information.

In this sense we may say that there is a universality of man; but it is not given, it is perpetually being made. I build the universal in choosing myself; I build it in understanding the configuration of every other man, whatever age he might have lived in. This absoluteness of choice does not do away with the relativeness of each epoch. At heart, what existentialism shows is the connection between the absolute character of free involvement, by virtue of which every man realizes himself in realizing a type of mankind, an involvement always comprehensible in any age whatsoever and by any person whatsoever, and the relativeness of the cultural ensemble which may result from such a choice; it must be stressed that the relativity of Cartesianism and the absolute character of Cartesian involvement go together. In this sense, you may, if you like, say that each of us performs an absolute act in breathing, eating, sleeping, or behaving in any way whatever. There is no difference between being free, like a configuration, like an existence which chooses its essence, and being absolute. There is no difference between being an absolute temporarily localized, that is, localized in history, and being universally comprehensible.

TRANSLATOR'S NOTE

1. *Les Chemins de la Liberté,* M. Sartre's projected trilogy of novels, two of which, *L'Age de Raison* (*The Age of Reason*) and *Le Sursis* (*The Reprieve*), have already appeared.—Translator's note.

WHAT IS PHENOMENOLOGY?

Maurice Merleau-Ponty

What is phenomenology? It may seem strange that this question has still to be asked half a century after the works of Husserl. The fact remains that it has by no means been answered. Phenomenology is the study of essences; and according to it, all problems amount to finding definitions of essences: the essence of perception, or the essence of consciousness, for example. But phenomenology is also a philosophy which puts essences back into existence, and does not expect to arrive at an understanding of man and the world from any starting point other than that of their 'facticity'. It is a transcendental philosophy which places in abeyance the assertions arising out of the natural attitude, the better to understand them; but it is also a philosophy for which the world is always 'already there' before reflection begins—as an inalienable presence; and all its efforts are concentrated upon re-achieving a direct and primitive contact with the world, and endowing that contact with a philosophical status. It is the search for a philosophy which shall be a 'rigorous science', but it also offers an account of space, time and the world as we 'live' them. It tries to give a direct description of our experience as it is, without taking into account of its psychological origin and the causal explanations which the scientist, the historian or the sociologist may be able to provide. Yet Husserl in his last works mentions a 'genetic phenomenology',[1] and even a 'constructive phenomenology'.[2] One may try to do away with these contradictions by making a distinction between Husserl's and Heidegger's phenomenologies; yet the whole of *Sein und Zeit* springs from an indication given by Husserl and amounts to no more than an explicit account of the 'natürlicher Weltbegriff' or the 'Lebenswelt' which Husserl, towards the end of his life, identified as the central theme of phenomenology, with the result that the contradiction reappears in Husserl's own philosophy. The reader pressed for time will be inclined to give up the idea of covering a doctrine which says everything, and will wonder whether a philosophy which cannot define its scope deserves all the discussion which has gone on around it, and whether he is not faced rather by a myth or a fashion.

Even if this were the case, there would still be a need to understand the prestige of the myth and the origin of the fashion, and the opinion of the responsible philosopher must be that *phenomenology can be practised and identified as a manner or style of thinking, that it existed as a movement before arriving at complete awareness of itself as a philosophy.* It has been long on the way, and its

Reprinted by permission of Humanities Press International, Inc., Atlantic Highlands, NJ, from Maurice Merleau-Ponty, "Preface," in Merleau-Ponty, *Phenomenology of Perception,* trans. Colin Smith, pp. vii–xxi. London: Routledge & Kegan Paul, 1962.

adherents have discovered it in every quarter, certainly in Hegel and Kierkegaard, but equally in Marx, Nietzsche and Freud. A purely linguistic examination of the texts in question would yield no proof; we find in texts only what we put into them, and if ever any kind of history has suggested the interpretations which should be put on it, it is the history of philosophy. We shall find in ourselves, and nowhere else, the unity and true meaning of phenomenology. It is less a question of counting up quotations than of determining and expressing in concrete form this *phenomenology for ourselves* which has given a number of present-day readers the impression, on reading Husserl or Heidegger, not so much of encountering a new philosophy as of recognizing what they had been waiting for. Phenomenology is accessible only through a phenomenological method. Let us, therefore, try systematically to bring together the celebrated phenomenological themes as they have grown spontaneously together in life. Perhaps we shall then understand why phenomenology has for so long remained at an initial stage, as a problem to be solved and a hope to be realized.

It is a matter of describing, not of explaining or analysing. Husserl's first directive to phenomenology, in its early stages, to be a 'descriptive psychology', or to return to the 'things themselves', is from the start a rejection of science. I am not the outcome or the meeting-point of numerous causal agencies which determine my bodily or psychological make-up. I cannot conceive myself as nothing but a bit of the world, a mere object of biological, psychological or sociological investigation. I cannot shut myself up within the realm of science. All my knowledge of the world, even my scientific knowledge, is gained from my own particular point of view, or from some experience of the world without which the symbols of science would be meaningless. The whole universe of science is built upon the world as directly experienced, and if we want to subject science itself to rigorous scrutiny and arrive at a precise assessment of its meaning and scope, we must begin by reawakening the basic experience of the world of which science is the second-order expression. Science has not and never will have, by its nature, the same significance *qua* form of being as the world which we perceive, for the simple reason that it is a rationale or explanation of that world. I am, not a 'living creature' nor even a 'man', nor again even 'a consciousness' endowed with all the characteristics which zoology, social anatomy or inductive psychology recognize in these various products of the natural or historical process—I am the absolute source, my existence does not stem from my antecedents, from my physical and social environment; instead it moves out towards them and sustains them, for I alone bring into being for myself (and therefore into being in the only sense that the word can have for me) the tradition which I elect to carry on, or the horizon whose distance from me would be abolished—since that distance is not one of its properties—if I were not there to scan it with my gaze. Scientific points of view, according to which my existence is a moment of the world's, are always both naïve and at the same time dishonest, because they take for granted, without explicitly mentioning it, the other point of view, namely that of consciousness, through which from the outset a world forms itself round me and begins to exist for me. To return to things themselves is to return to that world which precedes knowledge, of which knowledge always *speaks,* and in relation to which every scientific schematization is an abstract and derivative sign-language, as is geography in relation to the countryside in which we have learnt beforehand what a forest, a prairie or a river is.

This move is absolutely distinct from the idealist return to consciousness, and the demand for a pure description excludes equally the procedure of analytical reflection on the one hand, and that of scientific explanation on the other. Descartes and particularly Kant *detached* the subject, or consciousness, by showing that I could not possibly apprehend anything as existing unless I first of all experienced myself as existing in the act of apprehending it. They presented consciousness, the absolute certainty of my existence for myself, as the condition of there being anything at all; and the act of relating as the basis of relatedness. It is true that the act of relating is nothing if divorced from the spectacle of the world in which relations are found; the unity of consciousness in Kant is achieved simultaneously with that of the world. And in Descartes methodical doubt does not deprive us of anything, since the whole world, at least in so far as we experience it, is reinstated in the *Cogito,* enjoying equal certainty, and simply labelled 'thought about . . .' But the relations between subject and world are not strictly bilateral: if they were, the certainty of the world would, in Descartes, be immediately given with that of the *Cogito,* and Kant would not have talked about his 'Copernican revolution'. Analytical reflection starts from our experience of the world and goes back to the subject as to a condition of possibility distinct from that experience, revealing the all-embracing synthesis as that without which there would be no world. To this extent it ceases to remain part of our experience and offers, in place of an account, a reconstruction. It is understandable, in view of this, that Husserl, having accused Kant of adopting a 'faculty psychologism'[3], should have urged, in place of a noetic analysis which bases the world on the synthesizing activity of the subject, his own *'noematic reflection'* which remains within the object and, instead of begetting it, brings to light its fundamental unity.

The world is there before any possible analysis of mine, and it would be artificial to make it the outcome of a series of syntheses which link, in the first place sensations, then aspects of the object corresponding to different perspectives, when both are nothing but products of analysis, with no sort of prior reality. Analytical reflection believes that it can trace back the course followed by a prior constituting act and arrive, in the 'inner man'—to use Saint Augustine's expression—at a constituting power which has always been identical with that inner self. Thus reflection itself is carried away and transplanted in an impregnable subjectivity, as yet untouched by being and time. But this is very ingenuous, or at least it is an incomplete form of reflection which loses sight of its own beginning. When I begin to reflect my reflection bears upon an unreflective experience; moreover my reflection cannot be unaware of itself as an event, and so it appears to itself in the light of a truly creative act, of a changed structure of consciousness, and yet it has to recognize, as having priority over its own operations, the world which is given to the subject, because the subject is given to himself. The real has to be described, not constructed or formed. Which means that I cannot put perception into the same category as the syntheses represented by judgements, acts or predications. My field of perception is constantly filled with a play of colours, noises and fleeting tactile sensations which I cannot relate precisely to the context of my clearly perceived world, yet which I nevertheless immediately 'place' in the world, without ever confusing them with my daydreams. Equally constantly I weave dreams round things. I imagine people and things whose presence is not incompatible with the context, yet who are not in fact involved in it: they are ahead of reality, in the realm of the imaginary. If the reality of my perception were based solely on the intrinsic coherence of 'representations', it ought to be for ever hesitant and, being wrapped up in my conjectures on probabilities, I ought to be ceaselessly taking apart misleading syntheses, and reinstating in reality stray phenomena which I had excluded in the first place. But this does not happen. The real is a closely woven fabric. It does not await our judgement before incorporating the most surprising phenomena, or before rejecting the most plausible figments of our imagination. Perception is not a science of the world, it is not even an act, a deliberate taking up of a position; it is the background from which all acts stand out, and is presupposed by them. The world is not an object such that I have in my possession the law of its making; it is the natural setting of, and field for, all my thoughts and all my explicit perceptions. Truth does not 'inhabit' only 'the inner man',[4] or more accurately, there is no inner man, man is in the world, and only in the world does he know himself. When I return to myself from an excursion into the realm of dogmatic common sense or of science, I find, not a source of intrinsic truth, but a subject destined to be in the world.

All of which reveals the true meaning of the famous phenomenological reduction. There is probably no question over which Husserl has spent more time—or to which he has more often returned, since the 'problematic of reduction' occupies an important place in his unpublished work. For a long time, and even in recent texts, the reduction is presented as the return to a transcendental consciousness before which the world is spread out and completely transparent, quickened through and through by a series of apperceptions which it is the philosopher's task to reconstitute on the basis of their outcome. Thus my sensation of redness is *perceived* as the manifestation of a certain redness experienced, this in turn as the manifestation of a red surface, which is the manifestation of a piece of red cardboard, and this finally is the manifestation or outline of a red thing, namely this book. We are to understand, then, that it is the apprehension of a certain *hylè,* as indicating a phenomenon of a higher degree, the *Sinngebung,* or active meaning-giving operation which may be said to define consciousness, so that the world is nothing but 'world-as-meaning', and the phenomenological reduction is idealistic, in the sense that there is here a transcendental idealism which treats the world as an indivisible unity of value shared by Peter and Paul, in which their perspectives blend. 'Peter's consciousness' and 'Paul's consciousness' are in communication, the perception of the world 'by Peter' is not Peter's doing any more than its perception 'by Paul' is Paul's doing; in each case it is the doing of pre-personal forms of consciousness, whose communication raises no problem, since it is demanded by the very definition of consciousness, meaning or truth. In so far as I am a consciousness, that is, in so far as something has meaning for me, I am neither here nor there, neither Peter nor Paul; I am in no way distinguishable from an 'other' consciousness, since we are immediately in touch with the world and since the world is, by definition, unique, being the system in which all truths cohere. A logically consistent transcendental idealism rids the world of its opacity and its transcendence. The world is precisely that thing of which we form a representation, not as men or as empirical subjects, but in so far as we are all one light and participate in the One without destroying its unity. Analytical reflection knows nothing of the problem of other minds, or of that of the world, because it insists that with the first glimmer of consciousness there appears in me theoretically the power of reaching some universal truth, and that the other person, being equally without thisness, location or body, the Alter and the Ego are one and the same in the true world which is the unifier of minds. There is no difficulty in understanding how *I* can conceive the Other, because the I and consequently the Other are not conceived as part of the woven stuff of phenomena; they have validity rather than existence. There is nothing hidden behind these faces and gestures, no domain to which I have no access, merely a little shadow which owes its very existence to the light. For Husserl, on the contrary, it is well known that there is a problem of other people, and the *alter ego* is a paradox. If the other is truly for himself alone, beyond his being for me, and if we are for each other and not both for God, we must necessarily have some appearance for each other. He must and I must have an outer appearance, and there must be, besides the perspective of the For Oneself—my view of myself and the other's of himself—a perspective of For Others—my view of others and theirs of me. Of course, these two perspectives, in each one of us, cannot be simply juxtaposed, *for in that case it is not I that the other would see, nor he that I should see.* I must be the exterior that I present to others, and the body of the other must be the other himself. This paradox and the dialectic of the Ego and the Alter are possible only provided that the Ego and the Alter Ego are defined by their situation and are not freed from all inherence; that is, provided that philosophy does not culminate in a return to the self, and that I discover by reflection not only my presence to myself, but also the possibility of an 'outside spectator'; that is, again, provided that at the very moment when I experience my existence—at the ultimate extremity of reflection—I fall short of the ultimate density which would place me outside time, and that I discover within myself a kind of internal weakness standing in the way of my being totally individualized: a weakness which exposes me to the gaze of others as a man among men or at least as a consciousness among consiousnesses. Hitherto the *Cogito* depreciated the perception of others, teaching me as it did that the I is accessible only to itself, since it defined *me* as the thought which I have of myself, and which clearly I am alone in having, at least in this ultimate sense. For the 'other' to be more than an empty word, it is necessary that my existence should never be reduced to my bare awareness of existing, but that it should take in also the awareness that *one* may have of it, and thus include my incarnation in some nature and the possibility, at least, of a historical situation. The *Cogito* must reveal me in a situation, and it is on this condition alone that transcendental subjectivity can, as Husserl puts it,[5] *be* an intersubjectivity. As a meditating Ego, I can clearly distinguish from myself the world and things, since I certainly do not exist in the way in which things exist. I must even set aside from myself my body understood as a thing among things, as a collection of physico-chemical processes. But even if the *cogitatio,* which I thus discover, is without location in objective time and space, it is not without place in the phenomenological world. The world, which I distinguished from myself as the totality of things or of processes linked by causal relationships, I rediscover 'in me' as the permanent horizon of all my *cogitationes* and as a dimension in relation to which I am constantly situating myself. The true *Cogito* does not define the subject's existence in terms of the thought he has of existing, and furthermore does not convert the indubitability of the world into the indubitability of thought about the world, nor finally does it replace the world itself by the world as meaning. On the contrary it recognizes my thought itself as an inalienable fact, and does away with any kind of idealism in revealing me as 'being-in-the-world'.

It is because we are through and through compounded of relationships with the world that for us the only way to become aware of the fact is to suspend the resultant activity, to refuse it our complicity (to look at it *ohne mitzumachen,* as Husserl often says), or yet again, to put it 'out of play'. Not because we reject the certainties of common sense and a natural attitude to things—they are, on the contrary, the constant theme of philosophy—but because, being the presupposed basis of any thought, they are taken for granted, and go unnoticed, and because in order to arouse them and bring them to view, we have to suspend for a moment our recognition of them. The best formulation of the reduction is probably that given by Eugen Fink, Husserl's assistant, when he spoke of 'wonder' in the face of the world.[6] Reflection does not withdraw from the world towards the unity of consciousness as the world's basis; it steps back to watch the forms of transcendence fly up like sparks from a fire; it slackens the intentional threads which attach us to the world and thus brings them to our notice; it alone is consciousness of the world because it reveals that world as strange and paradoxical. Husserl's transcendental is not Kant's and Husserl accuses Kant's philosophy of being 'worldly', because it *makes use* of our relation to the world, which is the motive force of the transcendental deduction, and makes the world immanent in the subject, instead of *being filled with wonder* at it and conceiving the subject as a process of transcendence towards the world. All the misunderstandings with his interpreters, with the existentialist 'dissidents' and finally with himself, have arisen from the fact that in order to see the world and grasp it as paradoxical, we must break with our familiar acceptance of it and, also, from the fact that from this break we can learn nothing but the unmotivated upsurge of the world. The most important lesson which the reduction teaches us is the impossibility of a complete reduction. This is why Husserl is constantly re-examining the possibility of the reduction. If we were absolute mind, the reduction would present no problem. But since, on the contrary, we are in the world, since indeed our reflections are carried out in the temporal flux on to which we are trying to seize (since they *sich einströmen,* as Husserl says), there is no thought which embraces all our thought. The philosopher, as the unpublished works declare, is a perpetual beginner, which means that he takes for granted nothing that men, learned or otherwise, believe they know. It means also that philosophy itself must not take itself for granted, in so far as it may have managed to say something true; that it is an ever-renewed experiment in making its own beginning; that it consists wholly in the description of this beginning, and finally, that radical reflection amounts to a consciousness of its own dependence on an unreflective life which is its initial situation, unchanging, given once and for all. Far from being, as has been thought, a procedure of idealistic philosophy, phenomenological reduction belongs to existential philosophy: Heidegger's 'being-in-the-world' appears only against the background of the phenomenological reduction.

A misunderstanding of a similar kind confuses the notion of the 'essences' in Husserl. Every reduction, says Husserl, as well as being transcendental is necessarily eidetic. That means that we cannot subject our perception of the world to philosophical scrutiny without ceasing to be identified with that act of positing the world, with that interest in it which delimits us, without drawing back from our commitment which is itself thus made to appear as a spectacle, without passing from the *fact* of our existence to its *nature,* from the Dasein to the Wesen. But it is clear that the essence is here not the end, but a means, that our effective involvement in the world is precisely what has to be understood and made amenable to conceptualization, for it is what polarizes all our conceptual particularizations. The need to proceed by way of essences does not mean that philosophy takes them as its object, but, on the contrary, that our existence is too tightly held in the world to be able to know itself as such at the moment of its involvement, and that it requires the field of ideality in order to become acquainted with and to prevail over its facticity. The Vienna Circle, as is well known, lays it down categorically that we can enter into relations only with meanings. For example, 'consciousness' is not for the Vienna Circle identifiable with what we are. It is a complex meaning which has developed late in time, which should be handled with care, and only after the many meanings which have contributed, throughout the word's semantic development, to the formation of its present one have been made explicit. Logical positivism of this kind is the antithesis of Husserl's thought. Whatever the subtle changes of meaning which have ultimately brought us, as a linguistic acquisition, the word and concept of consciousness, we enjoy direct access to what it designates. For we have the experience of ourselves, of that consciousness which we are, and it is on the basis of this experience that all linguistic connotations are assessed, and precisely through it that language comes to have any meaning at all for us. 'It is that as yet dumb experience . . . which we are concerned to lead to the pure expression of its own meaning.'[7] Husserl's essences are destined to bring back all the living relationships of experience, as the fisherman's net draws up from the depths of the ocean quivering fish and seaweed. Jean Wahl is therefore wrong in saying that 'Husserl separates essences from existence'.[8] The separated essences are those of language. It is the office of language to cause essences to exist in a state of separation which is in fact merely apparent, since through language they still rest upon the antepredicative life of consciousness. In the silence of primary consciousness can be seen appearing not only what words mean, but also what things mean: the core of primary meaning round which the acts of naming and expression take shape.

Seeking the essence of consciousness will therefore not consist in developing the *Wortbedeutung* of consciousness and escaping from existence into the universe of things said; it will consist in rediscovering my actual presence to myself, the fact of my consciousness which is in the last resort what the word and the concept of consciousness mean. Looking for the world's essence is not looking for what it is as an idea once it has been reduced to a theme of discourse; it is looking for what it is as a fact for us, before any thematization. Sensationalism 'reduces' the world by noticing that after all we never experience anything but states of ourselves. Transcendental idealism too 'reduces' the world since, in so far as it guarantees the world, it does so by regarding it as thought or consciousness of the world, and as the mere correlative of our knowledge, with the result that it becomes immanent in consciousness and the aseity of things is thereby done away with. The eidetic reduction is, on the other hand, the determination to bring the world to light as it is before any falling back on ourselves has occurred, it is the ambition to make reflection emulate the unreflective life of consciousness. I aim at and perceive a world. If I said, as do the sensationalists, that we have here only 'states of consciousness', and if I tried to distinguish my perceptions from my dreams with the aid of 'criteria', I should overlook the phenomenon of the world. For if I am able to talk about 'dreams' and 'reality', to bother my head about the distinction between imaginary and real, and cast doubt upon the 'real', it is because this distinction is already made by me before any analysis; it is because I have an experience of the real as of the imaginary, and the problem then becomes one not of asking how critical thought can provide for itself secondary equivalents of this distinction, but of making explicit our primordial knowledge of the 'real', of describing our perception of the world as that upon which our idea of truth is for ever based. We must not, therefore, wonder whether we really perceive a world, we must instead say: the world is what we perceive. In more general terms we must not wonder whether our self-evident truths are real truths, or whether, through some perversity inherent in our minds, that which is self-evident for us might not be illusory in relation to some truth in itself. For in so far as we talk about illusion, it is because we have identified illusions, and done so solely in the light of some perception which at the same time gave assurance of its own truth. It follows that doubt, or the fear of being mistaken, testifies as soon as it arises to our power of unmasking error, and that it could never finally tear us away from truth. We are in the realm of truth and it is 'the experience of truth' which is self-evident.[9] To seek the essence of perception is to declare that perception is, not presumed true, but defined as access to truth. So, if I now wanted, according to idealistic principles, to base this *de facto* self-evident truth, this irresistible belief, on some absolute self-evident truth, that is, on the absolute clarity which my thoughts have for me; if I tried to find in myself a creative thought which bodied forth the framework of the world or illumined it through and through, I should once more prove unfaithful to my experience of the world, and should be looking for what makes that experience possible instead of looking for what it is. The self-evidence of perception is not adequate thought or apodeictic self-evidence.[10] The world is not what I think, but what I live through. I am open to the world, I have no doubt that I am in communication with it, but I do not possess it; it is inexhaustible. 'There is a world', or rather: 'There is the world'; I can never completely account for this ever-reiterated assertion in my life. This facticity of the world is what constitutes the *Weltlichkeit der Welt,* what causes the world to be the world; just as the facticity of the *cogito* is not an imperfection in itself, but rather what assures me of my existence. The eidetic method is the method of a phenomenological positivism which bases the possible on the real.

We can now consider the notion of intentionality, too often cited as the main discovery of phenomenology, whereas it is understandable only through the reduction. 'All consciousness is consciousness of something'; there is nothing new in that. Kant showed, in the *Refutation of Idealism,* that inner perception is impossible without outer perception, that the world, as a collection of connected phenomena, is anticipated in the consciousness of my unity, and is the means whereby I come into being as a consciousness. What distinguishes intentionality from the Kantian relation to a possible object is that the unity of the world, before being posited by knowledge in a specific act of identification, is 'lived' as ready-made or already there. Kant himself shows in the *Critique of Judgement* that there exists a unity of the imagination and the understanding and a unity of subjects *before the object,* and that, in experiencing the beautiful, for example, I am aware of a harmony between sensation and concept, between myself and others, which is itself without any concept. Here the subject is no longer the universal thinker of a system of objects rigorously interrelated, the positing power who subjects the manifold to the law of the understanding, in so far as he is to be able to put together a world—he discovers and enjoys his own nature as spontaneously in harmony with the law of the understanding. But if the subject has a nature, then the hidden art of the imagination must condition the categorial activity. It is no longer merely the aesthetic judgement, but knowledge too which rests upon this art, an art which forms the basis of the unity of consciousness and of consciousnesses.

Husserl takes up again the *Critique of Judgement* when he talks about a teleology of consciousness. It is not a matter of duplicating human consciousness with some absolute thought which, from outside, is imagined as assigning to it its aims. It is a question of recognizing consciousness itself as a project of the world, meant for a world which it neither embraces nor possesses, but towards which it is perpetually directed—and the world as this pre-objective individual whose imperious unity decrees what knowledge shall take as its goal. This is why Husserl distinguishes between intentionality of act, which is that of our judgements and of those occasions when we voluntarily take up a position—the only intentionality discussed in the *Critique of Pure Reason*—and operative intentionality (*fungierende Intentionalität*), or that which produces the natural and antepredicative unity of the world and of our life, being apparent in our desires, our evaluations and in the landscape we see, more clearly than in objective knowledge, and furnishing the text which our knowledge tries to translate into precise language. Our relationship to the world, as it is untiringly enunciated within us, is not a thing which can be any further clarified by analysis; philosophy can only place it once more before our eyes and present it for our ratification.

Through this broadened notion of intentionality, phenomenological 'comprehension' is distinguished from traditional 'intellection', which is confined to 'true and immutable natures', and so phenomenology can become a phenomenology of origins. Whether we are concerned with a thing perceived, a historical event or a doctrine, to 'understand' is to take in the total intention—not only what these things are for representation (the 'properties' of the thing perceived, the mass of 'historical facts', the 'ideas' introduced by the doctrine)—but the unique mode of existing expressed in the properties of the pebble, the glass or the piece of wax, in all the events of a revolution, in all the thoughts of a philosopher. It is a matter, in the case of each civilization, of finding the Idea in the Hegelian sense, that is, not a law of the physico-mathematical type, discoverable by objective thought, but that formula which sums up some unique manner of behaviour towards others, towards Nature, time and death: a certain way of patterning the world which the historian should be capable of seizing upon and making his own. These are the *dimensions* of history. In this context there is not a human word, not a gesture, even one which is the outcome of habit or absent-mindedness, which has not some meaning. For example, I may have been under the impression that I lapsed into silence through weariness, or some minister may have thought he had uttered merely an appropriate platitude, yet my silence or his words immediately take on a significance, because my fatigue or his falling back upon a ready-made formula are not accidental, for they express a certain lack of interest, and hence some degree of adoption of a definite position in relation to the situation.

When an event is considered at close quarters, at the moment when it is lived through, everything seems subject to chance: one man's ambition, some lucky encounter, some local circumstance or other appears to have been decisive. But chance happenings offset each other, and facts in their multiplicity coalesce and show up a certain way of taking a stand in relation to the human situation, reveal in fact an *event* which has its definite outline and about which we can talk. Should the starting-point for the understanding of history be ideology, or politics, or religion, or economics? Should we try to understand a doctrine from its overt content, or from the psychological make-up and the biography of its author? We must seek an understanding from all these angles simultaneously, everything has meaning, and we shall find this same structure of being underlying all relationships. All these views are true provided that they are not isolated, that we delve deeply into history and reach the unique core of existential meaning which emerges in each perspective. It is true, as Marx says, that history does not walk on its head, but it is also true that it does not think with its feet. Or one should say rather that it is neither its 'head' nor its 'feet' that we have to worry about, but its body. All economic and psychological explanations of a doctrine are true, since the thinker never thinks from any starting-point but the one constituted by what he is. Reflection even on a doctrine will be complete only if it succeeds in linking up with the doctrine's history and the extraneous explanations of it, and in putting back the causes and meaning of the doctrine in an existential structure. There is, Husserl says, a 'genesis of meaning' (*Sinngenesis*),[11] which alone, in the last resort, teaches us what the doctrine 'means'. Like understanding, criticism must be pursued at all levels, and naturally, it will be insufficient, for the refutation of a doctrine, to relate it to some accidental event in the author's life: its significance goes beyond, and there is no pure accident in existence or in coexistence, since both absorb random events and transmute them into the rational.

Finally, as it is indivisible in the present, history is equally so in its sequences. Considered in the light of its fundamental dimensions, all periods of history appear as manifestations of a single existence, or as episodes in a single drama—without our knowing whether it has an ending. Because we are in the world, we are *condemned to meaning,* and we cannot do or say anything without its acquiring a name in history.

Probably the chief gain from phenomenology is to have united extreme subjectivism and extreme objectivism in its notion of the world or of rationality. Rationality is precisely measured by the experiences in which it is disclosed. To say that there exists rationality is to say that perspectives blend, perceptions confirm each other, a meaning emerges. But it should not be set in a realm apart, transposed into absolute Spirit, or into a world in the realist sense. The phenomenological world is not pure being, but the sense which is revealed where the paths of my various experiences intersect, and also where my own and other people's intersect and engage each other like gears. It is thus inseparable from subjectivity and intersubjectivity, which find their unity when I either take up my past experiences in those of the present, or other people's in my own. For the first time the philosopher's thinking is sufficiently conscious not to anticipate itself and endow its own results with reified form in the world. The philosopher tries to conceive the world, others and himself and their interrelations. But the meditating Ego, the 'impartial spectator' (*uninteressierter Zuschauer*)[12] do not rediscover an already given rationality, they 'establish themselves',[13] and establish it, by an act of initiative which has no guarantee in being, its justification resting entirely on the effective power which it confers on us of taking our own history upon ourselves.

The phenomenological world is not the bringing to explicit expression of a pre-existing being, but the laying down of being. Philosophy is not the reflection of a pre-existing truth, but, like art, the act of bringing truth into being. One may well ask how this creation is *possible,* and if it does not recapture in things a pre-existing Reason. The answer is that the only pre-existent Logos is the world itself, and that the philosophy which brings it into visible existence does not begin by being *possible;* it is actual or real like the world of which it is a part, and no explanatory hypothesis is clearer than the act whereby we take up this unfinished world in an effort to complete and conceive it. Rationality is not a *problem.* There is behind it no unknown quantity which has to be determined by deduction, or, beginning with it, demonstrated inductively. We witness every minute the miracle of related experiences, and yet nobody knows better than we do how this miracle is worked, for we are ourselves this network of relationships. The world and reason are not problematical. We may say, if we wish, that they are mysterious, but their mystery defines them: there can be no question of dispelling it by some 'solution', it is on the hither side of all solutions. True philosophy consists in relearning to look at the world, and in this sense a historical account can give meaning to the world quite as 'deeply' as a philosophical treatise. We take our fate in our hands, we become responsible for our history through reflection, but equally by a decision on which we stake our life, and in both cases what is involved is a violent act which is validated by being performed.

Phenomenology, as a disclosure of the world, rests on itself, or rather provides its own foundation.[14] All knowledge is sustained by a 'ground' of postulates and finally by our communication with the world as primary embodiment of rationality. Philosophy, as radical reflection, dispenses in principle with this resource. As, however, it too is in history, it too exploits the world and constituted reason. It must therefore put to itself the question which it puts to all branches of knowledge, and so duplicate itself infinitely, being, as Husserl says, a dialogue or infinite meditation, and, in so far as it remains faithful to its intention, never knowing where it is going. The unfinished nature of phenomenology and the inchoative atmosphere which has surrounded it are not to be taken as a sign of failure, they were inevitable because phenomenology's task was to reveal the mystery of the world and of reason.[15] If phenomenology was a movement before becoming a doctrine or a philosophical system, this was attributable neither to accident, nor to fraudulent intent. It is as painstaking as the works of Balzac, Proust, Valéry or Cézanne—by reason of the same kind of attentiveness and wonder, the same demand for awareness, the same will to seize the meaning of the world or of history as that meaning comes into being. In this way it merges into the general effort of modern thought.

NOTES

1. *Méditations cartésiennes,* pp. 120 ff.
2. See the unpublished *6th Méditation cartésienne,* edited by Eugen Fink, to which G. Berger has kindly referred us.
3. *Logische Untersuchungen, Prolegomena zur reinen Logik,* p. 93.
4. In te redi; in interiore homine habitat veritas (Saint Augustine).
5. *Die Krisis der europäischen Wissenschaften und die transzendentale Phänomenologie,* III (unpublished).
6. *Die phänomenologische Philosophie Edmund Husserls in der gegenwärtigen Kritik,* pp. 331 and ff.
7. *Méditations cartésiennes,* p. 33.
8. *Réalisme, dialectique et mystère,* l'Arbalète, Autumn, 1942, unpaginated.
9. *Das Erlebnis der Wahrheit* (*Logische Untersuchungen, Prolegomena zur reinen Logik*) p. 190.
10. There is no apodeictic self-evidence, the *Formale und transzendentale Logik* (p. 142) says in effect.
11. The usual term in the unpublished writings. The idea is already to be found in the *Formale and transzendentale Logik,* pp. 184 and ff.
12. *6th Méditation cartésienne* (unpublished).
13. Ibid.
14. 'Rückbeziehung der Phänomenologie auf sich selbst,' say the unpublished writings.
15. We are indebted for this last expression to G. Gusdorf, who may well have used it in another sense.

NIETZSCHE, GENEALOGY, HISTORY

Michel Foucault

1. Genealogy is gray, meticulous, and patiently documentary. It operates on a field of entangled and confused parchments, on documents that have been scratched over and recopied many times.

On this basis, it is obvious that Paul Ree was wrong to follow the English tendency in describing the history of morality in terms of a linear development—in reducing its entire history and genesis to an exclusive concern for utility. He assumed that words had kept their meaning, that desires still pointed in a single direction, and that ideas retained their logic; and he ignored the fact that the world of speech and desires has known invasions, struggles, plundering, disguises, ploys. From these elements, however, genealogy retrieves an indispensable restraint: it must record the singularity of events outside of any monotonous finality; it must seek them in the most unpromising places, in what we tend to feel is without history—in sentiments, love, conscience, instincts; it must be sensitive to their recurrence, not in order to trace the gradual curve of their evolution, but to isolate the different scenes where they engaged in different roles. Finally, genealogy must define even those instances where they are absent, the moment when they remained unrealized (Plato, at Syracuse, did not become Mohammed).

Genealogy, consequently, requires patience and a knowledge of details and it depends on a vast accumulation of source material. Its "cyclopean monuments"[1] are constructed from "discreet and apparently insignificant truths and according to a rigorous method"; they cannot be the product of "large and well-meaning errors."[2] In short, genealogy demands relentless erudition. Genealogy does not oppose itself to history as the lofty and profound gaze of the philosopher might compare to the molelike perspective of the scholar; on the contrary, it rejects the metahistorical deployment of ideal significations and indefinite teleologies. It opposes itself to the search for "origins."

2. In Nietzsche, we find two uses of the word *Ursprung*. The first is unstressed, and it is found alternately with other terms such as *Entstehung, Herkunft, Abkunft, Geburt*. In *The Genealogy of Morals,* for example, *Entstehung* or *Ursprung* serve equally well to denote the origin of duty or guilty conscience;[3] and in the discussion of logic or knowledge in *The Gay Science,* their origin is indiscriminately referred to as *Ursprung, Entstehung,* or *Herkunft*.[4]

The other use of the word is stressed. On occasion, Nietzsche places the term in opposition to another: in the first paragraph of *Human, All Too Human* the miraculous origin (*Wunderursprung*) sought by metaphysics is set against the analyses of historical philosophy, which poses questions *über Herkunft und Anfang. Ursprung* is also used in an ironic and deceptive manner. In what, for instance, do we find the original basis (*Ursprung*) of morality, a foundation sought after since Plato? "In detestable, narrowminded conclusions. *Pudenda origo*."[5] Or in a related context, where should we seek the origin of religion (*Ursprung*), which Schopenhauer located in a particular metaphysical sentiment of the hereafter? It belongs, very simply, to an invention (*Erfindung*), a sleight-of-hand, an artifice (*Kunststück*), a secret formula, in the rituals of black magic, in the work of the *Schwarzkünstler*.[6]

One of the most significant texts with respect to the use of all these terms and to the variations in the use of *Ursprung* is the preface to the *Genealogy*. At the beginning of the text, its objective is defined as an examination of the origin of moral preconceptions and the term used is *Herkunft*. Then, Nietzsche proceeds by retracing his personal involvement with this question: he recalls the period when he "calligraphied" philosophy, when he questioned if God must be held responsible for the origin of evil. He now finds this question amusing and properly characterizes it as a search for *Ursprung* (he will shortly use the same term to summarize Paul Ree's activity).[7] Further on, he evokes the analyses that are characteristically Nietzschean and that began with *Human, All Too Human*. Here, he speaks of *Herkunfthypothesen*. This use of the word *Herkunft* cannot be arbitrary, since it serves to designate a number of texts, beginning with *Human, All Too Human*, which deal with the origin of morality, asceticism, justice, and punishment. And yet, the word used in all these works had been *Ursprung*.[8] It would seem that at this point in the *Genealogy* Nietzsche wished to validate an opposition between *Herkunft* and *Ursprung* that did not exist ten years earlier. But immediately following the use of the two terms in a specific sense, Nietzsche reverts, in the final paragraphs of the preface, to a usage that is neutral and equivalent.[9]

Why does Nietzsche challenge the pursuit of the origin (*Ursprung*), at least on those occasions when he is truly a genealogist? First, because it is an attempt to capture the exact essence of things, their purest possibilities, and their carefully protected identities, because this search assumes the existence of immobile forms that precede the external world of accident and succession. This search is directed to "that which was already there," the image of a primordial truth fully adequate to its nature, and it necessitates the removal of every mask to ultimately disclose an original identity. However, if the genealogist refuses to extend his faith in metaphysics, if he listens to history, he finds that there is "something altogether different" behind things: not a timeless and essential secret, but the secret that they have no essence or that their essence was fabricated in a piecemeal fashion from alien forms. Examining the history of reason, he learns that it was born in an altogether "reasonable" fashion—from chance;[10] devotion to truth and the precision of scientific methods arose from the passion of scholars, their reciprocal hatred, their fanatical and unending discussions, and their spirit of competition—the personal conflicts that slowly forged the weapons of reason.[11] Further, genealogical analysis shows that the concept of liberty is an "invention of the ruling classes"[12] and not fundamental to man's nature or at the root of his attachment to being and truth. What is found at the historical beginning of things is not the inviolable identity of their origin; it is the dissension of other things. It is disparity.

History also teaches how to laugh at the solemnities of the origin. The lofty origin is no more than "a metaphysical extension which arises from the belief that things are most precious and esential at the moment of birth."[13] We tend to think that this is the moment of their greatest perfection, when they emerged dazzling from the hands of a creator or in the shadowless light of a first morning. The origin always precedes the Fall. It comes before the body, before the world and time; it is associated with the gods, and its story is always sung as a theogony. But historical beginnings are lowly: not in the sense of modest or discreet like the steps of a dove, but derisive and ironic, capable of undoing every infatuation. "We wished to awaken the feeling of man's sovereignty by showing his divine birth: this path is now forbidden, since a monkey stands at the entrance."[14] Man originated with a grimace over his future development; and Zarathustra himself is plagued by a monkey who jumps along behind him, pulling on his coattails.

The final postulate of the origin is linked to the first two in being the site of truth. From the vantage point of an absolute distance, free from the restraints of positive knowledge, the origin makes possible a field of knowledge whose function is to recover it, but always in a false recognition due to the excesses of its own speech. The origin lies at a place of inevitable loss, the point where the truth of things corresponded to a truthful discourse, the site of a fleeting articulation that discourse has obscured and finally lost. It is a new cruelty of history that compels a reversal of this relationship and the abandonment of "adolescent" quests: behind the always recent, avaricious, and measured truth, it posits the ancient proliferation of errors. It is now impossible to believe that "in the rending of the veil, truth remains truthful; we have lived long enough not to be taken in."[15] Truth is undoubtedly the sort of error that cannot be refuted because it was hardened into an unalterable form in the long baking process of history.[16] Moreover, the very question of truth, the right it appropriates to refute error and oppose itself to appearance, the manner in which it developed (initially made available to the wise, then withdrawn by men of piety to an unattainable world where it was given the double role of consolation and imperative, finally rejected as a useless notion, superfluous, and contradicted on all sides)—does this not form a history, the history of an error we call truth? Truth, and its original reign, has had a history within history from which we are barely emerging "in the time of the shortest shadow," when light no longer seems to flow from the depths of the sky or to arise from the first moments of the day.[17]

A genealogy of values, morality, asceticism, and knowledge will never confuse itself with a quest for their "origins," will never neglect as inaccessible the vicissitudes of history. On the contrary, it will cultivate the details and accidents that accompany every beginning; it will be scrupulously attentive to their petty malice; it will await their emergence, once unmasked, as the face of the other. Wherever it is made to go, it will not be reticent—in "excavating the depths," in allowing time for these elements to escape from a labyrinth where no truth had ever detained them. The genealogist needs history to dispel the chimeras of the origin, somewhat in the manner of the pious philosopher who needs a doctor to exoricse the shadow of his soul. He must be able to recognize the events of history, its jolts, its surprises, its unsteady victories and unpalatable defeats—the basis of all beginnings, atavisms, and heredities. Similarly, he must be able to diagnose the illnesses of the body, its conditions of weakness and strength, its breakdown and resistances, to be in a position to judge philosophical discourse. History is the concrete body of a development, with its moments of intensity, its lapses, its extended periods of feverish agitation, its fainting spells; and only a metaphysician would seek its soul in the distant ideality of the origin.

3. *Entstehung* and *Herkunft* are more exact than *Ursprung* in recording the true objective of genealogy; and, while they are ordinarily translated as "origin," we must attempt to reestablish their proper use.

Herkunft is the equivalent of stock or *descent;* it is the ancient affiliation to a group, sustained by the bonds of blood, tradition, or social class. The analysis of *Herkunft* often involves a consideration of race[18] or social type.[19] But the traits it attempts to identify are not the exclusive generic characteristics of an individual, a sentiment, or an idea, which permit us to qualify them as "Greek" or "English"; rather, it seeks the subtle, singular, and subindividual marks that might possibly intersect in them to form a network that is difficult to unravel. Far from being a category of resemblance, this origin allows the sorting out of different traits: the Germans imagined that they had finally accounted for their complexity by saying they possessed a double soul; they were fooled by a simple computation, or rather, they were simply trying to master the racial disorder from which they had formed themselves.[20] Where the soul pretends unification or the self fabricates a coherent identity, the genealogist sets out to study the beginning—numberless beginnings whose faint traces and hints of color are readily seen by an historical eye. The analysis of descent permits the dissociation of the self, its recognition and displacement as an empty synthesis, in liberating a profusion of lost events.

An examination of descent also permits the discovery, under the unique aspect of a trait or a concept, of the myriad events through which—thanks to which, against which—they were formed. Genealogy does not pretend to go back in time to restore an unbroken continuity that operates beyond the dispersion of forgotten things; its duty is not to demonstrate that the past actively exists in the present, that it continues secretly to animate the present, having imposed a predetermined form to all its vicissitudes. Genealogy does not resemble the evolution of a species and does not map the destiny of a people. On the contrary, to follow the complex course of descent is to maintain passing events in their proper dispersion; it is to identify the accidents, the minute deviations—or conversely, the complete reversals—the errors, the false appraisals, and the faulty calculations that gave birth to those things that continue to exist and have value for us; it is to discover that truth or being do not lie at the root of what we know and what we are, but the exteriority of accidents.[21] This is undoubtedly why every origin of morality from the moment it stops being pious—and *Herkunft* can never be—has value as a critique.[22]

Deriving from such a source is a dangerous legacy. In numerous instances, Nietzsche associates the terms *Herkunft* and *Erbschaft*. Nevertheless, we should not be deceived into thinking that this heritage is an acquisition, a possession that grows and solidifies; rather, it is an unstable assemblage of faults, fissures, and heterogeneous layers that threaten the fragile inheritor from within or from underneath: "injustice or instability in the minds of certain men, their disorder and lack of decorum, are the final consequences of their ancestors' numberless logical inaccuracies, hasty conclusions, and superficiality."[23] The search for descent is not the erecting of foundations: on the contrary, it disturbs what was previously considered immobile; it fragments what was thought unified; it shows the heterogeneity of what was imagined consistent with itself. What convictions and, far more decisively, what knowledge can resist it? If a genealogical analysis of a scholar were made—of one who collects facts and carefully accounts for them—his *Herkunft* would quickly divulge the official papers of the scribe and the pleadings of the lawyer—their father[24]—in their apparently disinterested attention, in the "pure" devotion to objectivity.

Finally, descent attaches itself to the body.[25] It inscribes itself in the nervous system, in temperament, in the digestive apparatus; it appears in faulty respiration, in improper diets, in the debilitated and prostrate body of those whose ancestors committed errors. Fathers have only to mistake effects for causes, believe in the reality of an "afterlife," or maintain the value of eternal truths, and the bodies of their children will suffer. Cowardice and hypocrisy, for their part, are the simple offshoots of error: not in a Socratic sense, not that evil is the result of a mistake, not because of a turning away from an original truth, but because the body maintains, in life as in death, through its strength or weakness, the sanction of every truth and error, as it sustains, in an inverse manner, the origin—descent. Why did men invent the contemplative life? Why give a supreme value to this form of existence? Why maintain the absolute truth of those fictions which sustain it? "During barbarous ages . . . if the strength of an individual declined, if he felt himself tired or sick, melancholy or satiated and, as a consequence, without desire or appetite for a short time, he became relatively a better man, that is, less dangerous. His pessimistic ideas could only take form as words or reflections. In this frame of mind, he either became a thinker and prophet or used his imagination to feed his superstitions."[26] The body—and everything that touches it: diet, climate, and soil—is the domain of the *Herkunft*. The body manifests the stigmata of past experience and also gives rise to desires, failings, and errors. These elements may join in a body where they achieve a sudden expression, but as often, their encounter is an engagement in which they efface each other, where the body becomes the pretext of their insurmountable conflict.

The body is the inscribed surface of events (traced by language and dissolved by ideas), the locus of a dissociated Self (adopting the illusion of a substantial unity), and a volume in perpetual disintegration. Genealogy, as an analysis of descent, is thus situated within the articulation of the body and history. Its task is to expose a body totally imprinted by history and the process of history's destruction of the body.

4. *Entstehung* designates *emergence,* the moment of arising. It stands as the principle and the singular law of an apparition. As it is wrong to search for descent in an uninterrupted continuity, we should avoid thinking of emergence as the final term of an historical development; the eye was not always intended for contemplation, and punishment has had other purposes than setting an example. These developments may appear as a culmination, but they are merely the current episodes in a series of subjugations: the eye initially responded to the requirements of hunting and warfare; and punishment has been subjected, throughout its history, to a variety of needs—revenge, excluding an aggressor, compensating a victim, creating fear. In placing present needs at the origin, the metaphysician would convince us of an obscure purpose that seeks its realization at the moment it arises. Genealogy, however, seeks to reestablish the various systems of subjection: not the anticipatory power of meaning, but the hazardous play of dominations.

Emergence is always produced through a particular stage of forces. The analysis of the *Entstehung* must delineate this interaction, the struggle these forces wage against each other or against adverse circumstances, and the attempt to avoid degeneration and regain strength by dividing these forces against themselves. It is in this sense that the emergence of a species (animal or human) and its solidification are secured "in an extended battle against conditions which are essentially and constantly unfavorable." In fact, "the species must realize itself as a species, as something—characterized by the durability, uniformity, and simplicity of its form—which can prevail in the perpetual struggle against outsiders or the uprising of those it oppresses from within." On the other hand, individual differences emerge at another stage of the relationship of forces, when the species has become victorious and when it is no longer threatened from outside. In this condition, we find a struggle "of egoisms turned against each other, each bursting forth in a splintering of forces and a general striving for the sun and for the light."[27] There are also times when force contends against itself, and not only in the intoxication of an abundance, which allows it to divide itself, but at the moment when it weakens. Force reacts against its growing lassitude and gains strength; it imposes limits, inflicts torments and mortifications; it masks these actions as a higher morality, and, in exchange, regains its strength. In this manner, the ascetic ideal was born, "in the instinct of a decadent life which . . . struggles for its own existence."[28] This also describes the movement in which the Reformation arose, precisely where the church was least corrupt;[29] German Catholicism, in the sixteenth century, retained enough strength to turn against itself, to mortify its own body and history, and to spiritualize itself into a pure religion of conscience.

Emergence is thus the entry of forces; it is their eruption, the leap from the wings to center stage, each in its youthful strength. What Nietzsche calls the *Entstehungsherd*[30] of the concept of goodness is not specifically the energy of the strong or the reaction of the weak, but precisely this scene where they are displayed superimposed or face-to-face. It is nothing but the space that divides them, the void through which they exchange their threatening gestures and speeches. As descent qualifies the strength or weakness of an instinct and its inscription on a body, emergence designates a place of confrontation but not as a closed field offering the spectacle of a struggle among equals. Rather, as Nietzsche demonstrates in his analysis of good and evil, it is a "non-place," a pure distance, which indicates that the adversaries do not belong to a common space. Consequently, no one is responsible for an emergence; no one can glory in it, since it always occurs in the interstice.

In a sense, only a single drama is ever staged in this "non-place," the endlessly repeated play of dominations. The domination of certain men over others leads to the differentiation of values;[31] class domination generates the idea of liberty;[32] and the forceful appropriation of things necessary to survival and the imposition of a duration not intrinsic to them account for the origin of logic.[33] This relationship of domination is no more a "relationship" than the place where it occurs is a place; and, precisely for this reason, it is fixed, throughout its history, in rituals, in meticulous procedures that impose rights and obligations. It establishes marks of its power and engraves memories on things and even within bodies. It makes itself accountable for debts and gives rise to the universe of rules, which is by no means designed to temper violence, but rather to satisfy it. Following traditional beliefs, it would be false to think that total war exhausts itself in its own contradictions and ends by renouncing violence and submitting to civil laws. On the contrary, the law is a calculated and relentless pleasure, delight in the promised blood, which permits the perpetual instigation of new dominations and the staging of meticulously repeated scenes of violence. The desire for peace, the serenity of compromise, and the tacit acceptance of the law, far from representing a major moral conversion or a utilitarian calculation that gave rise to the law, are but its result and, in point of fact, its perversion: "guilt, conscience, and duty had their threshold of emergence in the right to secure obligations; and their inception, like that of any major event on earth, was saturated in blood."[34] Humanity does not gradually progress from combat to combat until it arrives at universal reciprocity, where the rule of law finally replaces warfare; humanity installs each of its violences in a system of rules and thus proceeds from domination to domination.

The nature of these rules allows violence to be inflicted on violence and the resurgence of new forces that are sufficiently strong to dominate those in power. Rules are empty in themselves, violent and unfinalized; they are impersonal and can be bent to any purpose. The successes of history belong to those who are capable of seizing these rules, to replace those who had used them, to disguise themselves so as to pervert them, invert their meaning, and redirect them against those who had initially imposed them; controlling this complex mechanism, they will make it function so as to overcome the rulers through their own rules.

The isolation of different points of emergence does not conform to the successive configurations of an identical meaning; rather, they result from substitutions, displacements, disguised conquests, and systematic reversals. If interpretation were the slow exposure of the meaning hidden in an origin, then only metaphysics could interpret the development of humanity. But if interpretation is the violent or surreptitious appropriation of a system of rules, which in itself has no essential meaning, in order to impose a direction, to bend it to a new will, to force its participation in a different game, and to subject it to secondary rules, then the development of humanity is a series of interpretations. The role of genealogy is to record its history: the history of morals, ideals, and metaphysical concepts, the history of the concept of liberty or of the ascetic life; as they stand for the emergence of different interpretations, they must be made to appear as events on the stage of historical process.

5. How can we define the relationship between genealogy, seen as the examination of *Herkunft* and *Entstehung,* and history in the traditional sense? We could, of course, examine Nietzsche's celebrated apostrophes against history, but we will put these aside for the moment and consider those instances when he conceives of genealogy as "wirkliche Historie," or its more frequent characterization as historical "spirit" or "sense."[35] In fact, Nietzsche's criticism, beginning with the second of the *Untimely Meditations,* always questioned the form of history that reintroduces (and always assumes) a suprahistorical perspective: a history whose function is to compose the finally reduced diversity of time into a totality fully closed upon itself; a history that always encourages subjective recognitions and attributes a form of reconciliation to all the displacements of the past; a history whose perspective on all that precedes it implies the end of time, a completed development. The historian's history finds its support outside of time and pretends to base its judgments on an apocalyptic objectivity. This is only possible, however, because of its belief in eternal truth, the immortality of the soul, and the nature of consciousness as always identical to itself. Once the historical sense is mastered by a suprahistorical perspective, metaphysics can bend it to its own purpose and, by aligning it to the demands of objective science, it can impose its own "Egyptianism." On the other hand, the historical sense can evade metaphysics and become a privileged instrument of genealogy if it refuses the certainty of absolutes. Given this, it corresponds to the acuity of a glance that distinguishes, separates, and disperses, that is capable of liberating divergence and marginal elements—the kind of dissociating view that is capable of decomposing itself, capable of shattering the unity of man's being through which it was thought that he could extend his sovereignty to the events of his past.

Historical meaning becomes a dimension of "wirkliche Historie" to the extent that it places within a process of development everything considered immortal in man. We believe that feelings are immutable, but every sentiment, particularly the noblest and most disinterested, has a history. We believe in the dull constancy of instinctual life and imagine that it continues to exert its force indiscriminately in the present as it did in the past. But a knowledge of history easily disintegrates this unity, depicts its wavering course, locates its moments of strength and weakness, and defines its oscillating reign. It easily seizes the slow elaboration of instincts and those movements where, in turning upon themselves, they relentlessly set about their self-destruction.[36] We believe, in any event, that the body obeys the exclusive laws of physiology and that it escapes the influence of history, but this too is false. The body is molded by a great many distinct regimes; it is broken down by the rhythms of work, rest, and holidays; it is poisoned by food or values, through eating habits or moral laws; it constructs resistances.[37] "Effective" history differs from traditional history in being without constants. Nothing in man—not even his body—is sufficiently stable to serve as the basis for self-recognition or for understanding other men. The traditional devices for constructing a comprehensive view of history and for retracing the past as a patient and continuous development must be systematically dismantled. Necessarily, we must dismiss those tendencies that encourage the consoling play of recognitions. Knowledge, even under the banner of history, does not depend on "rediscovery," and it emphatically excludes the "rediscovery of ourselves." History becomes "effective" to the degree that it introduces discontinuity into our very being—as it divides our emotions, dramatizes our instincts, multiplies our body and sets it against itself. "Effective" history deprives the self of the reassuring stability of life and nature, and it will not permit itself to be transported by a voiceless obstinacy toward a millenial ending. It will uproot its traditional foundations and relentlessly disrupt its pretended continuity. This is because knowledge is not made for understanding; it is made for cutting.

From these observations, we can grasp the particular traits of historical meaning as Nietzsche understood it—the sense which opposes "wirkliche Historie" to traditional history. The former transposes the relationship ordinarily established between the eruption of an event and necessary continuity. An entire historical tradition (theological or rationalistic) aims at dissolving the singular event into an ideal continuity—as a teleological movement or a natural process. "Effective" history, however, deals with events in terms of their most unique characteristics, their most acute manifestations. An event, consequently, is not a decision, a treaty, a reign, or a battle, but the reversal of a relationship of forces, the usurpation of power, the appropriation of a vocabulary turned against those who had once used it, a feeble domination that poisons itself as it grows lax, the entry of a masked "other." The forces operating in history are not controlled by destiny or regulative mechanisms, but respond to haphazard conflicts.[38] They do not manifest the successive forms of a primordial intention and their attraction is not that of a conclusion, for they always appear through the singular randomness of events. The inverse of the Christian world, spun entirely by a divine spider, and different from the world of the Greeks, divided between the realm of will and the great cosmic folly, the world of effective history knows only one kingdom, without providence or final cause, where there is only "the iron hand of necessity shaking the dice-box of chance."[39] Chance is not simply the drawing of lots, but raising the stakes in every attempt to master chance through the will to power, and giving rise to the risk of an even greater chance.[40] The world we know is not this ultimately simple configuration where events are reduced to accentuate their essential traits, their final meaning, or their initial and final value. On the contrary, it is a profusion of entangled events. If it appears as a "marvelous motley, profound and totally meaningful," this is because it began and continues its secret existence through a "host of errors and phantasms."[41] We want historians to confirm our belief that the present rests upon profound intentions and immutable necessities. But the true historical sense confirms our existence among countless lost events, without a landmark or a point of reference.

Effective history can also invert the relationship that traditional history, in its dependence on metaphysics, establishes between proximity and distance. The latter is given to a contemplation of distances and heights: the noblest periods, the highest forms, the most abstract ideas, the purest individualities. It accomplishes this by getting as near as possible, placing itself at the foot of its mountain peaks, at the risk of adopting the famous perspective of frogs. Effective history, on the other hand, shortens its vision to those things nearest to it—the body, the nervous system, nutrition, digestion, and energies; it unearths the periods of decadence and if it chances upon lofty epochs, it is with the suspicion—not vindictive but joyous—of finding a barbarous and shameful confusion. It has no fear of looking down, so long as it is understood that it looks from above and descends to seize the various perspectives, to disclose dispersions and differences, to leave things undisturbed in their own dimension and intensity. It reverses the surreptitious practice of historians, their pretension to examine things furthest from themselves, the grovelling manner in which they approach this promising distance (like the metaphysicians who proclaim the existence of an afterlife, situated at a distance from this world, as a promise of their reward). Effective history studies what is closest, but in an abrupt dispossession, so as to seize it at a distance (an approach similar to that of a doctor who looks closely, who plunges to make a diagnosis and to state its difference). Historical sense has more in common with medicine than philosophy; and it should not surprise us that Nietzsche occasionally employs the phrase "historically and physiologically,"[42] since among the philosopher's idiosyncracies is a complete denial of the body. This includes, as well, "the absence of historical sense, a hatred for the idea of development, Egyptianism," the obstinate "placing of conclusions at the beginning," of "making last things first."[43] History has a more important task than to be a handmaiden to philosophy, to recount the necessary birth of truth and values; it should become a differential knowledge of energies and failings, heights and degenerations, poisons and antidotes. Its task is to become a curative science.[44]

The final trait of effective history is its affirmation of knowledge as perspective. Historians take unusual pains to erase the elements in their work which reveal their grounding in a particular time and place, their preferences in a controversy—the unavoidable obstacles of their passion. Nietzsche's version of historical sense is explicit in its perspective and acknowledges its system of injustice. Its perception is slanted, being a deliberate appraisal, affirmation, or negation; it reaches the lingering and poisonous traces in order to prescribe the best antidote. It is not given to a discreet effacement before the objects it observes and does not submit itself to their processes; nor does it seek laws, since it gives equal weight to its own sight and to its objects. Through this historical sense, knowledge is allowed to create its own genealogy in the act of cognition; and "wirkliche Historie" composes a genealogy of history as the vertical projection of its position.

6. In this context, Nietzsche links historical sense to the historian's history. They share a beginning that is similarly impure and confused, share the same sign in which the symptoms of sickness can be recognized as well as the seed of an exquisite flower.[45] They arose simultaneously to follow their separate ways, but our task is to trace their common genealogy.

The descent (*Herkunft*) of the historian is unequivocal: he is of humble birth. A characteristic of history is to be without choice: it encourages thorough understanding and excludes qualitative judgments—a sensitivity to all things without distinction, a comprehensive view excluding differences. Nothing must escape it and, more importantly, nothing must be excluded. Historians argue that this proves their tact and discretion. After all, what right have they to impose their tastes and preferences when they seek to determine what actually occurred in the past? Their mistake is to exhibit a total lack of taste, the kind of crudeness that becomes smug in the presence of the loftiest elements and finds satisfaction in reducing them to size. The historian is insensitive to the most disgusting things; or rather, he especially enjoys those things that should be repugnant to him. His apparent serenity follows from his concerted avoidance of the exceptional and his reduction of all things to the lowest common denominator. Nothing is allowed to stand above him; and underlying his desire for total knowledge is his search for the secrets that belittle everything: "base curiosity." What is the source of history? It comes from the plebs. To whom is it addressed? To the plebs. And its discourse strongly resembles the demagogue's refrain: "No one is greater than you and anyone who presumes to get the better of you—you who are good—is evil." The historian, who functions as his double, can be heard to echo: "No past is greater than your present, and, through my meticulous erudition, I will rid you of your infatuations and transform the grandeur of history into pettiness, evil, and misfortune." The historian's ancestry goes back to Socrates.

This demagogy, of course, must be masked. It must hide its singular malice under the cloak of universals. As the demagogue is obliged to invoke truth, laws of essences, and eternal necessity, the historian must invoke objectivity, the accuracy of facts, and the permanence of the past. The demagogue denies the body to secure the sovereignty of a timeless idea and the historian effaces his proper individuality so that others may enter the stage and reclaim their own speech. He is divided against himself: forced to silence his preferences and overcome his distaste, to blur his own perspective and replace it with the fiction of a universal geometry, to mimic death in order to enter the kingdom of the dead, to adopt a faceless anonymity. In this world where he has conquered his individual will, he becomes a guide to the inevitable law of a superior will. Having curbed the demands of his individual will in his knowledge, he will disclose the form of an eternal will in his object of study. The objectivity of historians inverts the relationships of will and knowledge and it is, in the same stroke, a necessary belief in Providence, in final causes and teleology—the beliefs that place the historian in the family of ascetics. "I can't stand these lustful eunuchs of history, all the seductions of an ascetic ideal; I can't stand these whited sepulchres producing life or those tired and indifferent beings who dress up in the part of wisdom and adopt an objective point of view."[46]

The *Entstehung* of history is found in nineteenth-century Europe: the land of interminglings and bastardy, the period of the "man-of-mixture." We have become barbarians with respect to those rare moments of high civilization: cities in ruin and enigmatic monuments are spread out before us; we stop before gaping walls; we ask what gods inhabited these empty temples. Great epochs lacked this curiosity, lacked our excessive deference; they ignored their predecessors: the classical period ignored Shakespeare. The decadence of Europe presents an immense spectacle (while stronger periods refrained from such exhibitions), and the nature of this scene is to represent a theater; lacking monuments of our own making, which properly belong to us, we live among crowded scenes. But there is more. Europeans no longer know themselves; they ignore their mixed ancestries and seek a proper role. They lack individuality. We can begin to understand the spontaneous historical bent of the nineteenth century: the anemia of its forces and those mixtures that effaced all its individual traits produced the same results as the mortifications of asceticism; its inability to create, its absence of artistic works, and its need to rely on past achievements forced it to adopt the base curiosity of plebs.

If this fully represents the genealogy of history, how could it become, in its own right, a genealogical analysis? Why did it not continue as a form of demagogic or religious knowledge? How could it change roles on the same stage? Only by being seized, dominated, and turned against its birth. And it is this movement which properly describes the specific nature of the *Entstehung:* it is not the unavoidable conclusion of a long preparation, but a scene where forces are risked in the chance of confrontations, where they emerge triumphant, where they can also be confiscated. The locus of emergence for metaphysics was surely Athenian demagogy, the vulgar spite of Socrates and his belief in immortality, and Plato could have seized this Socratic philosophy to turn it against itself. Undoubtedly, he was often tempted to do so, but his defeat lies in its consecration. The problem was similar in the nineteenth century: to avoid doing for the popular asceticism of historians what Plato did for Socrates. This historical trait should not be founded upon a philosophy of history, but dismantled beginning with the things it produced; it is necessary to master history so as to turn it to genealogical uses, that is, strictly anti-Platonic purposes. Only then will the historical sense free itself from the demands of a suprahistorical history.

7. The historical sense gives rise to three uses that oppose and correspond to the three Platonic modalities of history. The first is parodic, directed against reality, and opposes the theme of history as reminiscence or recognition; the second is dissociative, directed against identity, and opposes history given as continuity or representative of a tradition; the third is sacrificial, directed against truth, and opposes history as knowledge. They imply a use of history that severs its connection to memory, its metaphysical and anthropological model, and constructs a counter-memory—a transformation of history into a totally different form of time.

First, the parodic and farcical use. The historian offers this confused and anonymous European, who no longer knows himself or what name he should adopt, the possibility of alternate identities, more individualized and substantial than his own. But the man with historical sense will see that this substitution is simply a disguise. Historians supplied the Revolution with Roman prototypes, romanticism with knight's armor, and the Wagnerian era was given the sword of a German hero—ephemeral props that point to our own unreality. No one kept them from venerating these religions, from going to Bayreuth to commemorate a new afterlife; they were free, as well, to be transformed into street-vendors of empty identities. The new historian, the genealogist, will know what to make of this masquerade. He will not be too serious to enjoy it; on the contrary, he will push the masquerade to its limit and prepare the great carnival of time where masks are constantly reappearing. No longer the identification of our faint individuality with the solid identities of the past, but our "unrealization" through the excessive choice of identities—Frederick of Hohenstaufen, Caesar, Jesus, Dionysus, and possibly Zarathustra. Taking up these masks, revitalizing the buffoonery of history, we adopt an identity whose unreality surpasses that of God who started the charade. "Perhaps, we can discover a realm where originality is again possible as parodists of history and buffoons of God."[47] In this, we recognize the parodic double of what the second of the *Untimely Meditations* called "monumental history": a history given to reestablishing the high points of historical development and their maintenance in a perpetual presence, given to the recovery of works, actions, and creations through the monogram of their personal essence. But in 1874, Nietzsche accused this history, one totally devoted to veneration, of barring access to the actual intensities and creations of life. The parody of his last texts serves to emphasize that "monumental history" is itself a parody. Genealogy is history in the form of a concerted carnival.

The second use of history is the systematic dissociation of identity. This is necessary because this rather weak identity, which we attempt to support and to unify under a mask, is in itself only a parody: it is plural; countless spirits dispute its possession; numerous systems intersect and compete. The study of history makes one "happy, unlike the metaphysicians, to possess in oneself not an immortal soul but many mortal ones."[48] And in each of these souls, history will not discover a forgotten identity, eager to be reborn, but a complex system of distinct and multiple elements, unable to be mastered by the powers of synthesis: "it is a sign of superior culture to maintain, in a fully conscious way, certain phases of its evolution which lesser men pass through without thought. The initial result is that we can understand those who resemble us as completely determined systems and as representative of diverse cultures, that is to say, as necessary and capable of modification. And in return, we are able to separate the phases of our own evolution and consider them individually."[49] The purpose of history, guided by genealogy, is not to discover the roots of our identity but to commit itself to its dissipation. It does not seek to define our unique threshold of emergence, the homeland to which metaphysicians promise a return; it seeks to make visible all of those discontinuities that cross us. "Antiquarian history," according to the *Untimely Meditations,* pursues opposite goals. It seeks the continuities of soil, language, and urban life in which our present is rooted and, "by cultivating in a delicate manner that which existed for all time, it tries to conserve for posterity the conditions under which we were born."[50] This type of history was objected to in the *Meditations* because it tended to block creativity in support of the laws of fidelity. Somewhat later—and already in *Human, All Too Human*—Nietzsche reconsiders the task of the antiquarian, but with an altogether different emphasis. If genealogy in its own right gives rise to questions concerning our native land, native language, or the laws that govern us, its intention is to reveal the heterogenous systems which, masked by the self, inhibit the formation of any form of identity.

The third use of history is the sacrifice of the subject of knowledge. In appearance, or rather, according to the mask it bears, historical consciousness is neutral, devoid of passions, and committed solely to truth. But if it examines itself and if, more generally, it interrogates the various forms of scientific consciousness in its history, it finds that all these forms and transformations are aspects of the will to knowledge: instinct, passion, the inquisitor's devotion, cruel subtlety, and malice. It discovers the violence of a position that sides against those who are happy in their ignorance, against the effective illusions by which humanity protects itself, a position that encourages the dangers of research and delights in disturbing discoveries.[51] The historical analysis of this rancorous will to knowledge reveals that all knowledge rests upon injustice (that there is no right, not even in the act of knowing, to truth or a foundation for truth) and that the instinct for knowledge is malicious (something murderous, opposed to the happiness of mankind). Even in the greatly expanded form it assumes today, the will to knowledge does not achieve a universal truth; man is not given an exact and serene mastery of nature. On the contrary, it ceaselessly multiplies the risks, creates dangers in every area; it breaks down illusory defences; it dissolves the unity of the subject; it releases those elements of itself that are devoted to its subversion and destruction. Knowledge does not slowly detach itself from its empirical roots, the initial needs from which it arose, to become pure speculation subject only to the demands of reason; its development is not tied to the constitution and affirmation of a free subject; rather, it creates a progressive enslavement to its instinctive violence. Where religions once demanded the sacrifice of bodies, knowledge now calls for experimentation on ourselves,[52] calls us to the sacrifice of the subject of knowledge. "The desire for knowledge has been transformed among us into a passion which fears no sacrifice, which fears nothing but its own extinction. It may be that mankind will eventually perish from this passion for knowledge. If not through passion, then through weakness. We must be prepared to state our choice: do we wish humanity to end in fire and light or to end on the sands?"[53] We should now replace the two great problems of nineteenth-century philosophy, passed on by Fichte and Hegel (the reciprocal basis of truth and liberty and the possibility of absolute knowledge), with the theme that "to perish through absolute knowledge may well form a part of the basis of being."[54] This does not mean, in terms of a critical procedure, that the will to truth is limited by the intrinsic finitude of cognition, but that it loses all sense of limitations and all claims to truth in its unavoidable sacrifice of the subject of knowledge. "It may be that there remains one prodigious idea which might be made to prevail over every other aspiration, which might overcome the most victorious: the idea of humanity sacrificing itself. It seems indisputable that if this new constellation appeared on the horizon, only the desire for truth, with its enormous prerogatives, could direct and sustain such a sacrifice. For to knowledge, no sacrifice is too great. Of course, this problem has never been posed."[55]

The *Untimely Meditations* discussed the critical use of history: its just treatment of the past, its decisive cutting of the roots, its rejection of traditional attitudes of reverence, its liberation of man by presenting him with other origins than those in which he prefers to see himself. Nietzsche, however, reproached critical history for detaching us from every real source and for sacrificing the very movement of life to the exclusive concern for truth. Somewhat later, as we have seen, Nietzsche reconsiders this line of thought he had at first refused, but directs it to altogether different ends. It is no longer a question of judging the past in the name of a truth that only we can possess in the present; but risking the destruction of the subject who seeks knowledge in the endless deployment of the will to knowledge.

In a sense, genealogy returns to the three modalities of history that Nietzsche recognized in 1874. It returns to them in spite of the objections that Nietzsche raised in the name of the affirmative and creative powers of life. But they are metamorphosized; the veneration of monuments becomes parody; the respect for ancient continuities becomes systematic dissociation; the critique of the injustices of the past by a truth held by men in the present becomes the destruction of the man who maintains knowledge by the injustice proper to the will to knowledge.

NOTES

1. *The Gay Science,* 7.
2. *Human, All Too Human,* 3.
3. *The Genealogy,* II, 6, 8.
4. *The Gay Science,* 110, 111, 300.
5. *The Dawn,* 102.
6. *The Gay Science,* 151, 353; and also *The Dawn,* 62; *The Genealogy,* I, 14; *Twilight of the Idols,* "The Great Errors," 7.
7. Paul Ree's text was entitled *Ursprung der Moralischen Empfindungen.*
8. In *Human, All Too Human,* aphorism 92 was entitled *Ursprung der Gerechtigkeit.*
9. In the main body of *The Genealogy, Ursprung* and *Herkunpt* are used interchangeably in numerous instances (I, 2; II, 8, 11, 12, 16, 17).
10. *The Dawn,* 123.
11. *Human, All Too Human,* 34.
12. *The Wanderer and His Shadow,* 9.
13. Ibid., 3.
14. *The Dawn,* 49.
15. *Nietzsche contra Wagner,* p. 99.
16. *The Gay Science,* 265 and 110.
17. *Twilight of the Idols,* "How the world of truth becomes a fable."
18. For example, *The Gay Science,* 135; *Beyond Good and Evil,* 200, 242, 244; *The Genealogy,* I, 5.
19. *The Gay Science,* 348–349; *Beyond Good and Evil,* 260.
20. *Beyond Good and Evil,* 244.
21. *The Genealogy,* III, 17. The *abkunft* of feelings of depression.
22. *Twilight,* "Reasons for philosophy."
23. *The Dawn,* 247.
24. *The Gay Science,* 348–349.
25. Ibid., 200.
26. *The Dawn,* 42.
27. *Beyond Good and Evil,* 262.
28. *The Genealogy,* III, 13.
29. *The Gay Science,* 148. It is also to an anemia of the will that one must attribute the *Entstehung* of Buddhism and Christianity, 347.
30. *The Genealogy,* I, 2.
31. *Beyond Good and Evil,* 260; cf. also *The Genealogy,* II, 12.
32. *The Wanderer,* 9.

33. *The Gay Science,* 111.
34. *The Genealogy,* II, 6.
35. Ibid., Preface, 7; and I, 2. *Beyond Good and Evil,* 224.
36. *The Gay Science,* 7.
37. Ibid.
38. *The Genealogy,* II, 12.
39. *The Dawn,* 130.
40. *The Genealogy,* II, 12.
41. *Human, All Too Human,* 16.
42. *Twilight,* 44.
43. Ibid., "Reason within philosophy," 1 and 4.
44. *The Wanderer,* 188.
45. *The Gay Science,* 337.
46. *The Genealogy,* III, 26.
47. *Beyond Good and Evil,* 223.
48. *The Wanderer* (Opinions and Mixed Statements), 17.
49. *Human, All Too Human,* 274.
50. *Untimely Meditations,* II, 3.
51. Cf. *The Dawn,* 429 and 432; *The Gay Science,* 333; *Beyond Good and Evil,* 229–230.
52. *The Dawn,* 501.
53. Ibid., 429.
54. *Beyond Good and Evil,* 39.
55. *The Dawn,* 45.

DECONSTRUCTION AND THE OTHER

Jacques Derrida

Richard Kearney: The most characteristic feature of your work has been its determination to 'deconstruct' the Western philosophy of presence. I think it would be very helpful if you could situate your programme of deconstruction in relation to the two major intellectual traditions of Western culture—the Hebraic and the Hellenic. You conclude your seminal essay on the Jewish philosopher, Emmanuel Lévinas, with the following quotation from James Joyce's *Ulysses:* 'GreekJew is JewGreek'. Do you agree with Lévinas that Judaism offers an alternative to the Greek metaphysics of presence? Or do you believe with Joyce that the Jewish and Greek cultures are fundamentally intertwined?

Jacques Derrida: While I consider it essential to think through this copulative synthesis of Greek and Jew, I consider my own thought, paradoxically, as neither Greek nor Jewish. I often feel that the questions I attempt to formulate on the outskirts of the Greek philosophical tradition have as their 'other' the model of the Jew, that is, the Jew-as-other. And yet the paradox is that I have never actually invoked the Jewish tradition in any 'rooted' or direct manner. Though I was born a Jew, I do not work or think within a living Jewish tradition. So that if there is a Judaic dimension to my thinking which may from time to time have spoken in or through me, this has never assumed the form of an explicit fidelity or debt to that culture. In short, the ultimate site (*lieu*) of my questioning discourse would be neither Hellenic nor Hebraic if such were possible. It would be a non-site beyond both the Jewish influence of my youth and the Greek philosophical heritage which I received during my academic education in the French universities.

Kearney: And yet you share a singular discourse with Lévinas—including notions of the 'other', the 'trace' and writing as 'difference', etc.—which might suggest a common Judaic heritage.

Derrida: Undoubtedly, I was fascinated and attracted by the intellectual journey of Lévinas, but that was not because he was Jewish. It so happens that for Lévinas there is a discrete continuity between his philosophical discourse qua phenomenologist and his religious language qua exegete of the Talmud. But this continuity is not immediately evident. The Lévinas who most interested me at the outset was the philosopher working in phenomenology and posing the question of the 'other' to phenomenology; the Judiac dimension remained at the stage a discrete rather than a decisive reference.

This interview took place in Paris in 1981. Reprinted by permission of Manchester University Press, from Jacques Derrida, "Deconstruction and the Other," in *Dialogues with Contemporary Continental Thinkers,* ed. Richard Kearney, pp. 107–126. Manchester, England: Manchester University Press, 1984.

You ask if Judaism offers an alternative to the Greek philosophy of 'presence'. First we must ascertain what exactly we mean by 'presence'. The French or English words are, of course, neither Greek nor Jewish. So that when we use the word we presuppose a vast history of translation which leads from the Greek terms *ousia* and *on* to the Latin *substantia, actus,* etc. and culminates in our modern term 'presence'. I have no knowledge of what this term means in Judaism.

Kearney: So you would account yourself a philosopher above all else?

Derrida: I'm not happy with the term 'philosopher'.

Kearney: Surely you are a philosopher in that your deconstruction is directed primarily to philosophical ideas and texts?

Derrida: It is true that 'deconstruction' has focused on philosophical texts. And I am of course a 'philosopher' in the institutional sense that I assume the responsibilities of a teacher of philosophy in an official philosophical institution—*l'Ecole Normale Supérieure.* But I am not sure that the 'site' of my work, reading philosophical texts and posing philosophical questions, is itself properly philosophical. Indeed, I have attempted more and more systematically to find a non-site, or a non-philosophical site, from which to question philosophy. But the search for a non-philosophical site does not bespeak an anti-philosophical attitude. My central question is: from what site or non-site (*non-lieu*) can philosophy as such appear to itself as other than itself, so that it can interrogate and reflect upon itself in an original manner? Such a non-site or alterity would be radically irreducible to philosophy. But the problem is that such a non-site cannot be defined or situated by means of philosophical language.

Kearney: The philosophy of deconstruction would seem, therefore, to be a deconstruction of philosophy. Is your interest in painting, psychoanalysis and literature—particularly the literary texts of Jabes, Bataille, Blanchot, Artaud and Mallarmé—not an attempt to establish this non-philosopical site of which you speak?

Derrida: Certainly, but one must remember that even though these sites are non-philosophical they still belong to our Western culture and so are never totally free from the marks of philosophical language. In literature, for example, philosophical language is still present in some sense; but it produces and presents itself as alienated from itself, at a remove, at a distance. This distance provides the necessary free space from which to interrogate philosophy anew; and it was my preoccupation with literary texts which enabled me to discern the problematic of *writing* as one of the key factors in the deconstruction of metaphysics.

Kearney: Accepting the fact that you are seeking a non-philosophical site, you would, I presume, still acknowledge important philosophical influences on your thought. How, for example, would you situate your strategy of deconstruction in respect to the phenomenological movement?

Derrida: My philosophical formation owes much to the thought of Hegel, Husserl and Heidegger. Heidegger is probably the most constant influence, and particularly his project of 'overcoming' Greek metaphysics. Husserl, whom I studied in a more studious and painstaking fashion, taught me a certain methodical prudence and reserve, a rigorous technique of unravelling and formulating questions. But I never shared Husserl's pathos for, and commitment to, a phenomenology of presence. In fact, it was Husserl's method that helped me to suspect the very notion of presence and the fundamental role it has played in all philosophies. My relationship with Heidegger is much more enigmatic and extensive: here my interest was not just *methodological* but *existential.* The themes of Heidegger's questioning always struck me as necessary—especially the 'ontological difference', the reading of Platonism and the relationship between language and Being. My discovery of the genealogical and genetic critique of Nietzsche and Freud also helped me to take the step beyond phenomenology towards a more radical, 'non-philosophical' questioning, while never renouncing the discipline and methodological rigour of phenomenology.

Kearney: Although you share Heidegger's task of 'overcoming' or 'deconstructing' Western metaphysics, you would not, presumably, share his hope to rediscover the 'original names' by means of which Being could be thought and said?

Derrida: I think that there is still in Heidegger, linked up with other things, a nostalgic desire to recover the proper name, the unique name of Being. To be fair, however, one can find several passages in which Heidegger is self-critical and renounces his nostalgia: his practice of cancelling and erasing the term in his later texts is an example of such a critique. Heidegger's texts are still before us; they harbour a future of meaning which will ensure that they are read and reread for centuries. But while I owe a considerable debt to Heidegger's 'path of thought' (*chemin de pensée*), we differ in our employment of language, in our understanding of language. I write in another language—and I do not simply mean in French rather than in German—even though this 'otherness' cannot be explained in terms of philosophy itself. The difference resides outside of philosophy, in the non-philosophical site of language; it is what makes the poets and writers that interest me (Mallarmé, Blanchot, etc.) totally different from those that interest Heidegger (Hölderlin and Rilke). In this sense my profound rapport with Heidegger is also and at the same time a non-rapport.

Kearney: Yes, I can see that your understanding of language as 'differance' and 'dissemination' is quite removed from Heidegger's notion of language as the 'house of Being', that which 'recalls and recollects' and 'names the Holy'. In addition, while Heidegger is still prepared to use such philosophical concepts as *Being* and *existence* to express his thought, you have made it clear that the operative terms in your language—e.g. deconstruction, differance, dissemination, trace and so on—are basically 'non-concepts', 'undecidables'. What exactly do you mean by 'non-concepts' and what role do they play in your attempt to deconstruct metaphysics?

Derrida: I will try to reconstitute the argument by means of which I advanced the notion of a non-concept. First, it doesn't have the logical generality which a philosophical concept claims to have in its supposed independence from ordinary or literary language. The notion of 'differance', for example, is a non-concept in that it cannot be defined in terms of oppositional predicates; it is neither *this* nor *that*; but rather this *and* that (e.g. the act of differing and of deferring) without being reducible to a dialectical logic either. And yet the term 'differance' emerges and develops as a determination of language from which it is inseparable. Hence the difficulty of translating the term. There is no conceptual realm beyond language which would allow the term to have a univocal semantic content over and above its inscription in language. Because it remains a trace of language it remains non-conceptual. And because it has no oppositional or predicative generality, which would identify it as *this* rather than *that*, the term 'differance' cannot be defined within a system of logic—Aristotelian or dialectical—that is, within the logocentric system of philosophy.

Kearney: But can we go beyond or deconstruct the logocentric system of metaphysics without employing the terminology of metaphysics? Is it not only *from the inside* that we can undo metaphysics by means of stratagems and strategies which expose the ambiguities and contradictions of the logocentric system of presence? Does that not mean that we are condemned to metaphysics even while attempting to deconstruct its pretensions?

Derrida: In a certain sense it is true to say that 'deconstruction' is still in metaphysics. But we must remember that if we are indeed *inside* metaphysics, we are not inside it as we might be *inside* a box or a milieu. We are still *in* metaphysics in the special sense that we are *in* a determinate language. Consequently, the idea that we might be able to get outside of metaphysics has always struck me as naive. So that when I refer to the 'closure' (*clôture*) of metaphysics, I insist that it is not a question of considering metaphysics as a circle with a limit or simple boundary. The notion of the limit and boundary (*bord*) of metaphysics is itself highly problematic. My reflections on this problematic have always attempted to show that the limit or end of metaphysics is not linear or circular in any indivisible sense. And as soon as we acknowledge that the limit-boundary of metaphysics is divisible, the logical rapport between inside and outside is no longer simple. Accordingly, we cannot really say that we are 'locked into' or 'condemned to' metaphysics, for we are, strictly speaking, neither inside nor outside. In brief, the whole rapport between the inside and the outside of metaphysics is inseparable from the question of the finitude and reserve of metaphysics as language. But the idea of the finitude and exhaustion (*épuisement*) of metaphysics does not mean that we are incarcerated in it as prisoners or victims of some unhappy fatality. It is simply that our belonging to, and inherence in, the language of metaphysics is something that can only be rigorously and adequately thought about from *another* topos or space where our problematic rapport with the boundary of metaphysics can be seen in a more radical light. Hence my attempts to discover the non-place or *non-lieu* which would be the 'other' of philosophy. This is the task of deconstruction.

Kearney: Can literary and poetic language provide this *non-lieu* or *u-topos*?

Derrida: I think so; but when I speak of literature it is not with a capital L; it is rather an allusion to certain movements which have worked around the limits of our logical concepts, certain texts which make the limits of our language tremble, exposing them as divisible and questionable. This is what the works of Blanchot, Bataille or Beckett are particularly sensitive to.
Kearney: What does this whole problematic of the closure of Western 'logocentric' philosophy and of the limits of our language tell us about the modern age in which we live? Is there a rapport between deconstruction and 'modernity' in so far as the latter bespeaks a crisis of scientific foundations and of values in general, a crisis occasioned by the discovery that the absolute origin that the Western tradition claimed to have identified in the 'logos' is merely the trace of an absence, a nothingness?
Derrida: I have never been very happy with the term 'modernity'. Of course, I feel that what is happening in the world today is something unique and singular. As soon, however, as we give it the label of 'modernity', we inscribe it in a certain historical system of evolution or progress (a notion derived from Enlightenment rationalism) which tends to blind us to the fact that what confronts us today is *also* something ancient and hidden in history. I believe that what 'happens' in our contemporary world and strikes us as particularly new has in fact an essential connection with something extremely old which has been covered over (*archi-dissimulê*). So that the new is not so much that which occurs for the first time but that 'very ancient' dimension which recurs in the 'very modern'; and which indeed has been signified repetitively throughout our historical tradition, in Greece and in Rome, in Plato and in Descartes and in Kant, etc. No matter how novel or unprecedented a modern meaning may appear, it is never exclusively *modernist* but is also and at the same time a phenomenon of *repetition*. And yet the relationship between the ancient and the modern is not simply that of the implicit and the explicit. We must avoid the temptation of supposing that what occurs today somehow pre-existed in a latent form, merely waiting to be unfolded or explicated. Such thinking also conceives history as an evolutionary development and excludes the crucial notions of rupture and mutation in history. My own conviction is that we must maintain two contradictory affirmations at the same time. On the one hand we affirm the existence of ruptures in history, and on the other we affirm that these ruptures produce gaps or faults (*failles*) in which the most hidden and forgotten archives can emerge and constantly recur and work through history. One must surmount the categorical oppositions of philosophical logic out of fidelity to these conflicting positions of historical discontinuity (rupture) and continuity (repetition), which are neither a pure break with the past nor a pure unfolding or explication of it.
Kearney: How do you explain the way in which philosophy has altered and changed from one historical epoch to the next? How do you explain, for example, the difference between Plato's thought and your own?
Derrida: The difference between our modes of thought does not mean that I or other 'modern' thinkers have gone beyond Plato, in the sense of having

succeeded in exhausting all that is contained in his texts. Here I return to what I was describing as the 'future' of a Heideggerian text. I believe that all of the great philosophical texts—of Plato, Parmenides, Hegel or Heidegger, for example—are still *before* us. The future of the great philosophies remains obscure and enigmatic, still to be disclosed. Up to now, we have merely scratched the surface. This opaque and inexhaustible residue of philosophical texts, which I call their 'future', is more predominant in Greek and German philosophy than in French. I have a profound respect for the great French thinkers, but I have always had the impression that a certain kind of rigorous analysis could render their texts accessible and exhaustible. Before a Platonic or Heideggerian text, by contrast, I feel that I am confronting an abyss, a bottomless pit in which I could lose myself. No matter how rigorous an analysis I bring to bear on such texts, I am always left with the impression that there is something *more* to be thought.

Kearney: What exactly is the inexhaustible richness which these great texts possess and which continues to fascinate us throughout the centuries?

Derrida: The temptation here is to offer a quick and simple response. But having taught philosophy for over twenty years, I must honestly say that now, less than ever, do I know what philosophy is. My knowledge of what it is that constitutes the essence of philosophy is at zero degree. All I know is that a Platonic or Heideggerian text always returns us to the beginning, enables us to *begin* to ask philosophical questions, including the question: what is philosophy?

Kearney: But surely it must be possible to say *what* philosophy is by way of distinguishing it from other scientific disciplines such as economics, sociology, the natural sciences, or even literature? Why learn philosophy at all, in schools, universities or in the privacy of one's study, if it is impossible to say what it is or what function it serves? If deconstruction prevents us from asserting or stating or identifying anything, then surely one ends up, not with 'differance', but with indifference, where nothing is anything, and everything is everything else?

Derrida: It is as impossible to say what philosophy *is not* as it is to say what it *is*. In all the other disciplines you mention, there is philosophy. To say to oneself that one is going to study something that is *not* philosophy is to deceive oneself. It is not difficult to show that in political economy, for example, there is a philosophical discourse in operation. And the same applies to mathematics and the other sciences. Philosophy, as logocentrism, is present in every scientific discipline and the only justification for transforming philosophy into a specialized discipline is the necessity to render explicit and thematic the philosophical subtext in every discourse. The principal function which the teaching of philosophy serves is to enable people to become 'conscious', to become aware of what exactly they are saying, what kind of discourse they are engaged in when they do mathematics, physics, political economy, and so on. There is no system of teaching or transmitting knowledge which can retain its coherence or integrity without, at one moment or another, interrogating itself philosophically, that is, without acknowledging its subtextual premisses; and this may even include an interrogation of unspoken political interests or traditional values. From such an interrogation each society draws its own conclusions about the worth of philosophy.

Kearney: How, for example, can political economy interrogate itself philosophically?

Derrida: First, all of the major concepts which constitute the discourse of economics are philosophical, and particularly such concepts as 'property', 'work' or 'value'. These are all 'philosophemes', concepts inaugurated by a philosophical discourse which usually go back to Greece or Rome, and kept in operation by means of this discourse, which refers back at first, as does philosophy itself, to the 'natural languages' of Greece and Rome. Consequently, the economic discourse is founded on a logocentric philosophical discourse and remains inseparable from it. The 'autonomy' which economists might subsequently like to confer on their discipline can never succeed in masking its philosophical derivation. Science is never purely objective, nor is it merely reducible to an instrumental and utilitarian model of explanation. Philosophy can teach science that it is ultimately an element of language, that the limits of its formalization reveal its belonging to a language in which it continues to operate despite its attempts to justify itself as an exclusively 'objective' or 'instrumental' discourse.

Kearney: Is the logocentric character of science a singularly European phenomenon?

Derrida: Logocentrism, in its developed philosophical sense, is inextricably linked to the Greek and European tradition. As I have attempted to demonstrate elsewhere in some detail, logocentric philosophy is a specifically Western response to a much larger necessity which also occurs in the Far East and other cultures, that is, the phonocentric necessity: the privilege of the voice over writing. The priority of spoken language over written or silent language stems from the fact that when words are spoken the speaker and the listener are supposed to be simultaneously present to one another; they are supposed to be the same, pure unmediated presence. This ideal of perfect self-presence, of the immediate possession of meaning, is what is expressed by the phonocentric necessity. Writing, on the other hand, is considered subversive in so far as it creates a spatial and temporal distance between the author and audience; writing presupposes the absence of the author and so we can never be sure exactly what is meant by a written text; it can have many different meanings as opposed to a single unifying one. But this phonocentric necessity did not develop into a systematic logocentric metaphysics in any non-European culture. Logocentrism is a uniquely European phenomenon.

Kearney: Does this mean that other cultures do not require deconstruction?

Derrida: Every culture and society requires an internal critique or deconstruction as an essential part of its development. *A priori,* we can presume that non-European cultures operate some sort of autocritique of their own linguistic concepts and foundational institutions. Every culture needs an element of self-interrogation and of distance from itself, if it is to transform itself. No culture is closed in on itself, especially in our own times when the impact of European civilization is so all-pervasive. Similarly, what we call the deconstruction of our own Western culture is aided and abetted by the fact that Europe has always registered the impact of heterogeneous, non-European influences. Because it has always been thus exposed to, and shadowed by, its 'other', it has been compelled to question itself. Every culture is haunted by its other.

Kearney: Did the arrival of Judeo-Christianity represent such a radicalizing 'alterity' for the Graeco-Roman civilization? Did it challenge the homogeneity of the Western metaphysics of presence?

Derrida: I'd be wary of talking about Judeo-Christianity with a capital J and C. Judeo-Christianity is an extremely complex entity which, in large part, only constituted itself qua Judeo-Christianity by its assimilation into the schemas of Greek philosophy. Hence what we know as Christian and Jewish theology today is a cultural ensemble which has already been largely 'Hellenized'.

Kearney: But did not Judaism and Christianity represent a heterogeneity, an 'otherness' before they were assimilated into Greek culture?

Derrida: Of course. And one can argue that these original, heterogeneous elements of Judaism and Christianity were never completely eradicated by Western metaphysics. They perdure throughout the centuries, threatening and unsettling the assured 'identities' of Western philosophy. So that the surreptitious deconstruction of the Greek *Logos* is at work from the very origin of our Western culture. Already, the translation of Greek concepts into other languages—Latin, Arabic, German, French, English, etc.—or indeed the translation of Hebraic or Arabic ideas and structures into metaphysical terms, produces 'fissures' in the presumed 'solidity' of Greek philosophy by introducing alien and conflicting elements.

Kearney: The logocentrism of Greek metaphysics will always be haunted, therefore, by the 'absolutely other' to the extent that the *Logos* can never englobe everything. There is always something which escapes, something different, other and opaque which refuses to be totalized into a homogeneous identity.

Derrida: Just so—and this 'otherness' is not necessarily something which comes to Greek philosophy from the 'outside', that is, from the non-Hellenic world. From the very beginnings of Greek philosophy the self-identity of the *Logos* is already fissured and divided. I think one can discern signs of such fissures of 'difference' in every great philosopher: the 'Good beyond Being' (*epekeina tes ousias*) of Plato's *Republic,* for example, or the confrontation with the 'Stranger' in *The Sophist* are already traces of an alterity which refuses to be totally domesticated. Moreover, the rapport of self-identity is itself always a rapport of violence with the other; so that the notions of property, appropriation and self-presence, so central to logocentric metaphysics, are essentially dependent on an oppositional relation with otherness. In this sense, identity *presupposes* alterity.

Kearney: If deconstruction is a way of challenging the logocentric pretensions of Western philosophy, and by implication of the sciences it has founded, can

it ever surmount its role of iconoclastic negation and become a form of affirmation? Can your search for a non-site or *u-topos,* other than the *topos* of Western metaphysics, also be construed as a prophetic utopianism?
Derrida: I will take the terms 'affirmation' and 'prophetic utopianism' separately. Deconstruction certainly entails a moment of affirmation. Indeed, I cannot conceive of a radical critique which would not be ultimately motivated by some sort of affirmation, acknowledged or not. Deconstruction always presupposes affirmation, as I have frequently attempted to point out, sometimes employing a Nietzschean terminology. I do not mean that the deconstructing *subject* or *self* affirms. I mean that deconstruction is, in itself, a positive response to an alterity which necessarily calls, summons or motivates it. Deconstruction is therefore vocation—a response to a call. The other, as the other than self, the other that opposes self-identity, is not something that can be detected and disclosed within a philosophical space and with the aid of a philosophical lamp. The other precedes philosophy and necessarily invokes and provokes the subject before any genuine questioning can begin. It is in this rapport with the other that affirmation expresses itself.

As to the question of prophecy, this is a much more obscure area for me. There are certainly prophetic effects (*effets*): but the language of prophecy alters continually. Today the prophets no longer speak with the same accents or scenography as the prophets in the Bible.
Kearney: Lévinas has suggested that the contemporary deconstruction of philosophy and the sciences is symptomatic of a fundamental crisis of Western culture, which he chooses to interpret as a prophetic and ethical cry. Would you agree?
Derrida: Certainly prophets always flourish in times of socio-historical or philosophical crisis. Bad times for philosophy are good times for prophecy. Accordingly, when deconstructive themes begin to dominate the scene, as they do today, one is sure to find a proliferation of prophecies. And this proliferation is precisely a reason why we should be all the more wary and prudent, all the more discriminating.
Kearney: But here we have the whole problem of a criterion of evaluation. According to what criterion does one discriminate between prophecies? Is this not a problem for you since you reject the idea of a transcendental *telos* or *eschaton* which could provide the critical subject with an objective or absolute yardstick of value?
Derrida: It is true that I interrogate the idea of an *eschaton* or *telos* in the absolute formulations of classical philosophy. But that does not mean I dismiss all forms of Messianic or prophetic eschatology. I think that all genuine questioning is summoned by a certain type of eschatology, though it is impossible to define this eschatology in philosophical terms. The search for objective or absolute criteria is, to be sure, an essentially philosophical gesture. Prophecy differs from philosophy in so far as it dispenses with such criteria. The prophetic word is its own criterion and refuses to submit to an external tribunal which would judge or evaluate it in an objective and neutral fashion. The

prophetic word reveals its own eschatology and finds its index of truthfulness in its own inspiration and not in some transcendental or philosophical criteriology.

Kearney: Do you feel that your own work is prophetic in its attempt to deconstruct philosophy and philosophical criteria?

Derrida: Unfortunately, I do not feel inspired by any sort of hope which would permit me to presume that my work of deconstruction has a prophetic function. But I concede that the style of my questioning as an exodus and dissemination in the desert might produce certain prophetic resonances. It is possible to see deconstruction as being produced in a space where the prophets are not far away. But the prophetic resonances of my questioning reside at the level of a certain rhetorical discourse which is also shared by several other contemporary thinkers. The fact that I declare it 'unfortunate' that I do not personally feel inspired may be a signal that deep down I still hope. It means that I am in fact still looking for something. So perhaps it is no mere accident of rhetoric that the search itself, the search without hope for hope, assumes a certain prophetic *allure*. Perhaps my search is a twentieth century brand of prophecy? But it is difficult for me to believe it.

Kearney: Can the theoretical radicality of deconstruction be translated into a radical political praxis?

Derrida: This is a particularly difficult question. I must confess that I have never succeeded in directly relating deconstruction to existing political codes and programmes. I have of course had occasion to take a specific political stand in certain codable situations, for example, in relation to the French university institution. But the available codes for taking such a political stance are not at all adequate to the radicality of deconstruction. And the absence of an adequate political code to translate or incorporate the radical implications of deconstruction has given many the impression that deconstruction is opposed to politics, or is at best apolitical. But this impression only prevails because all of our political codes and terminologies still remain fundamentally metaphysical, regardless of whether they originate from the right or the left.

Kearney: In *The Revolution of the Word,* Colin McCabe employed your notions of deconstruction and dissemination to show how James Joyce recognized and revealed the inner workings of language as a refusal of identity, as a process of 'differance' irreducible to all of our logocentric concepts and codes. In *Ulysses* this process of 'differance' is epitomized by Bloom, the vagrant or nomad who obviates and subverts the available codes of identity—religious, political or national. And yet, McCabe argues, the Joycean refutation of all dogmatic or totalizing forms of identity is itself a political stance—an anti-totalitarian or anarchic stance.

Derrida: This is the politics of exodus, of the emigré. As such, it can of course serve as a political ferment or anxiety, a subversion of fixed assumptions and a privileging of disorder.

Kearney: But does the politics of the emigré necessarily imply inaction and non-commitment?

Derrida: Not at all. But the difficulty is to gesture in opposite directions at the same time: on the one hand to preserve a distance and suspicion with regard to the official political codes governing reality; on the other, to intervene here and now in a practical and *engagé* manner whenever the necessity arises. This position of dual allegiance, in which I personally find myself, is one of perpetual uneasiness. I try where I can to act politically while recognizing that such action remains incommensurate with my intellectual project of deconstruction.
Kearney: Could one describe the political equivalent of deconstruction as a disposition, as opposed to a position, of responsible anarchy?
Derrida: If I had to describe my political disposition I would probably employ a formula of that kind while stressing, of course, the interminable obligation to work out and to deconstruct these two terms—'responsible' and 'anarchy'. If taken as assured certainties in themselves, such terms can also become reified and unthinking dogmas. But I also try to re-evaluate the indispensable notion of 'responsibility'.
Kearney: I would now like to turn to another theme in your work: the deconstructive role of the 'feminine'. If the logocentric domination of Western culture also expresses itself as a 'phallogocentrism', is there a sense in which the modern movement to liberate women represents a deconstructive gesture? Is this something which Nietzsche curiously recognized when he spoke of 'truth becoming woman'; or Joyce when he celebrated the 'woman's reason' of Molly Bloom in *Ulysses* and Anna Livia Plurabelle in *Finnegans Wake?* Is the contemporary liberation of woman's reason and truth not an unveiling of the hitherto repressed resources of a non-logocentric *topos*?
Derrida: While I would hesitate to use such terms as 'liberation' or 'unveiling', I think there can be little doubt that we are presently witnessing a radical mutation of our understanding of sexual difference. The discourses of Nietzsche, Joyce and the women's movement which you have identified epitomize a profound and unprecedented transformation of the man–woman relationship. The deconstruction of phallogocentrism is carried by this transformation, as are also the rise of psychoanalysis and the modernist movement in literature. But we cannot objectify or thematize this mutation even though it is bringing about such a radical change in our understanding of the world that a return to the former logocentric philosophies of mastery, possession, totalization or certitude may soon be unthinkable. The philosophical and literary discoveries of the 'feminine' which you mention—and even the political and legal recognition of the status of women—are all symptoms of a deeper mutation in our search for meaning which deconstruction attempts to register.
Kearney: Do you think then that this mutation can be seen and evaluated in terms of an historical progress towards the 'good', towards a 'better' society?
Derrida: This mutation is certainly experienced as 'better' in so far as it is what is desired by those who practically dispose of the greatest 'force' in society. One could describe the transformation effected by the feminine as 'good' with-

out positing it as an *a priori* goal or telos. I hesitate to speak of 'liberation' in this context, because I don't believe that women are 'liberated', any more than men are. They are, of course, no longer 'enslaved' in many of the old sociopolitical respects, but even in the new situation woman will not ultimately be any freer than man. One needs another language, besides that of political liberation, to characterize the enormous deconstructive import of the feminine as an uprooting of our phallogocentric culture. I prefer to speak of this mutation of the feminine as a 'movement' rather than as an historical or political 'progress'. I always hesitate to talk of historical progress.

Kearney: What is the relationship between deconstruction and your use of poetic language, particularly in *Glas*? Do you consider *Glas* to be a work of philosophy or of poetry?

Derrida: It is neither philosophy nor poetry. It is in fact a reciprocal contamination of the one by the other, from which neither can emerge intact. This notion of contamination is, however, inadequate, for it is not simply a question of rendering both philosophy and poetry *impure*. One is trying to reach an additional or alternative dimension beyond philosophy and literature. In my project, philosophy and literature are two poles of an opposition and one cannot isolate one from the other or privilege one over the other. I consider that the limits of philosophy are also those of literature. In *Glas,* consequently, I try to compose a *writing* which would traverse, as rigorously as possible, both the philosophical and literary elements without being definable as either. Hence in *Glas* one finds classical philosophical analysis being juxtaposed with quasi-literary passages, each challenging, perverting and exposing the impurities and contradictions in their neighbour; and at some point the philosophical and literary trajectories cross each other and give rise to something else, some *other* site.

Kearney: Is there not a sense in which philosophy for you is a form of literature? You have, for example, described metaphysics as a 'white mythology', that is, a sort of palimpsest of metaphors (*eidos, telos, ousia*) and myths (of return, homecoming, transcendence towards the light, etc.), which are covered over and forgotten as soon as philosophical 'concepts' are construed as pure and univocal abstractions, as totalizing universals devoid of myth and metaphor.

Derrida: I have always tried to expose the way in which philosophy is literary, not so much because it is *metaphor* but because it is *catachresis.* The term metaphor generally implies a relation to an original 'property' of meaning, a 'proper' sense to which it indirectly or equivocally refers, whereas *catachresis* is a violent production of meaning, an abuse which refers to no anterior or proper norm. The founding concepts of metaphysics—*logos, eidos, theoria,* etc.—are instances of *catachresis* rather than metaphors as I attempted to demonstrate in 'White Mythology' (*Marges de la philosophie*). In a work such as *Glas,* or other recent ones like it, I am trying to produce new forms of *catachresis,* another kind of writing, a violent writing which stakes out the faults (*failles*) and

deviations of language; so that the text produces a language of its own, in itself, which while continuing to work through tradition emerges at a given moment as a *monster,* a monstrous mutation without tradition or normative precedent.
Kearney: What then of the question of language as reference? Can language as mutation or violence or monstrosity refer to anything other than itself?
Derrida: There have been several misinterpretations of what I and other deconstructionists are trying to do. It is totally false to suggest that deconstruction is a suspension of reference. Deconstruction is always deeply concerned with the 'other' of language. I never cease to be surprised by critics who see my work as a declaration that there is nothing beyond language, that we are imprisoned in language; it is, in fact, saying the exact opposite. The critique of logocentrism is above all else the search for the 'other' and the 'other of language'. Every week I receive critical commentaries and studies on deconstruction which operate on the assumption that what they call 'post-structuralism' amounts to saying that there is nothing beyond language, that we are submerged in words—and other stupidities of that sort. Certainly, deconstruction tries to show that the question of reference is much more complex and problematic than traditional theories supposed. It even asks whether our term 'reference' is entirely adequate for designating the 'other'. The other, which is beyond language and which summons language, is perhaps not a 'referent' in the normal sense which linguists have attached to this term. But to distance oneself thus from the habitual structure of reference, to challenge or complicate our common assumptions about it, does not amount to saying that there is *nothing* beyond language.
Kearney: This could also be seen as a reply to those critics who maintain that deconstruction is a strategy of nihilism, an orgy of non-sense, a relapse into the free play of the arbitrary.
Derrida: I regret that I have been misinterpreted in this way, particularly in the United States, but also in France. People who wish to avoid questioning and discussion present deconstruction as a sort of gratuitous chess game with a combination of signs (*combinatoire de signifiants*), closed up in language as in a cave. This misinterpretation is not just a simplification; it is symptomatic of certain political and institutional interests—interests which must also be deconstructed in their turn. I totally refuse the label of nihilism which has been ascribed to me and my American colleagues. Deconstruction is not an enclosure in nothingness, but an openness towards the other.
Kearney: Can deconstruction serve as a method of literary criticism which might contribute something positive to our appreciation of literature?
Derrida: I am not sure that deconstruction can function as a literary *method* as such. I am wary of the idea of methods of reading. The laws of reading are determined by the particular text that is being read. This does not mean that we should simply abandon ourselves to the text, or represent and repeat it in a purely passive manner. It means that we must remain faithful, even if it implies a certain violence, to the injunctions of the text. These injunctions will differ

from one text to the next so that one cannot prescribe one general method of reading. In this sense deconstruction is not a method. Nor do I feel that the principle function of deconstruction is to contribute something to literature. It does, of course, contribute to our epistemological appreciation of texts by exposing the philosophical and theoretical presuppositions that are at work in every critical methodology, be it Formalism, New Criticism, Socialist Realism or a historical critique. Deconstruction asks *why* we read a literary text in this particular manner rather than another. It shows, for example, that New Criticism is not *the* way of reading texts, however enshrined it may be in certain university institutions, but only one way among others. Thus deconstruction can also serve to question the presumption of certain university and cultural institutions to act as the sole or privileged guardians and transmitters of meaning. In short, deconstruction not only teaches us to read literature more thoroughly by attending to it *as language,* as the production of meaning through *differance* and dissemination, through a complex play of signifying traces; it also enables us to interrogate the covert philosophical and political presuppositions of institutionalized critical methods which generally govern our reading of a text. There is in deconstruction something which challenges every teaching institution. It is not a question of calling for the destruction of such institutions, but rather of making us aware of what we are in fact doing when we subscribe to this or that institutional way of reading literature. Nor must we forget that deconstruction is itself a form of literature, a literary text to be read like other texts, an interpretation open to several other interpretations. Accordingly, one can say that deconstruction is at once extremely *modest* and extremely *ambitious.* It is ambitious in that it puts itself on a par with literary texts, and modest in that it admits that it is only one textual interpretation among others, written in a language which has no centralizing power of mastery or domination, no privileged metalanguage over and above the language of literature.

Kearney: And what would you say to those critics who accuse you of annihilating the very idea of the human subject in your determination to dispense with all centralizing agencies of meaning, all 'centrisms'?

Derrida: They need not worry. I have never said that the subject should be dispensed with. Only that it should be deconstructed. To deconstruct the subject does not mean to deny its existence. There are subjects, 'operations' or 'effects' (*effets*) of subjectivity. This is an incontrovertible fact. To acknowledge this does not mean, however, that the subject is what it *says* it is. The subject is not some meta-linguistic substance or identity, some pure *cogito* of self-presence; it is always inscribed in language. My work does not, therefore, destroy the subject; it simply tries to resituate it.

Kearney: But can deconstruction, as the disclosure of language as *differance,* contribute to the *pleasure* of reading, to our appreciation of the living *texture* of a literary text? Or is it only an intellectual strategy of detection, of exposing our presuppositions and disabusing us of our habitual illusions about reading?

Derrida: Deconstruction gives pleasure in that it gives desire. To deconstruct a text is to disclose how it functions as desire, as a search for presence and fulfilment which is interminably deferred. One cannot read without opening oneself to the desire of language, to the search for that which remains absent and other than oneself. Without a certain love of the text, no reading would be possible. In every reading there is a *corps-à-corps* between the reader and text, an incorporation of the reader's desire into the desire of the text. Here is pleasure, the very opposite of that arid intellectualism of which deconstruction has so often been accused.

PHILOSOPHY AS STAND-IN AND INTERPRETER

Jürgen Habermas

Master thinkers have fallen on hard times. This has been true of Hegel ever since Popper unmasked him in the forties as an enemy of the open society. It has also been intermittently true of Marx. The last to denounce Marx as a false prophet were the New Philosophers in the seventies. Today even Kant is affected by this decline. If I am correct, he is being viewed for the first time as a *maître penseur,* that is, as the magician of a false paradigm from the intellectual constraints of which we have to escape. Though among a philosophical audience there may still be a majority of scholars whose image of Kant has stayed the same, in the world outside his reputation is being eclipsed, and not for the first time, by Nietzsche.

Historically, Kantian philosophy marks the birth of a new mode of justification. Kant felt that the physics of his time and the growth of knowledge brought by it were important developments to which the philosopher had to respond. For Kant, the new science represented not some philosophically indifferent act of life but proof of man's capacity to know. Specifically, the challenge Newtonian physics posed for philosophy was to explain how empirical knowledge is at all possible, an explanation that could not itself be empirical but had to be transcendental. What Kant calls "transcendental" is an inquiry into the *a priori* conditions of what makes experience possible. The specific upshot of Kant's transcendental inquiry is that those conditions are identical with the conditions of possible objects of experience. The first job for the philosopher, then, is to analyze the concepts of objects as we "always already" intuitively use them. Transcendental analysis is a nonempirical reconstruction of the *a priori* achievements of the cognizing subject, achievements for which there is no alternative: No experience shall be thought possible under *different* conditions. Transcendental justification has nothing to do with deduction from first principles. Rather, the hallmark of the transcendental justification is the notion that we can prove the nonsubstitutability of certain mental operations that we always already (intuitively) perform in accordance with rules.

As a master thinker, Kant fell into disfavor because he used transcendental justification to found the new discipline of epistemology. In so doing, he redefined the task, or vocation if you like, of philosophy in a more demanding way. There are two principal reasons why the Kantian view of philosophy's vocation has a dubious ring today.

The first reason has directly to do with the foundationalism of epistemol-

Reprinted by permission of The Massachusetts Institute of Technology and the author, from Jürgen Habermas, "Philosophy as Stand-In and Interpreter," in Habermas, *Moral Consciousness and Communicative Action,* trans. Christen Lenhardt and Shierry Weber Nicholsen, pp. 1–20. Cambridge, Massachusetts: The MIT Press, 1987.

ogy. In championing the idea of a cognition *before* cognition, Kantian philosophy sets up a domain between itself and the sciences, arrogating authority to itself. It wants to clarify the foundations of the sciences once and for all, defining the limits of what can and cannot be experienced. This is tantamount to an act of showing the sciences their proper place. I think philosophy cannot and should not try to play the role of usher.

The second reason lies in the fact that transcendental philosophy refuses to be confined to epistemology. Above and beyond analyzing the bases of cognition, the critique of pure reason is also supposed to enable us to criticize the abuses of this cognitive faculty, which is limited to phenomena. Kant replaces the substantive concept of reason found in traditional metaphysics with a concept of reason the moments of which have undergone differentiation to the point where their unity is merely formal. He sets up practical reason, judgment, and theoretical cognition in isolation from each other, giving each a foundation unto itself, with the result that philosophy is cast in the role of the highest arbiter for all matters, including culture as a whole. Kantian philosophy differentiates what Weber was to call the "value spheres of culture" (science and technology, law and morality, art and art criticism), while at the same time legitimating them within their respective limits. Thus Kant's philosophy poses as the highest court of appeal vis-à-vis the sciences and culture as a whole.[1]

There is a necessary link between the Kantian foundationalism in epistemology, which nets philosophy the unenviable role of usher, and the ahistoricity of the conceptual system Kant superimposes on culture, which nets philosophy the equally undesirable role of a judge parceling out separate areas of jurisdiction to science, morality, and art.

> Without the Kantian assumption that the philosopher can decide *questiones juris* concerning the rest of culture, this self-image collapses. . . . To drop the notion of the philosopher as knowing something about knowing which nobody else knows so well would be to drop the notion that his voice always has an overriding claim on the attention of the other participants in the conversation. It would also be to drop the notion that there is something called "philosophical method" or "philosophical technique" or "the philosophical point of view" which enables the professional philosopher, ex officio, to have interesting views about, say, the respectability of psychoanalysis, the legitimacy of certain dubious laws, the resolution of moral dilemmas, the soundness of schools of historiography or literary criticism, and the like.[2]

Richard Rorty's impressive critique of philosophy assembles compelling metaphilosophical arguments in support of the view that the roles Kant the master thinker had envisaged for philosophy, namely those of usher and judge, are too big for it. While I find myself in agreement with much of what Rorty says, I have trouble accepting his conclusion, which is that if philosophy forswears these two roles, it must also surrender the function of being the "guardian of rationality." If I understand Rorty, he is saying that the new modesty of philosophy involves the abandonment of any claim to reason—the very claim that has marked philosophical thought since its inception. Rorty not only argues for the demise of philosophy; he also unflinchingly accepts the end of the belief that ideas like truth or the unconditional with their transcending power are a necessary condition of humane forms of collective life.

Implied by Kant's conception of formal, differentiated reason is a theory of modernity. Modernity is characterized by a rejection of the substantive rationality typical of religious and metaphysical worldviews and by a belief in procedural rationality and its ability to give credence to our views in the three areas of objective knowledge, moral-practical insight, and aesthetic judgment. What I am asking myself is this: Is it true that this (or a similar) concept of modernity becomes untenable when you dismiss the claims of a foundationalist theory of knowledge?

What follows is an attempt to narrate a story that might help put Rorty's criticism of philosophy in perspective. Granted, by going this route I cannot settle the controversy. What I can do is throw light on some of its presuppositions. At the outset (section 1 below) I will look at Hegel's critique of Kantian foundationalism and the substitution of a dialectical mode of justification for Kant's transcendental one. Next (section 2) I will retrace some of the lines of criticism and self-criticism that have emerged in the Kantian and Hegelian traditions. In section 3 I will dwell on a more radical form of criticism originating in pragmatist and hermeneuticist quarters, a form of attack that repudiates Kant and Hegel simultaneously. Section 4 deals with thinkers, respectable ones no less, who respond to this situation by annulling philosophy's long-standing claim to reason. In conclusion (section 5) I will argue that philosophy, while well advised to withdraw from the problematic roles of usher (*Platzanweiser*) and judge, can and ought to retain its claim to reason, provided it is content to play the more modest roles of stand-in (*Platzhalter*) and interpreter.

1

Hegel fashioned his dialectical mode of justification in deliberate opposition to the transcendental one of Kant. Hegel—and I can only hint at this here—agrees with those who charge that in the end Kant failed to justify or ground the pure concepts of the understanding, for he merely culled them from the table of forms of judgment, unaware of their historical specificity. Thus he failed, in Hegel's eyes, to prove that the *a priori* conditions of what makes experience possible are truly necessary. In his *Phenomenology of Spirit* Hegel proposes to correct this flaw by taking a genetic approach. What Kant regarded as a unique (Copernican) turn to transcendental reflection becomes in Hegel a general mechanism for turning consciousness back upon itself. This mechanism has been switched on and off time and time again in the development of spirit. As the subject becomes conscious of itself, it destroys one form of consciousness after another. This process epitomizes the subjective experience that what initially appears to the subject as a being in itself can become content only in the forms imparted to it by the subject. The transcendental philosopher's experience is thus, according to Hegel, reenacted naively whenever an in-itself becomes a for-the-subject. What Hegel calls "dialectical" is the reconstruction of this recurrent experience and of its assimilation by the subject, which gives rise to ever more complex structures. Hegel goes beyond the particular manifestation of consciousness that Kant analyzed, attaining in the end knowledge that has become autonomous, that is, absolute knowledge. This highest vantage point enables Hegel, the phenomenologist, to witness the genesis of structures of consciousness that Kant had assumed to be timeless.

Hegel, it should be noted, exposes himself to a criticism similar to the one he levels against Kant. Reconstructing successive forms of consciousness is one thing. Proving the necessity of their succession is quite another. Hegel is not unaware of this gap, and he tries to close it by logical means, thereby laying the basis for a philosophical absolutism that claims an even grander role for philosophy than did Kant. In Hegel's *Logic* philosophy's role is to effect an encyclopedic conceptual synthesis of the diffuse chunks of content thrown up by the sciences. In addition, Hegel picks up Kant's latent theory of modernity, making it explicit and developing it into a critique of the diremptive, self-contradictory features of modernity. It is this peculiar twist that gave philosophy a new world-historical relevance in relation to culture as a whole. And this is the stuff of which the suspect image of Hegel as a master thinker is made.[3]

The metaphilosophical attack on the *maîtres penseurs*, whether its target be Hegel's absolutism or Kant's foundationalism, is a recent phenomenon. Antecedents of it can be found in the strands of self-criticism that have run through Kantianism and Hegelianism for quite some time. I shall comment briefly on two lines of self-criticism that I think complement each other in an interesting way.

2

In reference to Kant's transcendental philosophy there are today three distinct critical positions: the analytic one of Strawson, the constructivist one of Lorenzen, and the critical-rationalist one of Popper.

Analytic philosophy appropriates Kant by jettisoning any claim to ultimate justification (*Letztbegründung*). From the very outset it drops the objective Kant had in mind when he deduced the pure concepts of the understanding from the unity of self-consciousness. The analytic reception of Kant is confined to comprehending those concepts and rules that underlie experience insofar as it can be couched in elementary propositions. The analysis focuses on general, indispensable, conceptual preconditions that make experience possible. Unable to prove the objective validity of its basic concepts and presuppositions, this analysis nevertheless makes a universalistic claim. Redeeming it involves changing Kant's transcendental strategy of justification into a testing procedure. If the hypothetically reconstructed conceptual system underlying experience as such is valid, not a single intelligible alternative to it can possibly exist. This means any alternative proposal will be scrutinized with a view to proving its derivative character, that is, with a view to showing that the alleged alternative inevitably utilizes portions of the very hypothesis it seeks to supplant. A strategy of argumentation like this tries to prove that the concepts and presuppositions it singles out as fundamental cannot be dispensed with. Turned modest, the transcendental philosopher of the analytic variety takes on the role of the skeptic who keeps trying to find counterexamples that might invalidate his theories.[4] In short, he acts like a hypothesis-testing scientist.

The *constructivist position* tried to compensate for the justificatory shortfall that has now opened up from the perspective of transcendental philosophy in the following way. It concedes from the start that the basic conceptual organization of experience is conventional while at the same time putting a constructivist critique of language in the service of epistemology.[5] Those conventions are considered valid that are generated methodically and therefore transparently. It should be clear that this approach lays, rather than uncovers, the foundations of cognition.

On the face of it, the *critical-rationalist position* breaks completely with transcendentalism. It holds that the three horns of the "Münchhausen trilemma"—logical circularity, infinite regress, and recourse to absolute certitude—can only be avoided if one gives up any hope of grounding or justifying whatsoever.[6] Here the notion of justification is being dislodged in favor of the concept of critical testing, which becomes the critical rationalist's equivalent for justification. In this connection I would argue that criticism is itself a procedure whose employment is never presuppositionless. That is why I think that critical rationalism, by clinging to the idea of irrefutable rules of criticism, allows a weak version of the Kantian justificatory mode to sneak into its inner precincts through the back door.[7]

Self-criticism in the Hegelian tradition has developed along lines parallel to the self-criticism among Kantians. Again, three distinct positions might be said to be represented by the young Lukács and his materialist critique of epistemology, which restricts the claim to justification of dialectics to the man-made world and excludes nature; by K. Korsch's and H. Freyer's practicism, wherein the classical relation of theory and practice is stood on its head and the "interested" perspective of creating a society of the future informs the theoretical reconstruction of social development; and finally by the negativism of Adorno, who finds in comprehensive logic of development only the proof that it is impossible to break the spell of an instrumental reason gone mad.

I cannot examine these positions here. All I shall do is to point out certain interesting parallels between the Hegelian and Kantian strands of self-criticism. The self-criticism that begins by doubting the Kantian transcendental deduction and the self-criticism that begins by doubting Hegel's passage to absolute knowledge have this in common: they reject the claim that the categorical makeup and the pattern of development of the human spirit can be proved to be necessary. With regard to constructivism and practicism a similar convergence occurs: both are involved in a shift from rational reconstruction to creative praxis, which is to make possible a theoretical recapitulation of this praxis. Critical rationalism and negativism, for their part, share something too, which is that they reject transcendental and dialectical means of cognition while at the same time using them in a paradoxical way. One may also view these two attempts at radical negation as showing that these two modes of justification cannot be abolished except on penalty of self-contradiction.

My comparison between parallel self-critical strategies to restrict the justificatory claims of transcendental and dialectical philosophies gives rise to the following question: Do these self-limiting tendencies merely reinforce each other, encouraging the skeptic to reject justification all the more roundly? Or does the retrenchment on either side to a position of diminished justificatory objectives and strategies represent a precondition for viewing them not as opposites but as supplementing each other? I think the second possibility deserves serious consideration. The genetic structuralism of Jean Piaget provides an instructive model along these lines, instructive for all philosophers, I think, but particularly those who want to remain philosophers. Piaget conceives "reflective abstraction" as that learning mechanism which explains the transition between cognitive stages in ontogenetic development. The end point of this development is a decentered understanding of the world. Reflective abstraction is similar to transcendental reflection in that it brings out the formal elements hidden in the cognitive content, identifies them as the schemata that underlie the knowing subject's action, differentiates them, and reconstructs them at the next highest stage of reflection. Seen from a different perspective, the same learning mechanism has a function similar to Hegel's power of negation, which dialectically supersedes self-contradictory forms of consciousness.[8]

3

The aforementioned six positions in the tradition of Kant and Hegel stick to a claim to reason, however small in scope, however cautious in formulation. It is this final intention that sets off Popper and Lakatos from a Feyerabend and Horkheimer and Adorno from a Foucault. They still say *something* about the indispensible conditions of claims to the validity of those beliefs we hold to be justified, claims that transcend all restrictions of time and place. Now any attack on the master thinkers questions this residual claim to reason and thus in essence makes a plea for the abolition of philosophy. I can explain this radical turn by talking briefly about a wholly different criticism, one that has been raised against both Kant *and* Hegel.

Its proponents can be found in *pragmatism* and *hermeneutic philosophy*. Their doubts concerning the justificatory and self-justificatory potential of philosophy operate at a more profound level than do the self-criticisms within the Kantian and Hegelian traditions. They step resolutely outside the parameters set by the philosophy of consciousness and its cognitive paradigm, which stresses the perception and representation of objects. Pragmatism and hermeneutics oust the traditional notion of the solitary subject that confronts objects and becomes reflective only by turning itself into an object. In its place they put an idea of cognition that is mediated by language and linked to action. Moreover, they emphasize the web of everyday life and communication surrounding "our" cognitive achievements. The latter are intrinsically intersubjective and cooperative. It is unimportant just how this web is conceptualized, whether as "form of life," "lifeworld," "practice," "linguistically mediated interaction," a "language game," "convention," "cultural background," "tradition," "effective history," or what have you. The important thing is that these commonsensical ideas, though they may function quite differently, attain a status that used to be reserved for the basic concepts of epistemology. Pragmatism and hermeneutics, then, accord a higher position to acting and speaking than to knowing. But there is more to it than that. Purposive action and linguistic communication play a qualitatively different role from that of self-reflection in the philosophy of consciousness. They have no justificatory function any more save one: to expose the need for foundational knowledge as unjustified.

Charles S. Peirce doubted that radical doubt is possible. His intentions were the same as those of Dilthey, who doubted that neutrality in interpretive understanding is possible. For Peirce problems always arise in a specific situation. They come to us, as it were. We do not go to them, for we do not fully control the totality of our practical existence. In a similar vein Dilthey argues that we cannot grasp a symbolic expression unless we have an intuitive preunderstanding of its context, for we do not have unlimited freedom to convert the unproblematic background knowledge of our own culture into explicit knowledge. Every instance of problem solving and every interpretation depend on a web of myriad presuppositions. Since this web is holistic and particularistic at the same time, it can never be grasped by an abstract, general analysis. It is from this standpoint that the myth of the given—that is, the distinctions between sensibility and understanding, intuition and concept, form and content—can be debunked, along with the distinctions between analytic and synthetic judgments, between *a priori* and *a posteriori*. These Kantian dualisms are all being dissolved, a fact that is vaguely reminiscent of Hegel's metacritique. Of course, a full-fledged return to Hegel is made impossible by the contextualism and historicism to which the pragmatist and hermeneutic approaches subscribe.

There is no denying that pragmatism and hermeneutics represent a gain. Instead of focusing introspectively on consciousness, these two points of view look outside at objectifications of action and language. Gone is the fixation on the cognitive function of consciousness. Gone too is the emphasis on the representational function of language and the visual metaphor of the "mirror of nature." What takes their place is the notion of justified belief spanning the whole spectrum of what can be said—of what Wittgenstein and Austin call illocutionary force—rather than just the contents of fact-stating discourses. "Saying things is not always saying how things are."[9]

Do these considerations strengthen Rorty's interpretation of pragmatism and hermeneutics, which argues for the abnegation by philosophical thought of any claim to rationality and indeed for the abnegation of philosophy per se? Or do they mark the beginning of a new paradigm that, while discarding the mentalistic language game of the philosophy of consciousness, retains the justificatory modes of that philosophy in the modest, self-critical form in which I have presented them? I cannot answer this question directly for want of compelling and simple arguments. Once again, the answer I will give is a narrative one.

4

Marx wanted to supersede (*aufheben*) philosophy by realizing it—so convinced was he of the truth of Hegelian philosophy, whose only fault was that concept and reality cleaved unbearably, a fault that Hegel studiously overlooked. The corresponding, though fundamentally different, present-day attitude toward philosophy is the dismissive goodbye and good riddance. These farewells take many forms, three of which are currently in vogue. For simplicity's sake I will call them the therapeutic, the heroic, and the salvaging farewell.

Wittgenstein championed the notion of a *therapeutic* philosophy, therapeutic in the specific sense of self-healing, for philosophy was sick to the core. Wittgenstein's diagnosis was that philosophy had disarrayed language games that function perfectly well in everyday life. The weakness of this particular farewell to philosophy is that it leaves the world as it is. For the standards by which philosophy is being criticized are taken straight from the self-sufficient, routinized forms of life in which philosophy happens to survive for now. And what about possible successors? Field research in cultural anthropology seems to be the strongest candidate to succeed philosophy after its demise. Surely the history of philosophy will henceforth be interpreted as the unintelligible doings of some outlandish tribe that today is fortunately extinct. (Perhaps Rorty will one day be celebrated as the path-breaking Thucydides of this new approach, which incidentally could only get under way after Wittgenstein's medicine had proved effective.)

There is a sharp contrast between the soft-spoken farewell of the therapeutic philosopher and the noisy demolition undertaken by someone like Georges Bataille or Heidegger. Their goodbye is *heroic*. From their perspective too, false habits of living and thinking are concentrated in elevated forms of philosophical reflection. But instead of accusing philosophy of homely category mistakes or simple disruptions of everyday life, their deconstruction of metaphysics and objectivating thought has a more incisive, epochal quality. This more dramatic farewell to philosophy does not promise a cure. Rather, it resembles Hölderlin's pathos-laden idea of a rescue attempt *in extremis*. The devalued and discredited philosophical tradition, rather than being replaced by something even more valueless than itself, is supposed to give way to a *different* medium that makes possible a return to the immemorial—to Bataille's sovereignty or Heidegger's Being.

Least conspicuous, finally, is the *salvaging* type of farewell to philosophy. Contemporary neo-Aristotelians best exemplify this type insofar as they do exegeses that are informed by hermeneutics. Some of their work is unquestionably significant. But all too often it departs from pure interpretation in an effort to salvage some old truth or other. At any rate, this farewell to philosophy has a disingenuous ring: While the salvager keeps invoking the need to preserve philosophy, he wants to have nothing to do with its systematic claims. He does not try to make the ancients relevant to the discussion of some subject matter. Nor does he present the classics as a cultural treasure prepared by philosophy and history. What he does is to appropriate by assimilation texts that we once thought to embody knowledge, treating them instead as sources of illumination and edification.

Let us return for a moment to the critique of Kant, the master thinker, and in particular to his foundationalism in epistemology. Clearly, present-day philosophies of the sort just described wisely sidestep the Kantian trap. The last thing they think they can do is show the natural sciences to their proper place. Contemporary poststructuralist, late-pragmatist, and neohistoricist tendencies share a narrow objectivistic conception of science. Over against scientific cognition they carve out a sphere where thought can be illuminating or awakening instead of being objective. These tendencies prefer to sever all links with general, criticizable claims to validity. They would rather make do without notions like consensus, incontrovertible results, and justified beliefs. Paradoxically enough, whereas they make these (unnecessary) sacrifices, they somehow keep believing in the authority and superiority of philosophical insights: their own. In terms of their views on science, the philosophers of the definitive farewell agree with the existentialist proposal (Jaspers, Sartre, Kolakowski) for a division of labor that puts science on one side and philosophical faith, life, existential freedom, myth, cultivation, or what have you, on the other. All these juxtapositions are identical in structure. Where they differ is in their assessment of what Max Weber termed the cultural relevance of science, which may range from negative to neutral to positive. As is well known, Continental philosophy has a penchant for dramatizing the dangers of objectivism and instrumental reason, whereas Anglo-American philosophy takes a more relaxed view of them.

With his distinction between normal and abnormal discourse, Richard Rorty has come up with an interesting variation on the above theme. In times of widely acknowledged theoretical progress, normality takes hold of the established sciences. This means methods become available that make problem solving and dispute settling possible. What Rorty calls commensurable discourses are those discourses that operate with reliable criteria of consensus building. In contrast, discourses are incommensurable or abnormal when basic orientations are contested. Generally, abnormal conversations tend to pass over into normal ones, their ultimate purpose being to annul themselves and to bring about universal agreement. Occasionally, however, abnormal discourses stop short of taking this self-transcending step and are content with "interesting and fruitful disagreement." That is, they become *sufficient unto themselves.* It is at this point that abnormal discourses take on the quality that Rorty calls "edifying." According to him, philosophy as a whole verges on edifying conversation once it has sloughed off all pretensions to problem solving. Such philosophical edification enjoys the benefits of all three types of farewell: therapeutic relief, heroic overcoming, and hermeneutic reawaking. It combines the inconspicuously subversive force of leisure with an elitist notion of creative linguistic imagination and with the wisdom of the ages. The desire for edification, however, works to the detriment of the desire for truth: "Edifying philosophers can never end philosophy, but they can help prevent it from attaining the secure path of a science."[10]

I am partly sympathetic to Rorty's allocation of roles, for I agree that philosophy has no business playing the part of the highest arbiter in matters of science and culture. I find his argument unconvincing all the same. For even a philosophy that has been taught its limits by pragmatism and hermeneuticism will not be able to find a resting place in edifying conversation *outside* the sciences without immediately being drawn back into argumentation, that is, justificatory discourse.

The existentialist or, if you like, exclusive division of labor between philosophy and science is untenable. This is borne out by the particular version of discourse theory Rorty proposes. Ultimately, there is only one criterion by which beliefs can be judged valid, and that is that they are based on agreement reached by argumentation. This means that *everything* whose validity is at all disputable rests on shaky foundations. It matters little if the ground underfoot shakes a bit less for those who debate problems of physics than for those who debate problems of morals and aesthetics. The difference is a matter of degree only, as the postempiricist philosophy of science has shown. Normalization of discourse is not a sufficiently trenchant criterion for distinguishing science from edifying philosophical conversation.

5

To those who advocate a cut-and-dried division of labor, research traditions representing a blend of philosophy and science have always been particularly offensive. Marxism and psychoanalysis are cases in point. They cannot, on this view, help being pseudosciences because they straddle normal and abnormal discourse, refusing to fall on either side of the dividing line. On this point Rorty speaks the same language as Jaspers. What I know about the history of the social sciences and psychology leads me to believe that hybrid discourses such as Marxism and psychoanalysis are by no means atypical. To the contrary, they may well stand for a type of approach that marks the beginning of new research traditions.

What holds for Freud applies to all seminal theories in these disciplines, for instance, those of Durkheim, Mead, Max Weber, Piaget, and Chomsky. Each inserted a genuinely philosophical idea like a detonator into a particular context of research. Symptom formation through repression, the creation of solidarity through the sacred, the identity-forming function of role taking, modernization as rationalization of society, decentration as an outgrowth of reflective abstraction from action, language acquisition as an activity of hypothesis testing—these key phrases stand for so many paradigms in which a philosophical idea is present in embryo while at the same time empirical, yet universal, questions are being posed. It is no coincidence that theoretical approaches of this kind are the favorite target of empiricist counterattacks. Such cyclical movements in the history of science, incidentally, do not point to a convergence of these disciplines in one unified science. It makes better sense to view them as stages on the road to the philosophization of the sciences of man (*Philosophischwerden der Humanwissenschaften*) than as stages in the triumphal march toward objectivist approaches, such as neurophysiology, that quaint favorite child of the analytic philosophers.

What I have said lies mainly in the realm of speculative conjecture. But unless I am completely mistaken, it makes sense to suggest that philosophy, instead of just dropping the usher role and being left with nothing, ought to exchange it for the part of stand-in (*Platzhalter*). Whose seat would philosophy be keeping; what would it be standing in for? Empirical theories with strong universalistic claims. As I have indicated, there have surfaced and will continue to surface in nonphilosophical disciplines fertile minds who will give such theories a try. The chance for their emergence is greatest in the reconstructive sciences. Starting primarily from the intuitive knowledge of competent subjects—competent in terms of judgment, action, and language—and secondarily from systematic knowledge handed down by culture, the reconstructive sciences explain the presumably universal bases of rational experience and judgment, as well as of action and linguistic communication. Marked down in price, the venerable transcendental and dialectical modes of justification may still come in handy. All they can fairly be expected to furnish, however, is reconstructive hypotheses for use in empirical settings. Telling examples of a successful cooperative integration of philosophy and science can be seen in the development of a theory of rationality. This is an area where philosophies work as suppliers of ideas without raising foundationalist or absolutist claims à la Kant or Hegel. Fallibilistic in orientation, they reject the dubious faith in philosophy's ability to do things single-handedly, hoping instead that the success that has for so long eluded it might come from an auspicious matching of different theoretical fragments. From the vantage point of my own research interests, I see such a cooperation taking shape between philosophy of science and history of science, between speech act theory and empirical approaches to pragmatics of language, between a theory of informal argumentation and empirical approaches to natural argumentation, between cognitivist ethics and a psychology of moral development, between philosophical theories of action and the ontogenetic study of action competences.

If it is true that philosophy has entered upon a phase of cooperation with the human sciences, does it not run the risk of losing its identity? There is some justification in Spaemann's warning "that every philosophy makes a practical and a theoretical claim to totality and that not to make such a twofold claim is to be doing something which does not qualify as philosophy."[11] In defense, one might argue that a philosophy that contributes something important to an analysis of the rational foundations of knowing, acting, and speaking does retain at least a thematic connection with the whole. But is this enough? What becomes of the theory of modernity, what of the window on the totality of culture that Kant and Hegel opened with their foundational and hypostatizing concepts of reason? Down to Husserl's *Crisis of the European Sciences,* philosophy not only usurped the part of supreme judge, it also played a directing role. Again, what happens when it surrenders the role of judge in matters of science as well as culture? Does this mean philosphy's relation to the totality is severed? Does this mean it can no longer be the guardian of rationality?

The situation of culture as a whole is no different from the situation of science as a whole. As totalities, neither needs to be grounded or justified or given a place by philosophy. Since the dawn of modernity in the eighteenth century, culture has generated those structures of rationality that Max Weber and Emil Lask conceptualized as cultural value spheres. Their existence calls for description and analysis, not philosophical justification.

Reason has split into three moments—modern science, positive law and posttraditional ethics, and autonomous art and institutionalized art criticism—but philosophy had precious little to do with this disjunction. Ignorant of sophisticated critiques of reason, the sons and daughters of modernity have progressively learned to differentiate their cultural tradition in terms of these three aspects of rationality such that they deal with issues of truth, justice, and taste discretely rather than simultaneously. At a different level, this shift toward differentiation produces the following phenomena: (1) The sciences disgorge more and more elements of religion, thus renouncing their former claim to being able to interpret nature and history as one whole. (2) Cognitivist moral theories disgorge issues of the good life, focusing instead strictly on deontological, generalizable aspects of ethics, so that all that remains of "the good" is the just. (3) With art it is likewise. Since the turn to autonomy, art has striven mightily to mirror one basic aesthetic experience, the increasing decentration of subjectivity. It occurs as the subject leaves the spatiotemporal structures of everyday life behind, freeing itself from the conventions of everyday perception, of purposive behavior, and of the imperatives of work and utility.

I repeat, these eminent trends toward compartmentalization, constituting as they do the hallmark of modernity, can do very well without philosophical justification. But they do pose problems of mediation. First, how can reason, once it has been thus sundered, go on being a unity on the level of culture? And second, how can expert cultures, which are being pushed more and more to the level of rarefied, esoteric forms, be made to stay in touch with everyday communication? To the extent to which philosophy keeps at least one eye trained on the topic of rationality, that is, to the extent to which it keeps inquiring into the conditions of the unconditional, to that extent it will not dodge the demand for these two kinds of efforts at mediation.

The first type of problem of mediation arises within the spheres of science, morals, and art. In this area we witness the rise of countermovements. For example, in human sciences nonobjectivist approaches bring moral and aesthetic criticism into play without undermining the primacy of issues of truth. Another example is the way in which the discussion of ethics of responsibility and ethics of conviction and the expanded role of utilitarian considerations within universalist ethics have brought the calculation of consequences and the interpretation of needs into play—and these are perspectives situated rather in the domains of the cognitive and the expressive. Let us finally look at postmodern art as the third example. It is characterized by a strange simultaneity of realistic, politically committed schools on the one hand and authentic followers of that classical modernism to which we owe the cystallization of the specific meaning of the aesthetic on the other. In realistic and politically committed art, elements of the cognitive and the moral-practical come into play once again, but at the level of the wealth of forms unloosed by the avant-garde. To that extent they act as agents of mediation. Counterdevelopments like these, it seems, mitigate the radical differentiation of reason and point to its unity. Everyday life, however, is a more promising medium for regaining the lost unity of reason than are today's expert cultures or yesteryear's classical philosophy of reason.

In everyday communication, cognitive interpretations, moral expectations, expressions, and evaluations cannot help overlapping and interpenetrating. Reaching understanding in the lifeworld requires a cultural tradition that ranges across *the whole spectrum*, not just the fruits of science and technology. As far as philosophy is concerned, it might do well to refurbish its link with the totality by taking on the role of interpreter on behalf of the lifeworld. It might then be able to help set in motion the interplay between the cognitive-instrumental, moral-practical, and aesthetic-expressive dimensions that has come to a standstill today like a tangled mobile.[12] This simile at least helps identify the issue philosophy will face when it stops playing the part of the arbiter that inspects culture and instead starts playing the part of a mediating interpreter. That issue is how to overcome the isolation of science, morals, and art and their respective expert cultures. How can they be joined to the impoverished traditions of the lifeworld, and how can this be done without detriment to their regional rationality? How can a new balance between the separated moments of reason be established in communicative everyday life?

The critic of the master thinkers will likely express his alarm one more time. What in the world, he will ask, gives the philosopher the right to offer his services as a translator mediating between the everyday world and cultural modernity with its autonomous sectors when he is already more than busy trying to hold open a place for ambitious theoretical strategies within the system of the sciences? I think pragmatism and hermeneutics have joined forces to answer this question by attributing epistemic authority to the community of those who cooperate and speak with one another. Everyday communication makes possible a kind of understanding that is based on claims to validity and thus furnishes the only real alternative to exerting influence on one another in more or less coercive ways. The validity claims that we raise in conversation—that is, when we say something with conviction—transcend this specific conversational context, pointing to something beyond the spatiotemporal ambit of the occasion. Every agreement, whether produced for the first time or reaffirmed, is based on (controvertible) grounds or reasons. Grounds have a special property: they force us into yes or no positions. Thus, built into the structure of action oriented toward reaching and understanding is an element of unconditionality. And it is this unconditional element that makes the validity (*Gültigkeit*) that we claim for our views different from the mere de facto acceptance (*Geltung*) of habitual practices.[13] From the perspective of first persons, what we consider justified is not a function of custom but a question of justification or grounding. That is why philosophy is "rooted in the urge to see social practices of justification as more than just such practices."[14] The same urge is at work when people like me stubbornly cling to the notion that philosophy is the guardian of rationality.

NOTES

1. "The critique . . . arriving at all its decisions in the light of fundamental principles of its own institution, the authority of which no one can question, secures to us the peace of a legal order, in which our disputes have to be conducted solely by the recognized methods of legal action." Kant, *Critique of Pure Reason,* trans. N. Kemp Smith, p. 601.
2. Richard Rorty, *Philosophy and the Mirror of Nature* (Princeton, 1979), pp. 392ff.
3. Rorty approvingly paraphrases a dictum by Eduard Zeller: "Hegelianism produced an image of philosophy as a discipline which somehow both completed and swallowed up the other disciplines, rather than *grounding* them. It also made philosophy too popular,

too interesting, too important, to be properly professional; it challenged philosophy professors to embody the World-Spirit, rather than simply getting on with their *Fach*." Rorty (1979), p. 135.

4. G. Schönrich, *Kategorien und transzendentale Argumentation* (Frankfurt, 1981), chapter 4, pp. 182ff; R. Bittner, "Transzendental," in *Handbuch philosophischer Grundbegriffe*, vol. 5 (Munich 1974), pp. 1524ff.
5. C. F. Gethmann and R. Hegselmann. "Das Problem der Begründung zwischen Dezisionismus and Fundamentalismus." *Zeitschrift für allegemeine Wissenschaftstheorie* 8 (1977): 432ff.
6. H. Albert, *Treatise on Critical Reason* (Princeton, 1985).
7. H. Lenk, "Philosophische Logikbegründung und rationaler Kritizismus," *Zeitschrift für philosophische Forschung* 24 (1970): 183ff.
8. T. Kesselring, *Entwicklung and Widerspruch—Ein Vergleich zwischen Piagets genetischer Erkenntnistheorie und Hegels Dialektik* (Frankfurt, 1981).
9. Rorty (1979), p. 371.
10. Rorty (1979), p. 372.
11. R. Spaemann, "Der Streit der Philosophen," in H. Lübbe, ed., *Wozu Philosophie?* (Berlin, 1978), p. 96.
12. J. Habermas, "Modernity versus Postmodernity," *New German Critique* 22 (1981): 3–14.
13. See J. Habermas, *Theory of Communicative Action* (Boston, 1984), vol. 1. pp. 114ff.
14. Rorty (1979), p. 390.

PART IV

PROSPECTS FOR PHILOSOPHY

The final three selections present recent reactions to the philosophical positions represented in this book. They deal with the roles of subjectivity and objectivity in the methods and products of philosophy. They deal with the very meanings of such terms. Richard Rorty develops a neo-pragmatic approach heavily influenced by John Dewey. Characterized roughly, Rorty comes down on the side of the acceptance of subjectivity and the rejection of objectivity. His views are affiliated with contemporary continental philosophy. Ernest Sosa and Hilary Putnam settle on the side of objectivity and realism, although these terms take on special meanings in either case. In this section, the fundamental question of how one goes about *defending* one's philosophical method gets special emphasis. Sosa, in particular, faces head-on the threat of circularity in arguments meant to defend a philosophical method, or a philosophy of philosophy.

In "Pragmatism and Philosophy," Richard Rorty characterizes pragmatists as doubting that there is anything to say about truth, goodness, or other traditional objects of philosophical inquiry, because the history of attempts to do so has failed. Pragmatists reject the set of questions coming from what they call the Platonic tradition; they want to "change the subject." Rorty recommends philosophy (with a lower case "p") as merely the attempt to see how *things,* in the broadest possible sense of the term, *hang together,* in the broadest possible sense of the expression. He objects to Philosophy that (a) asks questions about the *nature* or *essence* of certain normative notions and (b) searches for Truth, Goodness, Rationality, etc. He rejects the division of true statements into mere opinion and genuine knowledge and rejects the correspondence theory of truth.

Rorty claims that pragmatism is a position toward which both current analytic and continental philosophy are developing. An important part of this position is the Deweyan notion of language as a part of human behavior rather than a *tertium quid* between Subject and Object. There is no way to break out of language-as-a-whole and compare it with something else; we develop and improve it strictly from within. This anti-Platonist insistence on the ubiquity of language is the common ground between pragmatism, recent analytic philosophy, and recent French and German philosophy. It is the claim that there is no way to get behind language to something that "grounds" it.

There has recently been a resurgence of realism, and Rorty claims that the real debate between the pragmatist and the realist is not over what our *intuitions* are about truth or goodness but what the *status* of those intuitions is. The realist uses them as natural starting points for philosophy, but the pragmatist suggests doing what we can to *stop* having those intuitions and start having "better" ones. He claims that philosophy should not try to find natural starting points from all cultural traditions, but should only compare and contrast cultural traditions.

If we follow the pragmatist's advice to reject Philosophy, we shall produce a culture where no particular portion of that culture would be singled out as the most Rational. To the Philosopher, such a culture seems morally humiliating, because it acknowledges no Truth, but the pragmatist thinks that a post-Philosophical culture is good to seek.

In "Serious Philosophy and Freedom of Spirit," Ernest Sosa aims to defend serious, or realist, philosophy against some recent attacks from such philosophers as Rorty, Derrida, and Foucault.

Serious philosophy here means the Platonic tradition that is committed to an objective, conceiver-independent yet knowable reality. This reality provides the objects of knowledge but also constraining starting points and methods for reason. "Free-spirited philosophy" is the name Sosa borrows from Nietzsche's "The Free Spirit" to name antirealism, subjectivism, historical relativism and similar views. One representative of the type is textualism.

Sosa gives special attention to two central arguments that the free spirits bring against seriousness. The first is an argument for *phronesis* and against *theoria,* claiming there can be no strictly formal method for calculating answers to questions of value. Sosa responds that *theoria* can produce partial success, even though it has limitations. Some possible answers can be determinately ruled out, even if it is the case that no one answer is forced on us objectively.

The second argument from the free spirits claims that we should reject serious philosophy because it has failed, over the course of many centuries, to be successful and to produce any agreement regarding its promised results. Sosa contends that agreement alone is not a good criterion for success since there can be widespread agreement on what is false. He suggests that agreement is important only in so far as it is *best explained* by the *correctness* of its object.

Sosa insists that philosophy has to seek norms for criticizing certain cultural products (our own or others) as wrong. Sosa candidly admits that at some level such a search *must* begin begging the question of what justifies our acceptance of certain general principles of justification. He suggests that at this level of conflicting normative principles, we can appeal to a "deeper *phronesis*" that can assess even the most fundamental norms of a community.

Sosa objects to Rorty's strategy of questioning the *status* of certain intuitions leading to traditional philosophy. He says that we can equally well reject *any* field of thought by rejecting the intuitions proper to that field, without thereby *saying* anything about the status of that field. Further, such rejection itself relies on other intuitions that are on an exactly equal standing. He recommends that instead of eliminating objectivity for the sake of communal solidarity, we value both; that instead of rejecting *theoria* for *phronesis,* we need both; and that agreement should not be an end in itself, because it can be had in systems of massive error and evil.

In "Why Is a Philosopher?" Hilary Putnam defends his distinctive version of ("internal") realism and the philosophical method resulting from it. He identifies positivism as the central movement in analytic philosophy from 1930 to about 1960, and relativism as the central movement in recent French philosophy. He thinks that the problem of intentionality or representation is the main problem leading people either to relativism or positivism, and he claims that the "new realism" he and Kripke developed solves this problem.

Positivism sidestepped the problem of the correctness, or referential character, of language and focused instead on the nature of confirmation. Putnam thinks this approach leads ultimately to solipsism. In response, he developed a version of realism that avoids many problems of traditional realist philosophies. His realism is based on a theory of direct reference that explains the reference of a word in terms of social practices, past and present, including the role of specialists in determining references of words. It also recognizes the contribution of the environment to fixing the meaning of our words.

Given his theory of reference, Putnam explains his "internal realism." It says that reference is internal to "texts or theories" but also that there can be better or worse "texts" relative to one's historical situation and purposes. According to this realism, answers to questions can be right in a non-subjective way that goes beyond mere justification. Putnam identifies truth with *idealized* justification. His definition of *truth* leads him to blur the distinction between fact (or truth) and value (especially the epistemic value of justification). Epistemic virtues such as reasonableness are at the heart of judgments of fact.

Putnam ends by explaining that he is not a relativist because he does not want to put "the grand projects of Metaphysics and Epistemology" away forever. He wants only to declare a moratorium on them, because attempts at generating totalistic explanations have always failed.

PRAGMATISM AND PHILOSOPHY

Richard Rorty

1. PLATONISTS, POSITIVISTS, AND PRAGMATISTS

A pragmatist theory says that truth is not the sort of thing one should expect to have a philosophically interesting theory about. For pragmatists, "truth" is just the name of a property which all true statements share. It is what is common to "Bacon did not write Shakespeare," "It rained yesterday," "E equals mc^2," "Love is better than hate," "*The Allegory of Painting* was Vermeer's best work," "2 plus 2 is 4," and "There are nondenumerable infinities." Pragmatists doubt that there is much to be said about this common feature. They doubt this for the same reason they doubt that there is much to be said about the common feature shared by such morally praiseworthy actions as Susan leaving her husband, America joining the war against the Nazis, America pulling out of Vietnam, Socrates not escaping from jail, Roger picking up litter from the trail, and the suicide of the Jews at Masada. They see certain acts as good ones to perform, under the circumstances, but doubt that there is anything general and useful to say about what makes them all good. The assertion of a given sentence—or the adoption of a disposition to assert the sentence, the conscious acquisition of a belief—is a justifiable, praiseworthy act in certain circumstances. But, *a fortiori*, it is not likely that there is something general and useful to be said about what makes all such actions good—about the common feature of all the sentences which one should acquire a disposition to assert.

Pragmatists think that the history of attempts to isolate the True or the Good, or to define the word "true" or "good" supports their suspicion that there is no interesting work to be done in this area. It might, of course, have turned out otherwise. People have, oddly enough, found something interesting to say about the essence of Force and the definition of "number." They might have found something interesting to say about the essence of Truth. But in fact they haven't. The history of attempts to do so, and of criticisms of such attempts, is roughly coextensive with the history of that literary genre we call "philosophy"—a genre founded by Plato. So pragmatists see the Platonic tradition as having outlived its usefulness. This does not mean that they have a new non-Platonic set of answers to Platonic questions to offer, but rather that they do not think we should ask those questions anymore. When they suggest that we not ask questions about the nature of Truth and Goodness, they do not invoke a theory about the nature of reality or knowledge or man which says

Reprinted by permission of the University of Minnesota Press and the author, from Richard Rorty, "Introduction: Pragmatism and Philosophy," in Rorty, *Consequences of Pragmatism: Essays 1972–1980*, pp. xiii–xlvii. Minneapolis: University of Minnesota Press, 1982.

that "there is no such thing" as Truth and Goodness. Nor do they have a "relativistic" or "subjectivist" theory of Truth or Goodness. They would simply like to change the subject. They are in a position analogous to that of secularists who urge that research concerning the Nature, or the Will, of God does not get us anywhere. Such secularists are not saying that God does not exist, exactly; they feel unclear about what it would mean to affirm His existence, and thus about the point of denying it. Nor do they have some special, funny, heretical view about God. They just doubt that the vocabulary of theology is one we ought to be using. Similarly, pragmatists keep trying to find ways of making antiphilosophical points in nonphilosophical language. For they face a dilemma: if their language is too unphilosophical, too "literary," they will be accused of changing the subject; if it is too philosophical it will embody Platonic assumptions which will make it impossible for the pragmatist to state the conclusion he wants to reach.

All this is complicated by the fact that "philosophy," like "truth" and "goodness," is ambiguous. Uncapitalized, "truth" and "goodness" name properties of sentences, or of actions and situations. Capitalized, they are the proper names of objects—goals or standards which can be loved with all one's heart and soul and mind, objects of ultimate concern. Similarly, "philosophy" can mean simply what Sellars calls "an attempt to see how things, in the broadest possible sense of the term, hang together, in the broadest possible sense of the term." Pericles, for example, was using this sense of the term when he praised the Athenians for "philosophizing without unmanliness" (*philosōphein aneu malakias*). In this sense, Blake is as much a philosopher as Fichte, Henry Adams more of a philosopher than Frege. No one would be dubious about philosophy, taken in this sense. But the word can also denote something more specialized, and very dubious indeed. In this second sense, it can mean following Plato's and Kant's lead, asking questions about the nature of certain normative notions, (e.g., "truth," "rationality," "goodness") in the hope of better obeying such norms. The idea is to believe more truths or do more good or be more rational by knowing more about Truth or Goodness or Rationality. I shall capitalize the term "philosophy" when used in this second sense, in order to help make the point that Philosophy, Truth, Goodness, and Rationality are interlocked Platonic notions. Pragmatists are saying that the best hope for philosophy is not to practise Philosophy. They think it will not help to say something true to think about Truth, nor will it help to act well to think about Goodness, nor will it help to be rational to think about Rationality.

So far, however, my description of pragmatism has left an important distinction out of account. Within Philosophy, there has been a traditional difference of opinion about the Nature of Truth, a battle between (as Plato put it) the gods and the giants. On the one hand there have been Philosophers like Plato himself who were otherworldly, possessed of a larger hope. They urged that human beings were entitled to self-respect only because they had one foot beyond space and time. On the other hand—especially since Galileo showed how spatio-temporal events could be brought under the sort of elegant mathematical law which Plato suspected might hold only for another world—there have been Philosophers (e.g., Hobbes, Marx) who insisted that space and time make up the only Reality there is, and that Truth is Correspondence to *that* Reality. In the nineteenth century, this opposition crystallized into one between "the transcendental philosophy" and "the empirical philosophy," between the "Platonists" and the "positivists." Such terms were, even then, hopelessly vague, but every intellectual knew roughly where he stood in relation to the two movements. To be on the transcendental side was to think that natural science was not the last word—that there was more Truth to be found. To be on the empirical side was to think that natural science—facts about how spatio-temporal things worked—was all the Truth there was. To side with Hegel or Green was to think that some normative sentences about rationality and goodness corresponded to something real, but invisible to natural science. To side with Comte or Mach was to think that such sentences either "reduced" to sentences about spatio-temporal events or were not subjects for serious reflection.

It is important to realize that the empirical philosophers—the positivists—were still doing Philosophy. The Platonic presupposition which unites the gods and the giants, Plato with Democritus, Kant with Mill, Husserl with Russell, is that what the vulgar call "truth"—the assemblage of true statements—should be thought of as divided into a lower and an upper division, the division between (in Plato's terms) mere opinion and genuine knowledge. It is the work of the Philosopher to establish an invidious distinction between such statements as "It rained yesterday" and "Men should try to be just in their dealings." For Plato the former sort of statement was second-rate, mere *pistis* or *doxa.* The latter, if perhaps not yet *epistēmē,* was at least a plausible candidate. For the positivist tradition which runs from Hobbes to Carnap, the former sentence was a paradigm of what Truth looked like, but the latter was either a prediction about the casual effects of certain events or an "expression of emotion." What the transcendental philosophers saw as the spiritual, the empirical philosophers saw as the emotional. What the empirical philosophers saw as the achievements of natural science in discovering the nature of Reality, the transcendental philosophers saw as *banausic,* as true but irrelevant to Truth.

Pragmatism cuts across this transcendental/empirical distinction by questioning the common presupposition that there is an invidious distinction to be drawn between kinds of truths. For the pragmatist, true sentences are not true because they correspond to reality, and so there is no need to worry what sort of reality, if any, a given sentence corresponds to—no need to worry about what "makes" it true. (Just as there is no need to worry, once one has determined what one should do, whether there is something in Reality which makes that act the Right one to perform.) So the pragmatist sees no need to worry about whether Plato or Kant was right in thinking that something nonspatio-temporal made moral judgments true, nor about whether the absence of such a thing means that such judgments are "merely expressions of emotion" or "merely conventional" or "merely subjective."

This insouciance brings down the scorn of both kinds of Philosophers upon the pragmatist. The Platonist sees the pragmatists as merely a fuzzy-minded sort of positivist. The positivist sees him as lending aid and comfort to Platonism by leveling down the distinction between Objective Truth—the sort of true sentence attained by "the scientific method"—and sentences which lack the precious "correspondence to reality" which only that method can induce. Both join in thinking the pragmatist is not really a philosopher, on the ground that he is not a Philosopher. The pragmatist tries to defend himself by saying that one can be a philosopher precisely by being anti-Philosophical, that the best way to make things hang together is to step back from the issues between Platonists and posivitists, and thereby give up the presuppositions of Philosophy.

One difficulty the pragmatist has in making his position clear, therefore, is that he must struggle with the positivist for the position of radical anti-Platonist. He wants to attack Plato with different weapons from those of the positivist, but at first glance he looks like just another variety of positivist. He shares with the positivist the Baconian and Hobbesian notion that knowledge is power, a tool for coping with reality. But he carries this Baconian point through to its extreme, as the positivist does not. He drops the notion of truth as correspondence with reality altogether, and says that modern science does not enable us to cope because it corresponds, it just plain enables us to cope. His argument for the view is that several hundred years of effort have failed to make interesting sense of the notion of "correspondence" (either of thoughts to things or of words to things). The pragmatist takes the moral of this discouraging history to be that "true sentences work because they correspond to the way things are" is no more illuminating than "it is right because it fulfills the Moral Law." Both remarks, in the pragmatist's eyes, are empty metaphysical compliments—harmless as rhetorical pats on the back to the successful inquirer or agent, but troublesome if taken seriously and "clarified" philosophically.

2. PRAGMATISM AND CONTEMPORARY PHILOSOPHY

Among contemporary philosophers, pragmatism is usually regarded as an outdated philosophical movement—one which flourished in the early years of this century in a rather provincial atmosphere, and which has now been either refuted or *aufgehoben*. The great pragmatists—James and Dewey—are occasionally praised for their criticisms of Platonism (e.g., Dewey on traditional conceptions of education, James on metaphysical pseudo-problems). But their anti-Platonism is thought by analytic philosophers to have been insufficiently rigorous and by nonanalytic philosophers to have been insufficiently radical. For the tradition which originates in logical positivism the pragmatists' attacks on "transcendental," quasi-Platonist philosophy need to be sharpened by more careful and detailed analysis of such notions as "meaning" and "truth." [1] For the anti-Philosophical tradition in contemporary French and German thought which takes its point of departure from Nietzsche's criticism of both strands in nineteenth-century Philosophical thought—positivistic as well as transcendental—the American pragmatists are thinkers who never really broke out of positivism, and thus never really broke with Philosophy.[2]

I do not think that either of these dismissive attitudes is justified. On the account of recent analytic philosophy which I offered in *Philosophy and the Mirror of Nature,*[3] the history of that movement has been marked by a gradual "pragmaticization" of the original tenets of logical positivism. On the account of recent "Continental" philosophy which I hope to offer in a book on Heidegger which I am writing,[4] James and Nietzsche make parallel criticisms of nineteenth-century thought. Further, James's version is preferable, for it avoids the "metaphysical' elements in Nietzsche which Heidegger criticizes, and, for that matter, the "metaphysical" elements in Heidegger which Derrida criticizes. On my view, James and Dewey were not only waiting at the end of the dialectical road which analytic philosophy traveled, but are waiting at the end of the road which, for example, Foucault and Deleuze are currently traveling.

I think that analytic philosophy culminates in Quine, the later Wittgenstein, Sellars, and Davidson—which is to say that it transcends and cancels itself. These thinkers successfully, and rightly, blur the positivist distinctions between the semantic and the pragmatic, the analytic and the synthetic, the linguistic and the empirical, theory and observation. Davidson's attack on the scheme/content distinction,[5] in particular, summarizes and synthesizes Wittgenstein's mockery of his own *Tractatus,* Quine's criticisms of Carnap, and Sellar's attack on the empiricist "Myth of the Given." Davidson's holism and coherentism shows how language looks once we get rid of the central presupposition of Philosophy: that true sentences divide into an upper and a lower division—the sentences which correspond to something and those which are "true" only by courtesy or convention.

This Davidsonian way of looking at language lets us avoid hypostatizing Language in the way in which the Cartesian epistomelogical tradition, and particularly the idealist tradition which built upon Kant, hypostatized Thought. For it lets us see language not as a *tertium quid* between Subject and Object, nor as a medium in which we try to form pictures of reality, but as part of the behavior of human beings. On this view, the activity of uttering sentences is one of the things people do in order to cope with their environment. The Deweyan notion of language as tool rather than picture is right as far as it goes. But we must be careful *not* to phrase this analogy so as to suggest that one can separate the tool, Language, from its users and inquire as to its "adequacy" to achieve our purposes. The latter suggestion presupposes that there is some way of breaking out of language in order to compare it with something else. But there is no way to think about either the world or our purposes except by using our language. One can use language to criticize and enlarge itself, as one can exercise one's body to develop and strengthen and enlarge it, but one cannot see language-as-a-whole in relation to something else to which it applies, or for which it is a means to an end. The arts and the sciences, and philosophy as their self-reflection and integration, constitute such a process of enlargement and strengthening. But Philosophy, the attempt to say "how language relates to the world" by saying what *makes* certain sentences true, or certain actions or attitudes good or rational, is, on this view, impossible.

It is the impossible attempt to step outside our skins—the traditions, linguistic and other, within which we do our thinking and self-criticism—and compare ourselves with something absolute. This Platonic urge to escape from the finitude of one's time and place, the "merely conventional" and contingent aspects of one's life, is responsible for the original Platonic distinction between two kinds of true sentence. By attacking this latter distinction, the holistic "pragmaticizing" strain in analytic philosophy has helped us see how the metaphysical urge—common to fuzzy Whiteheadians and razor-sharp "scientific realists"—works. It has helped us be skeptical about the idea that some particular science (say physics) or some particular literary genre (say Romantic poetry, or transcendental philosophy) gives us that species of true sentence which is not *just* a true sentence, but rather a piece of Truth itself. Such sentences may be very useful indeed, but there is not going to be a Philosophical explanation of this utility. That explanation, like the original justification of the assertion of the sentence, will be a parochial matter—a comparison of the sentence with alternative sentences formulated in the same or in other vocabularies. But such comparisons are the business of, for example, the physicist or the poet, or perhaps the philosopher—not of the Philosopher, the outside expert on the utility, or function, or metaphysical status of Language or of Thought.

The Wittgenstein–Sellars–Quine–Davidson attack on distinctions between classes of sentences is the special contribution of analytic philosophy to the anti-Platonist insistence on the ubiquity of language. This insistence characterizes both pragmatism and recent "Continental" philosophizing. Here are some examples:

> Man makes the word, and the word means nothing which the man has not made it mean, and that only to some other man. But since man can think only by means of words or other external symbols, these might turn around and say: You mean nothing which we have not taught you, and then only so far as you address some word as the interpretant of your thought . . . the word or sign which man uses is the man himself. . . . Thus my language is the sum-total of myself; for the man is the thought. (Peirce)[6]
>
> Peirce goes very far in the direction that I have called the deconstruction of the transcendental signified, which, at one time or another, would place a reassuring end to the reference from sign to sign. (Derrida)[7]

> . . . *psychological nominalism,* according to which all awareness of sorts, resemblances, facts, etc., in short all awareness of abstract entities—indeed, all awareness even of particulars—is a linguistic affair. (Sellars)[8]
>
> It is only in language that one can mean something by something. (Wittgenstein)[9]
>
> Human experience is essentially linguistic. (Gadamer)[10]
>
> . . . man is in the process of perishing as the being of language continues to shine ever brighter upon our horizon. (Foucault)[11]
>
> Speaking about language turns language almost inevitably into an object . . . and then its reality vanishes. (Heidegger)[12]

This chorus should not, however, lead us to think that something new and exciting has recently been discovered about Language—e.g., that it is more prevalent than had previously been thought. The authors cited are making only *negative* points. They are saying that attempts to get back behind language to something which "grounds" it, or which it "expresses," or to which it might hope to be "adequate," have not worked. The ubiquity of language is a matter of language moving into the vacancies left by the failure of all the various candidates for the position of "natural starting-points" of thought, starting-points which are prior to and independent of the way some culture speaks or spoke. (Candidates for such starting-points include clear and distinct ideas, sense-data, categories of the pure understanding, structures of prelinguistic consciousness, and the like.) Peirce and Sellars and Wittgenstein are saying that the regress of interpretation cannot be cut off by the sort of "intuition" which Cartesian epistemology took for granted. Gadamer and Derrida are saying that our culture has been dominated by the notion of a "transcendental signified" which, by cutting off this regress, would bring us out from contingency and convention and into the Truth. Foucault is saying that we are gradually losing our grip on the "metaphysical comfort" which that Philosophical tradition provided—its picture of Man as having a "double" (the soul, the Noumenal Self) who uses Reality's own language rather than merely the vocabulary of a time and a place. Finally, Heidegger is cautioning that if we try to make Language into a new topic of Philosophical inquiry we shall simply recreate the hopeless old Philosophical puzzles which we used to raise about Being or Thought.

This last point amounts to saying that what Gustav Bergmann called "the linguistic turn" should not be seen as the logical positivists saw it—as enabling us to ask Kantian questions without having to trespass on the psychologists' turf by talking, with Kant, about "experience" or "consciousness." That was, indeed, the initial motive for the "turn," [13] but (thanks to the holism and pragmatism of the authors I have cited) analytic philosophy of language was able to transcend this Kantian motive and adopt a naturalistic, behavioristic attitude toward language. This attitude has led it to the same outcome as the "Continental" reaction against the traditional Kantian problematic, the reaction found in Nietzsche and Heidegger. This convergence shows that the traditional association of analytic philosophy with tough-minded positivism and of "Continental" philosophy with tender-minded Platonism is *completely* misleading. The pragmaticization of analytic philosophy gratified the logical positivists' hopes, but not in the fashion which they had envisaged. It did not find a way for Philosophy to become "scientific," but rather found a way of setting Philosophy to one side. This post-positivistic kind of analytic philosophy thus comes to resemble the Nietzsche–Heidegger–Derrida tradition in beginning with criticism of Platonism and ending in a period of doubt about their own status. Both are living between a repudiated past and a dimly seen post-Philosophical future.

3. THE REALIST REACTION (I): TECHNICAL REALISM

Before going on to speculate about what a post-Philosophical culture might look like, I should make clear that my description of the current Philosophical sense has been deliberately oversimplified. So far I have ignored the anti-pragmatist backlash. The picture I have been sketching shows how things looked about ten years ago—or, at least, how they looked to an optimistic pragmatist. In the subsequent decade there has been, on both sides of the Channel, a reaction in favor of "realism"—a term which has come to be synonymous with "anti-pragmatism." This reaction has had three distinct motives: (1) the view that recent, technical developments in the philosophy of language have raised doubt about traditional pragmatist criticisms of the "correspondence theory of truth," or, at least, have made it necessary for the pragmatist to answer some hard, technical questions before proceeding further; (2) the sense that the "depth," the human significance, of the traditional textbook "problems of philosophy" has been underestimated, that pragmatists have lumped real problems together with pseudo-problems in a feckless orgy of "dissolution"; (3) the sense that something important would be lost if Philosophy as an autonomous discipline, as a *Fach,* were to fade from the cultural scene (in the way in which theology has faded).

This third motive—the fear of what would happen if there were merely philosophy, but no Philosophy—is not simply the defensive reaction of specialists threatened with unemployment. It is a conviction that a culture without Philosophy would be "irrationalist"—that a precious human capacity would lie unused, or a central human virtue no longer be exemplified. This motive is shared by many philosophy professors in France and Germany and by many analytic philosophers in Britain and America. The former would like something to do that is not merely the endless, repetitive, literary-historical "deconstruction" of the "Western metaphysics of presence" which was Heidegger's legacy. The latter would like to recapture the spirit of the early logical positivists, the sense that philosophy is the accumulation of "results" by patient, rigorous, preferably cooperative work on precisely stated problems (the spirit characteristic of the younger, rather than of the older, Wittgenstein). So philosophy professors on the Continent are casting longing glares toward analytic philosophy—and particularly toward the "realist" analytic philosophers who take Philosophical problems seriously. Conversely, admirers of "Continental" philosophy (e.g., of Nietzsche, Heidegger, Derrida, Gadamer, Foucault) are more welcome in American and British departments of, e.g., comparative literature and political science, than in departments of philosophy. On both continents there is fear of Philosophy's losing its traditional claim to "scientific" status and of its relegation to "the merely literary."

I shall talk about this fear in some detail later, in connection with the prospects for a culture in which the science/literature distinction would no longer matter. But here I shall concentrate on the first and second motives I just listed. These are associated with two fairly distinct groups of people. The first motive is characteristic of philosophers of language such as Saul Kripke and Michael Dummett, the second with less specialized and more broadly ranging writers like Stanley Cavell and Thomas Nagel. I shall call those who turn Kripke's views on reference to the purposes of a realistic epistemology (e.g., Hartry Field, Richard Boyd, and, sometimes, Hilary Putnam) "technical realists." I shall call Cavell, Nagel (and others, such as Thompson Clarke and Barry Stroud) "intuitive realists." The latter object that the pragmatists' dissolutions of traditional problems are "verificationist": that is, pragmatists think our inability to say what would count as confirming or disconfirming a given solution to a problem is a reason for setting the problem aside. To take this view is, Nagel tells us, to fail to recognize that "unsolvable problems are not for that reason unreal." [14] Intuitive realists judge verificationism by its fruits, and argue that the pragmatist belief in the ubiquity of language leads to the inability to recognize that philosophical problems arise precisely where language is inadequate to the facts. "My realism about the subjective domain in all its forms," Nagel says, "implies a belief in the existence of facts beyond the reach of human concepts." [15]

Technical realists, by contrast, judge pragmatism wrong not because it leads to superficial dismissals of deep problems, but because it is based on a false, "verificationist" philosophy of language. They dislike "verificiationism" not because of its metaphilosophical fruits, but because they see it as a misunderstanding of the relation between language and the world. On their view, Quine and Wittgenstein wrongly followed Frege in thinking that meaning—something determined by the intentions of the user of a word—determines reference, what the word picks out in the world. On the basis of the "new theory of reference" originated by Saul Kripke, they say, we can now construct a better, non-Fregean picture of the word-world relationships. Whereas Frege, like Kant, thought of our concepts as carving up an undifferentiated manifold in accordance with our interests (a view which leads fairly directly to Sellars's "psychological nominalism" and a Goodman-like insouciance about ontology), Kripke sees the world as already divided not only into particulars, but into natural kinds of particulars and even into essential and accidental features of those particulars and kinds. The question "Is 'X is ϕ' *true*?" is thus to be answered by discovering what—as a matter of physical fact, not of anybody's intentions—'X' refers to, and then discovering whether that particular or kind is ϕ. Only by such a "physicalistic" theory of reference, technical realists say, can the notion of "truth as correspondence to reality" be preserved. By contrast, the pragmatist answers this question by inquiring whether, all things (and especially our purposes in using the terms 'X' and 'ϕ') considered, 'X is ϕ' is a more useful belief to have than its contradictory, or than some belief expressed in different terms altogether. The pragmatist agrees that if one wants to preserve the notion of "correspondence with reality" then a physicalistic theory of reference is necessary—but he sees no point in preserving that notion. The pragmatist has no notion of truth which would enable him to make sense of the claim that if we achieved everything we ever hoped to achieve by making assertions we might still be making *false* assertions, failing to "correspond" to something." [16] As Putnam says:

> The trouble is that for a strong antirealist [e.g., a pragmatist] *truth* makes no sense except as an intra-theoretic notion. The antirealist can use truth intra-theoretically in the sense of a "redundancy theory" [i.e., a theory according to which "S is true" means exactly, only, what "S" means] but he does not have the notion of truth and reference available extra-theoretically. But extension [reference] is tied to the notion of truth. The extension of a term is just what the term is *true of*. Rather than try to retain the notion of truth via an awkward operationalism, the antirealist should reject the notion of extension as he does the notion of truth (in any extra-theoretic sense). Like Dewey, he can fall back on a notion of 'warranted assertability' instead of truth. . . .[17]

The question which technical realism raises, then, is: are there technical reasons, within the philosophy of language, for retaining or discarding this extra-theoretic notion? Are there nonintuitive ways of deciding whether, as the pragmatist thinks, the question of what 'X' refers to is a sociological matter, a question of how best to make sense of a community's linguistic behavior, or whether, as Hartry Field says,

> one aspect of the sociological role of a term is the role that term has in the psychologies of different members of a linguistic community; another aspect, *irreducible to the first* [italics added], is what physical objects or physical property the term stands for.[18]

It is not clear, however, what these technical, nonintuitive ways might be. For it is not clear what data the philosophy of language must explain. The most frequently cited datum is that science *works, succeeds*—enables us to cure diseases, blow up cities, and the like. How, realists ask, would this be possible if some scientific statements did not correspond to the way things are in themselves? How, pragmatists rejoin, does *that* count as an explanation? What further specification of the "correspondence" relation can be given which will enable this explanation to be better than "dormitive power" (Molière's doctor's explanation of why opium puts people to sleep)? What, so to speak, corresponds to the microstructure of opium in this case? What is the microstructure of "corresponding"? The Tarskian apparatus of truth-conditions and satisfaction-relations does not fill the bill, because that apparatus is equally well adapted to physicalist "building-block" theories of reference like Field's and to coherentist, holistic, pragmatical theories like Davidson's. When realists like Field argue that Tarski's account of truth is merely a place-holder, like Mendel's account of "gene," which requires physicalistic "reduction to non-semantical terms," [19] pragmatists reply (with Stephen Leeds) that "true" (like "good" and unlike "gene") is not an explanatory notion.[20] (Or that, if it is, the structure of the explanations in which it is used needs to be spelled out.)

The search for technical grounds on which to argue the pragmatist-realist issue is sometimes endured artificially by the realist assuming that the pragmatist not only (as Putnam says) follows Dewey in "falling back on a notion of 'warranted assertibility' *instead* of truth" but uses the latter notion to *analyze the meaning* of "true." Putnam is right that no such analysis will work. But the pragmatist, if he is wise, will not succumb to the temptation to fill the blank in

S is true if and only if *S* is assertible ______

with "at the end of inquiry" or "by the standards of our culture" or with anything else.[21] He will recognize the strength of Putnam's "naturalistic fallacy" argument: Just as nothing can fill the blank in

A is the best thing to do in circumstances *C* if and only if ______
so, *a fortiori,* nothing will fill the blank in

Asserting *S* is the best thing to do in *C* if and only if ______

If the pragmatist is advised that he must not confuse the *advisability of asserting S* with the *truth of S,* he will respond that the advice is question-begging. The question is precisely whether "the true" is more than what William James defined it as: "the name of whatever proves itself to be good in the way of belief, and good, too, for definite, assignable reasons." [22] On James's view, "true" resembles "good" or "rational" in being a normative notion, a compliment paid to sentences that seem to be paying their way and that fit in with other sentences which are doing so. To think that Truth is "out there" is, on their view, on all fours with the Platonic view that The Good is "out there." To think that we are "irrationalist" insofar as it does not "gratify our souls to know/That though we perish, truth is so" is like thinking we are "irrationalist" just insofar as it does not gratify our moral sense to think that The Moral Law shines resplendent over the noumenal world, regardless of the vicissitudes of spatio-temporal lives. For the pragmatist, the notion of "truth" as something "objective" is just a confusion between

(I) Most of the world is as it is whatever we think about it (that is, our beliefs have very limited casual efficacy)

and

(II) There is something out there in addition to the world called "the truth about the world" (what James sarcastically called "this tertium quid intermediate between the facts *per se,* on the one hand, and all knowledge of them, actual or potential, on the other").[23]

The pragmatist wholeheartedly assents to (I)—not as an article of metaphysical faith but simply as a belief that we have never had any reason to doubt—and cannot make sense of (II). When the realist tries to explain (II) with

(III) The truth about the world consists in a relation of "correspondence" between certain sentences (many of which, no doubt, have yet to be formulated) and the world itself

the pragmatist can only fall back on saying, once again, that many centuries of attempts to explain what "correspondence" is have failed, especially when it comes to explaining how the final vocabulary of future physics will somehow be Nature's Own—the one which, at long last, lets us formulate sentences which lock on to Nature's own way of thinking of Herself.

For these reasons, the pragmatist does not think that, whatever else philosophy of language may do, it is going to come up with a definition of "true" which gets beyond James. He happily grants that it can do a lot of other things. For example, it can, following Tarski, show what it would be like to define a truth-predicate for a given language. The pragmatist can agree with Davidson that to define such a predicate—to develop a truth-theory for the sentences of English, e.g.—would be a good way, perhaps the only way, to exhibit a natural language as a learnable, recursive structure, and thus to give a systematic theory of meaning for the language.[24] But he agrees with Davidson that such an exhibition is *all* that Tarski can give us, and all that can be milked out of Philosophical reflection on Truth.

Just as the pragmatist should not succumb to the temptation to "capture the intuitive content of our notion of truth" (including whatever it is in that notion which makes realism tempting), so he should not succumb to the temptation held out by Michael Dummett to take sides on the issue of "bivalence." Dummett (who has his own doubts about realism) has suggested that a lot of traditional issues in the area of the pragmatist-realist debate can be clarified by the technical apparatus of philosophy of language, along the following lines:

> In a variety of different areas there arises a philosophical dispute of the same general character: the dispute for or against realism con-

> cerning statements within a given type of subject-matter, or, better, statements of a certain general type. [Dummett elsewhere lists moral statements, mathematical statements, statements about the past, and modal statements as examples of such types.] Such a dispute consists in an opposition between two points of view concerning the kind of meaning possessed by statements of the kind in question, and hence about the application to them of the notions of truth and falsity. For the realist, we have assigned a meaning to these statements in such a way that we know, for each statement, what has to be the case for it to be true. . . . The condition for the truth of a statement is not, in general, a condition we are capable of recognizing as obtaining whenever it obtains, or even one for which we have an effective procedure for determining whether it obtains or not. We have therefore succeeded in ascribing to our statements a meaning of such a kind that their truth or falsity is, in general, independent of whether we know, or have any means of knowing, what truth-value they have. . . .
>
> Opposed to the realist account of statements in some given class is the anti-realist interpretation. According to this, the meanings of statements of the class in question are given to us, not in terms of the conditions under which these statements are true or false, conceived of as conditions which obtain or do not obtain independently of our knowledge or capacity for knowledge, but in terms of the conditions which we recognize as establishing the truth or falsity of statements of that class.[25]

"Bivalence" is the property of being either true or false, so Dummett thinks of a "realistic" view about a certain area (say, moral values, or possible worlds) as asserting bivalence for statements about such things. His way of formulating the realist-vs.-anti-realist issue thus suggests that the pragmatist denies bivalence for all statements, the "extreme" realist asserts it for all statements, while the level-headed majority sensibly discriminate between the bivalent statements of, e.g., physics and the nonbivalent statements of, e.g., morals. "Bivalence" thus joins "ontological commitment" as a way of expressing old-fashioned metaphysical views in up-to-date semantical language. If the pragmatist is viewed as a quasi-idealist metaphysician who is ontologically committed only to ideas or sentences, and does not believe that there is anything "out there" which makes any sort of statement true, then he will fit neatly into Dummett's scheme.

But, of course, this is not the pragmatist's picture of himself. He does not think of himself as *any* kind of a metaphysician, because he does not *understand* the notion of "there being ________ out there" (except in the literal sense of 'out there' in which it means "at a position in space"). He does not find it helpful to explicate the Platonist's conviction about The Good or The Numbers by saying that the Platonist believes that "There is truth-or-falsity about

_______, regardless of the state of our knowledge or the availability of procedures for inquiry." The "is" in this sentence seems to him just as obscure as the "is" in "Truth is so." Confronted with the passage from Dummett cited above, the pragmatist wonders how one goes about telling one "kind of meaning" from another, and what it would be like to have "intuitions" about the bivalence or nonbivalence of kinds of statements. He is a pragmatist just because he doesn't have such intuitions (or wants to get rid of whatever such intuitions he may have). When he asks himself, about a given statement *S*, whether he "knows what has to be the case for it to be true" or merely knows "the conditions which we recognize as establishing the truth or falsity of statements of that class," he feels as helpless as when asked, "Are you really in love, or merely inflamed by passion?" He is inclined to suspect that it is not a very useful question, and that at any rate introspection is not the way to answer it. But in the case of bivalence it is not clear that there is another way. Dummett does not help us see what to count as a good argument for asserting bivalence of, e.g., moral or modal statements; he merely says that there are some people who do assert this and some who don't, presumably having been born with different metaphysical temperaments. If one is born without metaphysical views—or if, having become pessimistic about the utility of Philosophy, one is self-consciously attempting to eschew such views—then one will feel that Dummett's reconstruction of the traditional issues explicates the obscure with the equally obscure.

What I have said about Field and about Dummett is intended to cast doubt on the "technical realist's" view that the pragmatist-realist issue should be fought out on some narrow, clearly demarcated ground within the philosophy of language. There is no such ground. This is not, to be sure, the fault of philosophy of language, but of the pragmatist. He refuses to take a stand—to provide an "analysis" of "*S* is true," for example, or to either assert or deny bivalence. He refuses to make a move in *any* of the games in which he is invited to take part. The *only* point at which "referential semantics" or "bivalence" becomes of interest to him comes when somebody tries to treat these notions as explanatory, as not *just* expressing intuitions but as doing some work—explaining, for example, "why science is so successful." [26] At this point the pragmatist hauls out his bag of tried-and-true dialectical gambits.[27] He proceeds to argue that there is no pragmatic difference, no difference that makes a difference, between "it works because it's true" and "it's true because it works"—any more than between "it's pious because the gods love it" and "the gods love it because it's pious." Alternatively, he argues that there is no pragmatic difference between the nature of truth and the test of truth, and that the test of truth, of what statements to assert, is (except maybe for a few perceptual statements) not "comparison with reality." All these gambits will be felt by the realist to be question-begging, since the realist intuits that some differences can be real *without* making a difference, that sometimes the *ordo essendi* is *different* from the *ordo cognoscendi*, sometimes the nature of X is *not* our test for the presence of Xness. And so it goes.

What we should conclude, I think, is that technical realism collapses into intuitive realism—that the *only* debating point which the realist has is his conviction that the raising of the good old metaphysical problems (are there *really* universals? are there *really* casually efficacious physical objects, or did we just *posit* them?) served some good purpose, brought something to light, was important. What the pragmatist wants to debate is just this point. He does not want to discuss necessary and sufficient conditions for a sentence being true, but precisely *whether* the practice which hopes to find a Philosophical way of isolating the essence of Truth has, in fact, paid off. So the issue between him and the intuitive realist is a matter of what to make of the history of that practice—what to make of the history of Philosophy. The real issue is about the place of Philosophy in Western philosophy, the place within the intellectual history of the West of the particular series of texts which raise the "deep" Philosophical problems which the realist wants to preserve.

4. THE REALIST REACTION (II): INTUITIVE REALISM

What really needs debate between the pragmatist and the intuitive realist is *not* whether we have intuitions to the effect that "truth is more than assertability" or "there is more to pains than brain-states" or "there is a clash between modern physics and our sense of moral responsibility." *Of course* we have such intuitions. How could we escape having them? We have been educated within an intellectual tradition built around such claims—just as we used to be educated within an intellectual tradition built around such claims as "If God does not exist, everything is permitted," "Man's dignity consists in his link with a supernatural order," and "One must not mock holy things." But it begs the question between pragmatist and realist to say that we must find a philosophical view which "captures" such intuitions. The pragmatist is urging that we do our best to *stop having* such intuitions, that we develop a *new* intellectual tradition.

What strikes intuitive realists as offensive about this suggestion is that it seems as dishonest to suppress intuitions as it is to suppress experimental data. On their conception, philosophy (not merely Philosophy) requires one to do justice to *everybody's* intuitions. Just as social justice is what would be brought about by institutions whose existence could be justified to every citizen, so intellectual justice would be made possible by finding these which everyone would, given sufficient time and dialectical ability, accept. This view of intellectual life presupposes either that, contrary to the prophets of the ubiquity of language cited above, language does *not* go all the way down, or that, contrary to the appearances, all vocabularies are commensurable. The first alternative amounts to saying that some intuitions, at least, are *not* a function of the way one has been brought up to talk, of the texts and people one has encountered. The second amounts to saying that the intuitions built into the vocabularies of Homeric warriors, Buddhist sages, Enlightenment scientists, and contemporary French literary critics, are not really as different as they seem—that there are common elements in each which Philosophy can isolate and use to formulate theses which it would be rational for all these people to accept, and problems which they all face.

The pragmatist, on the other hand, thinks that the quest for a universal human community will be self-defeating if it tries to preserve the elements of every intellectual tradition, all the "deep" intuitions everybody has ever had. It is not to be achieved by an attempt at commensuration, at a common vocabulary which isolates the common human essence of Achilles and the Buddha, Lavoisier and Derrida. Rather, it is to be reached, if at all, by acts of making rather than of finding—by poetic rather than Philosophical achievement. The culture which will transcend, and thus unite, East and West, or the Earthlings and the Galactics, is not likely to be one which does equal justice to each, but one which looks back on both with the amused condescension typical of later generations looking back at their ancestors. So the pragmatist's quarrel with the intuitive realist should be about the *status* of intuitions—about their *right* to be respected—as opposed to how particular intuitions might be "synthesized" or "explained away." To treat his opponent properly, the pragmatist must begin by admitting that the realistic intuitions in question are as deep and compelling as the realist says they are. But he should then try to change the subject by asking, "And what should we *do* about such intuitions—extirpate them, or find a vocabulary which does justice to them?"

From the pragmatist point of view the claim that the issues which the nineteenth century enshrined in its textbooks as "the central problems of philosophy" are "deep" is simply the claim that you will not understand a certain period in the history of Europe unless you can get some idea of what it was like to be preoccupied by such questions. (Consider parallel claims about the "depth" of the problems about Patripassianism, Arianism, etc., discussed by certain Fathers of the Church.) The pragmatist is even willing to expand his range and say, with Heidegger, that you won't understand the West unless you understand what it was like to be bothered by the kinds of issues which bothered Plato. Intuitive realists, rather than "stepping back" in the historicist manner of Heidegger and Dewey, or the quasi-anthropological manner of Foucault, devote themselves to safeguarding the tradition, to making us even more deeply Western. The way in which they do this is illustrated by Clarke's and Cavell's attempt to see "the legacy of skepticism" not as a question about whether we can be sure we're not dreaming but as a question about what sort of being could ask itself such a question.[28] They use the existence of figures like Descartes as indications of something important about *human beings,* not just about the modern West.

The best illustration of this strategy is Nagel's way of updating Kant by bringing a whole series of apparently disparate problems under the rubric "Subjective-Objective," just as Kant brought a partially overlapping set of problems under the rubric "Conditioned-Unconditioned." Nagel echoes Kant in saying:

> It may be true that some philosophical problems have no solution. I suspect that this is true of the deepest and oldest of them. They show us the limits of our understanding. In that case such insight as we can achieve depends on maintaining a strong grasp of the problem instead of abandoning it, and coming to understand the failure of each new attempt at a solution, and of earlier attempts. (That is why we study the works of philosophers like Plato and Berkeley, whose views are accepted by no one.) Unsolvable problems are not for that reason unreal.[29]

As an illustration of what Nagel has in mind, consider his example of the problem of "moral luck"—the fact that one can be morally praised or blamed only for what is under one's control, yet practically nothing is. As Nagel says:

> The area of genuine agency, and therefore of legitimate moral judgment, seems to shrink under this scrutiny to an extensionless point. Everything seems to result from the combined influence of factors, antecedent and posterior to action, that are not within the agent's control.[30]

Nagel thinks that a typically shallow, verificationist "solution" to this problem is available. We can get such a solution (Hume's) by going into detail about what sorts of external factors we do and don't count as diminishing the moral worth of an action:

> This compatibilist account of our moral judgments would leave room for the ordinary conditions of responsibility—the absence of coercion, ignorance, or involuntary movement—as part of the determination of what someone has done—but it is understood not to exclude the influence of a great deal that he has not done.[31]

But this relaxed, pragmatical, Humean attitude—the attitude which says that there is no deep truth about Freedom of the Will, and that people are morally responsible for whatever their peers tend to hold them morally responsible for—fails to explain why there has been *thought* to be a problem here:

> The only thing wrong with this solution is its failure to explain how skeptical problems arise. For they arise not from the imposition of an arbitrary external requirement, but from the nature of moral judgment itself. Something in the ordinary idea of what someone does must explain how it can seem necessary to subtract from it anything that merely happens—even though the ultimate consequence of such subtraction is that nothing remains.[32]

But this is not to say that we need a metaphysical account of the Nature of Freedom of the sort which Kant (at least in some passages) seems to give us. Rather,

> . . . in a sense the problem has no solution, because something in the idea of agency is incompatible with actions being events or people being things.[33]

Since there is, so to speak, nothing *else* for people to be but things, we are left with an intuition—one which shows us "the limits of our understanding," and thus of our language.

Contrast, now, Nagel's attitude toward "the nature of moral judgment" with Iris Murdoch's. The Kantian attempt to isolate an agent who is not a spatio-temporal thing is seen by Murdoch as an unfortunate and perverse turn which Western thought has taken. Within a certain post-Kantian tradition, she says:

> Immense care is taken to picture the will as isolated. It is isolated from belief, from reason, from feeling, and is yet the essential center of the self. . . .[34]

This existentialist conception of the agent as isolated will goes along, Murdoch says, with "a very powerful image" of man which she finds "alien and implausible"—one which is "a happy and fruitful marriage of Kantian liberalism with Wittgensteinian logic solemnized by Freud." [35] On Murdoch's view,

> Existentialism, in both its Continental and its Anglo-Saxon versions, is an attempt to solve the problem without really facing it: to solve it by attributing to the individual an empty lonely freedom. . . . What it pictures is indeed the fearful solitude of the individual marooned upon a tiny island in the middle of a sea of scientific facts, and morality escaping from science only by a wild leap of will.[36]

Instead of reinforcing this picture (as Nagel and Sartre do), Murdoch wants to get behind Kantian notions of will, behind the Kantian formulation of an antithesis between determinism and responsibility, behind the Kantian distinction between the moral self and the empirical self. She wants to recapture the vocabulary of moral reflection which a sixteenth-century Christian believer inclined toward Platonism would have used: one in which "perfection" is a central element, in which assignment of moral responsibility is a rather incidental element, and in which the discovery of a self (one's own or another's) is the endless task of love.[37]

In contrasting Nagel and Murdoch, I am not trying (misleadingly) to enlist Murdoch as a fellow-pragmatist, nor (falsely) to accuse Nagel of blindness to the variety of moral consciousness which Murdoch represents. Rather, I want to illustrate the difference between taking a standard philosophical problem (or cluster of interrelated problems such as free will, selfhood, agency, and responsibility) and asking, on the one hand, "What is its essence? To what ineffable depths, what limit of language, does it lead us? What does it show us about *being human?*" and asking, on the other hand, "What sort of people would see these problems? Why, insofar as we are gripped by these problems, do we see them as deep rather than as *reductiones ad absurdum* of a vocabulary? What does the persistence of such problems show us about *being twentieth-century Europeans?*" Nagel is certainly right, and splendidly lucid, about the way in which a set of ideas, illustrated best by Kant, shoves us toward the notion of something called "the subjective"—the personal point of view, what science doesn't catch, what no "stepping back" could catch, what forms a limit to the understanding. But how do we know whether to say, "So much the worse for the solubility of philosophical problems, for the reach of language, for our 'verificationist' impulses," or whether to say, "So much the worse for the Philosophical ideas which have led us to such an impasse"?

The same question arises about the other philosophical problems which Nagel brings under his "Subjective-Objective" rubric. The clash between "verificationist" and "realist" intuitions is perhaps best illustrated by Nagel's celebrated paper "What Is It Like to Be a Bat?" Nagel here appeals to our intuition that "there is something which it is like" to be a bat or a dog but nothing which it is like to be an atom or a brick, and says that this intuition is what contemporary Wittgensteinian, Rylean, anti-Cartesian philosophy of mind "fails to capture." The culmination of the latter philosophical movement is the cavalier attitude toward "raw feels"—e.g., the sheer phenomenological qualitative ipseity of pain—suggested by Daniel Dennett:

> I recommend giving up incorrigibility with regard to pain altogether, in fact giving up *all* "essential" features of pain, and letting pain states be whatever "natural kind" states the brain scientists find (if they ever do find any) that normally produce all the normal effects. . . . One of our intuitions about pain is that whether or not one is in pain is a brute fact, not a matter of decision to serve the convenience of the theorist. I recommend against trying to preserve that intuition, but if you disagree, whatever theory I produce, however predictive and elegant, will not be in your lights a theory of pain, but only a theory of what I illicitly choose to *call* pain. But if, as I have claimed, the intuitions we would have to honor were we to honor them all do not form a consistent set, there can be no true theory of pain, and so no computer or robot could instantiate the true theory of pain, which it would have to do to feel real pain. . . . The inability of a robot model to satisfy all our intuitive demands may be due not to any irredeemable mysteriousness about the phenomenon of pain, but to irredeemable incoherence in our ordinary concept of pain.[38]

Nagel is one of those who disagrees with Dennett's recommendation. His anti-verificationism comes out most strongly in the following passage:

> . . . if things emerged from a spaceship which we could not be sure were machines or conscious beings, what we were wondering would have an answer even if the things were so different from anything we were familiar with that we could never discover it. It would depend on whether there was something it was like to be them, not on whether behavioral similarities warranted our saying so. . . .
>
> I therefore seem to be drawn to a position more 'realistic' than Wittgenstein's. This may be because I am drawn to positions more realistic than Wittgenstein's about everything, not just the mental. I believe that the question about whether the things coming out of the spaceship are conscious *must* have an answer. Wittgenstein would presumably say that this assumption reflects a groundless confidence that a certain picture unambiguously determines its own application. That is the picture of something going on in their heads (or whatever they have in place of heads) that cannot be observed by dissection.
>
> Whatever picture I may use to represent the idea, it does seem to me that I know what it means to ask whether there is something it is like to be them, and that the answer to that question is what determines whether they are conscious—not the possibility of extending mental ascriptions on evidence analogous to the human case. Conscious mental states are real states of something, whether they are mine or those of an alien creature. Perhaps Wittgenstein's view can accommodate this intuition, but I do not at the moment see how.[39]

Wittgenstein certainly *cannot* accommodate this intuition. The question is whether he should be asked to: whether we should abandon the pragmatical "verificationist" intuition that "every difference must *make* a difference" (expressed by Wittgenstein in the remark "A wheel that can be turned though nothing else moves with it, is not part of the mechanism")[40] or instead abandon Nagel's intuition about consciousness. We certainly *have* both intuitions. For Nagel, their compresence shows that the limit of understanding has been reached, that an ultimate depth has been plumbed—just as the discovery of an antinomy indicated to Kant that something transcendental had been encountered. For Wittgenstein, it merely shows that the Cartesian tradition has sketched a compelling picture, a picture which "held us captive. And we could not get outside it, for it lay in our language and language seemed to repeat it to us inexorably." [41]

I said at the beginning of this section that there were two alternative ways in which the intuitive realist might respond to the pragmatist's suggestion that some intuitions should be deliberately repressed. He might say either that language does not go all the way down—that there is a kind of awareness of facts which is not expressible in language and which no argument could render dubious—or, more mildly, that there is a core language which is common to all traditions and which needs to be isolated. In a confrontation with Murdoch one can imagine Nagel making the second claim—arguing that even the kind of moral discourse which Murdoch recommends must wind up with the same conception of "the isolated will" as Kantian moral discourse. But in a confrontation with Dennett's attempt to weed out our intuitions Nagel must make the first claim. He has to go all the way, and deny that our knowledge is limited by the language we speak. He says as much in the following passage:

> If anyone is inclined to deny that we can believe in the existence of facts like this whose exact nature we cannot possibly conceive, he should reflect that in contemplating the bats we are in much the same position that intelligent bats or Martians would occupy if they tried to form a conception of what it was like to be us. The structure of their own minds might make it impossible for them to succeed, but we know they would be wrong to conclude that there is not anything precise that it is like to be us. . . . We know they would be wrong to draw such a skeptical conclusion because we know what it is like to be us. And we know that while it includes an enormous amount of variation and complexity, and *while we do not possess the vocabulary to describe it adequately,* its subjective character is highly specific, and in some respects describable in terms that can be understood only by creatures like us [italics added].[42]

Here we hit a bedrock metaphilosophical issue: can one ever appeal to nonlinguistic knowledge in philosophical argument? This is the question of whether a dialectical impasse is the mark of philosophical depth or of a bad language, one which needs to be replaced with one which will not lead to such impasses. *That* is just the issue about the status of intuitions, which I said above was the real issue between the pragmatist and the realist. The hunch that, e.g., reflection upon anything worthy of the name "moral judgment" will eventually lead us to the problems Nagel describes is a discussable question—one upon which the history of ethics can shed light. But the intuition that there is something ineffable which it is like to be us—something which one cannot learn about by believing true propositions but only by *being* like that—is not something on which anything could throw further light. The claim is either deep or empty.

The pragmatist sees it as empty—indeed, he sees many of Nagel's discussions of "the subjective" as drawing a line around a vacant place in the middle of the web of words, and then claiming that there is something there rather than nothing. But this is not because he has independent arguments for a Philosophical theory to the effect that (in Sellars's words) "All awareness is a linguistic affair," or that "The meaning of a proposition is its method of verification." Such slogans as these are not the result of Philosophical inquiry into Awareness or Meaning, but merely ways of cautioning the public against the Philosophical tradition. (As "No taxation without representation" was not a discovery about the nature of Taxation, but an expression of distrust in the British Parliament of the day.) There are no fast little arguments to show that there are no such things as intuitions—arguments which are themselves based on something stronger than intuitions. For the pragmatist, the *only* thing wrong with Nagel's intuitions is that they are being used to legitimize a vocabulary (the Kantian vocabulary in morals, the Cartesian vocabulary in philosophy of mind) which the pragmatist thinks should be eradicated rather than reinforced. But his *only* argument for thinking that these intuitions and vocabularies should be eradicated is that the intellectual tradition to which they belong has not paid off, is more trouble than it is worth, has become an incubus. Nagel's dogmatism of intuitions is no worse, or better, than the pragmatist's inability to give noncircular arguments.

This upshot of the confrontation between the pragmatist and the intuitive realist about the status of intuitions can be described either as a conflict of intuitions about the importance of intuitions, or as a preference for one vocabulary over another. The realist will favor the first description, and the pragmatist, the second. It does not matter which description one uses, as long as it is clear that *the issue is one about whether philosophy should try to find natural starting-points which are distinct from cultural traditions, or whether all philosophy should do is compare and contrast cultural traditions.* This is, once again, the issue of whether philosophy should be Philosophy. The intuitive realist thinks that there is such a thing as Philosophical truth because he thinks that, deep down beneath all the texts, there is something which is not just one more text but that to which various texts are trying to be "adequate." The pragmatist does not think that there is anything like that. He does not even think that there is anything isolable as "the purposes which we construct vocabularies and cultures to fulfill" against which to test vocabularies and cultures. But he does think that in the process of playing vocabularies and cultures off against each other, we produce new and better ways of talking and acting—not better by reference to a previously known standard, but just better in the sense that they come to *seem* clearly better than their predecessors.

5. A POST-PHILOSOPHICAL CULTURE

I began by saying that the pragmatist refused to accept the Philosophical distinction between first-rate truth-by-correspondence-to-reality and second-rate truth-as-what-it-is-good-to-believe. I said that this raised the question of whether a culture could get along without Philosophy, without the Platonic attempt to sift out the merely contingent and conventional truths from the Truths which were something more than that. The last two sections, in which I have been going over the latest round of "realist" objections to pragmatism, has brought us back to my initial distinction between philosophy and Philosophy. Pragmatism denies the possibility of getting beyond the Sellarsian notion of "seeing how things hang together"—which, for the bookish intellectual of recent times, means seeing how all the various vocabularies of all the various epochs and cultures hang together. "Intuition" is just the latest name for a device which will get us off the literary-historical-anthropological-political merry-go-round which such intellectuals ride, and onto something "progressive" and "scientific"—a device which will get us from philosophy to Philosophy.

I remarked earlier that a third motive for the recent anti-pragmatist backlash is simply the hope of getting off this merry-go-round. This hope is a correlate of the fear that if there is nothing quasi-scientific for philosophy as an academic discipline to do, if there is no properly professional *Fach* which distinguishes the philosophy professor from the historian or the literary critic, then something will have been lost which has been central to Western intellectual life. This fear is, to be sure, justified. If Philosophy disappears, something will have been lost which was central to Western intellectual life—just as something central was lost when religious intuitions were weeded out from among the intellectually respectable candidates for Philosophical articulation. But the Enlightenment thought, rightly, that what would succeed religion would be *better*. The pragmatist is betting that what succeeds the "scientific," positivist culture which the Enlightenment produced will be *better*.

The question of whether the pragmatist is right to be so sanguine is the question of whether a culture is imaginable, or desirable, in which no one—or at least no intellectual—believes that we have, deep down inside us, a criterion for telling whether we are in touch with reality or not, when we are in the Truth. This would be a culture in which neither the priests nor the physicists nor the poets nor the Party were thought of as more "rational," or more "scientific" or "deeper" than one another. No particular portion of culture would be singled out as exemplifying (or signally failing to exemplify) the condition to which the rest aspired. There would be no sense that, beyond the current intra-disciplinary criteria, which, for example, good priests or good physicists obeyed, there were other, transdiciplinary, transcultural, ahistorical criteria, which they also obeyed. There would still be hero-worship in such a culture, but it would not be worship of heroes as children of the gods, as marked off from the rest of the mankind by closeness to the immortal. It would simply be admiration of exceptional men and women who were very good at doing the quite diverse kinds of things they did. Such people would not be those who knew a Secret, who had won through to the Truth, but simply people who were good at being human.

A fortiori, such a culture would contain nobody called "the Philosopher" who could explain why and how certain areas of culture enjoyed a special relation to reality. Such a culture would, doubtless, contain specialists in seeing how things hung together. But these would be people who had no special "problems" to solve, nor any special "method" to apply, abided by no particular disciplinary standards, had no collective self-image as a "profession." They might resemble contemporary philosophy professors in being more interested in moral responsibility than in prosody, or more interested in the articulation of sentences than in that of the human body, but they might not. They would be all-purpose intellectuals who were ready to offer a view on pretty much anything, in the hope of making it hang together with everything else.

Such a hypothetical culture strikes both Platonists and positivists as "decadent." The Platonists see it as having no ruling principle, no center, no structure. The positivists see it as having no respect for hard fact, for that area of culture—science—in which the quest for objective truth takes precedence over emotion and opinion. The Platonists would like to see a culture guided by something eternal. The positivists would like to see one guided by something temporal—the brute impact of the way the world is. But both want it to be *guided,* constrained, not left to its own devices. For both, decadence is a matter of unwillingness to submit oneself to something "out there"—to recognize that beyond the languages of men and women there is something to which these languages, and the men and women themselves, must try to be "adequate." For both, therefore, Philosophy as the discipline which draws a line between such attempts at adequacy and everything else in culture, and so between first-rate and second-rate truth, is bound up with the struggle against decadence.

So the question of whether such a post-Philosophical culture is desirable can also be put as the question: can the ubiquity of language ever really be taken seriously? Can we see ourselves as never encountering reality *except under a chosen description*—as, in Nelson Goodman's phrase, making worlds rather than finding them.[43] This question has nothing to do with "idealism"—with the suggestion that we can or should draw metaphysical comfort from the fact that reality is "spiritual in nature." It is, rather, the question of whether we can give up what Stanley Cavell calls the "possibility that one among endless true descriptions of me tells who I am." [44] The hope that one of them will do just that is the impulse which, in our present culture, drives the youth to read their way through libraries, cranks to claim that they have found The Secret which makes all things plain, and sound scientists and scholars, toward the ends of their lives, to hope that their work has "philosophical implications" and "universal human significance." In a post-Philosophical culture, some other hope would drive us to read through the libraries, and to add new volumes to the ones we found. Presumably it would be the hope of offering our descendants a way of describing the ways of describing we had come across—a description of the descriptions which the race has come up with so far. If one takes "our time" to be "our view of previous times," so that, in Hegelian fashion, each age of the world recapitulates all the earlier ones, then a post-Philosophical culture would agree with Hegel that philosophy is "its own time apprehended in thoughts." [45]

In a post-Philosophical culture it would be clear that this is *all* that philosophy can be. It cannot answer questions about the relation of the thought of our time—the descriptions it is using, the vocabularies it employs—to something which is not just some alternative vocabulary. So it is a study of the comparative advantages and disadvantages of the various ways of talking which our race has invented. It looks, in short, much like what is sometimes called "culture criticism"—a term which has come to name the literary–historical–anthropological-political merry-go-round I spoke of earlier. The modern Western "culture critic" feels free to comment on anything at all. He is a prefiguration of the all-purpose intellectual of a post-Philosophical culture, the philosopher who has abandoned pretensions to Philosophy. He passes rapidly from Hemingway to Proust to Hitler to Marx, to Foucault to Mary Douglas to the present situation in Southeast Asia to Ghandi to Sophocles. He is a name-dropper, who uses names such as these to refer to sets of descriptions, symbol-systems, ways of seeing. His specialty is seeing similarities and differences between great big pictures, between attempts to see how things hang together. He is the person who tells you how all the ways of making things hang together hang together. But, since he does not tell you about how all *possible* ways of making things hang together *must* hang together—since he has no extra-historical Archimedean point of this sort—he is doomed to become outdated. Nobody is so passé as the intellectual czar of the previous generation—the man who redescribed all those old descriptions, which, thanks in part to his redescription of them, nobody now wants to hear anything about.

The life of such inhabitants of Snow's "literary culture," whose highest hope is to grasp their time in thought, appears to the Platonist and the positivist as a life not worth living—because it is a life which leaves nothing permanent behind. In contrast, the positivist and the Platonist hope to leave behind true propositions, propositions which have been shown true once and for all—inheritances for the human race unto all generations. The fear and distrust inspired by "historicism"—the emphasis on the mortality of the vocabularies in which such supposedly immortal truths are expressed—is the reason why Hegel (and more recently Kuhn and Foucault) are *bêtes noires* for Philosophers, and especially for spokesmen for Snow's "scientific culture."[46] (Hegel himself, to be sure, had his Philosophical moments, but the temporalization of rationality which he suggested was the single most important step in arriving at the pragmatist's distrust of Philosophy.)

The opposition between mortal vocabularies and immortal propositions is reflected in the opposition between the inconclusive comparison and contrast of vocabularies (with everybody trying to *aufheben* everybody else's way of putting everything) characteristic of the literary culture, and rigorous argumentation—the procedure characteristic of mathematics, what Kuhn calls "normal" science, and the law (at least in the lower courts). Comparisons and contrasts between vocabularies issue, usually, in new, synthetic vocabularies. Rigorous argumentation issues in agreement in propositions. The really exasperating thing about literary intellectuals, from the point of view of those inclined to science or to Philosophy, is their inability to engage in such argumentation—to agree on what would count as resolving disputes, on the criteria to which all sides must appeal. In a post-Philosophical culture, this exasperation would not be felt. In such a culture, criteria would be seen as the pragmatist sees them—as temporary resting-places constructed for specific utilitarian ends. On the pragmatist account, a criterion (what follows from the axioms, what the needle points to, what the statute says) *is* a criterion because some particular social practice needs to block the road of inquiry, halt the regress of interpretations, in order to get something done.[47] So rigorous argumentation—the practice which is made possible by agreement on criteria, on stopping-places—is no more *generally* desirable than blocking the road of inquiry is generally desirable.[48] It is something which it is convenient to have if you can get it. If the purposes you are engaged in fulfilling can be specified pretty clearly in advance (e.g., finding out how an enzyme functions, preventing violence in the streets, proving theorems), then you *can* get it. If they are not (as in the search for a just society, the resolution of a moral dilemma, the choice of a symbol of ultimate concern, the quest for a "postmodernist" sensibility), then you probably cannot, and you should not try for it. If what you are interested in is *philosophy*, you *certainly* will not get it—for one of the things which the various vocabularies for describing things differ about is the purpose of describing things. The philosopher will not want to beg the question between these various descriptions in advance. The urge to make philosophy into Philosophy is to make it the search for some final vocabulary, which can somehow be known in advance to be the common core, the truth of, all the other vocabularies which might be advanced in its place. This is the urge which the pragmatist thinks should be repressed, and which a post-Philosophical culture would have succeeded in repressing.

The most powerful reason for thinking that no such culture is possible is that seeing all criteria as no more than temporary resting places, constructed by a community to facilitate its inquiries, seems morally humiliating. Suppose that Socrates was wrong, that we have *not* once seen the Truth, and so will not, intuitively, recognize it when we see it again. This means that when the secret police come, when the torturers violate the innocent, there is nothing to be said to them of the form "There is something within you which you are betraying. Though you embody the practices of a totalitarian society which will endure forever, there is something beyond those practices which condemns you." This thought is hard to live with, as is Sartre's remark:

> Tomorrow, after my death, certain people may decide to establish fascism, and the others may be cowardly or miserable enough to let them get away with it. At that moment, fascism will be the truth of man, and so much the worse for us. In reality, things will be as much as man has decided they are.[49]

This hard saying brings out what ties Dewey and Foucault, James and Nietzsche, together—the sense that there is nothing deep down inside us except what we have put there ourselves, no criterion that we have not created in the course of creating a practice, no standard of rationality that is not an appeal to such a criterion, no rigorous argumentation that is not obedience to our own conventions.

A post-Philosophical culture, then, would be one in which men and women felt themselves alone, merely finite, with no links to something Beyond. On the pragmatist's account, positivism was only a halfway stage in the development of such a culture—the progress toward, as Sartre puts it, doing without God. For positivism preserved a god in its notion of Science (and in its notion of "scientific philosophy"), the notion of a portion of culture where we touched something not ourselves, where we found Truth naked, relative to no description. The culture of positivism thus produced endless swings of the pendulum between the view that "values are merely 'relative' (or 'emotive,' or 'subjective')" and the view that bringing the "scientific method" to bear on questions of political and moral choice was the solution to all our problems. Pragmatism, by contrast, does not erect Science as an idol to fill the place once held by God. It views science as one genre of literature—or, put the other way around, literature and the arts of inquiries, on the same footing as scientific inquiries. Thus it sees ethics as neither more "relative" or "subjective" than scientific theory, nor as needing to be made "scientific." Physics is a way of trying to cope with various bits of the universe; ethics is a matter of trying to cope with other bits. Mathematics helps physics do its job, literature and the arts help ethics do its. Some of these inquiries come up with propositions, some with narratives, some with paintings. The question of what proposition to assert, which pictures to look at, what narratives to listen to and comment on and retell, are all questions about what will help us get what we want (or about what we *should* want).

The question of whether the pragmatist view of truth—that it is not a profitable topic—is itself *true* is thus a question about whether a post-Philosophical culture is a good thing to try for. It is not a question about what the word "true" means, nor about the requirements of an adequate philosophy of language, nor about whether the world "exists independently of our minds," nor about whether the intuitions of our culture are captured in the pragmatists' slogans. There is no way in which the issue between the pragmatist and his opponent can be tightened up and resolved according to criteria, agreed to by both sides. This is one of those issues which puts everything up for grabs at once—where there is no point in trying to find agreement about "the data" or about what would count as deciding the question. But the messiness of the issue is not a reason for setting it aside. The issue between religion and secularism was no less messy, but it was important that it got decided as it did.

If the account of the contemporary philosophical scene which I have offered here is correct, then the issue about the truth of pragmatism is the issue which all the most important cultural developments since Hegel have conspired to put before us. But, like its predecessor, it is not going to be resolved by any sudden new discovery of how things really are. It will be decided, if history allows us the leisure to decide such issues, only by a slow and painful choice between alternative self-images.

NOTES

1. A. J. Ayer, *The Origins of Pragmatism* (San Francisco: Freeman, Cooper, 1968) is a good example of the point of view.
2. For this attitude, see Habermas' criticism of Peirce in *Knowledge and Human Interests* (Boston: Beacon Press, 1968), chap. 6, esp. p. 135.
3. Richard Rorty, *Philosophy and the Mirror of Nature* (Princeton: Princeton University Press, 1979).
4. To appear in the Cambridge University Press *Modern European Philosophy* series.
5. See Davidson, "On the Very Idea of a Conceptual Scheme," *Proceedings and Addresses of the American Philosophical Association,* 47 (1973–74): 5–20. See also my discussion of Davidson in chap. 6 of *Philosophy and the Mirror of Nature,* and in "Transcendental Arguments, Self-Reference and Pragmatism" (*Transcendental Arguments and Science,* ed. P. Bieri, R. P. Horstmann, and L. Krüger [Dordrecht: Reidel, 1979]), pp. 77–103.
6. *Collected Papers of Charles Sanders Peirce,* ed. Charles Hartshorne, Paul Weiss, and Arthur Burks (Cambridge, Mass.: Harvard University Press, 1933–58), 5.313–314.
7. Jacques Derrida, *Of Grammatology* (Baltimore: Johns Hopkins University Press, 1976), p. 49.
8. Wilfrid Sellars, *Science, Perception and Reality* (London: Routledge and Kegan Paul, 1967), p. 160.
9. Ludwig Wittgenstein, *Philosophical Investigations* (New York: Macmillan, 1953), p. 18.
10. Hans-Georg Gadamer, *Philosophical Hermeneutics* (Berkeley: University of California Press, 1976), p. 19.
11. Michel Foucault, *The Order of Things* (New York: Random House, 1973), p. 386.
12. Martin Heidegger, *On the Way to Language* (New York: Harper and Row, 1971), p. 50.
13. See Hans Sluga, *Frege* (London: Routledge and Kegan Paul, 1980), Introduction and chap. 1, for a discussion of Frege's neo-Kantian, anti-naturalistic motives.
14. Thomas Nagel, *Mortal Questions* (Cambridge: Cambridge University Press, 1979), p. xii.
15. Ibid., p. 171.
16. See Hilary Putnam's definition of "metaphysical realism" in these terms in his *Meaning and the Moral Sciences* (London: Routledge and Kegan Paul, 1978), p. 125.
17. Hilary Putnam, *Mind, Language and Reality* (Cambridge: Cambridge University Press, 1975), p. 236.
18. Hartry Field, "Meaning, Logic and Conceptual Role," *Journal of Philosophy,* LXXIV (1977): 398.
19. Field, "Tarski's Theory of Truth," *Journal of Philosophy,* LXIX (1972): 373.
20. Putnam attributes this point to Leeds in his *Meaning and the Moral Sciences,* p. 16. Field would presumably reply that it *is* explanatory because we use people's beliefs as indicators of how things are in the world. (See "Tarski's Theory of Truth," p. 371, and also Field, "Mental Representations," in *Readings in Philosophical Psychology,* ed. Ned Block, vol. 2 [Cambridge, Mass.: Harvard University Press, 1981], p. 103, for this argument.) The pragmatist should rejoin that what we do is not to say, "I shall take what Jones says as,

ceteris paribus, a reliable indication of how the world is," but rather to say, "I shall, *ceteris paribus,* say what Jones says."

21. Many pragmatists (including myself) have not, in fact, always been wise enough to avoid this trap. Peirce's definition of truth as that to which inquiry will converge has often seemed a good way for the pragmatist to capture the realists' intuition that Truth is One. But he should not try to capture it. There is no more reason for the pragmatist to try to assimilate this intuition than for him to accept the intuition that there is always One Morally Best Thing To Do in every situation. Nor is there any reason for him to think that a science in which, as in poetry, new vocabularies proliferate without end, would be inferior to one in which all inquirers communicated in The Language of Unified Science. (I am grateful to discussions with Putnam for persuading me to reject the seductions of Peirce's definition—although, of course, Putnam's reasons for doing so are not mine. I am also grateful to a recent article by Simon Blackburn, "Truth, Realism, and the Regulation of Theory," *Midwest Studies in Philosophy,* V [1980]: 353–371, which makes the point that "It may be that the notion of improvement [in our theories] is sufficient to interpret remarks to the effect that my favorite theory may be wrong, but not itself sufficient to justify the notion of a limit of investigation" [p. 358].)
22. William James, *Pragmatism and the Meaning of Truth* (Cambridge, Mass.: Harvard University Press, 1978), p. 42.
23. Ibid., p. 322.
24. Note that the question of whether there can be a "systematic theory of meaning for a language" is ambiguous between the question "Can we give a systematic account of what the user of a given natural language would have to know to be a competent speaker?" and "Can we get a philosophical semantics which will provide a foundation for the rest of philosophy?" Michael Dummett runs these two questions together in a confusing way when he says that Wittgenstein's metaphilosophical view that philosophy cannot be systematic presupposes that there can be no "systematic theory of meaning." (Dummett, *Truth and Other Enigmas* [Cambridge, Mass.: Harvard University Press, 1978], p. 453). Dummett says, rightly, that Wittgenstein has to admit

> that the fact that anyone who has a mastery of any given language is able to understand an infinity of sentences of that language . . . can hardly be explained otherwise than by supposing that each speaker has an implicit grasp of a number of general principles governing the use in sentences of words in the language. (Ibid., p. 451)

and thus is committed to such a "systematic theory." But by granting that this is the only explanation of the fact in question, one is not committed to thinking, with Dummett, that "philosophy of language is the foundation for all the rest of philosophy" (Ibid., p. 454). One might, with Wittgenstein, *not* see philosophy as a matter of giving "analyses," and thus might deny the presupposition of Dummett's claim that "the correctness of any piece of analysis carried out in another part of philosophy cannot be fully determined until we know with reasonable certainty what form a correct theory of meaning for our language must take" (Ibid.). This latter remark is Dummett's only explication of the sense in which philosophy of language is "foundational" for the rest of philosophy. As I tried to argue in chap. 6 of *Philosophy and the Mirror of Nature,* the fact that philosophical semantics grew up in the bosom of metaphilosophy does not mean that a mature and successful semantics—a successful "systematic theory of meaning for a language"—would necessarily have any metaphilosophical import. Children often disown their parentage. Dummett is certainly right that Wittgenstein's work does not "provide a solid foundation for future work in philosophy" in the sense in which the positivists hoped (and Dummett still hopes) that Frege's work does (Ibid., p. 452). But only someone antecedently convinced that semantics must give philosophers guidance about how to "analyze" would blame this lack of a foundation on the fact that Wittgenstein fails to "provide us with any outline of what a correct theory of meaning would look like" (Ibid., p. 453). Wittgenstein believed, on nonsemantical grounds, that philosophy was not the sort of thing that had foundations, semantical or otherwise.

25. Dummett, *Truth and Other Enigmas,* p. 358.
26. On the claim that pragmatism cannot explain why science works (elaborated most fully in a forthcoming book by Richard Boyd), see Simon Blackburn, "Truth, Realism, and the Regulation of Theory" (cited in n. 21 above), esp. pp. 356–360. I agree with Blackburn's final conclusion that ". . . realism, in the disputed cases of morals, conditionals, counterfactuals, mathematics, can only be worth defending in an interpretation which makes it non-controversial" (p. 370).
27. This bag of tricks contains lots of valuable antiques, some bequeathed to the pragmatist by Berkeley *via* the British Idealists. This association of pragmatism with Berkeley's arguments for phenomenalism has led many realists (Lenin, Putnam) to suggest that pragmatism is (a) just a variant of idealism and (b) inherently "reductionist." But an argument for Berkeleian phenomenalism requires not only the pragmatic maxim that things are what they are known as, but the claim (deservedly criticized by Reid, Green, Wittgenstein, Sellars, Austin, *et al.*) that we can make sense of Berkeley's notion of "idea." Without this latter notion, we cannot proceed further in the direction of the British Idealist claim that "reality is spiritual in nature." Failure to distinguish among Berkeley's premises has led to a great deal of realist rhetoric about how pragmatists think reality is "malleable," do not appreciate the brutishness of the material world, and generally resemble idealists in not realizing that "physical things are externally related to minds." It must be confessed, however, that William James did sometimes say things which are susceptible to such charges. (See, e.g., the disastrously flighty passage at p. 125 of *Pragmatism.* Dewey occasionally wandered down the same gar en path.) As for reductionism, the pragmatist reply to this charge is that since he regards all vocabularies as tools for accomplishing purposes and none as representations of how things really are, he cannot possibly claim that "X's *really are* Y's," although he *can* say that it is more fruitful, for certain purposes, to use Y-talk than to use X-talk.
28. See Thompson Clarke, "The Legacy of Skepticism," *Journal of Philosophy,* LXIX (1972): 754–769, esp. the concluding paragraph. This essay is cited by both Cavell and Nagel as making clear the "depth" of the tradition of epistemological skepticism.
29. Nagel, *Mortal Questions,* p. xii.
30. Ibid., p. 35.
31. Ibid., pp. 35–36.
32. Ibid., p. 36.
33. Ibid., p. 37.
34. Iris Murdoch, *The Sovereignty of Good* (New York: Schocken, 1971), p. 8.
35. Ibid., p. 9.
36. Ibid., p. 27.
37. Ibid., pp. 28–30.
38. Daniel Dennett, *Brainstorms* (Montgomery, Vt.: Bradford Books, 1978), p. 228.
39. Nagel, *Mortal Questions,* pp. 182–193.
40. Wittgenstein, *Philosophical Investigations,* I, sect. 271.
41. Ibid., I, sect. 115.
42. Nagel, *Mortal Questions,* p. 170.

43. See Nelson Goodman, *Ways of Worldmaking* (Indianapolis: Hackett, 1978). I think that Goodman's trope of "many worlds" is misleading and that we need not go beyond the more straightforward "many descriptions of the same world" (provided one does not ask, "And what world is *that?*"). But his point that there is no way to compare descriptions of the world in respect of adequacy seems to me crucial, and in the first two chapters of this book he makes it very vividly.

44. Stanley Cavell, *The Claim of Reason* (Oxford: Oxford University Press, 1979), p. 388.

45. Hegel, *Philosophy of Right*, trans. T. M. Knox (Oxford: Oxford University Press, 1952), p. 11. This passage, like the famous one which follows ("When philosophy paints its grey in grey, then has a shape of life grown old. By a philosophy's grey on grey it cannot be rejuvenated but only understood. The owl of Minerva spreads its wings only with the falling of the dusk.") is not typical of Hegel, and is hard to reconcile with much of the rest of what he says about philosophy. But it perfectly represents the side of Hegel which helped create the historicism of the nineteenth century and which is built into the thinking of the present-day literary intellectual.

46. The opposition between the literary and the scientific cultures which C. P. Snow drew (in *The Two Cultures and the Scientific Revolution* [Cambridge: Cambridge University Press, 1959]) is, I think, even deeper and more important than Snow thought it. It is pretty well co-incident with the opposition between those who think of themselves as caught in time, as an evanescent moment in a continuing conversation, and those who hope to add a pebble from Newton's beach to an enduring structure. It is not an issue which is going to be resolved by literary critics learning physics or physicists reading the literary quarterlies. It was already drawn in Plato's time, when physics had not yet been invented, and when Poetry and Philosophy first squared off. (I think, incidentally, that those who criticize Snow along the lines of "not just *two* cultures, but many" miss his point. If one wants a neat dichotomy between the two cultures he was talking about, just ask any Eastern European censor which Western books are importable into his country. The line he draws will cut across fields like history and philosophy, but will almost always let physics in and keep highbrow novels out. The nonimportable books will be the ones which might suggest new vocabularies for self-description.)

47. There are, of course, lots of criteria which cut across all divisions between parts of culture—e.g., the laws of logic, the principle that a notorious liar's reports do not count as evidence, and the like. But these do not possess some special authority by virtue of their universality, any more than the set consisting of the fulcrum, the screw, and the lever is privileged by virtue of contributing to every other machine.

48. Peirce said that "the first rule of reason" was "Do not block the way of inquiry" (*Collected Papers,* 1.135). But he did not mean that one should always go down any road one saw—a point that comes out in his emphasis on "logical self-control" as a corollary of "ethical self-control." (See, e.g., *Collected Papers,* 1.606.) What he was getting at in his "rule of reason" was the same point as he makes about the ubiquity of language—that we should never think that the regress of interpretation can be stopped once and for all, but rather realize that there may always be a vocabulary, a set of descriptions, around the corner which will throw everything into question once again. To say that obedience to criteria is a good thing *in itself* would be like saying that self-control is a good in itself. It would be a species of Philosophical puritanism.

49. Jean-Paul Sartre, *L'Existentialisme est un Humanisme* (Paris: Nagel, 1946), pp. 53–54.

SERIOUS PHILOSOPHY AND FREEDOM OF SPIRIT

Ernest Sosa

Philosophers have long taken sides in a great divide by adopting one or more of a set of views that tend to go together:

FREEDOM	SERIOUSNESS
Subjectivism	Objectivism
Relativism	Absolutism
Antirealism	Realism
Historicism	Universalism

On the left is "free-spirited philosophy"; on the right "serious philosophy."

I wish to lay out a view of seriousness, and to consider recent attacks on that view from the side of the free spirited: deconstruction and textualism, hermeneutics, critical theory, and the new pragmatism. Without defining what all forms of freedom have in common, I shall draw from them a combined critique against seriousness. I will also examine, occasionally and in passing, positive ideas conjured up by the free. But mainly I wish to consider their combined critique of seriousness.

The combined critique—labeled here "free spirit" for convenience—is not one that *all* "free spirits" would accept. But all sides do contribute, some more extensively than others. Moreover, the influence of free spirits extends far beyond academic philosophy. It is found not only in historical studies, with Michel Foucault, but also in literary and critical theory, now widespread, with Jacques Derrida, Richard Rorty, and less serious cohorts. An allied phenomenon in legal scholarship is the critical legal studies movement, whose theorist Roberto Unger[1] preaches the sway of ideology over all value and norm, and the optionality and groundlessness of all politico-legal frameworks; and also advocates constant change and revision—framework shattering (groundlessly for its own sake, presumably).

I. SERIOUS PHILOSOPHY

Serious philosophy here means the Platonic tradition committed to an objective reality knowable to mind but independent from being known or conceived or otherwise minded—independent anyhow from its *human* minding. This makes room for idealism, and allows even Berkeley his rightful place

Reprinted by permission of the *Journal of Philosophy* and the author, from Ernest Sosa, "Serious Philosophy and Freedom of Spirit," *Journal of Philosophy* 84 (1987), pp. 707–726.

in that tradition. Berkeleyan spirits, from God on down, really do their minding without that minding requiring for its reality the support of any minding directed upon it; in that sense, therefore, it has a reality independent of being minded. The same is true for the Cartesian cogito, and for much axiology or ethics whose foundation for the good or the right resides in human preference and allows that goodness and rightness such objectivity as may lie in the reality of such preference—a preference which might exist in itself and unminded.

According to serious philosophy, moreover, objective reality provides us not only with objects of knowledge, but also with constraining starting points and obligatory methods for reason. These ultimate starting points and ultimate methods define an ahistorical framework that determines the legitimate use of reason and fixes the conditions and extent of rationality, knowledge, goodness, and rightness.

Some would think such philosophy positively *dour.* One or another element would be denied not only by free spirits but by many who view themselves as serious but not dour.[2] For example, many would reject moral realism and evaluative objectivity generally, while accepting objective facts of nature or mathematics. Others would reject realism wholesale with regard to values, nature, *and* mathematics. Logical positivists once rejected all realism by rejecting the very question of realism as a worthless pseudoquestion. But the question has proved hardier and more intriguing than its detractors. Today realism is again widely debated across the whole field of philosophy, and even moral realism once more elicits serious attention.

Serious philosophy and its free-spirited opposition lie at opposite ends of a spectrum, therefore, and no *pure* exemplar of either may be accepted by anyone today. I have chosen to compare extremes for the sake of a starker, more dramatic contrast. And, for convenience, I shall classify a philosophy as free spirited if it contains some significant admixture of the pure article.

"Is there a single major school or movement of philosophy—analytic or continental—which today approaches the serious end of our spectrum?" Suppose there is not. Why should one care? Schools and movements attract the public eye by dramatic opposition to the conventional wisdom. The latter, by contrast, is seldom unified into any explicit, concise formulation, and even more seldom is it baptized with any catchy label.

The present paper may be viewed as pitting analytic philosophy against all other philosophy. But that is a twofold mistake. Too much of analytic philosophy is not serious; think of the varieties of neopragmatism, only the most abandoned of which is considered explicitly here. And too much of all other philosophy is not free; think of institutional Thomism or Marxism. Free-spirited philosophy is certainly represented within analysis, as is serious philosophy outside analysis. Our lines of controversy are *not* drawn geographically or ideologically.

A final preliminary caveat: no proof is offered here for the tradition of seriousness, nor even weighty reasons in its favor. I wish rather to consider reasoning aimed in recent years *against* that tradition.

This introductory section has made the following six points:

(a) Serious philosophy encompasses Platonic traditions of objective realism.
(b) It believes in real objects of knowledge and in objective methods for reason.
(c) Seriousness and freedom lie at opposite ends of a spectrum; most of us fall somewhere in the middle.
(d) Perhaps no celebrated school or movement lies today near the serious end—but that is of limited importance.
(e) The division between seriousness and freedom is not geographical or ideological.
(f) No positive argument for seriousness shall be offered here—only a defense against attacks from the side of freedom.

II. PHILOSOPHY FOR FREE SPIRITS

It is a main traditional goal of serious philosophy to uncover more and more of the objective framework of reason. What can possibly remain for philosophy to do if we reject the very existence of such a framework? What remains is, of course, the task of free-spirit philosophy, variegated as it is bound to be. In the book of some free spirits, the Word was not only in the beginning, but is even—incredibly—said to be *everything.*[3] Free spirits are often textualists, readers and authors who live for the conversation, the only point of which, insofar as it has any extrinsic point at all, is to go on and on without end. Free-spirit philosophers do try to understand how things in the broadest sense of the term hang together in the broadest sense of the expression. And they claim to be aided in that endeavor by their lighter metaphysical baggage and their less ambitious epistemological commitments. Such free spirits would function in society as all-purpose critics or utility intellectuals, renouncing any shared disciplinary matrix and any common professional purpose.

So much for a life and direction found more lovely and apt by free spirits of our day. Here now is their brief against seriousness.

III. OBJECTIONS TO THE TRADITION OF SERIOUSNESS

It has been charged that only an unwarranted fear supports the tradition of serious philosophy, a threatening either/or: either there is the fixed, binding framework of reason, or we face intellectual and moral arbitrariness and chaos. According to some, it is this Cartesian anxiety[4] that needs to be exorcised. Once emancipated from that dichotomy, we may then move beyond objectivism and relativism, a task more practical than theoretical. What the world needs now is a profound recognition that the proper end of man is not to mirror passively any dead objective reality, but to work actively for solidarity among the living.[5]

Two chief arguments urged by free spirits deserve serious attention. The first is an argument against theoria and for phronesis, against the possibility of algorithmic calculation on any question of values, be it practical or theoretical, and in favor of deliberation and wise judgment. The second flows from the alleged failure of serious philosophy. "Given its total lack of success," we are told, "it is time to put a stop to its pretensions. Epistemology in particular deserves to be laid to rest, for its oft-repeated lie that it would found culture if allowed the time and attention." We consider these two arguments in turn.

IV. FIRST ARGUMENT AGAINST SERIOUSNESS: PHRONESIS VERSUS THEORIA

Invective now converges from all sides on the project of legitimizing or founding segments of our culture. For example, we are told that justice and freedom are incommensurable, and that there is no true principle that can give general priority to either over the other, nor is there any that will show us in advance how to resolve all possible conflicts, nor even all likely or actual ones. It is also well known that the judge and the legislator receive from ethics or morality no universal principles from which it might always be possible to deduce the right verdict or legislation. Deliberation requires, on the contrary, the pondering of reasons in favor and against, and the estimation of their respective combined weights as well as an assessment of the balance. All of that seems to me both true and important. If to found or legitimize requires providing axioms or even just coherent and general theories that would logically imply all that is to be founded, humanity is obviously in no position to "found" either law or morality or science. And, if we did manage to provide such a foundation for any of our science, that would just be to succeed with more and better science. One thing should be clear, nevertheless, for science as well as for law and morality: even if our success to date has been modest, that does not show we ought to quit. Where would physics be if Galileo, Newton, and Einstein had yielded to such reasoning? *Besides,* suppose that *fundamentally* there are *several* incommensurable factors; and suppose it to be quite *impossible* to arrive at a general and coherent theory that will logically imply a decision for all issues which might possibly or even probably come before us. Even so, it does not follow we ought to find for freedom and against seriousness. Fundamental factors that weigh for or against when one evaluates or deliberates may after all be factors whose validity, though incommensurable, is yet objective, absolute, and universal. Each fundamental factor, whether positive or negative, may have its own vectorial character objectively, absolutely, and universally.

So much in regard to the values and reasons that enter deliberation and evaluation. Let us next consider more generally the nature and validity of our beliefs.

"Accuracy, consistency, scope, simplicity, and fruitfulness" are values that, according to Thomas Kuhn,[6] inform scientific theory choice. When these values are in conflict, says Kuhn, rational scientists may still disagree in their judgments without showing any lack of information or failure of intellect. What Kuhn has claimed about science is found by Hans-Georg Gadamer (with inspiration from Aristotle) all over our lives and culture, and is accordingly made a major theme of his philosophy over nearly the full stretch of a long career. Deliberation and practical judgment are different in kind from mechanical proof or algorithmic calculation. A proper model is the judge invoking precedents, and not the accountant doing his sums. If you solemnly promised to be on time for a meeting but then your child needs some medicine and might be helped by getting it early, and you cannot both be on time and give the medicine early, what are you to do? Is there any rule to recall from mother's knee, or draw from religion, or get from our shared fund of wisdom, to solve our problem algorithmically? Can we even hope to *invent* a rule with any plausibility at all? Not when crucial factors seem in the relevant sense incommensurable. How solemn was the promise? How important is the meeting? How weighty is the claim of the group on one's loyalty? How serious is the child's illness? What are the possible consequences? What risks or discomforts are implied by delaying? How assured can we be of these matters? However assured we may be, there is simply no hope for algorithmic calculation on our choice as parent. The factors involved do not severally admit each its own metric, much less a common metric that would permit calculation—none accessible to us, anyhow, either now or in our most remote horizon. In such matters, we simply have no substitute for deliberation and choice by a wise and sensitive judge, no substitute for phronesis rather than theoria.

Even *if* we grant that our lack is not merely epistemic, that no increase in intelligence or information would help (which seems less than certain and obvious), what follows? Just because reason is not in a straightjacket, do we infer it can jump to the moon? That would be lunacy indeed. We have long known that reality is not determinate, not at least in terms accessible to our limited brains. When does night begin, or even twilight? When does baldness begin, or even thinness of hair? Such questions are to be met at every turn, whether we notice them or not. In the absence of any sharp difference between baldness and nonbaldness, there is yet the clear difference between a shiny pate and a full head of hair. Day turns into night at no precise instant, but noon differs *toto caelo* from midnight.

Accordingly, if the Cartesian anxiety is the fearsome either/or that requires algorithmic determinacy on pain of chaos, it might be possible to exorcise it by reflecting on how obvious it is that right now nearly everywhere we find neither the determinacy nor the chaos. From the fact that no one alternative is forced objectively, it is a fallacy to infer that no alternative is objectively foreclosed. And, if Buridan's ass is regarded as absurd and his predicament repugnant to reason, that may call for edifying therapy, but who among us is today so radical a devotee of reason? [7]

Naturally, the application of phronesis in particular situations cannot take place in a logical vacuum. Deliberative reason needs pertinent values to weigh, and factual assumptions in whose light to apply them. Where can the free spirit turn for such values and assumptions? Why does one accept that a promise was made or that a child is ill? Why suppose that such factors are relevant to one's decision? Gadamer speaks for many when he appeals here to the lore of the tribe, to tradition and precedent. And it is, of course, undeniable that we are creatures of our time and group, schooled in its way of life and informed by its habits of thought from the dawn of our reason. But our question requires not sociology or anthropology, but philosophy. We wish to know *not only* how we get to be the way we are. We wish to know whether and why it is good or right or fitting for us to be that way. We wish to know not only how we get to believe that a high thermometer reading means a high fever and a high fever an illness. We wish to know also whether and why it is that deriving our belief that way makes it an appropriate thing to believe. We wish to know not only how we get to believe that having promised is a good reason for keeping one's promise, but also whether and why that is a good thing to believe.

Getting to know how we acquire our commonsensical or scientific beliefs does perhaps give us a large part of the answer to philosophical questions about the nature and justification of our beliefs. But it cannot possibly be the whole answer, since plenty of superstitious and evil beliefs also get acquired all the time, and they too admit sociological or anthropological explanation. Plenty of evil and superstitious beliefs get acquired by imbibing tradition and the lore of a tribe. Nazi ideology, South African apartheid, and the mountain people's form of life are only three notorious examples.[8] So it is natural for us to wonder what the difference is, to wonder what we can say most generally to explain what makes our way better than theirs (in *some* respects anyhow), and our body of beliefs more credible. It might be difficult to generalize, but, if there really are general differences, as undeniably there are, it should be possible to state them and give them some degree of systematic order, and to provide answers with some degree of generality about the superiority of one system over the others. It is true that, at some level, there will be no real alternative to simply reaffirming the content of one's own system and hence begging the question *if* one is engaged in debate. But that does not mean one necessarily acts inappropriately in doing so, any more than reaffirming the law of contradiction would be inappropriate in the face of its denial. Some questions demand begging. This response has been called "too easy," but it is hard to fathom what that could mean. Suppose we reach a position to say that, at bottom, it is always factor *F* that makes a belief of our own justified, whatever the belief might be. *F* might be thought to be experience, or intuition, or convention, or pragmatic working, or coping, or coherence, or perhaps a combination of logic and observation—if we are lucky it will be something simple and unified. And suppose we are then challenged to explain what justifies us in holding that very belief. What can we possibly say in reply except that here again it is the presence of factor *F*? Will someone object that we beg the question and argue in a circle? The answer is, of course, that we do, but that, at this level of generality, it simply cannot be helped, and that regretting it is as bad as regretting that we cannot make a round cube.[9]

At just this point in the argument, there is a great temptation to say that, fundamentally, it is all relative and that factor *F* is just *our* basic source of justification, that others may differ, and, if so, to each his own. And this trend, once begun, extends easily to truth and morality as well. Now, if the claim is that there is no truth, justification, goodness, or rightness, *period,* but only justification, etc., *relative* to system *Si* (for *S*1, *S*2, . . .), then our justification for our own system is just relative to itself, and that is just to say that it affirms its own justification, truth, or what have you, that it affirms this at least implicitly, by implication. But, of course, many radically different and seemingly clashing systems can do the same, including that of the Nazis, that of the present South-African leadership, and perhaps even that of the mountain people. Whence the need to burden our own system with an axiom that there is no justification (truth, etc.) except relative to a system, in the sense that there is not even the very notion of justification (truth, etc.) on its own, *period*? That is just self-destructive and unnecessarily so. If all I say when I say that our system is justified (etc.) is that it is justified (etc.) relative to itself, and, if all this amounts to is that it approves of itself, either explicitly or implicitly, and, if many clashing systems do the same, how then can my commitment to our system be anything more than arbitrary willfulness? And, if that is its status, how can the justification of anything relative to such a system rise above that level of arbitrary willfulness? Where would the extra increment of justification come from? And how could it possibly make up the lack in its fundamental principles, the principles relative to which one must attain whatever justification one ever does attain?

Gadamer would offer the following defense:

> It is a grave misunderstanding to assume that emphasis on the essential factor of tradition which enters into all understanding implies an uncritical acceptance of tradition and sociopolitical conservatism. . . . In truth the confrontation of our historic tradition is always a critical challenge of this tradition. . . . Every experience is such a confrontation.[10]

But, as Richard Bernstein argues in response, we are left wondering what one might appeal to in a critique of one's own tradition:

> The claim that Gadamer makes about Aristotle's understanding of natural law (the universal element) as something that is essentially open to interpretation and that is only specified when mediated in a concrete ethical situation that demands choice and decision is paradigmatic, for Gadamer, of the application of all ethical principles and norms. But as Aristotle stresses, and Gadamer realizes, phronesis presupposes the existence of nomoi (funded laws) in the polis or

> community. This is what keeps phronesis from degenerating into the mere cleverness or calculation that characterizes the deinos (the clever person). Given a community in which there is a living, shared acceptance of ethical principles and norms, then *phronesis* as the mediation of such universals in particular situations makes good sense.
>
> The problem for us today, the chief characteristic of our hermeneutical situation, is that we are in a state of great confusion and uncertainty (some might even say chaos) about what norms or "universals" ought to govern our practical lives. Gadamer realizes—but I do not think he squarely faces the issues that it raises—that we are living in a time when the very conditions required for the exercise of *phronesis*—the shared acceptance and stability of universal principles and laws—are themselves threatened (or do not exist). . . .
>
> Furthermore, Gadamer does not adequately clarify the type of discourse that is appropriate when questions about the validity of basic norms (universals) are raised. How is such recognition and agreement to be achieved? When there is serious disagreement about what norms ought to be binding, should all participants be able to have a say? When pressed about these conditions, Gadamer frequently deals with a different issue. He tells us that such universals are inherited from tradition, that they are essentially open, that their meaning can be specified only in application to concrete, practical situations. But this does not clarify the issue of what we are to do in a situation in which there is confusion or conflict about which norms or universals are appropriate, or how we are to evaluate a situation in which we question the validity of such norms (op. cit., pp. 154–158).

If phronesis is, by definition, the application of laws already accepted in the community, it is of no use in deciding an issue for which there are no pertinent laws, which in a given community might even include the issue of how to overcome some perceived defect in a basic law. Moreover, if phronesis is so defined, how can one even make sense of the very notion of a defect in a basic law?

Is there not indeed a deeper phronesis which is not to be defined as the application of already accepted rules or laws, but is rather to be employed in the assessment of even the most fundamental community *mores*? Is there not deliberation, weighing of relevant values and reasons, even on matters untouched by such mores, or at least on matters that admit plenty of factors whose pertinence does not derive from any commonly accepted rule or law?

What is more, and what seems crucial here, are there not two fundamentally different sorts of laws? There are laws whose ultimate legitimacy and foundation lie simply in community agreement, so that, if the community had opted for requiring the opposite behavior, then that would have been the required behavior in the circumstances, with just as much legitimacy and foundation. For example, whether we should drive on the right or, on the contrary, should drive on the left depends simply on what rule the community adopts. But whether one should kill someone else at random and in cold blood just for the fun of it does not seem the same sort of question. Refraining from such activity is not a requirement that derives its force merely from the arbitrary conventions of one's tribe. Here we have a sort of Euthyphro question: Are the mores good because they prescribe the good, or is the good good because it is prescribed by the mores? To which we may well say: some of each. It all depends, for example, on whether it is driving or murder under discussion.

If there is nothing beyond the individual or collective will, if there is no way to understand how such will could possibly *go wrong*—since there is nothing with which it needs to agree—then what possible sense could there be in our "state of great confusion and uncertainty (some might even say chaos) about what norms or 'universals' ought to govern our practical lives"? Either there is something beyond that decision, relative to which it can be evaluated, or it makes no apparent sense for us to worry over which decision to take or which rule or convention to adopt, since whatever it turns out to be would be right by definition.

V. SECOND ARGUMENT AGAINST SERIOUSNESS: DISAGREEMENT

The second main argument against serious philosophy calls it a monumental failure that has had its chance and deserves no more attention, since it has not "paid off." And just why has it failed, why has it worked so poorly? The fundamental reason to which the rhetoric of failure reduces here is our remarkable lack of agreement both diachronically and synchronically. But why exactly is agreement so important? Is any institution or activity within which we fail to reach substantial agreement one to be rejected and abandoned? Is any institution or activity that yields extensive agreement to be embraced? In that competition, Athens is no match for Sparta, and fanatical cults deserve our respect and support.

Clearly it cannot be agreement per se that is relevant and important. But then what sort of agreement shall it be? One plausible restriction is anathema to the free: that it be agreement whose existence is best explained by the correctness of its object. But really that is nothing special about agreement in particular; it is rather a feature shared by our legitimate faculties and methods generally: including perception and memory, for example. Agreement that *p*, ostensible perception that *p*, ostensible memory that *p*—the acceptability of such profferings is always aided by the explicability of the proffering through the truth of what is proffered. In a fuller treatment of the topic, the variety of threads whose interweaving makes up a living tradition would deserve unraveling. Suffice it here to distinguish rules like those which specify the side of the road one is to use, again, from rules such as the moral and legal injunction against premeditated murder. The former rules are just arbitrary conventions which clearly might have been the reverse with no loss, but the latter rules are more than just conventions to facilitate interaction in keeping with ethnocentric goals. (More on agreement below.)

Serious philosophers believe in a reality independent of being minded by us, though one knowable by us. That reality is said to provide us not only with objects of knowledge, but also with compelling starting points of reason, along with its obligatory methods. And these starting points and methods are supposed to constitute a framework of reason that determines the conditions and extent of rationality, knowledge, goodness, and rightness. Finally, uncovering more and more of this framework is held to be a main goal of philosophy. Thus, for the serious, there are facts of nature and of logic not derived from anyone's thoughts or decisions, and there are moral desiderata with a status and validity not derived merely from the individual or social will (each of which might conceivably have willed quite differently, and each of which might even have willed in a way opposed to the way in which they do in fact will). For example, it is a fact of nature that the earth is round, and the earth might have been round even if there never had evolved or otherwise existed any people or other finite thinkers. As for a particular simple fact of logic, take the principle of identity that nothing is diverse from itself: even if there never had been finite thinkers at all, still nothing would have been diverse from itself. Finally, inflicting pain just for the sake of doing so, just for its own sake, is something that would have been evil even if we all had converted to some cult that urged the opposite.

Free spirits are radically opposed to the spirit of seriousness. For the free there is absolutely nothing independent of the collective will of the tribe: neither natural facts, nor facts of logic, nor moral desiderata. How, then, can they respond to the intuition that the roundness of the earth and the impossibility of self-diversity are independent facts whose status does not derive from anyone's acceptance or desire? The earth might still have been round even if life had never evolved and there never had existed any finite thinkers at all. And the earth was round and its surface layers contained various distinct substances even before the evolution of life (not to mention thought or consciousness). Otherwise how to explain such evolution? For life and consciousness to have evolved, must there not have been some pre-existing substances, or at the very least must there not have been some pre-existing events or processes not yet involving life or consciousness, namely the evolutionary events or processes that led eventually to life or consciousness? And however imperfectly known by us, those events must have had some definite nature and character, if we are to suppose that they would causally explain how it is that out of them life or consciousness eventually evolved.[11]

VI. WHAT TO MAKE OF OUR INTUITIONS?

Speaking of intuitions, a leading free spirit argues as follows:

> [The neopragmatist's] *only* argument for thinking that these intuitions and vocabularies should be eradicated is that the intellectual tradition to which they belong has not paid off, is more trouble than it is worth, has become an incubus. . . . Dogmatism of intuitions is no worse, or better, than the pragmatist's inability to give noncircular arguments.
>
> This upshot of the confrontation between the pragmatist and the intuitive realist about the status of intuitions can be described either as a conflict of intuitions about the importance of intuitions, or as a preference for one vocabulary over another. The realist will favor the first description, and the pragmatist, the second. It does not matter which description one uses, as long as it is clear that *the issue is one about whether philosophy should try to find natural starting-points which are distinct from cultural traditions, or whether all philosophy should do is compare and contrast cultural traditions.* . . . The intuitive realist thinks that there is such a thing as Philosophical truth because he thinks that, deep down beneath all the texts, there is something which is not just one more text but that to which various texts are trying to be "adequate." The pragmatist does not think that there is anything like that. He does not even think that there is anything isolable as "the purposes which we construct vocabularies and culture to fulfill" against which to test vocabularies and cultures. But he does think that in the process of playing vocabularies and cultures off against each other, we produce new and better ways of talking and acting—not better by reference to a previously known standard, but just better in the sense that they come to *seem* clearly better than their predecessors.[12]

"What really needs debate between the pragmatist and the intuitive realist," says Rorty, "is *not* whether we have intuitions to the effect that 'truth is more than assertability' or 'there is more to pains than brain-states' or 'there is a clash between modern physics and our sense of moral responsibility.' Of *course* we have such intuitions. How could we escape having them? We have been educated within an intellectual tradition built around such claims. . . . So the pragmatist's quarrel with the intuitive realist should be about the *status* of intuitions—about their *right* to be respected—as opposed to how particular intuitions might be 'synthesized' or 'explained away'. To treat his opponent properly, the pragmatist must begin by admitting that the realistic intuitions in question are as deep and compelling as the realist says they are. But he should then try to change the subject by asking, 'And what should we *do* about such intuitions—extirpate them, or find a vocabulary which does justice to them?' " (XXIX).

But that is not really to change the subject; what one should do is always part of the subject. And there is indeed a beautifully simple and conclusive way to end the problems of life: to bite the bullet and put it in one's brain. Short of that one can opt for the simple life of a monk, or a flower child, or a soldier, or any of a thousand others. Many are the ways to deaden oneself to the tortures of philosophy, but the more drastic deaden one also to its consolations. And, if one stops short of the final solution, then how far short? And on what basis? Again and again we are put through the litany of tradition, solidarity, community, forms of life, etc. Only two of the greatest will have none of this: one appeals directly to God through subjective truth, the other rejects the "herd" for the will to power of the superman.

Of course one can stop thinking about philosophy. How many ever really start? One can also stop thinking about history and geography and astronomy. One can refuse to look through telescopes, or to inspect maps, or to pore over documents. Is *that* all worth the trouble? And, if we are steadfast, we shall have little to say and little to worry about concerning the heavens, or the oceans, or the historical past. And, to lighten our burden of ignorance, we might even deny that there really are any such things, or better yet purge our language of all pertinent vocabulary. One might even just take a personal vow, and let the community do as it will. Again, why the obsession with solidarity, why the fetish of community agreement? Indeed, why believe in a community at all? Once we reject belief in an independent earth, and belief in an independent law of identity, and belief in the independent evil of pure malice, who can support a belief in others independent of oneself? What then am I to believe? That all the others are dependent on myself and my thought? Maybe the superman can manage that, or those who are willful enough to derive the very divinity from their subjective truth. The rest of us are not that egocentric. So how then are we to think of this community whose form of life is supposed the bedrock of our being, solidarity with which is exalted as the true meaning of our lives? Is each of its members dependent on the thought and vocabulary of all the others? And are all the others dependent on each?

That is, of course, a fatal flaw of any facile idealism. But, if we urge it against neopragmatism, we shall be missing the point. For the point now is not that the earth is dependent on us and our form of life. When realism is rejected by the neopragmatist, it is not rejected in favor of idealism or neutral monism or any other traditional "ism."[13]

VII. NEOPRAGMATISM

Whatever some cohorts may be up to, the neopragmatist rejects realism not in favor of some alternative metaphysical "ism," but only because the terms of the debate are rejected. So we must not press our neopragmatist to explain the ontological status of his community. The very notion of ontological status is now rejected, and cannot be brought against him without begging the question. There is the earth and there is also the community, and it is not true to say that the earth is independent of the community and its vocabulary and its form of life, nor that the community's members are independent of each other. Nor, of course, is there any dependence either, in *any* direction. Instead, the very notion of dependence is rejected along with its useless and outmoded way of thought. Naturally, that does not mean we stop believing in the earth, or denying self-diversity, or rejecting pure malice as unqualifiedly evil.[14] We just stop accepting the notion of metaphysical necessity, and, once necessity is rejected, metaphysical modality is rejected, and with metaphysical modality goes metaphysical dependence as well.[15]

But again we must return to our question: Is not *any* field of thought rejectable by rejecting the intuitions proper to that field? Take away the data and you clear away the theory. Take away the telescope, and even Galileo is helpless. Take away the documents, and even Gibbon is silenced. Take away modal intuitions, and even Leibniz is powerless.

There is anyhow, finally, the whole question of how to make sense of improving our practice, whether moral or intellectual. If the will, individual or collective, is the only "foundation" of practice; if, better, there is no such thing as a foundation of practice, if there is just what we do, period, then in what conceivable sense can we be *wrong* at any point in any of our practice? Even if we contradict ourselves, why not affect a Whitmanesque insouciance, and let it go at that? If our body of beliefs has no room for modality, how can it frame to itself the *possibility* that it is somewhere wrong? And the same goes for moral practice.

Finally, what are the prospects for philosophy if we abandon the spirit of seriousness and adopt the spirit of freedom? The free spirit often remains philosopher enough to make a general proposal. Rorty's neopragmatism, for example, is a philosophy of coping, and of seeing how "things hang together," a notion from Wilfrid Sellars which he repeatedly employs. And here is the sort of thing we are told. First, with regard to coping:

> The pragmatist does not think that there is anything . . . isolable as "the purposes which we construct vocabularies and cultures to fulfill" against which to test vocabularies and cultures. But he does think that in the process of playing vocabularies and cultures off against each other, we produce new and better ways of talking and acting—not better by reference to a previously known standard, but just better in the sense that they come to seem *clearly better than their predecessors.*[16]

As for hanging together:

> Pragmatism denies the possibility of getting beyond the Sellarsian notion of "seeing how things hang together"—which, for the bookish intellectual of recent times, means seeing how all the various vocabularies of all the various epochs and cultures hang together . . . In a post-Philosophical culture it would be clear that that is *all* that philosophy can be. It cannot answer questions about the relation of the

> thought of our time—the description it is using, the vocabularies it employs—to something which is not just some alternative vocabulary.[17]

Finally, in a recent pronouncement, Rorty throws into prominence the importance now assigned to *play*:

> My hope is that now, at the end of the century, we philosophers may be in a position to regain Hegel's sense of cultures and languages as matching themselves against past and future cultures and languages rather than against such extra-human forces as God, the moral law, or "the real world." This sense of ourselves as engaged in a process of reweaving our beliefs and desires rather than trying to bring these into conformity with something else lets us reappropriate Schiller's sense of play as the highest possibility for human life.[18]

Play is perhaps the highest possibility for some free spirits, but more serious philosophers could not be expected to agree. And, if to cope is just to be content or satisfied by your lights or by those of your culture, and, if that is our worthiest objective by the philosophy of coping, how can that philosophy stand up to the soft sell of the hidden persuaders, or the hard boot of political tyranny? The philosophy of coping has no way to conceive how we could be driven from the sunlight to a hideously worse piglife in a cave if the herdsmen take care to make us well satisfied: more satisfied and less dissatisfied than we are now in any case, impoverished though our lives would become. Feeling good and, with foreshortened horizons, quite content, we would even be denied the concepts to be *able* to feel discontent in a great variety of dimensions previously accessible to us. Our lives would still be *better,* since they would come to *seem* clearly better.

"The Philosophy of Coping," it might be replied, "has the internal resources to cope with our objections. The hidden persuaders and the tyrannical boot have a very delicate job to do. They cannot just excise historical memory, for this would not leave room for the situation of their victims to seem better than what went before. The victims must be allowed to retain the capacity for comparative historical judgment. But they cannot be allowed too much historical memory, lest they recall enough to recognize their loss. Even supposing a job so delicate to be actually practicable, the copers might still cope by noting the repugnancy of the outcome *from our present perspective.*"

The power of charisma (Hitler, Mussolini, Reverend Jones), the effects of fads and fashions on human preference, the plasticity of taste (the phenomenon of acquired taste, for instance)—anyone impressed by such phenomena will be less sanguine about the scope of unscrupulous power and authority. Suppose now that the greater value of "new and better ways of talking and acting" does derive simply from their coming "to *seem* clearly better than their predecessors." How then am I *now* to choose between receiving *A* or *B* at *t,* if both (i) now I prefer receiving *A* at *t,* but (ii) now I also know that, at *t,* I would prefer receiving *B?* Are (i) and (ii) so much as rationally compatible? We need to hear more from neopragmatism.

As for hanging together, what is that supposed to be? Historically, one associates this, first of all, with that apotheosis of modality which is objective idealism, with its coherence theory of everything. But that will hardly appeal to those who refuse to look above the concrete and contingent. With the rejection of modality we lose our best account of logical implication or entailment, without which we are clueless on how to understand coherence; and, if hanging together is not coherence, then what grasp are we left on what it might be? Is it something one should want to understand or describe at all, much less make the focus of one's lifework as philosopher?

VIII. SUMMARY

Free spirits reject the basis for serious philosophy by rejecting its key concept of necessity, and with it all logical modality. Candor compels the recognition that we do have modal intuitions, but these the free spirit would ignore or eradicate. For they are worthless fragments if detached from the intellectual tradition that gives them a place. And that whole tradition is to be deconstructed or demolished in favor of something more streamlined and functional, something that anyhow will "pay off" better. Exactly why, pray, has the tradition not "paid off"? Two main reasons are offered. *First,* the tradition has yielded only Derrida's "diaspora of institutes and languages, . . . the publications and techniques that follow on each other," [19] a Babel of journals and societies, schools and movements. *That* is not the way to scientific objectivity and progress. *Second,* the tradition's reason, bound by objective axioms and algorithms, is no longer credible. Phronesis—weighing of reasons, judgment—displaces calculation and deduction as a better understanding of how we arrive at beliefs and decisions responsibly and justifiably. Relevant facts are, of course, still needed along with relevant values as inputs to our use of phronesis, even if such values conflict incommensurably. But these factual and evaluative inputs derive for the free spirit from the tribe and not from any objective reality; they come rather with our Gadamerian "prejudices and traditions." Accordingly, we must dedicate ourselves not to reflecting dead reality but to improving dialogic community, not to objectivity but to solidarity.

I argue to the contrary. *First,* the dichotomy of objectivity or solidarity is false. We want *both* inquiry *and* community, and often we want each in part for the sake of the other. *Second,* a sane acceptance of phronesis does not mean that abstractly *anything goes,* and that *only* the individual or tribal will can appropriately determine what goes in the here and now. Historicism and relativism are just blantant nonsequiturs from the denial of algorithmic determinacy. *Third,* why the fetish of community agreement? On our best present bet, that commits us to Big Brother and the police state. There are many valuable institutions within which agreement is not on the horizon—not only those of politics, but also those of psychiatry and other branches of medicine, for example—and agreement even in the sciences is a shifting matter of degree. There is institutionalized agreement within the great religions, indeed more than in any science, but not among them. Do we decide conflicts by counting heads? Agreement is not an end in itself, and, even if it were, it would not warrant just any means, not, for example, the lobotomy of hard questions whose depth eludes agreement. *Finally,* we can, of course, close our eyes to the intuitive data of philosophy, or allow Big Brother to brainwash them away. But what would that show? And how can we possibly defend the denial of intuitive data except by leaning on other intuitive data? So far the free spirit leans on the denial of algorithic calculation and, often, on the adoption of agreement and solidarity as our primordial goal. But this yields the arguments already considered, and we offer now our response in dialogic solidarity.

NOTES

1. "The Critical Legal Studies Movement," *Harvard Law Review,* XCVI (1983); and *Passion: An Essay on Personality* (New York: The Free Press, 1984).
2. Even Habermasian critical theory is a special case. It is very hard to place, partly because it vacillates on whether to go transcendental. As Raymond Geuss shows, Jürgen Habermas changes his mind already in the mid 1960s; see *The Idea of a Critical Theory* (New York: Cambridge, 1981), p. 64: "In some of his earliest essays Habermas follows Adorno and holds a contextualist view of reflection; then, sometime in the mid 1960s, he seems to have been frightened by the specter of relativism, and retreated into a kind of transcendentalism." This is then supported textually.
3. According to Derrida, "there is nothing outside the text," and "there has never been anything but writing." *Of Grammatology,* G. C. Spivak, trans. (Baltimore, Johns Hopkins University Press, 1976), pp. 158/9. Derrida's pronouncements find an echo in Rorty's introduction to his *Consequences of Pragmatism* (Minneapolis: University of Minnesota Press, 1982), p. xxxvii: "the intuitive realist thinks that there is such a thing as Philosophical truth because he thinks that, deep down beneath all the texts, there is something which is not just one more text but that to which various texts are trying to be 'adequate'. The pragmatist does not think that there is anything like that."
4. In Richard Bernstein's apt phrase: *Beyond Objectivism and Relativism* (Philadelphia: University of Pennsylvania Press, 1983), p. 18.
5. Compare Rorty, "Solidarity or Objectivity?" *Nanzan Review of American Studies,* VI (1984). The theme of a philosophy of solidarity is drawn by Bernstein from the writings of Hannah Arendt, Gadamer, Habermas, and Rorty. See "Praxis, Practical Discourse, and Judgment," *Consequences,* pp. 171–233.
6. "Objectivity, Value Judgment, and Theory Choice," in *The Essential Tension* (Chicago: University Press, 1977).
7. Martha Nussbaum also draws inspiration from Aristotle for her theme of the place and nature of phronesis. Important here are her recent paper, "The Discernment of Perception: An Aristotelian Conception of Private and Public Rationality," *Proceedings of the Boston Area Colloquium in Ancient Philosophy,* I (1985): 151–201; and her book, *Fragility of Goodness: Luck and Ethics in Greek Tragedy and Philosophy* (New York: Cambridge, 1985).
8. All three are tarred, though not with the same brush. Cf. Colin Turnbull's *The Mountain People* (New York: Simon and Schuster, 1972).

9. That reasons inevitably give out is a familiar theme of the later Wittgenstein. But does that impose relativity to a form of life? And, if there is no way to understand how a private party could be wrong except by reference to a public form of life, what is the gain really if there is still no way to understand how the *group* could be wrong? Or shall we postulate a group of groups? And where do we appeal above the highest metagroup? Could this be a new argument for God, or is it rather the same old idea of God as the necessary ever-present thinker of ideas? See Kripke's *Wittgenstein on Rules and Private Language* (Cambridge, Mass.: Harvard, 1982), for reflections (and variations?) on the theme from Wittgenstein.

10. "The Problem of Historical Consciousness," in Paul Rabinow and William M. Sullivan, eds., *Interpretive Social Science: A Reader* (Berkeley, Calif.: University Press, 1979), p. 108.

11. Lucid defenses of strong realism are offered by William Alston in "Yes, Virginia. There is a Real World," *Proceedings and Addresses of the American Philosophical Association,* LI (1979): 779–808; and by Alvin Plantinga in "How to be an Anti-Realist," *Proceedings and Addresses of the American Philosophical Association,* LVI (1982): 47–70. Plantinga also offers a way to accommodate some degree of antirealism by appeal to theology. And a further interesting *via media* is due to Hilary Putnam, *Reason, Truth and History* (New York: Cambridge, 1981).

12. Rorty, *Consequences,* p. xxxvii.

13. Other free spirits may stay closer to the tradition, however, at least in the way suggested by Derrida when he writes that the "step 'outside philosophy' is much more difficult to conceive than is generally imagined by those who think they made it long ago, with cavalier ease, and who in general are swallowed up in metaphysics in the entire body of discourse which they claim to have disengaged from it" (p. 288). Compare also: "the passage beyond philosophy does not consist in turning the page of philosophy (which usually amounts to philosophizing badly), but in continuing to read philosophers *in a certain way*" (p. 284). (Apparently, though "there has never been anything but writing," there is now to be no more writing, at least not by those who move beyond philosophy, since they shall stick to *reading in a certain way.*) An example of the step "outside philosophy" into the jaws of metaphysics may be the pronouncement that the subject itself "is not at the center . . . but on the periphery, with no fixed identity, forever decentered, *defined* by the states through which it passes" [Gilles Deleuze and Félix Guattari, *Anti-Oedipus: Capitalism and Schizophrenia* (Minneapolis: University of Minnesota Press, 1983). p. 20; my emphasis.] Shades of Hume's bundle theory, through the neutral monism of James and Russell, on to Derek Parfit's process selves. *That* debate is about as serious as can be.

14. But, if we do believe in the earth and its roundness, then is there not after all, in our view, something distinct from all the texts, namely the earth and its being round (approximately), such that, if a text says that the earth is flat, then because the earth is round (which is no text) that text is inadequate (*contra* Derrida and Rorty above, and textualists generally)? And, if we do reject pure malice as unqualifiedly evil, and, if we approve of health and physical well being as so far unqualifiedly good, are these not after all purposes relative to which we may evaluate anything, including the construction of vocabularies or cultures? See again Derrida and Rorty, above. And compare Arthur Danto's "Philosophy, as/and/of Literature," *Proceeding of the and Addresses of the American Philosophical Association* LVIII, I (1984): 5–20: "it is altogether compatible with being united through a network of reciprocal effects that a literary work should refer, as it were extratextually, though the reference may be complicated as much by intra as by intertextual references. The *Prelude* and *Finale of Middlemarch* refer reciprocally, as well as to the novel they frame, and both refer or allude to Saint Theresa, herself not a text save in so wide a sense as to make . . . [a textualist theory that would admit her as just a plain text, a] theory timid and disappointing" (p. 13).

15. By *metaphysical modality* I mean the notions of necessity, possibility, etc. studied and systematized by the discipline of modal logic. The notions of metaphysical dependence and ontological status are closely related to the metaphysical modalities, if not even definable in their terms.
16. *Consequences,* p. xxxvii.
17. Ibid., pp. xxxix–xl.
18. "From Logic to Language to Play," *Proceedings and Addresses of the American Philosophical Association,* LIX (1986): 747–753. (An address at the Guadalajara Congress of the Interamerican Society of Philosophy.)
19. *Writing and Difference,* Alan Bass, trans. (Chicago: University Press, 1978), p. 81.

WHY IS A PHILOSOPHER?

Hilary Putnam

The great founders of analytic philosophy—Frege, Carnap, Wittgenstein, and Russell—put the question "How does language 'hook on' to the world?" at the very center of philosophy. I have heard at least one French philosopher say that Anglo-Saxon philosophy is "hypnotized" by this question. Recently a distinguished American philosopher[1] who has come under the influence of Derrida has insisted that there is no "world" out there for language to hook on *to*; there are only "texts." Or so he says. Certainly the question "How do texts connect with other texts?" exerts its own fascination over French philosophy, and it might seem to an American philosopher that contemporary French philosophy is "hypnotized" by *this* question.

My aim in recent years has not been to take sides in this debate about which the question should be, for it has come to seem to me that both sides in this quarrel are in the grip of simplistic ideas—ideas which do not work, although this is obscured by the fact that thinkers of genius have been able to erect rich systems of thought, great expressions of the human metaphysical urge, on these shaky foundations. Moreover, it has come to seem to me that these ideas are intimately related, that the great differences in style between French (and more generally continental) philosophy and Anglo-Saxon philosophy conceal deep affinities.

RELATIVISM AND POSITIVISM

To engage in a broad but necessary oversimplification, the leading movement in analytic philosophy was logical positivism (not from the beginning of analytic philosophy, but from 1930 to about 1960). This movement was challenged by "realist" tendencies (myself and Kripke), by "historicist" tendencies (Kuhn and Feyerabend), and by materialist tendencies. I will not take the risk of identifying the leading movement in French philosophy today, but if logical positivist ideas were for a long time (thirty crucial years) at the center of "Anglo-Saxon" philosophy, *relativist* ideas were (and perhaps continue to be) at the center of French philosophy. This may seem surprising because philosophers in all countries regularly remark that positivist and relativist ideas are self-refuting (and they are right to do so). But the fact of self-contradiction does not seem to stop or even slow down an intellectual fashion, partly because it is a fashion, and partly for the less disreputable reason that people don't want to stop it as long as interesting work is being produced under its aegis. Nevertheless, in my recent work[2] I have been trying to stop these fashions because they begin to threaten the possibility of a philosophical enterprise that men and women of good sense can take seriously.

Relativists do not, indeed, generally go quite all the way. Paul Feyerabend *is* willing to go all the way, that is, as far as to refuse to admit *any* difference between saying "It is raining" and "I *think* it is raining" (or whatever). For Feyerabend *everything* he thinks and says is merely an expression of his own subjectivity at the instant. But Michel Foucault claims that he is not a relativist; we simply have to wait for the future structuralist Copernican Revolution (which we cannot yet predict in any concrete detail) to explain to us how to avoid the whole problem of realism versus relativism.[3] And Richard Rorty[4] simultaneously denies that there *is* a problem of truth (a problem of "representation") at all and insists that some ideas do, and some do not, "pay their way."

If there is such a thing as an idea's paying its way, that is, *being right,* there is, inevitably, the question of the *nature* of this "rightness." What makes speech more than just an expression of our momentary subjectivity is that it can be appraised for the presence or absence of this property—call it "truth," or "rightness," or "paying its way," or what you will. Even if it is a culturally relative property (and what relativist really thinks that relativism is only *true-for-my-subculture?*), that does not exempt us from the responsibility of saying *which* property it is. If being true (or "paying one's way" as an idea) is just being successful by the standards of one's culture peers, for example, then the entire past becomes a sort of logical construction out of one's own culture.

It is when one notices this that one also becomes aware how very *positivist* the relativist current really is. Nietzsche himself (whose *Genealogy of Morals* is the paradigm for much contemporary relativist-cum-poststructuralist writing) is at his most positivist when he writes about the nature of truth and value. It seems to me that what bothers both relativists and positivists about the problem of representation is that representation—that is to say, intentionality—simply does not fit into our reductive post-Darwinian picture of the world. Rather than admit that that picture is only a partial truth, only an abstraction from the whole, both positivists and relativists seek to content themselves with oversimplified, in fact with patently absurd, answers to the problem of intentionality.[5]

LOGICAL EMPIRICISM AND THE REALIST REACTION

In the United States, these relativist and historicist views were virtually ignored until the 1960s. The dominant currents in the forties and fifties were empiricist currents—the pragmatism of John Dewey and (much more) the logical empiricism transported to the United States by Rudolf Carnap, Hans

Reichenbach, and others. For these latter philosophers the problem of the nature of truth took a back seat to the problem of the nature of confirmation.

The primary kind of *correctness* and *incorrectness* that a sentence possesses was thought to be the amount of inductive support the sentence receives on the basis of the evidence as the speaker perceives and remembers that evidence. For Quine, who has many affinities to these philosophers, although he must be counted as a postpositivist, *truth* is not a property at all; "to say a sentence is true is merely to reaffirm the sentence." (Quine also says that the only truth he recognizes is "immanent truth"—truth from within the evolving doctrine. Note how very "French" this sounds!) But if truth and falsity are not properties at all—if a sentence is "right" or "wrong" in a *substantive* sense only epistemically (only in the sense of being confirmed or disconfirmed by the present memories and experiences of a speaker)—then how do we escape from solipsism? Why isn't this picture *precisely* the picture of solipsism-of-the-present-instant? (To say that it is only a *methodological* solipsism is hardly a clear answer. It sounds as if saying that there are past times, other speakers, and truths which are not confirmed right now is correct "speaking with the vulgar" but not really the right standpoint thinking as a philosopher.)

Perhaps on account of these questions, by the end of the 1960s I began to revive and elaborate a kind of realism (joined by Saul Kripke, who I learned in 1972 had been working along similar lines). Our realism was not simply a revival of past ideas, however, because it consisted in large part in an attack on conceptions which had been central to realism from the seventeenth century on.

THE THEORY OF DIRECT REFERENCE

The seventeenth century thought of concepts as entities immediately available to the mind, on the one hand, and capable of fixing reference to the world, on the other. On this picture, the concept *gold,* for example, is in the mind of any speaker (even if he uses a Greek word, or a Latin word, or a Persian word) who can refer to gold; the "extension," or reference, of the world "gold," or "chrysos," or whatever, is determined by the concept. This picture of language is both individualistic (each speaker has the mechanism of reference of every word he uses in his own head) and aprioristic (there are "analytic truths" about the natural kinds we refer to, and these are "contained in our concepts").

It is not hard to see that this picture does violence to the facts of language use and conceptual thought, however. Few speakers today can be certain that an object is gold without taking the object to a jeweler or other expert. The reference of our words is often determined by other members of the linguistic community to whom we are willing to defer. There is a *linguistic division of labor* which the traditional picture entirely ignores.[6]

Kripke pointed out[7] that this linguistic division of labor (or "communication" of "intentions to refer," in his terminology) extends to the fixing of the reference of proper names. Many people cannot give an identifying description of the prophet Moses, for example. (The description "the Hebrew prophet who was known as 'Moses' " is not even correct; in Hebrew, Moses is called "Mosheh," not Moses.) This does not mean that those people are not *referring* when they speak of "the prophet Moses"; we understand that they are referring to a definite historical figure (assuming Moses actually existed). Experts today can tell us that that figure was called (something like) "Mosheh," but that is not an identifying description of Moses. There might have been Hebrew prophets who have been forgotten who were called "Mosheh," and the actual "Mosheh" might have had an Egyptian name which became corrupted to "Mosheh" centuries later. The "right" Mosheh or Moses is the one at the end of a *chain,* a chain leading backward in time. Or, to put it the right way around, the "right" Moses—the one we are referring to—is the one at the *beginning of a history,* a history which causally underpins our present uses and which is knitted together by the intention of speakers to refer to the person whom previous speakers referred to.

We may use descriptions to indicate to whom or to what we mean a word to refer, but even when those descriptions are correct they do not become *synonymous* with the word. Words acquire a kind of "direct" connection with their referents, not by being attached to them with metaphysical glue but by being used to name them even when we suppose the identifying description may be false, or when we consider hypothetical situations in which it is false. (We have already had an example of this: we can refer to Moses as "Moses" even when we know that this was not the name he actually bore. And I can explain which Richard Nixon I mean by saying "the one who was president of the United States" and then go on to imagine a situation in which "Richard Nixon was never elected president of the United States." I repeat, calling these cases "cases of direct reference" is merely denying that the name—"Moses" or "Richard Nixon"—is synonymous with a description: "the Hebrew prophet named 'Moses' or "the president of the United States named 'Richard Nixon.' " The mechanisms by which this "direct reference" is established are just the opposite of direct, involving chains of linguistic communication and division of linguistic labor as they do.)

A second way in which the seventeenth-century model of reference as fixed by concepts in individual minds does violence to the facts is, perhaps, more subtle. The reference of our words is determined (in some cases) by the nonhuman environment as well as by other speakers. When I speak of "water" I mean to be speaking of the liquid that falls as rain in *our* environment, the one that fills the lakes and rivers *we* know, and so forth. If somewhere in the universe there is a Twin Earth where everything is much as it is here *except* that the liquid that plays the role of "water" on Twin Earth is not H_2O but XYZ, then that does not falsify *our* statement that "water is H_2O." What we refer to as "water" is whatever liquid is of the composition, and so on, of *our* paradigmatic examples of water. Discovering that composition or the laws of behavior of the substance may lead scientists to say that some liquid which a layman would take to be water is not really water at all (and the layman would defer to this judgment). In this way, the reference of the terms "water," "leopard," "gold," and so forth is partly fixed by the substances and organisms themselves. As the pragmatist Charles Peirce put it long ago, the "meaning" of these terms is open to indefinite future scientific discovery.

Recognizing these two factors—the division of linguistic labor and the contribution of the environment to the fixing of reference—goes a long way toward overcoming the individualistic and aprioristic philosophical Weltanschauung that has long been associated with realism. If what a term refers to depends on other people and on the way the entire society is embedded in its environment, then it is natural to look with skepticism at the claim that armchair "conceptual analysis" can reveal anything of great significance about the nature of things. This kind of "realism" goes with a more fallibilistic spirit in philosophy. However, the traditional problems connected with realism are thereby considerably sharpened.

BRAINS IN A VAT

The new realism gives up the idea that our mental representations have any *intrinsic* connection with the things to which they refer. This can be seen in the examples of Twin Earth mentioned earlier: our "representations" of water (prior to learning that *water is H_2O/water is XYZ*) may have been phenomenologically identical with the Twin Earthers' "representations," but according to the "theory of direct reference" we were referring to H_2O (give or take some impurities) all along, and the Twin Earthers were referring to XYZ all along. The difference in the reference was, so to speak, "sleeping" in the substance itself all along, and was awakened by the different scientific discoveries that the two cultures made. There is no magical connection between the phenomenological character of the representation and the set of objects the representation denotes.

Now, imagine a race of people who have been literally created by a mad super-scientist. These people have brains like ours, let us suppose, but not bodies. They have only the illusion of bodies, of an external environment (like ours), and so on; in reality they are brains suspended in a vat of chemicals. Tubes connected to the brains take care of the circulation of blood, and wires connected to the nerve endings produce the illusion of sensory impulses coming to the "eyes" and "ears" and of "bodies" executing the motor commands of these brains. A traditional skeptic would have used this case (which is just the scientific version of Descartes's demon) to show that we may be radically deceived about the existence of an external world at all like the one we think we inhabit. The major premise in this skeptical argument is that the race we just imagined is a race of beings who *are* radically wrong in their beliefs. But are they?

It certainly seems that they are. For example, these people believe: "We are not brains in a vat. The very supposition that we might be is an absurd philosopher's fantasy." And obviously they *are* brains in a vat. So they are wrong. But not so fast!

If the Brain-in-a-Vatists' word *vat* refers to what *we* call "vats" and the Brain-in-a-Vatists' word *in* refers to spatial containment and the Brain-in-a-Vatists' word *brain* refers to what we call "brains," then the sentence "We are brains in a vat" has the same truth-condition for a Brain-in-a-Vatist as it would have for one of us (apart from the difference in the reference of the pronoun *we*). In particular, it is (on this supposition) a true sentence, since the people who think it are, in fact, brains spatially contained in a vat, and its negation, "We are not brains in a vat," is a false statement. But, if there is no intrinsic connection between the word *vat* and what are called "vats" (any more than there is an intrinsic connection between the word *water* and the particular liquid, H_2O, we call by that name), why should we not say that what the word *vat* refers to in Brain-in-a-Vatish is phenomenological appearances of vats and not "real" vats? (And similarly for *brain* and *in*.) Certainly the *use* of *vat* in Brain-in-a-Vatish is dependent on the presence or absence of phenomenological appearances of vats (or of features in the program of the computer that controls the "vat reality"), and *not* on the presence or absence of real vats. Indeed, if we suppose that there aren't any real vats in the mad scientist's world except the one that the brains are in, then it seems as if there is no connection, causal or otherwise, between actual vats and the use of the word *vat* in Brain-in-a-Vatish (except that the brains wouldn't be able to use the word *vat* if the one real vat broke—but this is a connection between the one real vat and *every* word they use, not a differential connection between real vats and uses of the word *vat*.)

This reflection suggests that when the Brains-in-a-Vat think "we are brains in a vat" the truth-condition for their utterance must be that they are *brains-in-a-vat in the image,* or something of that kind. So this sentence would seem to be *false,* not true, when *they* think it (even though they are brains in a vat from *our* point of view). It would seem that they are *not* deceived—they are not thinking anything radically false. Of course there are truths that they cannot even express; but that is, not doubt, true of every finite being. The very hypothesis of "radical deception" seems to depend on the idea of a predetermined, almost magical, connection betweens words or thought-signs and external objects that Transcendental Realism depends on.

Indeed, symbolic logic tells us that there are many different "models" for our theories and many different "reference relations" for our languages.[8] This poses an ancient problem: *if there are many different "correspondences" between thought-signs or words and external objects, then how can any one of these be singled out?*

A clever form of this problem (which, of course, goes back to the Middle Ages) is due to Robert Nozick (unpublished communication). Let C_1 and C_2 be two different "correspondences" (reference relations, in the sense of model theory) between our signs and some fixed set of objects. Choose them so that the same sentences come out true no matter whether we interpret our words as "referring" to what they correspond to in the sense of C_1 or as referring to what they correspond to in the sense of C_2. That this can be done—that there are alternative ways of putting our signs in correspondence with things which leave the set of true sentences invariant—was emphasized by Quine in his famous doctrine of Ontological Relativity.[9] Now, imagine that God arranged things so that when a man uses a word he refers to the things which correspond-C_1 to that word (the things which are the "image" of the word under the relation C_1) while when a woman uses a word she refers to the things which correspond-C_2 to that word. Since the truth-conditions for whole sentences are unaffected, no one would ever notice! So how do we know (how can we even give sense to the supposition) that there *is* a determinate correspondence between words and things?

There are many quick answers to this question. Thus, a philosopher is likely to say, "When we come to learn the use of the word *vat* (or whatever), we don't merely associate the word with certain visual sensations, certain tactile sensations, and so forth. We are *caused* to have those sensations, and the beliefs which accompany those sensations, by certain external events. Normally those external events involve the presence of vats. So, indirectly, the word *vat* comes to be associated with vats."

To see why this answer fails to speak to what puzzles us, imagine it being given first by a man and then by a woman. When the woman says this she is pointing out that certain ones of a speaker's beliefs and sensations are in a certain relation—the relation *effect*$_2$—to certain external events. In fact, they are caused$_2$ by the presence$_2$ of vats$_2$. When a male philosopher says this, he is pointing out that the same beliefs and impressions are caused$_1$ by the presence$_1$ of vats$_1$. Of course, they are both right. The word *vat* is "indirectly associated" with vats$_2$ (in the way pointed out by the woman) and also "indirectly associated" with vats$_1$ (in the way pointed out by the man). We still have not been given any reason to believe in the One metaphysically singled out correspondence between words and things.

Sometimes I am accused (especially by members of the materialist current in analytic philosophy) of caricaturing the realist position. A realist, I am told, does not claim that reference is fixed by the connection in our theory between the *terms* "reference," "causation," "sensation," and so on; the realist claims that reference is "fixed by causation itself." Here the philosopher is ignoring his own epistemological position. He is philosophizing as if naive realism were true for him, or, equivalently, as if he and he alone were in an *absolute* relation to the world. What *he* calls "causation" really is causation, and *of course* there is somehow a singled-out correspondence between the word and one definite relation in his case. But how this can be so is just the question at issue.

INTERNAL REALISM

Must we then fall back into the view that "there is only the text"? That there is only "immanent truth" (truth *according* to the "text")? Or, as the same idea is put by many analytic philosophers, that "is true" is only an expression we use to "raise the level of language"? Although Quine, in particular, seems tempted by this view (supplemented by the idea that a pure cause-effect story is a complete scientific and philosophical description of the use of a language), the problem with such a view is obvious. If the cause-effect description is complete, if all there is to say about the "text" is that it consists in the production of noises (and subvocalizations) according to a certain causal pattern; if the causal story is not to be and need not be supplemented by a normative story; if there is no substantive property of either warrant or truth connected with assertion—then there is no way in which the noises that we utter or the inscriptions we write down or the subvocalizations that occur in our bodies are more than expressions of our subjectivity. As Edward Lee put it in a fine paper on Protagoras and Plato,[10] a human being resembles an animal producing various cries in response to various natural contingencies, on such a view, or better, a plant putting forth now a leaf and now a flower. Such a story leaves out that we are *thinkers.* If such a story is right, then not only is representation a myth; the very idea of thinking is a myth.

In response to this predicament, the predicament of being asked to choose between a *metaphysical* position on the one hand and a group of *reductionist* positions on the other, I was led to follow Kant in distinguishing between two sorts of realism (whether Saul Kripke, whose work I alluded to earlier, would follow me in *this* move I rather doubt). The two sorts I called "metaphysical realism" and "internal realism." [11] The metaphysical realist insists that a mysterious relation of "correspondence" is what makes reference and truth possible; the internal realist, by contrast, is willing to think of reference as internal to "texts" (or theories), *provided* we recognize that there are better and worse "texts." "Better" and "worse" may themselves depend on our historical situation and our purposes; there is no notion of a God's-Eye View of Truth here. But the notion of a right (or at least a "better") answer to a question is subject to two constraints: (1) *Rightness is not subjective.* What is better and what is worse to say about most questions of real human concern is not just a matter of *opinion.* Recognizing that this is so is the essential price of admission to the community of sanity. If this has become obscured, it is in part because the tides of philosophical theory have swept so high around the words *subjective* and *objective.* For example, both Carnap and Husserl have claimed that what is "objective" is the same as what is "intersubjective," that is, in principle public. Yet this principle itself is (to put it mildly) incapable of "intersubjective" demonstration. That anyone interested in philosophy, politics, literature, or the arts should really equate being the better opinion with being the "intersubjective" truth is really quite amazing! (2) *Rightness goes beyond justification.* Although Michael Dummett[12] has been extremely influential in advocating the sort of non–metaphysical-realist and non–subjectivist view of truth that I have been putting forward, his formula that "truth is justification" is misleading in a number of ways, which is why I have avoided it in my own writings. For one thing, it suggests something which Dummett indeed believes and I do not: that one can *specify* in an effective way what the justification conditions for the sentences of a natural language are. Second, it suggests something on which Dummett's writing is rather ambiguous: that there is such a thing as *conclusive* justification, even in the case of empirical sentences. My own view is that truth is to be identified with idealized justification, rather than with justification-on-present-evidence. "Truth" in this sense is as context-sensitive as *we* are. The assertability conditions for an arbitrary sentence are not surveyable.

If assertability conditions are not surveyable, how do we learn them? We learn them by acquiring a practice. What philosophers in the grip of reductionist pictures miss is that what we acquire is not a knowledge that can be applied as if it were an algorithm. The impossibility of formalizing the assertability conditions for arbitrary sentences is just the impossibility of formalizing human rationality itself.

THE FACT-VALUE DICHOTOMY

If I dared to be a metaphysician, I think I would create a system in which there were nothing but obligations. What would be metaphysically ultimate, in the picture I would create, would be what we *ought* to do (ought to say, ought to think). In my fantasy of myself as a metaphysical super-hero, all "facts" would dissolve into "values." That there is a chair in this room would be analyzed (metaphysically, not conceptually—there is no "language analysis" in this fantasy) into a set of obligations: the obligation to think that there is a chair in this room if epistemic conditions are (were) "good" enough, for example. (In Chomskian language, one might speak of "competence" instead of "obligation": there is the fact that an ideally "competent" speaker would say (think) *there is a chair in this room* if conditions were sufficiently "ideal.") Instead of saying with Mill that the chair is a "permanent possibility of sensations," I would say that it is a *permanent possibility of obligations.* I would even go so far as to say that my "sense-data," so beloved of generations of empiricists, are nothing but permanent possibilities of obligations, in the same sense.

I am not, alas! so daring as this. But the reverse tendency—the tendency to eliminate or reduce everything to description—seems to me simply perverse. What I do think, even outside of my fantasies, is that fact and obligations are thoroughly interdependent; there are no facts without obligations, just as there are no obligations without facts.

This is, in a way, built into the picture of truth as (idealized) justification. To say that a belief is justified is to say that it is what we ought to believe; justification is a normative notion on the face of it. Positivists attempted to sidestep this issue by saying that which definition of justification (which definition of "degree of confirmation") one accepts is conventional, or a matter of utility, or, as a last resort, simply a matter of accepting a "proposal." But proposals presuppose ends or values; and it is essential doctrine for positivism that the goodness or badness of ultimate ends and values is entirely subjective. Since there are no universally agreed upon ends or values with respect to which positivist "proposals" are *best,* it follows from the doctrine that the doctrine itself is merely the expression of a subjective preference for certain language forms (scientific ones) or certain goals (prediction). We have the strange result that a completely consistent positivist must end up as a total relativist. He can avoid inconsistency (in a narrow deductive sense), but at the cost of admitting that all philosophical propositions, including his own, have no rational status. He has no answer to the philosopher who says, "I know how you feel, but, you know, positivism isn't *rational in my system.*"

Metaphysical realists attempted to deal with the same issue by positing a total logical cleavage between the question of what is *true* and the question of what is *reasonable to believe.* But what is *true* depends on what our terms *refer to,* and—on any picture—determining the reference of terms demands sensitivity to the referential intentions of actual speakers and an ability to make nuanced decisions as to the best reconstruction of those intentions. For example, we say that the term "phlogiston" did not refer to anything. In particular, it did not refer to valence electrons, although a famous scientist (Cyril Stanley Smith) once joked that "there really is such a thing as phlogiston; it turns out that phlogiston is valence elctrons." We regard it as reasonable of Bohr to keep the same word, "electron" (*Elektron*), in 1900 and in 1934, and thereby to treat his two very different theories, his theory of 1900 and his theory of 1934, as theories which described the same objects and unreasonable to say that "phlogiston" referred to valence electrons.

Of course, a metaphysical realist might be a realist about reasonableness *as well as* a realist about truth. But that is, in a way, my point: neither a positivist nor a metaphysical realist can avoid absurdities if he attempts to deny any objectivity whatever to the question of what constitutes *reasonableness.* And *that* question, metaphysically speaking, is a typical *value* question.

The argument I have just briefly sketched (it is developed at length in my book *Reason, Truth, and History*) has been called a "companions in the guilt" argument. The structure is: "You say [imagine this addressed to a philosopher who believes in a sharp fact-value dichtomy] that value judgments have no objective truth-value, that they are pure expressions of preference. But the reasons that you give—that there are disagreements between cultures (and within one culture) over what is and is not valuable; that these controversies cannot be settled "intersubjectively"; that our conceptions of value are historically conditioned; that there is no "scientific" (reductive) account of what value *is*—all apply immediately, and without the slightest change, to judgments of justification, warrant, reasonableness—to epistemic values generally. So, if you are right, judgments of epistemic justification (warrant) are also entirely subjective. But judgments of coreferentiality, and hence of reference and truth, depend on judgments of reasonableness. So instead of giving us a fact-value *dichotomy,* you have given us a reason for abandoning epistemic concepts, semantic concepts, indeed, abandoning the notion of a *fact* altogether." Put more simply, the point is that no conclusion should be drawn from the fact that we cannot give a "scientific" explanation of the possibility of values until we have been shown that a "scientific" explanation of the possibility of reference, truth, warrant, and so on, is possible. And the difficulties with the correspondence theory suggest that to ask for this latter is to ask for a we-know-not-what.

WHY AM I NOT A RELATIVIST?

My failure to give any metaphysical story at all, or to explain even the possibility of reference, truth, warrant, value, and the rest, often evokes the question: "But then, why aren't you a relativist too?" I can sympathize with the question (and even with the querulousness which often accompanies it) because I can sympathize with the urge to *know,* to *have* a totalistic explanation which includes the thinker in the act of discovering the totalistic explanation in the totality of what it explains. I am not saying that this urge is "optional," or that it is the product of events in the sixteenth century, or that it rests on a false presupposition because there aren't really such things as truth, warrant, or value. But I am saying that the project of providing such an explanation has failed.

It has failed not because it was an illegitimate urge—what human pressure could be more worthy of respect than the pressure to *know*?—but because it goes beyond the bounds of any notion of explanation that we have. Saying this is, perhaps, not putting the grand projects of Metaphysics and Epistemology away for good—what another millennium, or another turn in human history as profound as the Renaissance, may bring forth is not for us today to guess—but it is saying that the time has come for a moratorium on Ontology and a moratorium on Epistemology. Or rather, the time has come for a moratorium on the kind of ontological speculation that seeks to describe the Furniture of the Universe and to tell us what is Really There and what is Only a Human Projection, and for a moratorium on the kind of epistemological speculation that seeks to tell us the One Method by which all our beliefs can be appraised.

Saying "a moratorium on those projects" is, in fact, the opposite of relativism. Rather than looking with suspicion on the claim that some value judgments are reasonable and some are unreasonable, or some views are true and some false, or some words refer and some do not, I am concerned with bringing us back to precisely these claims, which we do, after all, constantly make in our daily lives. Accepting the "manifest image," the *Lebenswelt,* the world as we actually experience it, demands of us who have (for better or for worse) been philosophically trained that we both regain our sense of mystery (for it *is* mysterious that something can both be *in* the world and *about* the world) and our sense of the common (for that some ideas are "unreasonable" is, after all, a *common* fact—it is only the weird notions of "objectivity" and "subjectivity" that we have acquired from Ontology and Epistemology that make us unfit to dwell in the common).

Am I then leaving anything at all for philosophers to do? Yes and no. The very idea that a poet could tell poets who come after him "what to do" or a novelist could tell novelists who come after him "what to do" would and should seem absurd. Yet we still expect philosophers not only to achieve what they can achieve, to have insights and to construct distinctions and follow out arguments and all the rest, but to tell philosophers who come after them "what to do." I propose that each philosopher *ought* to leave it more problematic what is left for philosophy to do. If I agree with Derrida on anything it is on this: that philosophy is writing, and that it must learn now to be a writing whose authority is always to be won anew, not inherited or awarded because it is philosophy. Philosophy is, after all, one of the humanities and not a science. But that does not exclude anything—not symbolic logic, or equations, or arguments, or essays. We philosophers inherit a field, not authority, and that is enough. It is, after all, a field which fascinates a great many people. If we have not entirely destroyed that fascination by our rigidities or by our posturings, that is something for which we should be truly grateful.

NOTES

1. Richard Rorty. See Richard Rorty, *Philosophy and the Mirror of Nature* (Princeton: N.J.: Princeton University Press, 1979) and Rorty, *Consequences of Pragmatism* (Minneapolis: University of Minnesota Press, 1982).
2. See Hilary Putnam, *Reason, Truth, and History* (Cambridge: Cambridge University Press, 1982) and Putnam, *Realism and Reason* (Cambridge: Cambridge University Press, 1983).
3. See Michael Foucault, *The Order of Things* (New York: Vintage Books, 1970), especially the concluding discussion of the human sciences.
4. See the works cited in note 1.
5. For a more detailed discussion see Hilary Putnam, *Reason, Truth, and History,* especially chap. 5, and "Why Reason Can't Be Naturalized," in *Realism and Reason.*
6. On this, see "The Meaning of 'Meaning,' " in Hilary Putnam, *Mind, Language, and Reality* (Cambridge: Cambridge University Press, 1975); see also "Explanation and Reference" in the same volume.
7. See Saul Kripke, *Naming and Necessity* (Cambridge, Mass.: Harvard University Press, 1982; lectures given at Princeton University in 1972).
8. See my paper "Models and Reality" in Hilary Putnam, *Realism and Reason* (first published in *Journal of Symbolic Logic,* 45 [1980]: 464–482).
9. See W. V. Quine, *Ontological Relativity and Other Essays* (New York: Columbia University Press, 1969).
10. Edward N. Lee, "Hoist with His Own Petard," in *Exegesis and Argument: Studies in Greek Philosophy Presented to Gregory Vlastos,* ed. E.N. Lee, A. P. D. Mourelatos, and R. M. Rorty (Assen: Van Gorcum, 1973).
11. See the essay titled, "Realism and Reason" in Hilary Putnam, *Meaning and the Moral Sciences* (London: Routledge and Kegan Paul, 1976).
12. See Michael Dummett, "What Is a Theory of Meaning? II," in *Truth and Meaning,* ed. G. Evans and J. McDowell (Oxford: Oxford University Press, 1976).

BIBLIOGRAPHY

1. BOOKS AND ANTHOLOGIES

Austin, J. L. *How to Do Things with Words.* Edited by J. O. Urmson. Cambridge, Mass.: Harvard University Press, 1962.

_____ . *Philosophical Papers.* Third edition. Edited by J. O. Urmson and G.J. Warnock. Oxford and New York: Oxford University Press, 1979.

Ayer, A. J. *The Central Questions of Philosophy.* London: Weidenfeld and Nicolson, 1973.

_____ . *Language, Truth, and Logic.* Second Edition. New York: Dover, 1946.

_____ . *The Meaning of Life.* New York: Charles Scribner's Sons, 1990.

_____ . *Metaphysics and Common Sense.* San Francisco: Freeman, Cooper and Company, 1970.

_____ . *Philosophical Essays.* London: Macmillan, 1954.

Ayer, A. J., *et. al. The Revolution in Philosophy.* London: Macmillan, 1956.

Ayer, A. J., ed. *Logical Positivism.* New York: The Free Press, 1959.

Baynes, Kenneth, James Bohman, and Thomas McCarthy, eds. *After Philosophy: End or Transformation?* Cambridge, Mass.: The MIT Press, 1987.

Bell, David and Neil Cooper, eds. *The Analytic Tradition: Meaning, Thought and Knowledge.* Oxford: Blackwell, 1990.

Bergmann, Gustav. *The Metaphysics of Logical Positivism.* Madison, Wisconsin: University of Wisconsin Press, 1967.

Black, Max. *Language and Philosophy.* Ithaca, New York: Cornell University Press, 1949.

Black, Max, ed. *Philosophical Analysis: A Collection of Essays.* Englewood Cliffs, New Jersey: Prentice-Hall, 1950.

Blanshard, Brand. *Reason and Analysis.* La Salle, Illinois: Open Court, 1962.

Bontempo, Charles and S. Jack Odell, eds. *The Owl of Minerva: Philosophers on Philosophy.* New York: McGraw-Hill, 1975.

Butler, R. J., ed. *Analytical Philosophy.* Oxford: Blackwell, 1963.

Carnap, Rudolf. *The Logical Syntax of Language.* Translated by Amethe Smeaton, Countess von Zeppelin. London: Kegan Paul, 1937.

_____ . *The Logical Structure of the World & Pseudoproblems in Philosophy.* Translated by Rolf A. George. Berkeley and Los Angeles: University of California Press, 1967.

Castañeda, Hector-Neri. *On Philosophical Method.* Bloomington: Noûs Publications, Number 1, Indiana University Publications, 1980.

Caton, Charles Edwin, ed. *Philosophy and Ordinary Language.* Urbana, Illinois: University of Illinois Press, 1963.

Chappell, V. C., ed. *Ordinary Language: Essays in Philosophical Method.* New York: Dover, 1964.

Chisholm, Roderick. *The Problem of the Criterion.* Milwaukee, Wisconsin: Marquette University Press, 1973.

Chisholm, Roderick, *et al. Philosophy.* Englewood Cliffs, New Jersey: Prentice-Hall, 1964.

Cohen, Avner and Marcelo Dascal, eds. *The Institution of Philosophy: A Discipline in Crisis?* La Salle, Illinois: Open Court, 1989.

Cohen, L. Jonathan. *The Dialogue of Reason: An Analysis of Analytic Philosophy.* Oxford: Clarendon Press, 1986.

Collingwood, R. G. *An Essay on Philosophical Method.* Oxford: Clarendon Press, 1933.

Culler, Jonathon. *On Deconstruction: Theory and Criticism after Structuralism.* Ithaca, N.Y.: Cornell University Press, 1982.

Dasenbrock, Reed Way, ed. *Redrawing the Lines: Analytic Philosophy, Deconstruction, and Literary Theory.* Minneapolis: University of Minnesota Press, 1989.

Derrida, Jacques. *Margins of Philosophy.* Translated by Alan Bass. Chicago: University of Chicago Press, 1982.

———. *Of Grammatology.* Translated by Gayatri Chakravorty Spivak. Baltimore: Johns Hopkins University, 1976.

———. *Positions.* Translated by Alan Bass. Chicago: University of Chicago Press, 1981.

Descombes, Vincent. *Modern French Philosophy.* Translated by L. Scott-Fox and J. M. Harding. Cambridge: Cambridge University Press, 1980.

Dewey, John. *Reconstruction in Philosophy.* Boston: Beacon Press, 1948.

Ducasse, C. J. *Philosophy as a Science: Its Matter and Its Methods.* New York: Oskar Piest, 1941.

Dummett, Michael. *The Logical Basis of Metaphysics.* Cambridge, Mass.: Harvard University Press, 1991.

Fetzer, James, ed. *Principles of Philosophical Reasoning.* Totowa, New Jersey: Rowman & Allanheld, 1984.

Feyerabend, Paul. *Against Method.* London: New Left Books, 1975.

Foucault, Michel. *Final Foucault.* Edited by James Bernauer and David Rasmussen. Cambridge, Mass.: The MIT Press, 1988.

———. *Politics, Philosophy, Culture: Interviews and Other Writings of Michel Foucault, 1977–1984.* Edited by Lawrence D. Kritzman. New York: Routledge, 1988.

———. *Power/Knowledge: Selected Interviews and Other Writings.* Edited by C. Gordon. New York: Pantheon, 1980.

Griffiths, A. Phillips, ed. *Contemporary French Philosophy.* Cambridge: Cambridge University Press, 1987.

Habermas, Jürgen. *The Philosophical Discourse of Modernity.* Translated by Frederick Lawrence. Cambridge, Mass.: The MIT Press, 1987.

———. *Postmetaphysical Thinking: Philosophical Essays.* Translated by William Mark Hohengarten. Cambridge, Mass.: The MIT Press, 1992.

_____. *Theory and Practice.* Translated by John Viertel. Boston: Beacon Press, 1973.
Hacking, Ian. *Why Does Language Matter to Philosophy?* Cambridge: Cambridge Univeristy Press, 1975.
Hare, R. M. *Essays on Philosophical Method.* Berkeley and Los Angeles: University of California Press, 1971.
Heidegger, Martin. *The Basic Problems of Phenomenology.* Revised edition. Translated by Albert Hofstadter. Bloomington: Indiana University Press, 1988.
_____. *Being and Time.* Translated by John Macquarrie and Edward Robinson. Oxford: Blackwell, 1967.
_____. *On Time and Being.* Translated by Joan Stambaugh. New York: Harper, 1974.
Horstmann, Rolf-Peter, Peter Bieri, and Lorenz Kruger, eds. *Transcendental Arguments and Science.* Boston: D. Reidel, 1979.
Husserl, Edmund. *Cartesian Meditations: An Introduction to Phenomenology.* Translated by Dorion Cairns. The Hague: Nijhoff, 1973.
_____. *The Crisis of European Sciences and Transcendental Phenomenology.* Translated by David Carr. Evanston: Northwestern University Press, 1970.
_____. *The Idea of Phenomenology.* Translated by William P. Alston and George Nakhnikian. The Hague: Nijhoff, 1964.
_____. *Ideas: A General Introduction to Pure Phenomenology.* Translated by W. R. Boyce. New York: Collier Books, 1967.
_____. *Phenomenology and the Crisis of Philosophy.* Translated by Quentin Lauer. New York: Harper, 1965.
James, William. *Pragmatism* and *The Meaning of Truth.* Cambridge, Mass.: Harvard University Press, 1975.
Kekes, John. *The Nature of Philosophy.* Oxford: Blackwell, 1980.
Lazerowitz, Morris. *Philosophy and Illusion.* London: George Allen & Unwin, 1968.
_____. *Studies in Metaphilosophy.* London: Routledge & Kegan Paul, 1964.
Lazerowitz, Morris and Alice Ambrose. *Necessity and Language.* London: Croom Helm, 1985.
Lewis, H. D., ed. *Clarity is Not Enough: Essays in Criticism of Linguistic Philosophy.* London: Allen & Unwin, 1963.
_____, ed. *Contemporary British Philosophy* (Third and Fourth Series). London: George Allen & Unwin, 1961 and 1976.
Lyotard, Jean-François. *The Postmodern Condition.* Translated by Geoff Bennington and Brian Massumi. Minneapolis: University of Minnesota Press, 1984.
Malachowski, Alan, ed. *Reading Rorty: Critical Responses to "Philosophy and the Mirror of Nature" (and Beyond).* Oxford: Blackwell, 1990.
Moore, G. E. *Lectures on Philosophy.* Edited by Casimir Lewy. London: George Allen & Unwin, 1966.
_____. *Philosophical Studies.* London: Kegan Paul, 1922.
_____. *Some Main Problems of Philosophy.* New York: Macmillan, 1953.
Montefiore, Alan, ed. *Philosophy in France Today.* Cambridge: Cambridge University Press, 1983.

Moser, Paul. *Philosophy After Objectivity.* Oxford and New York: Oxford University Press, 1993.

Muirhead, J. H., ed. *Contemporary British Philosophy* (First and Second Series). London: George Allen & Unwin, 1924 and 1925.

Nielsen, Kai. *After the Demise of the Tradition: Rorty, Critical Theory, and the Fate of Philosophy.* Boulder, Colorado: Westview Press, 1991.

Nietzsche, Friedrich. *Beyond Good and Evil.* Translated by R. J. Hollingdale. London and New York: Penguin Books, 1973.

_____. *On the Genealogy of Morals.* Translated by Walter Kaufmann and R. J. Hollingdale. New York: Vintage Books, 1967.

_____. *Philosophy and Truth.* Translated and edited by Daniel Breazeale. Atlantic Highlands, N. J.: Humanities Press, 1979.

Norris, Christopher. *The Contest of Faculties: Philosophy and Theory after Deconstruction.* London: Methuen, 1985.

_____. *The Deconstructive Turn.* London: Methuen, 1983.

Norton, Bryan, *Linguistic Frameworks and Ontology: A Re-Examination of Carnap's Metaphilosophy.* The Hague: Mouton, 1977.

Okrent, Mark. *Heidegger's Pragmatism: Understanding, Being, and the Critique of Metaphysics.* Ithaca: Cornell University Press, 1988.

Pap, Arthur. *Semantics and Necessary Truth: An Inquiry into the Foundations of Analytic Philosophy.* New Haven: Yale University Press, 1958.

Passmore, John Arthur. *Philosophical Reasoning.* Second edition. London: Duckworth, 1970.

Putnam, Hilary. *Philosophical Papers, vol. 3: Realism and Reason.* Cambridge; Cambridge University Press, 1983.

_____. *Realism With a Human Face.* Edited by James Conant. Cambridge, Mass.: Harvard University Press, 1990.

_____. *Reason, Truth, and History.* Cambridge: Cambridge University Press, 1981.

Quine, W. V. *Ontological Relativity and Other Essays.* New York: Columbia University Press, 1969.

_____. *Pursuit of Truth.* Cambridge, Mass.: Harvard University Press, 1990.

_____. *Theories and Things.* Cambridge, Mass.: Harvard University Press, 1981.

_____. *Word and Object.* Cambridge, Mass.: The MIT Press, 1960.

Rajchman, John and Cornel West, eds. *Post-Analytic Philosophy.* New York: Columbia University Press, 1985.

Reichenbach, Hans. *The Rise of Scientific Philosophy.* Berkeley and Los Angeles: University of California Press, 1951.

Rescher, Nicholas. *The Strife of Systems: An Essay on the Grounds and Implications of Philosophical Diversity.* Pittsburgh: University of Pittsburgh Press, 1985.

_____. *Methodological Pragmatism.* Oxford: Blackwell, 1977.

Rescher, Nicholas, ed. *The Heritage of Logical Positivism.* Lanham: University Press of America, 1985.

Rorty, Richard. *Consequences of Pragmatism: Essays 1972–1980.* Minneapolis: University of Minnesota Press, 1982.

_____. *Contingency, Irony, and Solidarity.* Cambridge: Cambridge University Press, 1989.
_____. *Essays on Heidegger and Others: Philosophical Papers, Volume 2.* Cambridge: Cambridge University Press, 1991.
_____. *Objectivity, Relativism, and Truth: Philosophical Papers, Volume 1.* Cambridge: Cambridge University Press, 1991.
_____. *Philosophy and the Mirror of Nature.* Princeton: Princeton University Press, 1979.
Rorty, Richard, ed. *The Linguistic Turn: Recent Essays in Philosophical Method.* Chicago, University of Chicago Press, 1967.
Russell, Bertrand. *The Philosophy of Logical Atomism.* La Salle, Illinois: Open Court, 1985.
_____. *The Problems of Philosophy.* Oxford and New York: Oxford Univesity Press, 1912.
Ryle, Gilbert. *Dilemmas.* Cambridge: Cambridge University Press, 1954.
Ryle, Gilbert, ed. *Contemporary Aspects of Philosophy.* Stocksfield, England: Oriel Press, 1976.
Sartre, Jean Paul. *Being and Nothingness: An Essay on Phenomenological Ontology.* Translated by Hazel E. Barnes. New York: Philosophical Library, 1956.
_____. *Search for a Method.* Translated by Hazel E. Barnes. New York: Knopf, 1963.
Schlick, Morzit. *Philosophical Papers, Volume I (1901–1922).* Edited by Henk L. Mulder and Barbara F. B. van de Velde-Schlick. Translated by Peter Heath. Dordrecht: D. Reidel, 1979.
_____. *Philosophical Papers, Volume II (1925–1936).* Edited by Henk L. Mulder and Barbara F. B. van de Velde-Schlick. Translated by Peter Heath. Dordrecht: D. Reidel, 1979.
Shanker, Stuart, ed. *Philosophy in Britain Today.* London: Croom Helm, 1986.
Silverman, Hugh J. and Donn Welton, eds. *Postmodernism and Continental Philosophy.* Albany, N.Y.: State University of New York Press, 1988.
Stich, Stephen. *The Fragmentation of Reason.* Cambridge, Mass.: The MIT Press, 1990.
Strawson, P. F. *Individuals: An Essay in Descriptive Metaphysics.* London: Methuen, 1959.
_____. *Analysis and Metaphysics.* Oxford and New York: Oxford University Press, 1992.
Unger, Peter. *Philosophical Relativity.* Minneapolis: University of Minnesota Press, 1984.
Urmson, J. O. *Philosophical Analysis: Its Development Between the Two World Wars.* Oxford: Clarendon Press, 1956.
Waismann, Friedrich. *How I See Philosophy.* Edited by Rom Harré. London: The Macmillan Press Ltd; New York: St. Martin's Press, 1968.
_____. *Ludwig Wittgenstein and the Vienna Circle.* Edited by Brian McGuiness. Translated by Joachin Schulte and Brian McGuiness. Oxford: Blackwell, 1979.

———. *The Principles of Linguistic Philosophy.* Edited by Rom Harré. London: The Macmillan Press Ltd; New York: St. Martin's Press, 1965.
Wang, Hao. *Beyond Analytic Philosophy: Doing Justice to What We Know.* Cambridge, Mass.: The MIT Press, 1986.
Warnock, G. J. *English Philosophy Since 1900.* Oxford and New York; Oxford University Press, 1958.
White, Morton. *Toward Reunion in Philosophy.* Cambridge, Mass.: Harvard University Press, 1956.
Wittgenstein, Ludwig. *The Blue and Brown Books.* Oxford: Blackwell, 1958.
———. *On Certainty.* Edited by G. E. M. Anscombe and G. H. von Wright. Translated by Denis Paul and G. E. M. Anscombe. Oxford: Blackwell, 1969.
———. *Philosophical Grammar.* Edited by Rush Rhees. Translated by Anthony Kenny. Oxford: Blackwell, 1974.
———. *Philosophical Investigations.* Edited by G. E. M. Anscombe and Rush Rhees. Translated by G. E. M. Anscombe. Oxford: Blackwell, 1953.
———. *Philosophical Remarks.* Edited by Rush Rhees. Translated by R. Hargreaves and R. White. Oxford: Blackwell, 1975.
———. *Tractatus Logico-Philosophicus.* Translated by D. F. Pears and B. F McGuinness. London: Routledge & Kegan Paul, 1961.
———. *Zettel.* Edited by G. E. M. Anscombe and G. H. von Wright. Translated by G. E. M. Anscombe. Oxford: Blackwell, 1967.

2. ARTICLES AND CHAPTERS

Alston, William. "Are Positivists Metaphysicians?" *Philosophical Review* 63 (1954), 43–57.
———. "Ontological Commitments." *Philosophical Studies* 9 (1958), 8–17.
Ambrose, Alice. "The Defense of Common Sense." *Philosophical Investigations* 1 (1978), 1–13.
———. "Linguistic Approaches to Philosophical Problems." *Journal of Philosophy* 49 (152), 289–301.
Audi, Robert. "The Applications of Conceptual Analysis," *Metaphilosophy* 14 (1983), 87–106.
———. "Realism, Rationality, and Philosophical Method." *Proceedings and Address of the American Philosophical Association* 61, Supplementary Volume (1987), 65–74.
Ayer, A. J. "The Claims of Philosophy." *Polemic* no. 7 (1947), 18–33.
———. "Demonstration of the Impossibility of Metaphysics." *Mind* 43 (1934), 335–345.
———. "Does Philosophy Analyse Common Sense?" *Proceedings of the Aristotelian Society, Supplementary Volume* 16 (1937), 162–176.
———. "Metaphysics and Common Sense." In *Metaphysics,* edited by W. E. Kennick and Morris Lazerowitz. Englewood Cliffs, New Jersey: Prentice-

Hall, 1966. Reprinted in A. J. Ayer, *Metaphysics and Common Sense,* 64–81. San Francisco: Freeman, Cooper and Company, 1970.
_____. "Philosophy and Language." An Inaugural lecture delivered before the University of Oxford on 3 November 1960. Oxford: Clarendon Press, 1960.
_____. "Philosophy and Ordinary Language." *Pakistan Philosophical Congress* 5 (1958), 131–154.
_____. "Philosophy and Science." *Ratio* 5 (1963), 156–167.
_____. "Philosophy as Elucidating Concepts." In *The Nature of Philosophical Inquiry,* edited by Joseph Bobick, 101–117. Notre Dame: University of Notre Dame Press, 1970.
_____. "The Vienna Circle." *Midwest Studies in Philosophy* 6 (1981), 173–187.
_____. "What Can Logic Do for Philosophy? (Part III)." *Proceedings of the Aristotelian Society, Supplementary Volume* 22 (1948), 167–178.
Ayer, A. J. and Frederick Copleston, "Logical Positivism—A Debate." In *A Modern Introduction to Philosophy,* edited by Paul Edwards and Arthur Pap, 726–756. New York: The Free Press, 1957.
Baker, Gordon. "φιλοσοφία: ει'κὼν καὶε'ιδος (Philosophy: Simulacrum and Form)." In *Philosophy in Britain Today,* edited by S. G. Shanker, 1–57. London: Croom Helm, 1986.
Bambrough, Renford. "Unanswerable Questions." *Proceedings of the Aristotelian Society, Supplementary Volume* 40 (1966), 151–172.
Bealer, George. "The Philosophical Limits of Scientific Essentialism." In *Philosophical Perspectives, 1: Metaphysics,* edited by James Tomberlin, 289–365. Atascadero, California: Ridgeview, 1987.
Bennett, Jonathan. "Analytic-Synthetic." *Proceedings of the Aristotelian Society* 59 (1958–1959), 163–188.
_____. "Wisdom and Analytic Philosphy." *Analyse & Kritik* 4 (1982), 98–101.
Bergmann, Gustav. "Ineffability, Ontology, and Method." *Philosophical Review* 69 (1960), 18–40.
_____. "Sense Data, Linguistic Conventions and Existence." *Philosophical of Science* 14 (1947), 152–163.
_____. "Two Cornerstones of Empiricism." *Synthese* 8 (1950–51), 435–452.
_____. "Two Types of Linguistic Philosophy." *Review of Metaphysics* 5 (1952), 417–438.
Black, Max. "How Can Analysis be Informative?" *Philosophy and Phenomenological Research* 6 (1946), 628–631.
_____. "Is Analysis a Useful Method in Philosophy?" *Proceedings of the Aristotelian Society, Supplementary Volume* 13 (1934), 53–64.
_____. "Linguistic Method in Philosophy." *Philosophy and Phenomenological Research* 8 (1948), 635–649.
_____. "The 'Paradox of Analysis'." *Mind* 53 (1944), 263–267.
_____. "The 'Paradox of Analysis' Again: A Reply." *Mind* 54 (1945), 272–273.
_____. "Philosophical Analysis." *Proceedings of the Aristotelian Society* 33 (1932–33), 237–258.

Blanshard, Brand. "In Defence of Metaphysics." In *Metaphysics,* edited by W. E. Kennick and M. Lazerowitz, 331–355. Englewood Cliffs, New Jersey: Prentice-Hall, 1966.

———. "The Philosophy of Analysis." *Proceedings of the British Academy* 38 (1952), 39–69.

Blumberg, Albert and Herbert Feigl. "Logical Positivism." *Journal of Philosophy* 28 (1931), 281–296.

Broad, C. D. "Critical and Speculative Philosophy." In *Contemporary British Philosophy* (First Series), edited by J. H. Muirhead, 75–100. London: George Allen & Unwin, 1924.

———. "Some Methods of Speculative Philosophy." *Proceedings of the Aristotelian Society, Supplementary Volume* 21 (1947), 1–32.

Carnap, Rudolf. "The Elimination of Metaphysics Through Logical Analysis of Language." Translated by A. Pap, in *Logical Positivism,* edited by A. J. Ayer, 60–81. New York: The Free Press, 1959. (Originally published as "Überwindung der Metaphysik durch Logische Analyse der Sprache." *Erkenntnis* 2 (1932), 219–241).

———. "Empiricism, Semantics and Ontology." *Revue Internationale de Philosophie* 4 (1950), 20–40.

———. "On the Character of Philosophic Problems." Translated by W. M. Malisoff. *Philosophy of Science* 1 (1934), 5–19.

———. "Philosophy and Logical Syntax." In *Readings in Twentieth Century Philosophy,* edited by William P. Alston and George Nakhnikian, 424–460. London: Free Press, 1963.

———. "Remarks on the Paradox of Analysis: A Reply to Leonard Linsky." *Philosophy of Science* 16 (1949), 347–350.

Castañeda, Hector-Neri, "Philosophical Refutations." In *Principles of Philosophical Reasoning,* edited by James H. Fetzer, 227–258. Totowa, New Jersey: Rowman & Allanheld, 1984.

———. "Philosophy as a Science and as a Worldview." In *The Institution of Philosophy,* edited by Avner Cohen and Marcelo Dascal, 35–60. La Salle, Illinois: Open Court, 1989.

Chisholm, Roderick. "Comments on the 'Proposal Theory' of Philosophy." *Journal of Philosophy* 49 (1952), 301–306.

———. "Philosophers and Ordinary Language." *Philosophical Review* 60 (1951), 317–328.

———. "What is a Transcendental Argument?" *Neue Hefte für Philosophie* 14 (1978) 19–22.

Chisholm, Roderick and Richard Potter. "The Paradox of Analysis: A Solution." *Metaphilosophy* 12 (1981), 1–6.

Church, Alonzo. "On the Paradox of Analysis." *Journal of Symbolic Logic* 11 (1946), 132–133.

Coffa, Alberto. "From Geometry to Tolerance." In *From Quarks to Quasars,* edited by Robert G. Colodny, 3–70. Pittsburgh: University of Pittsburgh Press, 1986.

Cohen, L. Jonathan. "Are Philosophical Theses Relative to Language?" *Analysis* 9 (1949), 72–77.

_____. "How Empirical is Contemporary Logical Empiricism?" *Philosophia* 5 (1975), 299–317.

Copi, Irving. "Language Analysis and Metaphysical Inquiry." *Philosophy of Science* 16 (1949), 65–70.

_____. "Philosophy and Language." *Review of Metaphysics* 4 (1951), 427–437.

Copleston, Frederick. "Ayer and World Views." In *A. J. Ayer Memorial Essays,* edited by A. Phillips Griffiths, 63–76. Cambridge: Cambridge University Press, 1991.

_____. "The Function of Metaphysics." *Philosophy* 28 (1953), 3–15.

_____. "A Note on Verification." *Mind* 59 (1950), 522–528.

_____. "The Philosophical Relevance of Religious Experience." *Philosophy* 31 (1956) 229–243.

_____. "The Possibility of Metaphysics." *Proceedings of the Aristotetian Society* 50 (1950), 65–82.

_____. "The Question of Recurrent Problems in Philosophy." In *History of Philosophy in the Making,* edited by Linus J. Thro, 197–211. Washington: University Press of America, 1982.

Cornman, James. "Language and Ontology." *Australasian Journal of Philosophy* 41 (1963), 291–305.

_____. "Uses of Language and Philosophical Problems." *Philosophical Studies* 15 (1964), 11–16.

Derrida, Jacques. "Deconstruction and the Other." In *Dialogues with Contemporary Continental Thinkers* ed., Richard Kearney, 107–126. Manchester: Manchester University Press, 1984.

_____. "The Supplement of Copula: Philosophy *Before* Linguistics." In *Textual Strategies,* ed., J. V. Harari, 82–120. Ithaca, New York: Cornell University Press, 1979.

Dewey, John. "Experience and Philosophic Method." In Dewey, *Experience and Nature,* Second Edition, 1–36. La Salle, Illinois: Open Court, 1929.

_____. "The Development of American Pragmatism." *Studies in the History of Ideas, Volume II,* 351–377. New York: Columbia University Press, 1925. Reprinted in *John Dewey, The Later Works, 1925–1953,* Volume 2: 1925–1927, edited by Jo Ann Boydston, 3–21. Carbondale and Edwardsville: Southern Illinois University Press, 1984.

Ducasse, C. J. "Philosophy Can Become a Science." *Revue Internationale de Philosophie* 15 (1959), 3–16.

_____. "Reality, Science and Metaphysics." *Synthese* 8 (1949–51), 9–21.

_____. "The Subject-Matter Distinctive of Philosophy." *Philosophy and Phenomenological Research* 6 (1946), 417–420.

Dummett, Michael. "Can Analytical Philosophy be Systematic, and Should it Be?" In *Hegel-Studien, Beiheft 17: Ist systematische Philosophie möglich?,* edited by Dieter Henrich, 305–326. Bonn: Bouvier Verlag Herbert Grundmann, 1977.

Ewing, A. C. "Is Metaphysics Impossible?" *Analysis* 8 (1948), 33–38.

———. "Meaninglessness." *Mind* 46 (1937), 347–364.

———. "The Necessity of Metaphysics." In *Contemporary British Philosophy* (Third Series), edited by H. D. Lewis, 141–164. London: George Allen & Unwin, 1956.

Feigl, Herbert. "De Principiis Non Disputandum . . . ?" In *Philosophical Analysis,* edited by Max Black, 113–147. Englewood Cliffs, New Jersey: Prentice-Hall, 1950.

———. "Scientific Method Without Metaphysical Presuppositions." *Philosophical Studies* 5 (1954), 17–29.

Foucault, Michel. "Nietzsche, Genealogy, History." In Foucault, *Language, Counter-Memory, Practice,* 139–164. Ithaca: Cornell University Press, 1977.

Gadamer, Hans-Georg. "The History of Concepts and the Language of Philosophy." *International Studies in Philosophy* 18 (1986), 1–16.

———. "On the Origins of Philosophical Hermeneutics." In Gadamer, *Philosophical Apprenticeships,* 177–193. Cambridge, Mass.: The MIT Press, 1985.

Gallie, W. B "Essentially Contested Concepts." *Proceedings of the Aristotelian Society* 56 (1955–56), 167–198.

Geach, P. T. "On What There Is." *Proceedings of the Aristotelian Society, Supplementary Volume* 25 (1951), 125–136.

Gellner, Ernest. "Three Contemporary Styles of Philosophy." In *Philosophy In Britain Today,* edited by Stuart Shanker, 98–117. London: Croom Helm, 1986.

Grice, H. P., D. F. Pears, and P. F. Strawson. "Metaphysics." In *The Nature of Metaphysics,* edited by D. F. Pears, 1–22. London: Macmillan, 1957.

Habermas, Jürgen. "Philosophy as Stand-In and Interpreter." In Habermas, *Moral Consciousness and Communicative Action,* 1–20. Cambridge, Mass.: The MIT Press, 1987.

Hacking, Ian. "Is the End in Sight for Epistemology?'" *Journal of Philosophy* 77 (1980), 579–587.

———. "Michel Foucault's Immature Science." *Nous* 13 (1979), 39–51.

Hampshire, Stuart. "Are All Philosophical Questions Questions of Language?" *Proceedings of the Aristotelian Society, Supplementary Volume* 22 (1948) 31–48.

———. "Changing Methods in Philosophy." *Philosophy* 26 (1951), 142–145.

———. "The Progress of Philosophy." *Polemic,* no. 5 (1946), 22–32.

Hare, R. M. "Are Discoveries About the Uses of Words Empirical?" *Journal of Philosophy* 54 (1957), 741–750.

———. "Philosophical Discoveries." *Mind* 69 (1960), 145–162.

———. "A School for Philosophers." *Ratio* 2 (1960), 107–120.

Hempel, Carl. "Problems and Changes in the Empiricist Criterion of Meaning." *Revue Internationale de Philosophie* 4 (1950), 41–63.

Henle, Paul. "Do We Discover Our Uses of Words?" *Journal of Philosophy* 54 (1957), 750—758.

Hintikka, Jaakko. "Intuitions and Philosophical Method." *Revue Internationale de Philosophie* 35 (1981), 74–90.

_____. "Questioning as a Philosophical Method." In *Principles of Philosophical Reasoning,* edited by James H. Fetzer, 25–43. Totowa, New Jersey: Rowman & Allanheld, 1984.

James, William. "What Pragmatism Means." In *The Works of Wiliam James—Pragmatism,* edited by Frederick Burkhardt, 27–44. Cambridge, Mass.: Harvard University Press, 1975.

Kenny, Anthony. "Wittgenstein and the Nature of Philosophy." In *Wittgenstein and His Times,* edited by Brian McGuiness, 1–26. Chicago: University of Chicago Press, 1982.

Kim, Jaegwon. "Rorty on the Possibility of Philosophy." *Journal of Philosophy* 77 (1980), 588–597.

Kneale, William. "What Can Logic do for Philosophy? (Part II)." *Proceedings of the Aristotelian Society, Supplementary Volume* 22 (1948), 155–166.

Körner, Stephen. "The Meaning of Some Metaphysical Propositions." *Mind* 57 (1948), 275–293.

_____. "On Some Methods and Results of Philosophical Analysis." In *Philosophy in Britain Today,* edited by Stuart G. Shanker, 154–170. London: Croom Helm, 1986.

_____. "Philosophical Problems and Methods." In Körner, *What is Philosophy?* London: Penguin, 1969.

_____. "Some Remarks on Philosophical Analysis." *Journal of Philosophy* 54 (1957), 758–766.

_____. "Some Types of Philosophical Thinking." In *British Philosophy in the Mid-Century: A Cambridge Symposium,* edited by C. A. Mace, 113–131. London: George Allen & Unwin, 1957.

Kyburg, Henry. "Scientific and Philosophical Argument." In *Principles of Philosophical Reasoning,* edited by James H. Fetzer, 131–150. Totowa, New Jersey: Rowman & Allanheld, 1984.

Langford, C. H. "The Notion of Analysis in Moore's Philosophy." In *The Philosophy of G. E. Moore,* edited by P. A. Schilpp, 319–342. La Salle, Illinois: Open Court, 1968.

Lewis, C. I. "Introduction: About Philosophy in General and Metaphysics in Particular, the Proper Method of Philosophy." In Lewis, *Mind and the World Order,* 2–35. New York: Charles Scribner's Sons, 1929.

Lowe, Victor. "Lewis' Conception of Philosophy." In *The Philosophy of C. I. Lewis,* edited by P. A. Schilpp, 23–59. La Salle, Illinois: Open Court, 1968.

Luckhardt, C. G. "Philosophy in the Big Typescript." *Synthese* 87 (1991), 255–272.

MacIntyre, Alasdair. "Philosophy: Past Conflict and Future Direction." *Proceedings and Addresses of the American Philosophical Association* 61, Supplement (1987), 81–87.

_____. "Philosophy and its History." *Analyse & Kritik* 4 (1982), 102–104.

McKeon, Richard. "Philosophy and Method." *Journal of Philosophy* 48 (1951), 653–682.

Malcolm, Norman. "Defending Common Sense." *Philosophical Review* 58 (1949), 201–220.

_____. "Moore and Ordinary Language." In *The Philosophy of G. E. Moore,* edited by P. A. Schilpp, 343–368. La Salle, Illinois: Open Court, 1968.

_____. "Philosophy for Philosophers." *Philosophical Review* 60 (1951), 329–340.

Maxwell, Grover and Herbert Feigl. "Why Ordinary Language Needs Reforming." *Journal of Philosophy* 58 (1961), 488–498.

Merleau-Ponty, Maurice. "Philosophy and Non-Philosophy Since Hegel." *Telos* 29 (1976), 43–105.

_____. "Preface: What is Phenomenology?" In Merleau-Ponty, *Phenomenology of Perception,* vii–xxi. London: Routledge, 1962.

Moore, G. E. "A Defence of Common Sense." In *Contemporary British Philosophy* (Second Series), edited by J. H. Muirhead, 193–223. London: George Allen & Unwin, 1925.

_____. "Philosophical Methods." Part III, chapter 5 of Moore, *Lectures on Philosophy. London: George Allen & Unwin, 1966.*

_____. "A Reply to My Critics." In *The Philosophy of G. E. Moore,* edited by P. A. Schilpp, 535–677. La Salle, Illinois: Open Court, 1968.

_____. "What is Philosophy?" In Moore *Some Main Problems of Philosophy,* 1–27. London: George Allen & Unwin, 1953.

Nagel, Ernest. "On the Method of 'Verstehen' as the Sole Method of Philosophy." *Journal of Philosophy* 50 (1953), 154–157.

Pap, Arthur. "The Philosophical Analysis of Natural Language." *Methodos* 1 (1949), 344–369.

Passmore, John. "Philosophy and Scientific Method." *Proceedings of the Aristotelian Society* 49 (1948–49), 17–32.

_____. "The Place of Argument in Metaphysics." In *Metaphysics: Readings and Reappraisals,* edited by W. E. Kennick and M. Lazerowitz, 356–365. Englewood Cliffs, New Jersey: Prentice-Hall, 1966.

Peirce, Charles Sanders. "What Pragmatism Is." *Monist* 15 (1905), 161–181.

Pettit, Philip. "On Phenomenology as a Methodology of Philosophy." In *Linguistic Analysis and Phenomenology,* edited by Wolfe Mays and S. C. Brown, 241–255. New York: Macmillan, 1972.

Popper, K. R. "The Demarcation Between Science and Metaphysics." In *The Philosophy of Rudolf Carnap,* edited by P. A. Schilpp, 183–226. La Salle, Illinois: Open Court, 1963.

_____. "How I See Philosophy." In *The Owl of Minerva: Philosophers on Philosophy,* edited by Charles J. Bontempo and S. Jack Odell, 41–55. New York: McGraw-Hill, 1975.

_____. "The Nature of Philosophical Problems and Their Roots in Science." *British Journal for the Philosophy of Science* 3 (1952), 124–156.

_____. "On the Status of Science and of Metaphysics." *Ratio* 1 (1958), 97–115.

_____. "What Can Logic Do for Philosophy? (Part I)." *Proceedings of the Aristotelian Society, Supplementary Volume* 22 (1948) 141–154.

_____. "What is Dialectic?" *Mind* 49 (1940), 403–426.

Price, H. H. "The Appeal to Common Sense (I & II)." *Philosophy* 5 (1930), 24–35, 191–202.

_____. "Clarity is Not Enough." *Proceedings of the Aristotelian Society, Supplementary Volume* 19 (1945), 1–31.

Putnam, Hilary. "A Comparison of Something with Something Else." *New Literary History* 17 (1985), 61–79.

_____. "The Realist Picture and the Idealist Picture." In *Philosophy and Culture, VI,* edited by Venant Cauchy, 204–211. Montreal: Ed Montmorency, 1986.

_____. "Why is a Philosopher?" In *The Institution of Philosophy,* edited by Avner Cohen and Marcelo Dascal, 61–75. La Salle, Illinois: Open Court, 1989. Reprinted in Putnam, *Realism With a Human Face,* edited by James Conant, 105–119. Cambridge, Mass.: Harvard Univesity Press, 1990.

Quine, W. V. "Epistemology Naturalized." In Quine, *Ontological Relativity,* 69–90. New York: Columbia University Press, 1969.

_____. "Linguistics and Philosophy." In *Language and Philosophy,* edited by Sidney Hook, 95–98. New York: New York University Press, 1969.

_____. "On Austin's Method." In *Symposium of J. L. Austin,* edited by K. T. Fann, 86–90. London: Routledge & Kegan Paul, 1969.

_____. "On Carnap's Views on Ontology." *Philosophical Studies* 2 (1951), 65–72. Reprinted in Quine, *The Ways of Paradox,* 126–134. New York: Random House, 1966.

_____. "On What There Is." *Review of Metaphysics* 2 (1948), 21–38. Reprinted in Quine, *From a Logical Point of View,* second edition, 1–19. New York: Harper, 1961.

_____. "Ontology and Ideology." *Philosophical Studies* 2 (1951), 11–15.

_____. "The Pragmatists' Place in Empiricism." In *Pragmatism: Its Sources and Prospects.* Edited by Robert J. Mulvaney and Philip M. Zeltner. Columbia, S.C.: University of South Carolina Press, 1981.

_____. "Semantic Ascent." In Quine, *Word and Object,* 270–276. Cambridge, Mass.: The MIT Press, 1960.

_____. "Truth by Convention." In *Philosophical Essays for A. N. Whitehead,* edited by O. H. Lee, 90–124, New York: Longmans, 1936. Reprinted in Quine, *The Ways of Pardox,* 70–99. New York: Random House, 1966.

_____. "Two Dogmas of Empiricism." *Philosophical Review* 60 (1951), 20–43. Reprinted in Quine, *From a Logical Point of View,* second edition, 20–46. New York: Harper, 1961.

Ramsey, Frank. "Philosophy." In Ramsey, *The Foundations of Mathematics,* edited by R. B. Braithwaite, 263–269. London: Kegan Paul, 1931. Reprinted in Ramsey, *Philosophical Papers,* edited by D. H. Mellor, 1–7. Cambridge: Cambridge University Press, 1990.

Reichenbach, Hans. "Rationalism and Empiricism: An Inquiry into the Roots of Philosophical Error." *Philosophical Review* 57 (1948), 330–346.

Rescher, Nicholas. "Aporetic Method in Philosophy." *Review of Metaphysics* 41 (1987), 283–297.

_____. "Discourse on a Method." *Methodos* 11 (1959), 81–89.

_____. "Philosophical Disagreement: An Essay Towards Orientational Pluralism in Metaphilosophy." *Review of Metaphysics* 32 (1978), 217–251.

Rhees, Rush. "Unanswerable Questions." *Proceedings of the Aristotelian Society, Supplementary Volume* 40 (1966), 173–186.

Rorty, Richard. "The Historiography of Philosophy: Four Genres." In *Philosophy in History,* edited by Richard Rorty, J. B. Schneewind and Q. Skinner, 49–76. New York: Cambridge University Press, 1984.

_____. "Introduction: Pragmatism and Philosophy." In Rorty, *Consequences of Pragmatism,* xiii–xlvii. Minneapolis: University of Minnesota Press, 1982.

_____. "Metaphilosophical Difficulties of Linguistic Philosophy." Introduction to *The Linguistic Turn,* edited by Richard Rorty, 1–39. Chicago: University of Chicago Press, 1967.

_____. "Philosophy without Principles." *Critical Inquiry* 11 (1985), 459–465. Reprinted in *Against Theory: Literary Studies and the New Pragmatism,* edited by W. J. T. Mitchell, 132–138. Chicago: University of Chicago Press, 1985.

_____. "Pragmatism, Relativism, and Irrationalism." *Proceedings and Addresses of the American Philosophical Association* 53 (1980), 719–738.

_____. "A Reply to Six Critics." *Analyse & Kritik* 6 (1984), 78–98.

_____. "Solidarity or Objectivity?" *Nanzan Review of American Studies* 6 (1984). Reprinted in *Post-Analytic Philosophy,* edited by J. Rajchman and C. West, 3–19. New York: Columbia University Press, 1985.

_____. "Transcendental Arguments, Self-Reference and Pragmatism." In *Transcendental Arguments and Science,* edited by P. Bieri, R. P. Horstmann and I. Krüger, 77–103. Dordrecht: D. Reidel, 1979.

Russell, Bertrand. "The Cult of 'Common Usage'." *The British Journal for the Philosophy of Science* 3 (1953), 303–307.

_____. "Language and Metaphysics." In Russell, *An Inquiry into Meaning and Truth,* 429–438. New York: W. W. Norton, 1940.

_____. "Logic as the Essence of Philosophy." In Russell, *Our Knowledge of the External World,* 42–69. London: George Allen & Unwin, 1914.

_____. "Logical Atomism." In Russell, *Logic and Knowledge: Essays 1901–1950.* Edited by Robert Charles Marsh, 323–343. London: George Allen & Unwin; New York Macmillan, 1956. Reprinted in Bertrand Russell, *The Philosophy of Logical Atomism.* La Salle, Illinois: Open Court, 1985.

_____. "Logical Positivism." *Revue Internationale de Philosophie* 4 (1950), 3–19.

_____. "On Scientific Method in Philosophy." In Russell, *Mysticism and Logic,* 97–124. London: George Allen & Unwin, 1929.

_____. "Philosophical Analysis." *Hibbert Journal* 54 (1955–56), 319–329.

Ryle, Gilbert. "Categories." *Proceedings of the Aristotelian Society* 38 (1937–38), 189–206.

_____. "Fifty Years of Philosophy and Philosophers." *Philosophy* 51 (1976), 381–389.

_____. "Ordinary Language." *Philosophical Review* 62 (1953), 167–186.

_____. "Philosophical Arguments." Gilbert Ryle's Inaugural Lecture at Oxford University, copyright 1946 by the Clarendon Press. Reprinted in *Logical*

Positivism, edited by A. J. Ayer, 327–344. New York: The Free Press, 1959.
_____. "Proofs in Philosophy." *Revue Internationale de Philosophie* 8 (1954), 150–157.
_____. "Systematically Misleading Expressions." *Proceedings of the Aristotelian Society* 32 (1931–32), 139–170.
_____. "Taking Sides in Philosophy." *Philosophy* 12 (1937), 317–332.
Sellars, Wilfrid. "Philosophy and the Scientific Image of Man." In Sellars, *Science, Perception and Reality,* 1–40. London: Routledge & Kegan Paul, 1963.
Smart, J. J. C. "Plausible Reasoning in Philosophy." *Mind* 66 (1957), 75–78.
_____. "The Province of Philosophy." In Smart, *Philosophy and Scientific Realism,* 1–15. London: Routledge & Kegan Paul, 1963.
Sosa, Ernest. "Classical Analysis." *Journal of Philosophy* 80 (1983), 695–710.
_____. "Serious Philosophy and Freedom of Spirit." *Journal of Philosophy* 84 (1987), 707–726.
Strawson, P. F. "Analysis, Science, and Metaphysics." In *The Linguistic Turn,* edited by Richard Rorty, 312–320. Chicago: University of Chicago Press, 1967.
_____. "Construction and Analysis." In A. J. Ayer, *et al., The Revolution in Philosophy,* 97–110. London: Macmillan, 1956.
Waismann, Friedrich. "How I See Philosophy." In Waismann, *How I See Philosophy,* edited by Rom Harré, 1–38. London: The Macmillan Press Ltd; New York: St. Martin's Press, 1968.
Williams, Bernard. "Metaphysical Arguments." In *The Nature of Metaphysics,* edited by D. F. Pears, 39–60. London: Macmillan, 1957.
Wittgenstein, Ludwig. "Philosophy." Edited by Heikki Nyman. Translated by C. G. Luckhardt and M. A. E. Aue. *Synthese* 87 (1991), 3–22. This is an English translation of "Philosophie," ed. Heikki Nyman *Revue Internationale de Philosophie* 43 (1989), 177–203.
_____. "Wittgenstein's Notes for Lectures on 'Private Experience' and 'Sense Data'." Edited by Rush Rhees. *Philosophical Review* 77 (1968), 271–320.

ORIGINS OF THE SELECTIONS

1. Charles S. Peirce, "What Pragmatism Is." From Charles Hartshorne and Paul Weiss, eds., *Collected Papers of Charles Sanders Peirce,* Volume 5: *Pragmatism and Pragmaticism* (Cambridge, Massachusetts: The Belknap Press of Harvard University Press, 1934), pp. 272–292.
2. William James, "What Pragmatism Means." From Frederick Burkhardt, ed., *The Works of William James—Pragmatism* (Cambridge, Mass.: Harvard University Press, 1975), pp. 27–44.
3. John Dewey, "The Development of American Pragmatism." From Jo Ann Boydston, ed., *John Dewey, the Later Works, 1925–1953,* Volume 2: 1925–1927 (Carbondale and Edwardsville, Illinois: Southern Illinois University Press, 1984), pp. 3–21.
4. C. I. Lewis, "The Proper Method of Philosophy." From Lewis, *Mind and the World Order* (New York: Charles Scribner's Sons, 1929), pp. 2–35.
5. Bertrand Russell, "Logical Atomism." From Russell *Logic and Knowledge: Essays 1901–1950,* ed. Robert Charles Marsh (London: George Allen & Unwin, Ltd.; New York: The Macmillan Company, 1956), pp. 323–343.
6. G. E. Moore, "What is Philosophy?" From Moore, *Some Main Problems of Philosophy* (London: George Allen & Unwin; New York: The Macmillan Company, 1953), pp. 1–27.
7. Ludwig Wittgenstein, "Philosophy." From an English translation by C. G. Luckhardt and M. A. Aue in *Synthese* 87 (1991), 3–22.
8. A. J. Ayer and F. C. Copleston, "Logical Positivism—A Debate." From Paul Edwards and Arthur Pap, eds., *A Modern Introduction to Philosophy* (New York: The Free Press, 1957), pp. 726–756.
9. Rudolf Carnap, "Empiricism, Semantics, and Ontology." From *Revue Internationale de Philosophie* 4 (1950), 20–40.
10. Friedrich Waismann, "How I See Philosophy." From Waismann, *How I See Philosophy,* ed. Rom Harré (London: Macmillan and Co. Ltd.; New York: St. Martin's Press, 1968), pp. 1–38.
11. Roderick Chisholm, "Philosophers and Ordinary Language." From *The Philosophical Review* 60 (1951), 317–28.
12. Karl Popper, "The Nature of Philosophical Problems and Their Roots in Science." From *The British Journal for the Philosophy of Science* 3 (1952), 124–56.
13. W. V. Quine, "Semantic Ascent." From Quine, *Word and Object* (Cambridge, Mass.: The MIT Press, 1960), pp. 270–276.
14. Michael Dummett, "Can Analytical Philosophy Be Systematic, and Should It Be?" From *Hegel-Studien,* Beiheft 17 (1977), 305–26.
15. Friedrich Nietzsche, "On the Prejudices of Philosophers." From Nietzsche, *Beyond Good and Evil* (London and New York: Penguin Books, 1973), pp. 33–54.

16. Edmund Husserl, "Phenomenology and Philosophy." From Husserl, *The Idea of Phenomenology* (The Hague: Martinus Nijhoff, 1964), pp. 1–12, and Husserl, *The Crisis of European Sciences and Transcendental Phenomenology* (Evanston: Northwestern University Press, 1970), pp. 335–341.
17. Martin Heidegger, "The End of Philosophy and the Task of Thinking." From Heidegger, *On Time and Being* (New York: Harper & Row, 1972), pp. 55–73.
18. Jean-Paul Sartre, "Existentialism." From Sartre, *Existentialism and Human Emotions* (New York: Philosophical Library, 1957), pp. 12–40.
19. Maurice Merleau-Ponty, "What is Phenomenology?" From Merleau-Ponty, *Phenomenology of Perception* (London: Routledge & Kegan Paul, 1962), pp. vii–xxi.
20. Michel Foucault, "Nietzsche, Genealogy, History." From Foucault, *Language, Counter-Memory, Practice* (Ithaca: Cornell University Press, 1977), pp. 139–64.
21. Jacques Derrida, "Deconstruction and the Other." From Richard Kearney, ed., *Dialogues with Contemporary Continental Thinkers* (Manchester: Manchester University Press, 1984), pp. 107–126.
22. Jürgen Habermas, "Philosophy as Stand-In and Interpeter." From Habermas, *Moral Consciousness and Communicative Action* (Cambridge, Mass.: The MIT Press, 1987), pp. 1–20.
23. Richard Rorty, "Pragmatism and Philosophy." From Rorty, *Consequences of Pragmatism* (Minneapolis: University of Minnesota Press, 1982), pp. xiii–xlvii.
24. Ernest Sosa, "Serious Philosophy and Freedom of Spirit." From *The Journal of Philosophy* 84 (1987), pp. 707–726.
25. Hilary Putnam, "Why is a Philosopher?" From Putnam, *Realism With a Human Face*, ed. James Conant (Cambridge, Mass.: Harvard University Press, 1990), pp. 105–119.

INDEX